Property and Industrial Organization in Communist and Capitalist Nations

INDIANA UNIVERSITY

International Development Research Center

Studies in Development

No. 1

WORLD POPULATION—THE VIEW AHEAD
(ed.) Richard N. Farmer, John D. Long, George J. Stolnitz

No. 2

SOCIALIST MANAGEMENT AND PLANNING:
TOPICS IN COMPARATIVE SOCIALIST ECONOMICS
by Nicolas Spulber

No. 3

THE UN AND THE PALESTINIAN REFUGEES:
A STUDY IN NONTERRITORIAL ADMINISTRATION
by Edward H. Buehrig

No. 4

SOVIET AND EAST EUROPEAN FOREIGN TRADE (1946–1969):
STATISTICAL COMPENDIUM AND GUIDE
by Paul Marer

No. 5

RURAL POLITICS AND SOCIAL CHANGE IN
THE MIDDLE EAST
(ed.) Richard Antoun, Iliya Harik

No. 6

MODERNIZATION WITHOUT REVOLUTION:
LEBANON'S EXPERIENCE
By Elie Adib Salem

No. 7

PROPERTY AND INDUSTRIAL ORGANIZATION
IN COMMUNIST AND CAPITALIST NATIONS
by Frederic L. Pryor

FREDERIC L. PRYOR

Property and Industrial Organization in Communist and Capitalist Nations

INDIANA UNIVERSITY PRESS

Bloomington and London

International Development
Research Center

Directors:
George J. Stolnitz, 1966–1972
William J. Siffin, 1972–

Studies in Development: No. 7

BY THE SAME AUTHOR

The Communist Foreign Trade System
(also Spanish and Japanese translations)
Public Expenditures in Communist and Capitalist Nations

ᴄᴄ

Published in Canada by Fitzhenry & Whiteside Limited, Don Mills, Ontario
Library of Congress catalog card number: 73–75400
ISBN: 0–253–34621–5
Manufactured in the United States of America

TO

Lucius Clay
the late James B. Donovan
Thomas L. Farmer
and Wolfgang Vogel

Strangers to each other
who together once helped
an unknown student.

CONTENTS

APPENDICES

A. Research Notes

B. Statistical Notes

TABLES

Text Tables

Appendix Tables

Chart

Foreword

This newest of the Center's Studies in Development series effects a rare marriage among the concerns of comparativist economics, the evidence of key institutional trends in socialist and capitalist groupings of nations, and the methods of sophisticated theoretical-statistical analysis. As in the author's pioneering 1968 study, *Public Expenditures in Communist and Capitalist Nations,* a few key aspects of any economic system's mode of operation become the basis for a sweeping probe and interpretation. In the earlier work, the theme was fiscal allocations to each of an array of central social goals. Here the focus upon property and industrial organization, themselves no small subjects, leads us to even broader realms: the macro-scale efficiency and equity effects of alternative systemic arrangements. These basic issues are clarified and illuminated through analyses of within-group variation, between-group contrasts and similarities, probable main causes of systemic characteristics, and likely implications for change.

Professor Pryor's work is one of an interrelated series of volumes and reports that emerge from a major research program on East European economic transitions and performance of the International Development Research Center. These works constitute a significant body of literature concerning a region of considerable immediate importance in its own right, one whose evolution and development may well have outreaching implications for "third world" approaches to modernization and one which in any event will play a rapidly growing role in the future of international political and economic interaction.

George J. Stolnitz
Director, 1967–1972

May 1973

ACKNOWLEDGMENTS

The International Development Research Center (IDRC) of Indiana University financed and provided research facilities for this study as part of its group project on the economies of East Europe. I would like to express my deepest appreciation to George J. Stolnitz, former director of the IDRC, for his assistance and encouragement during the long gestation of this book. I would also like to thank Gustav Ranis, director of the Yale Economic Growth Center, for providing research facilities for several summers of work on this project.

I have been fortunate to receive an enormous amount of help from friends and colleagues. For reading and commenting upon the entire manuscript I would like to thank Robert W. Campbell, David Granick, Vaclav Holešovský, Paul Marer, John M. Montias, Egon Neuberger, Alec Nove, Mary S. Pryor, Millard H. Pryor, Sr., and Stephen Sacks. I also owe a great debt of gratitude to a great number of friends who read and criticized single chapters. These include R. Albert Berry, Richard N. Cooper, Clement Cottingham, Jr., Irvin Grossack, Harry Harding, Jr., Kenneth G. Lieberthal, Samuel Loescher, Joseph C. Miller, Hans Oberdiek, Howard Pack, Peter Pashigian, Merton Peck, Roland Pennock, Frank Pierson, Dieter Renning, Bernard Saffran, Frederic M. Scherer, David G. Smith, Leon Smolinski, Margaret Tuke, Otakar Turek, Klaus Wittich, and Arthur W. Wright. Further, I would like to express my appreciation to those who rendered valuable assistance in other ways, especially to: Linda Baker, Richard B. Caves, Janet Chapman, George Dalton, Carol Hopkins, Anton Kausal, Michael Kelcy, Iwan Koropeckyj, Jon Lax, Staffen B. Linder, Richard Portes, Millard H. Pryor, Jr., and Geoffrey Shepherd.

I would like to thank the following journals for their permission to use materials they originally published: For part of Chapter II, the *Weltwirtschaftliches Archiv,* 2, 1970, pp. 159–88; for material now in Chapter III, the *Slavic Review,* September, 1972; for material in Chapter IV, the *American Economic Review,* 1, 1973; for parts of Chapter V, the *Economic Journal,* June, 1972, pp. 547–66; for part of Chapter VI, the *Review of Economics and Statistics,* May, 1972, pp. 130–40; for part of Chapter VIII, the *Jahrbuch der Wirtschaft Osteuropas.* An earlier version of Chapter VII appeared in *Studies in Comparative Communism,* April, 1970, pp. 31–65.

Finally, I would like gratefully to acknowledge the help of my wife, who not only assisted in the preparation of some of the tables but also read and made perspicacious comments on the roughest drafts of this manuscript.

If I have made mistakes in this study, it is probably because I would not, or could not, take the advice of all those mentioned who were so generous with their time and assistance.

Property and
Industrial Organization
in Communist and
Capitalist Nations

CHAPTER I

Introduction

Guarda com' entri e di ti fide:
Non t'inganni l'ampiezza dell' entrare!
Dante[1]

A. The Major Themes

What factors determine the boundary between the sectors of public and private ownership? Is individual wealth becoming more concentrated? Are public and private ownership and control separated and if so, how does this affect production? Are we entering a technocratic era where only the mammoth enterprise is a viable economic unit? How does centralization of decision-making in an economic organization affect its performance?

Scholarly questions such as these, which probe into the issues of socialism, inequality, managerialism, bureaucracy, and centralization, have raised political and moral passions for many decades. Disparate as

---

1. "Watch how you enter and in whom you trust; do not let the wideness of the portal deceive you!" Dante Alighieri, *La divina commedia: Inferno,* Canto V.

I

they may appear on the surface, they are closely related in that all deal
with particular economic aspects of property and industrial organization.
Since these questions are discussed at length in the following chapters,
it is useful to survey the most important themes of this study to see how
they are related.

1. Property

The underlying theme of this book is property and it is well to begin with
a brief definition. "Property" is a bundle of rights or a set of relations
between people with regard to some good, service, or "thing"; such rights
must have economic value and must be enforced in some societally recognized manner.

This concept of property, focusing on positive rather than moral
rights, has been given alternative labels such as "economic power," "decision-making," or "control." It is specified broadly here so that functional equivalents can be designated in widely different economic systems.
It includes not only ownership in a traditional sense but also various
types of bureaucratic rights (e.g., giving orders to subordinates) and
rights that are enforced by social custom or through informal arrangements as well as by legal means. Although such a broad concept raises
many theoretical issues requiring attention (some of which are discussed
below), it also allows a wide range of empirical and theoretical studies
that utilize the techniques of economic analysis. Various aspects of property in this broad sense have, of course, been intensively explored by
social scientists and jurists. But in economics the concept has been considerably neglected.

In most of the literature of orthodox Western economics, there
seems to be an important implicit assumption by most economists that
property has little influence on the functioning of the economy. Part of
the reason for this assumption is their very narrow definition of property
which primarily concerns ownership. Another part lies in the difficulty
of dealing quantitatively with some central aspects of the subject. And
perhaps a final explanation is that most economic analyses presuppose
one particular institutional arrangement of property so that effects of
changing property rights are neglected.

Lack of attention to the general concept of property has not, of
course, precluded exploration of important aspects of the topic. Indeed,
many questions dealt with in the field of industrial organization, in the
study of income and wealth, and in economic anthropology concern certain aspects of property. Nevertheless, the lack of interest in the more

general concept has led to the neglect of important interrelations between these fields.

Among unorthodox Western economists, especially institutionalists, property does indeed form a subject of interest. But lacking sharp analytic tools, their empirical investigations have been primarily descriptive and, moreover, often carried out within a legal rather than an economic framework.

Among Marxist economists, the situation appears at first sight quite different. Marx himself formulated a number of important theorems about the development of property in capitalism (e.g., that property will become concentrated in fewer and fewer hands; or that productive units will become increasingly bigger and fewer in number until the economy consists of only a few gigantic enterprises), as well as a number of hypotheses about the effects of such developments (e.g., that wage earners will receive an ever smaller share of total income; or that business cycles will increase in severity). Engels made additional contributions, especially in his writings on the development of property rights in primitive tribes. But most modern Marxists have hesitated to develop these ideas into a more general theory of property that would cover bureaucratic types of property rights in centrally planned economies or property phenomena in capitalism that appear strongly to contradict Marx's original hypotheses.

Approaching economic aspects of property by empirically analyzing important rights permits us to unify analyses of a great many different situations that have previously been considered unrelated and, in addition, to focus on a number of hitherto neglected economic phenomena. Cases in point that are treated below include investigations of the major factors underlying public ownership in different economic sectors, trends in concentration of private ownership, divergencies in the changing patterns of ownership and control, and the major factors determining different types of centralization of control. Thus, through both empirical and theoretical exploration of the concept of property, I hope to achieve a more abstract level of economic analysis that, among other things, will allow discussion of economies in East and West Europe in the same breath.

Let me also emphasize that I have no global "theory of property" such as propounded by Marx or other social scientists of the last few centuries who have attempted to cast their analytic nets over the entire ebb and flow of history. Rather, various chapters of this book deal primarily with middle-level hypotheses about particular aspects of property. In this way I follow the advice of Francis Bacon who wrote over three hundred years ago: "For the lowest axioms differ but slightly from bare experience, while the highest and most general (which we now have) are notional and abstract and without solidity. But the middle are the true and solid and living axioms, on which depend the affairs and fortune of men. . . ."[2]

Economic science is not yet sufficiently advanced for a general theory of property, just as there is no widely held unified field theory in physics; but this should not prevent us from analyzing a range of hypotheses that are of considerable concern and from which more all-embracing theories can be built in the future. At the same time, evidence is also brought forward in this book against premature global theories of property that have been proposed in the past and which have served, I feel, as fetters to the advancement of research on property.

2. Industrial Organization

Many of the traditional questions investigated in the field of industrial organization concern aspects of property, defined in the broad sense discussed above. For instance, investigation of the size distribution of decision-making units (e.g., enterprises) provides important insights into the distribution and concentration of economic power. Exploration of the separation of ownership and control yields important evidence on the degree to which certain property rights are exercised by those (e.g., managers) other than owners.

For the most part, analysts of industrial organization have confined their attentions to one or at most two countries. Although it would seem clear that perspective would require extensive comparisons and analysis of the organization of industry in many nations, just one such broad scale comparison has yet been written in English,[3] and this study was unfortunately limited by the unavailability of basic data that have subsequently been published.

In the following chapters data from many countries are presented on the sizes of manufacturing establishments and enterprises, the relative degree of monopoly, the degree to which enterprises maintain their relative size rank, locational aspects of manufacturing, and the relative decision-making powers of managers in different nations. In some cases, existing theories can be utilized to explain the results; in other cases, new hypotheses are proposed and tested; while in still other cases, no satisfactory explanation can be found and the results of the empirical analyses

2. Francis Bacon, *Novum Organum,* Book I, Aphorism CIV, as translated in James Spedding, *et al.,* eds., *The Works of Francis Bacon* (London: 1875), Vol. IV, p. 97.

3. Joe S. Bain, *International Differences in Industrial Structure* (New Haven: 1966). While this book was in press, I came across a new study by Louis Phlips, *Effects of Industrial Concentration: A Cross-Section Analysis of the Common Market* (Amsterdam: 1971).

are presented for stimulus to others. In all cases it is my hope to broaden the study of industrial organization by widening the empirical base on which generalizations and theories are based.

3. Economic Systems

Since economic systems are often defined by criteria based on property (e.g., predominant mode of ownership of the means of production) or industrial organization (e.g., dependence on markets), attention to similarities and differences of economic systems is an integral part of this study. Further, since property rights limit the choices facing decision-makers within particular economic institutions, the empirical analysis of economic systems permits the examination of certain theories about property that can be studied in no other way.

The field of comparative economic systems, at least in the West, generally deals with economic institutions; and theory in the field stresses the assumption that such institutions display a certain economic logic that cannot be adequately analyzed by the tools of other social science disciplines.[4] It is surprising that empirical study of economic systems, particularly from a comparative point of view, have been neglected by scholars in the West, even though political interest in such matters has been high.[5]

Major benefits of comparative analysis of economic systems should, it seems to me, be gained by focusing on two broad questions of inquiry: What are the factors influencing the origin, development, and continued existence of particular economic institutions? And what are the effects of particular institutions on the operation of the economy? Unfortunately, current writings in the field have, for the most part, done little to answer these questions. A glimpse at the literature sheds light on the reasons underlying this sad state of affairs.

Briefly, the scholarly literature appears as an inverted pyramid. At the top are scores of essays on "the scope and method of comparative economics." Whenever a conference in the West is held on comparative economics, it always seems to focus on this subject; whenever a professor of comparative economics is feeling in ill-humor, he writes a "scope and methods" paper telling other comparativists what kind of research to carry out. (Lest I appear too severe, let me add that I have also published such essays and would like to record a public *mea culpa* at this time.)

4. This is argued at some length by Peter Wiles, *The Political Economy of Communism* (Cambridge, Mass.: 1962), Chapter 1.
5. One manifestation of this neglect can be seen in the new *International Encyclopedia of the Social Sciences* which has no entry dealing with comparative economic systems.

Further down are a small group of theoretical studies, either explorations of concepts (e.g., such as "centralization") or developments of models (e.g., of the differential response to price changes of profit-maximizing capitalist and cooperative enterprises). And finally, at the bottom are a few isolated studies that empirically compare economies with different institutions and try to analyze the degree to which these institutions influence economic performance (e.g., growth of G.N.P., fluctuations in production, relative importance of different manufacturing industries, and level of public expenditures).

For the field to experience any progress, the pyramid should, of course, be turned right side up so that the largest number of studies would be empirical. To those writing "scope and method" papers, we should reiterate C. Wright Mills's *cri de coeur,* "Every man his own methodologist! Methodologist! Get to work!"[6] Although discussions of problems of analytic method are sometimes valuable, a prerequisite for participation should be good-conduct medals gained in the battle of empirical research.

Such a reallocation of research efforts is easier to prescribe than to carry out and anyone proposing such changes should also be prepared to provide a concrete example of how such work should be done. This study tries, therefore, to broaden the empirical base of comparative economic systems by specific empirical exploration of actual institutions and economies. Such a task requires original research on a number of countries and I have tried to include many in East Europe where, in contrast to the West, most private ownership of the means of production has been abolished. Thus the East European nations provide a particularly telling test of the usefulness of the approach toward property and industrial organization developed in the following chapters.

B. Certain Implications of the Definition of Property

Although each term in the definition of property offered above can be explicated, such discussion beyond several brief explanatory remarks does not seem necessary.[7] A number of aspects of the concept of property are developed and refined in succeeding chapters in the context of empirical work where their relevance can be most clearly seen, especially in the analysis of centralization of property rights in Chapter VIII.

In the discussion immediately below I distinguish between two important subsets of property rights—namely, income and control rights—

6. C. Wright Mills, *The Sociological Imagination* (New York: 1961), p. 123.

7. A short explication is presented in Appendix A-1 to clear up certain apparent ambiguities.

around which the book is organized. Certain advantages and disadvantages of my definition of property are then briefly outlined. Later in the chapter I explore empirically the alleged correlation between income and control rights.

1. Subsets of Property Rights

One particularly important subset of property rights is the right to use a particular good, service, or thing to obtain income (either monetary or in the form of goods or services) other than by means of labor. Such income rights are sometimes designated by the term "ownership," although the latter term has certain broader connotations. The income derived from the holding of these rights can be obtained through particular types of levies (e.g., taxes, rents, lease payments and so forth)[8] or by using the good, service, or thing to produce something that is sold on the market for profit. Further, for ownership to exist, such income rights need not be actually utilized but need only be potentially usable; for instance, I have income rights or "own" a piece of land, even if I let it lie fallow, as long as it is *possible* for me to rent the land to someone else and receive income. Such a definition of ownership is somewhat different from the more common definition that focuses on the holder of a legal instrument or document containing provisions that can be enforced through the courts since many types of income rights rest on more informal understandings. The inadequacy of the more common or legal approach can be shown in an example from East Europe. Of the various nations only the government of the Soviet Union holds formal title to all agricultural land within its boundaries, yet agricultural institutions, policies, and income-distribution mechanisms were very similar in every nation of the region during the fifties.

Another particularly important subset of property rights is the right of use (or disposition) of goods, services, or "things" with regard to production and exchange which I designate below as "control rights" (and which others have called "decision-making," "economic-power," or "custodial rights"). Such control rights may either arise directly from

8. From such an approach it might be argued that the United States government has half ownership rights in United States corporations since corporate profit taxes are roughly 50 percent; but this type of argument neglects the incidence of such taxes. Although there is considerable dispute in the economic literature on the incidence of profit taxes, it appears that a very large share of corporate income taxes are passed on to the consumers or the workers, so that after-tax corporate profits are not greatly affected by the tax. Such considerations obviously complicate the exact determination of income rights, but somehow tax incidence must be taken into account in discussions of such matters.

ownership or may be delegated to their holder by others, or may adhere to an office which the holder occupies.

Control implies an asymmetric power relation in which a single person or group (the property-right holder) forces or induces other people to do what they ordinarily would not for the benefit of the controller. Control can be exercised in different ways, such as giving orders, manipulating incentives, or affecting the way in which decisions are made by others. Thus a manager of an enterprise possesses control rights in that he can effectively direct the actions of many others, exercising by virtue of his office many powers with which he can secure conformity to his desires including the right to dismiss from employment recalcitrant individuals. It is important to realize that the manager may have such control rights independently of whether he has any personal ownership in the enterprise.

Centralization is a critical concept of control rights and has many different dimensions which are explored later in this book. In place of a detailed investigation at this point, an analogy may provide a flavor of the concept: Centralization is to the distribution of control rights as inequality is to the distribution of ownership rights. The various investigations of industrial organization in this book were selected primarily to gather important evidence on the centralization of the economy.

In order to study the distribution of control rights, we must examine effective decision-making powers at different levels of the economy, the rules and procedures by which decisions are made, and the ways in which decision-making powers of different individuals or groups are coordinated with each other. To accomplish this end in the following chapters, I explore empirically the separation of ownership and control, the sizes of production establishments and enterprises, the degree of enterprise monopoly and competition, and, for nations in Eastern Europe, changes in decision-making rules. The conclusions from these studies are then used in Chapter VIII to generalize about different types of centralization in various economies and economic systems.

Ownership and control rights have certain "formal" relationships to each other. For example, in capitalist economies the shareholders allegedly select the enterprise manager who is "responsible" to them and administers the enterprise according to their desires. In socialist economies the enterprise managers are allegedly responsible to the "people" and are supposed to manage the enterprise according to their desires, as articulated by the representatives of the "people" in the government. But whether ownership and control are correlated in fact is a question for empirical research.

For certain purposes it is also useful to distinguish other subsets of property rights (e.g., the right of final destruction may, in some cases, usefully be separated from control rights). The essays in this study center mainly around income and control rights, however.

2. Advantages and Disadvantages of the Definition of Property

The definition of property that is used in this discussion has three important advantages for economic analysis over more restricted definitions:

First, it focuses on relations between men, rather than on particular goods, services, or "things" involved in the economic process. That is, such an emphasis forces our attention on the organization of economic activity, rather than only on the particular activity itself (production, consumption, exchange). Underlying this is an assumption that must be made explicit: The alleged distinction between the relationships of "man and objects" and "man and man" is overdrawn since in most cases a relationship between "man and objects" defines a relationship between men. This approach focuses thus on "things" existing not independently of men but in their role as social entities.

Second, the definition views property in its manifestation as an aspect of economic power; and the set of property rights possessed by an individual defines, as noted above, his realm of significant choices. The alleged impersonal rules or constitutions by which certain economic activities are regulated are power relationships and the degree to which a person can use such rules to exercise his will defines his property relations. Since economics deals with problems of maximization under conditions of constrained choice, the analytic tools of economics can be applied in examining behavior with different amounts of property. Focusing on sets of choice allows us to disentangle various semantic traps that arise in analyzing situations where the manager of an enterprise which is owned by the government may have more property rights than an owner-manager of a "private" enterprise which is constrained by multitudinous governmental restrictions.

Finally, the definition stresses the importance of economic values involved in property and this, in turn, should make us more sensitive to problems involving the interrelations between the distribution of particular property rights and the distribution of welfare.

Several disadvantages of the definition must also be noted:

First, the definition is extremely broad so that we run the double danger in our analyses of diffuseness and incompleteness.

Second, the definition covers a number of concepts which are used with more restricted meanings and which are associated with analyses of particular problems. Thus we are substituting one word ("property") for more common words and concepts and run the danger of confusing the reader.[9] This is particularly true with regard to ownership and control rights, concepts which—as noted above—cover only part of what is included under my broader concept of property.

Third, the boundaries of the concept are not clearly defined and many problems (e.g., the distinction between *dominium* and *imperium*) are left untouched. A complete theory of property would undoubtedly have to handle such cases, but for the succeeding chapters in this study, exploration of such distinctions is quite unnecessary.

Finally, the definition is strictly formal and content must be poured in for it to be analytically useful.[10] That is, I have offered a definition unrelated to any particular situation or theory and any hypothesis to be tested must be derived from further theoretical and empirical considerations. In succeeding chapters I present a wide variety of theoretical approaches and hypotheses which relate to, but do not spring directly from, the property definition.

Of course, the only way we can determine whether the advantages of the definition outweigh the disadvantages is through an evaluation of the ways in which the definition can be usefully employed in particular propositions about economic phenomena. My case for the usefulness of the concept lies in the empirical analyses in this and the following chapters.

C. Aspects of Ownership

By examining the alleged correlation between ownership (or income rights) and other important property rights with which economic systems are designated, we can both clarify the property concept and, at the same time, expose several important implicit assumptions that often accom-

9. Joseph Schumpeter, *Capitalism, Socialism, and Democracy,* 3rd ed. (New York: 1950), p. 189 used this objection to avoid any use of the term "property."

Those readers objecting to my use of the term "property" to cover the powers adhering to various positions within a bureaucracy can mentally substitute "decision-making powers" for "property" whenever it appears in the text. I prefer the term "property" because it more strongly connotes the inequality of power between people than the more neutral term "decision-making powers." Of course, power in hierarchies (control rights) has many more different aspects than power arising from ownership (income rights), but both cover a single fundamental social inequality between individuals.

10. In an early work Karl Marx [*The Poverty of Philosophy,* Chapter 2, Section 4] warned his readers against defining property as an "independent relation" and urged them to focus their attention on actual property and social relations instead. But an abstract definition helps to delineate those actual relationships on which the observer should focus.

pany the concept of economic system. Although carrying out this task requires drawing upon detailed statistical materials, the results have considerable importance for the structuring of the analysis in the rest of the book.

1. Ownership and the Classification of Economic Systems

Ever since Karl Marx (who coined the term "capitalism"), the notion of an "economic system" has often been tied to the predominant form of ownership prevailing in the economy. In "capitalism," income stemming from the ownership of the means of production accrues primarily to individuals; in "socialism," such income accrues to the government. Many Marxists hold the level of development and ownership of the means of production to be the two most important factors explaining the behavior of economic systems and, therefore, stress heavily the importance of classifying economic systems according to these criteria. Many non-Marxists, on the other hand, stress the importance of considering other aspects of the economy and have developed alternative types of classifications of economic systems. The differences between these two approaches cannot be resolved on a highly abstract level, since the "proper" classification of economic systems depends on the questions which the analyst is trying to answer and the type of results he obtains from different types of analytical schemas. Although such commonsense advice has often been offered, it is often forgotten and, as a result, the labels of economic systems have proliferated and the battle continues.[11]

Socialist and capitalist nations are often contrasted in a number of ways other than by ownership of the means of production. Decision-making autonomy on the part of production units is supposed to be smaller under socialism; that is, in socialist economies the enterprises and the government are alleged to share more control rights concerning the processes of production so that it is said that there is greater governmental planning and administration of the economy and "interference" with enterprise decisions. Such activity by the government can occur along many dimensions which are explored in later chapters; for simplicity (perhaps over simplicity) in the present discussion, we consider autonomy and "interference" as points along a single continuum which is defined below. Another alleged distinction between capitalism and socialism is that in the latter economies the share of current consumption financed and directly determined by the government is supposed to be larger so that an individual's power to determine his own consumption pattern is

---

11. Some attempt to relate the various labels of economic systems is presented in Appendix A-1, Section D.

smaller. The distribution of income is also said to be more equal under socialism which, in turn, reflects one aspect of the distribution of decision-making power in the consumption sphere. Vaguer differences are also sometimes cited, e.g., under socialism man is less alienated from his fellow man and exploitation of man by man occurs on a smaller scale. (These propositions cannot be easily tested empirically and usually evidence on such matters is essentially foreign to the empirical approach employed in this study.)

What is the relationship between these various criteria of socialism? Often there is the following implicit assumption: Among certain nations at particular times there is a general predisposition toward the exercising of property rights by governmental agencies, rather than by private individuals or groups, and it is likely that many of the different character-istics of socialism occur together. This notion can be restated as the following testable hypothesis: If "socialism" is a "seamless web," then a high degree of public ownership should be accompanied by other mani-festations of the exercise of property rights by the government, including a high ratio of public expenditures to the total gross national product and a high degree of governmental economic planning and administration of the economy. An empirical test of this "socialist web" hypothesis is pre-sented below.

An examination of the "socialist web" hypothesis is really an analysis of the degree to which certain types of property rights are correlated on a macro-economic level. (On a more micro-economic level this correla-tion between different types of property rights, namely income rights and control rights, is examined with regard to industrial enterprises in Chapter IV.) If this "socialist web" hypothesis does not prove successful in ex-plaining empirical differences between nations with different degrees of private or government ownership, then the usefulness of a classification system of economic systems that is based primarily on ownership is open to doubt. That is, if the distribution of particular property rights does not stand in a one-to-one relationship with the distribution of ownership (and the level of economic development), then a typology of economic systems based primarily on ownership may conceal more interesting and important phenomena than it illuminates.

In trying to examine such matters empirically, we can also gain cer-tain insights into other important questions. For instance, to what degree is public ownership linked with the level of economic development? Does a polity face a few "grand alternatives" in the structure of its economy because different property rights are correlated? Or does a polity face a wide number of choices along the dimensions of socialism that are men-tioned above?

2. *Some Data on Public Ownership in Different Nations*

Although empirical examination of the "socialist web" hypothesis has considerable importance, the very difficult, if mundane, problem of obtaining the proper data must first be briefly discussed. Comparable information on public ownership in different nations is extremely difficult to locate and, unfortunately, the definitions used in the available data do not correspond exactly to the definition proposed above. More specifically, the empirical materials employ a more formal legal definition for determining ownership. In addition, difficult valuational problems arise, particularly with regard to land and other types of nonreproducible wealth and to patents and other types of nontangible wealth.

Two types of measures have been used to gather ownership data for a sample of nations: First, a number of calculations have been made of the share of government ownership in the tangible reproducible wealth, both including and excluding housing. Second, it has been possible to calculate the share of the labor force working in facilities owned by the government. Although assets, not labor, are owned, the latter measure has the advantage of being more readily available and, in addition, on a more disaggregated basis. If we are interested in the organization of men and the division of the labor force in publicly and privately owned productive units, such a measure is also more appropriate. Relevant data for twenty-one economically developed or semideveloped nations are presented in Table I–I.

In interpreting the data, several features are worth noting. The rank orders of nations with either of the two wealth measures are relatively similar; in addition, the rank orders of nations using the four different labor-force measures are also similar (although to a lesser degree). Further, the labor and the wealth measures also show roughly similar results and, for the five countries for which both types of measures are available (the United States, Japan, France, Yugoslavia, and the Soviet Union), these rank orders are practically the same (only the United States and Japan change relative positions in several comparisons). If more countries were available for such a comparison, it is probable that these similarities in rank orders of public ownership measures would persist.

Second, for a single country the values of the various percentage measures are very different. In most cases the share of government ownership of wealth is considerably higher than the share of the labor force in governmentally owned facilities, primarily because much governmental wealth is in social overhead capital (roads, harbors, transportation facilities) that have a very high capital/labor ratio. The labor-force measures

TABLE 1–1

The Relative Importance of Government Ownership in East and West[a]

Country	Ratio of Economically Active Population in Governmentally Owned Enterprises and Facilities to Total Economically Active					Percentage Share of Government Ownership of Reproducible Tangible Wealth		
	Year	*Total*	*Total Material Sectors*	*Total Except Agriculture, Forestry, Fishing*	*Total Material Sector Except Agriculture, Forestry, Fishing*	*Year*	*Total*	*Total Excluding Housing*
West Germany	1950	9%	7%	12%	10%	1955	28%	33%
Japan	1960	10	5	14	9			
Switzerland	1960	11	8	12	9			
United States	1960	15	5	16	6			
Belgium						1955	15	22
Canada						1950	15	26
Netherlands						1955	18	23
Norway						1952	23	31
Australia								
South Africa								
France	1954	17	10	22	15	1953	23	31
Sweden	1960	20	6	22	7	1956	33	43
Israel	1959	24	8	28	11	1955	34	39
United Kingdom	1962	25	17	26	19	1954	48	59

Yugoslavia	1953	30	18	75	80	1953	63	79
Austria	1966	31	27	33	30			
Finland	1965	34	25	36	26			
Bulgaria	1956	37	27	92	88			
Poland	1960	48	40	84	86			
Soviet Union	1959	59	49	96	95	1960	75	87
East Germany	1964	71	69	80	84			

a. Government ownership excludes all producer cooperatives and enterprises managed by labor unions. For Yugoslavia, however, the enterprises managed by Workers' Councils are included as governmental property because profit redistribution to workers in 1953, the year for which the data are available, was still very limited. In the labor-force measure, government-owned enterprises and facilities include all such units in which the government ownership share is 50 percent or more, which means that in East Germany, the half-state enterprises are included in the government sector.

"Material" sectors include utilities, transportation and communication, construction, manufacturing and mining, and agriculture, forestry and fishing.

Reproducible tangible wealth is measured net of depreciation (except for the Soviet Union). It includes structures, equipment, and inventories (including cattle) and excludes land, timber stocks, consumer durables, military assets, and foreign assets. The data for France and the Netherlands have a slight upward bias (in comparison with that of other nations) because of inclusion of the value of land in government assets. Certain other slight incomparabilities exist that are discussed in the original source. The percentages excluding housing make no adjustments for subtracting governmentally owned housing from total governmental assets except for Yugoslavia and the Soviet Union, where the relative share of public to total housing assets is relatively large.

The capital stock data come from Th.D. van der Weide, "Statistics of National Wealth for Eighteen Countries," in Raymond Goldsmith and Christopher Saunders, eds., *The Measurement of National Wealth: Income and Wealth*, Series VIII, (International Association for Research in Income and Wealth), (London: 1959), Table 1. The Yugoslavia data are supplemented by statistics from Ivo Vinski, "The National Wealth of Yugoslavia at the End of 1953," Tables 1 and 2 in the same volume. The Soviet data come from statistics presented by Norman M. Kaplan, "Capital Stock," in Abram Bergson and Simon Kuznets, *Economic Trends in the Soviet Union* (Cambridge, Mass.: 1963), pp. 96–150.

For the labor force measurement, the estimates for Austria and Finland are not calculated directly but from value added and aggregate wage data respectively. Other small incomparabilities as well as details on sources and method of calculation are discussed in Chapter III where the data are disaggregated so that sectoral comparisons can be made.

differ in magnitude among each other because of the relative importance of agriculture (the least nationalized sector in most economies)[12] and the size of the armed forces (which greatly affects the share of the government in the service sector).

The relative degree of nationalization shows an enormous variation among nations, ranging in the total asset measure from 15 to 75 percent public ownership and in the total labor-force measure from 9 to 71 percent. Other measures of public ownership show even greater ranges: from 22 to 87 percent of public ownership in wealth excluding housing, and from 6 to 95 percent in the material sector excluding agriculture, forestry, and fishing.

Except for the two labor-force measures excluding agriculture, the nations in the sample are scattered relatively continuously over the different scales. Although the nominally "socialist" nations (Bulgaria, East Germany, Poland, the Soviet Union, and Yugoslavia) show a greater *average* degree of public ownership than the nominally "capitalist" nations, the range among nations with the same nominal system is sometimes greater than differences between the averages for the two systems; indeed, using the labor-force measure, several "capitalist" nations have a higher share of economically active population in the public sector than Yugoslavia (although this is primarily due to the very high proportion of the Yugoslav labor force in agriculture, which is predominantly private).

Only when we exclude the agricultural sector in examining the ownership patterns do there appear two clusters of nations where the differences between the averages of the capitalist and socialist nations are considerably greater than the range of variation within each group. It is probably on the basis of this particular type of indicator that the general consensus about extreme differences in ownership patterns between the two systems has arisen.

What is the relationship between the degree of public ownership and the level of economic development? It is well known that as the level of economic development rises, the proportion of the labor force and of total assets accounted for by the agricultural sector declines. As I show in the next chapter, agriculture is one of the sectors with the least government ownership. Thus as economic development proceeds, the relative degree of public ownership in an economy rises because of shifts in the relative proportion of labor and assets in the different sectors of the economy, other things remaining equal: an automatic "march into socialism," as it were. But does this *ceteris paribus* condition actually hold?

12. This matter is explored in detail in Chapter II. The very large Soviet private sector in agriculture (labor-force measure) is mostly accounted for by female dependents of collective farm and factory workers who cultivate small private plots and who, incidentally, account for a large share of total Soviet agricultural production and sales in many food items.

Propositions linking the degree of public ownership and the relative degree of economic development can be tested using information of single nations over a period of time or looking at a group of nations at a single point in time. And in examining time-series data, it is useful to distinguish between the very long-run and shorter periods within this.

Over the very long run there should be little doubt that the degree of public ownership of tangible, reproducible wealth or the proportion of the labor force working in governmentally owned facilities has risen. Obviously the degree of public ownership has greatly increased in the nations of Eastern Europe since important waves of nationalization occurred as the economic system was changing. Long time-series data for several Western nations such as the United States and the United Kingdom also suggest an analogous phenomenon has occurred, albeit to a much lesser extent.[13]

In the short run, however, trends are quite mixed. After the postwar wave of nationalization, the extent of public ownership has remained relatively steady or has declined in some Western nations such as Austria or the United Kingdom.[14] In other Western countries such as the United States, the relative share of government ownership (as shown in the data presented in the next chapter) has increased. (It is ironic that such "creeping socialism" occurred no less fast during the Eisenhower administration than during the Roosevelt and Truman administration from 1940 to 1952). In still other Western countries, other types of ownership change, especially through the introduction (or attempted introduction) of profit-sharing, schemes, have occurred.[15] In East Europe most of the

13. For the United States see Raymond W. Goldsmith, *The National Wealth of the United States in the Postwar Period* (Princeton: 1962) which contains data for the period 1900 to 1958; and for the United Kingdom estimates can be made from the data of C. H. Feinstein, *Domestic Capital Formation in the United Kingdom, 1920–1938* (Cambridge, Eng.: 1965).

14. Data for the United Kingdom can be found in a number of publications of the Central Statistical Office such as "Employment in the Public and Private Sectors of the Economy in Great Britain, 1949–1959," *Economic Trends,* November 1960, pp. 6–8. For Austria, time-series estimates have been made by Dr. Anton Kausel of the Öesterreichisches Institut für Wirtschaftsforschung.

15. The most revolutionary attempted change in property rights in Europe in the last decade occurred in France in August 1967, when President de Gaulle instituted a compulsory profit-sharing scheme in firms with one hundred employees or more. (These events are summarized by Salomon Wolff, " 'Participation'—de Gaulle's Formula for Industrial Peace," *Swiss Review of World Affairs,* XVIII, September 1968, pp. 9–11.) Although this move was opposed by both unions and property owners, it gave the workers ownership rights that are unprecedented in the West. In addition, Worker Councils were to be established so that the workers could participate in important policy decisions affecting their work situation. (These moves were prompted by de Gaulle's adherence to the doctrines of "solidarism," ideas that were popular in France before World War I.) After the election of President Pompidou, the implementation of these ideas was abandoned and

governments have followed a deliberate policy of increasing the share of government ownership, although in certain particular sectors of the economy, this trend has been slowed down or even reversed (if only to a small degree).

Using the cross-section data based on various measures that are presented in Table 1–1, no simple monotonic function linking the degree of public ownership and the relative degree of economic development can be seen. The discrepancies in results using time-series and cross-section data are due to a number of economic, political, and social forces that have received relatively little systematic investigation and that deserve considerable study before a full-fledged positive theory of nationalization can be devised.

The data in Table 1–1 also lead to several other conclusions: One, a commonplace, is that few economies approach "pure" capitalism or socialism, but rather contain mixtures of several different types of ownership. Thus the choices facing a polity with regard to public ownership may lie along a continuum, rather than at the extreme points of the public-ownership spectrum. Furthermore, in specifying economic systems in terms of ownership, it is important to declare explicitly which sectors are included in the comparison. Finally, the results suggest caution in generalizing about the behavior of actual economies on the basis of one or two theoretical models of "pure" systems of socialism and capitalism.

3. Relationship Between Ownership and Other Property Rights

To test the "socialist web" hypothesis we need now to devise indicators for other dimensions of socialism and then to measure their intercorrelations. Since traditional theory tells us little about what indicators to select, we must proceed intuitively and choose the most commonly mentioned dimensions. When the tests are performed, we find empirically that the "socialist web" hypothesis is quite inadequate.

Before turning to the empirical comparisons, it is useful to look more carefully at the distinctions between the various dimensions of capitalism and socialism that are briefly discussed above. One distinction is between public ownership of the means of production and public expenditures, i.e., those current expenditures of a nation for goods and services financed through its governmental budget. In Table 1–2 the possible combinations of these activities are shown.

Separation of ownership and financing suggests, in turn, that government ownership of the means of production does not necessarily mean

---

little effective support for their resuscitation appears on the horizon. The military leaders heading the Peruvian government tried to implement a mild form of solidaristic ideas in the early 'seventies.

TABLE 1–2
Four Types of Government Activities[a]

Ownership of the Means of Production	Financing of Current Expenditures	Examples Occurring in Both the United States and the Soviet Union
Public	Public	Public education
Public	Private	Electricity sold to private individuals by publicly owned electric companies
Private	Public	Government purchases of pictures from ataliers of private artists for public museums
Private	Private	Private purchases of vegetables in farmers' markets

a. This table is taken from Frederic L. Pryor, *Public Expenditures in Communist and Capitalist Nations* (Homewood, Ill.: 1968), p. 27. A more elaborate typology is presented in the same source in Appendix E-1, p. 437.

that the government exercises completely arbitrary control over what is produced; more specifically, if there are any constraints on enterprise decision-making (e.g., the enterprise must show a profit), the governmentally owned enterprise must produce to a certain extent what private individuals would like to buy. Similarly, if the government purchases goods or services from private enterprises or individuals and then gives them away, it has a certain power in determining the structure of production. Problems arise with this simple distinction once we begin to consider possibilities of governmental organs ordering state enterprises to finance certain expenditures out of sales or enterprises forcing (by threat of bankruptcy) governmental organs to finance expenditures which are against the desires of state officials.

Measuring the extent of governmental ownership or public financing (i.e., the ratio of publicly financed goods and services for current consumption to the total amount of produced goods and services) is considerably easier than measuring the extent of governmental planning and administration of the economy or the decision-making autonomy of enterprises (freedom from governmental "interference"). For instance, in trying to make certain quantitative comparisons, we might calculate the percent of total production in sectors in which the government "interferes" through such means as placing quantitative restrictions on production or setting up price controls. Such a method raises, however, considerable problems where qualitative aspects of such controls differ over time or between nations; and the most useful quantitative comparisons can be made most directly in cases where the institutional matrix between cases being compared is quite similar. (A case study of the degree of socialism in the United States from 1950 through 1966 using data on government ownership, expenditures, and regulated industries is presented in Appendix A-2 to illustrate such a procedure.)

Although difficulties in making international quantitative comparisons of government planning and administration seem great, we can still adequately test the "socialist web" hypothesis using two different methods.

One way is to select for comparison nations for which it is not necessary to quantify the relative extent of government administration since the facts are "obvious." For instance, we "know" that government economic administration in East Europe is much greater than in West Europe; hence we can then test to see if the ratio of public expenditures and other indicators of socialism are higher in the former group of nations, which the "socialist web" hypothesis would lead us to believe. Since public-expenditure ratios are also related to the relative level of economic development, it is necessary to take the relative per capita gross national products into analytical account. Comparable public-expenditure data for five pairs of nations in East and West Europe are presented in Table 1–3; each pair of nations has roughly the same development level.

The public-expenditure ratios for the two groups of nations are not significantly different. Holding the per capita G.N.P. and other determinants of current public expenditures constant (using regression techniques) does not change this conclusion. Furthermore, disaggregation of the expenditures data into individual functional components reveals many more similarities than differences.[16] We can thus conclude that among the nations in the sample a relatively higher degree of public ownership is not correlated with a higher degree of current governmental expenditures.[17] On the other hand, the relative degree of public ownership and the relative degree of governmental planning and administration of the economy are correlated, at least in this sample. Thus some indicators of socialism appear correlated while others do not.

It would, of course, be desirable to test the congruence between governmental ownership and governmental administration and planning with a more sensitive test, especially since it is possible that the government could have a high degree of ownership and yet completely delegate

16. Such an exercise is carried out by Pryor.

17. Using a much larger sample the same conclusion is obtained by Denis A. Flagg and Virginia G. Flagg, "An Empirical Application of Measures of Socialism to Different Nations," *Western Economic Journal*, VIII, September 1970, pp. 233–40.

TABLE 1–3

Ratios of "Current Adjusted Budgetary Expenditures" to Factor Price Gross National Product in 1962[a]

"Capitalist" Nations	Ratio	"Socialist" Nations	Ratio
West Germany	30%	East Germany	33%
Austria	28	Czechoslovakia	30
Ireland	18	Hungary	17
Italy	28	Poland	20
Greece	20	Bulgaria	22
Unweighted average	24.8	Unweighted average	24.4
Standard deviation	4.8	Standard deviation	6.1

a. "Adjusted budgetary expenditures" cover eight functions—(political administration, diplomacy and foreign aid, military, internal security, education, health, welfare, and research and development). Removal of welfare expenditures does not change the conclusions.

The pairs of nations are arranged roughly in order of descending per capita G.N.P.

The ratio of the socialist nations has an upward bias because of the omission of interest and rental payments in the gross national product. I do not believe that this bias is great enough to change the generalizations in the text.

The data come from Pryor, p. 61. The same source also contains data on the level of development and similar indicators to demonstrate the relative comparability of the nations.

Inclusion of the United States among the capitalist nations and the Soviet Union and Yugoslavia among the socialist nations reduces the unweighted average of the former nations to 24.5; but also reduces the average for the latter group of nations to 24.2. Inclusion of the three additional nations does not change any of the conclusions in the text either.

the exercise (or custody) of the property rights with regard to production to a hired manager, as in an extreme form of market socialism.

A second test of the "socialist web" hypothesis that can take into account relative degrees of governmental planning and administration can be made only for a group of developed Western nations. The relative degree of governmental planning and administration of the economy along a single aggregative dimension is derived from the results of a poll of twenty-two specialists in comparative economic systems who have made qualitative judgments of these matters on a four-point scale for various economies.[18] Since truth does not necessarily reside in majority opinion, we can object to the results; unfortunately, this is the only quantitative rating of the degree of government planning and administration of the economy that is available.

18. The results of this survey were presented by Myron H. Ross, "Fluctations in Economic Activity," *American Economic Review,* LV, March 1965, pp. 158–61.

Using the three indicators of "socialism," namely the relative share of government ownership, current public expenditures for goods and services in the G.N.P., and the relative importance of governmental planning, the "socialist web" hypothesis would lead us to predict a clustering of nations into two categories: one in which the nations rated low on all three criteria; and the other in which the nations rated high on all three. In Table 1–4 I present the relevant data according to these three indicators; the first and the last categories represent the extreme cases that provide the test for the theory.

Assuming that my various indicators for dimensions of socialism are adequate, several important conclusions can be drawn from the table:

First, the twelve nations are spread over the spectrum with six out of the eight categories containing at least one nation. As predicted, there is a clustering of nations in the top and bottom categories which contain one-half of the nations in the sample. While this suggests that the "socialist web" hypothesis contains a grain of truth, predictions based on the hypothesis are correct only 50 percent of the time.

Second, the congruence between nations differs, depending on the choice of indicators. Between the relative degree of public ownership and the relative degree of governmental planning and administration, ten of the twelve nations have the same rating; between relative public ownership and relative public expenditures, eight of the twelve nations are the same; and between relative public expenditures and relative governmental planning and administration, only six of the twelve nations are the same. The last two results can be due strictly to chance.

The low degree of association between public expenditures on the one hand and either government ownership or government planning and administration on the other hand gives additional empirical support to the conclusion derived from Table 1–3 where nations in East and West Europe are compared. The stronger relationship between government ownership and government planning and administration of the economy does not seem surprising, but it is important to emphasize that the correlation is far from perfect.

Third, the mediocre showing of the "socialist web" hypothesis means that the exercise of particular property rights by various governments cannot be adequately predicted by knowledge of one such property right; and, further, for many purposes classification of economic systems using one criterion may not be very useful. In other words, an economic theory of property is much more than a study of ownership and a single-criterion approach toward property and economic systems leaves much unanalyzed that examination of other types of property rights shows to be essential for a broader understanding of the functioning of an economy.

Much, of course, remains to be explored in the relationships between ownership and other property rights or between ownership and economic system. The empirical exercise carried on above has been intended to clear away some dead wood from the subject so that the investigations of income rights or ownership pursued in later chapters can proceed more quickly.

TABLE 1–4

Combinations of Indicators of "Socialism" with Examples from West Europe and North America[a]

Degree of Public Ownership	Extent of Current Public Expenditures	Degree of National Planning	Examples
Relatively high	Relatively high	Relatively high	France, Norway, Sweden
Relatively high	Relatively high	Relatively low	Austria
Relatively high	Relatively low	Relatively high	Netherlands, United Kingdom
Relatively high	Relatively low	Relatively low	
Relatively low	Relatively high	Relatively high	
Relatively low	Relatively high	Relatively low	Canada, West Germany
Relatively low	Relatively low	Relatively high	Belgium
Relatively low	Relatively low	Relatively low	Greece, Switzerland, United States

a. It must be emphasized that the placing of each country along a "socialist-nonsocialist continuum" for each criterion is made only by reference to the sample. There are twelve nations in the sample and the dividing line is drawn between the 6th and 7th nations in each ranking. If different nations are included in the sample, then the various nations may fit into different categories.

The relative degree of public ownership is determined from data from Table 1–1 using both the total-asset and the total labor-force indicators. For Greece, an inference is made that government assets are relatively small from data presented in Chapter II. The dividing line is between Norway and the Netherlands (relatively high) and Canada (relatively low).

The relative extent of public expenditures is determined from the ratio of current governmental consumption expenditures plus transfers to households to the gross national product in factor prices. The data are for the year 1962 and come from United Nations, *Yearbook of National Account Statistics 1967* (New York: 1968). The dividing line is between 26 and 27 percent and, in terms of nations, between Norway (relatively high) and the United Kingdom (relatively low).

The relative degree of national economic planning comes from a series of ratings presented by Ross and is discussed in the text. Switzerland was not included in this survey but I have judged it to have a relatively low degree of governmental national economic planning and administration. The dividing line is between Belgium (relatively high) and Austria (relatively low).

D. Bureaucratic Decision-making and Property

A large majority of the production decisions in modern economies, capitalist or socialist, are made by hired managers, rather than by the actual owners of the means of production. If we are trying to develop a theory of property, we must pay close attention to the exercising of control rights by bureaucrats. Such a task raises many problems and the purpose of this brief discussion is to illustrate on a micro-economic level the most severe difficulties. In investigating bureaucracies, two problems immediately arise.

First, although many control rights exercised by a bureaucracy are individually held (albeit in a conditional manner), others are exercised by groups in extremely complex ways. Hence, to determine responsibility for particular decisions by individuals or groups may be quite difficult.

Second, the utilization of many property rights within an administrative hierarchy to achieve a particular goal is no automatic matter and, indeed, may require considerable effort. Many a high official or functionary has tried to exercise a particular property right and has found that his commands have been subverted and that he has been totally unable to enforce "his rights." Problems of enforcement, particularly where state power cannot be relied upon, raises numerous difficulties concerning incentives, authority, information, and leadership.

In looking at property rights exercised within any given organization, we can ask a wide variety of questions about the pattern of these rights as well as questions about the impact of such patterns on the actual production decisions that are made. In order to provide specific examples of these questions and, at the same time, to show the relevance of empirical studies of organizations to be presented in later chapters, I would like to examine briefly different patterns of property rights in seemingly similar enterprises in two nations. To make the discussion more specific, I have selected twenty-five important enterprise decisions and designate in Table 1–5 whether each decision is formally made by the enterprise manager and his subordinates, or by the workers and their representatives, or by some higher authority (or the market), or by some combination of these three groups.

The overall patterns in the table are quite clear: Control rights (or decision-making) appears more centralized in some sense in the Soviet Union than in Yugoslavia. In the Soviet Union the bulk of the twenty-five decisions appears to be made by higher organs (e.g., the *Glavk* or the Ministry) and the manager's major role appears to be transmitting such decisions to the proper enterprise personnel and taking responsibility for their implementation. In Yugoslavia, the pattern is quite different. Most of the decisions are formally made by a Workers' Council, with the

TABLE 1–5

*Formal Decision-making Powers in Government-owned
Coal Mining Enterprises in Two Nations*[a]

Country	Soviet Union			Yugoslavia		
Decision level	H	M	W	H	M	W
Decision						
Production						
1. Overall volume of production	H					W
2. Assortment of coal produced	H				M	
3. Non-coal goods produced	H					W
4. Total labor to be used	H	M			M	W
5. Types of labor to be employed		M			M	
6. Labor productivity norms	H				M	
7. Major raw materials to be used	H				M	
8. Production techniques	H	M			M	W
9. Important buyers of products	H	M			M	
10. Important suppliers of raw materials	H	M			M	
Financial						
1. Goals for total profit or loss	H					W
2. Goals for total wage bill	H				M	W
3. Wage rate	H			H	M	W
4. Goals for total costs of materials	H			H	M	
5. Goals for overall costs	H					W
6. Major investments	H					W
7. Investment finance sources	H			H	M	
8. Prices	H			H	M	W
9. Working capital	H					W
10. Type of accounting system	H			H		
Organizational						
1. Most important organizational changes	H	M			M	W
2. Management techniques		M			M	
3. Selection of key personnel	H	M			M	
4. Methods of labor relations	H			H	M	W
5. Types of bonuses	H	M		H	M	W

H = higher authority;

M = enterprise manager and his subordinates;

W = councils of workers' representatives or unions.

a. For the Soviet Union and Yugoslavia I consider such enterprises in the middle and late 1960s; much more information concerning these economies and the enterprises at that time are presented in Chapter VII.

In the table the higher authorities include planning organs, ministries, intermediate organs, or city and regional economic organs. Further, this table covers only the most important decisions; no matter how centralized a production hierarchy may be, the enterprise managers are permitted to make certain production decisions.

To compile this table I relied on a wide range of sources too numerous to mention and, in addition, received some helpful assistance from various members of the East European team of the International Development Research Center of Indiana University.

manager's formal role limited to relatively unimportant or technical decisions and the presentation of materials to the council for approval. The organization of public enterprises in other countries is still different. For example, in West Germany most of the decisions in the few publicly owned mining enterprises appear to be made by the enterprise director alone or, in certain cases, with the concurrence of boards containing worker representatives (e.g., *Aufsichtsrat*). In the United Kingdom, a different pattern can be found in the mining sector where all publicly owned coal mines are operated as a single enterprise (the Coal Board) which operates under the aegis of Parliament.

However, we cannot easily make firm judgments about the exercising of property rights from the formal decision-making powers because of the importance of informal procedures as well. In the Soviet Union higher authorities may lack relevant information for independent decision-making and may merely "ratify" the managers' own desires; or they may be unable to enforce their decisions so that the managers go their own way. Conversely, the managers' formal powers may turn out to be limited because of informal constraints that are placed on their exercise of their formal property rights.[19] In the United Kingdom, the enterprise manager's formal (and legal) decision-making powers may be illusory, for we read: "Ministers not only exert a continuous general supervision over the [public] corporations, but they also intervene to alter or influence specific decisions or major policies; and no Board today would take such a decision without first 'clearing' it with the Ministry."[20] In other words, we have an extralegal system of sharing control rights or, at least, a much more restricted set of control rights exercised by the Coal Board than formal powers would suggest. Finally, for Yugoslavia we have considerable evidence that although the Workers' Councils have great formal authority, in most production decisions the manager very much has his own way.[21]

19. A manager may have the formal right to determine the enterprise labor force, but if the total wage bill and the average wage rates are determined from above (which was the case in the Soviet Union), the manager's sphere of independent decision-making (i.e., his control rights) is limited.

Of course, the degree of control a superior has over a subordinate depends greatly on the information system, the system of incentives, and the system of sanctions. Thus property rights are determined by many aspects of the system that are not "formal" or "legal."

20. C.A.R. Crosland, "The Private and Public Corporations in Great Britain," in E. S. Mason, ed., *The Corporation in Modern Society* (Cambridge, Mass.: 1959), pp. 260–77.

21. Such evidence is presented in Jiri Kolaja, *Workers' Councils: The Yugoslav Experience* (New York: 1965) and Josip Zupanov, "The Distribution of Control in some Yugoslav Industrial Organizations as Perceived by Members," in Arnold S. Tannenbaum, ed., *Control in Organization* (New York: 1968).

Such an exercise illustrates well the complex ways in which control rights may be shared and the fluidity of rights arising because of difficulties of enforcing them.[22] These difficulties are compounded when we try to determine the impact of particular property-right patterns on production decisions, for we must have considerably more data, especially to discover how particular decisions concerning certain rights are coordinated. Despite the difficulty in carrying out such a task, we must begin to tackle such matters if we are to gain insight into the determinants of organizational behavior or the impact of particular patterns of control rights on the success or failure of particular systems. Different types of attempts to attack such problems are found throughout this study.

Given differences in the patterns of control rights exercised by different groups, what differences arise in the actual behavior of an organization? For the most part this question has been attacked in terms of the incentives facing the single major decision-maker. However, in situations where various groups with different incentives interact and exercise control rights together, the traditional approach may be insufficient. Because of important environmental differences facing organizations in various countries, this problem is perhaps most adequately investigated by looking at the differential behavior of organizations with different control-right patterns within the same economy. The effects of different degrees of enterprise centralization on enterprise behavior or the effects of manager-domination rather than owner-domination of enterprises are examined in later chapters.

E. Theories of Property

A brief review of different propositions about property gives insight into the variety of property theories and permits perspective to be gained on the various studies presented in this book.

First, it is important to distinguish positive and normative theories of property. Positive theories link particular features of property to types of human behavior in a manner that can be empirically tested. For instance, Schiller once declared, "Man must have something to call his own, or he will murder and burn,"[23] a proposition that can be tested with data on criminal activity by those who do and do not own property. Nor-

---

22. Interesting case studies of the organization and administration of nationalized enterprises in various Western nations are presented in W. G. Friedmann and J. F. Garner, eds., *Government Enterprise: A Comparative Study* (New York: 1970).

23. "Etwas muss er sein eigen nennen, oder der Mensch wird morden und brennen." Friedrich Schiller, *Wallensteins Lager,* 1st Part.

mative theories apply value judgments to manifestations of property and focus on the "ought" or the "should"; they cannot be easily tested empirically. An example is Proudhon's famous declaration, "Property is theft,"[24] a statement about the moral worth of existing ownership relationships that was not (I think) meant literally. Although positive and normative realms of discourse may not be as distinct as economists like to believe, it is analytically useful to attempt to separate them. In this study I try to focus exclusive attention on positive theories in order to develop verifiable propositions about the operation of economic systems as they currently are; I leave normative considerations of such systems to the discussions of philosophers, poets, revolutionaries, and exploiters.

Positive theories of property are usually concerned with one of two types of questions: First, what factors explain the emergence, distribution, or pattern of particular property relations ("developmental theories")? Second, what are the effects of particular types and patterns of property rights on individual or group behavior ("impact theories")? Particular theories of societal change that include both developmental and impact hypotheses of property can be designated as "laws of motion" and are the final aim of property theories.

A large number of developmental theories have linked the emergence, distribution, or pattern of property to economic development. Marx, for instance, predicted a centralization of capital accompanying higher levels of development and Engel's theory of the origins of private property relates the emergence of slavery to the degree to which production in a society exceeds the biological minimum.[25] A number of continental economists, particularly Germans in the nineteenth century, proposed stage theories that sought to link the predominant form of property relations to the level of economic development and defined particular "stages" through which all economies must pass.[26] Modern Western

24. "La propriete, c'est le vol." Pierre Joseph Proudhon, *Qu'est-ce que la propriete?*

25. Karl Marx, *Capital,* Vol. I (Moscow: 1961); and Friedrich Engels, *The Origin of the Family, Private Property, and the State* (New York: n.d.). Engel's approach receives a modern quantitative extension in Frederic L. Pryor, "Property Rights and Economic Development," *Economic Development and Cultural Change,* XXI, April 1972, pp. 200–30, a study originally written for this volume.

26. For a review of such theories see Bert F. Hoselitz, "Theories of Stages of Economic Growth," in Bert F. Hoselitz, ed., *Theories of Economic Growth* (Glencoe, Ill.: 1960), pp. 193–238. Many of these stage theories do not, however, focus on property rights. The Marxist stage theory, which is the most persistent in linking property and development is in some disarray, particularly because crucial issues concerning two of the five stages (namely slave holding and feudal societies) have not been successfully resolved after Marx's *Grundrisse der Kritik der politischen Oekonomie* (East Berlin: 1953; earlier editions appeared in the 1930s) was unearthed and published. The

theories along these lines include the hypothesis of Adolf A. Berle and Gardiner C. Means that, with rising levels of economic development, a separation occurs between ownership and control of productive enterprises in capitalist economies;[27] or Kenneth Boulding's hypothesis that a rising level of economic development has been accompanied by a fall in the costs of maintaining organizations and, as a result, property is becoming increasingly concentrated in the hands of leaders of large organizations.[28] This list could be considerably lengthened but is sufficient to give a concrete notion of this genre of developmental theories.

A second type of developmental theory relates the emergence, distribution, or pattern of property rights to particular features of the economy other than development. These include Steven Cheung's hypothesis linking the relative prevalence of sharecropping and quit-rent tenure arrangements to the degree of fluctuations of various crops;[29] Evsey Domar's theory showing the relationship of serfdom or slavery to the existence of a rent-receiving class and the availability of empty fertile agricultural land;[30] hypotheses on the determinants of the distribution of property rights (power and rewards) in work organizations;[31] or hypotheses about the emergence of particular property rights to different types of externalities.[32] Again, the literature on such matters is large and embraces very different theoretical approaches.

Impact theories of property focus on the effects of particular property patterns. One type of such theory deals with the influence of particular property rights or property institutions on production behavior. Included in this category are theories that assume maximization behavior

---

state of Marxist theory on these matters is chronicled by Eric J. Hobsbawn in his "Introduction" to his edited edition of Marx's *Precapitalist Economic Formations* (New York: 1965).

27. Adolf A. Berle and Gardiner C. Means, *The Modern Corporation and Private Property* (New York: 1933).

28. Kenneth Boulding, *The Organizational Revolution* (New York: 1953).

29. Steven N. S. Cheung, *The Theory of Share Tenancy* (Chicago: 1970).

30. Evsey Domar, "The Causes of Slavery or Serfdom: A Hypothesis," *Journal of Economic History*, XXX, March 1970.

31. For example, Stanley H. Udy, Jr., *Organization of Work* (New Haven: 1959).

32. An economist working along these lines is Harold Demsetz, "Toward a Theory of Property Rights," *American Economic Review*, LVII, May 1967, pp. 347–60. Several interesting hypotheses, especially in regard to food sharing in herding and agricultural societies, are discussed by Marshall D. Sahlins, "On the Sociology of Primitive Exchange," in Michael Banton, ed., *The Relevance of Models for Social Anthropology*, Association for Social Anthropology Monograph No. 1 (London: 1965), pp. 139–86 although the author does not conduct his argument using the term "externalities" or other economic jargon.

and inquire into the impact on production behavior of various land-tenure arrangements,[33] government regulations,[34] or taxes.[35] Other examples deal with maximization of variables other than total profits under different property arrangements in family enterprises,[36] capitalist corporate enterprises,[37] socialist firms,[38] different types of producer cooperatives,[39] or other production units.[40] As noted above, property rights serve

33. While this book was in press, an excellent survey article of a wide number of impact theories of property appeared by Eirik Furubotn and Svetozar Pejovich, "Property Rights and Economic Theory: A Survey of Recent Literature," *Journal of Economic Literature*, X, December 1972, pp. 1137–62. The citations in this and the following notes contain only those studies which I have found to be most representative of the genre. On a theoretical side the literature is summarized by Cheung, *Share Tenancy*, and Steven N. S. Cheung, "Private Property Rights and Sharecropping," *Journal of Political Economy*, LXXVI, November-December 1968, pp. 1107–23. There is also a considerable amount of empirical studies, e.g., William R. Cline, *Economic Consequences of a Land Reform in Brazil* (Amsterdam: 1970); Walter G. Miller, *et al.*, *Relative Efficiencies of Farm Tenure Classes in Intrafirm Resource Allocation*, North Central Regional Publication No. 84, Iowa Agricultural Experiment Station Bulletin 461 (Iowa: 1958), or Virgil L. Hurlburt, *Uses of Farm Resources as Conditioned by Tenure Arrangements*, North Central Regional Publication No. 151, Nebraska College of Agriculture Research Bulletin 215 (Nebraska: 1964).

34. There are a number of theoretical studies such as H. Averch and L. Johnson, "The Firm under Regulatory Constraint," *American Economic Review*, LXX, December 1962, pp. 1052–69; or L. G. Telser, "On the Regulation of Industry," *Journal of Political Economy*, LXXVII, November-December 1969, pp. 937–52. On the empirical side, much less has been done; one notable exception to this generalization is an article by George J. Stigler and Claire Friedland, "What Can Regulators Regulate? The Case of Electricity," *The Journal of Law and Economics*, V, October 1962, pp. 1–16.

35. The public finance literature has a plethora of such studies, and more appear each year. Empirical testing of the various hypotheses has considerably lagged the theoretical work, however.

36. Enormous battles, especially between economic historians, have arisen concerning the family firm, what exactly it is maximizing, and what its behavior is under certain circumstances. These are summarized by Arthur Schweitzer, "Comparative Enterprise and Economic Systems," *Explorations in Economic History*, March 1970, pp. 413–32.

37. There is a growing literature about whether corporate managers maximize sales, profits, or something else, of which three pioneering books are: William Baumol, *Business Behavior, Value and Growth* (New York: 1959); Robin Marris, *The Economic Theory of Managerial Capitalism* (New York: 1964); and Oliver E. Williamson, *The Economics of Discretionary Behavior: Managerial Objectives in a Theory of the Firm* (Englewood Cliffs: 1964).

38. E.g., Joseph S. Berliner, *Factor and Manager in the U.S.S.R.* (Cambridge, Mass.: 1957); Edward Ames, *Soviet Economic Processes* (Homewood, Ill.: 1965); or János Kornai and Th. Lipták, "A Mathematical Investigation of Some Economic Effects of Profit Sharing in Socialist Firms," *Econometrica*, XXX, January 1962, pp. 140–61.

39. A growing literature on these problems exists: Benjamin Ward, "The Firm in Illyria," *American Economic Review*, XLVIII, September

as constraints in many different kinds of maximization processes in the economy and analyses of such problems are as old as the economic literature.[41]

A second type of impact theory concerns the link between different types and patterns of property rights and the consequences for the behavior of the entire economy. Examples on the theoretical side of the economic literature are the Walrasian general equilibrium system, Marx's theory of crisis, or various attempts to work out micro-economic models of socialist economies.[42] Examples on the empirical side are studies of the difference in performance of capitalist and socialist economies (which are reviewed in Chapter VIII) or attempts by political scientists to link the distribution of property to the level of domestic violence.[43]

A large proportion of the propositions of these four different types of positive theories of property has not been adequately tested. Although this has been due in part to difficulties in quantification and of obtaining relevant data, other causal factors must also be taken into consideration. As suggested at the beginning of this chapter, comparative economists have generally preferred to focus on the "big picture" and to avoid quantitative work. Although in some circumstances theoretical analysis is very useful, it is often counter-productive if resting on an extremely narrow empirical base, the situation that now characterizes comparative economic systems. To avoid being open to such accusations myself, it is propitious to outline briefly what kinds of propositions about property

1958, pp. 566–89; Evsey Domar, "The Soviet Collective Farm as a Producer Cooperative," *American Economic Review,* LVI, September 1966, pp. 734–57; Amartya K. Sen, "Labor Allocation in a Cooperative Enterprise," *The Review of Economic Studies,* XXXIII, October 1966, pp. 361–71; Walter Y. Oi and E. M. Clayton, "A Peasant's View of a Soviet Collective Farm," *American Economic Review,* LVIII, March 1968, pp. 37–68; and Jaroslav Vanek, *The General Theory of Labor-Managed Market Economies* (Ithaca: 1970). As far as I know, not one proposition of this literature has been empirically tested. Certain case studies, e.g., Eliyahu Kanovsky, *The Economy of the Israeli Kibbutz* (Cambridge, Mass.: 1966) do provide a useful bit of realism to the discussion.

40. E.g., L. S. Shapley and Martin Shubik, "Ownership and the Production Function," *The Quarterly Journal of Economics,* LXXI, February 1967, pp. 88–111.

41. Adam Smith's *Wealth of Nations* (published 1776) is full of such propositions. In the organization theory literature, there is also a wide range of such theories; these are surveyed in James G. March, ed., *Handbook of Organizations* (Chicago: 1965). The most systematic large-scale approach I have seen in the organization theory literature is by James D. Thompson, *Organization of Action* (New York: 1967).

42. E.g., Ames, Vanek, or various models of the socialist business cycle.

43. An interesting empirical investigation along these lines is by Bruce M. Russett, "Inequality and Instability: The Relation of Land Tenure to Politics," *World Politics,* XVI, April 1964, pp. 442–55.

and industrial organization I plan to examine and how I will carry out their empirical analysis.

F. Plan of Attack and an Overview

Three methodological premises underlying all the empirical studies in the following chapters should be made explicit. First, in exploring economic institutions, comparative analyses of many nations is an extremely fruitful approach. To this end, I have tried to extend the analysis to as many economies as time and expertise allowed. Second, quantitative analysis usually permits more conclusive results than other types of argumentation. Therefore, I have tried to quantify particular aspects of property institutions, a task that has some obvious pitfalls but which, on the other hand, allows greater certainty if successful. Finally, the testing of hypotheses deduced from a set of assumptions is the most desirable method of examining the adequacy of a theory or a set of concepts. Whenever possible, therefore, I have tried to deduce and test the empirical consequences of the various theoretical ideas about property that are presented in each chapter.

There is nothing extraordinary about these three methodological premises in most fields of science. However, I make them explicit here because they are so seldom applied in the study of comparative economic systems.

A warning should be sounded about the data used for this study. The problems of obtaining comparable data are among the most serious difficulties that arise in trying to test propositions about property. For the most part I have confined myself to data from nations in West and East Europe and from a handful of developed nations on other continents, all of which publish relatively extensive information on their economies.

In order to lighten the burdens placed on the reader, all technical terms used in the analysis are defined in a glossary at the end. Notes on sources and methods of calculating many of the tables as well as most of the digressions and comments on arcane points are placed in a series of appendices. Although value judgments are impossible to avoid, especially in the choice of materials, I have tried to make them explicit. Finally, I have avoided political, social, and psychological speculations which may have great ethical appeal but which would divert our attention from the way in which actual economic systems and institutions evolve and how they really function.

This book is composed of a number of empirical studies, each of which can be read independently of the others, around the central theme of property and industrial organization in nations with different economic systems. The overall organization of the book is straightforward: The next three chapters focus on problems concerning income rights or ownership while the following four chapters center on problems concerning control rights, ending with an exploration of the concept of centralization and how it is manifested in different economies. The book ends with a chapter placing the various investigations of property in a broader context.

In order to indicate the type of propositions investigated, each of the chapters deserves brief discussion. In Chapter II, I examine which sectors and branches in various economies feature the highest degree of public ownership. A very clear pattern among nations emerges and a number of developmental hypotheses to explain this pattern are tested in order to isolate the most important causal forces. In Chapter III, I investigate the impact of the distribution of property on the distribution of income and, more specifically, try to show that the inequality of labor income is more important than property income in explaining differences in the inequality of income among capitalist and socialist nations. And in Chapter IV, I study on a micro-economic level patterns of the distribution of property, institutional factors underlying the distribution of ownership, and the relationship between ownership and control. In addition to these developmental hypotheses, I summarize the various attempts to determine the impact of the alleged separation of ownership and control on actual enterprise behavior.

The four essays on control rights focus on clusters of such rights that are useful to examine together. In Chapters V and VI, I explore the sizes and size distributions of industrial establishments and enterprises, both at a single point in time and also over the last half century. Size is defined not only in an absolute sense but also vis-à-vis relevant markets so that monopolization phenomena can be studied. A number of developmental hypotheses are tested. In Chapter VII, I examine the economic reforms carried out in Eastern Europe during the late sixties in order to determine the degree to which certain changes in control rights were correlated. And in Chapter VIII, I analyze the concept of centralization in order to investigate a number of developmental and impact hypotheses, especially concerning the role of economic system, on this important attribute of the pattern of control rights.

The final chapter serves to relate the various explorations of property rights to a broader view of economic systems. I distinguish three major elements of economic systems—the structures of property, motivation, and information—and try to show how study of their interrelations permits a more comprehensive investigation of the operation of economic systems. Using this framework I also investigate the alleged convergence of economic systems and show that most discussions of the question have omitted many important considerations, and that the case for convergence is quite unsatisfactory.

Property has many manifestations and can be viewed from many different perspectives. The only justification for its exploration by economists is the degree to which such an exercise can be used to answer important old economic questions or to raise new ones. This means that economists must be able to avoid following interpretations of the property concept which discourage empirical research and testing of hypotheses, a situation which has unfortunately occurred in some of the other social science disciplines. The admonition greeting Dante on his descent into the underworld, cited at the beginning of this chapter, is useful to observe for those wishing to explore the economics of property; the broadness of the concept should not blind us to the fact that economic analysis can best be served by carefully applying and interpreting the concept of property in particular ways. Now is the time to attempt this task.

CHAPTER II

The Pattern of Public Ownership in Developed Economies

> However, is it better for a city which is to
> regulate its life aright to have community in
> everything that it is possible to hold in com-
> mon, or better that it should have community
> only in some things and not in others?
>
> *Aristotle*[1]

A. Introduction

Although all economically developed economies have a mixture of private and public ownership of the means of production, the degree of public ownership and type of mix can differ widely. The purpose of this chapter is to explore systematically the relative degree of public ownership of the means of production (or, for short, nationalization) in different sectors and branches of a number of economies in a quantitative manner.

The analysis proceeds in two steps. Since there are a number of un-resolved theoretical issues concerning the factors determining which sectors and branches of the economy are most likely to be publicly or

---

1. Aristotle, *Politics,* Book 2, Chapter 1, paragraph 1 [translation by M. L. W. Laistner, *Greek Economics* (London: 1923)].

privately owned, these matters must be discussed. In the first part of the chapter I explore a number of current hypotheses about the most important factors underlying the pattern of nationalization such as the existence of economies of scale in particular industries or the special relationship of certain industries to national sovereignty. Although the various hypotheses are conceptually quite different, it turns out empirically that most point to economic phenomena relating to the specific aspects of the distinction between heavy and light industry.

Then I try to examine these determinants of nationalization quantitatively. In the second part of the chapter I empirically test particular hypotheses at several different levels of aggregation. For the sector level (e.g., agriculture, manufacturing, or construction), I supply data on nationalization and examine the hypotheses in an informal way since the requisite data for more exact statistical tests are not available. For the individual branches of mining and manufacturing (corresponding to the "two-digit" industries of the International Standard Industrial Classification) I present data for thirteen nations and put to statistical test most of the various hypotheses outlined in the theoretical section. From the ideas developed from examining on a cross-section basis the pattern of public ownership on both the sector and branch levels, several hypotheses are also proposed about how this pattern may vary over time; these are investigated empirically with time-series data for the United States.

B. Hypotheses

It is useful to distinguish between the motives or reasons for any particular act of nationalization and the underlying economic rationale that makes certain sectors or branches of the economy more prone to be nationalized than others. Although these two levels of analysis are sometimes related, the focus in this chapter is on the latter or more basic economic forces underlying public ownership.

As far as I have been able to determine, no one has yet advanced a general positive economic theory of public ownership that can be used for explaining differences in the relative degree of nationalization within and between nations.[2] Nevertheless, many economists have put forward ad hoc hypotheses to explain why this or that industry is or is not nation-

2. There are a number of institutional or legal theories about public ownership and nationalized industries, of which an elaborate example is provided by the Bulgarian jurist Konstatin Katzarov, *The Theory of Nationalization* (The Hague: 1964). Such studies are usually normative in character and, in any case, offer few clues why certain industries are publicly owned while others are not.

alized. As we will see, many of these hypotheses reflect different facets of the same general phenomenon and are, therefore, similar.

1. The most skeptical hypothesis is that no regularities in the degree of public ownership either between or within nations are observable since nationalization has come about for a variety of political and historical reasons that have little to do with any alleged underlying economic forces. There is considerable evidence to support this "null" hypothesis, since examples of nationalization of industry for apparently strictly political reasons are ubiquitous. The Soviet occupation of East Europe after World War II resulted in the nationalization of a large number of enterprises, especially those previously owned by Germans. After this same war, the French government nationalized most of the factories primarily owned by Nazi collaborators. In other countries, various political parties detected sinister characteristics in different industries, demanded their nationalization, and, in many cases, carried out their objectives.

Special historical factors also seem to play an important role in determining the pattern of nationalization. For instance, subsurface mineral rights have traditionally belonged to the crown in a number of continental European nations. In other cases governments have owned and operated particular industries as fiscal monopolies (e.g., alcohol, tobacco, and salt) for many centuries, acting on the belief that control of production or sales is a more effective way of raising state revenues than taxation. Another historical influence can be seen in Italy in the 1930s when the government seemed indiscriminately to take over ownership of large enterprises that were going bankrupt during the depression. Here again, although explanations can be given for each particular nationalization in a country, similarities among nations seem slight.

Turning to those hypotheses which allow some prediction of the extent and pattern of public ownership, certain difficulties arise because many of these hypotheses are not mutually exclusive. Nevertheless, three economic theories (concerning natural monopolies, externalities, and vertical mergers) and three political-economic theories (concerning unearned income, sovereignty, and "commanding heights") can be distinguished.

2. A standard textbook explanation of public ownership focuses upon economies of scale, "natural monopolies," and the optimal or minimum efficient sizes of enterprises. If the minimum efficient scale of production in a particular industry is such that an enterprise of this size would exercise considerable market power (monopoly power), then there is a tendency for the industry to be nationalized—especially if government regulation of the industry incurs certain technical difficulties. Two related factors are thus involved: economies of scale within the industry and the size of the market.

A variant of this argument is that government ownership of such natural monopolies occurs so that the government can obtain fiscal benefits by appropriating the monopoly profits. Given the poor profit performance of many public enterprises, this motive does not appear strong.

Industries in which economies of scale are said to be particularly important are utilities (water supply, electricity, sewage removal), communication (the postal and telephone systems), and transportation (especially railroads). Among particular branches of mining and manufacturing there are considerable controversies concerning the existence and importance of such factors, especially since technology and optimal capital intensities seem to be changing so rapidly. The conventional wisdom usually considers such scale factors to be more important in "heavy" than in "light" industry. Fortunately, we have a more solid base for analysis than these speculations since considerable data on such matters are available; they are presented when this hypothesis is tested.

3. A second standard economic argument is that nationalization is more likely when an industry has important positive or negative "externalities," either technological or pecuniary. These externalities are particular costs or benefits to society stemming from the production process that cannot be "properly" taken into account by a profit-motivated private entrepreneur. They are often of such a nature that it is administratively difficult for adequate indirect incentives to be set up by a public regulatory body to achieve a social optimum.

An example of a negative externality is water pollution by offshore oil drillers, the costs of which are not borne by the oil company. Most governments have shown themselves as yet incapable of properly preventing or controlling such matters. Many of the traditional examples of positive externalities are manifested in social overhead capital, e.g., multipurpose dam projects provide benefits which are difficult for private businesses to sell in order to make a profit. In many cases inducing businessmen to provide such services by means of a special system of taxes and subsidies would be an administrative nightmare. It has also been argued that such positive externalities appear in particular services such as high culture (e.g., operas), where quality for its own sake is important. Allegedly this cannot be achieved through private ownership which would be subsidized by the government since the owners would always have an incentive to reduce quality to obtain higher profits.

4. Implicit in a great many economic analyses of nationalization is an argument that public ownership is more likely to occur when there are conveniences of a vertical merger, i.e., when major cost savings arise when a production unit merges with either its major supplier of inputs or the major buyer of its output. The most extreme example of this occurs when the government is the sole buyer of a product made by a single

producer. Here the instabilities of such a bilateral monopoly situation are well known; allegedly such instabilities might be eliminated by nationalizing the monopolist supplier. In less extreme situations where the government is one of many buyers of a product made by a few producers and where negotiation and information costs are high, there may also be a tendency toward some nationalization so that such costs can be reduced or so that greater administrative simplicity may be achieved. In particular cases of such situations, the line between public and private sectors becomes sufficiently blurred (e.g., the attempt in the early 1970s by the United States Department of Defense to *give* the Lockheed Company over one half billion dollars of taxpayers' money on grounds of "national security" to stave off a pending bankruptcy of the company) that the ideological arguments for "private enterprise" for such industrial sectors become confounded. (On these and other grounds, John Kenneth Galbraith has proposed that the United States nationalize the companies that supply aircraft and missiles to the government.) Thus, if the transportation sector is nationalized, one could conclude from consideration of the conveniences of vertical mergers that ship- or locomotive-building enterprises might also be owned publicly. In certain situations such as printing, where the government is a large buyer but where there are many buyers and sellers, a vertical merger might also provide certain administrative savings (e.g., the cost of negotiating contracts), and a tendency toward nationalization might be present here as well.

One situation relating to this hypothesis deserves special attention: those cases where the government is the principal buyer of a good or service which is then distributed gratis to the public. For instance, although the economic logic for a policy to eliminate public schools and to give pupil grants to private schools seems very strong to some, only three economically developed nations in the world (Belgium, Ireland, and the Netherlands) actually operate such a system on an extensive scale. The alleged administrative or economic convenience of vertical mergers (of governmental buyers of education and various suppliers of educational services) might provide an insight into the reasons underlying the *status quo* in most nations. From such considerations it could be argued that there is a high degree of correlation between extensive public expenditure and ownership, a proposition that is a facet of the "socialist web" argument discussed and empirically explored in the previous chapter.

5. A political-economic argument concerning nationalization is that public ownership occurs more often in those industries where "unearned income" is important. Such income could arise from one or more of the following three different cases: a "natural monopoly" (see hypothesis 2 above); a monopoly arising from particular historical circumstances (this

would seem to be covered in the null hypothesis); and extra high economic rents arising from ownership of some property, the value of which often has relatively little to do with the individual merit or work or ability of the owners. The latter case would occur, for instance, in the case of valuable mineral resources which are discovered on a particular property and, indeed, this hypothesis suggests that nationalization might be relatively high in mining, even though the government did not "traditionally" own subsurface mineral rights.

6. Considerations of economic and political sovereignty can also be brought into the analysis of the pattern of public ownership. It is sometimes argued that a tendency toward nationalization exists in those industries that provide a base for great political or economic power that affects the security of the nation as a whole. This is especially true of the postal system (which, incidentally, is nationalized in every developed country of the world); the type of power base it provides is shown in certain ancient despotic societies where the Postmaster General was simultaneously the head of the internal security apparatus.[3] Similarly, defense is a vital aspect of political sovereignty and, therefore, most governmental leaders are loath to permit private armies in their territories or to allow the private accumulation of mortars, torpedoes, and other instruments of war. Since rapid transportation of troops is often a vital necessity, certain transportation industries might also be nationalized. The energy and fuel industries might be similarly viewed. Finally, in certain low-density countries the territorial integrity is served by governmental attempts to populate the border regions through its building of productive facilities.

Aside from these cases that deal primarily with internal political aspects of sovereignty, it can be argued that criteria can be established for economic sovereignty as well, if we define this concept in terms of lack of dependency on "outsiders." For a government this would mean that it would control or own the source of its most important inputs (either intermediate products or final goods); and for the nation as a whole, this would mean that those industries primarily engaged in supplying inputs for other industries would be nationalized. It is reported that certain Pakistan socialists were trying to make this argument more specific by recourse to certain calculations based on input-output tables; by means of a similar procedure I try to make the economic sovereignty argument more concrete in order to test its influence on nationalization in a later section of this chapter.

7. The sovereignty argument can be extended by reference to the "commanding heights" of the economy, or "vital industries" or "industries serving the nation as a whole."

3. Various facets of state ownership in such "oriental" economies are discussed by Karl A. Wittfogel, *Oriental Despotism: A Comparative Study of Total Power* (New Haven: 1957).

The doctrine of the "commanding heights" is primarily advanced by Marxists in their arguments concerning the preconditions for rapid national economic growth. More specifically, any nation wishing to experience such rapid growth must have a nationalized sector of a certain critical size and composition; otherwise, governmental direction of the economy is supposedly ineffective because of difficulties in implementing any major development plan. Underlying this argument is an assumption about the relative ineffectiveness of indirect, as opposed to direct measures, to encourage economic growth. Such a doctrine has, of course, some obvious difficulties, of which not the least is the problem of outlining adequate criteria to designate which specific industries are, or should be, publicly owned.[4]

Arguments for nationalization based on notions of "vital industries" or "industries serving the nation as a whole" are usually made by non-Marxist socialists. For instance, the United Kingdom Trade Unions Congress drafted a policy statement in 1944 which proclaimed a vital industries doctrine and which presented a specific list of such industries that was headed by fuel and power, and followed by transport, iron and steel, and textiles. Although various criteria used in this selection were presented, the deductions of these specific industries from such criteria were, to put it mildly, subjective.

Since these arguments do not lead to a specific designation of industries that are, or should be, nationalized, it is difficult to analyze their empirical importance. It might be argued that we should investigate the order in which industries were nationalized if and when the particular political groups advocating such doctrines came into power. For instance, after the Bolshevik revolution in Russia the sequence of nationalization occurred along the following lines: agricultural land; banks, maritime transport; foreign enterprises; large-scale industry (first iron and steel, then chemicals, oil, and textiles); insurance; and so forth. On the other hand, the order of nationalization followed by various Marxist parties in Eastern Europe after World War II was quite different.

Two major difficulties arise in studying the sequence in which industries are nationalized to gain insight into the economic forces underlying governmental ownership. First, distinguishing the relative roles of doctrine and political reality are almost impossible. The doctrine is vague and the administrative ability of a government to take over a particular industry may play the most important role in the process. Second, know-

---

4. Most standard Marxist texts are quite vague on the concrete meaning of "commanding heights." For instance, in O. W. Kuusinen, *et al., Fundamentals of Marxism-Leninism* (Moscow: n.d.), Chapter 22, references are made to "big industry" such as transport, banks, agricultural estates, and industries owned by foreigners. In other Marxist texts [e.g., Akademiia nauk SSSR, Institut economiki, *Politicheskaia ekonomiia, uchebnik* (Moscow: 1955)] the meaning of the concept is assumed, rather than discussed.

ing which industries are "commanding heights" does not really tell us
anything about the underlying economic factors leading to nationalization
(just as in the area of consumer economics, studying revealed preferences
does not explain the factors underlying the relative desires of buyers for
particular goods). A problem of circularity is also encountered, namely
using the pattern of nationalization to explain the pattern of nationalizing.

Since I cannot formulate the doctrine of the "commanding heights"
to yield any specific predictions as to which particular industries are
nationalized, further discussion of this hypothesis does not seem profitable
for this empirical study.

In short, to explain the extent and the pattern of public ownership,
we have a "null" hypothesis that no successful economic analysis can be
made and, in addition, five hypotheses permitting prediction about particular patterns that would be revealed from comparable data about
nationalization. Three of these stem from strictly economic arguments:
the natural monopolies, externalities, and vertical merger hypotheses; and
two of them stem from political-economic arguments: the unearned income and the sovereignty hypotheses.

Several peculiarities of these hypotheses must be immediately noted.
First, many of them spring from normative arguments about the failure to
reach some "social optimum" through private ownership. Although
normative arguments can be used to derive useful hypotheses about actual
states of affairs (e.g., Ricardo's normative theory of comparative advantage to predict actual trade patterns), we must exercise caution in
making this leap from normative to positive economics. Second, many
of the hypotheses are not mutually exclusive and it is quite possible to
have several of the economic forces leading to nationalization operating
at the same time. And finally, conclusive tests of many of these hypotheses
would require highly disaggregated data in order to minimize intercorrelations between the explanatory variables (e.g., in the communications
sector as a whole, economies of scale, externalities, conveniences of vertical mergers, and sovereignty aspects all seem to operate and lead toward
nationalization).

C. The Quantity and Quality of Data

Two types of distinct problems concerning data arise: those relating
to measurement of nationalization and those relating to the measurement
of variables to use in testing the various hypotheses. The former problems
are briefly discussed below; the latter are examined in the next section.

Surprising as it may seem, it is extremely difficult to determine the
share of public ownership of the means of production for most countries.
Although a considerable amount of data exists on scattered industries,

the comparability of such data is doubtful and it is dangerous to use such data in order to build up aggregates.[5] Therefore, it is necessary to adopt the alternative procedure of disaggregating data covering the entire economy and to try to circumvent a number of problems that are due to inadequacies in the official statistics.[6] The raw materials for the estimates presented below are primary sources from the various nations, supplemented by information received in response to letters of inquiry to governmental statistical offices of most developed nations; further details of the particular sources are supplied in Appendix B-2.

The most suitable measure for the degree of nationalization is the percentage of physical capital (land, buildings, machinery) in a nation that is owned by various bureaus and agencies at every level of government; however, except in a few nations such data are not available in a sufficient degree of detail to permit separation by industrial sectors and branches. Indeed, the only data available for comparisons of the degree of nationalization in different economic branches and sectors in many nations are the number of economically active population or the labor force in publicly owned establishments and units (including establishments owned 50 percent or more by any governmental agency), from which ratios to the total labor force can easily be calculated. Although assets, not labor, are nationalized, this imperfect measure provides the only method by which any comparative study of nationalization can be carried out. It must be emphasized that this labor measure—designated in the rest of the chapter as the "nationalization ratio"—does not correspond exactly to the definition of ownership that is presented in Chapter I and, furthermore, yields results that are numerically different from those based on other measures of public ownership such as the share of productive assets or even the share of production. Nevertheless, whatever measure of nationalization is selected, consistent conclusions about the relative degree of public ownership in different branches and sectors of the economy will probably be obtained.[7]

5. Building up estimates from scattered data has other difficulties, not the least of which is the sin of omission. For instance, my estimates of public ownership in France are considerably higher than those of Centre européen de l'enterprise publique, *Les enterprises publiques dans la Communauté Economique Européene* (Paris: 1967) which constructed its estimates from scattered data.

6. For instance, certain nations such as Italy include enterprises owned by local governments in the "private" sector in the official statistics; other nations such as Sweden put certain wholly or partially governmentally owned corporations in the "private" sector; while still other countries such as Canada publish few usable statistics on public ownership at all.

7. One indication of such consistent conclusions using different measures of public ownership may be seen in the comparisons that employ both labor and capital measures presented in Table 1-1.

Although I have made considerable effort to adjust the data for comparability, some problems remain. First, the concept of "public ownership" in the various national statistical sources is slippery. Although most national statistics use *de jure* ownership as the criterion for "public ownership," certain exceptions are made and in some of these cases I have had to follow the statistical practices of the nation (e.g., notably the Volkswagen Company in West Germany which was legally owned by no one in the early 1950s and, therefore, was not considered "public" in the national statistics) because of lack of sufficiently detailed information to make adjustments. In certain cases the national statistics deviated from the *de jure* ownership criterion in a manner to bring the definition of ownership closer to that presented in the previous chapter (e.g., the Soviet statistics place in the "private" sector those dependents of collective farm and factory workers who cultivate small "private" plots on land formally owned by the government but who retain all receipts from the sale of their products).

Second, only "governmental" or "quasi-governmental" units are considered "public" so that producer and consumer cooperatives or enterprises owned by labor unions or charitable groups are considered to be in the private sector.[8] Third, since the nationalization ratios are based on labor-force data, the statistical handling of part-time workers and unpaid family workers in the official statistics can affect the numerical height of the nationalization ratio although incomparabilities in this respect should play an important role only in agriculture and commerce.

I have tried to organize the data to correspond to the definitions of the International Standard Industrial Classification, but certain small incomparabilities remain. The most important is due to the somewhat different statistical sectoring principles used in East and West Europe. Further, in some cases I was forced to make rough estimations although these are primarily for quantitatively unimportant magnitudes.

Finally, although the data apply to different years this should not make much difference since the pattern of nationalization for the nations in the table changed very little in the period under consideration.

8. Although production in agricultural cooperatives in East Europe is controlled by the government through plans and other directives, the farmers (with the exception of those in the Soviet Union) formally "own" the land and must bear the risks arising from crop failures, etc. alone. Those who object to such a statistical procedure may consult Appendix A-3 where data on the ratio of the economically active population working in consumer or producer cooperatives to the total economically active population in the corresponding branch or sector are presented for a number of countries. It is noteworthy that these data show a very strong pattern and can be analyzed in a way similar to the way in which the nationalization ratios are examined in the rest of this essay.

In Table 2–1, I present data on the nationalization ratios for major economic sectors as well as for the entire economies of fifteen nations. For each country the rank order of the nationalization ratio for each sector was determined and then an average rank order of sectors for the entire sample of nations was calculated; the sectors in the table are listed according to this unweighted average with the sector with the highest relative degree of nationalization at the top of the table.

In Table 2–2, I present nationalization ratios for the major branches of mining and manufacturing, again with the specific branches listed according to the unweighted average rank order of nationalization ratios in the thirteen countries of the sample. In those cases where the available statistical materials combine two branches, such branches are indicated with asterisks or other signs.

D. Statistical Tests

1. Cross-section of Nations

The hypotheses are examined at three different levels of aggregation, namely the economy as a whole, large industrial sectors (manufacturing, agriculture, or construction), and individual branches of manufacturing. Before starting to analyze the data, two general precautions must be noted. First of all, the more disaggregated the data, the easier it is to carry out meaningful statistical tests of the hypotheses. Unfortunately, comparable data at a level of disaggregation greater than the twenty-one branches of mining and manufacturing are not available. Second, most of the hypotheses are stated in a manner to allow random factors to affect individual cases; therefore, this stochastic element must be taken into consideration in the choice of a statistical method.

a. *The entire economy.* Application of the various hypotheses to the relative degree of nationalization of the economy as a whole is quite difficult since most of the hypotheses refer to specific features of individual industries. However, the economies-of-scale or natural-monopolies argument does suggest that the smaller the domestic market, the more likely an enterprise with a minimum efficient size will exercise considerable monopolistic power and, hence, the more likely the industry is to be nationalized. As I show in Chapter V, a quite adequate measure of the "size of the domestic market" is the total gross national product measured in dollars. If this is true, then there might be some relationship between the G.N.P. and the aggregate level of nationalization—an hypothesis that can be easily tested.

TABLE 2–I

Nationalization Ratios for Major Economic Sectors in Fifteen Nations[a]

Economic Sector	West Germany 1950	Japan 1960	Switzerland 1960	United States 1960	France 1954	Sweden 1960	Israel 1959	United Kingdom 1962	Yugoslavia 1953[c]	Austria 1966[d]	Finland 1965[e]	Bulgaria 1956	Poland 1960	Soviet Union 1959	East Germany 1964
Total	9%	10%	11%	15%	17%	20%	24%	25%	30%	31%	34%	37%	48%	59%	71%
Total excluding agriculture, forestry, fishing	12	14	12	16	22	22	28	26	75	33	36	92	84	96	80
Utilities[b] (electricity, gas, water, sanitation)	43	20	60	28	83	71	100	} 70	100	100	53	100	100	100	100
Transportation and communication	74	42	63	18	69	53	32		100	78	59	100	96	100	96
Services (public administration, defense, professions, other)	33	40	31	46	41	56	61	87	86	59	77	97	90	98	84
Construction	0	14	6	12	1	12	6	8	100	4	31	96	90	100	67
Manufacturing and mining	1	0	1	1	8	4	2	9	72	25	14	85	83	93	84

| Commerce and finance | 0 | 0 | 2 | 1 | 5 | 5 | 1 | f | 79 | 18 | 3 | 96 | 53 | 92 | 55 |
| Agriculture, forestry, fishing | 2 | 1 | 3 | 1 | f | 5 | 1 | 2 | 3 | 6 | 17 | 6 | 8 | 14 | 17 |

a. The "nationalization ratio" is the ratio of the economically active population in publicly owned enterprises and units to the total economically active population in the corresponding branch or sector. Sources and methods are given in Appendix B-2.

b. For Bulgaria, East Germany, Poland, the Soviet Union and Yugoslavia, only electricity production is included and the other utilities are included in the services or in manufacturing.

c. Enterprises owned by Workers' Councils are considered as government ownership because profit distribution was still quite limited in 1953.

d. Ratios are calculated from G.N.P. data rather than from labor-force data.

e. Ratios are calculated from aggregate wage data rather than from labor-force data.

f. Not available, but an estimate made to calculate the total.

TABLE 2–2

Nationalization Ratios for Major Branches of Mining and Manufacturing[a]

Branch	ISIC No.	Japan 1960	Greece 1963	Switzerland 1960	United States 1960	West Germany 1950	Norway 1964	France 1954[b]	Israel 1965[c]	Finland 1963[d]	Poland 1960[b]	East Germany 1964[b]	Hungary 1966	Bulgaria 1956
Total		0%	0%	1%	1%	1%	6%	9%	9%	13%	79%	83%	84%	85%
Highest-range nationalization ratios														
Mining and quarrying	10–19	0	3	2	0	12	23	64*	24	59	100*	100*	100*	100*
Transport equipment	38	0	1	2*	6	3	15	17	25	34	95	99	97	93**
Middle-range nationalization ratios														
Petroleum and coal products	32	0	1	0	0	0	18	64*	0	65	100*	100*	100*	100*
Primary metals	34	0	0	0**	0	2	26	0	0	22	100	100	99	100
Chemicals	31	0	0	1	1	0	0	8	29	29	88	93	91**	96†
Printing and publishing	28	2	3	0	1	0	1	6	8	3	75	74	99	94
Machinery except electrical, transport	36	0	0	2*	0	1	0	7	11	19	96	82	92	93**
Tobacco products	22	100	1	0	0	0	0	99	5*	0	62**	96	98†	96‡‡
Stone, glass, clay products	33	0	0	0	0	1	2	0	10	1	87	91	97	96
Electrical machinery	37	0	0	2*	0	0	2	0	8	5	93	86	96	93**

Lowest-range nationalization ratios

Beverages	21	0	0	0	0*	0	8	0	5*	18	62**	91	98†	96‡‡
Metal products except machinery	35	0	0	0**	5	0	14	0	3	7	61	95	75	58
Food processing	20	0	0	1	0*	0	3	0	5*	0	62**	53	98†	96‡‡
Paper and pulp products	27	0	0	0	0	0	1	0	0	24	74	84	89	100
Textiles	23	0	0	0	0	0	1	0	5	0	94	86	98	92
Lumber products except furniture	25	0	0	0†	0	0	3	0**	2**	11	66†	58**	64‡‡	100
Rubber products	30	0	0	0	0	0	0	0	0	0	89	98	91**	96†
Miscellaneous	39	0	0	0	1	0	0	0	4	4	27	84	42	94
Clothing and footwear	24	0	0	2	0	0	1	0	6	1	39	70	50	38
Furniture	26	0	0	0†	0	0	0	0**	2**	4	66†	58**	64‡‡	62
Leather products except footwear	29	0	0	0	0	0	0	0	1	1	48	42	61	53

a. The "nationalization ratio" is defined in note a in Table 2–1 and in the text. In the data for certain countries several branches of mining and manufacturing are combined; in such cases the nationalization ratio for the combined branches is used for each separate branch and the branches that are combined are indicated with a typographic sign.

b. Mining and manufacturing are defined slightly differently than in Table 3–1.

c. These data are for a different year than the previous table and the sector is defined somewhat differently.

d. Ratios are calculated on labor force rather than aggregate wage data, as in Table 2–1.

Correlation tests between the gross national product and the aggregate degree of nationalization were carried out and no statistically significant relationship could be found. A number of other related hypotheses (some of which included the introduction of trade variables) were also tested and found wanting. Since none of the other hypotheses discussed could be used to find significant relationships between the degree of nationalization and important economic variables, we may conclude that the factors used to explain the pattern of nationalization among industries cannot be employed successfully to explain the overall degree of nationalization among nations and in this single instance, therefore, the "null" hypothesis cannot be rejected. However, for the relative degree of nationalization of sectors and branches, these economic factors appear to play a much more important role.

b. *Sectors of the economy.* In Table 2–1, the rank order of the various sectors appear quite similar and, indeed, the Kendall coefficient of concordance (which measures the extent to which the various rank orderings of all nations in the sample form a consistent pattern) is statistically significant at the .01 level.[9] The relatively highest nationalization ratios in each country usually occur in the utilities and in the transportation and communication sectors, while the lowest ratios appear in the agriculture, forestry and fishing, and in the commerce and finance sectors.

Now it does not seem likely that the political or historical factors influencing nationalization in specific cases would act in a sufficiently consistent manner in various nations to produce a general pattern of nationalization among various industries. Taking this and the null hypothesis into account, we would not expect to find any regularities among the rank orders of nationalization ratios. The marked pattern that is found in Table 2–1 leads us, therefore, to reject the null hypothesis. Isolating the actual causal factors is quite difficult since we lack comparable data with which to test systematically the various hypotheses; therefore, our discussion must be very informal and we must wait for the analysis of nationalization in branches of mining and manufacturing in order to perform statistical tests.

9. The coefficient of concordance is equal to 1.00 when the rank orderings of all countries are the same; and is equal to 0.00 when there is no systematic relationship between the rankings. This coefficient is analyzed by Maurice G. Kendall, *Rank Correlation Methods* (New York: 1962) and is used throughout this study along with Kendall rank order correlation coefficient. Both coefficients are nonparametric; that is, they can be used without having to worry about normality or other such distributional conditions of the data.

For the fifteen nations and seven sectoral rankings in Table 2–1, the coefficient of concordance is .69, which is statistically significant at the .01 level.

The relatively high degree of nationalization in utilities and in transportation and communication seems to be due to the economic considerations discussed with the hypotheses concerning economies of scale or natural monopolies, unearned income (arising from natural monopolies), externalities (primarily for transportation), and sovereignty (primarily for certain branches of communication). Similarly, the relatively low degree of nationalization in the agriculture, forestry, and fishing sectors also seems related to these four hypotheses for in this sector, neither considerations of scale, unearned returns, externalities, nor sovereignty seem important. In commerce, none of these four factors seems very important either.[10]

Economic considerations arising from cost savings in vertical mergers do not seem to account for either a high or low degree of nationalization in any of the seven sectors. In the three sectors that have not yet been mentioned, a number of complications arise that make it worthwhile to examine briefly each case separately.

For services, a part of the nationalization ratio is determined by the relative importance of personnel in public administration which, for reasons of sovereignty, belong to the public sector. (No modern country has yet hired a private enterprise "government management company" to run its major affairs.) The relative importance of the military forces is a second importance influence on the nationalization ratio and, thus, this ratio is high for countries with relatively large armed forces (e.g., the United States) and low for countries with small armies (e.g., West Germany, which had no army in 1950; the situation in this nation has since changed).[11] A final complicating factor is the certain arbitrariness of classification into the public and private sectors of particular types of service personnel. For instance, physicians working in a public hospital who are paid by the patients through the national health insurance system are usually placed in the "private" sector while other physicians in the same hospital who are paid by the hospital from funds obtained from the same source belong to the "public" sector. Thus in services, analysis of the nationalization ratio is impeded by three considerations which, to be overcome, require more disaggregated data than are now available.

For construction, the nationalization ratio shows considerable variation in rank among different nations. In certain nations such as the United

10. Although nationalization of banking may be related to "sovereignty" and factors of scale, bank personnel make up only a small part of the economically active population in the commerce and finance sector.

11. It might be noted that in 1950 East Germany had a "hidden army," the Kasernierte Volkspolizei, whose existence was in gross violation of the Potsdam agreement. East German complaints about West Germany violating this agreement with the formation of its army in later years represented a massive hypocrisy.

States where the ratio is higher than expected, most of the public construction units (e.g., the Army Corps of Engineers and city government construction units) are engaged in building public roads and offices and thus the vertical merger hypothesis seems relevant. In other countries, however, much public building is contracted out to private enterprises. Until more detailed data on particular branches of construction and the costs of administration are available, the exact importance of this vertical merger explanation cannot be known.

Analysis of nationalization in individual branches of mining and manufacturing is pursued below with detailed data and statistical tests. This discussion of factors underlying the relative degree of nationalization in the other economic sectors must be considered only as suggestive, since the requisite data for testing rigorously the various hypotheses are not available. Nevertheless, such a qualitative survey does provide insights into the striking pattern of relative sectoral nationalization ratios.

c. *Branches in mining and manufacturing.* Among the various branches in mining and manufacturing, the rank orders of nationalization ratios in Table 2–2 also show a marked pattern. This impression is confirmed by the coefficient of concordance, which is statistically significant at the .01 level.[12] The relatively highest nationalization ratios appear in the mining and in the transport equipment branches, while the relatively lowest ratios occur in certain branches of light industry such as leather products and clothing. The ranking of industrial branches is not greatly different than most would have expected; in addition, for the socialist nations the pattern is not so greatly distorted by the somewhat arbitrary division of productive facilities into state-owned and cooperative enterprises that one finds in the agricultural sector.

The strong pattern that emerges casts great doubt on the null hypothesis that economic factors do not play an important role in determining the relative degree of nationalization among branches of mining and manufacturing. In particular cases, of course, the influence of special historical factors can be seen (e.g., the high degree of nationalization in the tobacco industry in Japan and France), but such cases are not fre-

---

12. The coefficient of concordance is .26; although this is statistically significant at the .01 level, it is much lower than the concordance coefficient for the nationalization pattern for the economic sectors because of the great number of tie-ranks among branches for the nations with very little nationalization.

It is worth noting that the average rank orderings of relative nationalization of the capitalist nations (the first nine nations in the table) and the socialist nations (the last four nations in the table) are significantly related to each other.

quent enough to obscure the basic similarity in the rank orderings of the nationalization ratios.

In order to test the various hypotheses, it is necessary to develop some operational indices to reflect the most important considerations discussed in the theoretical section of this chapter. Devising such indices raises a number of problems and it is necessary to discuss briefly the nature of each index.

For testing the natural-monopolies argument, we have no direct measures of this factor. However, as I argued in the theoretical section, a key consideration underlying natural monopolies is important economies of scale and for this latter phenomenon several indices are available for the individual branches of mining and manufacturing. The most readily available seem related to production inputs, and in Table 2–3 I present the rank order of industries according to the amount of fixed capital in an average-size enterprise in the branch and, in addition, according to the number of workers and employees in such an average enterprise.[13] For natural monopolies leading to actual monopolies, we have considerable comparable information about the relative degree of industrial concentration (as measured by a weighted average of four-digit, four-firm concentration ratios) in the various branches of manufacturing for many countries, from which we derive the results.[14]

For testing the externalities hypothesis no direct or proxy measures for all branches are readily available. Therefore, this particular causal factor underlying the nationalization pattern must go untested. It must be added that if industrial branches are ranked intuitively along an externalities scale, the relationship between externalities and nationalization does not seem strong. For instance, rubber and paper manufacturing, both of which generate considerable air and water pollution, are relatively unnationalized while certain "clean" industries such as printing or manufacturing of electrical machinery are more nationalized.

In devising an appropriate index for testing the vertical mergers hypothesis, it appears reasonable to base the measure on the degree to which the products of a particular industrial branch are sold to the government. In Table 2–3, the rank order of industries according to such a criterion are presented. An alternative measure is the share of branch production that is sold not only to the government but also to the

13. The derivation of rankings of employment size of average size enterprises (the arithmetic average is used in the table) is described in Chapter VI. Estimation of the rankings of the capital required in average size enterprises is discussed in Appendix B-3 and B-4.

14. The estimation of this series from a twelve nation sample is discussed in Appendix B-10. These data are analyzed in great detail in Chapter VI.

nationalized enterprises, but this is extremely difficult to estimate and only a rough approximation can be calculated.[15]

The unearned income argument is concerned with monopoly gains arising either from the possession of particular resources or from highly concentrated market structures. Unfortunately we have no comparable data for the former; and for the latter, we have the data on the average degree of concentration that is also used for testing the natural monopolies argument. The unavailability of independent indicators for the unearned income and the natural monopolies hypotheses mean that these two arguments must be, in a sense, combined and tested together in Table 2–4.

The final hypothesis dealing with "economic sovereignty" also presents a number of difficulties for making adequate indices since the concept is generally used in an extremely unrigorous manner. Nevertheless, as I argue in the theoretical section, if we approach the concept by focusing on dependency on "outsiders," then concrete measures can be devised. In the table, two measures are presented: the first concerns the dependency of the government on inputs from particular branches of mining and manufacturing and is measured by the total volume of branch sales to the government; the second concerns the dependency of all industries in the economy on particular inputs and is measured by the volume of branch sales to all industries for usage as intermediate goods.[16] Since the two indices capture different aspects of the sovereignty argument, they are kept separate in the statistical tests performed in Table 2–4.

Different samples of nations were used in the calculation of each index, depending on the availability of appropriate data. For each index the various industries were ranked and an average ranking was calculated and is presented in Table 2–3. In order to show the relationship between these various indices and the relative degree of nationalization more clearly, the branches of mining and manufacturing in the table are arranged according to the descending average rank order of nationalization as determined by the thirteen nation sample in the previous table.

After defining and calculating these various indices to see which economic factors explain in the most satisfactory manner the relative degree of nationalization among various branches of mining and manu-

---

15. The derivation of these two series from data taken from input-output tables of eight nations is explained in Appendix B-6. These series are somewhat incomplete since we have no data on sales to nationalized enterprises within particular sectors. A first approximation to this wider concept of "sales to the government" can be made by including all sales to enterprises in the transportation, communication, and utility sectors, the sectors with relatively the greatest amount of nationalization. Such an alternative series is presented in Appendix B-6 as well.

16. The derivation of these two series from an eight nation sample is discussed in Appendix B-6.

facturing, we are ready to perform the statistical tests. But before turning to the results, one serious problem of interpretation arises, namely many of the explanatory variables are strongly related to each other.[17] As one might expect, the three variables used to test the natural monopolies hypothesis are highly correlated with each other. The first two of these three variables are also significantly related to the index for economic sovereignty (defined as volume of sales of a branch for intermediate usage, rather than to the government) and the concentration ratios variable is significantly correlated to the variable for economic sovereignty (defined as volume of sales of a branch to the government). Finally, the variable for testing the vertical merger hypothesis is significantly related to the variable for unearned income (the concentration ratios) and for economic sovereignty (defined as volume of sales of a branch to the government). Relevant data are presented in Table 2–4.

The vertical merger argument appears to be the only one which does not receive statistical confirmation.[18] The variables representing the natural monopoly, unearned income, and economic sovereignty arguments, all of which are related to each other, are all significantly related to the rank order of nationalization in the various branches of mining and manufacturing.[19] These various hypotheses appear, indeed, to be facets of the same general phenomenon—the degree to which a particular branch can be characterized as belonging to "heavy" or "light" industry, a matter discussed in greater detail below.

In order to see these relationships between relative nationalization and particular explanatory variables more clearly, it is useful to consider those industries with the highest and lowest nationalization ratios. In mining and quarrying, which are the most nationalized of the twenty-one branches, the unearned income and the sovereignty hypotheses seem most relevant. That is, the mining industry is often characterized by high windfall gains; further, its products (excepting fuels) are generally used as intermediate goods by other industries. In the relatively highly nationalized transport equipment and petroleum and coal product branches of manufacturing, the scales of production are relatively large (as reflected both by employment and capital), the percentages and the volumes of

17. A correlation matrix of the six variables is presented in Appendix B-5.

18. The alternative variable for the vertical mergers argument—the share of branch sales to the government sector plus utility, transportation, and communication branches—is also not significantly related to the rank order of nationalization ratios.

19. The rank order correlation coefficient between volume of branch sales to the government and the nationalization ratios is just a shade under statistical significance, but the alternative index for economic sovereignty is significantly related to nationalization.

TABLE 2–3

Rank Order of Possible Factors Underlying the Nationalization Pattern in Mining and Manufacturing[a]

Branch (Arranged in descending average degree of nationalization)	ISIC No.	In Average Size Enterprise		Percentage of Branch Sales to Government	Weighted Four-digit Four-firm Concentration Ratios	Volume of Branch Sales	
		Fixed Capital	Workers and Employees			To Government	To All Industries
Mining and quarrying	10–9	6.5	8	11	n.a.	9	3
Transport equipment	38	10	6.5	1	2	1	11
Petroleum and coal products	32	1	1	3	4	3	7
Primary metals	34	2	3	16	12	15	1
Chemicals	31	3	4	9	5	4	2
Printing and publishing	28	16	17	2	8	6	14
Machinery except electrical, transport	36	14	11	5	3	2	9
Tobacco products	22	4.5	2	21	1	21	21
Stone, glass, clay products	33	8.5	12	14	10	14	10
Electrical machinery	37	12	6.5	6	7	5	12
Beverages	21	8.5	14	20	15	19.5	18
Metal products except machinery	35	15	15	8	11	7	6
Food processing	20	13	13	17	13	11	5
Paper and paper products	27	4.5	10	12	14	12	8
Textiles	23	11	9	18	16	17	4

Lumber products except furniture	25	18	20	19	19	19.5	13
Rubber products	30	6.5	5	10	6	16	15
Miscellaneous products	39	17	16	4	9	8	16
Clothing and footwear	24	20	18	13	18	13	19
Furniture	26	21	21	7	20	10	20
Leather products except footwear	29	19	19	15	17	18	17

a. For the different variables, rank one designates the branch with the greatest amount of fixed capital, the greatest number of workers and employees, the highest percentage of branch sales to the government, the highest weighted four-digit, four-firm concentration ratio, and the highest volume of branch sales to the government and to all industries. These variables are discussed in the text and the sources are indicated in previous footnotes.

TABLE 2–4

Relationships between Relative Nationalization of Mining and
Manufacturing Branches to Possible Explanatory Variables[a]

Hypotheses To Be Tested	Variable	Kendall Rank Order Correlation Coefficient
Natural monopoly	Fixed capital in average size enterprise	.50*
Natural monopoly	Workers and employees in average size enterprise	.49*
Unearned income/ natural monopoly	Weighted four-digit concentration ratios of branch	.55*
Vertical merger	Percentage of branch sales to government	.20
Economic sovereignty	Volume of branch sales to government	.34
Economic sovereignty	Volume of branch sales to other branches for intermediate usage	.40*

a. The Kendall rank order correlation coefficient is equal to unity when the rank orders of the two variables are exactly the same; equal to minus unity when the rank orders are exactly reversed; and equal to zero when there is no positive or negative relation. The asterisk designates statistical significance at the .05 level.

branch sales to the government are high, and the industries are highly concentrated. In the primary metals branch, which is also highly nationalized, the scale of production is relatively large and volume of sales used as inputs for other industries is also relatively high. Turning to the three branches of mining and manufacturing that have the lowest nationalization ratios, it is readily apparent that these branches score relatively low in almost all cases according to all of the variables serving to test the different hypotheses. In the fourteen branches of industry between the extremes, the various factors important in the analysis of nationalization appear to offset each other. In any case, most of the hypotheses discussed appear to receive impressive confirmation.

Three remaining phenomena in Table 2–2 deserve brief mention. First, certain random elements appear noticeable. More specifically, in countries with relatively high nationalization ratios, one expects but does not find high nationalization ratios in particular industries (e.g., chemicals in Norway, basic metals in Israel). Some of these exceptions occur in industries that are relatively small in that particular country and that import most of their products.

Second, among nations on the fringes of the table—either with very high or low degrees of nationalization—certain irregularities from the general pattern of nationalization obtain. That is, if nationalization has not proceeded very far or has almost included the entire nonagricultural part of the economy, the pattern of public ownership deviates from the average rank order of nationalization ratios in a noticeable fashion. For instance, no nationalization of mining occurs in Japan, while a very high relative degree of nationalization in lumber products occurs in Bulgaria. Such irregularities suggest that the overall degree of nationalization may have some effect on the pattern of nationalization, but until we have data for more nations, this phenomenon cannot be more amply explored.

d. *A digression on "heavy" and "light" industry, relative unionization, and countervailing power.* The high degree of correlation of most of the explanatory variables in Table 2–4 suggests that these variables are indices of a more general phenomenon which, for lack of any better terminology, I label "heavy" and "light" industry. Although definitions of these terms are almost as numerous as the economists who use these loose designations, all definitions seem to point to the same subset of industries. If we collect and compare these definitions, "heavy" industry usually appears associated, on the input side, with large amounts of capital or large numbers of workers amassed within an average size enterprise and, on the output side, by a high degree of market control or monopoly. Although input and output size represent two very different kinds of economic power,[20] they usually appear together in the same industries. In contrast, "light" industries lack both manifestations of economic power, i.e., they have enterprises that are relatively small in terms of capital or manpower and that have little monopoly power. In the "heavy" industries, decision-making covers a broader range of alternatives (e.g., a wider range of price-output decisions) than in the "light" industries, where decisions are strongly limited by economic forces (e.g., a single market price). More descriptive than the terms "heavy" and "light" industries are, perhaps, "discretionary branches" and "market branches" of industry—terms which focus on the relative importance of different types of decision-making. Empirically determining the relative ranking of industries along a continuum of "heaviness" or "discretionary decision-making" is a relatively simple matter, at least as a first approxi-

20. Monopoly power is, of course, the bread-and-butter of industrial organization specialists; sheer size as a source of power is, however, often quite neglected. For a notable exception see George W. Stocking, "Conglomerate Bigness as a Source of Power," in Universities-National Bureau Committee for Economic Research, ed., *Business Concentration and Price Policy* (Princeton: 1955), pp. 331–61. These matters are discussed in considerably more detail in Chapter VIII.

mation, and involves merely the averaging of the rank orders of industries according to input and output measures of economic size. Such an exercise is carried out in Appendix B-7.

The correlation between branches of manufacturing and mining ranked along a scale of "heavy" and "light" industry and the ranking of these branches according to the relative level of nationalization is .63, which is higher than any of the individual series in Table 2–4. In addition, this "heaviness" ranking is significantly correlated with the ranking of industries according to relative wages and also according to the relative degree of unionization in the United States.[21] This complex of correlations is difficult to analyze because the major directions in which causal forces are operating are far from clear. Nevertheless, I would like to propose an explanation involving the rise of unionism and countervailing power which, although it cannot be easily proven, is consistent with the empirical evidence.

The argument starts with the observation that those branches of mining and manufacturing with relatively high or low wages are roughly the same in all countries; further, such a ranking of high and low wage industries appears both in nations with high and low degrees of unionization, with different degrees of public ownership, and in both centrally planned and market economies.[22]

This marked pattern can be attributed to two causal factors. The "heavy" and high-wage industries seem to have a greater proportion of skilled workers in their labor force than the "light" and low-wage industries. This interpretation receives additional support from the fact that the "heavy" industries also have the greatest relative number of research and development personnel.[23] (These industries also feature high capital/labor ratios, although this phenomenon may be a response to, rather than part of the cause of, the relatively high wages.) A second explanation is that the workers in these industries enjoy in the form of higher wages part of the economic power which the "heavy" industries gain through great size and (for market economies) a high degree of monopoly. Although available evidence makes it difficult to distinguish the relative importance of these two explanations, I believe that both play a role.

The second step of the argument focuses attention on the loss to workers when enterprises lay off men or reduce wages in periods of economic slowdown. Workers in the high-wage "heavy" industries have

21. See Appendix B-7 for these series and the Kendall rank order correlation coefficients.

22. These results are discussed in much greater detail in Chapter IV.

23. Some of the correlations are presented in Appendix B-7; others are discussed in Chapter VI. It should be emphasized that advanced technologies are not necessarily correlated with important economies of scale although this turns out to be the case empirically.

something extra-important to lose by suffering such wage cuts, namely their economic status among other workers. They have an incentive to band together, not only to protect themselves against "capital" but also to protect their position *vis-à-vis* other workers. Thus the correlation between unionization and relative position of the industry on a "heaviness" scale should come as no surprise, for high wages appear to be a property right that can be organizationally protected.

This correlation between relative unionization of various industries and their position on the "heaviness" scale supports a contention of John Kenneth Galbraith that a concentration of economic power on one side of the market (in this case, large companies on the labor market) is often accompanied by a concentration of power on the other side of the market (in this case, unionization).[24] We have, in other words, countervailing power. My approach is also consistent with the theories of various labor economists such as Selig Perlman or Frank Tannenbaum who have interpreted the rise of unionism in terms of defensive, rather than offensive, motives.[25] But my proposed mechanism is slightly different: To put the matter baldly, it was the high wages in "heavy" industry that brought about greater relative unionization, rather than the reverse.[26]

The complex of attributes of "heavy" industry that make it difficult to disentangle the causal forces underlying relative nationalization in different branches of mining and manufacturing leads us to some interesting propositions concerning relative unionization that are important for a positive theory of property. My approach suggests that the recent disregard of interpretations of unionization in terms of laborers' property rights to higher wages may be a step backward in understanding economic forces. Further, the evidence provided above suggests that professional economists have written off too quickly Galbraith's theory of countervailing power and that some of the flaws in his approach can be repaired. The technological-economic attributes of particular branches of mining and manufacturing that underlie the position of the industry along a

24. John Kenneth Galbraith, *American Capitalism: The Concept of Countervailing Power* (Boston: 1952), especially Chapter IX.

25. The views of the various exponents are neatly summarized in Mark Perlman, *Labor Union Theories in America* (Evanston: 1958).

26. One objection to Galbraith's theory of countervailing power has been raised by Albert Rees [*The Economics of Trade Unions* (Chicago: 1962), pp. 82–3] who argues that the first unions were organized in industries where most employers were small firms (e.g., printing, construction, bituminous coal mining, etc.), rather than in industries characterized by great size or a high degree of concentration. Part of this objection is beside the point since Galbraith was concerned about present conditions, not origins (and the factors making for a viable union in the early days of unionism were quite different than those needed to sustain it when the climate of opinion toward unions was more friendly).

"heavy-light" scale provide the key for showing a relationship between forces encouraging nationalization and unionization; they also tie Galbraith and an older tradition in the study of labor economics together.

e. *Summary.* Most of the hypotheses examined in the theoretical discussion seem to shed light on particular aspects of the pattern of public ownership, but at different levels of aggregation. The "null" hypothesis that economic forces do not play a causal role serves best for the overall degree of nationalization. In explaining the relative degree of nationalization among sectors within economies, the natural monopolies, unearned income, economic sovereignty, externalities, and vertical merger hypotheses all appear applicable; for lack of data with which to test these hypotheses, however, our conclusions on these matters must be tentative. In the analysis of nationalization patterns among the various branches of mining and manufacturing, considerations of natural monopolies, unearned income, and economic sovereignty appeared useful as explanatory factors. The correlation between indices representing these considerations make separation of their individual effects impossible; however, further reflection suggests that all of these considerations are but various facets of a more basic characteristic of individual branches of mining and manufacturing, namely the degree to which they represent "heavy" or "light" industries. Thus the distinction between "heavy" and "light" industry appears to be the most important consideration in predicting which branches of mining and manufacturing are relatively most nationalized, and the null hypothesis must be decisively rejected. Although ostensible motives or circumstances for nationalization have varied enormously in different countries at different times, the relative degree to which various sectors and branches of the economy are owned by the government is strongly influenced by some very clear economic and political-economic factors that have been outlined.

2.   *Implications for Changes over Time*

As noted in Chapter I, divergent trends in the overall level of nationalization have appeared in the postwar era. Although the various hypotheses discussed do not focus on processes of change as such, they should have certain implications for changes in the pattern of nationalization over time. How can we extend the cross-section results to time-series data? Although various approaches are conceivable, we are strongly limited in testing various hypotheses because of limitations of data and, therefore, must rely on extremely simple and informal procedures.

Perhaps the most simple approach to this problem is to compare changes in the pattern of nationalization in a particular country with the pattern of nationalization derived from the data from a large number of nations. If the initial impetus toward nationalization of certain sectors or branches of the economy of a particular nation includes many non-economic forces, then we would expect that the initial pattern of nation-alization might differ greatly from the "normal" pattern. Over time, how-ever, the government of that nation might make marginal decisions, based on economic considerations, about buying or selling particular facilities that might bring the pattern of nationalization closer to the pattern that seems to be due to the economic forces discussed above.

An example of this process can be seen from the data in Table 2–1 in which it appears that in Eastern Europe during the late fifties and early sixties nationalization in the sectors of agriculture, commerce and finance, and mining and manufacturing were most out of line with the pattern of sectoral nationalization in other nations. From this reasoning it seems likely that if denationalization were to occur at all, it would happen in these sectors; and, as a matter of fact, this prediction appears to have been borne out during the late sixties. More specifically, at this time private service trades and other types of private small-scale commerce and handicraft seemed to be increasing in relative importance in a num-ber of East European nations.[27] (It must be added, however, that de-nationalization did not occur in agriculture at this time; the denationaliza-tions in this sector that occurred in Yugoslavia and Poland took place in the fifties and were more of a decollectivization). With the outstanding exception of Cuba, no Western socialist nation appears to be taking immediate measures to eliminate private ownership in every sector of the economy.[28]

In order to test such an approach in a more rigorous fashion, we should have detailed data on the pattern of nationalization for many nations for a number of decades. Unfortunately, such data do not appear

27. Denationalization in Eastern Europe is analyzed in two articles by Michael Garmarnikow, "Another Step Toward Private Enterprise," *East Europe,* XVII, January 1968, pp. 2–9 and "The New Role of Private Enter-prise," *East Europe,* XVI, August 1967, pp. 2–10. These denationalizations are still extremely limited in scope and in no way change the basic operation of the economies of these nations.

28. Cuba's plans to quickly nationalize the entire economy are dis-cussed by René Dumont, *Cuba: Est-il socialiste* (Paris: 1970), pp. 135 ff. In another book, *Cuba: Socialism and Development* (New York: 1970), p. 132, Dumont argues: "Attributing excessive importance that collectivization of the means of production represents the only really important fact might be a matter for debate hereafter." He adds in a footnote that: "It remains essential nonetheless, in particular because of its irreversible nature." This last remark is debatable; it also does not take into account that an easing of the drive toward nationalization can bring about a faster growth of the private than of the public sector and thus reduce the degree of national-ization.

to exist, so we must be content with an illustrative example concerning the United States, one of the few nations for which such time-series information is readily available.

From the data in Table 2–1, it appears that the nationalization ratios for the United States are most out of line with the "average pattern" in the utilities and in the transportation and communication sectors. If nationalization were to increase in the United States, the changes should occur most markedly in these two sectors. Nationalization data for the period 1940 through 1970 yield interesting results and are presented in Table 2–5.

Comparison of relative changes are not meaningful because nationalization ratios are initially so low in several sectors; so we must examine only absolute changes in nationalization. Over the three decades the nationalization ratios increased most in absolute terms in three sectors: utilities, transportation and communication, and services. The change in services is unexpected and the major cause appears to be a shift within the service sector toward those branches which originally had higher nationalization ratios (e.g., education). The predictions of changes in the United States pattern of nationalization that are based on our hypotheses receive weak confirmation. Although this extension of the cross-section results to time-series changes is by no means completely conclusive, more presumptive evidence is added to the hypothesis con-

Table 2–5

*Trends in Sector Nationalization Ratios in the United States,
1940 through 1970*

Sector	1940	1950	1960	1970
Total	10%	12%	15%	19%
(Total excluding public administration and defense)	(5)	(6)	(8)	(12)
Utilities	24	25	28	32
Transportation and communication	12	15	18	21
Services, public administration, defense	33	42	46	48
(Services excluding public administration and defense)	(17)	(20)	(25)	(31)
Construction	13	10	12	11
Mining and manufacturing	1	1	1	2
Commerce and finance	0	1	1	2
Agriculture, forestry, fishing	0	1	1	3

cerning the importance of economic factors underlying the nationalization pattern.

E. Summary and Conclusions

This chapter has focused on one particular property right—ownership—and its distribution between the public and private sectors.

The underlying causal factors determining the relative extent of public ownership among nations seem to lie outside the sphere of economics. However, particular economic and political-economic factors appear as extremely important causal forces underlying the relative extent of public ownership in different sectors and branches of the economy.

More specifically, arguments concerning the greater probability of nationalization in sectors and branches showing natural monopolies, the presence of "unearned income," or factors related to "economic sovereignty" receive empirical confirmation; these three factors are related to each other and seem to be particular facets of the degree to which different branches of mining and manufacturing can be classified as belonging to "heavy" or "light" industries. In addition, I suggest that the presence of externalities may also play a certain role in the nationalization of particular sectors. Finally, the results from the cross-section analysis appear to have applicability in analyzing changes over time in the relative degree of nationalization in different sectors of the national economy.

Because of limitations of data, a number of aspects of the pattern of nationalization must remain insufficiently explored. Nevertheless, the results do show in a convincing manner the importance of economic factors in illuminating a phenomenon which has received relatively little empirical attention; nationalization is only one of a large number of property phenomena which have received extensive political but relatively little empirical analysis.

The results of this study of nationalization have significance for a number of both normative and positive analyses of property. Let me specifically note at this point an important implication for the theory of convergence of nations with different economic systems: Although the pattern of nationalization in countries with different economic systems may appear more similar in the future, the lack of important economic influences on the overall level of nationalization means that there are no direct economic impulses toward convergence along this dimension.

At least one important aspect of property, namely the relative degree of public ownership in different economic sectors, has proven quite amenable to a rough quantitative analysis. Undoubtedly, the analysis can be improved when better data are available. Other aspects of ownership, especially its impact on the distribution of income and the degree to which ownership is becoming concentrated, can also be illuminated through similar types of quantitative exploration, as we will see in the next few chapters. In considering the relative ease with which different facets of ownership can be analyzed—for ownership is a much more quantifiable aspect of property than control—the relative neglect of the subject by Western economists is not only surprising but also, unfortunately, alarming.

CHAPTER III

Property and Labor Incomes: Some Empirical Reflections

When men are rich, they are too proud to obey commands;
When poor, they are insensitive to shame.

The *Kuan-Tzu*[1]

The rich man in his castle, the poor man at his gate,
God made them, high or lowly, and ordered their estate.

C. F. Alexander[2]

A. Introduction

The impact of property income on the size distribution of income has been the subject of acute political controversy for many centuries; but the empirical investigations of such matters have unfortunately been meager.

1. Lewis Maverick, ed., *Economic Dialogues in Ancient China: The Kuan-Tzu* (New Haven: 1954), Essay 10.
2. Cecil Frances Alexander, "All Things Bright and Beautiful," a be-

In comparisons between East and West, it is a commonplace that the lack
of extensive property income is the major factor underlying the alleged
greater income equality in the socialist nations; but the actual situation is
not nearly so simple. The purpose of this chapter is to investigate empirically some of the major issues concerning the impact of ownership on income distribution.

If we consider total personal income to be composed of two parts—
originating from property and labor—then its variance can be attributed
to the variance of property and labor incomes separately and the correlation between these two types of income among individuals.[3] A more familiar approach toward the size distribution of income is to examine three
major factors: the relative shares of total property and labor incomes;
the dispersion around the mean of these two types of incomes; and the
correlation among individuals of the amounts of their property and labor
incomes. Since property income is much more unequally distributed in all
economies than labor income, the greater the share of property income,
or the greater the inequality of labor or property income, or the more
correlated these two types of income are, the more unequal the size distribution of total income will be (assuming, of course, other things remain the same). These three factors form the focus of the analysis of this
chapter.

In the following sections I will investigate the relative shares of property and labor income and show that the relative importance of the
former has been declining over time and that the latter now composes
roughly three-quarters of all income received. This means that any study
of the sources of income inequality must focus considerable attention on
the distribution of labor income. Through an analysis of the relative inequality of labor incomes in East and West plus data about the contribution of property income to total income inequality, I arrive at the tentative conclusion that differences in the size distribution of labor income in
capitalist and socialist nations are a somewhat more important source of
differences in total income equality than is the existence of property income. This is, of course, not an attempt to justify property income but
rather an attempt to place the controversy about the impact of property
income in the context of the facts of the matter.

---

loved hymn (but later removed) in the Anglican missal. Lest any reader
think that such sentiments were confined to the eastern side of the Atlantic,
he should be reminded that it was none other than Henry David Thoreau
who wrote (in *Walden,* Chapter 18), "The setting sun is reflected from the
windows of the alms house as brightly as from the rich man's abode."

3. A mathematical exposition of the components of variance is presented in Appendix A-4.

B. The Relative Importance of Property and Labor Incomes

1. Changes over Time

Classical economists such as Adam Smith or David Ricardo wrote a great deal about the increase of property income over time; unfortunately, their remarks were sufficiently imprecise that it is difficult to know what they really thought on such matters.[4] Since they viewed rents from land as the most important component of property income, their views have little relevance for modern controversies. More germane to our current discussions is the view of Karl Marx, who focused his attentions directly on profits and argued that the share of property income would increase in the long run (even though he recognized the existence of certain short-run offsets to this trend.)[5]

Most Marxists at the present time support Marx's proposition. Non-Marxist economists following the marginal productivity theory of distribution have generally thrown up their hands at the possibility of making any long-run predictions about relative shares. They seem to argue that the critical variable is a technological factor, namely the marginal rate of substitution between capital and labor, which cannot be specified for the future.

Depending on the assumptions, almost any change in relative shares of property income and labor income can be predicted. Rather than argue this question from a theoretical point of view, it seems more worthwhile to look at the available information on the matter. Data for the four leading capitalist nations, the United States, the United Kingdom, France, and West Germany are presented in Table 3–1.

In the United States, the United Kingdom, and France, the share of property income in the total national income has declined markedly,

4. In Ricardo's theory changes in factor shares depended on what we now label as the elasticity of substitution of capital for labor in an aggregate production function embracing the entire economy. Such an approach is, of course, basic to the modern neoclassical analysis of factor shares as well. A useful and simple mathematical analysis of Ricardo's long-run theory of factor shares is presented by Mark Blaug, *Economic Theory in Retrospect* (Homewood, Ill.: 1968), rev. ed., pp. 108–11.

5. Marx held very early that the ratio of property income to labor income would rise over time (e.g., in his 1847 lectures that are reprinted in *Wage-Labour and Capital*) and this idea is repeated in *Capital* in his discussion of the rise of the rate of surplus value which accompanies a rise in productivity and the expropriation of a higher percentage of labor power by the capitalists. Certain additional notes on Marx's theory are presented in Appendix A-8.

TABLE 3–1

Shares of Property Income in Total National Income Over a Half-century Period in Four Leading Capitalist Nations[a]

United States		United Kingdom		France		Germany	
Period	Property Share	Period	Property Share	Period	Property Share	Period	Property Share
1900–09	30.6%	1900–09	40.6%	1913	34.0%	1900–09	28.3%
1905–14	30.7	1905–14	42.3			1905–13	29.1
1910–19	31.9						
1915–24	29.8						
1920–29	28.4	1920–29	30.8	1920–29	30.7	1925–34	6.8
1925–34	26.8	1925–34	29.9	1929–38	28.4	1930–38	10.2
1930–39	23.4	1930–39	28.9				
1934–43	24.2	1935–44	27.6				
1939–48	24.3	1940–49	22.8				
1944–53	23.8						
1949–57	23.8	1949–54	20.5	1952–56	20.6	1950–59	26.5

a. Property and labor incomes are defined before taxes. The income concept is national income, rather than personal income (discussed in the text) because of problems of obtaining long-time series for the latter. The data are not comparable among nations nor with the data presented in Table 3–2.

For the United States, the data come from Irving B. Kravis, *The Structure of Income* (Philadelphia: 1962), p. 124. The data from 1900 to 1939 are based on the estimates of D. G. Johnson; the data from 1929–57, from the estimates of the United States Department of Commerce. Thirty-five percent of the income from unincorporated businesses (entrepreneurial income) is assigned to property income, a procedure also followed for the data of the United Kingdom and France.

For the United Kingdom and France the data come from Simon Kuznets, "Quantitative Aspects of the Economic Growth of Nations: IV. Distribution of National Income by Factor Shares," *Economic Development and Cultural Change*, VII, April 1959, Part II, pp. 86–8. The United Kingdom data are drawn primarily from estimates by Phyllis Deane; the French data are based on estimates of de Bernonville for the years 1913–39 and from United Nations estimates for the post-World War II period.

For Germany the data come from Walther G. Hoffman, *et al.*, *Das Wachstum der deutschen Wirtschaft seit der Mitte des 19. Jahrhunderts* (Berlin: 1965), p. 509, Columns 13 and 14. The estimates cover the geographical area of Germany at the particular cited dates; the postwar datum is only for West Germany. Although the property-income shares in the interwar period appear unreasonably low, they stem from Hoffman's particular method of estimating property income and making certain imputations. The Hoffman estimates are somewhat different (and more recent) than the Jostock and official estimates reported by

while in West Germany no general trend can be determined. Although severe difficulties arise in making such estimates—especially the division of income from unincorporated businesses or independent traders (or entrepreneurial income) into labor and property components—the trends are unmistakable. With few exceptions, data on property-income shares from other studies or for other nations show a similar decline.[6]

The causes underlying the decline in the relative importance of property income are obscure and cannot be isolated in this essay. Although such decline is correlated with a rising level of development, we cannot tell from the data whether this was due to, or accompanied by, a fall in profit rates, an increase in the intensity of the "class struggle," or a change in the production function. Nevertheless, it is the empirically determined trend that is of major interest for the analysis below.

2. Differences among Western Nations

By obtaining comparable data on components of national income for many nations, we can extend the empirical investigation. Data for most of the O.E.C.D. nations for two periods in the post-World War II period are presented in Table 3–2.

The share of property income varied between one-third and one-sixth of total national income in both time periods; however, in most of these nations this fraction lay between one-fourth and one-fifth. There is no apparent relation between the share of property income and either the level of economic development or the degree of public ownership. Between the two decades the share of property income appeared to decrease in most nations.

The data in Table 3–2 are calculated without removing direct taxes. If one subtracts direct business taxes from property income and social security taxes from labor income, the relative income shares are not essentially changed. (Other types of direct taxes cannot be removed without considerably more effort and a number of assumptions about tax incidence that are controversial. I do not believe, however, that any such

6. Studies of time-series data for various nations can be found not only in the sources cited in note a for Table 3–1, but also in a number of other studies of which Jean Marchal and Bernard Ducros, eds., *The Distribution of National Income* (London: 1968) is probably the most recent extensive study.

In the English language literature, the only recent major study showing that the share of property income has not fallen but risen is by Paul Baran and Paul Sweezy, *Monopoly Capitalism* (New York: 1966) and they use a method confusing the income and product side of the national accounts which has been severely (but justly, I feel) attacked by Raymond Lubitz, "Monopoly Capitalism and Neo-Marxism," *Public Interest*, XXI, Fall 1970, pp. 167–78.

calculation would change the nature of the conclusions drawn from the table.)

All in all, there appears to be little variation in the share of property income among nations and the exact causal factors underlying the small variations must remain unexplored. For the purpose of the analysis below, only the major trends are important.

3. Property Income in East Europe

Thus far we have directed our attention to property income in the West. It is now necessary to make a few brief remarks about such income in the socialist nations of East Europe.

TABLE 3–2

Shares of Property Income in Total National Income in Western Nations during the Mid-1950s and 1960s[a]

Country	1955–57	1965–67
United States	24.6%	24.7%
Switzerland	26.6	24.8
Sweden	22.9	20.7
Canada	25.3	24.6
Norway	32.8	27.5
France	20.1	21.0
United Kingdom	24.3	23.5
Belgium	27.2	22.8
Italy	29.7	22.6
Japan	23.8	29.1
Finland	27.7	25.5
Ireland	23.8	24.2
Spain	—	25.2
Unweighted average	25.7	24.3

a. Property and labor incomes are calculated before taxes. The data for the various nations are comparable with each other but are not comparable with the data of the previous table.

The countries are arranged according to descending per capita G.N.P. in 1962. The definition of national income follows the O.E.C.D. definition, but with the inclusion of interest on public debt and on consumer debt as part of property income (instead of treating them as transfer payments). Property income includes interest, rent and dividends to households, savings of corporations as well as direct taxes on corporations, government income from property and entrepreneurship, interest on public and consumer debt, and 25 percent of income of unincorporated business (e.g., farms).

The basic data come from O.E.C.D., *National Accounts of O.E.C.D. Countries, 1950–68* (Paris: n.d.). Percentages of property income for each year of the three-year periods were averaged. Certain small estimates had to be made. For the remaining O.E.C.D. nations, no data on income from unincorporated businesses comparable to the data of the nations in the table could be located.

Property income appears a relatively minor source of income in Eastern Europe. In the decade of the 1960s, explicit property income in these socialist nations arose primarily from interest on bank accounts and government bonds, but such income accounted for a miniscule part of total national income. Dividends were almost nonexistent, except in East Germany where a small number of "half-state" companies were allowed to exist. Profit-sharing schemes were introduced in many East European nations in the late 1960s, but except for Yugoslavia, the amounts involved were relatively minor. Thus, explicit property incomes were a small proportion of total national income and could not have served as an important source of income inequality.

Implicit property returns were perhaps most important in agriculture, where part of the income shared by cooperative farmers might be considered as rent on land; much of this implicit rent, however, was siphoned off by the government in the form of low fixed prices for agricultural goods sold to the government. Other implicit property returns were part of the returns from sales of home-grown foods and imputed rents from owner-occupied housing, but these sources of return on property were again relatively small.

Western recalculations of national incomes in various East European nations give quantitative expression to some of these qualitative judgments.[7] Since in total incomes the share of property incomes was quite small and seems to have been rather widely distributed, it is difficult to believe that property income contributed greatly to the inequality of income.

4. Several Conclusions

Several aspects of this discussion on the relative importance of property and labor income deserve emphasis.

First, since labor income in the West accounts for roughly 75 percent of national income, it is quite possible that the most important source of variations of personal income stems from labor, not property income (unless property income is extremely unequally distributed). If we are trying to compare income inequalities in the East and the West, it is not enough to look only at the existence of property income; we must explore the degree to which income inequality arises from labor income as well.

Second, although property income exists in Eastern Europe, it is highly doubtful that it is an important source of income inequality, especially outside of agriculture.

7. These include Abram Bergson, *The Real National Income of Soviet Russia Since 1928* (Cambridge, Mass.: 1961) and the various other studies of the Soviet Union and East Europe cited in note 15.

Third, it is puzzling that in the West an inverse relation between the level of development and the share of property income in the national income is manifested in the long run time-series data but does not appear in the cross-section data. One possible explanation is that the causal forces accompany the rise in the level of technology over time but do not operate at any particular point in time since in this situation the level of technological knowledge is roughly the same among all nations. Or if a bargaining theory of income shares has merit, the differences between the cross-section and the time-series data might be attributed to a worldwide increase in the power of labor *vis-à-vis* capital over time that is not correlated with the level of development at a single point in time. Although other explanations come to mind, they are not relevant for the empirical analysis below.

C. The Size Distribution of Labor Income

1. Some Theoretical Considerations

In the economic literature one finds a plethora of propositions about the determinants of the distribution of labor incomes.[8] Some of these propositions relate this distribution to particular macro-economic variables. For instance, after a certain point in the development process, labor incomes allegedly become increasingly more equally distributed as economic growth continues; or, the larger the nation, the greater is believed to be the separation of labor markets and, as well, the greater the inequality of labor incomes. Other propositions in the literature relate the distribution of labor incomes to particular micro-economic considerations (e.g., the role of human capital),[9] while still other propositions about labor income equality focus attention on particular institutional factors, such as particular types of "barriers," the role of government, and so forth.[10]

Unfortunately, there has been relatively little speculation on the impact of economic systems on the distribution of labor incomes and those propositions that can be found are quite contradictory. Some have argued that the distribution of labor income is more equal in socialism than in capitalism because of the more equal distribution of education and because the government is able to reduce the power that strong labor groups

8. These are summarized by Reder, "A Partial Survey of the Theory of Income Size Distribution," in Lee Soltow, ed., *Six Papers on the Size Distribution of Wealth and Income* (New York: 1969), pp. 205–55.

9. These are surveyed by Jacob Mincer, "The Distribution of Labor Incomes: A Survey with Special Reference to the Human Capital Approach," *Journal of Economic Literature,* VIII, March 1970, pp. 1–27.

10. See Appendix A-8 for a survey of these propositions.

("noncompeting groups") have to raise their incomes far above that received by the average worker.[11] Others have suggested that a socialist government's power to manipulate wages between industrial sectors so as to attract workers to particular priority sectors will lead to greater inequalities in labor income. Still others have suggested that socialist governments try harder than capitalist governments to obtain a more equal distribution of labor income in order to fulfill certain doctrinal commitments. Since all these arguments are based on what socialist governments "could" or "should" do, rather than what they are actually doing, they have an ideological tint that is out of place in positive economic analysis.

If we eliminate such propositions about the impact of economic systems on the distribution of labor incomes, we have nothing left from the theoretical literature on which to draw. Since I have no alternative model to propose, it seems most useful to turn to an empirical examination of these matters instead.

2. The Distribution of Labor Incomes in East and West

Comparable international data on the size distribution of labor incomes are not readily available. In addition, measures of inequality may vary considerably for the same population, depending on the unit of analysis (individuals, "adult units," spending units, families); the measure of income (gross income, money income, disposable money income, or income adjusted by certain "budget standards" that take into account family composition, age, or sex, etc. of the unit under analysis); the time period covered; the regions and sectors of the economy covered; the inclusion or exclusion of certain groups (e.g., the unemployed, the part-time worker, apprentices, seasonal workers, etc.); and the method of sampling (which especially affects the upper and lower tails of the distribution).[12]

Despite these difficulties, sufficient information is available for rough qualitative judgments. To ease discussion, three major factors are separated below: labor income differences in agricultural and nonagricultural sectors; labor income differences in different branches of manufacturing; and then the overall size distribution of nonagricultural labor income. The results of these analyses form a sufficiently consistent pattern to allow the generalization that labor earnings are probably more equally distributed in the East than in the West.

11. For instance, Abram Bergson, *The Structure of Soviet Wages* (Cambridge, Mass.: 1944), pp. 15–18.

12. Quantitative estimates of the impact of these factors are made by James N. Morgan, *et al., Income and Welfare in the United States* (New York: 1962), Chapter 20.

a. *Labor incomes in agricultural and nonagricultural sectors.* In nations where agriculture accounts for a relatively high proportion of the labor force, differences between average labor incomes in agriculture and in the rest of the economy make a great impact on the overall distribution of personal income. As development proceeds past a certain point, factor returns in the various sectors of the economy begin to converge and in developed economies, sectoral-income differences may not be an important determinant of inequality of personal income.[13] Nevertheless, the rate at which the income convergence occurs depends on a great number of factors that influence the migration from the country to the city, the terms-of-trade between the country and the city, and the absorption of rural labor into the urban economy. Making empirical comparisons of agricultural- and nonagricultural-labor incomes among nations raises a number of well-known difficulties, but two different important pieces of empirical evidence are available:

First, in Eastern Europe earnings of farm wage workers (primarily workers on state farms and machine-tractor stations) are usually 75 percent or more of average wages in manufacturing, while in most West European nations this ratio of relative wages is usually considerably less than 75 percent.[14] Of course, there are several important sources of incomparabilities: Different practices may be followed in evaluating wages-in-kind; the Western data often include wages of casual day laborers which are usually less than those of full-time agricultural workers; and the data from Eastern Europe cover only a small segment of total agricultural workers. Nevertheless, the wage ratio differences are sufficiently great in the two sets of nations that they must be taken into account in any overall evaluation of rural/urban income differentials.

Second, the ratio of total factor income returns per economically active worker in agricultural and nonagricultural sectors appears somewhat greater in the East than in the West.[15] For most Western Europe and the developed North American nations, the ratio of total factor returns

13. This is empirically analyzed by Simon Kuznets, "Quantitative Aspects of the Economic Growth of Nations: II. Industrial Distribution of National Product and Labor Force," *Economic Development and Cultural Change,* V, July 1956, Supplement. Data for labor incomes in agriculture and industry for 1938 are examined by J. R. Bellerby, *et al., Agriculture and Industry: Relative Income* (London: 1956) and show a different pattern, but the years selected for examination are somewhat unusual.

14. This may be seen by examining the relevant data in International Labour Office, *Yearbook of Labour Statistics* (Geneva: annual).

15. For the West, sector value-added and labor-force data were taken from: O.E.C.D., *National Accounts of O.E.C.D. Nations, 1958–67* (Paris: n.d.) and *Labor Force Statistics, 1956–1966* (Paris: 1968). For the East European nations excluding the Soviet Union, such data were taken from two essays in Joint Economic Committee, 91st Congress of the United States, *Economic Developments in Countries of Eastern Europe* (Washington, D.C.: 1970): Thad P. Alton, "Economic Structure and Growth in Eastern Europe,"

(property and labor incomes) per worker in agricultural to nonagricultural sectors falls between .40 and .60. For Eastern Europe the ratio of factor returns excluding rents in the two sectors also falls in the same range.[16] If rents were added, the ratio of factor returns in the two sectors would be somewhat higher than in the West.

From these two bits of evidence it seems likely that the ratio of average labor incomes in agricultural to that in nonagricultural sectors is as high or somewhat higher in the East than in the West. Such rough comparisons lead to the further conclusion that differences in average labor incomes in agricultural and nonagricultural sectors probably serve less as a source of total personal income inequality in the East than in the West, other things remaining equal. One important aspect in this *ceteris paribus* clause is differences in the degree of dispersion of labor incomes within the agricultural sector in East and West, a topic on which very little information is available.

b. *Labor earnings in different branches of mining and manufacturing.* Many Western observers of Eastern Europe have emphasized that although labor markets in East Europe are now relatively free of conscriptive devices, aggressive wages policies are followed by these nations to lure workers into certain designated priority branches; and, on the other hand, certain low priority industries (especially in the consumer goods branches) feature very low average wages. If this were the case, then one might suspect that the distribution of labor earnings in mining and manufacturing might be considerably more unequal in the East than in the West. Fortunately, data are readily at hand to examine these matters empirically.

The first step in the analysis is to compute and rank the average labor earnings in the various branches of mining and manufacturing

pp. 41–68; and Andrew Elias, "Magnitude and Distribution of the Labor Force in Eastern Europe," pp. 149–240. More detailed G.N.P. data for some of the East European nations are presented in Thad P. Alton, *et al., Czechoslovak National Income and Product in 1947–48 and 1955–56* (New York: 1962); *Hungarian National Income and Product in 1955* (New York: 1963); and *Polish National Income and Product in 1954, 1955, and 1956* (New York: 1965). For the Soviet Union, data were taken from Abraham S. Becker, *Soviet National Income, 1958–64* (Berkeley: 1969) and Joint Economic Committee, United States Congress, *New Direction in the Soviet Economy* (Washington, D.C.: 1966).

16. The data for the East European nations except the Soviet Union include imputed interest charges and exclude rents; from the more detailed data in Alton *et al.*, the interest imputations can be removed. The Soviet data were calculated with imputations for both rents and interest removed. The major biases remaining in the East European data are that differential income taxes to farmers and nonfarmers and differential retail prices paid by the two groups are not taken into account. On the other hand, the inclusion in the Western data of both rents and interest in agricultural value added, much of which does not accrue to the actual farmers, would undoubtedly more than offset the biases in the East European data.

TABLE 3–3

*Rankings of Average Wages and Salaries of Workers and Employees
in Mining and Manufacturing*[a]

ISIC No.	Industry	Average Rank Order (From Highest Average Earnings to Lowest)	
		West, 1963	*East, 1963–66*
32	Petroleum and coal products	1	3
34	Primary metals	2	2
31	Chemicals	3	7
38	Transport equipment	4	4
36	Machinery except electrical, transport	5	5
10–9	Mining	6	1
28	Printing	7	15
27	Paper products	8	12
37	Electrical machinery	9	6
30	Rubber products	10	8
21	Beverages	11	16.5
35	Metal products	12	10
33	Stone, glass, clay products	13	9
39	Miscellaneous industries	14	11
22	Tobacco	15	18
20	Food processing	16	16.5
26	Furniture	17	14
25	Lumber products except furniture	18	13
29	Leather products	19	19
23	Textiles	20	20
24	Clothing	21	21
Number of countries in sample		19	6
Coefficient of concordance (both statistically significant at .05 level).		.59	.80

a. Yugoslavia is omitted from the sample of Eastern nations because its relative wage structure is much more related to the pattern in the West than in the East. Sources and methods of calculation of the table are presented in Appendix B-12.

where these branches are defined in a relatively comparable manner. The average ranks for nations in the East and West are presented in Table 3–3.

From these data several important generalizations can be drawn: First, among the nations in both the West and the East, these rankings for the different countries are highly related to each other, with statistically significant concordance coefficients of .59 and .80 respectively.[17]

17. The greater similarity of wage structures in the East seems to be due to deliberate imitation of the Soviet Union by the other nations; for an interesting study of this process in China, see Peter Schran, "Unity and Diversity

Second, the rankings of relative branch earnings for the two groups of nations are also significantly related to each other with a Kendall rank order correlation coefficient of .67. This similarity in the pattern of relative branch wages and salaries within and between the East and the West should not be surprising since a very distinct pattern of relative branch earnings in mining and manufacturing has been found in both time-series and cross-section studies of Western nations by a number of economists.[18]

Third, East European workers and employees tend to receive relatively higher wages in mining, lumber products, and in the stone, glass, and clay products industries and relatively lower wages in printing, beverage, chemical, and paper industries. Except for mining, none of these relatively low- or high-wage industries fall into priority or nonpriority branches of industry. For the remaining branches average relative labor income patterns are very similar. Although the East European nations may follow an aggressive wage policy *vis-à-vis* a few priority industries, such policies do not appear to distort greatly the pattern of relative wages.

A second step is to estimate the degree of dispersion of earnings among branches of industries for each country and to compare them. Coefficients of variation (the standard deviation divided by the mean) were calculated on both an unweighted and weighted basis (using as weights the number of workers and employees in each branch) for every nation. The following regression was then computed:[19]

$$\text{In C.V.} = 2.455 - \underset{(.155)}{.1195} - \underset{(.166)}{.558^* \text{ In } (Y/P)}$$

Sample size = 24   Coefficient of determination = .39*

where C.V. = weighted coefficient of variation of average wages and salaries in various branches of mining and manufacturing.

S = dummy variable denoting economic system (0 = capitalist; 1 = socialist)

Y/P = per capita G.N.P. expressed in dollars.

of Russian and Chinese Industrial Wage Policies," *Journal of Asian Studies,* XXIII, Feb. 1964, pp. 245–51.

18. See, for instance: Walther G. Hoffman, *et al, Die branchenmaessige Lohnstruktur der Industrie: Ein intertemporaler und internationaler Vergleich* (Tuebingen: 1961); United Nations, Economic Commission for Europe, *Incomes in Postwar Europe* (Geneva: 1967); John T. Dunlop and Melvin Rothbaum, "International Comparison of Wage Structures," *International Labour Review,* LXXI, April 1955, pp. 347–63; or D. E. Cullen, "The Interindustry Wage Structure, 1899–1950," *American Economic Review,* XLVI, June 1956, pp. 353–70.

19. An asterisk denotes statistical significance at the .05 level. Yugoslavia is omitted from the regression because of problems regarding the handling of profit redistributions among the workers (for this, see Howard M.

As expected, the degree of dispersion between average branch wages and salaries decreases as the level of economic development increases; the coefficients of variation decline roughly 0.5 percent for each 1 percent increase in per capita G.N.P. Contrary to the results of Galenson and Fox (which are based on a much smaller sample),[20] no significant differences exist in dispersion of wages and salaries among branches between nations in the East and West when the level of development is held constant. We must therefore conclude that the "aggressive" nature of wage policies in Eastern Europe may have been overstated by Eastern Europeans and overemphasized by Western analysts of the East European scene. Further, we cannot expect differences in the dispersion of wages and salaries among the various branches of mining and manufacturing to affect significantly the relative degrees of inequality of the distribution of labor earnings in the East and West, at least in the mid-1960s for which the calculations were made.[21]

c. *Dispersion of wages and salaries of males outside of agriculture.* We now come to the crucial question of how income is differentiated within particular industries. One facet of this question is the degree to which "material incentives" are used to encourage production; another facet is the degree to which particular groups (e.g., white- and blue-collar groups) act as noncompeting wage groups; and a final facet is the degree of inequality of education (or human capital) among the labor force. For this human capital factor, there is considerable evidence (which is presented in Appendix A-10) that there are few important differences among nations with different economic systems, other things remaining equal. For the other considerations, however, we have little systematic evidence and must approach the topic differently.

Until recently few empirical studies were made of the distribution of labor earnings in Eastern Europe, even though data were available for most countries.[22] In order to take advantage of comparable data on the

---

Wachtel, "Workers' Management and Interindustry Wage Differentials in Yugoslavia," *Journal of Political Economy,* LXXX, May-June 1972, pp. 540–61); Denmark is omitted for technical reasons. For further details on the calculation, see Appendix B-12.

20. Walter Galenson and Alan Fox, "Earnings and Employment in Eastern Europe, 1957 to 1963," *The Quarterly Journal of Economics,* LXXXI, May 1967, pp. 220–40.

21. In earlier times this might not have been the case. For the Soviet Union, interesting analyses of wage policies in the early 1930s are made by Bergson, *The Structure . . . ,* and Rudolf Becker, *Sowjetische Lohnpolitik zwischen Ideologie und Wirtschaftsgesetz* (Berlin: 1965).

22. One pioneering micro-economic study based on unpublished data is by M. Gardner Clark, "Comparative Wage Structure in the Steel Industry of the Soviet Union and Western Countries," Industrial Relations Research Association, *Proceedings,* XIII, December 1970, pp. 366–88. For many years the most extensive study of Soviet wages was based on data for the early

distribution of wages and salaries in Western Europe, I follow closely an analytical method pioneered by Harold Lydall.[23]

Lydall plotted graphically the distribution of labor earnings and determined such earnings at particular percentiles (e.g., earnings in the 5th percentile are the earnings received by those whose labor incomes are greater than 95 percent of the rest of the labor force). He then calculated these earnings as a percentage of the median labor income. This procedure enabled him to compare a great deal of available wage data without the necessity of estimating wages and salaries of those at the extremes of the distribution, which would be necessary if Gini coefficients were calculated.

For simplicity, I follow Lydall and take the distribution of pretax-money wages and salaries of males who work for the entire period under examination in all occupations and industries outside of farming for the entire country. The available data for estimates for economically developed or semideveloped nations are presented in Table 3–4. However, caution must be exercised in interpreting the data for two reasons. First, the underlying data in certain cases are poor or were collected in unspecified ways; e.g., for certain East European nations we do not know whether bonuses were included or whether particular highly paid workers in the service sector were included.[24] Second, the method by which the published data were adjusted to the "standard definitions" is crude.

In order to draw certain general conclusions from the data—especially the influence of economic systems—it is useful to separate out the most important causal factors. For instance, it has often been claimed that the distribution of labor incomes becomes more equal as the level of development rises and for supporting evidence a number of institutional

1930s (Bergson, *The Structure . . .*). Recently several studies have appeared, of which a comparative study by Peter J. D. Wiles and Stefan Markowski, "Income Distribution Under Communism and Capitalism: Some Facts About Poland, the UK, the USA, and the USSR," *Soviet Studies,* XXII, January 1971, pp. 344–70, and April 1971, pp. 487–512 must be especially noted. It is difficult to compare the Wiles-Markowski results with mine below since they use different years, different data on income, and different analytical techniques. Roughly speaking, their data (Table 28) show the distribution of wages and salaries outside of agriculture in 1966 most unequal in the United Kingdom, followed closely behind by the Soviet Union and then Poland, while I find nonagricultural wage and salary incomes around 1960 most unequal in the Soviet Union, followed by the United Kingdom and Poland. Since considerable wage levelization occurred in the Soviet Union in the early 1960s, their results and mine are not necessarily inconsistent.

23. Harold Lydall, *The Structure of Earnings* (Oxford: 1968).

24. Indeed, one reason why the distribution of labor earnings in East Europe follows a log-normal, rather than a Pareto curve, may be because such bonuses—which are given to the top labor income receivers—are omitted. Additional doubts about the handling of bonuses come through Lydall's observation (pp. 150–1) that relative incomes of white-collar *vis-à-vis* blue-collar workers in Eastern Europe are much lower.

and economic factors can be mentioned. For instance, as the level of development of a nation rises, an increasingly larger percentage of the population receives primary, secondary, and higher education so that the distribution of education (and income arising from education) are less unequal; further, transmission of labor market information becomes less expensive and labor mobility increases so that wage differentials in different markets may diminish and barriers around noncompeting groups become less important; finally, as work between different groups becomes more interdependent and as the percentage of white-collar to blue-collar workers continues to rise, marginal productivity of individual workers or groups of workers becomes more difficult to calculate and wage differentials become increasingly more arduous to defend.

The size of a nation, as measured by the population, might influence labor earnings differentials in two different ways. First, as noted above, the larger the population the greater the number of regional labor markets and the greater the potential for considerable differences in wages for the same type of work. Second, as noted in Chapter VI, the larger the population (or total G.N.P.), the higher the percentage of the labor force working for a given number of big enterprises, which might introduce a "standardization effect" that would narrow differentials between

TABLE 3–4

Distribution of Labor Earnings Following the "Standard Definition"
in Twenty-two Nations[a]

Country	Year	Labor Earnings as Percentage of Median Income			
		5th Percentile	*10th Percentile*	*75 Percentile*	*85th Percentile*
Western nations					
United States	1959	206%	167%	75%	60%
New Zealand	1960/1	178	150	83	67
Australia	1959/60	185	157	84	66
Sweden	1959	200	165	78	62
Canada	1960/1	205	166	79	59
Belgium	1964	206	164	84	76
France	1963	282	205	73	60
United Kingdom	1960/1	200	162	80	71
West Germany	1957	205	165	77	55
Denmark	1956	200	160	82	65
Austria	1959/60	210	170	80	70
Finland	1960	250	200	73	56
Japan	1955	270	211	64	50
Spain	1964	220	180	75	62

TABLE 3–4 *continued*

*Distribution of Labor Earnings Following the "Standard Definition"
in Twenty-two Nations*[a]

Country	Year	Labor Earnings as Percentage of Median Income			
		5th Percentile	*10th Percentile*	*75 Percentile*	*85th Percentile*
Eastern nations					
Czechoslovakia	1964	165	145	85	79
East Germany	1959	180	151	86	77
Hungary	1964	180	155	83	74
Soviet Union	1959	245	195	69	61
Poland	1960	200	170	76	64
Bulgaria	1962	172	150	86	79
Yugoslavia	1963	200	166	80	71
Standardized for income and population					
($1000 G.N.P. per capita, 40,000,000 population)					
Western nations		238	189	71	58
Eastern nations		202	169	77	69
($2000 G.N.P. per capita, 40,000,000 population)					
Western nations		216	173	76	61
Eastern nations		184	155	82	73

a. The data in the first three columns for all countries except Bulgaria, East Germany, and the Soviet Union come from Lydall, p. 153; for the last column, adjustments of data presented by Lydall in Appendix 7 were made following the method he used for obtaining the data in the first three columns. The nondeveloped nations and the Netherlands (for which data were not comparable) were dropped from the analysis. For sources and estimation methods for Bulgaria, East Germany, and the Soviet Union, see Appendix B-13. The available data for Romania (see Appendix B-13) are in the same order of magnitude as the other East European nations.

The data for the "standardized" nations in East and West are obtained from a regression analysis explained in the text; the exact equations are presented in Appendix B-9.

regions and counteract the first mentioned factor. (It must be added that this "standardization effect" might be related to economic systems when wages are determined centrally, rather than reflecting supply and demand forces in each region.)

Using a regression analysis we can investigate the influence of per capita income, total population, economic system and other variables on the wage differentials data in Table 3–4. It turns out that the first three variables appear to play a statistically significant explanatory role while other variables tested were much less important.[25] The results of these calculations are used for the determination of the standardized wage distribution presented at the bottom of Table 3–4. A close examination of the various regressions allows several important conclusions to be drawn:

First, as expected the degree of inequality of labor earnings outside of agriculture declines as the level of development rises.

Second, the degree of labor income inequality increases as the population of a nation increases. Thus, the regional separation of labor markets appears to swamp the "standardization effect."

Third, the degree of inequality of labor income is greater in the West than in the East, other things being equal. If we calculate Gini coefficients of inequality, we find that the coefficients are about .06 greater in the Western nations than in the Eastern nations, which is a considerable and important difference.[26] There is some evidence that this greater equalization of income in the East may be due to a lower ratio of average earnings of white-collar to blue-collar workers.[27] Unfortunately, we know too little about wages and salaries in Eastern Europe to know if other causal factors may play an important role in these matters as well.

25. The regression equations for the pooled sample are given in Appendix B-9. Tests were carried out to see whether it is statistically legitimate to pool the data from the East and West and in each case it was. The regressions are calculated in logarithms in order to minimize the influence of extreme points; other forms of the regression were also calculated and, surprisingly, showed roughly the same results.

Other variables were also added to the regressions such as growth of G.N.P. It can be argued that the demand for skilled workers *vis-à-vis* unskilled workers changes if the economy is expanding rapidly and this would affect wage differentials, other things being equal; but these did not prove statistically significant determinants.

26. A Gini coefficient of inequality is calculated by lining up the income recipients from poorest to richest, determining the curve that indicates what percentage of total income is received by the poorest x percent (a Lorenz curve) and then estimating the "area of inequality" (the difference between this curve and a curve representing total income equality) as a fraction of the total area bounded by the curve representing total income equality. The Gini coefficient runs from 0.00 (total equality) to 1.00 (total inequality where one recipient receives all income).

In the calculations mentioned in the text the Gini coefficients for socialist and capitalist nations were, respectively .21 and .27 (when average income is $1000 and the nation has 40,000,000 people) and .18 and .24 (when average income is $2000 and the nation has 40,000,000 people). These Gini coefficients were calculated in two steps: First, wage differentials for two other percentiles (the 20th and the 95th) were estimated and regressions similar to those discussed in the above footnote were calculated. Second, I assumed that for nations in both the East and West, the average labor earnings of all workers above the 5th percentile were 16.7 percent higher than the labor earnings of those in the 5th percentile; and that the average earnings of all those below the 95th percentile were 10 percent below the earnings of those in the 95th percentile.

27. Lydall, pp. 150–1.

It is noteworthy that the Soviet Union appears to have the greatest inequality of labor incomes of any nation in the sample. We might expect such a result, given the Soviet Union's large size and relatively low degree of economic development in comparison to smaller and more developed nations such as Switzerland and Sweden. It must be emphasized that the Soviet economy experienced considerable wage levelization in the years following that for which data are presented in the table (1959) so that differences in wage inequality between the Soviet Union and other nations might have been smaller or eliminated by the late sixties. Finally, I must point out that generalizations about wage and salary inequalities in social-ism and capitalism that are based solely on data from the Soviet Union and the United States are very misleading; unfortunately, a number of commentators have chosen this procedure instead of employing the more arduous method of basing their generalizations on a larger sample.

d. *Other factors.* We cannot, of course, generalize quantitatively about the distribution of labor incomes of families (which is perhaps more interesting than that of individuals) from data on the distribution of individual labor incomes without additional information about unemploy-ment, earnings differentials between men and women, degree of moon-lighting, extent to which families where the head earns a particular in-come have two or more wage earners, correlation between level of wages of household heads and other working members of the family, and so forth. Nevertheless, certain qualitative judgments are relevant to take into consideration.

In Eastern Europe the participation rate of women in the labor force is higher than in the West, especially among women with small children. Among other reasons for this is the extensive network of day-care centers for children. The removal of a barrier for women working in Eastern Europe probably acts to make the distribution of family incomes *vis-à-vis* individual labor earnings somewhat more equal in the East than in the West. The role of the other factors mentioned in the previous paragraph should play a much less important role in East-West comparisons since they are very much less specifically related to economic system.

e. *A brief resume of empirical results.* Scattered data on relative aver-age labor earnings in agricultural and nonagricultural sectors lead to the tentative conclusion that the differences among nations in the East ap-peared to be equal to, or smaller than, such differences in the West. The data on individual labor incomes outside of agriculture show that other things being equal, the Gini coefficient of income inequality is consider-ably higher in the West than in the East. An argument is also presented above that the distribution of family incomes *vis-à-vis* individual incomes should be slightly more equal in the East than in the West.

Such conclusions can be brought together in a single tentative quantitative generalization: The Gini coefficient of inequality of family labor incomes is at least .06 higher in the West than in the East, other things remaining equal.[28] Because of uncertainties about the basic data on which particular generalizations are drawn, qualifying adjectives indicating this limitation must be attached to the overall generalization. With our present state of knowledge, it is doubtful that more can be said.

D. The Impact of Property Income on the Size Distribution of Income

Two factors need to be explored in this section: the inequality of property income in the population and the correlation between labor and property income among income recipients. It is convenient to discuss the second factor first.

If individual receipts of property and labor income are inversely related, then highly unequal distributions of property and labor income could offset each other and the overall distribution of total income could be relatively equal. Such a situation may have occurred in nineteenth-century China where it is reported that physical labor was so disdained that many of those receiving property income were willing to live on the verge of subsistence, rather than to soil their hands by work.[29] And in other agricultural societies, the landowners not only would not but, indeed, could not obtain labor income. (This tradition has been preserved for us in novels such as I.A. Goncharov's *Oblomov*.) But does an inverse relation between property and labor income exist in modern industrial societies?

Despite the publicity given to nonworking widows and orphans living off of property earnings or rich playboys, jet setters, the "beautiful people" and other dubious species of the idle rich, some indications point to a positive correlation between property and labor income. Certain positions with high labor income permit their holders to obtain the requi-

28. This result is qualitatively consistent with the scattered data on income distribution in the various East European nations (discussed in United Nations, E.C.E., *Incomes in Postwar Europe,* or presented in the various national statistical yearbooks of these nations) which I have not used in these comparisons because the manner in which they are calculated is not specified and they may be considerably less comparable with the Western data than the wage information.

29. Fei Hsiao-Tung, "Peasantry and Gentry: An Interpretation of Chinese Social Structure and Its Changes," *American Journal of Sociology,* LII, July 1946, pp. 1–17.

site information for quite profitable investments; similarly, certain positions paying high salaries are open primarily to those already possessing great wealth. But more to the point, casual observation suggests that most men enjoying high property incomes generally work in Western societies if for no other reason than to increase their wealth even more. Some recent data also support this contention.[30]

It should come as no surprise that in capitalist nations property holdings are quite unequally held. For the United States, for instance, the top 10 percent of all wealth holders own roughly 55 percent of total wealth, and the top 20 percent roughly 75 percent.[31] Measuring the impact of this inequality of wealth distribution on the distribution of income without taking into account either explicitly or implicitly the correlation between labor and property income slows only part of the picture. Fortunately, the available data allow us to handle matters in a better way.

Although considerable sample survey data of family income in the United States and developed Western nations have been collected, the published results seldom distinguish between property and labor income. The results cited below are an exception to this rule and come from a study by Professor Irving B. Kravis of income of United States urban consumer units in 1950.[32]

The Gini coefficient of income inequality was .35 for wages and salaries alone, and .36 when one-third of self-employment income was estimated as labor income (which I consider as a low estimate). Property income (interest, dividends, and rents) was much more unequally distributed with a Gini coefficient of .60. However, the Gini coefficient of total family income was .38 when all income (including transfers) was included. Exclusion of transfer payments (which are a more important share of the incomes of the poor) might raise the Gini coefficient of total family income another .01 or .02, which means that the existence of property income raises the Gini coefficient of income in equality roughly .03 to .05.[33]

30. See especially aggregated data that are presented and analyzed by Dorothy S. Projector, Gertrude S. Weiss, and Erling T. Thoresen, "Composition of Income as Shown by the Survey of Financial Characteristics of Consumers," in Soltow, ed., Table 3.

31. These data were taken from Lorenz curves of the wealth distribution for the mid-1950s presented by Robert J. Lampman, *The Share of Top Wealth Holders in National Wealth, 1922–56* (Princeton: 1962), Chapters 6 and 7. These data are consistent with the data concerning the distribution of property income presented by Kravis, p. 193, for urban consumer units in 1950.

32. Kravis, *The Structure of Income.* . . .

33. A roughly similar picture can be gained from the data presented by Projector, *et al*. Although this source has later data, the numbers are not presented in the proper form so that very exact comparisons can be made. The

To what extent can the results for the United States be generalized for other developed capitalist nations? In England the distribution of wealth appears more unequal than in the United States,[34] but the differences do not appear great enough to raise the Gini coefficient of income inequality more than .005. Further, it appears likely that the more unequal the distribution of wealth, the less the correlation between labor and property income so that total income inequality does not change to the same degree as does the inequality of property income. In developed capitalist economies, we can make the rough generous estimate that the existence of property income probably raises the Gini coefficient of income inequality .03 to .06.

E. Summary and Conclusions

From the analysis of the distribution of labor incomes, I contend that the incomes in socialist nations are more evenly distributed than those in capitalist nations and that the Gini coefficient of inequality of such incomes is, other things remaining the same, at least .06 less in East Europe. If agricultural incomes were much more unevenly distributed in East Europe than in the West, then the differences in the inequality of labor incomes in socialist and capitalist nations might be somewhat less. Unfortunately, we have little comparable information on the distribution of agricultural incomes.

From an exploration of the impact of property income in the United States, we arrive at the rough conclusion that in developed capitalist nations, the existence of property income increases the Gini coefficient of inequality of total income from .03 to .06. In Eastern Europe the impact of property income on the size distribution of income should be extremely small and should only have some effect in agriculture where collective farmers might obtain some differential rents.

From such considerations we can estimate that the Gini coefficient of total income inequality is at least .10 less in the East than in the West, other things remaining equal (e.g., level of economic development). Fur-

---

calculations of Gini coefficients including and excluding property income seem quite implausible (p. 111, where income inequality including property income is less than when property income is excluded) and I suspect that a numerical mistake was made.

34. International comparisons of wealth distributions are still in their infancy. Lampman, p. 212, shows that distribution of wealth in the United States is more equal than wealth in England and Wales. Certain data, discussed by Lampman, also suggest that the inequality of wealth holdings has gradually declined, a situation that is investigated with the aid of a simulation model in the next chapter.

ther, the greater inequality of labor income in the West is probably a somewhat more important source of income inequality between systems than the existence of property income. This tentative conclusion, let me add, runs quite contrary to the conventional (both Marxist and non-Marxist) wisdom on such matters that focuses almost exclusive attention on property as the chief causal factor underlying differences in income inequality between East and West.

It must be explicitly noted that the data do not indicate anything about the distribution of welfare because they include neither the impact of taxes nor government expenditures. But at least these data constitute a first step toward comparisons of the distribution of welfare. Further, as I mentioned, they cannot be used in any way either to justify or, for that matter, to criticize the existence of property income without additional analysis.

Such calculations are also important in obtaining a quantitative perspective on the impact of ownership on the distribution of income in comparison to other sources of inequality. Certainly within any modern economic system the inequality of labor income is vastly more important in determining the inequality of income than the inequality of wealth holdings. Even if we reduce the inequality of total income by controlling for age and that of employment status by calculating lifetime income distributions, it appears that labor income inequality is still the overwhelmingly most important factor underlying the inequality of total income.[35]

Although we see in this chapter that economic system, defined in terms of ownership of the means of production, does have an impact on the distribution of income, other factors also play an important role. For instance, the distribution of labor income is affected by the degree of economic development as well as the size of the economy. Although sources of labor income inequality have received considerable attention, factors underlying the distribution of ownership have been relatively neglected in the economic literature. This latter topic receives considerable attention in Chapter IV.

---

35. From the estimates of Robert Summers, *An Econometric Investigation of the Size Distribution of Lifetime Average Annual Income,* Technical Report No. 31, Department of Economics, Stanford University (Stanford: 1956), p. 110, a Gini coefficient of lifetime income of .21 can be calculated for the United States. Even if removal of property income would reduce this by .06 (a high guess), differences in labor incomes would still be the preponderant source of income inequalities. Further notes on quantitative effects are presented in Chapter IV, note 10.

Two Notes on the Distribution of Property Holding

Le mépris des richesses était dans les
philosophes un désir caché de venger
leur mérite de l'injustice de la fortune
par le mépris des mêmes biens dont elle
les privait . . .

La Rochefoucauld[1]

A. Introduction

The purpose of this chapter is to investigate some major factors influencing the distribution of property holding among individuals. From this investigation alleged trends in the concentration of property holding in the

1. François I de La Rochefoucauld, *Reflexions ou sentences et maximes morales,* Maxim No. 54: The scorn for wealth among philosophers was

hands of a small group of people can be viewed with greater perspective. In order to carry out this aim, it is necessary to examine separately particular subsets of property rights, namely ownership and control, for trends in concentration of these rights appear to differ. Further, the method of inquiry into these two subsets of rights differs considerably.

First, I analyze the size distribution of ownership and, to make the discussion more concrete, its influence on the distribution of income. For this purpose, I employ a simulation model and examine the effect of such socio-economic variables as the rules of inheritance, differential fertility among income classes, the pattern of marriages, and the intergenerational savings function on the distributions of wealth and income. Since adequate data on many of these variables are not available, most of this exercise must be carried out on a hypothetical level. The results point to the most important factors we must examine in future empirical research in order to understand the long-run forces that play an important role in determining the size distribution of ownership.

Following this discussion, I attempt to examine the distribution of control rights by exploring the degree to which ownership and control rights are correlated and the differences in distributional trends between these two types of property rights. Although no final answer on the distribution of control can be given, the broad outlines of the major problems are presented so as to introduce the more detailed research on this topic in further chapters. Finally, I summarize briefly the available evidence on the impact of the separation of ownership and control rights on actual management decisions of large enterprises with regard to profit making.

B. A Model of the Distribution of Ownership[2]

In analyzing the long-run determinants of the distribution of ownership, we must not only pay attention to socio-economic variables discussed in the literature such as the rules of inheritance, the pattern of mate selection, and the relative fertility of different income classes, but also to the reciprocal influences of the size distributions of income and ownership on each other.

---

a hidden desire to avenge their honor against the injustices of fate by despising the very things of which she deprived them.

2. The following analysis is a condensation of a more extensive treatment of these matters that has been published elsewhere. For further details, see Frederic L. Pryor, "Simulation of the Impact of Social and Economic Institutions on the Size Distribution of Income and Wealth," *American Economic Review*, LXXX, March 1973, pp. 50–73.

The model rests on the pioneering work of Guy H. Orcutt, *et al., Microanalysis of Socio-economic Systems: A Simulation Study* (New York: 1961).

To take all the major long-run factors influencing the size distributions of income and ownership into account is an extremely complicated
matter and we face two alternative research strategies: Either we model
these factors mathematically, which requires some drastic simplifications
in order to keep the equation system solvable; or we take more factors
into account by simulating their impact, a procedure which does not permit a completely general solution but which does permit us to investigate
numerous features of economic systems using parameters of particular
interest. The latter is adopted here and the results of long-run simulations
covering many generations are shown.

The simulation results presented in the various tables shows the size
distribution of income when the distribution of wealth reaches an equilibrium. To place this model in perspective, it is useful to note that the
variance of personal income can be derived from three sources arising
respectively from the variance in the distribution of labor income, of
property income, and of the interaction between these two variables.[3] In
this model variations of labor income are handled by assigning everyone
a lifetime income equal to the average lifetime income times a random
variable with a mean of unity and a specified standard deviation. Variations in property income stem only from differential holdings of wealth;
returns per unit of wealth are assumed equal. And finally, no correlation
is assumed between individual labor and property incomes. Thus the critical factor for a change in the distribution of income is a change in the
distribution of wealth which, in turn, is greatly influenced by the different
socio-economic variables that are investigated.

The results of the model allow us to pinpoint some important factors
influencing the concentration of income and wealth. Because the simulation model is complicated and the results are difficult to grasp easily, the
model is presented in several stages of increasing complexity.

Although other simulation models of income distribution have been made,
e.g., Hans-Juergen Krupp, *Theorie der personellen Einkommensverteilung*
(Berlin: 1968), these are considerably different from mine and, moreover,
focus primarily on short-run problems.

Several recent analytic approaches toward the distribution of wealth and
income touch on some of the problems discussed below. The most mathematical analysis is by Joseph E. Stiglitz, "The Distribution of Income and
Wealth among Individuals," *Econometrica*, XXXVII, July 1969, pp. 382–97;
a less formal analysis is by James E. Meade, *Efficiency, Equality, and the
Ownership of Property* (London: 1964).

3. The formula for this relationship is presented in Appendix A-4. This
approach neglects certain types of interactions such as those discussed by E.
Preiser ("Property and Power in the Theory of Distribution," *International
Economic Papers* No. 2, 1952, pp. 206–20) in which the distribution of income is affected by the elasticity of the labor supply which, in turn, is influenced by the distribution of wealth.

1. A Simple Simulation Model

The simulation model starts with one hundred unmarried people with an arbitrary initial distribution of ownership which is in the form of productive capital. These people are "put to work" and both lifetime labor and property incomes are generated by means of a production function and the assumption of full employment and of average factor payment equal to its marginal product. (A Cobb-Douglas function is used, which means that the shares of labor and property income remain the same over time.) The total amount of property income is divided among all wealth holders in amounts proportional to the quantity of wealth held by each; the total amount of labor income is distributed to the entire population by giving each a wage equal to the average wage times a normally distributed variable (which is supposed to represent a differential distribution of abilities such as intelligence and/or diligence).

The people in the model are then lined up according to income and marriages are arranged according to one of three different rules: (1) A person may only marry another person next to him on the income scale (this I call the "no-choice" rule); (2) the chances for a person marrying anyone else are equal (the "equal-choice" rule); (3) a person can marry anyone but the chances are greater if the two are closer to each other on the income distribution scale (the "limited-choice" rule).[4]

We then may have the government step in and redistribute income (either progressively or regressively). This is followed by the accumulation or disposal of family wealth (positive or negative savings) so that a prespecified ratio (by a formula discussed below) of family wealth (which is later inherited by the children) to family income is achieved; this intergenerational savings function is discussed in detail below. A simplifying assumption used in the model is that all wealth and net changes in wealth (net savings or dissavings) are in the form of productive capital which yields property income.

At this point the various families have children according to their income in the following manner. First, the families are divided into three groups according to whether they are among those with the highest family incomes, lowest incomes, or in-between. (The percentage of families falling in each group can be varied.) Then the number of children are

4. The probabilities of one person marrying another are, of course, changed whenever a couple is married and removed from the pool of eligibles. Therefore, the statement in the text must be considered as just approximately true. For the limited-choice model, the probability of marriage is inversely proportional to the difference in income rank between the two individuals. The calculations are simplified by not designating the sex of the individuals so that marriages between any two individuals may be possible.

specified for each group, e.g., the rich can be designated to have more or fewer children than the poor, or *vice-versa*. Polygamous situations can be approximated by specifying many children for the rich and no children for the poor, since in such societies it is believed that only the wealthier can afford to support many wives and the low-income men often do not marry.

The parents are then removed from the scene (husband and wife are assumed to have equal life spans) and family wealth is divided among the children according to one of three different rules: (1) One child can receive everything (the "primogeniture" rule);[5] (2) the property can be divided equally among all children (the "equal-division" rule); (3) the first child can receive half of the wealth and the remainder is divided equally among the rest (the "compromise" rule). At this point the government can also redistribute wealth (a sort of inheritance tax). We now have a group of people with a given distribution of wealth of productive capital whom we "put to work"; the process is repeated many times to see if a stable distribution of income and wealth is achieved.

With only a few exceptions (discussed below) the processes converge toward an "equilibrium distribution" of income and of ownership of wealth which, when attained, is maintained for all succeeding generations. In certain cases, however, the process is extremely slow and in order to avoid inordinate computer expenses, the following procedure was adopted: In every case the simulation was carried out twice, once starting from a highly unequal initial distribution of wealth (where the wealthiest 10 percent of individuals shares the total societal wealth in equal portions) and once starting from a relatively equal wealth distribution (where the wealthiest 75 percent of individuals shares the total wealth in equal amounts). Each simulation was then run for thirty generations (which represents 1,000 years if a generation is calculated as 33 1/3 years or 750 years if a generation is 25 years) and the end results of the simulations starting from different points were averaged; in almost all cases, the two end results were very similar to each other.

In the tables I present three measures of income inequality of the equilibrium size distribution of lifetime income: Gini coefficients (these are defined in note 26 of the previous chapter; the coefficient ranges from 0.00, which represents total equality, to 1.00, which represents total inequality); the share of total income earned by the richest 10 percent; and

5. I have used an extreme form of primogeniture in which the first child, regardless of sex, obtains the family's entire wealth. This variant of primogeniture leads to the most extreme wealth-holding inequalities and, in addition, is computationally simpler in that sexes do not need to be assigned to particular individuals for the model to work. A more usual case of primogeniture is, of course, when only the eldest son obtains the entire estate.

TABLE 4–1

Basic Equilibrium Patterns of the Distribution of Wealth

Inheritance Rules	Marriage Rules		
	No-choice	*Limited-choice*	*Equal-choice*
Primogeniture	Wealth concentrates to a single owner; fast convergence	Same as no-choice rule, but convergence is slower	Same as no-choice rule, but convergence is slower than other primogeniture situations
Equal-division	Wealth distribution remains the same as starting position	Wealth becomes evenly distributed but convergence is slow.	Wealth becomes evenly distributed; convergence is faster than with limited-choice rule

the antilog of the standard deviation of the logarithms of income (the "SD indicator"). In certain cases where it is useful to discuss relative speeds of convergence, the period is measured from the starting point to the point when an equilibrium Gini coefficient is achieved (plus or minus a small amount).[6]

2. *The Model without Capital Accumulation*

Before the numerical results are presented, certain features of the model may perhaps be better understood if we examine in a qualitative fashion the effect of certain variables.

If we take a situation where every family, regardless of income, has two children, where there is no variation in labor income (the random factor is not yet introduced), and where families do not add to or decrease their inherited wealth (i.e., family wealth is passed on unchanged, regardless of family income; such a situation occurs when land is the basic source of wealth and is not alienable), the observed patterns of convergence of the distribution of wealth are quite simple and are outlined in Table 4–1.

With primogeniture, wealth accumulates eventually into a single hand.[7] The speed of convergence is inversely proportional to the degree to which people choose marriage partners in other income brackets. With equal division of inherited property and with everyone marrying a person

6. The exact method employed is described in Appendix A-7.
7. If the eldest son variant of primogeniture is used, then, of course, this extreme result will not obtain.

next to him on the income distribution, it should be readily apparent that no change will occur in the size distribution of income and wealth—as long as all families continue to have two children. In the other two cases with equal division of inherited property, wealth eventually becomes completely equally distributed.

The compromise rule of inheritance, where the first child receives half of the property and the remainder is divided equally among the other children, is the same as the equal division rule (under the assumption of two-child families).

The speed of conversion to equilibrium depends, of course, on the distribution of wealth at the starting point and at equilibrium. Starting from a highly unequal distribution of income, convergence was found to be achieved in the primogeniture case in three to five generations; starting from the more equal distribution of wealth, convergence takes six to fifteen generations. For the equal-division cases when convergence occurs, the process generally takes somewhat longer. Although convergence speeds in these examples appear to have little economical meaning, they become important when governmental policy measures are introduced (i.e., redistribution of income and/or wealth) and certain goals of income distribution are set.

If we now introduce a random variable representing differential abilities so that labor incomes are the product of the average wage times a random variable (with a mean of unity), the basic patterns are modified in the following ways:

(a) The greater the variation in the random element, the more unequal the equilibrium income distribution becomes in those five cases in Table 4–1 where convergence is observed. This is because greater extremes in labor income are generated.

(b) In situations where people are allowed choice in marriage partners, the convergence process is speeded up where there is an equal-division inheritance rule and slowed down where there is primogeniture. This stems from the fact that there is a greater mixing of people of different wealth at the time of marriage (since the marriage rules are based on total income, not wealth alone). Where people marry those next to them on the income scale, a complication arises which is discussed below.

An important methodological point is that introduction of a random element raises difficulties in determining the exact equilibrium distribution of income. In interpreting the various tables presented below, small differences in the coefficients should be overlooked and, although data are presented in the third place, variations of 1 percent or less should be neglected.

Throughout the remaining simulations the random factor is set with a coefficient of variation of 15 percent, which is roughly similar to the variation of I.Q. test scores.

Differential fertility of income classes also affects the equilibrium distribution of ownership and income. In all cases primogeniture leads to a highly unequal income and ownership distribution since whatever the fertility pattern, only one child receives all the property. Similarly, in all cases where the rich have only one child (which leads automatically to primogeniture) highly unequal equilibrium income and ownership distributions are also generated.

In other primogeniture cases, differential fertility of income groups affects the end results considerably. In cases where fertility increases with income, the system should converge relatively quickly to fairly even distributions. (Such a situation allegedly occurred in past eras in oriental despotic societies where the rulers encouraged polygamy so that the rich would have a much higher fertility rate than other classes and, at the same time, forbade primogeniture; the end result was supposed to be an economy with a relatively even distribution of income and no independent bases of wealth with which to challenge royal authority.)[8]

Simulation results of different patterns of fertility among the income classes are presented in Appendix A-8. For simplicity, I assume that fertility is the same in all income classes, unless otherwise specified, for the rest of the chapter.

We are now ready to begin the quantitative investigation. In Table 4–2, the results for the most simple situation with different marriage and inheritance rules are presented. There is no accumulation of wealth for the society as a whole and each family passes on only that wealth which it inherits.

As expected, the inequality of income, as measured by the Gini coefficient, the standard deviation of the logarithms of income, and the income percentage of the richest families is higher with primogeniture than with the compromise or equal-division inheritance rules (which give the same answers because each family has only two children). As we can also expect, the equilibrium income distribution does not seem greatly affected by the marriage rules; in this simple model the major effect of the marriage rules appears on the speed at which equilibrium is achieved. Only in much more complicated models do the marriage rules appear to have much impact on the equilibrium size distribution of income. One puzzling phenomenon appears in the primogeniture case where the equilibrium income increases slightly in inequality as the choice of marriage partners is limited (moving from equal-choice to no-choice), using as a measure the share of income of the richest families, but decreases slightly in inequality, employing the standard deviation indicator. This is due most likely to a change in the shape of the distribution of income, with

8. Such systems are analyzed by Karl Wittfogel, *Oriental Despotism: A Comparative Study of Total Power* (New Haven: 1957).

slightly increasing inequality at the high income end and slightly decreasing inequality at the middle and lower income levels. (This particular result does not appear to be due to random factors since equilibrium was achieved from all starting points of the simulation and the various results given particular marriage and inheritance rules were very similar.)

In the simulation model a simple wealth redistribution process can be set up so that all inherited wealth is taxed a given percentage and then the total amount of taxed wealth is distributed equally among all individuals. If the tax rate is positive, then such a process is progressive because the least wealthy end up with a net gain in wealth while the most wealthy end up with a net loss. This manner of specifying a capital tax on inherited wealth allows the total amount of privately held wealth to remain constant.

The results of imposing a capital redistribution tax are presented in Table 4–3 and can be summarized quite easily: The greater the redistribution of wealth, the more equal the equilibrium distribution of income and wealth will be. This, of course, is not surprising. The equilibrium income distribution is most unequal for the primogeniture case and most equal when family property is evenly distributed among heirs, a result similar to the previous findings. The marriage rules again have a relatively small impact. It must be noted that with very high redistributions of wealth, the differences in the equilibrium distributions with the various marriage and inheritance rules are relatively small; it appears that after a certain point, the redistribution swamps the effects of other factors.

Since redistribution of wealth can be a deliberate tool of governmental policy, the rate of convergence to the equilibrium income distribution is of considerable interest. Several generalizations can be made. First, imposition of a redistribution of wealth greatly increases the speed of convergence; in almost all cases, convergence is achieved within five generations (with the major portion of the changes occurring in the first two generations). Second, convergence appears to be faster when the model is started with a relatively more unequal wealth distribution than with a relatively more equal wealth distribution. In other words, achieving a more equal distribution of income by means of a redistribution of wealth can be carried out more quickly in those cases where the difference between actual and desired distributions are greatest.

Introducing a redistributive income tax changes, of course, the equilibrium income distribution. In this case wealth is not affected; and since marriages are arranged according to relative income, this part of the system is not affected either. Under the assumptions in this section about no net intergenerational accumulations of family capital, the speed of convergence toward the equilibrium income distribution should not be affected. However, once we allow net intergenerational accumulation of

TABLE 4-2

Measures of Equilibrium Income Distribution
Assuming Different Marriage and Inheritance Rules

Assumptions: No net capital formation; no capital or income redistribution; all families have two children; standard deviation of the random element is .15; labor share of national income is 75 percent.

Inheritance Rules	No-choice			Marriage Rules Limited-choice			Equal-choice		
	Gini Coef.	S.D. of Logs. of Income	Income % of Top 10%	Gini Coef.	S.D. of Logs. of Income	Income % of Top 10%	Gini Coef.	S.D. of Logs. of Income	Income % of Top 10%
Primogeniture	.307	.383	34.4%	.308	.428	34.2%	.297	.446	33.5%
Compromise	a	a	a	.064	.116	11.9	.060	.110	11.8
Eq. div.	a	a	a	.064	.116	11.9	.060	.110	11.8

a. If the system starts from a highly unequal distribution of wealth, the equilibrium distribution of income is equal to its original value. If the system starts from a relatively equal wealth distribution where high-ability people with no property might marry low-ability people with property (since they would be next to each other on the income scale), then the equilibrium income distribution would be highly equal.

TABLE 4–3

Measures of Equilibrium Income Distribution
with Different Redistributions of Wealth

Assumptions: No net capital formation; all families have two children; standard deviation of random element is .15; labor share of national income is 75 percent.

Redistribution and Inheritance Rules	Marriage Rules								
	No-choice			Limited-choice			Equal-choice		
	Gini Coef.	S.D. of Logs. of Income	Income % of Top 10%	Gini Coef.	S.D. of Logs. of Income	Income % of Top 10%	Gini Coef.	S.D. of Logs. of Income	Income % of Top 10%
No redistribution of wealth									
Primog.	.307	.383	34.4%	.308	.428	34.2%	.297	.446	33.5%
Eq. div.	a	a	a	.064	.116	11.9	.060	.110	11.8
30 percent redistribution of wealth									
Primog.	.156	.274	18.5	.158	.276	18.4	.148	.256	16.5
Eq. div.	.061	.110	11.8	.063	.114	11.9	.063	.112	11.9
60 percent redistribution of wealth									
Primog.	.088	.158	12.8	.091	.162	12.9	.089	.158	12.8
Eq. div.	.062	.111	11.8	.062	.112	11.9	.064	.116	11.9
90 percent redistribution of wealth									
Primog.	.061	.109	11.8	.066	.118	12.0	.064	.116	11.9
Eq. div.	.062	.111	11.8	.062	.111	11.9	.062	.112	11.8

a. See note to Table 4–2.

capital based on family income, then an income redistribution could have a number of effects on total savings, growth, and convergence; this provides a much more interesting problem for analysis.

3. The Model with Capital Accumulation

Let us now allow the capital stock to change, while still keeping the total population constant, so that we can isolate some of the effects of different patterns of intergenerational savings and transfers. One of the most important results of the simulation exercise is to show that the shape of this function has crucial importance on the equilibrium income distribution. Before turning to the results, however, several theoretical questions deserve brief examination.

First, we must inquire about the nature of the intergenerational transfer function. Up to now this has been a *terra incognita* in the economic literature. Empirical data with which to derive such a function are unavailable and theorists who insist on deducing propositions about consumer behavior from the neoclassical axioms of rational choice have not been able to say anything about the matter. One reasonable assumption, which is reflected in numerous *obiter dicta* on the subject, is that the amount of wealth passed on by a husband and wife to their children is primarily a function of lifetime family income. It is on this basis that the model is changed below, although the shape of the function is still problematical and experiments are usefully carried out with several different formulae.

Second, once we introduce changes in the net capital stock, a problem arises because we must also take into consideration the possibility of multiple stable growth paths; thus the initial conditions of the system and the way in which the intergenerational transfer function are specified become important. In order to avoid such complications, care was exercised in designing the intergenerational transfer function so that only a single stable growth path, independent of the initial conditions, would be achieved. A number of tests were also made with different initial conditions (different initial capital stocks) in order to insure the correctness of the specification.

A third problem arises in the choice of the production function, i.e., the function showing the relationship between the capital and labor in the system and total production. All production functions used below exhibit diminishing returns which means, among other things, that the ratio of capital to labor asymptotically approaches a limit which represents a "steady-state" equilibrium where depreciation just equals gross savings and net capital formation is zero. Such diminishing returns can, however, be offset by technological change so that in "steady-state growth" production, the capital stock and the ratio of capital to labor rise at the same rate of growth. In this particular case (usually designated in the economic literature as Harrod-neutral growth), labor productivity (the ratio of output to the constant labor force) also rises at the same rate while capital productivity asymptotically approaches a constant.

One last precautionary note must be added. Although the analysis below focuses almost exclusively on income distribution, it must be emphasized that the various types of intergenerational transfer functions, production functions, and redistributions of wealth and income lead to quite different equilibrium levels of production. Although there are a number of propositions in the economic literature linking the inequality of income to the growth rate of production (e.g., the more unequal the distribution of income, the greater the aggregate production), the results below show numerous puzzling exceptions to such generalizations. For those interested in pursuing the relationship between income distribution, the saving function, and growth, some data on steady-state production equilibria are given in Appendix A-9.

Two types of intergenerational transfer functions are used in the analysis below. The first is a simple linear function where intergenerational transfers of a particular family are a proportion of lifetime income: $S = Yz$ (where $S =$ intergenerational transfers; $Y =$ family lifetime income; and z is the "savings constant" to be specified). If family income is low and inherited wealth is great, the intergenerational transfer might be less than the original inherited wealth, i.e., the family has "dipped into capital." A second type of intergenerational transfer function has a kink in it and is thus nonlinear; such transfers are a function of income over and above some socially determined "subsistence" level, below which no intergenerational savings are made (i.e., the family does not add to inherited wealth). Since negative intergenerational transfers (i.e., debts) are not permitted (although dipping into capital is allowed) the kink of the savings function occurs at $\overline{Y}$. The simple form selected for this nonlinear function is: $S = (Y - \overline{Y})z$, $S \geqq 0$.

A brief digression is necessary to clear up certain ambiguities surrounding the "subsistence level" concept. First, this is not necessarily the biological subsistence level nor does there need to be any explicit societal recognition that such a subsistence level actually exists. Rather, it is merely the income level below which families feel they *must* spend all of their income for consumption in order to try to achieve a certain standard of living and, as a result, have no surplus wealth to pass on to succeeding generations. (By "surplus" wealth I mean wealth over and above that which every parent is "required" by the society to transfer, e.g., certain minimum educational expenditures, expensive weddings, or in a few societies, a dowry.) If per capita income in the society rises and the socially determined subsistence level remains stationary, bare subsistence may eventually become such a small proportion of individual family income that the savings function is, for all intents and purposes, linear, i.e., the performance of the system asymptotically approaches that of a system with an intergenerational transfer function of $S = Yz$. On the other hand, the socially determined subsistence level can also rise as society's views of an adequate standard of living rise. Since this might be a reasonable approximation of reality, it is useful to tie the subsistence income to the rise in per capita income. For simplicity, I have set the "subsistence" income always equal to average per capital income which means that when a nonlinear intergenerational transfer function is used, only those families with incomes above the average pass on wealth to the succeeding generation. Finally, it must be noted that the socially determined subsistence level can rise faster than average income and in this strange case, with such a strong "demonstration effect," families might "dip into capital" (as long as they didn't run into debt) until little capital would be left in society as the "subsistence" level approaches the highest family incomes.

Experiments were also made with a third form of the intergenerational transfer function: $S = W + Yz$, where W is the wealth inherited by the mother and father of the family from their parents. This function implies that the wealth inherited by the children is always greater than the wealth inherited by the parents, no matter how low the family income might be because of the low labor incomes received by the parents. These experiments added little new knowledge and were abandoned. The results of simulation experiments using both linear and nonlinear intergenerational transfer functions for several different parameters of the savings coefficient (z) are presented in Table 4–4.

The nonlinear transfer function leads, as one might expect, to a much greater inequality of income than the linear function; for in the former case, only the richer segments of the population pass on wealth to their children and this, in turn, concentrates wealth and property income. With a simple linear function, the height of the savings coefficient (z) bution (the differences do not appear statistically significant) although, of course, a higher z leads to a higher steady-state production level. On does not appear to affect the inequality of the equilibrium income distri- the other hand, a higher savings coefficient does seem to affect the degree of income inequality when a nonlinear function is used, although the direction of the effect depends upon the particular measure of inequality that is chosen and the inheritance rule that is followed. These various results are also obtained when a wide variety of values for the parameters are selected.

TABLE 4–4

Measures of Equilibrium Income Distribution Assuming
Different Intergenerational Transfer Functions[a]

Assumptions: All families have two children; standard deviation of random element is .15; labor share of national income is 75 percent; no income or capital redistributions; no technical change; no negative transfers.

Abbreviations: S = intergenerational transfers; Y = personal income; $\overline{Y}$ = average income; z = a constant.

Transfer Functions and Inheritance Rules	No-choice			Marriage Rules Limited-choice			Equal-choice		
	Gini Coef.	S.D. of Logs. of Income	Income % of Top 10%	Gini Coef.	S.D. of Logs. of Income	Income % of Top 10%	Gini Coef.	S.D. of Logs. of Income	Income % of Top 10%
				$S = Yz$					
z = 1.5									
Primog.	.165	.294	15.0%	.165	.293	15.1%	.161	.287	14.8%
Eq. div.	.069	.123	12.1	.067	.120	12.0	.060	.110	11.8
z = 2.0									
Primog.	.167	.297	15.2	.169	.302	15.0	.162	.291	14.6
Eq. div.	.066	.118	12.0	.066	.118	12.0	.063	.113	11.9
z = 2.5									
Primog.	.165	.293	15.2	.170	.302	15.2	.164	.294	14.7
Eq. div.	.065	.118	12.0	.063	.114	11.9	.062	.111	11.9
				$S = (Y - \overline{Y})z$					
z = 2.0									
Primog.	.306	.382	34.1	.301	.378	33.8	.300	.452	33.7
Eq. div.	.293	.458	33.3	.266	.441	28.6	.206	.350	20.0
z = 2.5									
Primog.	.308	.383	34.0	.309	.384	34.3	.306	.427	34.0
Eq. div.	.296	.461	33.4	.260	.432	27.6	.199	.341	18.5

a. If the capital/output ratio is greater than unity, the average z coefficient must also be greater than unity if the capital stock in the economy is to be maintained. In the results reported in the table, z is placed larger than unity; using a Cobb-Douglas production function with a multiplicative constant to make the capital/output less than unity allows values of z less than unity as well (which makes more empirical sense). In such cases the impact of changing values of z would, of course, be the same as in the

With the introduction of intergenerational transfer functions based on income, we now have a situation where the marriage rules have a somewhat more important impact on the equilibrium income distribution than in the previous section where capital was passed on regardless of income. With primogeniture, the effect of the marriage rules is small in almost all cases (except with the S.D. indicator and the nonlinear transfer function). On the other hand, with equal division of property, especially with a nonlinear transfer function, the inequality of the equilibrium income distribution decreases as the marriage rule changes toward equal-choice.

Generalizing about the relationships between equilibrium income distribution, inheritance rules, and transfer functions is more difficult. With a linear intergenerational transfer function, primogeniture leads to a more unequal distribution of personal income than other inheritance rules; with a nonlinear transfer function, the results depend upon the measure of inequality chosen since the relationships between different parts of the income distribution are differentially affected. Thus no generalization is possible.

To summarize, with a linear transfer function where families at all income levels pass on wealth to the succeeding generation, the primary influence on the equilibrium distribution of income is the inheritance rules; and marriage rules or the height of the savings constant (z) have little effect. With a nonlinear intergenerational transfer function, the equilibrium income distribution is affected by the marriage rules, the inheritance rules, and the height of the savings constant. Generalization in these latter cases is difficult because the overall inequality and the shape of the income distribution curve change simultaneously.

If we now add to the analysis population growth which can arise from many different patterns of differential fertility, a large number of cases are open for exploration. Simplification can be achieved once we realize that introduction of population change has two major effects: It raises the absolute value of total production; and it allows different rates of growth of the capital/labor ratio to occur through changes in the denominator of the fraction, rather than in the numerator. Rather than multiply examples endlessly, it seems most useful to examine only several simple patterns of fertility in order to show how the system works. A financial constraint on this process of analysis must also be mentioned: The greater the number of people in the system, the more expensive the simulation becomes. The results reported in Table 4–5 are based on a system which began with only fifty people, had a 10 percent population growth (per generation), and ran for only twenty-five generations. This led to an eightfold increase in population and, as a result, almost a quadrupling of computer costs. (It must also be noted that in order to limit population growth, "poor" and "rich" families are defined as the 20 per-

TABLE 4-5

*Measures of Equilibrium Income Distribution with
Population Change and Different Fertility Patterns*

Assumptions: Standard deviation of random element is .15; Cobb-Douglas production function with labor share of national income is 75 percent; no technological change; no income or capital redistribution; no negative savings.

Abbreviations: S = intergenerational transfers; Y = personal income; $\overline{Y}$ = average income; z = a constant.

$$S = Yz, (z = 2.0)$$

Fertility Patterns and Inheritance Rules	Number of children Rich	Number of children M.C.	Number of children Poor	Marriage Rules — No-choice Gini Coef.	No-choice S.D. of Logs. of Income	No-choice Income % of Top 10%	Limited-choice Gini Coef.	Limited-choice S.D. of Logs. of Income	Limited-choice Income % of Top 10%	Equal-choice Gini Coef.	Equal-choice S.D. of Logs. of Income	Equal-choice Income % of Top 10%
Primog.	2	2	2	.167	.297	15.2%	.169	.302	15.0%	.162	.291	14.6%
Compr.				.066	.118	12.0	.066	.118	12.0	.063	.113	11.9
Eq. div.				.066	.118	12.0	.066	.118	12.0	.063	.113	11.9
Primog.	3	2	2	.182	.318	16.1	.178	.312	15.8	.175	.311	15.3
Compr.				.071	.129	12.2	.068	.122	12.0	.071	.130	12.2
Eq. div.				.065	.117	12.0	.069	.124	12.1	.066	.120	12.0
Primog.	2	2	3	.182	.319	16.0	.176	.309	15.9	.175	.311	15.3
Compr.				.075	.139	12.2	.076	.139	12.2	.073	.135	12.2
Eq. div.				.074	.136	12.2	.073	.132	12.2	.072	.131	12.2

$$\underline{S = (Y - \bar{Y})z, (z = 2.0)}$$

2 2									
2									
Primog.	.306	.382	34.1	.301	.378	33.8	.300	.452	33.7
Compr.	.293	.458	33.3	.266	.441	28.6	.206	.350	20.0
Eq. div.	.293	.458	33.3	.266	.441	28.6	.206	.350	20.0
3 2									
2									
Primog.	.314	.310	34.5	.313	.284	34.4	.309	.349	34.2
Compr.	.273	.437	30.2	.253	.413	26.5	.169	.293	17.4
Eq. div.	.230	.387	22.3	.185	.321	16.9	.127	.230	13.9
2 2									
3									
Primog.	.312	.285	34.4	.313	.297	34.4	.310	.370	34.2
Compr.	.309	.387	34.2	.296	.450	33.3	.194	.332	18.0
Eq. div.	.306	.391	34.0	.294	.460	33.0	.219	.369	20.8

cent of families on either end of the income distribution, while the "middle class" is the remaining 60 percent. Equilibrium gross national products are presented in Appendix A-8.)

The most surprising result appears where the transfer function is linear: Here differential fertility appears to have relatively little impact on the equilibrium distribution of income, a result which is somewhat different from the situation in Appendix A-8 where no net capital formation takes place. In the case of the nonlinear transfer function, on the other hand, the expected impact of differential fertility can be observed in nonprimogeniture situations, i.e., the equilibrium distribution appears more equal, the greater the number of children of the rich *vis-à-vis* other groups in the population.

It should also be noted that population growth gives rise to a somewhat more unequal equilibrium distribution of income than no population growth does and it seems likely that this effect would be greater if population growth were higher. Such a result may be tied up with the observed fact that with population growth, the equilibrium per capita income and the equilibrium capital/labor ratio are somewhat lower. In turn, this means that returns per unit of capital are higher and returns per unit of labor are lower. The exact interaction of these various factors is, however, complex.[9]

4. Application of the Model

Other kinds of phenomena can be examined with the model. We can, for instance, look at the effect of technological change or of trying different types of production functions. We must also note that the model cannot be directly applied to available data on the distributions of income and wealth because of certain biases arising from the simplifying assumptions that require special attention.

First, the model assumes that the labor income of an individual is not positively correlated with his parents' income. Since it is generally believed that there is, indeed, a positive correlation, this means that the

9. Some insight can be gained into these matters by starting from the formulae for the separation of the components of variance that are presented in Appendix A-4. In the case discussed in the text, $\bar{i}^2$ increases, Var (k) remains the same, the $\bar{k}^2$ Var(i) factor still remains zero (since there is no variation in return per unit of capital) and the covariance term remains roughly the same. Thus the overall variance in property income rises and this, in turn, leads to an increase in the variance of overall personal income. Certain other puzzling phenomena remain, particularly in the data for the nonlinear savings function; these are due in part to the fact that unlike most other simulations in this essay, equilibrium was achieved extremely slowly and often by the 25th generation (the cutoff point), this equilibrium point had not been reached.

results presented above have a bias toward equality. In future simulations this fact could either be built directly in the model (a procedure which would require considerably more memory capacity of a computer than the program used in this study) or introduced by using a different type of intergenerational savings function in which a fraction of the parents' income would be considered human capital transmitted to the children.

Second, the model assumes that labor income and property income are not correlated. But, as I argued in Chapter III, there is evidence to suggest that in advanced capitalist nations such as the United States, individual labor and property incomes are indeed positively correlated which means that the empirical results obtained with the simulation model show a bias toward equality. Repairing this fault in the model would not be difficult; labor income could be made a function of the random variable plus a given fraction of wealth.

Third, for technical reasons labor incomes in the model were bounded by limits of .5 and 1.5 of the average income and since capital accumulation is a function of total income, certain limits were placed on the amount of wealth that one individual may accumulate. Since this does not permit the existence of a Henry Kaiser, an H. Ross Perot, or a J. Paul Getty, who manage to accumulate enormous sums within a single lifetime, the results of the simulation model show a bias toward equality. This might be repaired in the model by designating one person in each generation who is destined to strike it rich at the expense of everyone else (who are "taxed" for this purpose).

Fourth, the distribution of income is calculated from labor and property income before family accumulation (or disaccumulation) takes place. This procedure omits a source making for greater income inequality, namely the income accruing to owners of recently accumulated wealth. In the model presented above, this should not make very much difference; but in a more complicated model, this factor must be taken into consideration. On a more general level, the simulation model is based on the assumption that capital accumulation for the entire society occurs through the net addition to inherited productive capital by various families in the system. An alternative method for achieving economic growth that does not involve inheritance occurs when claims on productive capital are accumulated through part of a person's lifetime and then are converted into consumption by the end of the person's life.[10] If generations overlap and if the maximum accumulated wealth is greater for each succeeding generation, then societal capital accumulation could occur without any inheritances. Such a process is occurring in part and the

---

10. Such a model is explored by James Tobin, "Life Cycle Saving and Balanced Growth," in William Fellner, *et al., Ten Economic Studies in the Tradition of Irving Fisher* (New York: 1967), pp. 231–57.

equilibrium income results of the simulation model would have a further bias toward equality. This factor could be incorporated into the model, but considerably more memory space in the computer would be required.

Fifth, in the results presented above, labor income is assumed to be a fixed percentage of total national income. However, as was shown in Chapter III, the share of labor income appears to be slowly increasing and, therefore, the long-run results presented in the above tables have a bias toward inequality.[11]

Sixth, the model takes only into account direct redistributional aspects of inheritance taxes. But inheritance taxes may discourage intergenerational transfers of wealth (except in nontaxable forms such as in education and health) which, in turn, might lead to greater equality than the results presented above. If such human capital can be acquired free from the government, then intergenerational transfers of wealth in high income families may be even more discouraged.

Seventh, the model is allowed to run to equilibrium which, in many cases, takes twenty or so generations. Much more useful for policy purposes would be examination of situations where, starting with the current size distribution of income and wealth, the model were allowed to run only for several generations. The purpose of letting equilibrium be achieved is to give some general results about the direction of change that may be of use to analysts facing many different size distributions of income and wealth.

Eighth, and finally, our knowledge about the actual parameters of the system that would influence the equilibrium size distribution of income and wealth is quite limited. Most important, we have no statistical idea about the shape of the intergenerational savings function which proves such a critical factor in determining the final equilibrium positions. We do not know the relative importance of more complicated inheritance arrangements where wealth is passed two generations away through particular types of trust arrangements. Our quantitative notions about marriage patterns and inheritance rules may be greater, but such matters still need considerable analysis before parameters can be derived for use in the model. Except for some imaginative work by Robert Summers, little

11. Some idea of the magnitude of this property income share effect can be gained from the following figures. If the standard deviation of labor income is 15 percent and if there is no property income, the Gini coefficient of income inequality is .086. Where the distribution of labor income is the same but property income accounts for 25 percent of total income, the distribution of total income depends on the inequality with which such wealth is held. If 75 percent of the population share the total income from wealth equally, the Gini coefficient is .10; and if 10 percent of the population share equally the total income from wealth, the Gini coefficient is .28. If the share of property income increased to 50 percent, both of the latter two Gini coefficients of income inequality would rise even higher.

has been done on calculating lifetime size distributions of income.[12] Thus even if the simulation model were more sophisticated, we would not have the requisite knowledge of the proper parameters for running the model for predictive purposes.

Despite the shortcomings in the model, one extremely important conclusion can nevertheless be drawn: A number of socio-economic factors such as the inheritance rules of the society, differential fertility rates among income classes, and the relationships between lifetime income and intergenerational savings strongly affect both the equilibrium distribution of wealth and income in a society. Thus the subject of income distribution is far from exhausted by pointing to the mere existence of private wealth and property income in an economy. In order to evaluate fully the impact of private ownership on the distribution of income, we need to know a considerable amount about long-run factors affecting the distribution of wealth. Like most good, honest, but platitudinous, advice this simple message is usually disregarded.

5. Some Speculations: A Digression

The results of the simulation model, even though biased, permit us to pose an answer to some puzzling questions regarding long-run changes in the inequality of the distribution of income and wealth that arise whenever we look at the scattered but available empirical evidence on such matters.

Among Western non-Marxist economists, there seems to be some agreement that the distribution of income and wealth of nations becomes increasingly unequal during the early stages of the development process but that after the development process is well underway, this distributional tendency is reversed and the income distribution becomes increasingly more equal. Empirical evidence supports this proposition. For instance, in the United States estimates of the distribution of wealth show an increasing inequality throughout the nineteenth century, reaching a high point at the turn of the century; since then, however, these data show that the inequality of wealth holding has declined so that the Gini coefficient of wealth inequality was roughly the same in 1962 as in 1860.[13] In this century the inequality of personal wealth holdings appears

12. Robert Summers, *An Econometric Investigation of the Size Distribution of Lifetime Average Annual Income,* Technical Report No. 31, Department of Economics, Stanford University (Stanford: 1956). I would like to thank Professor Summers for sending me a copy of this extremely useful study.

13. Lee Soltow, "Forward," in Soltow, ed. Supporting data come from Robert E. Gallman, "Trends in the Size Distribution of Wealth in the Nineteenth Century: Some Speculations," in Soltow, ed., pp. 1–25; Robert J.

to have decreased in the United Kingdom as well.[14] Finally, income inequality has decreased in a great many developed nations in the last thirty to sixty years and there appears to be an inverse relationship in the West between the level of development and the Gini coefficient of income inequality on both a time-series and a cross-section basis.[15] A number of theoretical arguments concerning the causes of such shifts in the distribution of income have been offered,[16] and to these I would like to add one more explanation based on the simulation results above.

In an economically highly underdeveloped nation the major source of wealth is land and inheritances consist primarily of intergenerational transfers of a fixed amount of land; the equilibrium distribution of income in such a case is described in Section B-2. As industrialization begins and accumulated industrial capital becomes an important source of wealth, it seems likely that the intergenerational transfer function approaches the nonlinear form described in Section B-3. This is because the biological level of subsistence is still a substantial proportion of average income and it is unlikely that people with relatively low incomes could pass on a very significant proportion of their lifetime incomes to their heirs, except perhaps, in the form of investment-in-kind on a farm. As per capita income rises, this biological subsistence income becomes an increasingly smaller share of average incomes and it seems likely that the

Lampman, *The Share of Top Wealth Holders in National Wealth, 1922–56* (Princeton: 1962); and James Smith, *Income and Wealth of Top Wealth Holders in the United States, 1958,* Ph.D. dissertation, University of Oklahoma (Ann Arbor: University Microfilms, n.d.).

14. Data are presented by Lampman, p. 214.

15. The four most extensive recent international comparisons of the size distribution of income are: Simon Kuznets, "Quantitative Aspects of the Economic Growth of Nations, VIII. Distribution of Income by Size," *Economic Development and Cultural Change,* XI, February 1962, Part 2; Kravis, Chapter 7; Lydall, (who only covers labor income); and Richard Weisskoff, *"Income Distribution and Economic Growth: An International Comparison,"* Ph.D. dissertation, Harvard University, 1969.

16. Simon Kuznets ("Economic Growth and Income Inequality," *American Economic Review,* XLV, March 1955, pp. 1–28) focuses on the shift from rural to urban areas as the most important causal factor. [This model is investigated more thoroughly on a theoretical level by Henri Theil, "Migration and Its Effect on Per Capita Income Inequality: Maxwell's Demon on Ellis Island," *Economics and Information Theory* (Chicago: 1967), pp. 114–20; and on an empirical level by Weisskoff]. Stiglitz bases an explanation for the same phenomenon on the relationship in the process of economic growth of the starting point to the equilibrium production level. R. Albert Berry ("Income and Wealth Distribution in the Development Process and their Relationship to Output Growth," Yale Economic Growth Center Discussion Paper No. 89) focuses on unemployment and changes in particular market imperfections. Others have focused on more political factors such as the increase of political mobilization accompanying economic development that leads to greater progressive redistribution of income and wealth by the government after a particular point of development.

income level below which no intergenerational transfers take place does not rise as fast as average income. If so, then the nonlinear intergenerational transfer function asymptotically approaches the linear case.

In such a situation, three stages in the distribution of wealth and income can be distinguished: a stagnant stage in which the distribution of wealth and income remain relatively constant; the initial stages of industrialization in which the distribution of wealth and income become increasingly more unequal (under the impact of a nonlinear intergenerational savings function); and a later stage of industrialization in which the distribution of wealth and income become more equal when the intergenerational transfer function becomes more linear.

Since we know very little about intergenerational transfers at any stage of development, this scenario of development must remain speculative; nevertheless, it does provide a focus for future empirical research.

6. An Overview

First, for a general theory of the size distribution of the ownership of wealth, we must take into account the influence of a great many socioeconomic variables such as the pattern of intergenerational transfers of wealth, the rules of inheritance in the society, the differential patterns of fertility of income classes, and the size distribution of income. It is impossible to generalize in a meaningful way about long-run changes in the size distributions of ownership and income in capitalism without specifying many more variables than economists have usually done. Blanket predictions about increasing concentration of income and wealth, e.g., the orthodox Marxist analysis of such problems, make too many implicit assumptions of a vital nature to be of much use.

Second, the simulation model presented above provides a useful starting point for a broader type of analysis of the distributions of income and wealth. On the theoretical side we need to consider many more complications than those presented in this essay; on the empirical side we need to have a much clearer picture of the critical parameters. The model does, however, point to one extremely important factor—the shape of the intergenerational savings function—which has been neglected by previous analyses and which I hope to have demonstrated is critical in predicting changes in the size distributions of income and the ownership of weath.

Third, certain factors in capitalist nations suggest that there are some powerful forces influencing the distribution of the ownership of wealth toward greater equality. Primogeniture, where it existed, appears to be becoming replaced by a more equal division of inherited wealth. Fertility differences between income classes appear to be narrowing, at least in some leading nations such as the United States. Various governments appear to be trying to enforce more progressive taxes on inherited wealth and, although in some countries such as the United States, many tax loopholes still exist, such measures appear to have had some impact on the distribution of ownership of wealth toward greater equality. And, as I argued in the speculative section, the shape of the intergenerational savings function may be becoming more linear.

Empirical evidence on the distribution of ownership of wealth shows that in the leading capitalist nations a certain equalizing trend is apparent, although the shift of the size distribution of ownership of wealth toward equality has been changing very slowly. In any case, the size distribution of the ownership of wealth is not becoming more unequal and the gloomy predictions of a number of nineteenth-century economists on such matters have not been fulfilled.

C. Ownership and Control

If ownership is not becoming more concentrated, what about control over the means of production (i.e., influence over the major policy decisions that are implemented within an enterprise)? Can we generalize about the distribution of control rights from data on the distribution of income rights or ownership, or are ownership and control in some manner separated?

In the first chapter, certain correlations between government ownership of the means of production and government control over the economy were explored. In this section, I examine the degree to which private ownership of enterprises (the right to receive income) is correlated with enterprise control.

If enterprise ownership and effective control are *not* separated, then a great number of people may participate in the policy making process, either directly or indirectly. On the other hand, if ownership and control are separated so that control over the enterprise lies essentially in the hands of the top managers, then control rights are probably held in many fewer hands than ownership rights so that a certain type of centralization of property along this dimension has occurred. Finally, if ownership and control are separated so that effective control of the enterprise lies in the hands of financial groups above the enterprise that control many such production units, then control rights in the economy are held in still fewer hands and greater centralization of property has occurred.

Whether ownership and control in mining and manufacturing enterprises are separated has given rise to a number of thorny theoretical and empirical questions that are discussed in turn below. Although individual cases where control of an enterprise lies in the hands of the owners, the managers, the middle-level bureaucrats of the enterprise, or supra-enterprise groups can be designated, it is necessary to investigate a large sample of enterprises. Having followed such a procedure below, the evidence for a separation of ownership and control appears more convincing than the opposite case. After a digression to explore whether ownership and control are also becoming separated in East Europe, I then attempt to assess the impact on the economy occurring when such property rights are held in different hands.

1. Some Theoretical Notes

The correlation between ownership and control of enterprises and the effect on enterprise behavior if such separation occurs have been discussed at least as far back as Adam Smith, who strongly believed that injurious consequences would occur in such cases. The idea that the separation of ownership and control would become a general phenomenon was analyzed by nineteenth-century economists including Marx who noted: "The capitalist mode of production has brought matters to a point where the work of supervision [is] entirely divorced from the ownership of capital. . . . [T]he mere manager who has no title whatever to the capital . . . performs all the real functions pertaining to the function [of] capitalism as such. . . ."[17] The idea that enterprise ownership and control are becoming increasingly separated has been explicated and developed by a wide number of social scientists with quite different political leanings including Rudolf Hilferding, V. I. Lenin, Alfred Marshall, Thorstein Veblen, John Maynard Keynes, Adolf A. Berle and Gardiner C. Means, James Burnam, Robert Aaron Gordon, Ralf Dahrendorf, and John Kenneth Galbraith.[18]

17. Karl Marx, *Capital,* Vol. III (Moscow: 1962), Chapter 23, pp. 379–80. (Originally published in 1894.)

18. Rudolf Hilferding, *Das Finanzkapital* (Frankfurt: 1968), (originally published, 1910); V. I. Lenin, *Imperialism, The Highest Stage of Capitalism* (Moscow: 1968), especially Chapter 3 (originally published, 1916); Alfred Marshall, *Industry and Trade* (London: 1920), Book 2; Thorstein Veblen, *Absentee Ownership and Business Enterprise in Recent Times* (New York: 1964) (originally published, 1923); John Maynard Keynes, "The End of Laissez Faire," in his *Essays in Persuasion* (New York: 1932), pp. 312–23 (essay originally published, 1923); Adolf A. Berle, Jr. and Gardiner C. Means, *The Modern Corporation and Private Property* (New York: 1933); James Burnham, *The Managerial Revolution* (New York: 1941); Robert Aaron Gordon, *Business Leadership in the Large Corporation* (Washington, D.C.: 1945); Ralf Dahrendorf, *Class and Class Conflict in Industrial Society* (Stanford: 1959); and John Kenneth Galbraith, *The New Industrial State* (Boston: 1967).

Three recent books on the subject of theoretical or empirical interest are: Robin Marris, *The Economic Theory of "Managerial" Capitalism* (New

On the other hand, a number of other social scientists have denied this separation, or claimed that the importance of the phenomenon is not great, or that attention to this separation draws our gaze away from much more important aspects of capitalism: among these are Paul Sweezy, C. Wright Mills, Ferdinand Lundberg, and certain Soviet economists such as Stanislav Menshikov.[19]

Those arguing the existence of a separation of ownership and control point to four major phenomena. First, as enterprises become larger, it becomes increasingly difficult for a single individual or group to own large proportions of voting stock. Stock holding has become splintered because of inheritance taxes; this splintering is further stimulated by the rise of the stock market that permits a person to reduce his asset risk arising in holding all wealth in one enterprise by diversifying his portfolio. With ownership of stock splintered, the managers of large corporations have found it increasingly easy to select the directors and to control the corporation through the proxies received from the stockholders. Second, corporate affairs have become so complicated that high profits can be obtained only if stockholders voluntarily hand over effective control to specialists, i.e., the managers. Third, the rise of financial intermediaries who control large blocks of stock directly or hold them in trust for individual stockholders or who have made large loans to particular corporations in return for partial control further splits actual ownership from effective control. Finally, when the enterprise is small and the stockholders are few, it is difficult to sell ownership shares and the individual stockholder is forced to take a more active role in the running of the enterprise to protect his own interests than in a situation where the enterprise is large, the market for ownership shares is active, and a person can sell his shares anytime he is discontented with any enterprise decision. That is, owners of enterprises with highly liquid ownership shares have an incentive to spend their efforts selecting profitable enterprises in which to buy shares, rather than participating in the decision-making process of the enterprises in which they own shares. Since the liquidity of ownership shares has risen over time with the development of various types of stock

York: 1964); Oliver E. Williamson, *The Economics of Discretionary Behavior: Managerial Objectives and the Theory of the Firm* (Chicago: 1967); and Robert J. Larner, *Management Control and the Large Corporation* (New York: 1970).

19. Paul M. Sweezy, "The Illusion of the Managerial Revolution," in his *The Present as History* (New York: 1953), pp. 39–67 (essay originally published, 1942); C. Wright Mills, *The Power Elite* (New York: 1956); Ferdinand Lundberg, *The Rich and the Super Rich* (New York: 1968); and Stanislav Menshikov, *Millionaires and Managers: Structure of U.S. Financial Oligarchy* (Moscow: 1969).

markets, forces encouraging the separation of ownership and control have increased as well.

A number of arguments against these contentions have been raised. First, it is said that this splintering of ownership has not really occurred. Second, if it has occurred, small blocks of stock can be used to gain control of the board of directors and such stockholders have no rational reason for giving full decision-making powers to hired managers who may have quite different goals than making the highest profit for the shareholders.[20] Third, the finance capitalists controlling the financial intermediaries and the largest stockholders of the big corporations are often the same people or have, at least, the same interests so that restrictions are placed on managerial decision-making. Finally, a separate argument (since it is somewhat contradictory to the other three) is that the managers may have effective control of the corporation but they have a sufficiently large ownership stake in the corporation and their compensation is sufficiently tied to profits that they are encouraged to maximize the same values as the owners; thus the separation of ownership and control makes no strong difference on the operation of the enterprise.

Some very serious issues are raised that can only be resolved empirically; other issues involve some theoretical points that require a much deeper analysis before they can be successfully resolved. Reluctantly leaving such theoretical issues to others, it seems most useful to survey the available empirical studies on these matters.

2. Some Data on the Separation of Ownership and Control

It is possible to follow two approaches in analyzing the separation of ownership and control empirically. On the one hand, we could start with a study of financial intermediaries, cartels, and other alleged supra-enterprise organizations, trace the links between these and particular enterprises, and then draw our conclusions. Particular attention would be paid to loans of such finance capitalists to enterprises, the holding of stock by financial intermediaries in enterprises, and the personnel of such intermediaries on the enterprises' boards of directors. On the other hand, we could start with a study of the enterprises directly to discover their degree of autonomy from or dependence on supra-enterprise organizations and owners.

Unfortunately, study of decision-making units in capitalism above the level of enterprise has not, to my knowledge, been carried out on a comparative basis for several nations and we are left with a series of na-

---

20. On this point see Galbraith, Marris, and Williamson.

tional case studies of varying degrees of quality.[21] Further, the actual role of these alleged higher decision-making levels is extremely difficult to assess and from similar evidence different analysts (or even the same analysts at different points in time[22]) have arrived at very different evaluations. In addition, some severe methodological pitfalls exist in many of the techniques employed in such analyses (e.g., the presence of a single bank representative on the board of directors of an enterprise has been used to designate bank "control").[23] Finally, the character of finance capital may differ enormously between nations; certain even casual knowledge of the West German and American economies reveals a much different role of bankers in the making of important enterprise decisions. For these reasons it seems more worthwhile to approach the matter by looking first at data for enterprises, especially since certain roughly comparable studies of different nations have been carried out.

If the directors of an enterprise exercise ultimate control of the business, and if these directors are selected by the stockholders, then it might be useful to examine the relative concentration of stock holdings in the hands of particular individuals or blocks who could exercise their votes in a manner to place their own representatives as directors. If stock holdings are sufficiently splintered, then managers who control the vote proxies can select their nominal superiors. Fortunately, comparable data are available for the largest enterprises in three countries. Companies are classified "private" if an individual or block controls 80 percent or more of the voting shares; as "majority ownership" if an individual or block controls 50 to 80 percent of the voting shares; "minority control" if the controlling group has 15 to 50 percent of the voting shares; "control through a legal device" if effective control is exercised by a financial intermediary voting stocks in trust or some similar arrangement; and "management control" if no single individual or block controls more than 15 percent of the stock. Relevant data are presented in Table 4–6.

21. The two best studies that I have seen are for Belgium [Federation générale du travail de Belgique, *Holdings et democratie economique* (Brussels: 1956)] and Sweden [Statens offentliga utredningar, Finansdepartementet, *Ägande och inflytande inom det private näringslivet,* Koncentrationsutredningen V (Stockholm: 1968)].

22. For the United States, Paul M. Sweezy defined eight "interest groups" in a government collection of studies on industrial organization (reprinted as "Interest Groups in the American Economy," in his *The Present as History,* pp. 158–88). In a later study, however, he reversed his position and emphasized that the major locus of power of American corporations lies inside rather than outside the corporation [Paul A. Baran and Paul M. Sweezy, *Monopoly Capital* (New York: 1966), Chapter 2.]

23. Menshikov uses the methodology and "finds" finance capital "control" of major corporations with the inclusion of a single employee of a bank on the boards of directors of particular corporations!

TABLE 4–6

Control Configurations in the Largest Domestically Privately Owned Mining and Manufacturing Enterprises in Three Nations[a]

Country	United States		United Kingdom		Australia
Date	1929	1963	1936	1951	1953
Number of enterprises in sample	106	117	50	50	20
	Percentage of Companies				
Private ownership	8%	0%	2%	0%	0%
Majority ownership	6	3	10	6	0
Minority control	32	15	12	8	15
Control through legal device	14	4	26	14	15
Management control	40	76	50	72	70
Total	100	100	100	100	100

a. Sources and data are given in Appendix B-30. Some data for Sweden are also available but could not be made comparable to those in the above table. According to the Statens offentliga utredningar, Finansdepartementet, management control occurs in a maximum of 13 percent of the largest ninety-seven enterprises (both nonfinancial and financial). One reason for this is the importance of a small number of extremely large financial groups (e.g., the Wallenberg family controls or shares in the control of fifty-four enterprises and the top seventeen financial groups control over 60 percent of the nonfinancial enterprises employing a labor force of over five hundred). Another reason is that the largest ninety-seven enterprises include some relatively small enterprises; management control appears higher among enterprises in the top twenty.

If the data are correct (and there is some controversy about this as I note below), then privately owned enterprises with "management control" comprise over two-thirds of all of the largest enterprises in the United States, the United Kingdom, and Australia at the present time. Further, the percentage of enterprises with such control has markedly increased over time, at least for the first two nations. (In Australia, the percentage of largest enterprises with management control appeared to remain roughly the same for a ten-year period, but this seems too short a period for meaningful comparisons to be made, given the nature of the underlying data.) Private, majority, and minority ownership are relatively unimportant and have been declining over the years. Control through a legal device (including control through finance capital) appears small and declining.

If this were all, we could conclude that ownership and control of large corporations are indeed separated, that control rights are held in many fewer hands than ownership rights, and that ownership might be becoming increasingly dispersed among the population while control might be becoming more concentrated. But matters are not, unfortunately, so simple.

First, such data have been considerably criticized.[24] For instance, in their assessment of control in a large number of particular corporations in the United States, the Soviet economist Stanislav Menshikov and the American economist Robert Larner (whose data are presented in Table 4–6 for the United States) differ enormously.[25] Larner worked from proxy statements submitted to the Securities and Exchange Commission plus additional materials relating to decision-making in the enterprise, while Menshikov laid crucial emphasis on the presence of one or two representatives of finance capital on the boards of directors. Although I find Larner's approach (the approach followed originally by Berle and Means) more convincing, both leave something to be desired.

Second, what do these data mean if there is a rapid turnover of top managers? For instance, Menshikov cites evidence that in a five-year period, 47 percent of the top executives in leading corporations were changed.[26] This type of evidence, of course, needs to be supplemented with evidence about the turnover of the entire management group since it contradicts the generally accepted notion that today's executives are men who have been in their respective enterprises for quite long periods of time. It might also be argued that the declining share of top managers serving simultaneously on the boards of directors of their own companies is another sign of declining management control.

Third, such structural data draw our attention away from participation by owners, managers, and financial intermediaries in any particular decision. That is, the types of decisions or the impact of these decisions are not specified. It may turn out, for instance, that the banker representative on the board of directors of an enterprise may have little influence except in the area of the financing of particular investments. Such an omission in our knowledge could be filled by careful analyses of the minutes of boards of directors from many enterprises, but such large scale systematic studies along these lines have not, as far as I have been able to find out, been carried out.

24. Disputes about the determination of managerial domination, even when the same methodology is employed, are endemic in the literature. For instance, with a different cut-off point between "minority control" and "managerial domination" considerably different results from those in Table 4–6 are obtained by Jean-Marie Chevalier, "The Problem of Control in Large Business Corporations," *Antitrust Bulletin,* Spring 1969, p. 165. For a brief summary of these disputes, see Larner, Chapter 2.

25. Menshikov, and Larner.

26. Menshikov, p. 129.

Fourth, the data on enterprises need to be supplemented by data on participation by financial intermediaries in enterprise decision-making from several standpoints. In the United States, at least, the degree to which financial intermediaries control voting shares of corporations is small, but has been increasing.[27] On the other hand, the degree to which enterprise investments are financed by loans from finance capitalists has remained roughly the same for a number of decades.[28] Although some influence of finance capital cannot be denied, what is the extent of this influence and the degree to which such financial groups set industrial policy or passively react to enterprise decisions, especially since enterprises can take advantage of competition between particular financial intermediaries? The notion that a small financial oligarchy sets major policy for the bulk of United States big business appears unrealistic and the evidence adduced to support this claim is quite unconvincing, at least at the present time.[29]

And finally, the interpretation of these data depends partly, at least, on differences in interest between managers and either owners or finance capitalists. With regard to the overlap of interests between owners and managers, several important arguments have been advanced. First, top managers may be wealthy men so that their "class interests" would be the same. Second, these managers may hold a sufficient amount of stock in the enterprise they head that their financial interests may be the same as the owners. And third, the compensation received by top corporate leaders may be highly dependent on the performance of the corporation as measured by profits.

Certainly the top managers of large corporations have usually amassed considerable assets.[30] Further, such top executives usually have large stock holdings in the companies they manage. For instance, in a study of ninety-four presidents of America's largest enterprises, Robert Larner found that the average market value of their stock in their companies was roughly $650,000 in 1962 to 1963; further, the expected divi-

27. Evidence on this matter is summarized briefly by Larner, Chapter 2.

28. For the United States, this is discussed in detail by John Lintner, "The Financing of Corporations," Edward S. Mason, ed., *The Corporation in Modern Society* (New York: 1966), pp. 166–201; some international comparisons over time of sources of enterprise finance are presented by Raymond W. Goldsmith, *Financial Structure and Development* (New Haven: 1969). This latter book is by far the best study of finance capital from a macro-economic standpoint that has yet appeared or probably will appear in a number of years.

29. This position is held by, among others, Menshikov; Victor Perlo, *The Empire of High Finance* (New York: 1957); and G. William Domhoff, *Who Rules America?* (Englewood Cliffs: 1967).

30. For considerable anecdotal evidence, see Menshikov, p. 90.

dend income from this stock ownership was roughly 40 percent of their total salary and bonuses.[31] (This evidence about total assets of corporate presidents must not be interpreted to mean necessarily that such men are wealthy, for we have no information on their liabilities. There is certain informal evidence suggesting that many of these men have borrowed considerable sums in order to be able to take advantage of the stock options that are offered them so that their net worth may be a small fraction of their total assets; nevertheless, it is their assets in which we are interested.)

In recent years, a considerable controversy has flared in the economic literature concerning the relationship between manager compensation and enterprise performance, as measured by profits or sales.[32] If manager compensation were related to sales and if there were a separation of interests between managers and owners, then we would expect managers to maximize sales at the expense of profits. The question can be resolved either by looking directly at managerial compensation or by looking at the alleged impact of managerial versus owner control on enterprise profits or sales. The former approach is discussed in the next paragraph; results following the latter approach are presented in a later section of this chapter.

Two major statistical problems arise in analyzing managerial compensation and enterprise performance in a direct fashion.[33] There is the difficulty of evaluating such payments as stock options, capital gains on enterprise stock, deferred compensation, and dividends from corporate stock holdings; failure to include these aspects of compensation along with direct salary and bonuses has marred a number of studies. There is also the problem of specifying the empirical investigation so that particular evidence of linkages between executive compensation and nonprofit goals can be picked up.[34] Although the most recent and comprehensive

31. Larner, Chapter 4.

32. The sales maximization hypothesis was advanced in particularly powerful form by William J. Baumol, *Business Behavior, Value, and Growth* (New York: 1959) and has been argued by a great many economists since then; another strong case is presented by Marris.

33. Recent studies of executive compensation include those of Robert Aaron Gordon; David Roberts, *Executive Compensation* (Glencoe, Ill.: 1959); Joseph W. McGuire, John S. Y. Chiu, and Alavar O. Elbing, "Executive Income, Sales, and Profits," *American Economic Review*, LII, September 1962, pp. 753–61; Leonard R. Burgess, *Top Executive Pay Package* (New York: 1963); Williamson, Chapter 7; Wilbur G. Lewellen, *Executive Compensation in Large Industrial Corporations* (New York: 1968); Wilbur G. Lewellen, "Management and Ownership in the Large Firm," *Journal of Finance*, XXIV, May 1969, pp. 299–322; Blaine Huntsman and Wilbur G. Lewellen, "Profits as a Managerial Objective: Some Empirical Evidence," paper presented at the Econometric Society annual meeting, New York City, December 1969; and Larner, Chapter 4.

34. This is difficult to discuss concisely, but two telling examples can be given. William G. Shepherd ("Market Power and Racial Discrimination in White-Collar Employment," *Antitrust Bulletin*, XIV, spring 1969, pp. 141–

econometric studies that have handled the valuation of managerial compensation correctly have indicated that such compensation is more highly influenced by profits (than by sales or other variables),[35] they have not included any but the most obvious nonprofit goals. The subject is far from closed until more comprehensive and more carefully specified econometric investigations are carried out.

What can we conclude from this welter of evidence, most of which is quite fragmentary? Despite the criticisms that can be leveled against the data presented in Table 4–6, it seems clear that there is a separation of ownership and control of large industrial enterprises in the West which is increasing over time. Although high managerial turnover, presence of banking representatives on boards of directors, and other evidence suggest that managerial control is not absolute, this does not mean that the nominal owners, i.e., the stockholders, have a more important voice. Evidence that managers are controlled by finance capitalists, who own large blocs of stock and vote the proxies of other stockholders as well, does not seem convincing in most cases. Although there may be a considerable identity of interest between the managers and stockholders, particularly since compensation of the former depends on enterprise profits, conflicts of interest between these two groups can also be specified in which it is highly likely that managerial interests are served over those of the stockholders. Any serious positive theory of property embracing major developments over time in the property structure of the West must take into account this separation of ownership and control.

3. Separation of Ownership and Control in East Europe?

What does the separation of ownership and control mean in a context where the government owns roughly three quarters or more of the means of production in the mining and manufacturing sector? Drawing a line between the "economic" and "political" spheres at the level between the enterprise and the next higher organ, two interpretations can be offered. First, separation could occur when enterprise managers have been able either to increase their autonomy from the political sphere or to increase

---

61) has found that the greater the degree of market power in an industry, the greater the racial discrimination (as manifested by a low percentage of Negro white-collar workers). Since such racial discrimination reduces profits (Negro workers can generally be hired for less pay than whites), real managerial compensation (compensation plus indulging his "taste for discrimination") is higher in more concentrated industries. Williamson, Chapter 7, also found that actual managerial compensation (as measured imperfectly by salary and bonus) is related to market concentration of the enterprise. Regression analyses of the relationship between managerial compensation and enterprise profits or sales that do not include such indicators of "discretionary income" by managers may be biased as a result.

35. Huntsman and Lewellen; and, to a partial extent, Larner, Chapter 4.

their political power at the expense of other power groups such as the
elite dominating the central government, a phenomenon I designate as
"managerialism." Second, this separation could occur when the enterprise
managers have greater decision-making autonomy and fewer direct interventions into production matters from superior organs, a phenomenon
reflecting certain aspects of decentralization. Each of these meanings of
the separation of ownership and control are briefly explored below.

From theoretical grounds a number of observers such as Raymond
Aron have argued that socialist managerialism will rise over time and the
"technological complexity will strengthen the managerial class at the expense of the ideologists and militants."[36] These matters are, of course,
difficult to analyze empirically. Close empirical studies of the Soviet
Union have shown, however, that the political power of the Soviet managers is quite weak, has always been weak, and that the alleged autonomy
of the economic from the political sphere has not occurred.[37] Although
the situation appears somewhat different in other East European nations,
it does not appear that industrial managers have been able effectively to
utilize their economic power to create an independent political force.

If we consider in this context separation of ownership and control
to mean a decentralization of production decisions from central governmental control to lower organs and the enterprises, then a more definite
answer can be given. The most difficult problem of investigating this matter is to distinguish the appearance of centralization from the reality.

In discussions of East European economies, greatest attention has
been paid to the planning system and the ways in which these plans are
implemented. But does this mean that the productive sphere is directed
from the highest organs? Naum Jasny has presented considerable documentation that up to the 1960s, Soviet long-run plans bore little relation
to reality and had even less influence on the course of events.[38] The evidence was based on a study of the manner in which the plans were made,
comparisons of plans and fulfillment, and an analysis of the way in which
operational decisions were actually made.

Another analyst has argued that even the yearly and quarterly plans

36. Raymond Aron, "Soviet Society in Transition," *Problems of Communism,* VI, November-December 1957.
37. This is the theme of a book by Jeremy R. Azrael, *Managerial Power
and Soviet Politics* (Cambridge, Mass.: 1966). For a study of the role of
local party and governmental officials in enterprise decision-making, see
Jerry Hough, *The Soviet Prefects: The Local Party Organization in Industrial
Decision-Making* (Cambridge, Mass.: 1969). Yugoslav social scientists have
worried a great deal about this problem in their own country; for one study
in English, see Eugen Pusic, "Territorial and Functional Administration in
Yugoslavia," *Administrative Science Quarterly,* XIV, March 1969, pp. 62–72.
38. Naum Jasny, "Soviet 'Perspective' Planning," in his *Essays on the
Soviet Economy* (New York: 1963), pp. 159–264.

have had little impact on the structure of production.[39] According to him, the crucial influence on the structure of production is the interaction of enterprises with each other (through such media as "pushers" (*tolkachi*) and illegal favors to obtain vital production inputs (*blat*)); and the ministries and higher planning agencies merely ratify enterprise decisions and serve as their supply agencies. Part of the impotence of the center is due to technical constraints on changing the production pattern in the short run, so that relatively little room for real choice exists while, at the same time, only the enterprises have the necessary information to make highly micro-economic decisions. Aside from theoretical arguments of this nature, additional evidence is provided in the form of isolated (and unguarded) statements of East European economists. Although such an hypothesis is provocative it is, I believe, quite overdrawn, especially if we take seriously into account the detailed case study materials of the operations of particular industries[40] or the importance of particular guides to production such as the bonus system which have been controlled by higher economic organs. It should be emphasized that the proposition about the relative importance or unimportance of short-term plans in the Soviet Union or other East European nations has never been very adequately tested, but perhaps such a test could be carried out in a manner similar to that with which Western economists have tried to gauge the impact of economic planning in the West.[41]

Although it is difficult to evaluate the degree of centralization along various dimensions in various East European economies at any single point in time, it is considerably easier to evaluate changes over time.[42] The major thrust of the reforms in most nations in East Europe during the 1960s was decentralization, as I argue in detail in later chapters.

39. Paul Craig Roberts, "The Polycentric Soviet Economy," *Journal of Law and Economics,* XII, April 1969, pp. 163–81. See also his book, *Alienation and the Soviet Economy* (Albuquerque: 1971).

40. E.g., János Kornai, op. cit., *Overcentralization in Economic Administration* (trans. by John Knapp) (London: 1959), for Hungarian light industry; or such case studies for the Soviet Union as: David Granick, *Soviet Metal-Fabricating and Economic Development* (Madison: 1967); or Robert W. Campbell, *The Economics of Soviet Oil and Gas* (Baltimore: 1968).

41. Some attempts have been made to gauge the impact of French long-run planning on the course of the economy. For instance Armand M. J. Van Nimmen, "French Planning: An Essay in Evaluation," Ph.D. dissertation, Columbia University, 1967 (Ann Arbor: University Microfilm, 1970) tried to measure the impact of French long-term plans by seeing whether the economy performed closer to the plan or closer to long-run trends. Although Van Nimmen's tests were relatively weak, he faced a difficult problem squarely that others have avoided.

42. This approach is emphasized by John Michael Montias, "A Framework for Theoretical Analysis of Economic Reforms in Soviet-Type Economies," in Morris Bornstein, ed., *Plan and Market: Economic Reforms in Eastern Europe* (New Haven: 1973).

The pattern of decentralization varied between nations. One set of nations formally reduced the powers of the central administrators and tried to introduce market mechanisms. Another set of nations attempted to decentralize by increasing the degree of participation of enterprise managers into the decision-making structure while still maintaining an administered economy. Since the various reforms are discussed in Chapter VII and are related to the concept of centralization in Chapter VIII, we defer further discussion until that time.

We can conclude that there has been a separation of ownership and control in East Europe, but this has followed the lines of decentralization of production decision-making, rather than the rise of socialist managerialism (in the special sense in which I have defined this term).

4. The Impact of the Separation of Ownership and Control: A Digression

If we accept the evidence presented earlier that a certain separation of ownership and control of industrial enterprises has occurred in the West, it seems reasonable to ask what difference it makes. For the last two centuries, economists have had strong opinions on these matters.

According to Adam Smith,

> The directors of [joint stock] companies, however, being the managers rather of other people's money than of their own, it cannot well be expected, that they should watch over it with the same anxious vigilance with which the partners in a private copartnery frequently watch over their own. Like the stewards of a rich man, they are apt to consider attention to small matters as not for their master's honour, and very easily give themselves a dispensation from having it. Negligence and profusion, therefore, must always prevail, more or less, in the management of the affairs of such a company.[43]

Almost two hundred years later John Kenneth Galbraith was inveighing against economists who believed this situation in large corporations would be any different, i.e., that managers would forsake their own self-interest to maximize the income of stockholders (a paradox he labeled the "approved contradiction").[44] Unfortunately, the identity of interest between the managers and the stockholders that I briefly discussed above muddies the theoretical picture.

43. Adam Smith, *The Wealth of Nations* (New York: 1937), Book V, Chapter 1, Part 3, Article 1.
44. Galbraith, *The New Industrial State*.

If managers in manager-dominated enterprises are pursuing different goals than the stockholders, then one would suspect that profit rates of these enterprises would be lower than those of owner-dominated enterprises, other things remaining the same.[45] The few empirical studies of these matters have focused primarily on profit rate differences between the two types of enterprises and their results deserve brief examination because quite different conclusions were reached.

In a study of average profit rates in forty-seven enterprises, David Kamerschen found in a multiple regression analysis no evidence that managerial control had any influence on the profit rate (profits as a percentage of net worth) after holding constant the concentration ratio of the major industry of the firm, the growth rate of the industry, the size of enterprise (as measured by assets or sales), and a number of other variables as well.[46] No corrections were made for heteroskedasticity or other statistical problems.

In a broader study of 187 enterprises for seven years (1292 observations in all), Robert Larner found in a multiple regression analysis only a very small influence of managerial control, after holding constant the concentration ratio of the major industry of the enterprise, the size of enterprise, the growth rate of the industry of the firm, and the ratio of equity to assets.[47] Manager-dominated enterprises had a profit rate after taxes that was roughly 0.5 percent lower than owner-dominated enterprises. Corrections were made for heteroskedasticity.

In a third study of seventy-two firms over a twelve-year period (864 observations in all), Monsen, Chiu and Cooley found in a three-way analysis of variance that manager-domination led to a posttax profit rate of 5.5 percent less than owner-domination, after holding the three-digit industry of the enterprise constant.[48]

All three studies suffer from certain sampling difficulties and a replication of the Larner study demonstrates the sensitivity of some of the calculated parameters to the enterprises that are included in the sample.[49] Further, although the first two studies used the same determinations of managerial domination, the study of Monsen, *et al.,* used different rat-

45. Theoretical demonstration of this proposition is offered by Williamson, and Marris.

46. David R. Kamerschen, "The Influence of Ownership and Control on Profit Rates," *American Economic Review,* LVIII, June 1968, pp. 432–47.

47. Larner, Chapter 3.

48. Joseph R. Monsen, John S. Chiu, and David E. Cooley, "The Effect of Separation of Ownership and Control on the Performance of the Large Firm," *The Quarterly Journal of Economics,* LXXXII, August 1968, pp. 435–51.

49. This exercise was carried out in an unpublished paper for an econometrics course at Swarthmore College by Andrew Pike.

ings. Further, in each study different variables were held constant so that the results cannot be easily compared; replication of the Larner study holding the industry variable constant (to approximate the Monsen, *et al.,* industry variable) changes the results and leads to manager-dominated enterprises showing a slightly higher profit rate than owner-dominated firms, although the difference is not significant.[50] Finally, such studies may not be looking at the proper performance variable; after all, stockholders care little about the relation of profit to net worth; their interest is in dividends and appreciation of the value of their shares.

Some of these difficulties (although not the last) are not so severe in a fourth study by John Shelton, who compared profit rates of identical restaurants of a large chain. In a sample of twenty-two restaurants, he found that profits were higher when the same restaurant was operated by franchise-owners than when it was operated by hired managers.[51] More specifically, the profit margin for the franchise-owners averaged 9.5 percent, while the profit margin for the company-appointed managers in the same restaurants averaged 1.8 percent. Although a great many variables are controlled in this experiment that are not in others, objections can be raised because the hired managers were not greatly familiar with the local scene and, furthermore, had a much shorter time horizon than the franchise-owners.

One last study of relevance deserves mention. David C. McClelland and his students gave a number of psychological tests to managers of different nations, both from private enterprises (where the managers may have had an ownership interest) and public enterprises.[52] Managers from public enterprises showed roughly the same degree of achievement and power motivation as the managers from private enterprises; there did not seem to be any innate psychological differences that would lead to different behavior in the two groups.

50. Pike's industry variable was broader than that used by Monsen, *et al.* Since Pike also used a four-firm, four-digit concentration ratio as another independent variable, this seems to serve as a good proxy for the narrower industry classification that Monsen, *et al.,* employed. The latter paper did not hold such variables as size of enterprise constant.

51. John P. Shelton, "Allocative Efficiency versus 'X-Efficiency': A Comment," *American Economic Review,* LVII, December 1967, pp. 1252–58.

52. David C. McClelland, *The Achieving Society* (New York: 1961), Chapter 7, especially Table 7–9. Differences between managers in private and public enterprises differed among countries and it is difficult to make overall conclusions. For instance, only in Italy did managers from public enterprises have significantly higher "achievement motivation" ("n Ach") than managers from private enterprises; similarly, only in the United States was the "power motivation" ("n power") of managers in private enterprises significantly higher than of those in public enterprises.

We thus have two studies in which manager-domination leads to little or no change in profit rates and two studies in which such manager-domination leads to considerably lower profits. In order to reconcile these conflicting results, needless to say, considerably more work needs to be done on the subject. The results from the psychological tests of managers does not reveal any significant psychological makeup of managers in different types of ownership situations so this should not affect the results either. Although the separation of ownership and control has increased over time in capitalist economies, we can draw no firm conclusions about what the effect of this has been on the economy; I strongly suspect that any unambiguous effect that may be isolated in future studies of the matter is likely to be small.

5. An Overview

There appears to be an increasing separation of ownership and control in mining and manufacturing enterprises in leading capitalist nations. The major decision-making powers of the enterprises and the power to select these decision-makers has apparently increasingly devolved from the stockholders to the managers, particularly in large corporations. Some evidence is also available that a part of such power has devolved from the enterprise managers to supra-enterprise groups, although the degree to which this has occurred is open to some doubt. The available empirical evidence on all these matters is, unfortunately, quite unsatisfactory and until efforts can be placed into studying in detail corporate decision-making processes (perhaps through examining corporation records such as minutes of meetings of the board of directors), we can never be completely sure of our conclusions on the matter. Comparative cross-national data concerning the control of enterprises is even more limited.

In East Europe a separation of ownership and control also appears to be taking place, at least in the sense that managers of enterprises have gained more power in making key decisions for their own enterprises.

The trend toward the separation of ownership and control in the West implies that control is becoming held in fewer hands. On the other side, in the East the trend implies that control is becoming held in more hands. The differential impact of the separation of ownership and control in the two economic systems stems, of course, from the different starting points within the two groups of economies. Let me further add that there is no implication in this argument that the two economic systems might become similar with regard to the distribution of control, for the situation is much more complicated than I have indicated above and discussion of these matters must await Chapters VIII and IX.

Finally, the impact of the separation of ownership and control is extremely difficult to gauge. Evidence on these matters for United States enterprises is very mixed and no firm conclusion can be drawn.

D. Summary and Conclusions

Many facets concerning the distribution of property have been discussed in this chapter. Three extremely important conclusions can be drawn.

First, both theoretical and empirical evidence points toward an increasing equality in the distribution of ownership of wealth in capitalist economies. Among the possible socio-economic variables contributing to this trend are a decline in the frequency of primogeniture, a change in the shape of the intergenerational savings function, and the impact of capital redistribution taxes.

Second, certain theoretical and empirical evidence presented shows that ownership and control of industrial enterprises are becoming increasingly separated over time in both capitalist and socialist economies. This means that we cannot use data about one subset of property rights to generalize about another subset.

Third, the control of the means of production of industrial enterprises is becoming concentrated into fewer hands in capitalist economies and thus the distribution of control is becoming more unequal. Thus opposite trends about ownership and control rights have been revealed for Western nations.

Before we can properly evaluate the meaning of these important changes in the distribution of property, we need to look at a number of other aspects of control rights. More specifically, we need to know more about the decision-making units such as industrial establishments and enterprises in which such control is exercised. In analyzing control patterns in East Europe, we need to know much more about the types of control rights in planned economies. And finally, we need to develop sharper analytic tools to handle concepts such as centralization. These problems form the focus of analysis for the next four chapters and extensive further discussion about the distribution of property holding will be deferred until the final chapter.

Despite difficulties in placing the major conclusions in perspective, many of the results of this chapter have interest and, indeed, certain policy implications. The distribution of wealth can be affected by redistributional taxes on income or wealth and can be investigated with the simulation model. And the distribution of control rights can be affected by measures, such as a graduated profits tax, that affect the sizes of enterprises and the degree to which ownership and control are separated. Although the size distributions of ownership and control rights can be affected by the same measures, the separation of these two types of property rights makes it imperative to consider the differential impact or particular policy instruments on the two distributions. The property atom has been split and we must forevermore avoid confounding or confusing the two parts.

CHAPTER V

The Size of Production Establishments in Mining and Manufacturing

And did the Countenance Divine
Shine forth upon our clouded hills?
And was Jerusalem builded here
Among these dark Satanic mills?

Blake[1]

A. Introduction

B. Some Important Theoretical
   Considerations
   1. The Effects of Economic
      Development
   2. The Effects of Market Size
   3. Other Factors
   4. A Brief Recapitulation

C. Some Statistical Problems
   1. Measurements of Average

Establishment Size
   2. Other Difficulties

D. Empirical Results of the Study
   of Establishment Size
   1. A Time-series Analysis
   2. A Cross-section Analysis of
      Western Nations
   3. Establishment Size in
      Eastern Europe

E. Summary and Conclusions

A. Introduction

The purpose of this and the following three chapters is to explore both theoretically and empirically some problems of control rights in production, i.e., effective decision-making power over the means of production.

1. William Blake, Preface to "Milton, A Poem in Two Books."

To provide a common empirical base for the various analyses I focus exclusively on the mining and manufacturing sector.

Production establishments and enterprises are key decision-making units in the mining and manufacturing sector and study of their size gives us insight into the distribution of control rights in the economy. As production units increase in size, the set of decision options or property rights available to top management increases in scope: Larger amounts of capital and numbers of workers are brought under its overall direction and new choices (e.g., more options for obtaining aid from governmental or banking agencies) become available. Thus the size distribution of production units has important implications for the centralization of control rights.

In this chapter I deal with the sizes of establishments; in the next chapter I carry out a similar analysis for production enterprises. In order to avoid confusion, a clear distinction between establishment and enterprise must now be made. An *establishment* is a business or industrial unit at a single physical location; it can consist of several "plants", "workshops", or "factories", as long as these are located together and under a single management. An *enterprise* (or *firm*) is a business organization consisting of one or more establishments under common ownership and control. It is a consolidated unit because wholly owned subsidiaries are included as part of the parent enterprise, even though for tax and other purposes such units may report on an unconsolidated basis.

Study of establishment and enterprise size is important for investigating many long-standing economic questions: If growth in the average size production unit exceeds the pace of economic development, then under certain conditions an economy can become dominated by monopolies and the long-term efficiency and stability of market allocations systems (either capitalist or socialist) are open to doubt. Evidence on production unit sizes can also be utilized in evaluating the degree to which economies of scale are realized in an economy. Information on establishment and enterprise size gives insight into the bureaucratization and centralization (and even, perhaps, of social stratification) of an economy, all of which are of considerable political and sociological interest. Size of production units also appears related to the degree of work satisfaction of the labor force and thus may have importance in determining some psychological characteristics on the population. Finally we obtain extremely useful data with which to assess the diffusion of control rights throughout the economy.

We can approach the subject in two ways. Many topics can be examined in the traditional framework of industrial organization and the functioning of exchange systems such as the market mechanism. However, we can also approach the subject from a morphological standpoint and analyze important facets of the organizational complexity of the manufacturing sphere from such size information.[2]

The two approaches are not mutually exclusive and certain more basic phenomena are examined in both. Economies of scale are one such factor. A major pillar of the argument that sizes of production establishments rise with the level of economic development is the notion that economies of scale are either unlimited or increase with a rising level of technology. Potential economies of administration are a second factor: If, for instance, the costs of maintaining an organization (administration costs) fall over time with a decline in transportation, communication, and data processing costs, then increasingly larger size organizations may become economically viable.

Questions regarding economies of scale can most expeditiously be studied through an analysis of the size of production establishments, while questions concerning economies of administration are most easily explored through study of the size of enterprises.[3] Size (particularly of enterprises) is considered not only in an absolute sense but also *vis-à-vis* the size of economies and markets in which the production units operate. Although it should be clear that there are important interactions between establishment and enterprise sizes, the underlying forces can be sufficiently disentangled to permit separate treatment of the two phenomena.

B. Some Important Theoretical Considerations

Theoretical analysis of establishment size depends very much on the measure of size that is employed. On the grounds of the availability of comparable data (see below), I have chosen in the empirical analysis to measure establishment size by the size of its labor force, rather than by output. This means that if the number of workers in an establishment decreases, establishment size decreases even though production has greatly increased because of the introduction of more capital intensive methods of production.

2. The theory underlying such a morphological approach is discussed by Herbert A. Simon, "The Architecture of Complexity," *Proceedings of the American Philosophical Society,* CVI, December 1962, pp. 467–82.

3. This is an oversimplification since certain interrelations exist between establishment size, economies of scale, and economies of administration. For instance, in a market economy enterprises gain certain "security" advantages by making a wide product line and this may, in certain circumstances, result in an enterprise administering a number of establishments that are highly specialized, but not necessarily of optimal scale. Other types of situations can also be imagined. Nevertheless, as the first approximation for conducting research on a topic that has received relatively little attention, the generalization in the text seems adequate.

Economists from Adam Smith to the present have been concerned with the economic and technological forces underlying economies or diseconomies of scale; and the economic literature abounds in theoretical analyses of such factors. Because of lack of comparable data for industries narrowly defined, we have relatively few empirical international comparisons of industrial establishment size and many of those available leave much to be desired.[4] If we focus our attention on average establishment size in the entire manufacturing sector or on industries broadly defined such as the two-digit ISIC (International Standard Industrial Classification) industrial classes, more comparable data are available; but many detailed technological or economic factors that are important in explaining establishment size in industries narrowly defined lose their critical explanatory role and more general (and less explored) forces assert themselves. Thus there seems to be a trade-off between availability of comparable data and specificity with which particular factors influencing establishment size can be designated.

The search for general causal factors underlying establishment size in industries broadly defined is nevertheless highly instructive and, indeed, can shed considerable light on problems dealing with narrowly defined industries. Such general forces influencing average establishment size include the level of economic development, the size of the market, population density, and economic system. The ways in which these influences are exercised on establishment size are explored below. At several places I also examine the effect of these causal factors on the "degree of agglomeration," which is the percentage of the labor force engaged in an average size (defined below) industrial establishment. This latter phenomenon is important in gaining an overall picture of trends in establishment size distribution and, in addition, foreshadows some of the analysis of monopoly that is presented in the next chapter.

1. The Effects of Economic Development

a. *Technology.* In the early stages of European and American industrialization, advanced technology appeared associated with increasing establishment size. The nineteenth-century polemics against the "dark, Satanic mills" were a literary reflection of this phenomenon. A number of reasons underlying such apparent growth of establishment size has been offered

---

4. For instance, L. Rostas (*Comparative Productivity in British and American Industry* [Cambridge, England: 1948]) attempts to show from a very small sample of United States, British, and Swedish establishments that such establishments in given industries are the same size. The similarities that he shows are not very impressive and, indeed, may be essentially fortuitous; in any case, he performs no statistical tests on the data.

of which the economies of power production and usage at a single location may be particularly important.

Whether establishment size has continued to increase in the twentieth century is more subject to debate; in the economic literature there is considerable controversy about this matter. Certain economists such as John Jewkes have argued that "there have in the past thirty or forty years been no very spectacular changes in size [of manufacturing establishments] . . .";[5] while others, such as P. Sargent Florence, have contended that "the average size of a factory is in fact slowly creeping up almost everywhere."[6]

One important theoretical consideration on this matter deserves immediate attention: If the average employment size of establishments in any given branch of industry is determined primarily by the level of technological knowledge available to all nations, then any difference in the average size of industrial establishments between countries can be explained by differences in the distribution of employment among industrial branches. If we also assume that the composition of industrial employment varies in a systematic way with changes in the level of development, then in the end we must attribute the differences in average size of establishments between countries to differences in their levels of development. Although this argument is based on a number of assumptions that have never been adequately demonstrated (e.g., that the optimum size establishment in a given industrial branch is independent of market size and/or conditions and depends solely on technological factors), it is often accepted. A less extreme restatement of this approach emphasizes similar relative differences of establishment sizes in different industrial branches among nations. Since this more moderate view underlies certain arguments below, it needs to be tested; and, fortunately, such a test is quite easy to carry out.

Broad technological factors seem to underlie the ISIC industrial classification, since the various industries are primarily grouped accord-

5. John Jewkes, "The Size of the Factory," *Economic Journal,* LXII, June 1952, pp. 237–51. Jewkes has stated his position more strongly in a later essay ("Are Economies of Scale Unlimited?" in E. A. G. Robinson, ed., *Economic Consequences of the Size of Nations* [New York: 1960], pp. 95–116) where he wrote: "If there are pervasive and powerful forces making for increased size of factories, then they cannot have been operating long, because so far they have produced no remarkable results. If, on the other hand, there are forces acting in this direction which are deep-seated and have been long in operation, they cannot be very powerful, because they have not produced conspicuous effects." Jewkes' position is supported by economists from the International Labour Office (see "The Size of Industrial Establishments," *International Labour Review,* LXXVIII, June 1956, pp. 634–44).

6. P. Sargent Florence, "The Size of the Factory: A Reply," *Economic Journal,* LXIV, September 1954, p. 628.

ing to types of processing (e.g., textile industry, clothing industry, rubber industry, primary metals industry), rather than types of products (e.g., electric and steam motors are in different branches; and so are paper and wooden boxes). This fortunate circumstance means that we can ignore, as a first approximation, the effects of a changing composition within the two-digit classes and compare the sizes of establishments between the various two-digit branches of mining and manufacturing. Data on the average rank order of size of industrial establishments in twenty-three developed or semideveloped Western nations according to four different measurements of average size (measured in terms of labor inputs and discussed in detail in Section C of this chapter) are presented in Table 5–1.

The coefficients of concordance, which measure the similarity of the rank ordering of the specific nations from which the average is derived, are statistically significant at the .01 level.[7] Thus, the rank orderings of size (relative sizes) of industrial establishments in the various two-digit ISIC industries are roughly similar in all nations, even though the average absolute size of establishments in a given branch varies greatly among nations. Furthermore, the rank orderings of average size are roughly the same for all four measures of average size. And finally, the results make intuitive sense: The largest establishments are found in the primary metals, rubber products (especially tires), and transport equipment industries and the smallest establishments are found in the leather product, lumber product (except furniture), and furniture and fixtures industries.[8]

---

7. The entropy and Niehans indices are discussed in detail in the section on statistical problems; their formulae are presented in notes 25 and 26 of this chapter. The twenty-three nations used in the calculations are listed in Table 5–4. The sources of data for the table are listed in Appendix B–18. A number of problems arose in the calculation of the concordance coefficients, especially where particular ISIC two-digit industries were not reported for particular nations or were combined with other two-digit industries; the adjustments that were made give a slight downward bias to the calculated concordance coefficient.

8. The relationship between establishment size and technology is usually investigated in a more explicit manner with the aid of production function estimates. Unfortunately, scale coefficients are extremely sensitive to the manner in which production functions are specified and this, in turn, is an unresolved and controversial matter about which there is a great deal of disagreement among experts (e.g., see Murray Brown, ed., *The Theory and Empirical Analysis of Production* [New York: 1967]). In comparing my relative size rankings of the United States with the scale calculations made from cross-state data by George H. Hildebrand and Liu Ta-Chung (*Manufacturing Production Functions in the United States, 1957* [Ithaca: 1965], pp. 109–10), the rank orders are not significantly correlated (either when the scale coefficients assuming constant technology or the "technological effect" are calculated). The Hildebrand-Liu results, which place food products as the industry with the greatest returns to scale and electrical machinery and equipment among those with the least returns to scale, may be due to their specification of the production function which assumes that the

TABLE 5-1

Average Rank Orders in the West of Industrial Establishment Size Measured in Terms of Employment[a]

ISIC No.	Name of Industry	Average Rank Orderings			Percentage of Labor Force in Establishments Over 1000
		Arithmetic	Entropy index	Niehans index	
34	Primary metals	1	1	1	1
22	Tobacco products	2	4	5	12
30	Rubber products	3	3	3	4
38	Transport equipment	4	2	2	2
32	Petroleum and coal products	5	7	9	8
37	Electrical goods and machinery	6	5	4	6
31	Chemicals	7	6	6	7
27	Paper and pulp products	8	9	11	10
23	Textiles	9	10	10	9
10–19	Mining	10	8	7	3
36	Machinery except electrical and transportation	11	11	8	5
33	Stone, glass, and clay products	12	12	12	11
20	Food processing	13	14	14.5	16
21	Beverages	14	15	16	18
35	Metal products except machinery	15	13	13	13
28	Printing and publishing	16	16	14.5	14
39	Miscellaneous products	17	17	17	15
24	Clothing and footwear	18	18	18	17
29	Leather products except footwear	19	19	20	21
25	Lumber products except furniture	20	20	19	19
26	Furniture and fixtures	21	21	21	20
	Number of nations in sample	23	23	23	14
	Coefficients of concordance	.89*	.86*	.80*	.54*

a. The concordance coefficient for the size indicator based on percentage of labor force employed in establishments over 1,000 is statistically significant but much lower than the rest because of the large number of tie scores for those industries in particular countries in which there were no manufacturing establishments of this size.

These results suggest that the influence of technology on average establishment size through the branch structure of employment may be an extremely important factor that must be explicitly taken into account in any empirical analysis of average establishment size. In the light of the effort it took me to carry out this injunction, it is ironic that the empirical analysis below shows that the effect of differences in branch employment structure is not an important determinant in international differences in average establishment size.

b. *Changes in capital intensity.* It is well known that economic development is accompanied by a rise in capital intensity, i.e., in a rise of the capital/labor ratio. Although we do not have adequate data on these matters for making cross-country comparisons, some indirect supportive evidence is supplied by the great differences in the price of capital (both the price of capital goods and the interest rate) *vis-à-vis* the price of labor in nations with different per capita incomes.[9] What effect could this difference in capital intensity have on the optimal scale of industrial establishments?

An intuitive way of looking at the problem is to consider what happens to the scale of an industrial establishment when the price of labor rises *vis-à-vis* the price of capital. Following the standard neoclassical axioms, individual establishments will find it profitable to substitute capital for labor.[10] *A priori,* however, we cannot tell whether the scale of production (as measured by output) will increase, or if it does increase, whether total labor inputs will increase. For this we must have highly specific information about the cost function. In centrally planned economies, planners need highly specific information about production functions to make rational decisions about changing establishment size with changes in capital intensity.[11] Unfortunately, we have detailed information neither

---

long-run cost curve is linear. This feature, it must be added, is characteristic of most production function calculations by others as well.

9. According to calculations that I made for the year 1955, the ratio of relative prices of capital goods to labor varies much more than per capita income when a group of West European nations and the United States are compared. For details of this calculation, see Statistical Appendix B-14.

10. For this analysis I am assuming away the "double-switching problem" and other nightmares popularized by the Cambridge school of capital theory. Empirical investigation of these matters by Frederic M. Scherer, *et al., The Economics of Multi-Plant Operation: An International Comparisons Study,* forthcoming, suggests that European manufacturers view the same production technologies as optimal as United States manufacturers, despite the differences in relative factor cost among the various nations.

11. The problem can be set up mathematically in the following way: Let the production function for a single establishment be $Q = f(K, L) = g(K/L, L)$, where Q is output, K = capital, and L = labor. The "g" function is merely the "f" function rewritten such that production is a function of

about costs nor about production functions and, as a result, cannot decide from theoretical considerations how changes in capital intensity accompanying economic development might influence establishment size.

c. *Other effects.* Other influences of the level of economic development on the size of establishments deserve brief mention. As the level of development increases and technology rises, transportation and communication costs fall. In addition, a higher level of economic development is associated with greater education and this, in turn, might allow cost savings in the supervision of production by permitting larger spans of control. The influences of these factors on the size of production establishments depend crucially on the manner in which these costs change *vis-à-vis* other costs; until this vital relationship is determined, we cannot predict whether establishment size will increase or decrease with a rising level of economic development. The logic behind this assertion may become clearer after the more extended treatment of transportation costs below.

Another set of considerations arise with the possibility of substituting capital for missing labor skills, a feature that may characterize some economically less developed nations. We do not have the data to test this notion.

d. *Final remarks.* Although we have a number of reasons for believing that economic development might have an important influence on the size of industrial establishments, not enough information is available to determine without empirical analysis whether such relationships actually exist and, if so, whether the relationships are direct or inverse. In the

---

capital intensity (K/L) and the total amount of labor, a reformulation that still makes total production a function of the total amount of capital and labor.

Let us now imagine a series of economies that have the same aggregate amounts of capital and labor and the same capital intensity in each establishment but are composed of different numbers of equal-size establishments. In the economy where production is highest, the average product of labor is also the highest since we are holding capital intensity constant. Thus if we wish to find the optimal-scale establishment, we find the derivative of the average product of labor, set it to zero, and solve. If we now wish to determine whether the scale increases or decreases when the capital intensity increases we differentiate the formula for the optimal-scale establishment and note the sign.

An alternative formulation of the problem would start from cost functions and then note the response when the relative price of labor *vis-à-vis* capital changes (which, in a market economy, could result from a change in the relative amounts of capital and labor).

In this brief analysis I am assuming continuity of the functions and other properties (e.g., U-shaped long run cost curves) that permit meaningful solutions to be obtained.

cross-section regression analysis presented below, an economic development variable is included in order to gain some empirical notion about the direction and magnitude of the influence of economic development on establishment size. Not surprisingly, no such influence can be found.

2. *The Effects of Market Size*

a. *Traditional arguments.* If there are no economies of scale, then establishment size is not related to market size, *ceteris paribus;* however, as the size of the market increases, we would expect the number of establishments to increase and the percentage of workers and employees in the total labor force engaged in a single establishment to decline. If there are economies of scale but the minimum-efficient-size (M.E.S.) establishment is not large enough to supply the entire market, then we would also not expect establishment size to be related to market size, *ceteris paribus.* Only if the M.E.S. establishment is larger than that needed to supply the entire domestic market and if exports are prohibited might we expect to find a relationship between establishment and market size.

If we assume that there are unutilized economies of scale such that larger size establishments have a cost savings over smaller establishments, and if competition is effective, the smaller establishments should either become larger or become unprofitable and disappear. Therefore, as long as there are unutilized economies of scale, the average size of establishments should increase over time in normal situations as establishment size is brought closer to the optimum. If we are trying to explain cross-section data where this time factor cannot be brought into the analysis in such a manner, then the argument must be slightly modified. If there are unutilized economies of scale in the manufacturing sector of a group of nations at a particular point in time, then we might expect that the process by which the small establishments are displaced by large establishments is furthest advanced in those nations with the largest market sizes. Such arguments linking establishments and market size are tenuous and much more direct links between the two phenomena can be established.

b. *Environmental considerations.* Let us assume a constant capital/labor ratio in production and then introduce certain nonproduction costs originating from the environment in which the establishment is located. A typical environmental cost is the cost of transporting the produced goods to the customer. If, for instance, the population of a country lives on a single straight road and the production establishment is located in the middle between the end points of the road, it should be clear that with each additional customer at the end points, transportation costs per unit of output become increasingly higher.[12] Even though the production unit may have enormous economies of scale, these may be more than offset by very high transportation costs so that it may be worthwhile to set up one or more additional establishments to service the far ends of the nation.

If we consider such activities of "overcoming the environment" in getting the product to the consumer as a type of production with its own production function, then we can easily determine the optimal scale by maximizing the value of net output, i.e., total valued output minus production costs of overcoming the environment.[13] The major conclusion of such an exercise can be intuitively grasped without any mathematics: the lower the costs of overcoming the environment, the larger the optimal scale of an industrial establishment.

What kind of deductions follow from this proposition? First, optimal size will be greater, the higher the population density. Second, the faster transportation or other costs of overcoming the environment fall with increasing scale of activity, the larger the optimal size (in employment or output) of production units. Or if transportation costs fall faster than production costs, in ordinary cases the optimal size of establishments increases; if the reverse should occur, in ordinary cases establishment sizes decrease, even if both production and environmental costs are declining absolutely with scale.

But other types of environmental barriers should be considered, of which trade barriers must count among the most important. The highest trade barriers are, of course, those arising at national boundaries where

12. If the population is distributed uniformly along the road, if each person on the road buys one unit of the product, and if it costs x units of resources to deliver a product one distance unit, then total transportation costs are: $(x)\ (p/4)\ (p + 2)$, where p is the number of persons buying the product. Thus it can be easily seen that average transportation costs per person increase as the number of people rises. If one complicates the model by considering an area where the population is distributed uniformly in circular arcs surrounding the production establishment and where transportation costs are proportional to the direct distance between the person and the point of production, transportation costs per person still rise as the number of people increase, albeit at a slower rate. (It must be added that the algebraic expression of the cost function is also considerably more complicated.)

13. Let us view the situation as a cost-minimization problem and start with a formula for total costs (T) as the sum of production costs (P) and costs of overcoming the environment (E). Both P and E are functions of the scale of activity and by differentiating the formula $T = P + E$ with respect to scale, we can determine the optimum scale.

Such a model has been used for numerous types of economic analyses and, recently, has also been used to analyze political centralization by Manfred Kochen and Karl W. Deutsch, "Toward a Rational Theory of Decentralization: Some Implications of a Mathematical Approach," *American Political Science Review*, LXIII, September 1969, pp. 734–49.

tariffs and other types of hindrances are applied. If such tariffs are infinitely high, then the size of production establishments in an exporting nation whose optimal employment is larger than that necessary to supply the domestic market is limited and we would expect the average employment size of establishments to be a function of a measure of total domestic production. If such trade barriers are of finite size, then we would still expect a positive relationship between the average employment size of establishments and the size of the domestic market. Only in the case where such international trade barriers are relatively unimportant would we expect the average employment size of establishments *not* to be related to the size of the domestic market. Other environmental barriers of a more political nature can also be analyzed in a similar manner and are brought into the analysis of several puzzling phenomena about establishment size in Eastern Europe.

This reasoning is predicated on the assumption that establishment size is not affected by changes in the assortment of products manufactured in a given establishment that conceivably might be associated with changes in the market size. Unfortunately, adequate statistics to test this important assumption are not available.

The impact of these environmental barriers on the degree of agglomeration (percentage of the labor force in an average size industrial establishment) is difficult to determine on an *a priori* basis. Theory tells us little about the numerical relation between the employment size of establishments and the total employment in the industry.

c. *The impact of enterprise administration costs.* Up to now I have implicitly assumed that the economy consists only of single establishment enterprises; it is now time to break this assumption.

Walter Eucken once made the theoretical assertion that in planned economies production units are generally larger because of simplicity of administration and lower costs of coordination.[14] An industrial enterprise is, of course, a small planned economy and on the basis of this proposition, one might suspect that establishment size might be larger in multi-establishment than in single establishment enterprises. Unfortunately, Eucken did not feel it necessary to argue this "obvious proposition" and his underlying rationale is quite unclear. Other economists have also argued that establishments in multi-establishment enterprises are larger

14. Walter Eucken, "On the Theory of the Centrally Administered Economy: An Analysis of the German Experience," *Economica*, N.S., XV, May 1948, pp. 79–100. A parallel argument was made by the Soviet economist V. Kvasha in *Voprosi ekonomiki*, No. 5, 1967, cited by Alec Nove, "Internal Economies," *Economic Journal*, LXXIX, December 1969, pp. 847–61.

than in single establishment enterprises but their explanations, e.g., "administrative convenience," have been similarly vague. A theoretical justification could be made that takes into account economies of different spans of control, costs of vertical information flows, etc., but this would take us far from the major theme of this study.

Whether it is true that establishment sizes are larger in multi-establishment enterprises is important because, as I show below, the degree to which an economy is characterized by multi-establishment enterprises is correlated with the size of the domestic market. It seems most simple to examine the relationship between establishment size and multi-establishment enterprises by referring to some detailed information for a single country for which data are plentiful.

For the United States considerable data on industrial establishment sizes on single and multi-establishment enterprises are readily available. Looking at mining and manufacturing enterprises with twenty or more manual and nonmanual workers, a very clear pattern emerges: Establishments in multi-establishment enterprises are over one-third larger in employment size than those in the single establishment enterprises.[15] Furthermore, the larger the size of the multi-establishment enterprise, the larger the size of individual establishments comprising the enterprise. For instance, the average establishment size in multi-establishment enterprises with 1,000 employees or more is almost 1.6 times as large as establishments in enterprises with 250 to 499 employees and almost 2.5 times as large as establishments in enterprises with 100 to 250 employees. A similar pattern appears in individual industrial branches.

Clearly industrial establishments are larger in multi-establishment enterprises. The importance of this observation becomes apparent when we examine the factors correlated with the degree to which economies are characterized by multi-establishment enterprises. One readily available measure of the degree of multi-establishment enterprises in a nation is the ratio of the average employment size of enterprises in the economy to the average employment size of establishments, which indicates the average number of establishments per enterprise: the higher the ratio, the greater the relative degree of multi-establishment enterprises.[16] Although

15. These and the following data come from the United States Bureau of the Census, *1963 Enterprise Statistics,* Part I (Washington, D.C.: 1968), Table 9. It should be noted that as the size of the multi-establishment enterprise rises, the average number of establishments per enterprise also rises. Much different evidence on these matters is also presented by Ralph L. Nelson, *Concentration in Manufacturing Industries in the United States* (New Haven: 1963), Chapter 4.

16. This ratio measures the average number of establishments per enterprise and, if every enterprise had the same number of establishments, it would reflect this phenomenon alone. However, most enterprises in Western economies are single-establishment units so that this ratio of enterprise to establishment size also partly reflects the penetration of the multi-estab-

this measure is certainly not ideal and has several problems associated with it, no better statistic can easily be calculated.

Using a ten-nation sample (this is discussed in the analysis of Table 6–1), we can see that the degree to which economies are characterized by multi-establishment enterprises is significantly and highly correlated with the size of the domestic market as measured by the G.N.P. A more concrete idea of this relationship can be seen in the cases of Japan and Switzerland: In comparison to Switzerland Japan has a much lower per capita G.N.P. but a much higher total G.N.P. (domestic market); Japan also has a much higher indicator of multi-establishment enterprises.

From the results of this empirical analysis, we can conclude that the average size of industrial establishments would be positively correlated to the size of the domestic market because larger national economies have higher degrees of multi-establishment enterprises.

d. *The impact of government policy.* Because of fear of balance of payments problems, many governments have encouraged import substitution which has led to domestic production of goods for which the nation has no comparative advantage; in many such cases this is manifested by investment in less than optimal size production units. Since the relative importance of foreign trade is greater in nations with small gross national products, balance of payment problems might loom larger in these nations and government policy makers would have greater temptations to follow import substitution policies. Thus establishment size might be linked with size of G.N.P. through the influence of governmental policy to forestall balance of payment difficulties.[17]

In nations with small domestic markets, the lack of governmental enforcement of cartel agreements might also induce enterprises to build less than optimal size new establishments in order to maintain their market share. In such economies, only strict enforcement of cartel agreements designating the years in which each enterprise could build a new establishment could lead to optimal size production units.[18]

e. *Summary.* We have three reasons for suspecting that average establishment size is positively related to the size of the domestic economy. First, there is a relationship between employment size of establishments and particular environmental barriers that are related to the economic size

---

lishment form of enterprise into the economy. The data on this measure and the correlation experiments are reported in detail in Chapter VI, Section B-2.

17. This hypothesis was suggested to me by Howard Pack, to whom I would like to express my appreciation. A case study of such import substitution policies and the impact on the organization of industry can be found in his book *Structural Change and Economic Policy in Israel* (New Haven: 1971).

18. This hypothesis is argued by Scherer, *et al.*, Chapter 3.

(G.N.P.) of the nation. Second, average employment size of an establishment is related to the degree of multi-establishment enterprises in the nation which, in turn, is related to the total value of the G.N.P. Third, average establishment size is related to the G.N.P. through the impact of governmental import substitution and cartel policies. If a positive relationship between establishment size and G.N.P. is empirically found, it is not possible to determine which one or more of the three explanations is most important in determining the results. Although this gives rise to problems of interpretation, it should not discourage us from determining whether any such relationship exists empirically.

3. Other Factors

a. *The effects of economic system.* The proposition by Eucken cited above was taken from his argument that in planned economies there is greater standardization of products and greater standardization of production methods so that production units would be larger and more similar to each other in size. We therefore have additional propositions about average sizes and size distributions of establishments in East and West which can be empirically tested. The statistical analysis of the impact of economic system is deferred until the examination of establishment size distributions in the West is completed in order to develop some comparative norms.

b. *The effects of population density.* In a nation with a relatively sparse population, transportation costs are considerably higher than in a densely populated nation, other things being equal. For goods where such transportation costs are important, we might predict establishment sizes to be smaller in nations with low population densities. For instance, in Great Britain, average establishment size in specific industries in the different counties is positively correlated with the population densities of these counties.[19] It could be argued that such a density factor might influence relative establishment sizes in the world economy as well. However, preliminary econometric work did not indicate that this was a significant explanatory variable of differences in establishment size among nations and it was dropped from the final analysis.

c. *Random factors and a Markov analysis.* In recent years economists have focused considerable attention on analyzing size distributions (of

---

19. Evidence on this matter is presented by P. Sargent Florence, *Investment, Location, and Size of Plant* (Cambridge, England: 1948). In such an analysis there is a problem of direction of causation since heavy industry (which is correlated with establishment size) may bring about high population density, rather than the reverse.

establishments, enterprises, incomes, cities, etc.) as the resultant of random processes operating within certain rules of transition.[20] The critical rules include the stochastic laws by which existing units grow or decline and the laws governing the birth of new units and the death of old units. With information about the laws of growth, natality (entry of new units), and mortality, the size distribution of the units can be determined by use of a Markov chain technique, and from this generalizations about the changing sizes of production units can be made. For instance, if we make the assumption that there are no long-run diseconomies of scale and that short-run gains from expanding existing establishments are greater than from creating new establishments, then conditions can easily be specified which would be consistent with both an expanding number of establishments as well as an increasing average size of establishment in a nation over time.[21]

We could also link market size with establishment size on a cross-section basis by adding the consideration that greater constraints are placed on establishment growth in a nation with a smaller market size. That is, if we start with two nations that have different market sizes but have similar size distributions of establishments (except that the nation with the larger market size will have a certain proportion of more establishments in any given establishment size category), the stochastic process determining the size distribution of establishments will lead under certain specified conditions to a larger number of large establishments in the nation with the larger market size.[22]

The problem with this Markov approach is that almost any result

20. For production units most such arguments are concerned with the size distribution of enterprises, rather than establishments, e.g., Herbert A. Simon and C. P. Bonini, "The Size Distribution of Business Firms," *American Economic Review*, XLVIII, September 1958 pp. 607–17; or Josef Steindl, *Random Processes and the Growth of Firms: A Study of the Pareto Law* (New York: 1965). Nevertheless, the stochastic process on which they are based can be employed in analyzing the distribution of establishments as well.

21. The short-run gains of expanding additional facilities, rather than building new plants, are that an experienced labor force is already at hand so that learning costs are lower and that overhead facilities can also be shared. Given such short-run gains, then a variety of sets of conditions can be specified so that a stochastic growth process of establishments can yield an increasing number of establishments and a rising average size, e.g., that new establishments are larger than the average establishment, or that the birth of new establishments of a given size is more than matched by the growth of the labor force of existing establishments, etc.

22. A rigorous proof of this proposition awaits a mathematician; this conclusion was derived from a number of numerical examples. It can also be argued that the size of the market affects the laws governing growth, natality, and mortality of establishments (with a ceiling of establishment growth in small markets and, at the same time, lower natality) which would result in a lower average establishment size in nations with smaller market sizes.

can be obtained if the laws of growth, natality, and mortality are specified in the proper manner; and since we know so very little about these laws at the present time, testable predictions cannot be made. If we use the resulting size distributions to deduce these laws, we assume the process which we are really trying to test and are therefore guilty of circular reasoning. Therefore, this approach is not further pursued here.

4. A Brief Recapitulation

This ends my survey of general explanatory factors for differences in establishment sizes in nations. The most promising variables to be examined are the level of economic development, market size, and economic system. However, it must be noted that we have several possible explanations for a relationship between establishment and market size which cannot be easily disentangled until greater attention is paid to the factors underlying them (e.g., cost functions of overcoming the environmental barriers, costs and benefits of large-scale administration; and impact of governmental policies).

C. Some Statistical Problems

1. Measurement of Average Establishment Size

An establishment is defined above as a "business or industrial unit at a single location; it can consist of several 'plants,' 'workshops' or 'factories' as long as these are located together and under a single management." Several obvious difficulties in obtaining comparable data using this definition can be seen. First, the "single location" and the "single management" criteria allow different interpretations. Second, if an establishment is producing two very different products, sometimes it is designated by national statistical offices as two establishments. (Such problems arise in cases of integrated production in the petro-chemical, oil, and metallurgical industries.) Third, the inclusion of particular "units" as separate establishments, especially if they are leased, used on a temporary basis, or used primarily for nonproduction purposes raises difficulties.

I believe that the most important incomparabilities in national data arise in the treatment of very small establishments. Such a problem influences greatly any analysis that is based on statistics of average size, a procedure that has been used in most studies up to now. The nature of the problem can be seen most clearly by examining some actual data.[23] For instance, in 1963 in the United States the average manufacturing

---

23. The data for this example come from United States Bureau of Census, *1963 Census of Manufacturing, Summary,* Vol. I (Washington, D.C.: 1966).

establishment had 53 employees. However, if we exclude establishments with under 5 employees, the average establishment had 82; and if we exclude those with under 20 employees, the average establishment had 152. The reason for such significant differences in the averages lies not in the importance of the share of the labor force employed by such tiny establishments, but in their number: establishments with under 5 employees constituted 37 percent of all United States manufacturing establishments in that year; and those with under 20 employees, 68 percent. A similar picture emerges when enterprise statistics are used.

Differences in the definitions used in counting the enterprises and establishments in a nation can greatly affect the number of units employing a very small number of employees and this, in turn, can radically affect the results of any analysis resting on comparisons of "average size." One procedure for minimizing such difficulties is to exclude establishments and enterprises with less than twenty employees—a method that is followed in this study—but additional problems also arise that require brief exploration.

What should be the measure of size used in the analysis? Several measures have been proposed—volume of output, value added, capital stock, labor force, or various combinations of these four; and, indeed, the proper measure that is selected depends partly on the problem under consideration. Although a great many considerations can be mentioned that point to one or another size indicator, one vital practical difficulty must be noted: If we wish to make comparisons between nations, the choice is limited by the available statistics and, indeed, only comparable data on the size distribution of enterprises and establishments by the labor force are available for a sufficient number of nations to make such comparisons very embracing. Or, in the words of an eminent authority in the field of industrial organization, labor measures of size are "usually the least objectionable of the indices [of size] made possible by official censuses."[24]

Use of such a labor force measure of size raises several difficulties in interpretation and calculation. Such a measure does not directly indicate scale (which is an output concept). On the other hand, if we are interested in the organization of the labor force in particular business units, then the labor input measure may be more useful than an output measure. Such a labor measure also says nothing about capital intensity (the capital/labor ratio) or other aspects of the organization of production. Third, the labor force measures used in the various national statistics are

24. P. Sargent Florence, *Investment, Location and Size of Plant*, p. 13. In this connection it should be noted that Scherer, *et al.*, examine in an international context twelve industries narrowly defined using output measures of size; they arrive at basically the same conclusions as I do regarding the central importance of market size as a determinant of establishment size.

not completely standardized. For this study both manual and nonmanual workers are included; therefore, estimates of nonmanual workers had to be made for several nations. Finally, because the size groupings of enterprises and establishments for most nations are relatively few, I had to forego detailed analysis of the distribution curve.

Another major problem concerns the particular statistic that is employed to designate the size distribution. This is, of course, a specific question in the more general problem of how an entire distribution can be characterized by a few statistics. The possibility of calculating the formula of the distribution and using the derived parameters is not feasible because of the limited number of size categories (i.e., limited number of degrees of freedom). The only other valid procedure is to calculate several different descriptive statistics of the distribution and to see whether the derived determinants of one statistic can be used in analyzing the behavior of the other descriptive statistics. To this end, four different characterizations of the size distribution are employed.

Two of the statistics of size are straightforward. The first is the arithmetic average of workers and employees in all establishments with a labor force of twenty or more; the second is the percentage of total labor force (including those in establishments under twenty) employed in establishments with a labor force of one thousand or more.

Two types of weighted averages, a Niehans index and an entropy index, are also employed. These measures have some useful properties that are fully described in the technical literature and proponents of both indices have provided evidence that they are better measures of "economic power" within a market than simple arithmetic averages.[25] The Niehans index is the sum of the sizes of the various establishments (with a labor force of twenty or more), weighted by the fraction of the labor force employed in all the particular units under consideration.[26] (The Niehans index is equal to the Herfindahl-Hirshman or "H" weighted average of

25. The two measures are compared and evaluated as measures of economic power by George Stigler, *The Organization of Industry* (Homewood, Ill.: 1968), Chapter 4. For a more sympathetic approach toward the entropy measure as a useful tool in the study of industrial organization, see Michael O. Finkelstein and Richard M. Friedberg, "The Application of the Entropy Theory of Concentration to the Clayton Act," *Yale Law Journal,* LXXVI, March 1967, pp. 677–717.

26. The Niehans measure is analyzed in detail by Jurg Niehans, "An Index of the Size of Industrial Establishments," *International Economic Papers,* VIII (London: 1958), originally published as "Eine Messziffer fuer Betriebsgroessen," *Zeitschrift fur die gesamte Staatswissenschaft,* CXI, March 1955. The formula for the index is:

$N = \Sigma s_i L_i$, where s_i is the share of the total relevant labor force in unit i and L_i is the labor force employed in that unit. (If establishment data are grouped, then the formula is modified in a simple manner).

the share of the labor force divided into the total labor force; its justification is considerably more elaborate and also independent of the discussion of the "H" measure.) This index has one disadvantage for empirical work in that it is sensitive to the manner in which size categories are defined in the upper ranges. The entropy measure is a multiplicative statistic employing the reciprocals of the shares of the total labor force employed in each unit (with a labor force of twenty or more) raised to the fractional power of this share.[27] To show how the different averages work, three numerical examples are presented in Table 5–2 and are briefly discussed below.

In all three examples there are five establishments employing a total of one thousand workers and employees, but the size distributions are different. In the first example, all five establishments are the same size and both the Niehans and the entropy indices of average size are the same as the arithmetic average. In the second example, the sizes are somewhat different, the entropy index is slightly greater than the arithmetic average, and the Niehans index is somewhat greater than the entropy index. In the third example, the size range is even more extreme and the two weighted averages are considerably greater than the arithmetic average. When establishment sizes are not the same, the Niehans index always yields a larger average than the entropy index which, in turn, is always greater than the arithmetic average. As the range of size variation increases, the differences between the results of the three indices become larger.

In the discussion below I test the same explanatory variables against all four measures of size; in most cases all four yield roughly the same results. This gives us some confidence in the results, so far as the mode of measurement is concerned.

The three averages are used in other ways in this study as well. The degree of agglomeration is determined by finding the share of the labor force engaged in an "average size" establishment. The reciprocal of this percentage yields the number of "average size" establishments that would employ the entire labor force and has been sometimes used by others for particular analytic purposes.[28]

27. The entropy measure is analyzed in detail by Henri Theil, *Economics and Information Theory* (Chicago: 1967). Its formula is:

$$E = L/(1/s_1)^{s_1} \; (1/s_2)^{s_2} \; (1/s_3)^{s_3} \; \ldots$$

or $\log E = \log L - \Sigma s_i \log (1/s_i)$

where L is the total relevant labor force and s_i is the share employed in a single productive unit.

28. This usage is discussed in greater detail by Morris A. Adelman, "Comment on the 'H' Concentration Measure as a Numbers-Equivalent," *The Review of Economics and Statistics*, LI, February 1969, pp. 99–101.

TABLE 5–2

Numerical Examples of Different Averages of Establishment Size

	Example 1	Example 2	Example 3
A. <u>Arithmetic Average</u>	Labor Force in Establishments	Labor Force in Establishments	Labor Force in Establishments
Establishment			
1	200	100	100
2	200	150	100
3	200	200	100
4	200	250	100
5	200	300	600
Total	1000	1000	1000
Arithmetic average	200	200	200
B. <u>Entropy Index</u>	Weight of Individual Components $-s_i\log(1/s_i)$	Weight of Individual Components $-s_i\log(1/s_i)$	Weight of Individual Components $-s_i\log(1/s_i)$
Establishment			
1	−.139794	−.100000	−.100000
2	−.139794	−.123586	−.100000
3	−.139794	−.139794	−.100000
4	−.139794	−.150515	−.100000
5	−.139794	−.177864	−.133180
Subtotal	−.698970	−.691759	−.533180
Log L	3.000000	3.000000	3.000000
Total	2.301030	2.308241	2.466890
Antilog of total (entropy index)	200	203.35	293.01
C. <u>Niehans Index</u>	Weight in Index of Single Unit s_iL_i	Weight in Index of Single Unit s_iL_i	Weight in Index of Single Unit s_iL_i
Establishment			
1	40	10.0	10
2	40	22.5	10
3	40	40.0	10
4	40	62.5	10
5	40	90.0	360
Total (Niehans index)	200	225.0	400

s_i = share of labor force of a particular establishment in the total labor force.
L = total labor force.

2. *Other Difficulties*

Measuring market size presents some practical difficulties that must be briefly mentioned. For an isolated nation without foreign trade, the potential size of the market can be measured by the value of national product. In comparing several such autarkical nations, the G.N.P. calculated in some common currency could be used as such a measure. In a situation with perfectly free trade and no transportation costs, the size of the market is the same for all nations—namely the world. In actuality, however, free trade does not exist and transportation costs are important; and, therefore it seems best to use as a measure of market size a measure of the G.N.P. together with a measure of the importance of foreign trade. Ideally, the ratio of value-added in exported manufacturing commodities to total value-added in manufacturing would be needed, but requisite data are not available. At an early stage of this investigation I experimented with three different approximations and selected the ratio of the value of mining and manufacturing exports to total value added domestically in these sectors, the measure with both the most theoretical appeal and the highest explanatory power. Its use is based on the reasonable assumption that the ratio of value-added to gross total value of production does not differ greatly among developed economies.

D. *Empirical Results of the Analysis of Establishment Size*

1. *A Time-series Analysis*

If we examine the size of establishments between two widely separated points in time, it should be clear that a number of factors discussed above may be at work: The level of economic development rises, population density increases, and the size of the market becomes larger. Disentangling these factors is complex, especially in view of the disagreement about the basic facts of the matter. In order to gain a clearer empirical picture, relevant data for six nations that are now economically developed are presented in Table 5–3.

The numbers in the table that are underlined show establishment size without adjustment for change in the composition of output; the other data show establishment size with adjustment made for changes in the share of employment among industries. Thus the arithmetic average size of Australian manufacturing establishments without adjustment rose from seventy-one to ninety-seven workers; if the 1907 composition of employment had been maintained, the rise would have been somewhat less, from seventy-one to ninety-one; if the 1961 employment composi-

TABLE 5-3

Employment Size of Manufacturing Establishments in the Early and Middle Twentieth Century in Six Nations[a]

Nation	Date	Arithmetic Average		Entropy Index		Niehans Index		Percentage of Labor Force in Establishments Over 1000
		Early year wght.	Late year wght.	Early year wght.	Late year wght.	Early year wght.	Late year wght.	
Australia	1907	71	74	101	105	137	145	n.a.
	1961	91	97	142	161	204	224	n.a.
France	1910	98	110	199	249	517	671	8.0
	1960	103	122	231	339	997	1620	20.3
Germany	1907	86	99	158	203	343	478	5.1
	1961	115	141	268	409	674	1054	27.7
South Africa	1907	92	74	142	133	192	182	n.a.
	1961	124	128	258	276	514	599	17.6
Switzerland	1905	83	92	150	196	293	421	n.a.
	1965	88	100	164	233	390	625	14.9
United States	1909	148	149	250	305	542	697	15.0
	1963	130	152	340	451	1111	1412	30.5

a. The estimates for the averages in the table were calculated in a three step procedure. First, the establishment data for each country were grouped as far as possible according to the ISIC industrial classification; in certain cases, however, two or more two-digit categories had to be combined. Second establishments with under twenty workers and employees were removed. Third, the size coefficients were calculated not only in the regular manner but also taking into account changes in industrial structure. The latter correction was made by multiplying the number of establishments and the total employment in each two-digit ISIC category by the ratio of total employment in one period to total employment in the other period for the particular industry and then summing to obtain an aggregate.

For all nations, workers and employees are included in the calculations. The sources of the data and certain additional notes are given in Appendix B-16.

tion among industrial branches had existed in 1907, the rise would have been from seventy-four to ninety-seven.

The empirical results are quite clear: in all countries average establishment size greatly increased over the half-century period.[29,30] If we hold the structure of employment among industries constant, this major conclusion is not changed although in most cases the increase in size was somewhat less; this means that at least a small part of the increase in establishment size can be attributed in most countries to a shift in production toward those industrial branches with relatively larger establishments.

29. My results differ from those of Jewkes, and the I.L.O. for several important reasons. First, their time periods cover about thirty years, while mine cover roughly fifty or sixty years. Second, Jewkes and the I.L.O. use arithmetic averages which, as noted above, are extremely sensitive to the large number of very small establishments. (The I.L.O. in some calculations removed establishments with less than ten workers and employees). Third, the I.L.O. also uses the percentage of workers and employees in establishments with more than a specified number but, I believe, misinterprets the data. For instance, three out of the four nations for which they have data show an increase in the labor force employed in establishments with more than one thousand workers and employees between 1920 and 1950; and five out of six nations show an increase in the labor force employed in establishments with more than five hundred workers and employees in the same period. The I.L.O. draws the conclusion that establishment size is not increasing primarily from the arithmetic averages, rather than from both sets of establishment size measures; what has happened, of course, is that the size distribution has shifted. My weighted averages, which place greater weight on large-size establishments, reflect the increase in the share of the labor force in large-size establishments.

30. There are several other Western nations for which some data over one-half century interval on the size distributions of establishments are available but which were not included in Table 5–3 for various reasons. I omitted Belgium because the available data are only for blue-collar workers (so that no account of the shift in white-collar to blue-collar workers could be taken into account) and, furthermore, contain some important incomparabilities. (See the explanatory notes in Institut national de statistique, "Evolution de concentration industrielle," *Études statistiques et econometrique,* June 1966.) I did not include Austria because the domestic market of the nation was reduced more than two-thirds after World War I. Some establishment data are also available for other countries such as Sweden and Italy but I could not find such data disaggregated by industry to a sufficient extent to hold employment structure constant. The United Kingdom data at my disposal did not prove sufficiently complete or comparable to warrant inclusion.

My results for Switzerland differ from those of Rolf Hasler, "Betriebsgroesse und Betriebskonzentration in der schweizerischen Industrie," *Schweizerische Zeitschrift fuer Volkswirtschaft und Statistik,* CII, June 1966, pp. 121–56, for three possible reasons. First, he based his calculations on "Fabrik" data, while mine are based on "Betrieb" data. Second, I have excluded all establishments with under twenty employees while he used a lower cut-off point. Third, he only used a Niehans index, which is quite sensitive to the manner in which the size data are grouped in the upper ranges. Since I was unable to obtain the sources from which he obtained his information, I cannot tell which of these three reasons is most important.

Inclusion of establishments with under twenty workers in the calculations might have revealed even greater increases. If an output measure would have been used as a measure of establishment size, the increase in size would have been much greater than shown in the table because output per worker increased greatly.

The percentage change of average size is greater using the Niehans index than the entropy index and larger using the entropy index than the arithmetic average. This phenomenon reflects two facts: Large establishments are more heavily weighted in the entropy and Niehans indices than in the unweighted arithmetic average, and a larger share of establishments fell into the larger size categories in the later years. Table 5–3 also shows that for each indicator, the ranking of nations according to establishment size has remained roughly the same over the half-century interval. Although one might suspect that there is some relationship between relative rates of change of establishment size and the initial size levels, the situation varies according to size indicator so that no definite conclusions can be drawn in this regard from the table.

Although the average employment size of manufacturing establishments has increased over the past half century, in most cases (Germany is the exception) the labor force in the manufacturing sector has increased even faster. Thus agglomeration (the percentage of the total manufacturing labor force employed in an average size establishment[31]) has decreased.

Is the increase in establishment size due to the increase in domestic market size accompanying economic development or to a rising level of technology or to other factors? If we use the relationship derived in the cross-section analysis between market size and establishment size as valid to describe such relations over time as well, then it seems likely that the rising level of technology probably acted in a manner to increase average establishment employment size, other things remaining equal. That is, the average establishment employment size increases over time at a somewhat faster rate than one would expect from the cross-section relationships derived below. This conclusion is, it must be emphasized, highly tentative since I have assumed that the cross-section relationship between establishment size and market size accurately describes this linkage over a long time interval as well, an assumption open to dispute.

31. Since the size coefficients were calculated for establishments with twenty or more workers and employees, only this restricted definition of the manufacturing labor force was used in making this comparison. For Germany, the entropy and Niehans indicators grew considerably faster than the labor force (possible reasons are explored in the next section). For other countries, the generalization holds for all three averages. It did not seem suitable to use the percentage indicators for these comparisons.

2. *A Cross-section Analysis of Western Nations*

If we take a group of nations at roughly the same time and make the reasonable assumption that the basic available technological knowledge necessary for manufacturing is roughly the same in all developed nations, then we can begin to separate the causal factors underlying establishment size that are discussed above. The relevant establishment data for such a study are presented in Table 5–4.

Two features of the data deserve brief mention. First, the rankings of countries according to establishment size are similar for all four indicators of size. Second, the ratio of the Niehans to the other two averages varies considerably. As explained above, this comes about because of

TABLE 5–4

Average Employment Size of Manufacturing Establishments in Western Nations[a]

Country	Year	Averages			Percentage of Labor Force in Establishments Over 1000
		Arith-metic	Entropy Index	Niehans Index	
Australia	1962	97	161	224	n.a.
Austria	1963	125	314	774	21.6
Belgium	1962	131	372	1311	22.8
Canada	1961	120	278	742	18.8
Denmark	1958	96	161	223	n.a.
Finland	1953	105	186	294	n.a.
France	1962	122	339	1620	20.3
West Germany	1961	141	409	1054	27.7
Greece	1963	80	112	137	n.a.
Ireland	1963	108	205	367	n.a.
Israel	1965	74	128	220	n.a.
Italy	1961	98	250	1039	13.8
Japan	1963	87	224	667	16.6
Netherlands	1962	106	268	879	17.6
New Zealand	1964	75	127	206	n.a.
Norway	1966	92	167	268	n.a.
Portugal	1958	94	159	304	6.9
South Africa	1962	128	276	599	17.6
Spain	1965	98	205	422	n.a.
Sweden	1961	107	224	586	17.0
Switzerland	1965	100	233	625	14.9
United Kingdom	1958	193	464	1188	32.0
United States	1963	152	451	1412	30.5

a. The data in the table cover ISIC industries 20 through 39. Sources and notes on the data are given in Appendix B-18.

differences in the range of establishment sizes in different nations: the
larger the spread between smallest and largest establishments, the greater
the divergence between size indicators. This accords with mathematical
expectations about such matters.

Of the four general determinants of establishment size that have
been discussed, only market size appears to be significantly related to the
establishment size indicators. Some relevant relationships are presented
in Table 5–5.

In all four cases the relationship between average establishment size
and the value of the G.N.P is statistically significant at the .05 level. For
the Niehans index, the second indicator of market size which takes
foreign trade considerations into account also plays a statistically significant role in determining establishment size.[32] In simple regressions with
other possible explanatory variables such as the level of economic development (per capita G.N.P.) or density, no statistically significant relationships were found (with one exception).[33] Inclusion of the per capita
income and density variables into the regressions with the market size
variables adds little explanatory power and the calculated regression
coefficients are not statistically significant. Nor do these conclusions
appear altered when the United States is removed from the sample and
the regressions are recalculated. If output measures of size were used
instead, I believe that a significantly positive relation with establishment
size would be found. Nevertheless, the results seem relatively unambiguous: Market size appears to be the crucial influence of the employment
size of manufacturing establishments.

Certain difficulties arise in interpreting these results since the way in
which G.N.P. (market size) influences establishment size is not clear.
Does market size act to limit the manufacturing establishments in each
of the particular branches? Or does it influence average establishment size
by affecting the composition of output such that nations with small
domestic markets do not have very much production in those industries

32. Regression results with the X ratio removed are reported in Appendix B-23.

33. Per capita G.N.P. is significantly related only to the percentage
indicator. The coefficient of determination in this case is slightly less than
when the percentage indicator is regressed against the two indicators of
market size and slightly more than when it is regressed against total income
alone. Further difficulties occur when this percentage indicator is regressed
against per capita income and both indicators of market size—the coefficient
of determination is statistically significant, but none of the individually
calculated regression coefficients are. These problems in interpretation arise
from a certain collinearity between the independent variables in the four-
teen-nation sample. Since such multicollinearity does not raise such problems
in the larger sample with the other size indicators and the results of these
indicators are relatively unambiguous, the interpretation in the text omits
consideration of the difficulties occurring with the percentage indicator.

TABLE 5–5

Relationship Between Establishment Size and Market Size Indicators[a]

	S	R²
ln A = 2.805 + .166* ln Y + .093 ln X	23	.36*
(.035) (.084)		
ln E = 1.070 + .273* ln Y + .241 ln X	23	.61*
(.049) (.117)		
ln N = 1.843 + .508* ln Y + .481* ln X	23	.67*
(.081) (.193)		
ln P = −1.948 + .296* ln Y + .327 ln X	14	.57*
(.082) (.186)		

where: A = arithmetic average of establishment size;
   E = entropy index of establishment size;
   N = Niehans index of establishment size;
   P = percentage of manufacturing labor force in establishments over 1000;
   Y = gross national product calculated with United States price weights in thousand United States dollars;
   X = ratio of nonagricultural merchandise exports to value-added in mining and manufacturing;
   S = number of nations in sample (size of sample);
   R² = coefficient of determination.

a. A specification of these relationships in logarithms gives in most cases a considerably higher coefficient of determination than when no transformation of the variables is carried out. Natural logarithms are used in the calculations.

The constant dollar gross national products were derived in a manner described in Frederic L. Pryor, *Public Expenditures in Communist and Capitalist Nations* (Homewood, Ill., 1968), Appendix B. The trade variables were calculated from data from United Nations, *Yearbook of International Trade Statistics* (New York: annual) and *Yearbook of National Account Statistics,* (New York: annual), supplemented by national data and, for Switzerland and New Zealand several estimates. The establishment size data come from Table 5–4.

The only other international comparison of establishment size of this nature that I could find was by M. M. Metwally, "A Comparison between Representative Size of Plant in Manufacturing Industries in Industrialized and Less Industrialized Countries," *Yorkshire Bulletin of Economic and Social Research,* XVII, November 1965, pp. 139–56. Our results are considerably different and are due, I feel, to his inappropriate statistical methods.

featuring large establishments, while, on the other hand, such industrial branches play a much more important role in domestic output of large nations? In other words, can the regression results be attributed to differences in production structure among nations with small and large markets?

The question can be easily decided by recalculating the establishment size averages when the assumption is made that the branch employment structure is the same for all nations. (This procedure is similar to assuming constant branch employment in the time-series analysis.) For this purpose I made two sets of calculations, one assuming that the two-digit ISIC branch employment structure was the same as that in the United States (a large, rich nation); the other, the same as that in Portugal (a small, poor nation).

Comparing the calculated regression coefficients assuming the United States branch employment structure, relatively little difference can be observed with the results in Table 5–5. For the arithmetic average, entropy index, and Niehans index, the calculated regression coefficients of the G.N.P. variable are less than 10 percent different, while for the percentage index, the difference is only slightly greater. If we use Portuguese branch employment weights, considerably more change is observable; further, the greatest reductions in calculated average establishment size appear in those countries with the largest national products. Nevertheless, all of the calculations are qualitatively similar in that most of the same statistically significant relationships appear between the same variables and, furthermore, no new significant relationships with other variables can be found.[34]

Thus we conclude that market size seems to affect the average size of establishments in all industries and that differences in the structure of output seem to play a relatively minor role. The conclusion is, of course, quite consistent with the theoretical explanations relating market size and establishment size.

Because the regressions in Table 5–5 are calculated in natural logarithms, the coefficients can be interpreted as elasticities, i.e., the percentage increase in establishment size accompanying a 1 percent increase in market size. It is noteworthy that in all four cases these elasticities are less than unity, i.e., that average establishment size increases more slowly than the G.N.P. This means that agglomeration decreases with market size. In order to investigate this phenomenon more directly, a number of regressions were calculated using the degree of agglomeration as the variable to be explained. The results can be easily summarized.[35]

As expected, the degree of agglomeration is inversely proportional to market size. However, there is also a statistically significant and positive relationship between the level of development and the degree of agglomeration, although the numerical value of the elasticity is lower than that of market size. Nevertheless, in order to make correct predictions

34. As expected, using both United States and Portuguese weights, the elasticity coefficients between market size and establishment size are generally lower than when no adjustments for industrial structure are carried out.
35. The results are presented in Appendix B-23.

about the degree of agglomeration, we must take into account both per capita and total G.N.P. If these cross-section regression results are valid for time-series, then we can also see why Germany, whose per capita G.N.P. rose relatively faster than its total G.N.P. *vis-à-vis* other nations (because Germany lost considerable population and territory in the two World Wars), might be an exception to the generalization that the degree of establishment agglomeration in a nation decreases over time.

In contrast to the time-series study, the cross-section analysis does permit us to disentangle some of the possible determinants of establishment size. Particular attention is given to the importance of market size as the critical determinant. These results, in turn, give us an empirical norm with which to explore the influence of one additional factor, that of economic system, on establishment size

3. Establishment Size in Eastern Europe

The combination of public ownership and central planning, as found in Eastern Europe, has bearing on two factors influencing establishment size. On the one hand, these nations have much less foreign trade than Western nations, other things remaining the same.[36] This would tend to reduce establishment size by reducing the size of the potential market. On the other hand, the production establishments in Eastern Europe (with the exception of Yugoslavia) received highly detailed plans and directives from superior agencies. (The situation after the reforms in the mid–1960s is analyzed in Chapter VII.) If the proposition by Eucken is correct, then this central planning factor would act to increase average establishment size. Although the foreign trade and central planning considerations act in opposite directions, it seems highly likely that the latter is considerably stronger than the former.

One important political factor also deserves attention: the degree to which the government has tolerated small-scale private and cooperative enterprises in the manufacturing sphere. As noted in the section on statistical problems, most manufacturing establishments in the West are quite small, even though they do not necessarily employ a very large share of the labor force. If for ideological reasons an East European government has acted to reduce the number of such small-scale enterprises, then the average size of production establishments may be quite large, even though central direction of the existing productive units may not

36. Results of a regression experiment demonstrating this phenomenon are reported in my "Comment on Montias," in Alan Brown and Egon Neuberger, eds., *International Trade and Central Planning* (Berkeley: 1968), pp. 163–4.

necessarily be very great. This political factor introduces difficulties into the analysis since we have no measure of its strength, other than indicators which we are trying to predict.

The most simple way to analyze the situation in East Europe is to compare the actual sizes of manufacturing establishments to that predicted by the equations derived from the data for Western nations. Certain problems arise since data on establishment sizes are not available for most East European nations (the published statistics focus much more on enterprise size instead). With a sample of only three East European nations, of which one is Yugoslavia, the results must be considered as suggestive rather than definitive. Relevant data on average establishment size of all manufacturing establishments (state, cooperative, and private) are given in Table 5–6.

Establishment sizes in Eastern Europe are very large in comparison with those in the West as presented in Table 5–4. Using information about the G.N.P. of these nations and the regression equations calculated with the Western data, we see that the actual establishment size is from two to four times larger than predicted! One part of Eucken's hypothesis appears validated. In comparing the cumulative size distributions (or in comparing the relative sizes of the arithmetic average, entropy index, and Niehans index), we see that the establishments are somewhat more similar in size and have a somewhat smaller range (i.e., the cumulative

TABLE 5–6

Manufacturing Establishment Size in Three East European Nations[a]

Nation	Date	Arithmetic Average		Entropy Index		Niehans Index		Percent of Labor Force in Establishments Over 1000	
		Actual	*Predicted*	*Actual*	*Predicted*	*Actual*	*Predicted*	*Actual*	*Predicted*
Hungary	1966	375	104	881	217	1779	468	40.0%	15.7%
Poland	1960	331	115	587	269	1592	692	39.5	18.9
Yugoslavia	1963	269	104	566	217	1064	468	33.1	15.6

a. Since data to calculate the trade ratios are not available, the predicted values are calculated from regressions based on domestic production alone that are reported in Appendix B-23. Since Yugoslavia and Hungary have roughly the same overall G.N.P. (although their per capita G.N.P.s and populations differ), their predicted values are roughly the same.

The sources of establishment data are given in Appendix B-18.

size distribution has a steeper slope) in the East than in the West; this partially validates the second part of Eucken's "standardization of production" hypothesis. Certain problems of interpretation of the data will still arise, however.

We know that central direction of manufacturing has been very much less in Yugoslavia than in Hungary and Poland (see Chapter VII) and from Eucken's hypothesis we would suspect that the ratio of actual establishment size would be closer to predicted establishment size in the former than in the latter two nations. Although this hypothesis is borne out when comparing Yugoslavia and Hungary, the ratio of actual to predicted establishment size is roughly the same in Poland and Yugoslavia. This latter result is difficult to understand but the explanation may lie in the fact that many Yugoslav manufacturing establishments were built when the central government still had considerable control over investment and smaller scale establishments were discouraged; only later was the investment function decentralized. It is also important to realize that the Polish government actively encouraged the formation of industrial cooperatives in order to absorb some of the rural unemployment and these cooperatives are relatively small in size (which would act to lower the average size of industrial establishments). These matters require much more thorough research before an adequate answer to the puzzles raised in the table can be resolved.

The discussion of East European establishment sizes has been in terms of administrative factors with implicit assumptions that technological factors play the same role in both East and West and that relative labor productivity between branches are roughly similar in the two areas as well. With the conclusion from Table 5–6 that East European manufacturing establishments are larger on the whole than those in the West, other things remaining the same, we can now examine such technological factors more closely.

If decisions about the sizes of industrial establishments had been made with some type of economic calculus so that economies of scale were taken into account in a systematic manner, then we would expect that relative establishment sizes in different industrial branches would be similar in East and West. If, on the other hand, such technological and economic factors were ignored and decisions about the establishment sizes were made on the basis of political or social criteria, then such similarity in establishment size rankings would not be expected. With the available data for the three countries, such a test is quite easy to make.[37]

37. In order to facilitate the comparisons, the two-digit data for the Western nations were grouped into sixteen industrial categories so that the industrial categories would be more similar to those in the East European

The results of such a comparison are clear and can be easily summarized. The rank orders of establishment sizes in the different industrial branches in the three East European nations are extremely similar, with concordance coefficients running from .89 to .92. The average rank order of establishment sizes in the East and West are significantly correlated (.05 level of significance) with Kendall rank order coefficients ranging from .57 to .75, depending on the size indicator.[38] The similarity of role of technological factors in determining relative establishment size in different industrial branches in East and West receives impressive confirmation.

The differences in the rank orders of establishment sizes in the East and the West are also interesting to investigate briefly and a simple hypothesis can be tested. For every industry there is a range of options facing those responsible for making decisions about establishment size. If an industry is characterized by a wider range of size options than average and if, as in East Europe, the decision-makers tend to choose among the largest size options (a key assumption), then establishments would show greater *relative* sizes in the East than in the West. Similarly, in those industries where there is a smaller range of technological options, the size of establishments would vary little in the East and the West and these industries would have *relatively* smaller size establishments (*vis-à-vis* establishments in other industries) in Eastern Europe.

A simple measure of range of technological options is the coefficient of variation of absolute size (standard deviation of size divided by the mean) calculated for the sample of Western nations. If we select those industries that average three ranks or more difference between the East and the West, we have five industries to investigate: those industrial branches in the East showing much greater relative establishment size—leather products (ISIC 29), mining (ISIC 10–19), and clothing (ISIC 24); and those industrial branches in the East showing much smaller establishment size—stone, glass, and clay products (ISIC 33) and miscellaneous products (ISIC 39). Because of incomparabilities in branch definition, leather products and miscellaneous products must be removed

---

data. The ranks were then recomputed and the comparisons discussed below were carried out. The data are presented in Appendix B-13.

38. For the arithmetic average indicator, the Kendall coefficient is .57; for the entropy indicator, .70; for the Niehans indicator, .75; and for the percentage indicator, .68.

John Michael Montias has pointed out to me that in some Eastern European nations, capital/labor ratios are higher in the priority industries and lower in the nonpriority industries than one would predict using data on these ratios from the West. This systematic bias might affect the relative employment sizes of establishments in different industries and lower the correlation of rank orderings of industries according to the capital/labor ratio from East and West. Despite this bias, the Kendall correlation coefficients are still statistically significant.

from consideration.[39] Mining establishments have the highest coefficient of variation of size in the West, while stone, glass, and clay products have one of the lowest.[40] Thus we can explain two out of the three industries where great differences in rank orders of establishment sizes occur in the East and the West. Combined with the results above, this means that we cannot only explain the overall similarity of rank orderings of relative establishment size in Eastern and Western Europe, but some of the most important differences as well. Although other more complex hypotheses about the differences in rank orders can be offered, none that were tested seemed as satisfactory as the simple hypothesis presented above.[41]

E. Summary and Conclusions

In this chapter I have examined the size distribution of production establishments in order to see how control rights are partitioned in the economy at this particular level of the organization of industry. The most important discovery is the positive relationship between establishment size and a single economic variable—the size of the entire market.

This relationship can be argued from three theoretical standpoints. The first approach is from considerations of the extent to which establishment size is limited by costs incurred in overcoming certain environmental barriers, of which barriers to foreign trade seem particularly important: The smaller the domestic market of the nation and the greater the barriers to trade, the smaller establishment size would be. The second theoretical approach starts from considerations of enterprise administration costs. Establishments in multi-establishment enterprises are larger than establishments which are enterprises in themselves; further, the larger the enterprise, the larger the different establishments composing it. Since the degree of multi-establishment enterprises is related to the size of the domestic market (which I discuss in detail in Chapter VI), we again would expect that nations with larger domestic markets would have

39. In the East, leather products include shoe manufacturing; in the West this is placed in clothing (ISIC 24). Since shoe manufacturing is an extremely important part of the leather products branch, this incomparability could not be overlooked. The miscellaneous products category is a residual and seems too heterogeneous to include in such comparisons when the rest of the industrial classification is not quite similar.

40. Data on these coefficients of variation for different industrial branches are given in Appendix B-21.

41. I expended considerable effort in developing a measure of the relation between size of establishment and average size of enterprise which could be used for investigating these size differences, but utilization of the results was quite unsatisfactory.

larger size industrial establishments. The third approach focuses on the impact of governmental policies, especially concerning import substitution and enforcement of cartel agreements, which link establishment and market sizes.

The data for sizes of manufacturing establishments in twenty-three nations in the West appear to confirm this hypothesized relation. Although we are unable to distinguish which of the three theoretical factors has a more important influence, the empirical results certainly suggest the fruitfulness of further investigation.

As Eucken predicted, the size of industrial establishments appeared larger in East Europe than in the West. In addition, the dispersion of establishment size was less in the former group of nations, which confirms a second part of Eucken's hypothesis. Hypotheses linking average establishment size to other factors appear much less promising, except for the influence of economic system.

Study of the share of the labor force employed in an average size establishment (agglomeration) has important implications not only for the study of the size distribution of control rights but also, in an indirect way, for the analysis of economic forces encouraging monopoly. The empirical analysis shows that agglomeration seems positively related to the degree of economic development and negatively related to the total gross national product. In normal circumstances, however, the latter appears more important so that the degree of establishment agglomeration is declining over time in most nations.

Looking at relative establishment sizes in individual industries, technological factors appear to play the critical role. In all nations the relative size rankings are roughly similar and differences in such rankings between the East and West can, in part, be explained by technological options open to the planners.

For the study of property, the various conclusions are extremely important. Although they show that we can expect industrial establishment sizes to increase in the future, they also indicate that the labor force may not become increasingly concentrated into a smaller number of such establishments. Further, the results allow us to isolate more precisely the effects of technological and organization factors when studying the growth of enterprises, a topic to which I turn in the following chapter. And finally, the analysis allows us to lay to rest a number of hoary myths about the sizes of production units that have been based on ideological considerations or on the analysis of the experiences of one nation examined from a limited perspective. The comparative analysis of establishment size in many nations permits a much more general analysis of causal forces influencing an important macro-structuring of property relations.

CHAPTER VI

The Size of Production Enterprises in Mining and Manufacturing

But with the beginning of wealth danger attends upon
every enterprise and no man knows where it is like
to stop . . . to wealth men have set themselves no clear
bounds; for those of us who now have most substance
redouble our zeal even more.

Solon[1]

A. Introduction

In both the East and the West the enterprise is a critical decision-making
unit in industry; for the study of the macro-structure of property rights
enterprises are more important to analyze than establishments. Although

1. Solon, *Fragments,* trans. by M. L. W. Laistner, *Greek Economics*
(London: 1923).

these notions are quite commonplace, much less research has been carried out on the sizes of enterprises than on the sizes of establishments. The difficulties facing the prospective researcher are twofold: On a theoretical level, he must wrestle with a great many thorny problems regarding economies of administration and other organizational phenomena; and on an empirical level, considerably less comparable data are available. The conclusions drawn in this chapter may be more startling than those of the previous chapter but, at the same time, are also more tentative.

To avoid confusion it is useful to repeat the definition of enterprise presented at the beginning of the last chapter. "An enterprise (or firm) is a business organization consisting of one or more establishments under common ownership and control. It is a consolidated unit because wholly owned subsidiaries are included as part of the parent enterprise, even though for tax or other purposes such units may report on an unconsolidated basis." Although this definition distinguishes between an establishment and an enterprise, it does not handle the problem of how to draw the line between enterprises and other decision-making units that in both the East and the West are above the enterprise in the hierarchy of industrial organizations. Units embracing one or more individual enterprises in various Western nations include cartels, holding companies, syndicates, *zaibatsu* (in Japan), "ententes" or "financial groups," and, on a governmental level, various industrial commissions and central planning organs. Decision-making units in the East include "associations," ministries, and central planning bureaus.

For the countries in the West the delineation between enterprises and these supra-enterprise organizations can be made on the basis of legal criteria for "center of ultimate legal responsibility"; although such a notion is vague, a common concept of "enterprise" appears to be held in all Western European nations. For the nations in East Europe, enterprise is sometimes defined as that organ where greatest responsibility is placed for fulfillment of production plans, but considerable ambiguity arises because some responsibility for plan fulfillment is placed on all levels of the industrial hierarchy. For instance, can we really consider the very large organizations resulting from mergers of enterprises in Hungary in the mid-1960s as "enterprises" anymore, or must we label them "associations"? For lack of detailed information concerning nodes of responsibility, I have had to follow the designation of "enterprise" that is used in each individual country.[2] This arbitrary procedure makes it imperative that enterprise size in the East and the West be considered separately.

2. Strictly speaking, an enterprise in East Europe is the smallest production unit on "economic accounting" (*khozraschet*), which means that it has a bank account, and its own income statement and that depreciation charges of fixed assets under the unit's control show up as costs in the unit's financial accounts. However, in some East European nations (e.g., Romania),

Aside from separating enterprises from supra-enterprise organizations, difficulties in obtaining comparable enterprise statistics also involve problems in handling partly owned subsidiaries and very small units of a temporary nature. Some of these problems can be eliminated by excluding from the calculation of the average size statistics enterprises with labor forces of less than twenty. With regard to other problems of comparability, national statistical sources seldom spell out their definitions in such sufficient detail that completely adequate adjustments for comparability can be made.

Size of enterprise has important implications in three areas of social and political concern. First is the basic problem of the concentration of economic power into large units, i.e., the increase in average enterprise employment size. Second is the problem of agglomeration: the degree to which manufacturing activities are becoming centered in a small number of units. Average enterprise employment size can increase, but if total industrial employment is growing faster, agglomeration can decrease. Third is the problem of monopoly: the degree to which sales in a particular market are accounted for by one or a few enterprises. It is quite possible for agglomeration to increase, but monopoly to decrease if the very largest enterprises begin to enter industries previously monopolized by others. These are three aspects of economic power which are also entwined with political power; and in this chapter all three aspects receive treatment. Before turning to the data, certain theoretical issues concerning the determinants of enterprise size require brief attention.

B. Some Important Theoretical Considerations

Two major sets of influences on enterprise size are explored below. First, I analyze economies of administration. A vital feature distinguishing industrial enterprises and establishments is the potentially important role of special economies of administration in the enterprises; for if these did not exist, a major justification of multi-establishment enterprises would be missing. Although data to examine economies of administration in a direct manner are unavailable, certain important clues are gained from such indirect methods as exploring the extent of multi-establishment enterprises or studying merger activities. I also analyze special influences

---

some intermediate organs appear to have taken over most of the decision-making powers of the enterprises under them and yet the separate enterprises maintain their status as units on "economic accounting." Further confusion arises because the central statistical offices of these nations are never very specific on how they define "enterprise" in their reports. As the economic reforms proceeded in the late sixties, these problems of definition increased; fortunately, the data used in this chapter come from a period in which these problems were not severe.

on enterprise size arising from the interacting links between establishment and enterprise size.

1. Economies of Administration

a. *A direct approach.* What are the economic advantages, where there are constant returns to scale in production, of an enterprise consisting of two establishments, each employing one thousand men, in comparison to a single-establishment enterprise with a labor force of one thousand? First, certain administrative overhead costs are supposed to embody economies of scale so that administrative expenditures do not rise as fast as manufacturing costs when production is increased.[3] Functional areas in which such economies of scale are said to be important are research and marketing. Other types of administrative economies are said to arise from assurance of input supplies, savings of information costs, internalization of certain externalities, and so forth.[4] Second, the larger the enterprise, the easier the massing of internal reserves for any particular project is supposed to be; in addition, in some market economies such as the United States it is known that the large enterprises can borrow funds at lower rates than small enterprises. Third, multi-establishment enterprises that embrace several different industries are alleged to have an advantage because research and development and other types of technical personnel with experience in one industry can be used to apply their knowledge in another industry of the enterprise more easily than a single industry enterprise can hire outside consultants. (This assumes an imperfect market for technical personnel).

However, several cogent arguments concerning diseconomies of multi-establishment enterprises also deserve mention. Increasing size of the enterprise is accompanied by greater complexity of decision-making and by more difficulty in coordination.[5] In addition, creation of a large bureaucracy is supposed to generate in many circumstances an autono-

3. Empirical evidence on this has been given by Seymour Melman, "Production and Administration Costs in Relation to Size of Firm," *Applied Statistics,* III, March 1954, pp. 1–11.

4. The "functional" economies are analyzed and emphasized by P. Sargent Florence, *Investment, Location, and Size of Plant* (Cambridge, Eng.: 1948); other types of administrative economies, especially particular externalities, are explored by Alec Nove," Internal Economies," *Economic Journal,* LXXIX, December 1967, pp. 847–61.

5. An interesting theoretical exploration of this problem (especially "combinatorial effects") is by William Baumol, "Interaction of Public and Private Decisions," in Howard Schaller, ed., *Public Expenditure Decisions in the Urban Community* (Baltimore: 1963). Other arguments about long-run rising average costs of a much vaguer sort are given in most standard economic textbooks; these are challenged by Peter Wiles, *Price, Cost, and Output* (New York: 1963).

mous impulse for unnecessary further expansion of the bureaucracy, i.e., certain Parkinson law phenomena might become more important.[6] Further, it is known that the higher the administrative pyramid, the higher are the salaries of the top managers and this, in turn, raises average unit costs.[7]

These types of arguments are interesting, but they raise two difficulties for empirical research. Very few propositions can be generated from them that can be tested with the available data. Direct measurement of some of the alleged advantages and disadvantages of enterprise size— especially those dealing with administrative costs—has not been satisfactorily carried out in the past, and the time-consuming task of making such measurements would take us too far from the central theme of this study.[8] Such difficulties call, therefore, for a more indirect approach to circumvent some of these problems.

b. *Evidence from multi-establishment enterprises.* Since the existence of economies of scale of administration is supposed to underlie the competitive advantage of multi-establishment enterprises (or, less strictly, to be thought of sufficient importance to encourage mergers of single establishment enterprises to form multi-establishment enterprises), it is useful to investigate such enterprises in some detail. Let us start by considering the degree to which an economy as a whole is characterized by such multiestablishment enterprises. Several hypotheses link the relative importance of multi-establishment enterprises to the level of economic development or to the size of the domestic market and each of these conjectures deserves attention.

A common assumption in the economic literature is that as the level of economic development rises, the "organizational structure" of the economy becomes more complex. This observation, sometimes given the pompous designation of the "law of decreasing social entropy," is the inverse of the second law of thermodynamics and is supposed to distinguish human society from nature.[9] Although this assertion has not been

6. Some counter-evidence on this matter is given by Frederic L. Pryor, *Public Expenditures in Communist and Capitalist Nations* (Homewood, Ill.: 1968), pp. 235–6.

7. This is briefly explored in a subsection of Appendix A-8.

8. The problem is compounded not only by lack of relevant and comparable input data but also by the measurement of exactly what is produced by "administration." Both economists and organization theorists have neglected attacking these extremely vital problems so that the field has been mainly preempted by business writers with a qualitative, rather than a quantitative, bent.

9. This proposition has been argued by a number of scholars, among whom is Norbert Wiener, *The Human Use of Human Beings: Cybernetics and Society* (Boston: 1950).

seriously examined in an empirical manner by tectologists,[10] three theoretical justifications can be offered. Some, such as Kenneth Boulding,
have argued that costs of communication and data processing, which
form a major portion of the costs of administration, fall dramatically
over time (i.e., fall *vis-à-vis* other costs of production) so that increasingly
larger and more complex organizations become economically feasible.[11]
A second (and partially overlapping) justification is offered by some who
assert that economies of scale can be found in administration and that,
over time, market forces act to assure the existence only of increasingly
larger enterprises. Since transportation costs act to limit increases in
establishment size, these administrative economies are manifested by a
rise in the relative importance of multi-establishment enterprises. (Such
an argument can be used for cross-section analysis with the additional
assumption that in the economically most highly developed nations, these
market forces have had the longest time to work themselves out.) Finally,
it can be argued that as the stock of human capital per worker increases,
problems of labor coordination and supervision—at least on the lower
levels of production—decrease more than other costs so that larger
organizations become economically feasible. It should be noted in conclusion that most of these are variants of the arguments grouped under
the rubric of "environmental barriers" that are discussed in the previous
chapter.

A number of hypotheses have been offered that link the relative importance of multi-establishment enterprises to the size of the domestic
market. A plausible justification for multi-establishment enterprises arising because of savings from lower administration costs limits these
savings primarily to production within the same industry. In a nation
with a small domestic market and with only one establishment in particular (narrowly defined) industries, a multi-establishment enterprise may
not generate the administrative savings occurring in a large nation where
a number of establishments in the same industry can be merged into an
enterprise. Other types of considerations leading to a correlation between
market size and the relative extent of multi-establishment enterprises rest
on characteristics of the banking and foreign trade sectors.[12]

10. "Tectology" is a word coined for the science of organization by
Aleksander Bogdanov (A. A. Malinovskii) in his book *Tektologiya,
voeobshchaya organnizatsionnaya nauka* (Petersburg, Moscow: 1922).
Bogdanov is the unacknowledged father of modern organization and general
systems theory; he analyzed the economy in terms of control over organization, rather than in terms of ownership, and is said to represent a neo-
Kantian revision of Marxism.

11. Kenneth Boulding, *The Organizational Revolution* (New York:
1953).

12. From financial considerations the following argument can be raised.
In a small nation where information about each enterprise is known to a

These hypotheses linking the degree to which economies are characterized by multi-establishment enterprises to the level of economic development or to the size of the market can be easily tested. Most enterprises in Western nations consist of a single establishment and only a small minority are composed of a large number of establishments. A simple measure of the degree to which an economy is composed of such multi-establishment enterprises is the ratio of the average size of enterprises to the average size of establishments. Although this statistic leaves something to be desired, data for more satisfactory measures cannot be easily obtained on a comparable basis. Relevant data are presented in Table 6–1 with the countries listed according to the descending value of their total G.N.P.s.

As one can see at a glance, an almost perfect relationship exists

---

large proportion of the financial community, enterprises may be able to obtain external finances from banks more easily than in a larger nation where the same proportion of the financial community does not have information about a single enterprise; because of this information gap, banks may be more ready to make loans to enterprises based on their size alone. Now the credit worthiness of large enterprises is, in a real sense, greater than that of small enterprises because of their larger cash reserves and the economies of scale of risk pooling (see note 20). But the differential in interest rates paid by large and small enterprises may not be so great in small nations where information problems are not so severe. The relatively greater availability of credit to large enterprises in large nations may act to increase their relative importance in the production sphere through the creation of more multi-establishment enterprises.

Several arguments link the degree of multi-establishment enterprises to foreign trade considerations. First, in a small nation where foreign trade is an extremely competitive force, entrepreneurs cannot afford to own particularly high cost establishments unless they can obtain and maintain high tariff barriers. In a large nation where imports are not such a strong competitive force and where informal agreements among manufacturers can be reached, an enterprise can consist of a series of establishments with varying costs without fearing bankruptcy. In other words, the difficulties of international collusion and the subsequently greater competition arising from foreign trade in smaller nations may force entrepreneurs to focus their attention on a smaller number of establishments. One method of testing this proposition is to compare the relative extent of multi-establishment enterprises in industries that have different degrees of tariff protection and compare these results with those of a nation where foreign trade and tariff protection is relatively unimportant. (For this proposition and method of testing, I would like to thank Professor John M. Montias.)

Another foreign trade argument stems from barriers to trade. If there are barriers in international trade among products in which a number of varieties can be produced, and if the minimum efficient scale for certain product lines is quite high, then only nations with large domestic markets may be able to support multi-establishment enterprises in which the complete product line is manufactured, while smaller nations may have single establishment enterprises producing only those parts of the product line in which economies of scale are not great. (For this proposition, I would like to thank Professor Richard E. Caves.)

TABLE 6–1

Extent of Multi-establishment Enterprises in Western Nations[a]

Country	Year	Ratio of Average Enterprise Size to Average Establishment Size		
		Arithmetic average	*Entropy index*	*Niehans index*
United States	1963	1.52	7.43	9.90
Japan	1963	1.25	2.15	4.54
West Germany	1961	1.16	1.88	3.73
France	1963	1.20	1.90	2.33
Italy	1961	1.14	1.74	3.36
Netherlands	1962	1.15	1.47	2.29
Belgium	1962	1.05	1.38	2.02
Switzerland	1965	1.12	1.36	2.00
Greece	1963	1.00	1.34	1.96
Portugal	1958	1.05	1.07	1.05

a. The data in this table were obtained by dividing average enterprise size (Table 6–5) by average establishment size (Table 5–4). The very low ratio for the arithmetic average for Greece is due either to a large number of small multi-establishment enterprises that have establishments with less than twenty workers and employees (e.g., small workshops) or to incomparabilities between the establishment and enterprise data.

between the degree of multi-establishment enterprises and the absolute value of the G.N.P., expressed in a common currency; the Kendall rank order correlation coefficients are statistically significant (.05 level) and are respectively .80, .96, and .96. A similar relationship appears to exist for individual industries. Although we cannot determine the most important causal forces, the hypothesis establishing a positive link between the degree of multi-establishment enterprises and the size of the domestic market seems validated. However, positive relationships also exist between the degree of multi-establishment enterprises and the per capita G.N.P., but the Kendall coefficients are much lower (respectively, .40, .47, and .38) and are not (except for the second) statistically significant (.05 level). This link with per capita income is probably due to the positive relationship between total and per capita G.N.P. that appears in this small ten-nation sample and should be ignored.

Further insight into economies of administration manifested in multi-establishment enterprises can be gained by looking at the degree to which particular industries are characterized by such enterprises. For instance, it is well known that each industry faces administrative-technical problems that are relatively specific to that industry. For instance, the chemical industry must employ a high percentage of engineers and scientists; the clothing industry must face a highly uncertain demand; the stone, glass, and clay products industry must deal with highly localized markets because of high costs of transportation. We know that different branches of industry have greatly different ratios of administrative to total personnel and that this pattern is similar in all developed nations.[13] If these administrative-technical problems limit enterprise size, or, at least, play a role in determining the size of a minimum efficient enterprise, then at least two important implications can be drawn: There should be a definite pattern of the degree to which industries are characterized by multi-establishment enterprises; and there should be a definite pattern of the relative sizes of enterprises. The former is examined in this section; the latter is examined in the following section.

In order to test whether the degree to which industries are characterized by multi-establishment enterprises follows a pattern, we calculate the ratios of average enterprise to establishment size for the individual two-digit industries for each of the ten nations and then compute an index of concordance.[14] For all three measures, the pattern is statistically significant, with concordance coefficients ranging from .28 to .43. In general, tobacco, mining, and chemicals have the highest degree of multi-establishment enterprises, while furniture, leather products, and metal products have the lowest degree. Thus among different industrial branches, administrative economies arising from multi-establishment enterprises are different and appear to be caused by particular factors of the various industrial environments.

To summarize, two important relationships emerge. First, the degree to which an economically developed economy in the West is characterized by multi-establishment enterprises appears related to the total size of the domestic market. Second, the rank order of industries according to the relative frequency of multi-establishment enterprises appears similar in these nations.[15] Such evidence suggests (but does not prove) the existence of economies of administration that arise from economic or technological considerations that are not specific to the process of administration per se.

13. Ranking industrial branches according to the ratio of operatives to total workers and employees for eighteen Western nations gives a statistically significant pattern; moreover, a very similar pattern appears when data for the East European nations are examined. Further details on this experiment are reported in Appendix B-15.

14. Data on these size rankings and more detailed results of these comparisons are given in Appendix B-22.

15. My empirical results are greatly different from those of an international comparison carried out by Joe S. Bain, *International Differences in Industrial Structure* (New Haven: 1966), Chapter 5. Such differences arise because Bain's sample is much smaller and he uses, I believe, less satisfactory statistical methods.

c. *Evidence from conglomerate merger activity.* Are there any "general" economies of scale of administration that arise strictly from the size of the administrative operations involved and do not originate from economic or technological aspects of the industry or from complementaries occurring from the production of related products? One attempt to answer this question on an empirical basis is to look at the results of conglomerate mergers when an enterprise in one industry merges with an enterprise in a completely different industry.

Although published information allows some estimation of the percentage of mergers that are complete failures,[16] it is not possible to study closely these "general" administration economies except with information supplied by the enterprises themselves. Of course, such survey data can give rise to certain biased results so that any small-scale investigation must be considered merely as an experiment from which conclusions must be drawn cautiously.

If "general" administrative economies are important, then conglomerate mergers should result in an increased market share and/or higher profits of the acquired company since certain cost advantages would be gained. Although comparable profit data are difficult to obtain because of proprietary secrets and changes in accounting methods, companies are willing to supply qualitative information on whether specific market shares have changed. I, therefore, selected every enterprise in the *Fortune* 500 that entered into an important conglomerate merger in 1961 or 1966 with another company whose sales data are public, wrote to the President or the Sales Vice President, and asked whether the overall market share of the acquired enterprise had increased, decreased, or remained the same. The response rate was roughly 50 percent. The results for the two years were sufficiently similar to allow the samples to be combined and the results are reported in Table 6–2.[17]

16. The results of one large-scale investigation is reported by John Bjorksten, "Merger Lemons," reported by the Subcommittee on Antitrust and Monopoly of the Committee on the Judiciary, United States Senate, *Economic Concentration: Hearings: Part 5, Concentration and Divisional Reporting* (Washington, D.C.: 1966), pp. 1940–7. Bjorksten produces evidence that at least one out of six mergers is a total failure, and, furthermore, that this figure represents a lower limit of merger failures.

17. Details of this study are presented in Appendix A-11.

Much more aggregative studies on the profitability of conglomerate mergers also have relevance to the study of general administrative costs. One interesting empirical study is by Samuel Richardson Reid, *Mergers, Managers, and the Economy* (New York: 1968). A number of other recent studies are summarized by John M. Blair, *Economic Concentration: Structure, Behavior, and Public Policy* (New York: 1972) pp. 186–95. In general these studies support my contention that general administrative economies obtained through mergers are probably very small or nil.

The market share of acquired enterprises increased in roughly 50 percent of the cases. If we take into account changes in the market share of acquired enterprises in the quinquennium preceding merger, then the table shows that mergers resulted in a favorable change in the market share direction (i.e., an increase in market share in cases where the share had previously been stable; or a stabilization of the market share in cases where the share had been decreasing) in only roughly 30 percent of all cases.

TABLE 6–2

Market Shares of Companies Acquired by Conglomerates
in the United States in 1961 and 1966

Market Share Change, Five Years Preceding Merger	Market Share in 1970 Compared to Year of Merger			
	Decreased	*Roughly Same*	*Increased*	*Total*
Decreased	0	3	6	9
Roughly Same	0	1	2	3
Increased	2	5	7	14
Undetermined	1	5	4	10
Total	3	14	19	36

Since there are several important sources of upward bias in these data (e.g., executives responsible for a merger might take a more rosy view of the results than the true facts, if they were available, might warrant), these percentage results may be interpreted as upper limits of mergers resulting in significant market share increases.

The results do not show a very impressive gain in market share arising from conglomerate mergers and we can tentatively conclude that general economies of administrative scale do not seem very important. It must be added that general diseconomies of administration do not appear important either since only 10 percent of the mergers resulted in a significant decline of market share.

Indeed, the results suggest that reasons other than increased gross profit rates might be the most important reason for business mergers, a conclusion which seems validated from a perusal of the merger literature which stresses the importance for mergers of certain financial reasons (e.g., using the high cash flow of one enterprise to finance the expansion of another; or increasing leverage on equity), personnel factors, various tax angles, and other such considerations. But for our purposes, the apparent relative unimportance of overall savings in administrative costs is the most important conclusion.

d. *A brief summary.* Although economies of administration acting to encourage multi-establishment enterprises cannot be measured directly, several important bits of indirect evidence are available. Data on ratios of operatives to the total labor force and ratios designating the degree of multi-establishment enterprises in particular industries show a sufficiently marked pattern to suggest that economies of administration in particular industrial environments are important determinants of enterprise size. On the other hand, the evidence from examining a series of conglomerate mergers suggests that "general" economies of administration that arise in the administrative process do not seem particularly important. Finally the hypotheses and empirical results that validate the correlation between domestic market size and degree of multi-establishment enterprises point toward a number of economy-wide forces influencing administration costs and enterprise size.

2. *Relationships Between Sizes of Enterprise and Establishments*

a. *Some direct relationships.* Since enterprises are composed of one or more establishments, an obvious proposition can be stated: Given the relative degree of multi-establishment enterprises, the nation with the larger industrial establishments will have larger industrial enterprises.

Furthermore, a nation with a higher degree of multi-establishment enterprises will have larger enterprises, not only because more establishments are combined in a single enterprise but also because, as shown in the previous chapter, establishments in multi-establishment enterprises are generally larger than single-establishment enterprises. Thus if we examine the relative sizes of establishments and enterprises, either across nations or across industries in a single nation, there should be strong correlations. Exploring these matters empirically provides further insight into these correlations, especially on the level of industrial branches.

Let us start by ranking the sizes of enterprises in the various two-digit industrial branches for various nations in the West. We find a very similar pattern among nations, with statistically significant concordance coefficients ranging from .62 to .74, depending on the measure of size.[18] The largest enterprises occur in the primary metals, transportation, and tobacco product branches; the smallest enterprises occur in the furniture and fixtures, wood products (excluding furniture), and leather product industries.

It is useful to examine these calculations of the relative ranking of industries according to the average size of enterprises with the ranking of industries by the average size of establishment (from Chapter V) and

18. These results are presented in Appendix B-19.

the ranking of industries according to the relative frequency of multi-establishment enterprises. We may suspect that these rankings for western nations are highly related; the correlation matrices of the three rankings are presented in Table 6–3.

All three of the rank orderings are significantly related to each other, as the theoretical considerations briefly discussed above would have us believe. The relationships between average enterprise and average establishment size appear strongest because there are several causal influences: directly from establishment size to enterprise size, and indirectly because average establishment size and degree of multi-establishment industry are related and the latter is related to enterprise size.

b. *Some theoretical parallels.* Several of the theoretical arguments used in analyzing establishment size can also be used for examining enterprise size.

First, Eucken's proposition (discussed in Chapter V) that production units in planned economies are larger and more standardized in size than in market economies is certainly relevant. This means not only that enterprises in Eastern Europe would be larger than those in Western Europe, other things remaining the same, but also, perhaps, that enterprises in economies with important supra-enterprise groups such as cartels or "financial groups" might also tend to be larger.

Second, "environment considerations" are of use in investigating not only establishment but enterprise size as well. Although transportation costs do not play the important role in enterprise size that they do in establishment size, other types of environmental barriers more important to enterprises can be specified.[19, 20] The analysis of such barriers provides

19. Transportation costs can have some influence on enterprise size, however. As I argued in Chapter V, establishments of multi-establishment enterprises are larger than those of single-establishment enterprises. But establishment size is not unlimited, for obtaining inputs from a wider area and supplying the product to customers in a wider area entails rising unit transportation costs. In so far as establishment size influences enterprise size, transportation costs play a role in enterprise size.

20. Three such barriers can be designated. First, environmental costs arise in situations where close contact with central governmental officials who regulate the industry is necessary for economic survival. In such cases, there may be considerable economies of scale and, thus, larger enterprises may have considerable economic and political advantage over smaller enterprises that cannot maintain so many contact men with the government.

Second, environmental costs arise from minimizing the effects of risk. One response to risk is small, flexible enterprises that can rapidly shift production from one good to another, a response that seems to have occurred in the textile and clothing industries. (An empirical investigation of these industries has been carried out by David Schwartzman, "Uncertainty and the Size of the Firm," *Economica*, N.S., XXX, August 1963, pp. 287–97, who measured uncertainty by the ratio of markdowns to total sales and

TABLE 6–3

Kendall Rank Order Correlation Coefficients between Average Rank Orderings of Industrial Branches according to Enterprise Size, Establishment Size, and Degree of Multi-establishment Enterprises For Western Nations[a]

	Arithmetic average			Entropy index			Niehans index		
	Avg. enter-prise size	Avg. estab-lishment size	Degree of multi-est. enterprises	Avg. enter-prise size	Avg. estab-lishment size	Degree of multi-est. enterprises	Avg. enter-prise size	Avg. estab-lishment size	Degree of multi-est. enterprises
Average enter-prise size	1.00	—	—	1.00	—	—	1.00	—	—
Average estab-lishment size	.88*	1.00	—	.89*	1.00	—	.91*	1.00	—
Degree of multi-establishment enterprises	.67*	.61*	1.00	.73*	.71*	1.00	.55*	.53*	1.00

a. The data for these rank order correlations come from Appendices B-17, B-19, and B-22. The asterisk denotes statistical significance at the .05 level.

insight into the response of enterprise size to particular situations but does not seem helpful in framing propositions linking enterprise size to particular macro-economic variables and, as a result, is not further pursued.

3. *Summary of Propositions*

Three propositions have emerged from the theoretical discussion:

First, average enterprise size is associated with market size because both establishment size and the degree of multi-establishment enterprises are correlated with market size and enterprise size.

Second, average enterprise size may also be associated with the level of development of the economy, primarily because there is a positive relation between multi-establishment enterprises and per capita G.N.P. This proposition is stated conditionally because this positive relationship is not strong.

Third, average enterprise size is associated with economic system and should be greater in centrally planned economies. Although this proposition is derived from Eucken's argument, additional evidence is provided by the empirical fact that establishment size, which is an important determinant of enterprise size, is larger in East than in West Europe.

C. Empirical Results of the Analysis of Enterprise Size

1. *Time-series*

It is a commonplace that average enterprise size has increased over the past half century; yet such statements in the economic literature are seldom backed by data for the simple reason that adequate data on the size distribution of enterprises are extremely difficult to locate for the

---

showed an inverse relation between average enterprise size and such uncertainty.) But another response is bigness where such risks can be pooled, for it is well known that there are important economies of scale in meeting risk. [A neat mathematical demonstration of this is given by Aryeh Dvoretzky, "Appendix to Chapter 5," in Don Patinkin, *Money, Interest, and Prices* (Evanston, Illinois: 1956)].

A third type of environmental cost arises in the formation of new enterprises when the costs may be sufficiently great that all an entrepreneur's economic activities are *per force* carried on under the organizational umbrella of a single enterprise, in contrast to a situation where an individual entrepreneur's activities may be spread over a large number of enterprises, in each of which different partners are participating and different sources of finance are tapped. In the former case, enterprise size is limited by the assets of a single group of men; while in the latter case, a wide variety of enterprises of different sizes are imaginable.

early part of the century. For Germany, where we have data on both enterprise and establishment size distributions, several generalizations can be made for the period between 1907 and 1961: the average size of enterprises in mining and manufacturing roughly quadrupled, while the prevalence of multi-establishment enterprises roughly doubled.[21] If data for other countries were available for the same time period, I have no doubt that they would yield the same picture.

The proposition that the process of enterprise growth has been accompanied by a relative agglomeration, i.e., that a given number of the largest enterprises are employing a larger percentage of the labor force or producing a larger percentage of total production, is a much different kind of proposition and is open to doubt. To be sure, certain theoretical justifications can be given: If economies of scale of administration are great so that large enterprises have a cost advantage over small enterprises; if mergers are more important among the largest than among the medium size enterprises; or if mergers among large enterprises occur at a rate above a critical ratio to new enterprise natality, then such agglomeration could also occur.

Fortunately, more empirical evidence bearing on this proposition is available than for the entire size distribution of enterprises. Certain relevant data for four nations are presented in Table 6–4.

In the United States, the relative importance of the 100 largest enterprises remained relatively constant for roughly half a century but has shown a rise in the relatively recent past.[22] In Germany there has been a dramatic rise in the relative importance of the largest enterprises, although certain data are available suggesting that this rise occurred primarily between 1907 and 1936 and that since then the relative importance of the

21. The 1907 data for Germany come from Kaiserliches Statistisches Amt, *Statistik des Deutschen Reiches,* Volumes 214–22 (Berlin: 1910). The 1961 data are for West Germany and come from Statistiches Bundesamt, *Statistisches Jahrbuch fuer die Bundesrepublik 1964* (Wiesbaden: 1964). The data for 1907 exclude home industry and, for establishments, exclude certain "Nebengeschaefte" which, however, are of little importance for establishments with over twenty employees and workers.

22. Considerable discussion in the literature about this question can be found, and my empirical results are controversial. The data of Gardiner Means ["Statement," in Subcommittee on Antitrust and Monopoly of the Committee on the Judiciary, United States Senate, *Economic Concentration.* Part 1 (Washington, D.C.: 1964), pp. 15–19] show a much faster rise than I do; so do the data of Frederic M. Scherer, *Industrial Market Structure and Economic Performance* (Chicago: 1970), p. 43. On the other hand the data of Morris Adelman ["Statement," in Subcommittee on Antitrust and Monopoly of the Committee on the Judiciary, p. 339] showed a smaller increase. Other estimates are presented by Blair, p. 64. The methods used in making these estimates differ considerably and, although I believe my calculations to be better, I cannot be completely without doubt on this matter.

TABLE 6–4

*Relative Importance Over Time of the Largest Enterprises
in Four Western Nations*[a]

	United States		Germany	Norway	Sweden
	Percentage of Assets		Percentage of employment in min. and mnf.	Percentage of employment in min. and mnf.	Percentage of employment in private sector
	In min. and mnf.	In mnf.			
Year	*Largest 100*	*Largest 100*	*Largest 100*	*Largest 50*	*Largest 50*
1907	—	—	7%	—	—
1909	41%	—	—	—	—
1919	37	—	—	—	—
1929	42	—	—	—	—
1930	—	—	—	29%	—
1935	43	—	—	—	—
1942	—	—	—	—	16%
1948	40	40%	—	25	—
1955	—	44	—	—	—
1960	—	—	—	—	18
1961	—	—	17	—	—
1964	—	—	—	—	20
1965	—	46	—	—	—
1968	—	50	—	—	—

a. The sources and estimation methods are presented in Appendix B-16.

largest enterprises has decreased.[23] The data for the two Scandinavian nations cover a much shorter period and show variable results, with the importance of the largest enterprises increasing in Sweden and decreasing in Norway.

Certain data of a less reliable nature on these matters are also available for other nations. In France the largest 50 and 100 private enterprises have shown a declining share of the gross assets of all "sociétiés" from 1912 to 1952. And in England, the market valuation of assets of the 50 and 100 largest enterprises as a share of such valuations for all quoted business units declined considerably between 1907 and 1950.[24]

23. Data on the "Grundkapital" of the largest stock companies for 1936 and 1958 are presented in "Die Unternehmen mit dem höchstem Aktien-kapital," *Frankfurter Allgemeine Zeitung,* November 7, 1959, p. 9. From this list all banks and financial companies were removed. Data on the capital stock are given in Walther G. Hoffman, *et al., Das Wachstum der deutschen Wirtschaft seit der Mitte des 19. Jahrhunderts* (West Berlin: 1965).

24. For France data are presented for 1912, 1936, and 1952 by Jacques Houssiaux, *Le pouvoir de monopol* (Paris: 1958), p. 292. Although the share

The situation in the last decade in Europe is difficult to summarize but it appears that the relative importance of the largest enterprises is increasing in most countries. One trend is quite certain: The share of sales accounted for in the Western world by multinational enterprises has risen so that for the capitalist system as a whole, the relative importance of the largest firms is rising.

From this welter of evidence we can conclude that although business enterprise has increased in average size over the past half century, the share accounted for by the largest enterprises does not show a general pattern of increase, although the situation differs somewhat from country to country. Further, although the share of the largest enterprises has probably increased in almost all economically developed Western nations in the past decade, past experience is not sufficient for believing that this trend will continue indefinitely in the future. Factors unique to the past decade may well extend in the future so that the relative importance of the largest enterprises may continue to increase; but these factors have yet to be systematically analyzed in the economic literature.

2. *A Cross-section Analysis of Western Nations*

The major hypothesis to be tested is that average enterprise size is related to market size; the justifications of this hypothesis are outlined at length above. A subsidiary proposition is that the level of economic development may also play a role. Relevant data to test these propositions are given in Table 6–5. Regressions showing the relationship between the

---

of the top fifty enterprises decreases from 52 percent to 43 percent, part of this is due to the fact that a larger share of total assets in mining and manufacturing are included in the denominator. Interpretive problems also arise because some of the largest enterprises in early years were later nationalized.

For the United Kingdom data on the sizes of market valuations of assets of the quoted business enterprises by size group from 1885 to 1950 are presented by P. E. Hart and S. J. Prais, "The Analysis of Business Concentration," *Journal of Royal Statistical Society*, Part 2, 1956, pp. 150–91. To calculate total assets of quoted enterprises I assumed that within each size-group the enterprises had assets equal to the geometric mean of the size-class end points. The assets accounted for by the top 50 and 100 were estimated from this distribution as well, with adjustments for size-groups that had to be divided. The share of the top 50 declined from 62 percent to 51 percent. More recent evidence from the United Kingdom Monopolies Commission, *General Observations on Mergers* (London: 1969) suggests that this trend has been sharply reversed. See also the evidence of Malcolm C. Sawyer, "Concentration of British Industry," *Oxford Economic Papers*, XXIII, November 1971, pp. 352–83.

Data on world multinational corporations come from Robert Rowthorn, *International Big Business 1957–1967: A Study of Comparative Growth*, University of Cambridge, Department of Applied Economics, Occasional Paper 24 (Cambridge, Eng.: 1971).

TABLE 6–5

*Average Employment Size of Manufacturing Enterprises
in Western Nations*[a]

Country	Year	Arith-metic Average	Entropy Index	Niehans Index	Percentage of Labor Force in Enterprises Over 1000 Employees
Belgium	1962	138	512	2647	28.5%
France	1963	147	644	3768	32.1
West Germany	1961	164	767	3932	36.9
Greece	1963	80	150	269	n.a.
Italy	1961	112	436	3486	21.9
Japan	1963	109	481	3028	32.7
Netherlands	1962	122	393	2013	24.4
Portugal	1958	99	170	318	7.6
Switzerland	1965	112	317	1247	20.2
United States	1963	231	3349	13976	59.6

a. The sources of data are given in Appendix B-20. Employment size is measured only within national boundaries.

four indicators of enterprise size and market size are presented in Table 6–6.

As predicted, a very strong positive relationship exists between market size and enterprise size, with over three-fifths of the variation of enterprise size accounted for by variation in market size. For the arithmetic average and the entropy indicator, this relationship is statistically significant only for the G.N.P. indicator of domestic market size; for the Niehans and percentage indicators, both variables for market size appear statistically significant. Testing the importance of the level of economic development raises difficulties because total and per capital G.N.P. are related in the small sample. Thus there appears to be a positive and significant relationship between enterprise size and per capita income but the correlation coefficients are lower than when market size indicators are used. When both variables are used, market size appears more important than per capita income.[25] Although market size appears to be the critical causal variable, we cannot definitely exclude the possibility that the level of development also plays a role.[26]

The response of enterprise size to an increase in gross national product (the calculated regression coefficient for Y) is larger for enter-

25. Such regressions are presented in Appendix B-24.
26. This is especially true for the percentage indicator where both market size and per capita production appear to be statistically significant causal variables.

TABLE 6–6

Relationships between Enterprise Size and Market Size Indicators

	S	R²
ln A = 1.882 + .173* ln Y + .065 ln X	10	.63*
(.060) (.138)		
ln E = −3.203 + .541* ln Y + .087 ln X	10	.82*
(.121) (.279)		
ln N = −7.785 + .919* ln Y + .682* ln X	10	.93*
(.105) (.243)		
ln P = −9.581 + .489* ln Y + .433* ln X	9	.93*
(.061) (.129)		

where A = arithmetic average of enterprise size in manufacturing;
     E = entropy index of enterprise size in manufacturing;
     N = Niehans index of enterprise size in manufacturing;
     P = percentage of labor force in enterprises over one thousand;
     Y = gross national products calculated with dollar price weight;
     X = ratio of nonagricultural merchandise exports to value-added in mining and manufacturing;
     S = number of nations in sample (sample size);
     R² = coefficient of determination;

     * = statistical significance at the .05 level.

prises than for establishments (Table 5–5), which gives additional evidence that the degree of multi-establishment enterprises is related to market size. It is noteworthy that the calculated coefficient increases as one moves from the arithmetic average to the entropy index of size to the Niehans index. This increase suggests that the slopes of the cumulative size distributions systematically change with market size so that the largest nations have the widest size variation and greatest importance of very large firms. In all three cases the calculated coefficient for the G.N.P. is less than unity, which means that a given percentage increase in the size of the domestic market is accompanied by a smaller percentage increase in enterprise size. Because the size distribution slopes are different and because the slope for the Niehans index is so close to unity, it is possible that degree of agglomeration, as measured by the relative importance of just the largest enterprises, may be positively related to market size (rather than negatively, when the degree of agglomeration is measured in the usual way).

A more direct analysis of this agglomeration phenomenon can be made by regressing the share of the manufacturing labor force accounted for by the average size enterprise (using the arithmetic, entropy, and Niehans size indicators). The results show the expected inverse relationship with total market size; if per capita G.N.P. is added as an additional explanatory variable to the agglomeration statistic, little additional explanatory power is gained except with the Niehans indicator.[27] Thus agglomeration also appears to be explained primarily by market size.

The positive relationship between enterprise size and market size can be due either to changes in the relative importance of employment in different industrial branches accompanying a change in G.N.P. or to changes in enterprise size for each branch. In a manner similar to the investigation of this problem for establishment sizes (in Chapter V), I recalculated the regressions for enterprise sizes using the assumptions that the labor force distribution by industry was the same in the United States and as in Portugal. The results are qualitatively similar to those in Table 6–6, i.e., roughly the same statistically significant and nonsignificant relationships were found with particular explanatory variables. Quantitatively, the response to changes in market size was somewhat less when United States or Portuguese industrial weights were used. Such results mean that although structural changes accompanying a rise in market size account for some part of the observed change in enterprise size, the major portion of the increase occurred through changes in enterprise size in each indutrial branch. In other words, changes in employment in different industrial branches accompanying changes in market size played a relatively small role in explaining the regression results presented in Table 6–6.

3. Enterprise Size in East Europe

We are now in a position to investigate enterprises in East Europe, using as a norm the results of such an investigation for the West. In order to be able to interpret the East European data, however, it is necesary to discuss briefly certain important aspects of the industrial organization of these nations in the light of some simple organizational considerations.

In East Europe, except for Yugoslavia, three major levels of authority can be distinguished for those enterprises under the aegis of the central government. The central authorities (the State Planning Commission and the Ministries) are at the highest level. Lower in the administrative ranking are the intermediate organs or associations (in several countries such as Hungary, these became unimportant in the late 1960s). And at the bottom level are the units designated as enterprises. (The entire industrial structure is discussed in much greater detail in Chapter VII.)

An analysis of the size of enterprises could start from several different considerations. We could simply test Eucken's proposition that enterprises in planned economies are larger and have a smaller range of

27. Such regressions are presented in Appendix B-24.

size than similar enterprises in market economies. The basic justification of this hypothesis is that, in nonmarket economies, coordination costs are high and significant savings can be gained by having the center deal with a relatively small number of decision-making units. Large-size enterprises would also mean that production in each would be less specialized so that enterprise managers would take over certain problems of coordinating production of intermediate and final products that, with smaller enterprises in a centrally administered economy, the central authorities would have to do. (Such considerations were apparently important factors in the Hungarian and Czechoslovak decisions in the late 1950s to consolidate many enterprises.) A more sophisticated approach to enterprise size would start from the fact that there are various types of costs to different shapes of the administrative pyramid and various sizes of decision-making units; but insufficient data are available on such cost parameters to permit empirical testing of any particular derived propositions so that this approach cannot be pursued. A third approach starts from some considerations about the degree to which the economy is characterized by multi-establishment enterprises and it is to this matter that I now turn.

For only three East European nations do we have data on the ratio of enterprise to establishment size with which to determine the relative degree of multi-establishment enterprises. For one of these nations, Yugoslavia, the problem is complicated by some changing rules on multi-establishment enterprises and it seems best to drop this case;[28] it might be worth noting, however, that the degree of multi-establishment enterprises appears very low. For the two remaining cases, Poland and Hungary,[29] several types of comparisons can be made. We saw for the West that the degree to which economies are characterized by multi-establishment enterprises depends on the absolute value of the G.N.P. and, for this reason, we would expect that the ratio of average enterprise size to average establishment size would be higher in Poland than in Hungary; however, the reverse is the case. In comparison with the West, the ratio for Poland appears quite in line with what we would predict from information about the G.N.P. (except for the Niehans indicator for which the

28. Complications arise because of the rules regarding the degree to which Worker Councils of particular establishments have autonomy over the Council of the entire enterprise. The data in Tables 7–6 and 7–7 cannot be compared to the data in Table 6–3 because the former statistics include mining enterprises while the latter exclude the mining branch.

29. The average size of enterprises in Hungary according to the four indicators are respectively 837, 2221, 4599, and 66.2 percent; in Poland, 375, 1925, 1974, and 50.4 percent. These include all manufacturing enterprises (state, cooperatives, and private) with over twenty employees and workers. These data are somewhat smaller than those presented in Tables 7–6 and 7–7 because the latter include mining enterprises which are much larger than manufacturing enterprises and which raise the average.

ratio is somewhat lower than predicted). For Hungary, on the other hand, the ratio is somewhat higher than we would predict from the Western data, but not greatly out of line except for the ratio derived from the arithmetic average. The relatively high degree to which Hungary is characterized by multi-establishment enterprises is the result of an enterprise consolidation program carried on during the late 1950s and early 1960s that brought about a considerable increase in average enterprise size.

For the Soviet Union and East Germany, we have qualitative indicators that the prevalence of multi-establishment enterprises might be low *vis-à-vis* Western nations; while for Czechoslovakia, where considerable enterprise consolidation has taken place, the degree to which the economy is characterized by multi-establishment enterprises is probably quite high. This variety of results seems due to the simple fact that the extent of multi-establishment enterprises is considered a policy instrument and that there is little agreement on its optimal use, a conclusion readily affirmed in conversation about the matter with East European economists.

To what degree has combining of establishments into enterprises been carried out in Eastern Europe to take advantage of the technological-administrative economies discussed above? Since such economies are difficult to measure and since the constant joining and separating of establishments seems to have been based more on political or personnel, rather than economic, considerations it does not seem likely that the pattern of the relative degrees of multi-establishment enterprises among different industrial branches would be very similar to the situation in the West where more attention may be paid to purely economic factors. This supposition is very easy to test and the results can be quickly summarized.[30] For Hungary, there is indeed some positive relation of the relative degree of multi-establishment enterprises in various industrial branches with the Western pattern although the correlation is not statistically significant with two of the three size indicators. For Poland, there is less relationship between the ranking of industries according to the relative prevalance of multi-establishment enterprises with either the West or with Hungary; indeed, the guiding arrangement principle of production units appears to be grouping together many small establishments into medium-size enterprises, while keeping the very large production establishments as single-establishment enterprises without paying any attention to the particular industrial branch in question.[31] In the reform discussions in Poland in 1971–72, voices were raised urging reconsideration of this policy.

30. The relevant data on this matter are presented in Appendix B-22.
31. The Poles publish a table showing the number of establishments per enterprise by employment size per enterprise [Głowny urząd statystyczny, *Statystyka przemysłu 1964* (Seria "Statystyka polski-materialy statystyczna," Zeszyt 1 (123) (Warsaw: 1966)] on which this generalization is based.

These results are not as clear as we would have hoped and in turning to the absolute size of enterprises, our predictions cannot be made with a high degree of confidence. One factor making for larger enterprise size in the East is the larger size of establishments. And in certain East European countries with relatively high prevalence of multi-establishment enterprises we would certainly expect larger enterprises than we would predict from regression formulae derived from the Western data. On the other hand, we do not know the degree to which a lower degree of multi-establishment enterprises might offset larger establishment sizes. The Eucken approach leaves no room for such doubts and confidently predicts that enterprise sizes in the East are much greater than those in the West and that there should be marked discrepancies between the actual data and the predicted enterprise sizes using the regression formulae derived from Western data. Relevant data on this matter are presented in Table 6–7.

In most countries of Eastern Europe, the data in the table show a very large enterprise employment size. Enterprises in Czechoslovakia and Hungary—two relatively small nations in terms of G.N.P.—are among the largest in the world.

With one exception (the Niehans indicator for the Soviet Union), the enterprises in Eastern Europe are very much larger than predictions based on regression equations derived from economically developed Western nations in Table 6–6. The relations between actual and predicted size are smallest in the Soviet Union, East Germany, and Yugoslavia—three nations where the relative importance of multi-establishment enterprises does not seem great. And the ratios of actual to predicted sizes are highest in Hungary and Czechoslovakia, where the relative importance of multi-establishment enterprises is much greater. The greatest differences between actual and predicted values appear with the arithmetic average because this indicator is the most sensitive to the relative lack of small enterprises in the East (especially those in the range of twenty to one hundred workers and employees) that one finds in the West.

In interpreting these data it must be noted that enterprise sizes were rapidly increasing in Eastern Europe during the early and mid-1960s. Such a rapid consolidation preceded the economic reforms in many of these nations and introduced certain difficulties in the implementation of the reforms by increasing the monopoly element in these economies. (Such matters are discussed in greater detail in Chapter VII.) In the late sixties enterprise size increased in East Germany and Romania for quite different reasons. In the former nation, a number of vertically integrated "combines" were formed by amalgamating existing enterprises; while in the latter nation, many enterprises in the same industry were combined into various "industrial centrals" which took over major enterprise decision-making powers. In April 1973 Soviet policy makers

announced plans to follow the Romanian example and horizontally combine all existing centrally directed enterprises into two hundred or so
super-enterprises in the next three years. If this Soviet policy measure is
actually implemented (a process which is quite problematic with Soviet
reform measures); it might prove quite difficult to dissolve such units in
the future. Will monopoly communism be the highest stage of socialism?

According to the proposition by Eucken the sizes of industrial enterprises in the planned economies of Eastern Europe should be much more
standardized than those in the West; and, indeed, this appears to be the
case. In the West the cumulative size distribution curves allegedly have
the property that they appear as straight lines when drawn on log-normal
graph paper.[32] If such an exercise is carried out for the cumulative size
distributions of enterprises in Eastern Europe, the curves appear roughly
straight as well, especially the upper tails. However, the slopes of these
cumulative curves are less steep than in the West which means that there
are fewer very small or very large enterprises in East Europe and that
enterprise sizes are more uniform than in the West. This may also be seen
for comparisons of actual to predicted enterprise size using different averages: the ratios are higher for the arithmetic average than for the
Niehans average, which means that there are fewer very small enterprises
as well as fewer very large enterprises in the East in comparison to the
West.

Turning now to the relative sizes of enterprises by industrial
branches, what predictions can be made? If, as in the West, the relative
size of establishments in the East is a more important determinant of
relative enterprise size than the relative degree of multi-establishment
enterprises in different industrial branches, then we have some confidence
that the rank orderings of relative enterprises by industry should be
roughly the same as those in the West since relative establishment sizes
by industrial branch are similar. It also seems likely that the relative
enterprise sizes by industry should be roughly similar in all East European
nations.

As we suspected, the rank orderings of relative enterprise sizes in
different industrial branches in the five East European nations for which
data are available are significantly related to each other, with coefficients

32. There is a large theoretical literature on these matters, but statistical
testing of the various propositions presents considerable difficulties (e.g.,
Richard E. Quandt, "On the Size Distribution of Firms," *American Economic
Review,* LVI, June 1966, pp. 416–33). The method used here was rough but
adequate for the purpose. The cumulative curves of the size distribution of
enterprises in East Europe were drawn on regular, semi-log, double-log, and
log-probability graph papers. Only on the latter grid did the curves approximate a straight line (visual check), and from there the generalizations in the
text were derived. For a more detailed study of these matters for Hungary,
see a forthcoming article by Richard Portes.

TABLE 6–7

Average Employment Sizes of Enterprise in Mining and Manufacturing in East Europe[a]

Country	Date	Arithmetic Average		Entropy Index		Niehans Index		Percentage of Labor Force in Enterprises Over 1000	
		Actual	Predicted	Actual	Predicted	Actual	Predicted	Actual	Predicted
Soviet Union	1964								
State enterprises		610	—	2017	—	5909	—	59.6%	—
All enterprises	1965	—	178	—	1544	—	10546	—	40.8%
Bulgaria									
State enterprises		533	—	1042	—	1779	—	47.0	—
All enterprises	1966	420	104	830	242	1566	781	41.6	16.7
Czechoslovakia									
State enterprises		2590	—	4111	—	5967	—	89.1	—
All enterprises	1965	1981	123	3689	431	5733	1756	84.9	27.0
East Germany									
State enterprises		605	—	1479	—	2929	—	64.3	—
All enterprises	1966	236	127	867	477	2418	2024	47.2	28.4
Hungary									
State enterprises		1595	—	3659	—	6176	—	82.5	—
All enterprises	1966	917	113	2285	318	5325	1147	66.2	21.4
Poland									
State enterprises		1016	—	1922	—	3137	—	71.1	—
All enterprises		612	130	1423	520	2720	2286	60.4	24.4

Romania	1966								
State enterprises		1244	—	1965	—	3095	—	70.3	—
All enterprises		1077	120	1789	392	2924	1538	61.7	21.3
Yugoslavia	1965								
State enterprises		574	—	1155	—	1874	—	57.2	—
All enterprises		402	113	989	317	1777	1143	50.4	16.4

a. Sources for the data are listed in Appendix B-20. The predicted size values are calculated from regressions based on Western nations presented in Appendix B-24, first set. Certain incomparabilities must be noted when interpreting the data:

The data include not only manufacturing but also mining and some utilities enterprises as well, giving them an upward bias since employment sizes in these industries appear larger than the average employment in manufacturing enterprises which the predicted values concern.

For the Soviet Union there are two uncertainties in the data. First, the number of enterprises had to be estimated and a possible error of ± 10 to 15 percent could have been introduced here. Second, it is not clear whether these cover just centrally directed enterprises or whether locally directed and even cooperative enterprises are included. It appears, however, that all state-owned enterprises are included, but that producer cooperatives are excluded.

For East Germany the state enterprises include nonhandicraft producer cooperatives as well.

For Yugoslavia, the state enterprises include nonhandicraft cooperatives.

For all nations except East Germany, private enterprises are very small and fall well under the limit of twenty workers and employees which is the cutoff point for the comparisons.

This table represents a revision of a previously published table in an article of mine in *Studies in Comparative Communism*, III, April 1970, pp. 310–65. Only small corrections were made with the data from the East European nations; however, the regressions from which predicted sizes of enterprises were calculated are considerably different because more nations and newer data are included in the present sample.

of concordance ranging from .55 to .70, depending on the measure of average enterprise size that is chosen.[33] In addition, the similarity of the average rank order of enterprise size by industrial branches to that in the West is also confirmed, with the Kendall rank order correlation coefficient of the rank orderings from the two groups of nations ranging from .62 to .77. Since the relative degree to which various industrial branches are characterized by multi-establishment enterprises does not seem similar in the East and the West, we must conclude that the similarity in relative enterprise sizes is due primarily to the influence of the similarity in the pattern of relative establishment sizes in the East and West. However, the correlation of rank orders of enterprise size in different industrial branches to the pattern in the West varied considerably among the East European nations, being highest in East Germany, followed by Hungary and Poland, and lowest in Czechoslovakia and Romania. Although a number of *ex post* rationalizations for these differences can be given, the necessary data with which the subject could be more thoroughly explored (namely size distributions of industrial establishments in various branches of manufacturing) are not available and I must reluctantly leave this matter unexplained.

In the East the rank orders of relative size are relatively higher than those in the West in the mining, leather product, and clothing industries; and are relatively lower in the rubber, chemical and petroleum products, food processing, and printing and publishing industries. Although it would be aesthetically neat to be able to predict this pattern in the same manner as we did for differences in relative establishment sizes between East and West, unfortunately the hypothesis that held for the establishment data cannot be successfully modified to explain this pattern among enterprises.[34]

The results of this empirical examination can be quickly summarized. Average enterprise size is considerably larger in East Europe than in West Europe. A major factor seems to be that production establishments are larger in the East. In certain East European nations such as Czechoslovakia and Hungary, the degree to which the economy is characterized by multi-establishment enterprises appears quite high so that these two countries have enterprises whose average sizes are among the largest in the world. Size variations of enterprises are, as expected, less in the East

33. The data on which the next two paragraphs are based are presented in Appendix B-19. Several difficulties arose in obtaining comparable data and for Romania I had to use only centrally directed state enterprises rather than all enterprises. In addition, data from somewhat different years were used: for Czechoslovakia, I chose 1965 because this was the year preceding a massive conglomeration of establishments into enterprises; the East German data are for 1966; the Hungarian data for 1965; the Polish data for 1960; and the Romanian data for 1966.
34. Data are presented in Appendix B-21.

than in the West. The rankings of relative sizes of enterprises by industrial branch show roughly the same pattern in both the East and the West. Since the relative degree to which different industrial branches are characterized by multi-establishment enterprises appears to differ in socialist and capitalist nations, the similarity in relative enterprise sizes in different branches appears to be due primarily to the similarity in rankings of relative establishment sizes which, in turn, is due to technological factors.

4. A Digression on Big Business

One aspect of the agglomeration of economic power that has received considerable attention in the popular press is the degree to which a given number of the largest enterprises account for total industrial sales or total employment of the labor force. The purpose of this digression is to present comparable data on these matters for a number of nations in the East and the West and to compare the results with the agglomeration regressions reported above.

If we examine the share of the total mining and manufacturing labor force employed by the top 200 enterprises in a large number of nations, a problem arises because we are examining a widely different percentage of enterprises in the various nations. One alternative procedure is to base the number of enterprises examined in each nation on the relative size of the manufacturing labor force. For instance, suppose we are analyzing the United States and another nation that has only 20 percent of the United States manufacturing labor force. When we examine the share of the labor force accounted for by the top 200 enterprises in the United States, we look at the top 40 (i.e., 20 percent) enterprises in the other nation. In the discussion below, the number of enterprises defined in this manner (to the top 200 enterprises in the United States) are designated as the "set of big businesses." In Table 6–8, data are presented on both the top 200 enterprises and the "set of big businesses" for eighteen nations which are arranged in descending order of total national product as measured in United States dollars.

For the Western nations the share of the labor force employed by the top 200 enterprises appears to be significantly related to the level of development; there appears to be no significant relationship with market size, either alone or with per capita G.N.P.[35] On the other hand, the share of labor force employed by the "set of big businesses" appears very much to be directly related with market size. Because of multicollinearity be-

35. See Appendix B-25 for regressions. This and the following generalizations differ from the conclusions of Frederic M. Scherer, *Industrial Market Structure and Economic Performance* (Chicago: 1970), pp. 44–5, who uses the biased estimation method discussed in note to Table 6–8. Scherer, however, explicitly notes that his data leave something to be desired.

TABLE 6–8

*Share of Labor Force in Mining and Manufacturing
Employed by the Largest Enterprises*[a]

Nation	Year	Top 200 Enterprises	"Set of Big Businesses"
West			
United States	1963	35%	35%
Japan	1963	24	19
West Germany	1961	24	18
France	1963	27	17
Italy	1961	19	13
Netherlands	1962	31	13
Belgium	1962	37	12
Switzerland	1965	27	7
Greece	1963	20	n.a.
Portugal	1958	*c.* 22	3
East			
Soviet Union	1964	14	16
Poland	1966	25	*c.* 10
East Germany	1965	29	11
Czechoslovakia	1966	56	*c.* 17
Romania	1966	42	11
Yugoslavia	1965	39	n.a.
Hungary	1966	63	16
Bulgaria	1965	47	*c.* 10

a. The "*c*" stands for *circa*. The data come from various official surveys
of enterprises listed in Appendix B-20. Several other economists have attempted to analyze this phenomenon using data from lists of the top 200
enterprises (e.g., from *Fortune*) and total manufacturing employment (determined from manufacturing establishments), but two upward sources of
bias appear. First, the employment contained in company lists include both
personnel working for the enterprise in foreign nations and also personnel
working in nonmanufacturing activities (e.g., transportation retail sales,
etc.). For the United States in 1963, determination of the ratio of manufacturing personnel employed by the largest 200 enterprises using such
unofficial data would be roughly 33 percent higher than the ratio computed
from the data contained in the United States Census Bureau, *Enterprise
Statistics.*

tween independent variables in the sample, we can not place complete
confidence in the results.

Although this second measure of agglomeration appears to yield
opposite results with those discussed above for Western nations, the results
are not necessarily inconsistent. The size distribution of enterprises could
be varied in such a manner that attention to just the upper tail of the distribution (Table 6–8) might give different results than analysis of various
weighted averages.

For the East European nations, no systematic relationships appear. We must, therefore, examine more closely the experience of each nation, a task pursued in Chapter VII.

Looking at the share of the labor force in mining and manufacturing in the top 200 enterprises, economic power in the West is agglomerated on the enterprise level to the greatest degree in Belgium and the United States. If we look at the "set of big businesses," such agglomeration is higher in the United States than in any nation in the entire sample, East or West. If we pair nations in the East and the West with roughly the same market size (same total G.N.P.), the share of the labor force in the top 200 enterprises is somewhat higher in East Europe but the share accounted for by the "top big businesses" is generally lower than in the West. This comes about from the above noted phenomenon that in the East the sizes of enterprises show less dispersion and the size distribution is less skewed than in the West.

If we look at the distribution of enterprises within the "top big businesses," we see that the size distributions in most Western nations seem to approximate a Pareto distribution and, moreover, have the same slope.[36] I can offer no satisfactory explanation for this surprising uniformity.

Although the data on the largest enterprises give results consistent with the generalization derived in other parts of this chapter, they are no easier to interpret in terms of the concentration of economic power because of the existence of higher organizations in the industrial hierarchy. I must, therefore, defer discussion of such matters until the concept of centralization is more thoroughly explored, the major task of Chapter VIII.

D. Enterprise Size and Market Structure

Up to now analytical attention has been focused primarily on size distributions and on the absolute sizes of establishments and enterprises. But it should be apparent that the sizes of enterprises *vis-à-vis* the sizes of the relevant markets have importance in determining the degree to which an economy is characterized by monopolies or oligopolies.

The purpose of this section is to compare the average degree of industrial concentration (or "monopolization") in the manufacturing sectors of a number of Western economies (comparable data are available only for Yugoslavia in Eastern Europe) and to examine the relative degree of concentration in individual branches. For the major industrial nations, I show not only that the average levels of concentration in the

36. Some data on this matter are presented in Appendix A-12.

manufacturing sector are the same, but also that concentration ratios are roughly the same in any specified four-digit industry.

1. *A Few Preliminary Remarks*

An implicit or explicit assumption in many discussions about the "monopoly problem" is that industrial concentration is lower in the United States than in other countries that have smaller domestic markets.[37] Underlying this assumption is the following type of argument: A single minimum efficient scale or optimal size enterprise may produce more than enough to supply the domestic market of a small nation, while in the United States, domestic consumption is equal in many cases to the production of several MES or optimal size firms; further, the minimum efficient or optimal scale of an enterprise is roughly the same in all developed nations; and finally, the relevant market facing the enterprise is related to the domestic G.N.P. and foreign trade is an irrelevant consideration.

These views have come under attack on several fronts. The minimum efficient or optimal scale may depend on relative factor prices as well as on size of domestic market.[38] Further, since many United States industries are regional, not national, the average degree of concentration in the United States is much higher than previously suspected when this phenomenon is properly taken into account;[39] after looking at these results for the United States the European industrial concentration data do not look so far out of line. Foreign trade considerations also seem too important to omit as many analysts have done. Although attempts have been recently made to construct coherent models taking all these various factors systematically into account, we have far to go to reach a satisfactory explanation.

In the industrial organization literature, one finds scattered comments about the degree to which given industries in different nations have

37. For instance, in an introduction to a presentation of French concentration ratios, Jacques Loup ("La concentration dans l'industrie française," *Études et conjoncture*, XXIV, February 1969) expressly notes that the United States concentration ratios are lower but does not bother to carry out any actual empirical comparisons which would, in point of fact, show the reverse conclusion (see Table 6–10).

38. This point was emphasized to me in correspondence by Peter Pashigian; for a detailed analysis of certain other critical aspects of the relationships between market size and monopoly, see his "The Effect of Market Size on Concentration," Report 6710, Center for Mathematical Studies in Business and Economics, University of Chicago; or his "Market Concentration in the United States and Great Britain," *Journal of Law and Economics*, XI, February 1968, pp. 299–319.

39. This is argued by William G. Shepherd, *Market Power and Economic Welfare* (New York: 1970).

similar degrees of concentration. Although it seems likely that more concentrated industries in one nation might also be more concentrated in another, a rigorous model of this phenomenon has not yet been presented either, and primary efforts have focused on explaining differences in industrial concentration between the United States and the United Kingdom.

The most important consideration to keep in mind during the analysis below is the empirical result presented earlier in this chapter: Average enterprise size appears related to the size of the market. This one major relation goes a long way in understanding the somewhat puzzling results presented below.

2. *The Empirical Results*

a. *The average degree of monopoly.* Our empirical knowledge about relative industrial concentration is small, especially since most international comparisons have been limited to the United States and the United Kingdom.[40] Using some newly released data, we can now extend such international comparisons.

The statistic used below to measure industrial concentration is the four-firm concentration ratio, i.e., the percentage of the value of shipments or production accounted for by the top four enterprises in a narrowly defined industry. In certain cases, which are designated, the concentration ratios are based on the percentage of employment in a particular industry that is accounted for by the largest four enterprises in an industry. Although there are certain well-known objections to the use of concentration ratios as a measure of monopoly, they provide the only available data with which any comparisons can be made.[41] The concentration ratios are calculated primarily for industries corresponding to the

40. Two recent international comparisons dealing with more than the United States and the United Kingdom deserve mention: Joe S. Bain, *International Differences in Industrial Structure* (New Haven: 1966); and Morris A. Adelman, "Monopoly and Concentration: Comparisons in Time and Space," in Tullio Bagiotti, ed., *Essays in Honor of Marco Fanno* (Padua: 1966). In neither study are global comparisons of industrial concentration calculated.

41. One objection to the use of four-firm concentration ratios is that the relative concentration in two industries might be reversed if a different cut-off point is used; empirical investigations using United States data show this objection to be of little consequence. Another criticism is that concentration ratios may understate concentration in regional industry since they are calculated on a national level; I try to make corrections in my analysis for this factor. Finally, many have argued that the four-digit classifications are too broad and that industries must be more narrowly defined. In many cases this is a quite valid objection but unfortunately this empirical investigation is limited by the data at hand.

four-digit classification in the United States industrial statistics reporting system; in certain cases, however, concentration ratios for five-digit industries (i.e., industries defined more narrowly) are used after appropriate adjustments are made.

Using pairs of concentration ratios for similarly defined industries of the United States and a given foreign country, I have computed weighted averages of overall concentration for the two countries. The results for all countries were then standardized by calculating the foreign average as a ratio of the respective United States average. The number of such pairs of concentration ratios in the weighted averages varied, ranging from 24 (the United States-Netherlands comparisons) to 107 (the United States-Sweden comparisons) and depended on the number of similarly defined industries for which I could find concentration data.

The indices (or weighted averages) were actually calculated in a two-step procedure because of weighting difficulties.[42] Where concentration ratios based on value of shipments were available, I used value-added weights to consolidate the ratios of individual industries into weighted averages for classes corresponding to the ISIC two-digit branches of manufacturing. These two-digit branch averages were then combined using value-added weights for the entire branch to calculate the aggregate measure for the entire manufacturing sector.[43] Where only concentration ratios from employment data are available, a similar two-step procedure was carried out using employment in individual industries and in the two-digit industrial branches as weights instead. For France both types of concentration ratios were available and the results were roughly the same.

There is, of course, an index-number problem in the choice of the national weights in the individual comparisons between the United States and different foreign nations. And, moreover, problems of interpretation arise whatever weights we select. In order to gauge quantitatively the magnitude of this problem, three different sets of indices were calculated for the two-country comparisons: one using United States value-added weights for the individual industries and two-digit branches; another using United States value-added weights for the individual industries but foreign value-added weights for the two-digit branches; and a third using foreign value-added weights for both individual industry and industrial

42. Weighted averages or indices of concentration have been analyzed and used by a number of economists. For a theoretical analysis of their construction, see Leonard W. Weiss, "Average Concentration Ratios and Industrial Performance," *Journal of Industrial Economics,* XI, March 1963, pp. 237–54.

43. Greater details on the construction of the averages are given in Appendix B-26. Value-added weights are used to aggregate concentration ratios within the two-digit branches in order to minimize differences in definition between weights that might occur because the degree of vertical integration of a particular industry is defined differently in the various national statistics.

branch weights.[44] Much less data are available for the third comparison but, as I show below, the results for all three calculations are roughly the same so that we can draw relatively unambiguous conclusions without worrying unduly about index-number effects.

A final problem arises in the treatment of regional industries and several choices of method are available. Rather than adjust the concentration ratios for each country to reflect whether regional industries are involved, I have chosen to omit from the indices those industries that can be classified as regional in the United States.[45] This procedure considerably reduces the size of the samples; in order to give some perspective on the effect of this measure, comparisons based on the raw data without such adjustments for regional industries are also presented.

The data in Table 6–9 show that three nations, France, West Germany, and Italy, have weighted concentration ratios somewhat lower than the United States, while an additional three, Japan, the Netherlands, and the United Kingdom, have weighted concentration ratios only slightly higher than the United States. In only five nations are concentration ratios clearly higher—namely Belgium, Canada, Sweden, Switzerland, and Yugoslavia. It is also noteworthy that concentration in Yugoslavia, a socialist nation which some have believed to be highly monopolized, has about the same degree of concentration as Sweden and Switzerland.

Unfortunately, no convenient tests of statistical significance can be performed on these doubly weighted averages in order to determine whether the differences are important. Nevertheless, the unweighted averages yield results quite similar in most cases to the weighted averages and for these we can perform significance tests. Some relevant data for the various nations excluding United States regional industries are presented in Table 6–10; similar results are obtained when other samples are used.

The data in Table 6–10 show that there are no statistical differences at the .05 level in the average aggregate concentration ratios of the United States and the following six nations: France, West Germany, Italy, Japan, the Netherlands, and the United Kingdom. In the remaining five nations the overall levels of concentration are higher.[45a]

44. This procedure had to be slightly modified in certain cases because of data deficiencies.

45. I have followed the designation of these industries (with several minor modifications) that is made by Shepherd, Appendix Table 8. It should be added that in the choice of comparable United States and United Kingdom industries, I also partly followed Shepherd's designation in his article "A Comparison of Industrial Concentration in the United States and Britain," *The Review of Economics and Statistics*, XVIII, February 1961, pp. 70–5, but included industries with low concentration ratios as well.

45a. These results appear to conflict with the conclusions drawn from a study of industrial concentration in several common market nations by Louis Phlips [*Effects of Industrial Concentration: A Cross-Section Analysis*

TABLE 6-9

Weighted Four-firm, Four-digit Aggregate Average Concentration Ratios as a Ratio of Weighted Concentration Ratios in the United States[a]

Country	Date	Type of Concentration Ratio	Size of "Basic Sample"	Branch and Sub-branch Weights		
				United States value-added or employed	*United States value-added or employed**	*Other Nations value-added or employed*
No Adjustments						
United States	1963	Both		1.00	1.00	1.00
Belgium	1963	Shipments	54	1.66	1.52	n.a.
Canada	1948	Employment	48	1.38	1.35	1.34
France	1963	Shipments	70	.93	.95	.92
West Germany	1963	Shipments	89	.94	.92	n.a.
Italy	1961	Employment	56	.89	.86	.83
Japan	1962	Shipments	70	1.14	1.11	n.a.
Netherlands	1963	Shipments	24	1.23	1.25	n.a.
Sweden	c. 1965	Shipments	107	1.54	1.55	1.41
Switzerland	1965	Employment	61	1.63	1.68	1.71
United Kingdom	1951	Shipments	101	1.20	1.13	1.14
Yugoslavia	1963	Shipments	42	1.47	1.41	n.a.
Omitting "Regional Industries"						
United States	1963	Both		1.00	1.00	1.00
Belgium	1963	Shipments	37	1.54	1.35	n.a.
Canada	1948	Employment	37	1.34	1.31	1.29
France	1963	Shipments	47	.85	.87	.85
West Germany	1963	Shipments	67	.91	.93	n.a.

Italy	1961	Employment	38	.82	.79
Japan	1962	Shipments	46	1.02	n.a.
Netherlands	1963	Shipments	16	1.10	n.a.
Sweden	c. 1965	Shipments	74	1.42	1.49
Switzerland	1965	Employment	39	1.51	1.72
United Kingdom	1951	Shipments	72	1.07	1.13
Yugoslavia	1963	Shipments	29	1.33	n.a.

*Branch weights are other nation value added or employed.

a. For the "type of concentration ratio," I have distinguished for simplicity only between those based on shipments and those based on employment. In the former class, I include those based on production, sales, and shipments and defined in either value or quantity terms.

The "basic sample" designates the number of comparable industries included in the comparison with the United States using United States weights for both sub-branch and branch weights. The number of comparable industries using foreign sub-branch weights is somewhat greater since a number of five-digit industries are included.

N.A. means not available.

To give some idea of the absolute values involved in the comparisons, the following data on United States weighted concentration ratios (using 427 four-digit industries) may be of interest (with weighted concentration ratios based on employment data in parentheses): no adjustments to the raw data, .39 (.30); adjustments made by excluding United States regional and local industries, .44 (.33). Shepherd makes different adjustments by including the regional and local industries, but increasing their concentration ratios and, in addition, adjusting the concentration ratios of certain industries to take into account the fact that they are too widely or narrowly defined. If we follow Shepherd's adjustments, the United States weighted concentration ratio rises to .58 (.44); this procedure is not, however, followed in the text.

Sources of data and methods of calculation are given in Appendix B-26. For some countries such as the United Kingdom, concentration data are available but data on the size distribution of enterprises are not sufficiently comparable for inclusion in the analysis of enterprise size.

TABLE 6–10

*Unweighted Averages of Aggregate Four-Firm, Four-Digit
Concentration Ratios (Excluding United States "Regional Industries")*[a]

Country	Size of Sample	Ratio of Foreign Mean to United States Mean	Difference Between Absolute Levels of Mean Concentration Ratios, Stated As Percentages
Belgium	37	1.46	18.41*
Canada	37	1.52	20.94*
France	47	.90	−5.26
West Germany	67	.98	−0.84
Italy	38	.97	−1.20
Japan	46	1.05	2.76
Netherlands	16	1.17	6.77
Sweden	74	1.58	27.63*
Switzerland	39	1.49	17.47*
United Kingdom	72	1.04	1.78
Yugoslavia	29	1.50	26.93*

*Designates statistical significance at .05 level.
a. Sources of data are the same as the previous table. The concentration ratios for each pair of comparisons are added without weighting one industry more than another.

From Table 6–9 it should be clear that the aggregate degree of concentration is related in some way to the overall market size, rather than to the level of economic development. The countries fall quite naturally into two groups: those with large dollar values of gross national production (the United States, France, West Germany, Italy, Japan, and the United Kingdom) and those with small dollar values of gross national production (Belgium, Canada, the Netherlands, Sweden, Switzerland,

---

for the Common Market (Amsterdam: 1971), Chpt. VI], a book I came across only when this study was in press. Phlips compared concentration by first calculating regressions relating concentration ratios in a given nation to the market sizes of the respective industries and then analyzing differences in the calculated regression coefficients for the various nations. In effect, he compared concentration among nations after trying to hold constant the size of markets in the industries of the different nations. His measure of market size (two variables: employment size in the industry and the arithmetic average employment size of firms in the industry) can be questioned. Further, his procedure of calculating a relation between concentration ratios and market size is based on some controversial assumptions (in general, this procedure assumes a certain similarity of production functions in different industries; with Phlip's market size variables, I believe a similarity of firm size distributions in different industries is assumed) about which doubts can be raised. The great differences in our statistical approaches toward measuring "average" concentration make our conflicting results quite incomparable.

and Yugoslavia). The countries in the first group have roughly the same concentration ratios; further, their overall levels of concentration are much lower than the nations in the second group (with the exception of the Netherlands). Dividing the groups of nations into those with relatively high and low per capita income admits of many more exceptions to any generalization. Using regression techniques to analyze the data yields the same conclusions.[46]

In interpreting these results one *caveat* must be emphasized: The data are related only to structural characteristics and not to the functioning of the individual economies. Before we can generalize from such structural information to the state of competition, we must have information about other considerations such as the degree of cartelization (or collusion) and the role of foreign trade. Since foreign trade plays a more important role in most foreign nations than in the United States, imports may provide an additional competitive element in these economies *vis-à-vis* the United States (assuming that tariff barriers are roughly similar); on the other hand, cartelization may be more important in these foreign nations as well. Credible conclusions about the relative state of competition in various nations can only be drawn from highly detailed studies in which these various factors can be properly weighted.[47]

b. *Concentration within particular industries.* The first step of analysis is to rank the various two-digit manufacturing branches in each of the

46. I calculated a number of such regressions, of which a typical one is:
In $C = 1.712 - .218^*$ In Y; $R^2 = .71$; $S = 11$ (the United States excluded)
$$(.047)$$
and where C = average aggregate concentration ratio, regional industries excluded, United States weights for both sub-branches and branches; and the rest of the symbols are the same as in Table 6–1. Changing the form of such regressions or adding additional independent variables does not substantially change the results.

47. Foreign trade considerations can be partly taken into account by calculating concentration ratios so as to include imports (see William G. Shepherd's forthcoming study using this approach) or by calculating international concentration ratios, so as to be able to take into account multinational enterprises (see Joseph Miller's forthcoming study using this approach). Nevertheless, we also need information concerning the degree to which tariffs protect domestic markets and the substitutability of foreign and domestic products before the competitive effect of foreign trade can be fully judged. Quantitatively determining the effect of formal and informal collusion, cartelization, and other such devices dampening the forces of competition is even more difficult. Effects of both foreign trade and domestic market considerations are analyzed in one manner by L. Esposito and F. F. Esposito, "Foreign Competition and Industrial Profitability," *Review of Economics and Statistics,* LIII, November 1971, pp. 343–53.

International comparisons of the effects of high concentration on particular performance variables for different common market nations are presented by Phlips, Part I.

twelve nations of the sample according to their weighted average concentration. The average rankings of such weighted average concentration estimates are presented in Table 6–11.

A very distinct pattern of relative concentration emerges and the concordance coefficient, which designates the degree to which the rank orderings of the various nations are similar, is statistically significant at the .01 level. Concentration in all nations is highest among the industries in the tobacco, transport equipment, machinery, and petroleum and coal product branches and lowest in the furniture, lumber products (except furniture), and clothing branches.

A more detailed comparison can be made by examining the relationship between individual comparable concentration ratios for the United States and for each of the foreign nations. The results of one set of such calculations is presented in Table 6–12.

The calculations show that in all cases there is a statistically sig-

TABLE 6–11

Average Rank Orderings of Weighted Concentration Ratios[a]

ISIC Number	Industry	Rank
22	Tobacco products	1
38	Transportation equipment	2
36	Machinery except electrical, transportation	3
32	Petroleum and coal products	4
31	Chemicals	5
30	Rubber products	6
37	Electrical equipment	7
28	Printing and publishing	8
39	Miscellaneous	9
33	Stone, glass, clay products	10
35	Metal products except machinery	11
34	Primary metals	12
20	Food processing	13
27	Paper products	14
21	Beverages	15
23	Textiles	16
29	Leather products	17
24	Clothing and shoes	18
25	Lumber products except furniture	19
26	Furniture and fixtures	20
Concordance coefficient		.51
Number of nations in sample		12

a. Weighted two-digit, four-firm concentration ratios were calculated for the twelve nations and then ranked; the average ranks for the manufacturing sector for the individual two-digit industries are presented in the table. The sources for the data are the same as the previous table.

TABLE 6–12

Relationships between United States and Foreign Four-Firm, Four-digit Concentration Ratios (Excluding United States "Regional Industries") [a]

Country		S	R^2
Belgium	F = .283* + .752* U (.095) (.216)	37	.26*
Canada	F = .220* + .973* U (.063) (.138)	37	.59*
France	F = .099 + .918* U (.073) (.125)	47	.55*
West Germany	F = .088 + .807* U (.053) (.095)	67	.53*
Italy	F = −.019 + 1.017* U (.053) (.118)	38	.67*
Japan	F = .162 + .754* U (.088) (.149)	46	.37*
Netherlands	F = .195 + .674* U (.107) (.241)	16	.36*
Sweden	F = .444* + .652* U (.044) (.083)	74	.46*
Switzerland	F = .290* + .674* U (.061) (.145)	39	.37*
United Kingdom	F = .227* + .541* U (.056) (.110)	72	.26*
Yugoslavia	F = .557* + .469* U (.073) (.119)	29	.36*

where F = foreign four-firm, four-digit concentration ratio;
U = United States four-firm, four-digit concentration ratio;
S = number of concentration ratios of different four-digit industries in sample;
R^2 = coefficient of determination.

a. Standard errors are placed below the calculated regression coefficients; asterisks denote statistical significance at the .05 level. The source of data is the same as in previous tables.

nificant (.05 level) relationship between the four-firm, four-digit concentration ratios in the United States and in the various foreign nations. The amount of variation of the foreign concentration ratios that is "explained" by variation in comparable United States ratios ranges from 26 to 67 percent.

The most striking results occur for France, West Germany, Italy, Japan, and the Netherlands; for these nations we cannot reject the hypothesis (at the .05 level of significance) that the concentration ratios in particular industries are numerically the same as in the United States (i.e., that the regression equation is: the foreign concentration ratio for industry X = 0.0 + 1.0 × United States concentration ratio for industry X)! Thus, for five of the six nations that have similar overall levels of concentration as the United States, the results appear caused by the fact that the concentration ratios for individual industries are similar as well. (The United Kingdom is the only exception.) These results are particularly impressive because there is a statistical bias in the regressions that leads to slopes less than unity, a positive constant coefficient, and an *underestimation* of the degree of equality between foreign and United States concentration ratios because concentration ratios are bounded between 0.00 and 1.00.[48] Investigation of the individual industries in which concentration ratios in the five nations differed significantly from those of the United States yielded no very interesting results.

For Belgium and Canada we cannot reject the hypothesis (at the .05 level) that the individual concentration ratios are equal to the individual United States ratios plus a constant; and, comparing Tables 6–9 and 6–12, we note that the constant in the regression is roughly equal to the difference between the overall levels of concentration in these nations and the United States. Thus for seven out of the eleven nations under examination (Belguim and Canada plus the five nations discussed in the previous paragraph,) the slope coefficient relating the United States and foreign concentration ratios for individual industries is not statistically different from unity.

For the remaining four nations (Sweden, Switzerland, the United Kingdom, and Yugoslavia), the pattern of relationship with United States concentration ratios is statistically significant but less easy to interpret, since, for a given industry, their concentration ratios are greater than those in the United States for industries with low concentration, and are lower than those in the United States in highly concentrated industries.[49]

The results show clearly that forces making for monopoly in a par-

48. The nature of this bias can be seen most clearly by starting with the full form of the calculated regression: $F = a + bU + u$, where u is a random disturbance. If U is very small, u will tend to be positive since F cannot be less than 0.00; if U is very large, u will tend to be negative since F cannot be greater than 1.00. This will lead to a positive intercept and a slope less than unity, even when the true relation is $F = 0.00 + 1.00$ U. Certain complicated statistical techniques such as probit analysis can be employed to get around this difficulty but for the purposes at hand these did not seem necessary. Several experiments were made to test the strength of the bias, e.g., the regressions were recalculated, omitting from the sample all industries in which the concentration ratio of one or both nations is a prespecified distance from 0.00 and 1.00. This seemed in most cases to yield roughly the same results as those presented in Table 6–12. The samples did not seem large enough to be able to be used to discriminate between different functional forms of the relationship between the concentration ratios of pairs of nations and, therefore, I chose the most simple relationship.

49. Pashigian, "Market Concentration in the United States and Great Britain," argues that the differences in concentration ratios for individual industries in the two nations can be explained by the relative sizes of the individual markets for these two countries.

ticular industry are similar in the twelve nations. A considerable amount of empirical work has been devoted to explaining such forces in the United States and much work needs to be done on other nations as well. The available international data do not permit adequate derivation of measures of barriers to entry that are independent of the concentration variable that we are trying to explain.[50] I did try to test a recently proposed hypothesis by L. G. Telser that the nature of the competitive process is such that concentration is related to the capital intensiveness of production by calculating a rank order correlation coefficient between relative concentration (Table 6–11) and relative capital/labor ratios,[51] but the calculated coefficient was low and not statistically significant. A quantitative international study of forces encouraging monopoly in particular industries must be put on the agenda of future research if we wish to fully understand industrial organization from a world standpoint.

3. *Some Interpretations*

For those who believe that the degree of industrial concentration is inversely related to market size, the results presented in this chapter provide an interesting paradox. The following remarks are intended to provide assistance in unraveling this problem.

First, the empirical results of this study are consistent with the proposition presented earlier in the chapter that average enterprise sizes (both in the manufacturing sector as a whole and also in individual industries) vary according to the market size in aggregate. If we look closely at the various indicators of enterprise size in the regressions reported in Table 6–6, we note that the greater the weight placed on the largest enterprise (the Niehans index places greater weight on the largest enterprises than the entropy index; and the entropy index places greater weight on these large enterprises than the arithmetic average), the closer the calcu-

---

50. I did find significant correlations between the rank order of concentration and rank orders of fixed capital in average size enterprises in the two-digit industries, or of workers and employees in average size enterprises (Table 2–3). Unfortunately, since absolute and relative enterprise size are highly correlated, such measures of barriers to entry are quite inadequate. From United States and Swiss industrial censuses, I found data on the ratio of research and development personnel to total personnel in the industry; and these data give some indication of the "degree of technical intensiveness" of an industry which, in turn, might reflect an important barrier to entry. Although such a rank ordering of industries is significantly correlated with the average rank ordering of concentration, the measure of this technological barrier is sufficiently imperfect to make interpretation of the results very uncertain.

51. This proposition has been argued on the basis of an interesting model of business behavior by L. G. Telser, "Cutthroat Competition and the Long Purse," *Journal of Law and Economics,* IX, October 1966, pp. 259–77. The capital/labor ratios come from Appendix B-3.

lated elasticity coefficient of average enterprise size to total G.N.P. is to unity. It thus appears from the regressions in Table 6–12 that the size of the largest enterprises could vary in certain ranges in rough proportion to the size of total G.N.P. which is quite consistent with the results that the average degrees of industrial concentration for many nations are roughly the same. The rise in industrial concentration in nations with small G.N.P.s would, according to this interpretation, reveal a non-linearity that is not reflected in the specification of the regressions in Table 6–6. Although questions about the functional form and the numerical value of coefficients linking average enterprise size and G.N.P. cannot be resolved with the small sample of nations having comparable data with which we have to work, the existence of a relationship between enterprise size and G.N.P. seems crucial in interpreting the empirical results presented in the last two sections of this study.

Second, the approach used in this chapter focuses the search for an explanation of the similarity of four-firm, four-digit concentration ratios in the largest industrial nations on those factors underlying the positive correlation between enterprise size and total G.N.P.: namely, the positive relationships between total G.N.P. and average establishment size and the degree to which industries are characterized by multi-establishment enterprises.

Third, alternative approaches toward an explanation that rely on the impact of differential tariffs or that start from Markov analyses of the growth of enterprises show little promise for helping us understand the results. Trying to explain the results of this study from the empirical analyses of concentration in a single country (that show an inverse relationship between market size and industrial concentration) with the addition of one or two more explanatory variables to take into account "international effects" does not seem very promising to me either. One explicitly acknowledged difficulty in all of these more intensive studies of market size and concentration is the difficulty in obtaining an adequate measure for market size.

Fourth, the results of this study of concentration may have one important implication on the analysis of production functions: namely, that the optimal or minimum efficient sizes of enterprises may not be invariant in all nations but may vary with size of the G.N.P. If the link between these results and production functions is denied, then some alternative explanation for the correlation between enterprise size and the G.N.P. must be specified. One possible alternative explanation that resorts to differences in relative factor prices to explain the conclusions about concentration was casually examined by the author, but the empirical results seemed sufficiently unpromising to encourage any greater efforts along these lines.

Fifth, the empirical results in this chapter, especially those showing great similarity in the degree of concentration in the group of largest nations, are the cross-section analogues to results reported by others showing that for individual nations, the degree of concentration has not changed greatly over long periods of time.[52] This numerical similarity of concentration at several points in time has never been adequately explained but implies a distinct relationship between average enterprise and market size, a relation that seems crucial to my results as well. It must be added that neither the time-series nor the cross-section comparisons of industrial concentration give insight into the exact nature of this relation between enterprise and market size, but merely demonstrate the existence of such a relation. However, recognizing the existence of some force is an important step in trying to assess its nature.

Finally, the similarity of industrial concentration in the largest nations at one point in time and the similarity of industrial concentration in particular nations over time makes us wonder whether antitrust legislation and enforcement, particularly in the United States, has been very effective.[53]

52. For the United States the key studies are by G. Warren Nutter, *The Extent of Enterprise Monopoly in the United States, 1899–1939* (Chicago: 1951) and Morris A. Adelman, "The Measurement of Industrial Concentration," *The Review of Economics and Statistics*, XXXIII, November 1951, pp. 269–96. [The relevant data are reprinted by the United States Bureau of the Census, *Historical Statistics of the United States, Colonial Times to 1957* (Washington, D.C.: 1960), p. 573.] These studies have received some criticism, e.g., Stanley Lebergott, "Has Monopoly Increased?" *The Review of Economics and Statistics*, XXXV, November 1953, pp. 349–51. Studies of the more recent period include those by William G. Shepherd, "Trends of Concentration in American Manufacturing Industry, 1947–58," *The Review of Economics and Statistics*, XLVI, May 1964, pp. 200–12; and Blair, Chapter 1, who argues that between 1963 and 1967, a slight but important increase in concentration occurred in American manufacturing.

For the United Kingdom data on these matters are analyzed by R. Evely and I. M. D. Little, *Concentration in British Industry* (Cambridge: 1960). Studies of the more recent period include William G. Shepherd, "Changes in British Industrial Concentration, 1951–58," *Oxford Economic Papers*, XVIII, March 1966, pp. 126–33; and Kenneth D. George, "Changes in British Industrial Concentration, 1951–58," *Journal of Industrial Economics*, XV, July 1967, pp. 200–11.

The Norwegian case is examined by Fröystein Wedervang, *Development of a Population of Industrial Firms* (Oslo: 1964), Chapter 6.

In the short run the degree of industrial concentration has apparently changed considerably in some nations; e.g., in Yugoslavia over a nine-year period, average concentration markedly declined. (Such data are analyzed by Stephen R. Sacks, "Changes in Industrial Structure in Yugoslavia, 1959–68," *Journal of Political Economy*, LXXX, May-June 1972, pp. 561–75.

53. This question has also been raised in the context of a comparison between United Kingdom and United States concentration by George Stigler, "The Economic Effects of the Anti-trust Laws," *Journal of Law and Economics*, IX, October 1966, pp. 225–58.

E. Summary and Conclusions

This chapter has focused on a consolidation of property rights into enterprises of different sizes. The analysis covers the absolute sizes of enterprises, their degree of agglomeration, and their degree of concentration in particular industries.

On an aggregate level the most important influences on the absolute size of enterprises appear to be the size of the domestic market, the economic system, and changes in the level of technology. The influence of the size of the market can be traced through the degree of multi-establishment enterprises and the size of production establishments. The pattern of relative enterprise size in different industries appears to rest primarily on technological factors for this pattern is very similar for nations in both the East and the West.

The degree of multi-establishment enterprises, at least in the West, rests partly on economies of administration. Although these are difficult to isolate and measure, they appear to stem from certain economic-technological factors peculiar to individual industries and are manifested in the strong pattern in the West of the relative degree of multi-establishment enterprises among different industrial branches. Although the direct relationship between domestic market size and the degree of multi-establishment enterprises is relatively clear, the causal linkages are difficult to uncover; they do not appear to be due to "general" economies of administration, at least insofar as these are manifested in conglomerate mergers. When higher administrative organs have the power to rearrange the number of establishments among enterprises, little can be said about the pattern or the degree of multi-establishment enterprises for those East European nations for which we have the relevant data.

The sizes of constituent industrial establishments in enterprises appear to play an even more important role in influencing the sizes of enterprises. There is a high degree of correlation in the patterns of relative enterprise and establishment sizes. Furthermore, establishment sizes appear strongly related to the size of the domestic market, at least in the West.

The economic system influences the sizes of enterprises in several ways, as predicted from theoretical considerations by Walter Eucken and verified by the data of this study. First, enterprises in the East are considerably larger in employment than predicted from the relationships derived with data from the West. This is probably due to the high costs of coordinating production in nonmarket economies; savings in such costs can be limited by reducing the number of enterprises with which the center deals and by placing some of the coordination of production and necessary inputs in the hands of directors of large, somewhat vertically integrated enterprises. Further, the size distribution of these enterprises under central planning is, as predicted, less extreme than in the West and a greater proportion of the enterprises are roughly the same size. The sample of nations was too small to test the impact of other types of institutional differences between countries, e.g., in the West, differences in antimonopoly enforcement; in the East, differences in the reliance on intermediate units between the center and the enterprises.

Finally, the rising level of technology over time seems to be associated with the rising absolute size of enterprises, independent of per capita income or the size of the domestic market. This is seen in the relative unimportance of per capita income in the cross-section analyses of enterprise size and the fact that the increasing size of the domestic market cannot explain all the size of enterprise growth over time. Such an inference is based, however, on the assumption that the influence of the market at a single point in time is the same as over a long-time period.

The degree of agglomeration (the size of the domestic market accounted for by an average size enterprise) appears to be inversely related to the size of the domestic market. The relationship varies for the different size indicators because the size distributions have a different slope so that for the very largest enterprises, the degree of agglomeration seems to be positively related to market size, at least at a single point in time.

Over the last half century the relative importance of the largest enterprises has increased in some Western countries such as the United States and appears to have decreased in others such as the United Kingdom and France. In most Western nations in the last decade, however, the relative importance of the largest enterprises, as measured by share of particular imputs, has appeared to increase. The inexorability of this latest trend, however, is open to doubt. Further, trends in agglomeration and in market concentration (monopoly) do not seem related to each other so that the two particular types of centralization of property rights do not necessarily reinforce each other.

In the analysis of the degree of monopoly on individual markets, I show that average concentration ratios are roughly the same for the largest countries and then rise for nations with smaller domestic markets. For five of the six largest nat'ons, the measure of concentration in particular industries appeared similar to that in the United States.

The empirical results of this chapter have ranged over a wide number of perennial questions of political economy—questions about the pattern of property rights that are usually argued by ideologists from debatable theoretical considerations rather than from any empirical standpoint that is based on a systematic sifting of the available facts. The approach of this chapter has allowed us to separate the influence of tech-

nological, economic, and systemic factors in many of these difficult ques-
tons. The most important implications of this analysis for such political-
economic considerations deal with concentration or the centralization of
property rights. The empirical results show that in one sense—namely
from the standpoint of the absolute sizes of enterprises—concentration of
property rights does appear to be associated with the level of economic
development and the size of the economy. In other senses—namely the
overall degree of agglomeration of enterprises or the degree of monopoly
—concentration of property rights in the economy as a whole does not
appear an inevitable aspect of industrialization in general or of capitalism
in particular. These considerations are discussed at greater length in
Chapter VIII when the concepts of centralization of property rights
receive more focused attention.

CHAPTER VII

Changes in Property Rights and Industrial Organization: East Europe in the 1960s

Rossiia predstavlalas' Ibragimu ogromnoi master-
ovoiu, gde dvizhuts'a odni mashinii, gde kazhdii
rabotnik podchinenii zavedennomu poriadku,
zan'at svoim d'elom.

Pushkin[1]

A. Introduction

Changes in decision-making powers of executives at different levels of a bureaucracy, changes in the industrial organization of a nation, or changes in the rules or procedures underlying interaction between eco-

1. Aleksandr Pushkin, "Arap petra velikovo," *Sochineniia*. "Russia appeared to Abraham as a gigantic workshop, where only machines moved and where each worker was occupied with his own job according to a fixed plan."

nomic units can all be classified as changes in property rights according to the broad meaning I am giving to this term. Analysis of the most important of these changes of the East European nations as they have moved from their Stalinist economic systems of the 1950s to a variety of different systems in the 1960s provides an opportunity to explore several new aspects of property rights.[2]

Most importantly, we can begin to examine more systematically the degree to which different types of changes in property rights are consistent or in harmony. That is, to what extent are changes in one area of property rights tied to changes in other areas in order to achieve the goals of the original changes? Further, we can study certain important implications of the analyses of the agglomeration of property rights that are carried out in Chapters V and VI.

On a more concrete level this investigation is aimed toward determining the degree to which the East European economic reforms in the late sixties represented either a move toward market socialism or a streamlining of the central administration of the economy. To realize these concrete and abstract purposes, it is necessary to examine closely a number of important features of the reforms in each nation; and in order to narrow the analysis to manageable proportions, several limits must be placed on the discussion.

First, I focus primarily on the changes that were actually taken through 1970. Of course, knowledge of the planned direction of change is important in interpreting whether certain measures were temporary or permanent or whether particular changes are to be understood as inconsistencies or as transitional steps. Nevertheless, many of the planned institutional changes of the past have never been realized and we are justified in maintaining a certain skepticism about the realization of future intentions.

Second, I consider almost exclusively the changes introduced from the mid-1960s to the end of the decade. Discussion of important reform drives that occurred in several East European nations in previous years (e.g., Poland in the mid-1950s; Czechoslovakia in the late 1950s) must be left for others. Although the reforms of the sixties were in no sense completed in the period under examination (particularly in Poland and Romania), the flow of changes do allow overall judgments to be passed on their main features.

2. Approaching the economic reforms of Eastern Europe from the standpoint of property rights is not an original approach and has been used by others, especially Svetozar Pejovich, *The Market-planned Economy of Yugoslavia* (Minneapolis: 1966) and numerous articles including his "Liberman's Reforms and Property Rights in the Soviet Union," *The Journal of Law and Economics,* XII, April 1969, pp. 155–62. The way in which I handle the analysis is, however, quite different.

Third, I focus almost exclusively on reforms in current production in the mining and manufacturing sectors, leaving aside reforms in agriculture, transportation, service, and other sectors of the economy as well as most reforms in investment decision-making, the banking system, and other such matters except insofar as they bear directly on problems of current industrial production.

The analysis turns first to structural elements of the system and then to functional elements. In the investigation of structural elements I examine the various types of decision-making units, the distribution of decision-making power among these units, and the sources of potential competition. Such a discussion presents a snapshot, as it were, of the static aspects of the distribution of control rights. In the investigation of functional elements I examine the mechanisms within the economy that influence the exercise of the property rights. In the final section I summarize the major trends and try to draw appropriate conclusions concerning the degree to which these nations face a spectrum of choices or only a few "grand alternatives" in trying to reform their economies.

B. The Chronological Sweep of the Reforms

Dating the start of the reform movement in Eastern Europe is difficult because the calls for important systemic changes in the economy by politicians, officials, journalists, and even economists were endemic after the mid-1950s. In the 1960s, serious discussion leading to important changes began roughly in 1961 and 1962 in Bulgaria, East Germany, and the Soviet Union and a year or so later in all other countries except Romania.[3]

Underlying the call for economic reforms and their later implementation were a complex series of political and economic factors that defy brief description. Particular attention, in both the East and the West, has been paid to the declining rates of economic growth between 1950 and 1965. In the second quinquennium of the 1950s, the growth rates of both material production (total production excluding services) and industrial

---

3. The Bulgarian reform discussion officially began after the Eighth Party Congress in November 1962 approved a resolution indicating the need for important changes. [J. F. Brown, *Bulgaria Under Communist Rule* (New York: 1970), pp. 160 ff.] The East German discussion took place primarily within the party and government organizations, with extensive experiments started in 1962; the Soviet reform discussion is more difficult to date since many of the participants had written repeatedly about the need for reform over the years. After a pause, however, more intense discussion began in 1962 again. [George Feiwel, *The Soviet Quest for Economic Efficiency* (New York: 1967).]

production were lower than in the first quinquennium in roughly half of the East European nations. Between 1960 and 1965 the growth rates of both material production and industrial production were lower still in all nations except Romania.[4] In addition, "labor reserves" (underemployed workers in agriculture and unemployed women in urban areas) became increasingly exhausted in all the nations, which meant that rapid increases in the work force could no longer be expected. Finally, as production became more varied and sophisticated, difficulties in planning and coordination became more acute; and policy makers began to rediscover the hoary notion that rapid economic growth depends not only on increases in inputs (labor and the means of production) but also on increases in productivity and efficiency. Theoretical discussion of such issues in East Europe occurred often in the framework of analyses of "extensive" and "intensive" growth patterns. Many economists and politicians in these nations came to the conclusion that the Stalinist model of economic administration and attendant policies (which laid primary stress on "extensive" growth) had outlived their usefulness. Additional support for the renewed interest in productivity and efficiency came from those who pointed to an alleged technology gap between the East and the West.

Important changes in economic administration were announced first in East Germany in mid-1963; actual changes began to be introduced in 1964 in that country and a year or so later in all other countries except, again, Romania. The actual timing of the most important changes is summarized in Table 7–1 which also details producer price reform.

Three critical questions of timing have to be faced by economic reformers. First, how long should experimentation with new forms and methods last? Here the reformers have to resolve the problem of how much information can be gained by having a small set of enterprises act according to one set of rules, while the rest of the economy follows another set. Bulgaria and East Germany had relatively extensive experimentation, while Czechoslovakia had relatively little. Second, at what speed should the reforms be introduced? Coherence is gained if all

4. Although this quantitative assessment is based on the official statistics of the various nations, Western estimates show roughly the same results. Relevant data for making such comparisons are presented in Harry G. Schaeffer, "Economic Reforms in the Soviet Union and East Europe: A Comparative Study," Research Papers in Theoretical and Applied Economics, Paper No. 28, Department of Economics, University of Kansas, April 1970; and Alan A. Brown and Paul Marer, "A Comparison of Economic Pressure Indicators in East Europe," Indiana University International Development Research Center Working Paper No. 7, 1970. The lateness of reform discussions and implementation in Romania should be apparent from the data; explaining the relative differences in the beginning of discussion and implementation in other countries does not seem worthwhile since events in all countries occurred quite closely in time to each other.

changes occur simultaneously; on the other hand, there is also much greater confusion and a much greater risk of failure. Hungary introduced most major changes at one time, while Poland spread its changes over a five-year interval.[5] Finally, to what degree should the major changes be followed by a stream of additional changes? Not allowing additional major changes for a while after the introduction of important changes permits greater coherence and greater time for the reformers to evaluate more carefully the effects of the reform; this approach, however, carries the price of rigidity. Hungarian and Yugoslavian reformers did not follow their major changes with other major changes, while Czechoslovakian reformers conceived of their reform as the introduction of a continual process of change.

As I document them below in great detail, the economic systems of the postreform East European nations can be divided into three groups. The first group consists of East Germany, Poland, Romania, and the Soviet Union. In these nations the changes were directed primarily toward improving the operation of the centrally planned and administered system. Of these nations, East Germany had the most far-reaching and consistent reforms. The second group consists of Hungary and Yugoslavia which had taken major steps toward achieving a type of market socialism. Yugoslavia had been moving in this direction for over a decade, while Hungary took the first important moves in this direction in the reform drive of the late sixties. A third group consists of Czechoslovakia and Bulgaria whose reforms were the most mixed: certain changes resembled those taken by the first group; other changes were similar to those taken by the second group. It is important to note that there is no correlation between the level of economic development of the different nations and the groups into which they can be classified.

The reform drives of the sixties also ended differently in the various nations. In Bulgaria the reforms were essentially revoked before they could be put into full operation. In the Soviet Union many of the projected reforms were not implemented and several reversals of important measures were taken, although the degree of abandonment was to a much lesser degree than in Bulgaria. The Czechoslovak reforms were cut back after the Soviet invasion and some important aspects were abandoned in

---

5. Although it may seem obvious that sudden and major changes lead to greater political instabilities, the reverse may actually be true. Hungary seemed to have few political tremors after its major changes in January 1968 while Poland suffered severe riots in December 1970 in Szczecin and Gdansk when a change in retail prices coincided with a change in the system of wage and bonus payments that had been gradually introduced in different industries throughout the economy. It is unclear to me whether the major difficulty lay in a lack of consistency between the two sets of measures or whether the timing of the introduction of these measures was poorly planned.

TABLE 7–1

A Chronology of Reforms in Mining and Manufacturing from 1964 Through 1970[a]

Country	Brief Characterization of Reform Motives	Initiation of Major Administrative Changes	Initiation of Reforms of Producer Prices
Soviet Union	Administrative streamlining	Changes introduced after September 1965 by groups of enterprises; roughly 75% of manufacturing labor force in reformed enterprises by January 1969. In 1969 and 1970 certain reform measures reversed	Simultaneous price reform in 1967, but preceded by selected changes
Bulgaria	Mixed motives in reform	Extensive experimentation in 1964 and 1965; changes introduced 1966 through 1968 by groups of enterprises. After July 1968, repudiation and retreat toward more administrative methods	Simultaneous price reform planned for 1967 but repeatedly delayed; unclear if carried out January 1969; new reform planned, January 1971; last reform, January 1962
Czechoslovakia	Toward market socialism	Series of changes introduced in 1965 and 1966 with latter year considered a "transitional" system. Major reforms in January 1967, but followed by further changes toward goal in 1968. After April 1969, roll-back of reforms, but only partial abandonment	Simultaneous price reform in January 1967
East Germany	Administrative streamlining	Changes introduced in the four-year period following July 1963. Extensive experimentation	Three-stage price reform carried out from 1964 through 1967. Price revision cycle began again in 1969
Hungary	Toward market socialism	Stream of minor changes introduced in 1966 and 1967; major changes in January 1968	Simultaneous price reform in January 1968

Poland	Administrative streamlining	Stream of minor changes after July 1965. Certain reforms rescinded after December 1970	Simultaneous reform of prices enterprises receive for goods, January 1967; no change in prices enterprises pay. Simultaneous general producer price reform, January 1971
Romania	Administrative streamlining	Reform plans announced in October 1967; earnest implementation begun in 1969 and 1970	Partial changes, 1970; last general producer price reform in 1963
Yugoslavia	Toward market socialism	Economic system already quite advanced toward market socialism. Series of changes introduced in rapid succession after July 1965	Simultaneous price changes in late 1965; followed by price freeze until 1967, when market principles introduced for many but not all goods

a. The "brief characterizations of reform motives" represent an overall judgment developed from the ideas presented throughout this chapter and are placed in this table without proof primarily to orient the reader to the more detailed analysis below. The information in this and the following tables has been gathered from hundreds of primary and secondary sources; little purpose would be served in detailing such sources for any but the most controversial or obscure bits of data.

the next two years. Finally the East Germans retreated from their reforms in 1969 and 1970, after having been unable to realize especially high plan goals during these two years. These four nations did not return to their previous systems but rather to points between their previous systems and their reform systems. The Hungarians, Romanians, and Yugoslavs continued in the early seventies to implement their reform plans although it must be added that the first two nations took their major reform steps only in the last few years of the sixties and that the Yugoslavs were running into their perpetual inflation and balance of payments problems. Finally Poland, which moved only slowly along its path of economic reform, began talking about instituting a series of new and far-reaching changes in the middle seventies, under the aegis of the new leadership of Edward Gierek.

From this brief survey it should be clear that the reform drives in the East European nations answered the various questions facing the reformers in much different ways, included quite different changes, and ended in very different ways.

C. Industrial Organization

The discussion below focuses on structural aspects of the distribution of control rights. After delineating the major decision-making units, I discuss the distribution of decision-making powers and the degree to which competition between enterprises can arise within such organizations of industry.

1. The Structure of the Industrial Hierarchy

As noted in previous chapters, the industrial organization of the East European nations features establishments and enterprises, as in the West. In addition, however, all have administrative units between the enterprises and the top economic organs (i.e., the ministries and planning commissions) that I designate with the neutral term of "associations." I discuss briefly in this section some formal aspects of the enterprises and associations.

The empirical investigations reported in Tables 5–6 and 6–7 show that the sizes of establishments and enterprises were very large in East Europe, if compared with their sizes in similar nations in the West. Furthermore, as I demonstrate in Table 7–2, the process of enterprise consolidation occurred rapidly in most countries in East Europe in the period immediately preceding or at the beginning of the reforms.

TABLE 7–2

*Changes in Employment Size of State Enterprises in East Europe
in the Early Sixties*[a]

Country	Years	Averages Arith-metic	Entropy index	Niehans index	Percentage of Labor Force in Enterprises over 1000 Persons
Soviet Union	1960	481	1814	3982	54.3
	1964	610	2017	5909	59.6
Bulgaria	1961	518	992	1700	43.2
	1965	533	1042	1779	47.0
Czechoslovakia	1960	2000	2909	4319	84.6
	1966	2590	4111	5967	89.1
East Germany	1960	503	1303	2678	60.9
	1965	605	1479	2929	64.3
Hungary	1960	818	1836	3929	58.8
	1966	1596	3659	6176	82.5
Poland	1960	719	1455	2555	64.9
	1966	1016	1922	3137	71.1
Romania	1960	869	1509	2660	57.6
	1966	1244	1965	3095	70.3
Yugoslavia	1960	457	921	1544	50.3
	1965	574	1155	1874	57.2

a. The data for the East European nations cover all publicly owned enterprises not only in the ISIC categories 10 through 39 but also in electricity generation and in certain utilities. The data for those countries including only blue-collar workers in their enterprise size distribution data have been adjusted to include white-collar workers as well. The handling of apprentices in the data is obscure in most countries, but for Czechoslovakia and East Germany, they are known to be excluded. The East German data exclude half-state enterprises; this form does not exist in the other nations. The East German data also include and the Soviet data probably include data for the producer cooperatives (which are excluded in the calculations for the other East European nations), but this should not greatly affect the results. In addition, the Soviet data required an estimation of the number of enterprises and these size estimates are subject to an error of ±15 percent.

For definitions of the various size indicators, see Chapter V; the data come from the sources listed in Appendix B-20.

According to the data, enterprise consolidation in the early 1960s proceeded the furthest in Czechoslovakia and Hungary. In the Soviet Union such consolidation appeared in the middle and late sixties under a very special guise—namely the creation of "ob'edin'eniye" and "firmy"—and although there is considerable dispute among Soviet economists about the theological essence of this institution, the major effect of the movement was the creation of large-size production units.[6] Enterprise consolidation of a different nature has also occurred in nations such as Romania where the associations have gained decision-making power at the expense of the enterprise.

Several implications of this trend can be drawn. The relatively large size of production enterprises or decision-making units makes monopolization easier if market competition were ever permitted (assuming, of course, that imports could not serve a competitive role). Further, the relatively large average size of an enterprise may decrease flexibility. It has been claimed by a number of economists (among them E.A.G. Robinson) that in industries with a high degree of demand uncertainty, large enterprises cannot compete successfully with small ones in market economies because of administrative inflexibilities.[7] Certain empirical evidence for the United States supports this contention.[8] If the East European economies were to move toward some form of market socialism, these two implications of enterprise size might have serious repercussions.

These problems have not gone unnoticed by East Europeans and in certain nations such as Hungary there is talk of enterprise "deglomeration measures." However, no East European nation has yet taken serious policy steps to discourage enterprise size (e.g., through either direct measures or such indirect as graduated taxes by size of enterprise).

In the industrial organization hierarchy, the association stands above the enterprise but below the ministry. In most East European countries the associations had existed before the reform and the reform

6. In discussing the nature of the "ob'edin'eniye" or "firmy," two problems arise. First, they have three different forms: (1) The component units lose all autonomy and operate as establishments; (2) some of the component units lose all autonomy, while others maintain their legal or economic and legal (and *khozraschōt*) identity; (3) all of the components maintain their economic and legal identity and the *ob'edin'eniye* function solely as coordinators. Second, at one time it was envisioned that the *ob'edin'eniye* would receive extra powers of decision-making (from the *glavk*) *vis-à-vis* regular enterprises but this does not seem to have occurred in the period under examination. My interpretation of the *ob'edin'eniye* follows that of I. Gromov and V. Ya. Kamenetskiy, *Proizvidstvenn'ye ob'edin'eniye v SSSR* (Moscow: 1967). In April 1973 Soviet policy makers announced plans to change the nature of *ob'edin'eniye* into super-enterprises, and to consolidate all existing enterprises into about two hundred of them.

7. E.A.G. Robinson, *The Structure of Competitive Industry* (New York: 1932). This assumes, of course, that the enterprise does not reduce uncertainty by gaining control of demand forces or by monopolizing the industry.

8. See especially David Schwartzman, "Uncertainty and the Size of the Firm," *Economica*, N.S., XXX, August 1963, pp. 287–97. Most industrial organization specialists have paid scant attention to this problem area and the Schwartzman article is the only recent quantitative study of such matters that I could find.

measures primarily changed their power. A summary of some major features of these associations is presented in Table 7–3.

In trying to understand the function of these associations, it is necessary to determine which of three different roles these organizations have played. They could have been simply agents of the central government (ministries and central planning bureaus) and acted as "transmission belts" between the center and the enterprises in the manner of the former ministerial departments; that is, interfering in the operations of the enterprises only with regard to and not independently of the orders received from above. Or they could have served the role of an "administrative cartel" (for lack of a better term), receiving orders from the center but also participating extensively in the administration of enterprises under their control independently of orders from above. Such "cartel" powers could be gained primarily at the expense of the center or at the expense of the enterprises. Or finally the associations could have received almost no orders from the center and acted either as agents of enterprises in the manner of American trade associations or else as very large independent trusts treating the units below them as "divisions," a situation that did not occur in any East European nation.

In the Stalinist model of industrial organization, associations were primarily agents of the center and, indeed, were parts of the ministries, a role which the *glavki* have continued to play in the Soviet Union. In Poland the associations were separate organizational units from the ministries but with only a small range of independent powers. The "cartel" role was more prominent in Romania and East Germany. In Romania the associations gained their "cartel" powers primarily at the expense of the enterprises and in many cases acted as one large enterprise with the former enterprises as "divisions." In East Germany the "cartel" powers were also strong but were gained primarily at the expense of the center. Only in Hungary and Yugoslavia did the associations have extremely limited powers which appeared to be granted primarily (but not exclusively) by the enterprises themselves (e.g., in Yugoslavia the chambers distributed certain scarce foreign currencies). In Czechoslovakia and Bulgaria the situation was much less defined. In Czechoslovakia the associations were primarily agents of the center until 1968 when the potential conflicts between "independent" enterprises and "dependent" associations became apparent. The Bulgarian literature on associations is extremely confusing since issues about association roles do not seem to have been faced; nevertheless, it appears that the associations were primarily agents of the center with certain "cartel" powers.

Most of the associations have been horizontal (i.e., combined enterprises producing roughly the same goods) and have covered the entire nation, although in Bulgaria, Czechoslovakia, Poland, and in Romania

TABLE 7-3

Associations in East Europe in the Mid- and Late 1960s[a]

Country	Name of Associations	Existed before Reform	Agent of Center; "Cartel"; or Agent of Enterprises	Industrial Type	On "Economic Accounting"	Number in Mining and Manufacturing
Soviet Union	Administration (*glavk*)	Yes	Agent of center	Horizontal	Some were; transition slow, however	?
Bulgaria	State economic association (D.S.O.)	No	Part agent of center; part "cartel" (role ambiguous)	Primarily horizontal	Yes	Originally 25–35; number later raised. Abolished, January 1971
Czechoslovakia	Productive economic unit (V.H.J.)	Yes	At first, center agent; 1968–69, more enterprise agent; unclear 1969–70	Mostly horizontal; 17 vertical or regional	Yes	85–90
East Germany	Associations of peoples' enter- prises (V.V.B.)	Yes	"Cartel"	Horizontal	Yes	80–85
Hungary	1. Intermediate (*eyesules*)	Yes	Agent of enterprise	Horizontal	?	?
	2. Trust (*troszt*)	Yes	Agent of enterprise	Horizontal	Apparently yes	?

Poland	Association (*zjednoczenia*)	Yes	Part agent of center; part "cartel"	Primarily horizontal; some regional	Yes	110–120; in flux, however
Romania	Industrial centers (C.I.)	No	Part agent of center; part "cartel"	Primarily horizontal but some vertical or mixed	Yes	197 set up by early 1970; but not all in mining or manufacturing
Yugoslavia	1. Economic chamber (P.K.)	Yes	Agent of enterprise	Horizontal	?	?
	2. Business association (P.U.)	Yes	Agent of enterprise	Horizontal	?	?

a. I have omitted reference in the table to "combines" which coordinated the efforts of certain enterprises with strong vertical ties to each other (e.g., coal and iron complexes) that exist in some of the nations such as the Soviet Union, Poland, and East Germany. (The East German combine appears to have certain horizontal elements as well.) The voluntary trade associations of East Germany (*Kontors*) and the equivalent organs in Czechoslovakia and Poland are also omitted, since their role and effect on decision-making was quite uncertain and because the range of their operations was limited primarily to several branches of manufacturing. The Soviet *ob'edin'eniye* are considered as enterprises and are not included in the table.

some have included only enterprises within a single region or combined enterprises of which one produced inputs for another.

Finally, most of the associations had or were moving toward "economic accounting" which means that they had an independent accounting system from the ministries and received the bulk of their funds from their constituent enterprises.

As associations gain independent decision-making powers, analysis of their role becomes increasingly difficult. Their relative decision-making powers have many implications, among which is an interesting impact on the sizes of enterprises. The more the associations act as a transmission belt so that the center must take into account individual enterprises in its plans, the greater the advantages of large enterprises so as to minimize the number of decision-making units with which the center must contend. The more the center deals with the enterprises through the associations, the less the administrative need for large enterprises. This rather elementary consideration does not seem to have been taken into consideration in most countries in the reform drives, however.

The role of associations in market systems also requires comment. The existence of associations acting as agents of the center would defeat the very purpose of market competition. In addition, associations acting as "cartels" could, in many circumstances, serve as centers of monopoly power and act as barriers to a functioning market system unless the association managers demonstrate an understanding of the operation of the entire economy, combined with a degree of social responsibility, that few industrial managers have yet possessed.[9] Associations that are independent of the center and acting as monopolies, a situation that did not arise in East Europe, might also alter considerably the nature of classical market competition. This latter possibility raises some fascinating problems which deserve a brief digression.

Traditional economic theory deals with situations in which large numbers of relatively small decision-making units interact; and traditional organization theory deals with the situation within one administrative hierarchy. But relatively little attention has been paid to the operation of an entire system composed of a relatively small number of decision-making units—which I shall call a "bloc economy"—with no effective higher authority. The blocs could be composed of a series of monopolies, each in a different industry; or a small number of large vertically integrated enterprises, each producing a wide number of finished products; or a small number of regional authorities representing all the enterprises in the area; or a small number of enterprises grouped accord-

---

9. Some monopoly powers can, of course, be limited by the central authorities. In Poland, for instance, the associations can regulate prices used in transactions between constituent enterprises, but not between these enterprises and the rest of the economy.

ing to sociological and political differences, as in Nazi Germany before 1937.[10]

If there is no central organization with power over these blocs, the economy and polity might function in a much different manner than they would in either a centrally planned or a market economy. We have, unfortunately, no adequate models of bloc economies that would allow us to predict and test this behavior.[11] Although it does not appear that such "bloc economies" were developing in East Europe (with the possible exception of international economic relations within the Council of Mutual Economic Assistance where the nations negotiated with each other over projects of allegedly common interest),[12] the possibility certainly has existed.

2. The Distribution of Decision-making Powers

Distribution of decision-making powers can only be investigated by focusing on particular types of decisions. Although many different decisions can be discussed in this regard, enterprise powers with regard to current input and output choices seem most appropriate for extensive treatment, especially if these decisions are broken up into major components. Relevant information on such matters is presented in Tables 7–4 and 7–5.

For both input and output decision-making by enterprises, the most critical question to ask of the reforms is to what degree the previous system of material balancing and central supply allocation of important raw

10. Arthur Schweitzer's theory of partial fascism [*Big Business and the Third Reich* (Bloomington, Ind.: 1964), Chapter 11] focuses on the relationships among four major blocs: the army, the police, the party, and big business. Within business, however, he also notes that there were several blocs, namely artisans, small businesses, and big business, and it was splits within the army and big business that allowed the Nazis to gain control over the economy after 1937.

11. A general theory on these matters might be developed either from some of the mathematical literature about the "core" of an economy or else from some of the speculations of Michael Polanyi about "polycentrism" (see *The Logic of Liberty* [Chicago: 1951]).

Among economists concerned with interest in concrete economic phenomena (rather than abstract mathematics or ideology) I have found little speculation about how "economies of monopolies" or other types of bloc economies would function. Three important exceptions to this generalization are: Joan Robinson, "A World of Monopolies," Chapter 27 in her *Economics of Imperfect Competition* (London: 1933); a model of price formation in a world of vertical monopolies that is discussed by Jan Tinbergen, *Economic Policy: Principles and Design* (Amsterdam: 1956); and Robin Marris, "Is the Corporate Economy a Corporate State," *American Economic Review,* LXII, May 1972, pp. 103–115.

12. For more details on the Council of Mutual Economic Assistance, see Frederic L. Pryor, *The Communist Foreign Trade System* (Cambridge, Mass.: 1963); or Michael Kaser, *Comecon,* 2nd ed. (London: 1967).

materials and intermediate goods has survived. The material balancing and central material allocation system was the keystone of the Stalinist economic administration designed to replace the "anarchy of the market" with "purposive and planned activity." It was the primary allocation device in all the East European nations except Yugoslavia until the reforms of the sixties. On the output side the material balance system meant that sellers were limited to their choice of products and customers; and on the input side this system was associated with obligatory input norms.

In the Soviet Union, Poland, and Romania, the former material balancing and central supply allocation system was continued intact with few changes. In East Germany and Bulgaria this allocation system was considerably reduced in scope (see Table 8–3 for East Germany) but in 1969 to 1970 such changes were reversed and in East Germany, at least, the step toward the former system was almost total. In Czechoslovakia and Hungary the material balancing and central allocation systems were almost completely eliminated although, in 1970, they seem to have been reintroduced in the former nation with a quite limited scope. Only in Yugoslavia, which abandoned the central allocation system over a decade ago, was such administrative allocation completely missing. It should be clear that the greater the remnants of the administrative allocation methods, the smaller the sphere for market activity.

The enterprise can receive several types of obligatory output targets. From the center or the associations (Table 7–4), aggregate targets include gross output goals (maintained primarily only in Romania) or aggregate sales, profit, or cost targets. (If two of the last three goals are explicitly given, there are severe limitations placed on the third as well.) Finally, on a more specific level we have output targets for major products or even more detailed product-mix goals. Until the reforms, the enterprises in all East European nations except Yugoslavia (where the enterprises already had extensive decision-making power) received such obligatory targets at regular intervals (three months or less).[13]

Leaving aside Yugoslavia (where the enterprises had considerable autonomy from the center before the reforms) and Romania (where the enterprises have apparently lost much of their autonomy to the new associations), in the other nations the enterprises gained in decision-making through the reforms. However, in the Soviet Union, East Germany, and Poland this broadening of enterprise property rights was relatively minor and more in the nature of a release from "petty tutelage" than a signifi-

13. Unfortunately, information about the frequency with which obligatory targets are given to enterprises is difficult to obtain for the postreform period, especially in the light of the experimentation and confusion that has occurred because of the reforms. Nevertheless, for those countries still with input targets, the quarterly plans do not appear to have been dropped.

TABLE 7–4

Indicators of Postreform Output Decision Powers of Enterprises in East Europe[a]

Country	Maintenance of Material Balancing and Central Supply Allocation System	Obligatory Enterprise Output Targets from Center or Associations			Comments
		Value Aggregates	Major Output Targets in Physical Units	Product Mix	
Soviet Union	Yes	Profits, sales	Yes	Yes, but less detailed	Fewer indicators; gross output target supposedly (but not actually)
Bulgaria	Yes, but reduced in scope	Sales	Primarily "basic goods"	Not clear	Fewer indicators; more planning from below until 1969
Czechoslovakia	Only few products, esp. in 1968; partial reintroduction in 1970	None until 1970	Formally few (violated in 1967) until 1970	No	Major expansion of enterprise decision power until mid-1969; binding goals then reintroduced
East Germany	Yes	Profits, costs	Yes	Yes, but supposedly less detailed	Gross output target dropped, relatively little change in enterprise autonomy
Hungary	Only few products	None	Only few products	No	Major expansion of enterprise decision powers; major decrease of power of center
Poland	Yes	Sales, costs	Yes	Yes, but supposedly less detailed	For some products, old indicators still used
Romania	Yes	Sales, profits, gross output	Yes	Yes	Enterprises have lost some decision-making power to associations
Yugoslavia	No	None	No	No	Little change from before reform

a. Targets for export production are discussed later in this section.

TABLE 7-5

Indicators of Postreform Input Decision Powers of Enterprises in East Europe[a]

Country	Average Enterprise Wage Payments	100% Guaranteed Wage Norms	Enterprise Labor Force	Enterprise Wage Fund	Material Norms from Center or Associations	Can Center or Associations Redistribute Working Capital among Enterprises?	Comments
Soviet Union	Yes	Apparently yes	No, but labor productivity norms	Yes	Yes, for improtant products	Yes	Obligatory targets less detailed than before
Bulgaria	Yes	No	Apparently no	Apparently no	Yes, for importants products	Apparently yes	Targets much less detailed than before, until 1969
Czechoslovakia	Yes	No	No	No	Only very few products	Yes, but very limited	Major change from previous system, until 1970
East Germany	Yes	Yes	?	Influenced by association	Yes	Apparently yes	Degree of VVB influence unclear
Hungary	Yes	Only workers	Some	Some	Only very few products	No	Major change from previous system
Poland	Yes	Probably yes	Ceilings	Ceilings	Yes	Apparently yes	Little real change from previous system
Romania	Yes	Yes	Ceilings	Yes	Yes	Yes	Apparently little real change
Yugoslavia	No	No	No	No	No	No	Little change from previous system

a. Norms of import use are discussed later in this section.

cant change. In Czechoslovakia and Hungary the enterprises experienced a much more extensive increase in power and approached (but not reached) the Yugoslav situation. Finally, in Bulgaria the enterprises appear to have gained in decision-making power but the exact division of powers between the enterprises and the associations is not clear, a factor that may have contributed to the retreat toward greater central influence after 1968.

Turning to input decisions (Table 7–5), it is useful to separate obligatory labor and wage targets from use-of-capital and material-input targets. The pattern of the reform is complex.

In all countries except Yugoslavia, the enterprises have had little role in the determination of their average wage payments, which have been decided at the center. Indeed, in many countries they have little role in determining average wages paid for particular types of work. In Czechoslovakia wages were supposed to be determined in conjunction with the enterprises and the labor unions, but such a system was not implemented. In Bulgaria, norms for average enterprise wages appeared to be imposed from above, although the logic of the reform did not at first point in this direction. In most of the nations, the "basic wage" has been guaranteed, so that if the enterprise performed poorly, it could not cut wages but had to look for other ways to meet its deficit. The implications of these wage-setting methods are difficult to trace, especially since the new wage systems have not been long in operation. However, if wages were settled outside, the enterprises (or even association) might set relative prices differently than if this were a matter between the enterprise and the workers, much as in the West.

It must be emphasized that if the average wage and the total wage fund are determined for the enterprises from above, the enterprises have only a narrow scope for decision-making in regard to their manpower. Such a situation occurred in the Soviet Union, Poland, Romania, and apparently in East Germany; while in the remaining countries, neither wage fund nor manpower targets were imposed. In Hungary changes in the wage fund were heavily taxed.

Obligatory material input-norms are, of course, tied in with the material balance and the central supply allocation systems. In Bulgaria, East Germany, Poland, and Romania, the associations were given a supply function which brought with it the power to set material norms for the subordinated enterprises; it further appears that these associations received aggregate input norms from the center which they fulfilled, so that in this sense they acted as transmission belts between the center and the enterprises. Nevertheless, the extent to which the association received such norms is quite unclear and we must be cautious in drawing quick conclusions.

In the Soviet Union the center tried to maintain strong powers in setting material input norms. Only in Czechoslovakia, Hungary, and Yugoslavia, which had more or less broken away from the former administrative allocation system, did the enterprises themselves have wide powers in selecting material inputs although, it must be added, in Czechoslovakia and Hungary certain informal rationing of scarce materials continued to exist.

The situation with regard to obligatory use-of-capital norms is unclear. For fixed capital a number of countries had norms tying capital to sales or output, but the extent to which these norms were enforced is difficult to ascertain. With regard to working capital, only enterprises in Hungary, Yugoslavia, and, to a more limited extent, Czechoslovakia had relatively strong control over such funds, while in the remaining countries the powers of the associations over such working capital appeared considerable.

In addition to the input norms, there were also controls on unit costs that were sometimes tied to input-norms or to the quotas of materials for production. The exact role of these controls and their actual enforcement differed in different years and can not be determined for most East European countries with any exactitude.

Tables 7–4 and 7–5 show consistent patterns for the postreform systems. Only enterprises in Czechoslovakia, Hungary, and Yugoslavia began to have that independence of decision-making for both inputs and outputs which is a prerequisite for the successful operation of a market system. In the remaining cases, the central administrative hierarchy maintained considerable power and the operation of market forces was therefore severely limited or extinguished. In this latter group of nations, the broadening of enterprise decision-making was slight.

In addition to a change in the degree of decision-making power of enterprises, which represented a change in managerial property rights, there was also a shift in power in most countries from the center (state planning office and ministries) to the associations. Public discussion about the associations mentioned seven major functions for them to fulfill (except in Hungary and Yugoslavia where the associations were weak) which previously had been either the prerogative of the center or else were fulfilled in part by agents of the center with relatively little public notice. These functions were the guiding of technological development of the industrial branch; the carrying out of market research; the drawing up of both long- and short-run branch plans; the distributing of investment funds; the fulfilling of foreign trade functions (see below); the obtaining of critical supplies for the constituent enterprises; and the carrying out of certain administrative and control tasks delegated by the center.

The degree to which the associations actually assumed such functions varied considerably among nations. In East Germany the involvement of the associations in these tasks has appeared the deepest and the Romanians seem to have patterned their reforms to some extent after the East German changes in this regard. In the Soviet Union, Bulgaria, and Poland the associations appeared to have considerably less delegated powers although for all countries a firm judgment on these matters is impossible to form. As noted, in Yugoslavia and Hungary the associations were weak and, moreover, were agents of the enterprises. In Czechoslovakia the associations appeared to have been losing power to the enterprises—at least until the end of 1968. Since the available materials on the actual functioning of the associations are extremely scant and opaque, these generalizations are based more upon vague impressions from the economic literature than upon precise information.

In any case, I believe the successful functioning of a socialist market system would require the withering away of the operational powers of the associations and a limiting of their activities to such matters as market research, product or process research and development, and other tasks traditionally fulfilled by trade associations and similar organizations in the West. If the associations increase in power and individual enterprises become similar to operating divisions of multidivisional corporations, the economy will be characterized not only by enormous agglomeration but also by a high degree of monopoly power in individual industries, a system which would probably have many negative features.

One last element of the distribution of property rights requires brief comment, namely the apparent increase in the sharing of decision-making powers in various industrial units through the introduction of various types of collegial arrangements or, in the terminology of Appendix A-1, corporate rights. Some measure of this phenomenon is given in Table 7–7.

In Yugoslavia the principle of one-man responsibility gave way in the early fifties to collective responsibility and in Czechoslovakia a move in this direction was cut short after the removal of Dubček in 1969. In Romania the enterprise manager was bound by the decisions of the collective body unless he successfully appealed its decision to the association. Considerable confusion about the function of these collective bodies arose and their form changed in 1971; in practice, one-man responsibility appears to have been preserved for the most part. In Hungary and Czechoslovakia there was considerable discussion about increasing the power of the trade unions and, in certain cases, assigning them a formal veto over certain types of management decisions; little seems to have come of these suggestions, however.

In most of the other countries the introduction of collegial elements

TABLE 7-6

Collegial Elements in Decision-making in East Europe

| Country | Intermediate Units | | Enterprises | | Party and union roles |
	One-man responsible	Advisory board and composition	One-man responsible	Worker Councils or advisory boards	
Soviet Union	Yes	No	Yes	No	Advisory
Bulgaria	Yes	Economic Council; included enterprise managers; abolished January 1971	Yes	Advisory Production Committees included workers; downgraded after 1968 and powers shared with union	Advisory
Czechoslovakia	Yes	Board of Directors; includes enterprise managers	Yes, but tried to change	Enterprise Councils (type of workers council) est. in 1968 in some enterprises; downgraded, 1969; discontinued, 1970	Union role strengthened; party role weakened until 1969
East Germany	Yes	Social Council; include "leading members of branch"; also outsiders	Yes	Advisory Production Committees which include workers	Advisory
Hungary	Yes	Advisory boards in some associations; composition unknown	Yes	Supervisory Board includes top enterprise personnel and outsiders	Advisory
Poland	Yes	Collegium; include enterprise managers	Yes	Advisory Workers Self-Management Conferences	Advisory
Romania	Yes, partly	Administration Council; include enterprise managers	Yes, partly	Board of Directors; also Enterprise Management Board with representatives chosen by Worker Assemblies	Advisory
Yugoslavia	No	?	No	Workers Council	Advisory

in decision-making appears to be small in actuality, for the various councils had only advisory powers.[14] The inclusion of managers on advisory boards of the associations could act to increase efficiency by saving certain types of information costs but the extent of such savings was probably small; in any case, little concrete information is yet available about the functioning of these advisory boards.

3. Sources of Potential Competition

Most descriptions of the organization of East European industry leave the impression that the industrial hierarchy was relatively monolithic and that few sources of potential competition could exist until the central administrative apparatus was deprived of its powers. This is not entirely true, however, for the state enterprises controlled by the center or by branch associations were not the only sources of supply in the East European nations. Alternative sources included industries outside the direct purview of the center or the associations (e.g., those enterprises controlled by local governments or cooperatives); secondary suppliers of particular products where such products were not included in the plan; and imports. The existence of such sources could have provided flexibility even when centrally controlled state enterprises had little decision-making autonomy and could have added limits to potential monopolistic behavior in cases where socialist market elements were introduced. Each of these sources of potential competition needs to be explored.

a. *Central versus noncentral industries.* The ministries and the associations have controlled only the "centrally administered" state enterprises (although the associations have had certain powers over local industries in East Germany). Alternative domestic sources of supply outside this hierarchy included the smaller enterprises that were controlled by local and provincial organs (including in the Soviet Union, the republics,

14. I have omitted discussion of changes in the role of the Communist party for this is an extremely intricate matter for which little information is available. In most of the nations the party's role did not appear to change greatly. In the late 1960s in Romania, however, Nicolae Ceauşescu tried to fuse party and state in the person of one man at key control points which greatly changed the party role and, perhaps, reduced collegiality although the extent to which this was carried out on the enterprise level before this policy was reassessed in the early 1970s is not known. In China during the 1960s collegiality increased with a rise in party control of enterprises, combined with a number of campaigns such as the "three taking-part-in" movement in which workers were urged to participate in enterprise decision-making. [For China, see Franz Schurmann, *Ideology and Organization in Communist China* (Berkeley: 1970), revised edition, Chapter 4; and Barry M. Richman, *Industrial Society in Communist China* (New York: 1969), Chapters 8 and 9.]

oblasti, kraia, and cities), producer cooperatives, small private enterprises, and (in East Germany only), the half-state enterprises. These served as a potential source of competition to the large central enterprises and are important to examine in a quantitative manner.

One available quantitative measure of the importance of these noncentral enterprises is the ratio of their work force to the total labor force in industry. Although such a measure has an upward bias because these noncentral industries employed more labor intensive technologies, no better comparative measurement can be devised. Using this indicator, a wide variation between the different countries can be observed.

The share of workers and employees in the noncentrally managed enterprises in mining and manufacturing during the mid-1960s was quite high in East Germany (36 percent), Poland (30 percent), and Hungary (27 percent) and was relatively low in Romania (16 percent) and Czechoslovakia (8 percent).[15] Although comparable data are not available for the remaining countries, scattered evidence suggests that such ratios for Bulgaria and the Soviet Union were closer to the first than the second group.[16]

For two countries, East Germany and Poland, disaggregated data are available so that the patterns for mining and manufacturing can be examined in detail. These data, along with other data on extrabranch production which are discussed below, are presented in Table 7–7. How might we explain the very striking pattern that is found in the percentage of workers and employees in noncentral enterprises in the different industrial branches?

As noted in Chapter II (Section D-1-d), industries can be arranged along a spectrum; at one end we have the "heavy" industries which are characterized by enterprises with large labor and capital inputs and a high degree of market concentration; at the other end are "light" industries which are characterized by enterprises with relatively small labor and

15. Except for Hungary the data are for 1966 and 1967 and come from the national statistical yearbooks. For Czechoslovakia an estimate of the private sector (which is extremely small) had to be made. The datum for Hungary is for 1960 and comes from the Hungarian Central Statistics Office, to which I would like to express my gratitude. For Hungary, data on workers and employees in producer cooperatives and the private sector are included in the yearbook.

16. For Bulgaria data are available on workers and employees in producer cooperatives and private enterprises and if we make the reasonable assumption that employment in locally controlled industries is roughly the same (which is the case for most other East European nations), then Bulgaria probably had between one-fourth and one-third of its industrial labor force in noncentral industries. For the Soviet Union producer cooperatives and private enterprises were quite unimportant, but it is known that the production directed by the various territorial units was significant.

capital inputs and a low degree of market concentration. One might suspect that the degree of central control would be higher in the "heavy" industries and that the degree of local control would be greater in the "light" industries. Statistical tests of this conjecture can be easily made.

For both East Germany and Poland, the share of noncentral industries was inversely and significantly (.05 level) related to the "heavy-light" industry rankings, with Kendall rank order correlation coefficients respectively .725 and .485. The importance of noncentral enterprises was highest in the clothing, leather products, and lumber and wood products and was lowest in such industries as primary metals, mining, and transport equipment; these two groups of industries form the opposite poles of the light-heavy spectrum. The conjecture is confirmed.

With the possible exception of those countries changing from a territorial to a ministerial command system, it is likely that the reforms of the mid-1960s had little effect on the relative importance of the noncentral enterprises. This can be seen from the data for the three countries for which time-series information is available. For East Germany the ratio representing the relative importance of noncentral enterprises was roughly the same in 1955 and 1966. It rose somewhat in the late 1950s when the nation adopted an industrial command system based partly on territories, rather than on ministries (an imitation of the Soviet *sovnarkhoz* experiment), but fell when this system was abandoned. For Czechoslovakia the ratio appeared roughly constant during the 1960s (unfortunately, data for the 1950s are not available). In Romania, the ratio fell considerably, primarily because the noncentral enterprise sector remained roughly the same in size while the centrally managed enterprises grew at a rapid rate.

Given this quantitative picture about the relative importance of the noncentral industries, we now turn to several factors that must be taken into account in interpreting the data.

First, because the data are available only at a high level of aggregation, we cannot be sure that the same products were manufactured in both central and noncentral industries. That is, the data in the table represent an upper limit to which the noncentral enterprises acted as an alternative supply source at that time. For such enterprises actually to have served as a source of competition might have required a considerable change in their product-mix which, in turn, would have meant that an accessible source for capital would have been a prerequisite for realizing their full competitive potential.

Second, these noncentral enterprises were generally small and had less capital equipment than centrally managed enterprises. They might have been able to serve as a source of flexibility to the economy, a role fulfilled by small-size enterprises in market economies. However, for pro-

TABLE 7-7

Potential Sources of Competition by Industrial Branch in East Europe[a]

Industry and ISIC Numbers[1]		Percentage of Workers and Employees in Noncentral Enterprises		Extrabranch production Ratios (Potential Intrahierarchical Competition)[4]	
		Poland 1967[2]	East Germany 1965[3]	East Germany 1965[5]	Hungary 1959[6]
10–19	Mining	0%	15%	12%	2%
20,21,22	Food processing, beverages, tobacco	74	71	8	1
23	Textiles	12	41	2	7
24	Clothing	91	82	9	5
25,26	Lumber and wood working	55	73	7	8
27	Paper and paper products	31	40	13	4
28	Printing and publishing	49	42	10	0
29	Leather and fur products	67	64	6	5
30	Rubber products	26	{16	{4	7
31,32	Chemicals, petroleum, and coal products	24			{8
33	Nonmetalic mineral products	36	37	9	5
34	Primary metals	0	4	13	7
35	Metal products except machines	42	49	36	72

ISIC					
36	Machinery except elec. and trans.	8	29	16	{8
38	Transport equipment	10	18	6	8
37	Electrical machinery	14	25	14	6
39	Other	92	22	8	2
	All mining and manufacturing[7]	31	37	10	14

a. The table notes are below.

(1) ISIC industrial numbers are only approximate since the available data are too highly aggregated to adjust to the exact ISIC categories.

(2) Metallurgy includes the mining of metallic ores; "other industries" is unspecified. Data for workers and employees in the central and noncentral industries come from Głowny urząd statystyczny, *Rocznik Statystyczny 1968* (Warsaw: 1968).

(3) "Other industries" are precision goods and optics; "wood products" include "cultural goods." Data are based on workers and employees in the mining and manufacturing industries and members of producer cooperatives and private enterprises in the manufacturing-handicraft sector. The data come from Staatliche Zentralverwaltung fuer Statistik, *Statistisches Jahrbuch der Deutschen Demokratischen Republik* (East Berlin) for 1966 and 1967.

(4) The exact concept is explained later in the text. The original tables for the two nations were published in value data and contained data only for the socialist (East Germany) or state (Hungary) industrial branches. Since comparable production data in the same prices for the private sector (and, for East Germany, industrial handicrafts) were not available, these ratios were weighted according to the workers and employees in the various socialist or state industries and were combined with employment data for the other sectors to calculate the total ratios. Underlying this procedure is the reasonable assumption that such "production overlap" occurs only in the state sector.

(5) The data come from the sources cited in note (3).

(6) The data come from the following publications of the Központi Statisztikai Hivatal: *A magyar népgazdasóg ágazati kapcsolatainak mérlege, 1959 évben* (Budapest: 1961); and *Statisztikai evkönyv 1959* (Budapest: 1960).

(7) The total ratios in the first two columns of this table are one percentage point higher than the aggregate data presented in the text because electricity production (which is completely centrally controlled) is omitted.

duction with economies of scale or highly capital intensive technique, the noncentral industries were likely to have had higher costs;[17] and additional investment and an active market for investment funds would have been required for them to be able to compete with larger enterprises.

Third, noncentral enterprises might have had lower priorities for receiving scarce materials. These local enterprises were incorporated in varying degrees into the central system of allocation of inputs and outputs and as long as this central allocation system continued, any effective competition of the local versus the centrally controlled enterprises was limited. If the central allocation system had been cut back in scope, this input-factor might not hinder so greatly the competitive power of the noncentral enterprises.

Finally, the degree to which noncentral enterprises could and did sell outside their immediate geographical area is not clear. If, however, there were limitations in the form of limited transportation facilities or limited sales access, then again the noncentral enterprises could not have effectively competed against either each other or the centrally directed enterprises.

b. *Intrahierarchical competition.* Even if production were completely controlled by central industrial ministries or associations arranged along product lines, competition could still arise if the enterprises under central organs produced goods that did not lie in their assigned sphere of responsibility and if there were no effective central coordination of such auxiliary production.

This kind of situation is more than a theoretical possibility, especially in light of the myriads of complaints about "ministerial autarky" that are found in the East European economic literature. For instance, in the Soviet Union only 20 percent of total instrument production was carried out in factories designated for this purpose; while in the United States, this ratio was over 70 percent. In Soviet machine-building plants, 99 percent produced their own cog wheels; 84 percent, diecastings; 71 percent, iron castings; and 57 percent, nonferrous castings.[18] In evaluating such scattered evidence, it is difficult to decide whether these results were due to an unwieldy system of central planning and the need to circumvent it or to some special features of the Soviet Union such as its vast geographical expanse and communication problems.

17. Such cost advantages of state over cooperative industry are shown for Poland by John Michael Montias, *Central Planning in Poland* (New Haven: 1961), p. 215.

18. These and other similar data are cited by Alexander Woroniak, "Industrial Concentration in Eastern Europe: The Search for Optimum Size and Efficiency," in a forthcoming volume of essays published by the List Gesellschaft.

One method of analyzing these matters empirically is to measure the degree to which East European enterprises are vertically integrated; but the standard statistic for this purpose (the ratio of value-added to total sales) cannot be used with confidence because of the distorted prices of intermediate goods in these countries.

A more promising way to attack this problem is to start with data on the value of production by industrial branch (where industrial branch is defined in terms of the establishments whose most important products are classified as belonging to this branch). We then determine the value of production of the various goods that are manufactured by establishments outside the designated branch and calculate the ratio of this to the total production value of the specified branch. For instance, if establishments whose major products are machines produce 1000 rubles of goods and if other establishments outside the branch produce 150 rubles of machines, then the calculated ratio (which I call the extrabranch production ratio, or the E.B.P. ratio) is 15 percent. Proper data on these matters are available only for East Germany and Hungary, but the results warrant examination. By classifying the data according to the ISIC two-digit categories, comparisons can also be made with selected Western nations. Relevant data are presented in Table 7–7.

In East Germany and Hungary the aggregate E.B.P. ratios, which reflect the potential intrahierarchical competition, were respectively 10 and 14 percent. The somewhat higher ratio in Hungary was probably due to the larger size enterprises in the latter nation in the early 1960s, as shown in Table 7–2. The enterprise consolidation occurring in Hungary between 1960 and 1966 also undoubtedly led to a considerable increase in the E.B.P. ratio. From remarks in the Soviet economic literature, it appears that the E.B.P. ratio was probably much greater in the Soviet Union than in these two East European nations, but without adequate data we cannot draw definite conclusions.

To place these results in perspective, it is useful to note that in the early 1960s, the E.B.P. ratio was 7 percent in West Germany and 13 percent in the United States (where conglomerate enterprises were relatively more important).[19] Even allowing for certain noncomparabilities of the data,[20] these results suggest that the East European nations were not

19. The Western data co..ie from the United States Bureau of the Census, *1963 Enterprise Statistics,* Part I (Washington, D.C.: 1968), Table 6; and Statistisches Bundesamt, *Statistisches Jahrbuch fuer die Bundesrepublik 1967* (Wiesbaden: 1967).

20. There are several sources of incomparability:

The West German and United States data define production by the "establishment method" while the exact East German and Hungarian methods are not clear.

The raw data for the four nations are presented with somewhat different

greatly out of line with Western nations in the early 1960s and that the problem of "ministerial autarky" was not too pronounced, at least in the two nations for which we have data.

The pattern of E.B.P. ratios by individual branches presented in Table 7–7 also yields interesting information. From a theoretical standpoint it is difficult to decide the most important causal factors underlying this pattern but, at least, we can make comparisons with Western nations to gain more perspective. The rank orderings of the E.B.P. ratios for West Germany, East Germany, and the United States are significantly correlated with each other,[21] which suggests a "natural" pattern: metal products and machinery are among those branches with the highest E.B.P. ratios, while textiles and leather products have the lowest ratios. It must be noted, however, that the rank order of the Hungarian E.B.P. ratios by branches is not significantly related to those of any of the other three countries, a result that may be due either to a helter-skelter consolidation of enterprises by the Hungarians during the late 1950s or to the fact that the "natural" ranking admits of many exceptions.

Turning briefly to time-series data on the E.B.P. ratios, which are available only for East Germany, we see little change in these ratios from the mid-1950s to the mid-1960s. Since the enterprise consolidation drive was not strong in this nation, we should not have expected much change. If time-series data were available for Hungary or Czechoslovakia, a different picture might emerge.

In interpreting the E.B.P. ratios in terms of a competitive potential, several important considerations must be taken into account. First, for extrabranch production to prove an effective alternative source of supply, the central organs should not have a hand in planning such production. In some cases (e.g., Czechoslovakia in 1960) the center did indeed attempt to plan such production while in other cases (e.g., East Germany in the late sixties) the center apparently was content to exercise more indirect control through the fostering of voluntary "trade associations" of producers of particular goods lying outside of the branch under which the products are classified. At least in the East German case, complaints about the operation of such "trade associations" suggests that central

---

branch definitions and, since most data are highly aggregated to start with, few adjustments could be made.

The original data for the four nations are presented at different degrees of aggregation. However, results from experiments with United States and East German data suggest that relative differences between nations at one degree of aggregation are the same at other degrees of aggregation as well. Therefore, the aggregate Western E.B.P. ratios presented in the text could be estimated at the same degree of aggregation as the East European data.

21. Kendall rank order correlation coefficients were calculated for each pair of nations, where the data were arranged according to the branch categories of the nation with the most aggregated raw data.

control over the secondary producers was not great; indeed, the existence of some extrabranch production might have been due to the desire of producers to circumvent central control. Although reliable information about the degree of central control over extrabranch production in various nations is extremely scanty, I have the impression that it is slight and that extrabranch production has served to escape control by the center.

Second, a branch making products "belonging" to another branch would have to have sufficient power to maintain such production within its branch after it had become an important source. That is, if an enterprise in branch A began producing in large quantities some goods from branch B, it would have to be able to withstand bureaucratic pressures to have such production transferred to some enterprise or to the association in branch B. Unfortunately, we have no reliable information about the relative strength of forces in such bureaucratic infighting.

c. *Foreign trade as a source of competition.* Although a single domestic enterprise may produce a particular good, competition can still arise if imports are freely available; furthermore, the possibilities of an enterprise achieving high rewards by exporting may also induce an improvement of product quality and, in special conditions, even the quantity of production for the domestic market. For trade to serve as such a competitive stimulus, however, two conditions must be fulfilled: The links between domestic producing units and foreign markets must be relatively direct and flexible; and foreign prices must have some relation to domestic prices.

In the system operating in the 1950s in all East European nations except Yugoslavia, the state foreign trade enterprises served as a barrier between domestic producers and the outside world; furthermore, it was thought a virtue to separate domestic and world prices. Foreign trade as a source of competition to domestic producers was practically excluded. In the postreform situation, foreign trade has still been one of the most regulated sectors of the economy; nevertheless, important structural changes have taken place which have increased the competitive potential of foreign trade. Information on these matters is presented in Table 7–8.

It should be clear that much more direct connections between domestic producers and foreign markets were created in most countries, with the Soviet Union as the most notable exception. In certain cases this was the result of physically relocating the foreign trade enterprises at the headquarters of an association (as in East Germany); in most cases this occurred by permitting some associations (and, in several nations some enterprises) to export and import directly rather than through the state foreign trade enterprises. Thus one prerequisite of a competitive role of foreign trade was fulfilled in most of these nations.

TABLE 7–8

Indicators of Foreign Trade Reforms in East Europe

Country	Direct Trading Arrangements		Obligatory Enterprise Targets				Role of Exchange Rate and Relations between Domestic and World Market Prices	Special Incentives for Exports
	Associations	Enterprises	Exports		Imports			
			value	physical	value	physical		
Soviet Union	No	No	Yes	Yes	?	?	Exchange rate relatively realistic; no other adjustment of domestic to world prices so that domestic and foreign prices still split	Special bonuses to managers; subsidies
Bulgaria	Yes Both granted rights; but limited in 1968 and abolished in 1970	Yes	Yes	Yes	Yes	?	From 1964–68 unrealistic exchange rate and split between domestic and foreign price structure maintained. Planned price reform supposed to link domestic and world prices	Enterprises can keep part of overplan export receipts; also subsidies
Czechoslovakia	Yes	Some	Yes	No	Yes	No	Shadow rate; also some attempt to align domestic and world prices of some exported and imported goods	Enterprises can keep part of export receipts; also subsidies
East Germany	Yes; co-responsible with F.T. ministry	A few	Yes but reduced	Yes	Yes?	Yes?	Shadow rate; no other adjustment of domestic to world prices	Enterprises can keep some of overplan export receipts; also special managerial bonuses and subsidies

Hungary	No	Many	No	No	No		Shadow rate; also some attempt to align domestic and world prices of exported and imported goods	Enterprises can keep part of export receipts; also special subsidies
Poland	Limited	A few	Yes	Yes but reduced	Yes	?	Shadow rate; split between foreign and domestic prices maintained until price reform of 1971 when a certain alignment of these prices took place	Special manager bonuses; also easier credit to exporting enterprises and subsidies
Romania	Yes	Yes	Yes	Yes	Yes	Yes	Unrealistic exchange rate and split between domestic and world prices maintained in most cases; however, some shadow rates used	Strong incentives
Yugoslavia	?	Yes, as before	No	No	No	No	Revaluation to realistic exchange rate; wide alignment of domestic and world prices	Enterprises can keep part of export receipts

The continual presence of obligatory foreign trade targets for production enterprises (in some cases, just in value terms) shows that the foreign trade sector was still highly controlled and the competitive potential of foreign trade was in part offset. Nevertheless, some flexibility was introduced in Czechoslovakia, East Germany, Hungary and Yugoslavia by permitting exporting enterprises to keep a certain share of foreign currency receipts for importing purposes. Furthermore, Czechoslovakia and Hungary tried to increase flexibility even further by abandoning detailed export and import controls, while Yugoslavia, which had accomplished such reforms many years ago, tried to dismantle most of the few controls that still existed. Nevertheless, because of balance of payments difficulties, Czechoslovakia had to maintain tighter controls than originally envisioned. Moreover, despite disclaimers to the contrary, important foreign currency rationing procedures continued to exist in both Czechoslovakia and Hungary,[22] which again modified the competitive potential of foreign trade.

Turning briefly to price considerations (which are discussed in greater detail in the section D), most countries introduced realistic exchange rates or shadow exchange rates to bring the general level of domestic and world prices into rough alignment. (In most nations with shadow rates, different rates were used for socialist and capitalist nations.) In addition, several nations, notably Czechoslovakia and Hungary (and Poland in 1971), attempted to go further and to equate individual domestic prices to world market prices, at least for those goods that were exported and imported. The extent to which these price measures were carried out is not certain, especially since such a practice would, given a fixed exchange or shadow rate, lead to the "importation of foreign inflations"; in Hungary, at least, the price agency later began to have doubts about this practice.

In Yugoslavia, which went furthest in introducing foreign trade as a source of competition to domestic production, the goal to equalize domestic and world market prices was a critical element of the reform. Indeed, the main strategic thrust of the Yugoslav reforms (which included a devaluation of the exchange rate, a price reform, the introduction of

22. For instance, in Hungary machinery imports from the West were subject to high duties and in those cases where the purchase was financed from the enterprise's investment fund, an advance deposit was originally required for a period of two·years amounting to 150 percent of the purchase price. If the import was financed from bank credit, bank authorization was required for the import. There were additional quantitative restrictions on the importation of some raw materials and intermediate products as well as on all consumer goods. (Bela Balassa, "Economic Reform in Hungary," IBRD Economics Department Working Paper No. 25, September 1968). The advance deposit was eliminated in January 1971.

new procedures by which prices were to be changed, and the goal to move toward full convertibility of the dinar) was primarily toward the utilization of foreign trade for a competitive role. Unfortunately, reintroduction of certain exchange controls after the reforms subverted to a certain extent this aim.

In Czechoslovakia and Hungary, foreign trade as a source of competition received recognition but considerably less emphasis in the actual reform measures. Convertibility of the currency as a goal was mentioned but placed in the indefinite future. Large numbers of exceptions in the equalization of domestic and foreign prices were granted, and many high policy makers did not completely accept the idea that foreign trade and the international market should have greater influence in the domestic economy. In the remaining nations the strict controls on foreign trade still served to insulate the domestic market from the potential competitive effects of imports. $W \partial G_s$

4. Summary

Viewing the postreform East European economies, three major structural barriers to market socialism have been analyzed.

First, in most countries the state enterprises had only limited independent powers of decision-making and various elements of the former administrative allocation methods still remained. Only in Czechoslovakia, Hungary, and Yugoslavia did the enterprises have considerable autonomy in the choices of inputs and outputs.

Second, in most countries the state enterprises were very large so that if central control were relaxed, they had quasi-monopolistic positions. Such tendencies toward monopoly were reinforced in many countries by the existence of associations with considerable administrative powers over the enterprises and, in some countries, considerable independence from the center. Czechoslovakia and Hungary, which were among the leaders in giving enterprises autonomy, had the largest state enterprises and, therefore, faced most directly the danger that their attempts toward some type of guided market socialism might result in some severe difficulties because of monopolistic practices by large state enterprises.

Third, the importance of these two factors was modified by certain alternative sources of supply. In regard to potential competition from noncentral enterprises, East Germany and Poland appeared high on the scale, while Romania and Czechoslovakia appeared low. Potential competition by enterprises in one branch producing goods that were primarily produced in another branch did not appear to be great. Foreign trade as a source of competitive pressure was quite unimportant in most countries except Czechoslovakia, Hungary, and Yugoslavia, and even in Czechoslovakia and Hungary, such foreign competitive pressures were limited.

In Poland and the Soviet Union the structural changes of the system appeared minor (except for the change from the "territorial" to "production" principle of administration in the Soviet Union) and the reforms were designed primarily to improve the functioning of the centrally administered system. The structural changes in East Germany and Romania were much more extensive, especially in the increase in decision-making powers of the associations, but the reforms had the same basic motives. In Bulgaria few of the major contemplated structural changes were introduced and allowed to function very long; and in Czechoslovakia, although major structural changes were introduced, inconsistencies between system parts were not resolved before the reforms began to be dismantled after the invasion. In both countries either reform motives were more mixed or else the reformers had to make more compromises. Only in Hungary and Yugoslavia were the reforms aimed unambiguously toward some form of market socialism and were the structural changes (which were major only in Hungary) introduced systematically to achieve this end.

D. Economic Mechanisms

The analysis of the postreform economic systems of East Europe has focused up to now primarily on organizational aspects and the distribution of control rights. For an analysis of property rights, however, this is only part of the story. More particularly, we must now consider the major influences on the ways in which these control rights were exercised, which focuses attention on information flows (particularly with regard to costs and prices) and incentives facing decision-makers. From such an analysis, insight can be gained into the adjustment mechanisms of these economies that brought about micro-economic balance, i.e., that equated supply for particular goods and services with their demand.

1. Reforms in Pricing and the Calculation of Costs

The role of the price system is crucial, not only in analyzing the degree to which market principles have actually been introduced in the economy but also in seeing how micro-economic imbalances might arise. Since the principles of price formation in most of the East European nations allegedly were based on their calculation of average production costs, it is useful to start with a brief summary of the cost side.

a. *Cost calculations.* In a perfectly functioning market, relative prices reflect relative opportunity costs; this means that in the calculation of costs for a particular good, the opportunity costs of the factors of production and intermediate products are taken properly into account. Relevant information on the principles of cost calculation in East Europe with regard to production factors is presented in Table 7–9.

By 1970 all nations except Poland had carried out a revaluation of assets or were taking steps toward this goal. Such a measure, combined with the use of new depreciation schedules (which most nations also introduced) led to a more accurate appraisal of one important cost element.

Moreover, all nations except Romania placed a charge on capital. However, except for certain branches of manufacturing in the Soviet Union and East Germany, this charge was relatively low. The degree to which such capital charges accurately reflected the true scarcity of capital is open to doubt.

These capital charges differed between nations in several important ways that deserve comment. In the Soviet Union and East Germany, the charge was differentiated by branch of manufacture, while in the other nations there was a greater degree of uniformity among branches. In some nations such as the Soviet Union, the charge was on the gross value of capital; however, in others, it was on the net (depreciated) value. In some nations such as Bulgaria and Hungary, fixed and circulating (inventories, etc.) capital were treated similarly, while in other nations such as Czechoslovakia and Poland, the charges on these two types of capital differed. Further, in all countries there was some spread in the interest rate structure on bank loans; compared to the charge on fixed capital, the loan charge was higher in nations such as Hungary and lower in nations such as East Germany.

Although before the reforms an interest charge on funds borrowed from the bank was a common feature, the reforms in all countries were aimed toward financing more investment through the banks rather than through grants from the government. This meant, of course, that new investment was forced to more than pay for itself which, in turn, was a considerable improvement over the prereform systems where there were few effective incentives from the cost side to prevent waste of investment grants.

Finally, in only three nations—the Soviet Union, Hungary, and Yugoslavia—were there formal rental charges on land and natural resources; in the Soviet Union the calculation as a charge per unit of production defeats part of the rationale for a lump sum rent. Other nations such as Czechoslovakia, East Germany, and Poland had differential prices for raw materials mined in different parts of the nation that served partly the

TABLE 7–9

Elements of Cost Calculations in the Postreform Systems in East Europe

Country	Revaluation of Assets	Charge on Capital in Mining and Manufacturing	Interest on Bank Loans	Rental Charges
Soviet Union	Planned; not sure if carried out	5 to 12% charge on fixed and circulating capital (gross value) and differentiated by industrial branch	Yes, and varied	Differential charges per unit of production for a few raw materials; also differentially set profit norms
Bulgaria	Planned by end of 1968; not sure if carried out	5% charge on fixed and circulating capital, but some branch exceptions; in 1968, rate lowered to 3% with some exceptions	Yes, and varied; raised in 1968	Has an excess profit tax that serves a similar function
Czecho-slovakia	Yes	6% charge on fixed capital (net value), but some exceptions; 2% on circulating capital	Yes, and quite varied	No, but differential zonal prices for raw materials
East Germany	Yes	0 to 9% charge on fixed capital (gross value) and circulating capital; differentiated by branch	Yes; 2 to 5%	No, but differential zonal prices for raw materials and differentially set profit norms
Hungary	Yes	5% uniform charge on fixed (gross value) and circulating capital, but some exceptions	Yes, roughly 8% but many exceptions	Yes

Poland	Only in 1960	5% charge on fixed capital (net value), but many exceptions; no charge on circulating capital	Yes, and varied	No, but differential zonal prices for raw materials; also differentially set profit norms
Romania	Yes, December 1968	None yet	Yes, and varied	None yet
Yugoslavia	Yes	4% on fixed and circulating capital and slight differentiation by branch. Was "higher" before, but more exceptions so that average was lower	Yes, and quite varied	Yes

same function as a rent calculated as a percent of production. Bulgaria had an excess profits tax that partly served a rental function, but it was not considered a cost element. In a similar manner the Soviet Union, East Germany, and Poland had obligatory profit-norms and payments to the state based on such norms that served in an imperfect manner to wipe out profits due to favorable location or other factors unrelated to enterprise production efforts; such profit deductions again were not formal cost elements (but, of course, were a "cost" when considered from the viewpoint of the net income left to the enterprise manager).

For determining the opportunity costs of production, the postreform methods of cost calculations represented a distinct improvement over previous methods except in Romania (which retained the old system) and Yugoslavia (where the prereform cost calculation rules were relatively "rational"). This evaluation is based mainly on their improved handling of capital charges, for several objections from an opportunity cost standpoint can still be raised: The capital charges did not necessarily represent the scarcity value of capital; the variation in capital charges introduced an element of arbitrariness; and the rental charges (or pseudo-rents) contained a number of additional distorting elements.

b. *Price calculations*. With such information on cost determination we can now turn to the methods by which prices were calculated. Primary attention in this section is paid to producer prices and we are particularly interested in determining the degree to which prices were based on marginal costs and fluctuated according to changing supply and demand relationships. Relevant information for the East European nations is given in Table 7–10. There are a number of complicated aspects of price building in these nations that require close attention.

There was considerable confusion with regard to the basic conception of price setting in certain East European nations. One Western commentator has noted that for Poland "according to the official theories, prices are supposed to be flexible and stable, to reflect demand and to direct demand, to redistribute income, to promote efficiency, and to preserve full employment by keeping in existence enterprises which incur losses."[23] Such a contradiction of goals has appeared in the price reforms of other countries as well. Nevertheless, certain types of principles can be discerned.

In all countries (except Yugoslavia) one basic aim of price formation of producer goods was to eliminate net subsidies to individual industrial branches (although not necessarily cross-subsidies within branches).[24]

23. Leon Smolinski, "Planning Reforms in Poland," *Kyklos,* September 1968, pp. 498–514.
24. Cross-subsidies are transfers of funds from profitable to unprofitable enterprises under the same ministerial control.

Basing prices on average branch costs was one method of achieving this aim although, of course, it defeated the aims of those favoring marginal cost pricing.

Price-setting was often accomplished by the application of the so-called one- or two-channel approaches, terms that require brief explanation. Much discussion of price-setting principles in the East European nations has been in terms of the proper method for distributing differences between prices and cost ("profits") among products, and schools have grown up favoring uniform markups of the wage fund, or of prime costs, or of fixed capital used in production. The so-called two-channel approach provides for a percentage markup of both the wage fund and total capital (usually fixed and circulating funds) and represents a compromise between two pricing schools.[25] Nevertheless, such a formula can be justified as providing an adjustment for the relative scarcity values of capital and labor. The "one-channel" approach provides for a markup on a single magnitude such as prime costs in East Germany. In all cases, however, it is argued that the markup should allow the final price to cover not only the costs of labor, depreciation, and intermediate products, but the interest on capital as well. In such a situation the distinction emphasized strongly by various East European commentators between price systems where the capital charges are "included as part of cost" or "deducted from profits" does not seem very important; the major effect of such differences in price-setting methods is not in the actual prices set (which should be similar) but rather in the calculation of bonus funds and taxes.

Both one- and two-channel pricing rules can give rise to many complications. If any markup of prime costs or wages is employed, then it is impossible to have uniform capital charges, profit rates, and markups over all industries without introducing taxes that vary according to industry. Otherwise, either the capital charge or the profit rate or the

---

The East German practice of using future cost norms (so-called progressive costs) might have been an exception to this attempt to eliminate net subsidies if such future cost norms were lower than current average costs. Without knowing the assumptions made about changes in productivity and wages, we cannot make a judgment about the impact of the price changes on net subsidies.

25. The different positions may be more easily seen with the use of formulae. Let P = price; F = fixed capital; D = depreciation; W = total wages; I = cost of intermediate goods; and a and b, constants. The above mentioned proposals for "single-channel prices" include: $P = W + D + I + (a)(W)$; $P = W + D + I + (a)(W + D + I)$; and $P = W + D + I + (a)(F)$. The two-channel formula is: $P = W + D + I + (a)(F) + (b)(W)$, where F may also include inventories. Some interesting but controversial remarks about the two-channel prices are made by Václav Holešovsky, "The Double-Channel Aberration in East European Price Formulas," in Hans Raupach, ed., *Jahrbuch der Wirtschaft Osteuropas,* Band 2 (Munich: 1971), pp. 329–43.

TABLE 7-10

Price Formation of Producer Goods in Mining and Manufacturing in the Postreform Systems in East Europe[a]

Country	Fixed Prices — Basic Principles	Fixed Prices — Calculation of profit rate	Fixed Prices — Who Sets	Different Categories of Price — Type	Different Categories of Price — Coverage of manufacturing sales	Comments
Soviet Union	Average branch cost	Percent of fixed and circulating capital, but varied by industry	Major prices, center; other prices, lower units with formula	Primarily fixed	Almost all	—
Bulgaria	Proposed average branch costs, one channel	Various proposals but no final decision by 1970	Primarily center	Originally proposed system like Czechoslovakian and Hungarian; fervor for flexible prices waned by 1968	Originally proposed fixed prices	Difficult to distinguish in literature between "ought" and "will be" of coming reform; repeated delays in implementation
Czechoslovakia	Average branch costs; two channels	Percent of fixed and circulating capital	Center and branches together	Fixed .... Upper ceiling .. Band .... Free	a b 64% 78% 15 {11 14 7 11	a = total industrial products b = all consumer goods in 1967, all prices frozen, but freeze later relaxed; price freeze again mid 1969
East Germany	Average branch costs; one channel	Percent of value added	Some center; most, lower units with formula	Primarily fixed	All	Cost norms for raw materials are projected costs

	Average branch costs	Percent of fixed and circulating capital	Center or enterprise following formula		a	b	c	
					30%	3%	20%	
Hungary	Average branch costs; two channels	Percent of fixed and circulating capital	Center or enterprise following formula	Fixed	30%	3%	20%	a = raw materials intermediate goods
				Upper ceiling	40	17	30	b = industrial end products
				Band	2	2	27	c = consumer industrial goods
				Free	28	78	23	
Poland	Average branch costs; one channel	Sometimes percent of value added; sometimes percent of prime costs	Primarily center	Primarily fixed	Almost all			1967 reform of prices from factory only; purchase prices unchanged
Romania	Proposed average branch cost; one channel	Various proposals	Proposed primarily center	Proposed primarily fixed	Proposed almost all			Price reform only in discussion phase; quite orthodox analysis
Yugoslavia	World market prices (converted at realistic exchange rate) or domestic market clearing price	Residual	Federal and republic units		All manufacturing production			All prices frozen until 1967
				Fixed	53%			
				Free	47			

a. Particular terms such as "one-channel" or "two channel" prices are explained in the text. It is hard to characterize Soviet prices as either one- or two-channel since they were supposed to cover bonuses which were based partly on the capital stock and partly on the wage bill but which did not conform to either the one-channel or two-channel formulae. The Polish reform of producer prices of January 1, 1971, set up a strange type of two-channel price, but for those goods that were exported or imported, different pricing principles were employed. Since the price reform falls outside of the period under consideration, I only include data on the 1967 reform.

The Czechoslovakian price coverage data come from Michael Garmarnikow, "Prices and the Market," *East Europe*, XV, May 1966, pp. 10–16; and Kurt Wessely, "Wirtschaftsreformen in der Tacheschoslovakei," in Karl C. Thalheim and Hans-Herman Höhmann, eds., *Wirtschaftsreformen in Osteuropa* (Cologne: 1968). Hungarian price coverage data come from Balassa, and Richard D. Portes, "Economic Reforms in Hungary," *American Economic Review*, LX, May 1970, pp. 307–13.

markup on prime costs or wages must vary by industry. Although this is a simple consideration, it did not seem to have been given its due weight in the new price systems introduced in the various nations. Even in the relatively careful price reforms in Czechoslovakia and Hungary, the combination of relatively uniform capital charges combined with two-channel prices (with uniform markups on the wage bill) gave rise to some difficult problems concerning the "fairness" of the residual funds that were left to enterprises in different industries. In countries such as East Germany, Poland, Romania, and the Soviet Union where the great bulk of any enterprise funds were siphoned back to the center this was not, of course, a problem.

With the exception of Yugoslavia most fixed prices of producer goods in the East European nations were designed primarily to reflect some notion of average domestic production costs, rather than an equilibrium between demand and cost forces. However, for some goods that were exported or imported, demand factors were introduced in price formation by abandoning the cost formula and pricing these products according to the world market price, converted to domestic prices by realistic exchange or shadow rates (see Table 7–8).

For the prices that were not fixed, i.e., those that were free or fluctuated between upper and lower limits (band prices) or fluctuated below a ceiling, demand factors played a much more important role. However, such variable prices appeared only in Czechoslovakia, Hungary, and Yugoslavia and in the first two nations only for a quite limited number of products. It must be added that all three countries announced their intention of decreasing the products in the fixed price category and increasing the sphere of the flexible price categories. If the Yugoslav experience is relevant for the other nations, inflationary forces often negate such intentions and force the return to centrally fixed prices.

As noted in Table 7–10, prices were set primarily by central authorities. Such a situation is not necessarily incompatible with the functioning of a market socialist system and, indeed, may be quite necessary as a method of countering potential monopolistic practices by individual large socialist enterprises. As an historical note it should be added that such central price-setting was a feature of Oskar Lange's 1938 model of market socialism although it should be added that Lange's model featured flexible prices with the central price board finding the equilibrium price by trial and error price-setting methods.[26]

Two features of the new pricing systems (again, with the exception of Yugoslavia) seem dysfunctional for any type of market socialism. First, there seemed little awareness in the various nations that because

26. Oskar Lange and Fred M. Taylor, *On the Economic Theory of Socialism* (Minneapolis: 1938).

prices reflected primarily average costs, amounts demanded might widely
exceed domestic production. In the absence of imports, either some types
of rationing system had to be introduced—which would lead back to the
previous administrative allocation system—or production had somehow
to be stimulated.

Second, the procedures for changing the fixed prices, either selected
or as a whole, seemed to be in a primitive state in almost all the East
European nations. Despite some recognition (particularly in East Germany and Hungary) that long-term fixed prices would hinder not only
the operation of a functioning market system but a centrally administered
economy as well, there was to be no continuing revision of the fixed price
system nor simple procedures by which single prices could be changed.
In East Germany, however, the subject did receive considerable discussion in the economic press and procedures along these lines were planned.
However, the retreat from the reform that occurred in 1969 to 1970 apparently forced a postponement of these measures.

From a more abstract viewpoint, these two dysfunctional elements
were the same; there was no adequate feedback mechanism between
prices and scarcities so that the burden of equalizing the amounts available and desired of particular raw materials and intermediate goods lay
either in changes of imports or informal rationing devices or some unspecified way of increasing domestic production.

In Yugoslavia the situation was different. A larger share of prices
was supposed to be market determined (although this aspect of the reform was subverted until 1967 by a price freeze). Moreover, procedures
for changing fixed prices were considerably simplified. And finally, world
market prices had a greater influence on domestic prices than in the other
East European nations.

Two final aspects of producer prices deserve consideration. First,
implementation of price-setting principles was a very difficult matter and
the goal of eliminating net branch subsidies (which may appear easy)
had not been reached by the seventies in any East European nation.

Second, timing of price and administrative reforms was important.
In Bulgaria, Poland, and Romania the price reforms lagged behind the
administrative reforms by many years. In situations combining decentralized authority (greater enterprise automony in decision-making) with irrational prices, the center could hardly expect that its notions about the
proper output and input mix would be realized; indeed, this was a major
lesson of the abortive reforms in Poland in the mid- and late 1950s. The
slowness in setting forth and implementing price reforms may, therefore,
be one of the most important reasons for the tardiness in implementing
other aspects of the reforms in Bulgaria and Poland (again!) in the mid-
1960s.

Up to now I have focused on producer prices; the retail price situation can be quickly summarized. In the Soviet Union, Bulgaria, East Germany, and Romania no drastic changes in retail prices were planned to accompany the changes in producer prices. The system of differential turnover taxes separating producer and retail prices, which resulted in greatly different price ratios in the two spheres, was essentially continued. The Poles introduced a partial reform of consumer prices in late 1970 in such a clumsy manner that major riots occurred and many of the changes were rescinded. The Czechoslovak, Hungarian, and Yugoslav reforms had the long-run goals of unifying the differential retail turnover tax into a more manageable single rate sales tax that would bring relative retail and producer prices into alignment. Yugoslavia progressed a significant way toward this goal (however, there were still some twenty categories of turnover taxes by the late 1960s, although the bulk of goods fell within just a few categories). The Hungarians took several important measures in this regard, but much remained to be done. The Czechoslovaks hardly began to implement this aspect of their price reform.

The lack of direct links between retail and producer prices means, of course, that consumer demand was only imperfectly transmitted to the producers and, furthermore, that large differences between amount demanded and domestic production could occur which, because of considerable barriers to consumer good imports, might not necessarily be closed.

2. Incentives Facing Enterprises and Associations

The adjustment mechanisms discussed above depended not only on prices but also on the incentives facing the producers. More particularly, we must also know to what degree decision-makers in enterprises and associations were motivated so that prices were important to them. It is to these matters that we now turn; analysis of bonuses to workers and changes in the wage systems are not directly relevant to this problem and must be left to others to discuss.

All nations in East Europe were moving away from the notorious gross output incentive system where primary bonuses and free funds at the disposal of enterprise managers depended on meeting the gross output goal measured in plan prices. And all nations began moving toward incentive systems which were based on actual sales and resulting profits. Nevertheless, the incentive systems varied considerably among nations; relevant information for middle managers is presented in Table 7–11.

In analyzing the incentive and bonus systems facing enterprise managers in East Europe, it is necessary to distinguish between "uniform" and "individualized" systems.[27] In the former system, enterprise pay-

27. I want to thank Otakar Turek for emphasizing this distinction to me.

ments to the state are in the nature of a tax; and the only way for the manager to increase his bonus is to maximize the relevant bonus indicators, e.g., to lower costs or to raise sales. Although the uniform system may have different rates for the various branches, the manager of a particular enterprise faces a set of fixed rates. In the latter system, the rates are determined for each enterprise and are usually designated so that the manager may achieve a certain maximum bonus and the remainder is returned to the state. One critical aspect of the system is that the manager may increase his bonus, not by improving the performance of the enterprise, but by bargaining with higher authorities to change his bonus rates. A second aspect of such a system is that the manager of an enterprise performing well may have a bonus that is smaller than a more poorly performing enterprise. With an individualized system, successful enterprises usually end up subsidizing poorly performing enterprises, while with a uniform system, the latter enterprises face bankruptcy. In short, the uniform system provides a certain market discipline, while the individualized system in practice has blunted such forces.

Among the East European nations four of the eight—Bulgaria, Czechoslovakia, Hungary, and Yugoslavia—introduced uniform systems. The discipline imposed by such systems was somewhat modified in Bulgaria and Czechoslovakia, where the associations were permitted a certain degree of cross-subsidization of enterprises under their jurisdiction (see Table 7–5). In Hungary the discipline imposed by the system was somewhat modified by special bonuses that were distributed by the center to only the top managers; however, the discipline of the system in Hungary was sufficiently strong that some bankruptcies (and forced reorganizations) were reported. In Yugoslavia such a uniform system has been in operation for many years. In the other four nations, the associations had considerable powers in the determination of bonus rates and were the administrative organ through which the incentive and bonus rates were individualized.

In understanding the role of the bonus and incentive systems, it is important to judge the simplicity of the formula by which the bonuses are determined; since the more complicated the formula, the more difficult it is to tell exactly what the manager is maximizing.[28] The formula for the

28. To determine exactly what the enterprise manager would do if he wished to maximize his own compensation is often difficult to carry out and, at this level of analysis, is omitted. For individual studies for Czechoslovakia, Hungary, and Yugoslavia by Václav Holešovsky, Bela Balassa, and Svetozar Pejovich see Morris Bornstein, ed., *Plan and Market: Eastern European Economic Reforms* (New Haven: 1973). For the Soviet Union, see Edward Ames, *Soviet Economic Processes* (Homewood, Ill.: 1965) or Gertrude E. Schroeder, "Soviet Economic 'Reforms': A Study in Contradictions," *Soviet Studies*, XX, July 1968, pp. 1–22. More general analyses may be found by Michael Keren, "Concentration and Efficiency in Eastern European Reforms," in Bornstein; Eirik Furubotn and Svetozar Pejovich, "Property

TABLE 7-11

Incentives and Bonus Systems for Middle Managers in the Postreform Systems in East Europe[a]

Country	Type of System	Complexity of System	Bonuses for Managers		Role of Plan	Rights of Disposal between Funds
			Basic Indicators	Basis of Bonus		
Soviet Union	Individualized	Baroque	Planned increase of profits; profit rates; must also fulfill certain output goals	Wage fund; total profits; changes in profits	Adjustments for overplan and underplan fufillment	Narrow limits
Bulgaria	Uniform	Simple, although enterprise profit tax system complex	Primarily disposable income	Disposable income	Little role except in determining excess profits tax	Wide limits
Czecho-slovakia	Uniform	Simple	Primarily disposable income	Disposable income	No role	Wide limits but subject to re-strictions based on short-term policy
East Germany	Individualized	Simple	Planned profits; overplan profits	Planned profits; overplan profits	Different bonus rates for plan and overplan profits	Narrow limits

Hungary	Uniform	Simple	Disposable income; assets	Disposable income, assets, wage fund	No role	Narrow limits
Poland	Individualized	Complicated	Rentability rate on gross profits; also other indicators such as net output value, wage fund, etc.	Varies according 50 indicators	Different rates for plan and overplan fulfillment	Narrow limits
Romania	Individualized, implementation started experimentally 1970	Appears complicated	Overplan profit	Profits, size of wage fund, other premia, fulfillment major plan goals	Only overplan profits; must fulfill major plan as well	?
Yugoslavia	Uniform	Simple	Disposable income	Disposable income	No role	Wide limits but ceilings

a. Of all elements of the reforms, the bonus systems appear as one of the most changeable; the table summarizes the situation around 1968.

The table contains bonus information for middle managers because for top managers the system contains certain items that have received very little public discussion. For instance, according to David Granick, managers in some nations not only received bonuses from enterprise funds that are governed by regulation (but which could be reduced on decision from higher authorities for "poor performance" which was determined subjectively and not necessarily related to any planned target) but also received (at least in East Germany, Hungary, and Romania) bonuses distributed out of the center's own bonus fund which was governed by subjective considerations.

The distinctions used in this table are explained in the text. Disposable income is used here to designate those funds remaining after costs of raw materials and intermediate goods, depreciation, taxes to the state and to the association, and wages were paid. Technically speaking, enterprise managers in Bulgaria, Czechoslovakia, and Yugoslavia were encouraged to maximize disposable income plus the wage fund, but since there were certain official or unofficial wage-norms which they had to meet, there was relatively little distinction between the two systems at the first level of approximation. If the two systems are described mathematically, however, the maximization results are somewhat different.

managerial bonus funds usually has three parts: the "basic indicators" from which the existence of bonuses or certain basic bonus rates are derived (e.g., the fulfillment of the sales plan); the bonus base, i.e., the aggregate to which certain bonus rates are applied so that the bonus can be calculated; and the adjustments of the bonus rates to take into account other goals such as plan fulfillment or quality factors. In the most simple systems, the bonus rates come from the outside and are applied to a single indicator such as disposable income; such simple systems are associated primarily with uniform systems. Complicated incentive plans are usually associated with individualized systems, although East Germany was an exception.

The most complicated managerial bonus system was that of the Soviet Union, and its designation in the table as "baroque" is no exaggeration. Indeed, its very complexity is one reason why no two Soviet descriptions of the system have been alike. In any case, without knowing the various rates and adjustment factors, it is impossible to judge exactly what the enterprise managers were maximizing. The other individualized systems are also difficult to describe briefly since the bonus systems varied among different branches. Again, without exact knowledge of rates, it is impossible to assess thoroughly the effects of such incentives.

Bulgaria, Czechoslovakia, Hungary and Yugoslavia based their managerial bonuses primarily on disposable income and made no distinction between fulfillment and overfulfillment of the plan. The other East European nations differentiated their bonus rates according to this distinction and permitted the managers to participate in the process by which the plan profit was set. However, there was a basic dilemma that must be noted: Allowing a higher bonus rate on overplan profits encouraged the managers to strive for a low plan; and allowing a lower bonus rate on overplan fulfillment may have discouraged efforts for achieving results very much higher than the plan, especially since the plan targets were raised each year, partly in accordance with current year results.

Another factor to consider about the bonus and incentive funds was the degree to which money could be transferred between bonus funds. In most of the countries such rights were quite limited; only in Bulgaria, Czechoslovakia, and Yugoslavia did enterprise decision-makers have wide discretionary rights to effect such transfers.

Although the incentive and bonus schemes of enterprise managers—can be thoroughly evaluated only in the context of the entire system—a

Rights and the Behavior of the Firm in the Socialist State," *Zeitschrift fuer Nationaloekonomie,* Winter 1970; or sources cited in note 38 of Chapter I. A good deal of the literature in the industrial organization field dealing with the behavior of regulated industries is also of relevance to these issues.

task that space does not permit—several important generalizations can nevertheless be made.

First, encouraging the manager to maximize disposable income in a system where prices do not serve very adequately as a measure of relative scarcity can lead to considerable waste, even though disposable income is determined in part by the results of actual sales. This is because the enterprise managers may have no stimulus to produce those products that are most vitally needed, but rather products which serve only as imperfect substitutes. In other words, the basic flaw of the fixed priced systems was not offset by the incentive system.

Second, indiscriminate use of subsidies can subvert the incentive system. For instance, tying bonuses partly to sales was a measure designed to reduce the large inventories of unsold and unwanted goods. Nevertheless, such inventories increased, rather than decreased, in Czechoslovakia in 1967, partly because authorities were willing to bail out faltering enterprises.

Third, the existence of "proper" incentives alone is no insurance of their adequacy, for the level and "objectivity" of the rates are equally important. Relatively little data are available to be able to judge whether the new bonuses are sufficiently large actually to encourage the desired managerial actions. The "objectivity" of the rates depends on the degree to which the manager had sufficient confidence that the structure would be similar enough in the future for him to undertake certain long-term measures. In other words, expectations concerning the incentive system are important in evaluating the system. Unfortunately, we have little adequate information about such matters as well.

Finally, all countries but Czechoslovakia announced their intention of placing all enterprises on the same incentive system. From a theoretical standpoint, this may not be correct. Different types of incentives may be necessary to induce optimal performance from enterprises with increasing and decreasing returns.[29] In Czechoslovakia the enterprises under two "heavy" industrial ministries were given somewhat different incentives, presumably to take this problem into account. And in Bulgaria and the Soviet Union, where different industries were placed under the new incentive system at different periods and where the process was apparently stopped in both countries before completion, this distinction between industries with increasing and decreasing returns also may have been taken into account. In any case, I strongly suspect that in future economic reforms in the East European nations, much more attention

---

29. An interesting theoretical model constructed along these lines is by Richard D. Portes, "Decentralized Planning Procedures and Centrally Planned Economies," forthcoming.

will be given to a careful differentiation of changes between the various industries in order to take account of such special features of particular industries.

In order to complete this analysis of incentive systems, the bonus system of the associations deserves brief comment. As noted in Table 7–3, the associations had "economic accounting" and received most of their funds from their constituent enterprises. There was considerable experimentation in the various countries with regard to association bonuses. In the Soviet Union, Bulgaria, East Germany, and Poland we know that such bonuses were tied in part to enterprise profits; in Czechoslovakia there was no unique prescription and some were based on the value-added of the constituent enterprises. However, other criteria for bonuses were also used; e.g., the Soviet Union had experimented with productivity increases as an indicator and East Germany had used a variety of indicators including sales, labor productivity, investment, and export criteria.

The type of association bonus system does not seem very important in an economy with considerable administrative elements; in a socialist market economy, however, basing association bonuses on enterprise profits would encourage monopolistic practices, especially if the association had price-setting powers. The problem of how to encourage the associations into "proper" activities has many theoretical difficulties, especially since in certain conceptions of market socialism (e.g., Lange's), the associations are supposed to act in order to offset external diseconomies that are not taken into proper account by the enterprise.[30] Such problems did not arise in Hungary and Yugoslavia, where the associations had almost no influence on production. In Czechoslovakia, where the association did have more power, the association bonuses were not supposed to be very large; and, moreover, the use of a value-added indicator for bonuses by some associations provided less incentive for monopolistic practices.

3. Decision-making and Information Channels

Since decision-making requires information, it is useful to pay brief attention to the channels of information to gain deeper understanding of adjustment mechanisms. The discussion below focuses on the relation between the flow of information and decision-making on three levels of the economy.

a. *Enterprise level.* At the enterprise level it is important to distinguish three different aspects of the flow of information.

30. These problems are elaborated in much greater detail by Abram Bergson, "Market Socialism Revisited," *Journal of Political Economy,* LXXV, October 1967, pp. 655–73.

First, we must consider the relationships between vertical, horizontal, and oblique flows of information. Vertical information-flows exist when a unit communicates with another by sending messages up the administrative hierarchy until the message reaches a level that has jurisdiction over both, and then it is sent down to the other. Horizontal information-flows exist when a unit that is neither superior nor subordinate to another unit communicates directly with it. An example of horizontal communication is direct communication between two production enterprises. Oblique information-flow is a special type of horizontal communication between two units that have either no common administrative superior (e.g., between a production enterprise and a private market research agency) or else a common administrative superior only at the very top of the system (e.g., between a production enterprise and a bank, where the only common superior is the Prime Minister).[31]

In all countries except Yugoslavia, where communications were primarily horizontal (especially oblique) before the reform, there was an increased emphasis on horizontal communication at the expense of vertical communication. This drive was manifested especially by the increased emphasis on "direct contacts" between enterprises in buying and selling so that higher units could be relieved of unnecessary paperwork. Oblique information channels were also increasing in importance, as enterprise contacts with banks, foreign trade enterprises, and research units became closer. Growing importance of horizontal (and especially oblique) flows is essential for the development of a market and, therefore, the reforms acted to surmount one of the barriers to market socialism.

A second important aspect of communication lines concerns the type of vertical channels between enterprises and the center. Four possible types are imaginable: The lines can be arranged on a "production" principle where enterprises communicate with ministries arranged according to groups of similar products; on a "territorial" principle where enterprises communicate with territorial agencies instead of ministries; on a "functional" principle where enterprises communicate with ministries arranged functionally (e.g., finance, research, production, sales, etc.); or on a "conglomerate" principle where enterprises communicate primarily with higher units in vertically integrated trusts. These four types of communication lines are not mutually exclusive and combinations or mixes can be employed effectively.

Each type of communication network within the industrial hierarchy has advantages and disadvantages which, in past years, have received

31. The concepts of horizontal and vertical communication channels are explored in much greater depth in a case study of Hungary by János Kornai, *Overcentralization in Economic Administration* (Oxford: 1959). The concept of the oblique communication channel is my own.

considerable analysis.[32] For our purpose it is worth noting that most vertical channels are inimical to a functioning market, and of the four types of vertical channels, the "production" channels are most likely to discourage market competition. It is this very channel which continued to remain strong in those nations that still maintained to a great extent the administrative allocation system, namely, the Soviet Union, Bulgaria, East Germany, Poland, and Romania.

A third and final aspect of the communication channels to be considered is the importance of parallel lines of information from the enterprise to the center, e.g., through the secret police or party hierarchies. It is necessary to note that in two of the three nations which attempted to move toward market socialism (Czechoslovakia and Yugoslavia), party controls of enterprise decision-making were curbed and such parallel communication channels were narrowed in order to strengthen the powers of the enterprise managers. There is a conflict between political and economic criteria in enterprise decision-making and for a market to function properly, economic criteria must be paramount (but not necessarily exclusive).

b. *Other economic organs.* Up to now I have focused almost exclusively on the production hierarchy; it is necessary to discuss briefly other institutions, in particular the banking system and the capital market, in the network of information that supplies the inputs for decision-making.

In all nations there was an attempt in the reforms to decrease the role of state grants of investment funds and to increase the importance of self-financed or bank-financed investments. Such a move was predicated on the belief that organs at the center did not have the proper information to make detailed investment decisions. Since a functioning market system requires the flow of capital to those sectors where investments with the highest social return could be obtained, it is useful to ask whether the information channels were sufficient to obtain this aim.

By reserving certain particularly important projects for financing from the state budget, there was an implicit assumption that with regard to gross shifts in the sectoral investment pattern, only the center had sufficient information to make such decisions. In cases where prices did not reflect scarcities, comparison of investment return calculations from different sectors would not bring about the proper investment pattern and,

---

32. E.g., Peter Wiles, *The Political Economy of Communism* (Cambridge, Mass.: 1962). An interesting mathematical analysis of the problem is presented by Michael Keren, "Industrial Versus Regional Partitioning of Soviet Planning Organization," *Economics of Planning,* IV, March 1964, pp. 143–60.

with its information about the supply and demand for critical raw materials and inputs, central agencies had the best information for such purposes. It must be added that the "best" information was not necessarily "sufficient" and the optimal allocation of even those investment funds allotted the center was not guaranteed.

The very important role that the associations played in investment decision in most countries through the administration of branch investment funds reflected in part sectoral decisions made by the center. If the center did not have sufficient information for comparing the relative payoffs of investments in various sectors, then certain mistakes of a more central method of allocating such funds would be repeated. On the other hand, it must be added that in regard to investment *within* a particular branch, giving the association greater decision-making autonomy cut down the costs of information transferral to the center and thus represented an improvement.

The increase in importance of enterprise self-financed or credit-financed investment was justified on three grounds. First, increasing the autonomy of investment decision-making by the enterprise would supposedly reduce the cost of information transfer and eliminate unnecessary red tape and delay. This argument is undoubtedly true. Second, the enterprises and banks allegedly had sufficient information to select those small investments with the highest social return. This argument seems dubious because of the distorted prices the enterprises faced and reported to the bank, from which the latter had to make allocation decisions. Finally, such a method of finance was supposed to encourage economical use of investment funds within the enterprise. This seems to have merit and may be the most important result of the entire change of investment financing in the reforms. Implementation of this increase in the relative importance of bank financing of investment was, however, somewhat slow in some East European nations.

One additional consideration of the banks' role in the investment process must be mentioned: They might not have had sufficient information at their disposal to allocate investment funds to increase, rather than decrease, competition. The Hungarians have attempted to overcome this difficulty by setting up broadly based advisory boards to the banks. But we must note at least the possibility that market competition might not be furthered by granting banks more decision-making autonomy.

This problem of information appears in a different guise in regard to other types of organs. For instance, there appeared to be quite insufficient communication channels between market-research and research and development agencies so that the choice of research and development projects was not necessarily optimal.

c. *Central governmental level.* One important possible restructuring of the information system employed by the central authorities could be to increase the frequency of communication between the center and the enterprises (e.g., by increasing the number of plan and counterplan proposals) in the drawing up of plans or the determination of policy measures to influence indirectly enterprise decision-making. On a very formal level, increasing such "iterations" could lead to the implementation of some sort of "two-level" planning or planning scheme using some type of decomposition algorithm that various mathematical economists have proposed.[33] But only two types of measures were taken along these lines at least for the short run. In countries such as East Germany and Romania, there was a much greater emphasis on having the enterprises obtain tentative supply commitments from other enterprises before sending back to the center a counterplan proposal, a measure to permit the equilibrating of material supply and demand in the plan more quickly (i.e., which speeds up the iteration process). Poland and East Germany (starting in 1969) replaced the discrete one-year plans with "rolling two-year" plans which permitted much more communication between the center and the enterprises in regard to the yearly plan because of the lengthening of the planning period. Tentative moves in regard to middle- and long-run planning in the same direction have also been called for.[34]

Another type of restructuring of the information system might be the setting up of various types of indicative planning schemes, but such measures were probably not seriously contemplated. Rather, the primary changes in the information systems appeared to be connected with the imposition of various degrees of market elements into the command system in most countries, which have been discussed.

The reforms were also not marked by any radical changes in the processing of information. Rather, information processing and planning methods seemed to have been changing independently of the reforms. Planners in all countries were experimenting with the use of more sophisticated planning methods, the processing of information via computers, and a wider application of mathematics and statistics. Although we can say that Czechoslovakia, Hungary, and Poland had the most sophisti-

33. E.g., Kornai and Lipták in János Kornai, *Mathematical Planning of Structural Decisions* (Amsterdam: 1967), Chapter 24; and Dantzig and Wolfe in George Dantzig, *Linear Programming and Extensions* (Princeton: 1963), Chapter 22.

34. Most of the East European nations announced much greater emphasis on middle- and long-term planning, including the use of so-called disaggregated rolling plans, i.e., multiyear plans for a particular period that are broken up by year and which are revised on a yearly basis. Most previous East European reform drives had called for similar action and such efforts had come to naught; therefore, skepticism is justified about whether this aspect of the mid-1960s reforms would be implemented.

cated literature on problems of mathematical planning, it appears that few of the East European nations actually employed these new methods very extensively.

The introduction of a guided market does not exclude the use of sophisticated central planning methods, especially in determining the use of the proper instruments to influence the direction of the market. The difficulty is that with the abandonment of direct administrative (command) allocation methods, there was incomplete replacement by the development of adequate policy instruments to influence either macro- or micro-economic developments indirectly.

One manifestation of this lack of information systems and policy instruments suitable for socialist market economies can be seen in the field of monetary policy. In potentially inflationary situations where the government wished to curb the least important investments, it had in most East European nations—at least up to the end of the decade—no sensitive policy instruments except for the imposition of quite arbitrary credit ceilings. If such measures are undesirable because of their bluntness or difficulty in enforcing, then inflation is the usual consequence because better policy tools are not used or available—a problem that plagued Yugoslavia for years and which caused considerable difficulties in Czechoslovakia in 1967 and 1968.

Another manifestation of this problem was in the sphere of fiscal policy. Although the central authorities in all East European nations had a great many taxes which they could manipulate to achieve particular goals in either guided market or administrative systems, they did not appear to have either well designed strategies or specialized information systems to allow them to use such measures effectively.

Extreme laissez faire protagonists have argued that a well-functioning market does not require central governmental fiscal action or other types of policy action. But as long as the policy-makers in those nations aiming toward some type of market socialism were unwilling to leave everything to the action of the market, they had to have effective policy tools and sufficient information to know when to use these tools. Unfortunately, these appeared to be missing. Or to put the matter in a somewhat different way, those reforms attempting to gain the advantages of both plan and market found that these could not be mechanically combined and their proper combination was difficult to determine.

4. Summary

The mechanisms of response of the post-reform economies in most of the East European nations to inefficiencies or to deficiencies in supply or demand left much to be desired on several accounts.

First, in all countries except Yugoslavia, prices were determined by average branch costs. Although these costs were probably closer to opportunity costs than before, such a price-setting principle neglected demand factors except insofar as such cost prices were modified by world market prices and imports could be obtained. The burden of equating amounts of commodities demanded to supply lay either on imports, or on informal rationing methods, or on central allocation methods. The efficiency of the allocation pattern resulting from the latter two methods leaves much to be desired.

Second, in those countries that had consciously tried to achieve some type of guided market socialism, managerial incentives were oriented toward the maximization of net enterprise income; because of deficiencies in the price system, maximization of such monetary profits did not necessarily lead to the most desirable output pattern. The system of allocating investment funds did not ensure that such funds would necessarily go to the most profitable sectors or to those places that would ensure the survival of market competition. Further, the central governments in these nations did not appear to have command over effective micro- or macroeconomic policy tools, nor did they appear to have effective strategies for interventions that would preserve, rather than throttle, competition.

Third, in those countries aiming toward a streamlining of the administrative system, many difficulties also appeared. Information systems left much to be desired. Administrative methods for the allocation of investment funds did not insure that the desired patterns would be obtained. Tools of intervention remained primarily direct and use of indirect measures, no matter how desirable they might seem (this was especially true in the East German literature) were undeveloped in most nations.

E. An Overview

Problems of reforming structures and mechanisms were formidable. A more detailed case study approach would reveal additional difficulties in carrying out the reforms, as well as a number of dysfunctional macroeconomic mechanisms (such as inventory cycles) that are difficult to deduce from the facts presented from the relatively broad perspective that I have chosen to take.

Leaving aside for a moment the reforms in Yugoslavia, which were *sui generis* (since that country did not start in the early 1960s with a Stalinist type system of economic administration), two quite different sets of postreform economic systems can be isolated. These can be represented by East Germany and Hungary which had the two most consistent systemic reforms of the seven nations we are now considering.

The East German reform represented an administrative streamlining with close attention paid to the use of administrative incentives and the channeling of information so that quick administrative measures could be taken to avert forthcoming crises. Indeed, many East German economists looked upon the act of economic reforms as an exercise in applied cybernetics. Although the East German economy ran into difficulties in 1970 and 1971, this seems to have been due primarily to inappropriate policy measures within the context of the reform;[35] in any case, the particular measures taken over the five-year period from 1964 through 1968 showed that the East Germans paid close attention to the consistency of various institutional changes.

The Hungarian reforms represented an important step toward some type of guided market socialism, with great emphasis placed on the market and the price system to influence the pattern of current production. At the time of writing, it seems too early to carry out a very profound evaluation of the impact of the Hungarian reforms, but preliminary indicators appear favorable.

Although the East German and the Hungarian reforms were the most coherent in Eastern Europe (again omitting Yugoslavia from consideration), they followed quite different strategies in their implementation. Hungary introduced most of the important reforms at a single date, while East Germany implemented its reforms in a series of planned phases stretching out over a number of years. But policy leaders in both nations had a clear idea of what they were about. This does not mean, of course, that these economies did not contain certain incongruities; for instance, we would expect the East German economy to be characterized by much larger production units than the Hungarian economy, but the reverse is actually the case. Nevertheless, the interrelation of different types of property rights were carefully considered. Using the East German and Hungarian economies as points of comparison, three groups of economic systems in East Europe can be distinguished.

The first group consists of the Soviet, Polish, and Romanian reforms which constituted primarily administrative streamlinings of the Stalinist system of economic administration. The reforms in these three nations were, however, neither as far reaching nor as consistent as those in East Germany. Although all administrative systems can live with certain inconsistencies, such lack of coherence can lead either to poor performance or to further changes in the system or else to a retreat to the previous system. In the case of Poland, if the late 1950s in that country can be characterized as a period of economic theory without change, the mid-

---

35. For an illuminating analysis of the rise and fall of the economic reforms in East Germany, see Michael Keren, "The New Economic System in the GDR: An Obituary," forthcoming.

and late 1960s can be characterized as a period of economic change without theory.[36] The difficulties in implementing such a reform in the late 1960s led to serious political problems, a change in personnel in leading positions, and an attempt in 1971 to 1972 to reform the reform. In the Soviet Union inconsistencies in the conception of the reforms led to only a partial implementation of the various measures and the reforms had relatively little apparent impact on the economy.[37] The Romanian reforms also appear to have lacked coherence and actual implementation; especially the transfer of ministerial powers to the associations appears to have been slower than planned. There are some important differences among the economic systems of the Soviet Union, Poland, Romania, and East Germany: they differ in the distribution of decision-making powers at various levels of the hierarchy, in consistency, and in effectiveness of adjustment mechanisms. Nevertheless, in comparison with the other economies under consideration they may all be characterized as variants of centrally administered economies.

Associated with Hungary as a second group is Yugoslavia, whose reform progressed in many ways much further toward market socialism. In Hungary policy-makers have expressed the desire to guide the market by some type of "visible hand"; although Yugoslav leaders appeared to have similar ideas a decade ago, the visible hand of the Yugoslav government in directing current production appears to have considerably withered in the last decade.[38] This experience of Yugoslavia raises serious questions concerning the degree to which the Hungarian economic system has institutional stability and whether Hungary will follow the Yugoslavian path in the years to come.

The third group of nations includes Bulgaria and Czechoslovakia. In the various tables of this chapter, the economies of the two nations

36. Smolinski.

37. Among the various discussions of the ways in which the Soviet reforms were thwarted, see Karl W. Ryavec, "Soviet Industrial Managers, Their Superiors, and the Economic Reforms: A Study of an Attempt at Planned Behavioral Change," *Soviet Studies,* XXI, October 1969, pp. 208–30; or Gertrude E. Schroeder, "Soviet Economic Reform at an Impasse," *Problems of Communism,* XX, July-August 1971, pp. 36–46. Among the evidence used by Schroeder are the results of a survey of 241 directors of enterprises on the impact of the reforms that are contained in *Ekonomika i organizatsiia promyshlennovo proizvodstva* (Novosibirsk), January 1970, pp. 101–7 in which a majority of managers saw few important changes in the reforms. Such evidence must be taken cautiously for in Hungary after the reforms, Granick reported that enterprise managers saw few important changes in certain areas such as supply, even though all input targets had been dropped. (David Granick, "Economic Reform in Hungary," forthcoming.)

38. See especially Egon Neuberger, "The Yugoslav Visible Hand: Why Is It No More?" in Janet G. Chapman and Chou Shun-hsin, eds., *The Economics of the Communist World,* forthcoming.

have sometimes been similar to those of Hungary and Yugoslavia and sometimes similar to those of East Germany, Poland, Romania, and the Soviet Union. The Czechoslovakian and Bulgarian reforms have been characterized by the greatest inconsistencies and, let me add, the greatest changes once the reforms were introduced. The original motives underlying the Bulgarian economic reforms appear mixed and the policy decisions of 1965 and 1966 to place greater emphasis on market elements were reversed in 1968. The Czechoslovakian policy-makers viewed their reforms as an ongoing process where important changes were made almost every year and thus made a virtue of continual systemic changes. Between 1967 and 1969 the economy appeared to be moving rapidly toward a system of guided market socialism, but various reform measures appeared to clash and a coherent economic system had not yet been achieved by the time of the Soviet invasion of August 1968 and the ascension to power of Gustav Husák in April 1969. Although the reform drive was blunted and a number of reversals were carried out, the situation in 1969 and 1970 was far from a return to the old system. In the early 1970s, however, changes in the Czechoslovakian economy (including a strengthening of the associations at the expense of the enterprises and reintroduction of tighter direct controls on production) appeared to be moving the economic system toward the East German, Polish, Romanian, and Soviet systems.

What are the directions of future changes? As I have indicated, the reform drive of the sixties has been blunted in most nations, and only the reforms in Hungary, Romania, and Yugoslavia (the first two reforms began quite late in the decade) continued full-force into the early seventies. But the retrenchment of some reforms (especially in East Germany) may be temporary and new reform drives in other countries (especially Poland) are gathering steam. Most East European nations began discussing new price reforms to be carried out in the mid-seventies.

A full evaluation of the reforms would require not only an assessment of the effects of the reforms on success indicators such as the growth rate or the balance of trade, but also a close evaluation of political trends which played such an important role in several nations.[39] Although such

39. In this regard Bulgaria is an extremely interesting case study. The relatively early date of reform discussion and experimentation was partly a reaction to the Stalinist-Maoist course steered by Valko Chervenkov and the economic repercussions of Bulgaria's great-leap-forward in 1959 and 1960. And, undoubtedly, the quick promulgation of the reform guidelines was, in part, an attempt to divert attention from the abortive *coup d'état* of April 1965. Between the announcement of the reform guidelines and the reform halt after the July 1968 plenum of the Central Committee, the influence of factional infighting on economic policy appeared important. Perhaps the relative strengths of the factions can be measured by looking at foreign trade:

an overall evaluation must be left for others, one extremely important economic consideration needs discussion, namely the degree to which system reformers are faced with several "grand alternatives" or with a spectrum of choices.

Many important economists have rejected the notion that there are only several distinct types of economic systems that nations may select; they argue, rather, that there is a wide variety of choices along a number of continuum that may be combined to form a functioning economic system.[40] Others, now a minority, argue that an economic system requires a certain coherence so that only particular choices can be combined to form a functioning economy. In other words, "mixed economies" may combine the worst, not the best elements, of other economic systems: Yugoslavia, which attempted in the 1950s and early 1960s to combine both plan and market economies ended up with the greatest economic fluctuations in Europe and the most unemployment,[41] combined with many striking examples of enormous static inefficiency.[42] Within the East European context the basic question underlying this dispute between the "grand alternatives" versus the "continuum" can be framed more concretely: To what extent can elements of administrative and market economies be combined? Or do nations simply have a real choice only between several distinct types of economic systems, with marginal variations permitted along with the basic choice?

Although evaluating the East European evidence on these matters is difficult, the facts presented in this chapter appear to point toward several "grand alternatives" rather than to a wide spectrum of choices. Leaving out of consideration the reforms of Hungary and Romania, which occurred most recently and have not had a chance to function very long, we have the experiences of six nations to consider.

The share of trade with the West rose rapidly in the mid-1960s, reaching a high point in 1966; thereafter the share of trade with the CMEA nations rose and in 1969 and 1970, a series of new joint Bulgarian-Soviet economic ventures and joint planning efforts were announced. These various events are discussed by J. F. Brown, Richard V. Burke, "The Politics of Economic Reform in Bulgaria and Romania," in Bornstein, ed.; and L. A. D. Dellin, "Bulgarian Economic Reform—Advance and Retreat," *Problems of Communism*, XIX, September-October 1970, pp. 44–53.

40. This case is argued in a convincing manner by Robert A. Dahl and Charles E. Lindblom, *Politics, Economics and Welfare* (New York: 1953), Chapter 1.

41. George J. Staller, "Fluctuations in Economic Activity: Planned and Free-Market Economies, 1950–60," *American Economic Review*, LIV, June 1964, pp. 385–95.

42. On the other hand, it must also be noted that Yugoslavia had the highest growth rate of aggregate production of any nation in Europe at that time.

East Germany, which had the most consistent administrative streamlining, only retreated from the reform when plan goals were considerably increased and subsequently unmet, which suggests that over-ambitious policies, rather than the system itself, were responsible for the reversal of the reform. In Poland and the Soviet Union, attempts to introduce a certain degree of enterprise autonomy in decision-making were reversed and supplanted by more traditional administrative methods of control because of inconsistencies in the system that I have discussed above. In contrast, Yugoslavia has been pushed by the *logique des choses* toward a freer market economy.[43]

The Bulgarian and Czechoslovak reforms, which contained the greatest admixture of administrative and market elements, did not prove stable and provided the most spectacular examples of reform reversals. But here, a problem of interpretation arises. The incomplete implementation of the Bulgarian reforms and their subsequent reversal appears to be associated with a serious political power struggle and the reversal of the Czechoslovakian economic reforms followed, of course, Soviet military and political intervention. Politics could be an independent cause of the institutional instability of mixed administrative-market economic systems; on the other hand, the political factors could have arisen as a result of the uncertainties created by such mixed economic systems. Unfortunately, the available evidence on these matters is still quite scanty.

My conclusions that the East European nations face several "grand alternatives" with regard to the system of resource allocation rather than a wide spectrum of choices must be viewed as quite tentative. Nevertheless, approaching the changes in economic systems from the point of view of this crucial question appears a profitable avenue for future research, for we need much more evidence on the performance and the institutional stability of mixed economies. The economic experiences of the East European nations as they continue their reforms or institute new reform drives during the next decade have crucial theoretical significance. If Western nations introduce further administrative elements into their economic systems, we will have additional useful evidence.

43. The situation has proceeded sufficiently far that in 1970 a draft bill was even prepared to establish a socialist bond market that would allow socialist enterprises to float certain types of securities.

CHAPTER VIII

Centralization of Property Rights

If we disregard due proportion by giving anything what is too much for it, too much canvas to a boat, too much nutriment to a body, too much authority to a soul, the consequence is always shipwreck; rankness runs in one case to disease, in the other to presumption, and its issue is crime.

Plato[1]

A. Introduction

B. Concepts or Indices of
   Centralization
   1. General Approach
   2. Ten Concepts of Centraliza-
      tion in Search of a Social
      Scientist
   3. Relationships between
      Concepts or Indices of
      Centralization

C. Developmental Propositions
   about Centralization
   1. Determinants of Spatial Cen-
      tralization in Mining and
      Manufacturing
   2. Determinants of Temporal
      Centralization in Mining

*and Manufacturing in
the West*
   3. The "Economic System"
      as a Determinant of
      Centralization
   4. The Level of Economic
      Development as a Determi-
      nant of Centralization in
      the West

D. Speculations about a Relationship between Income Equality
   and Centralization

E. Impact Propositions about
   Centralization
   1. Some Theoretical
      Approaches
   2. Some Empirical Approaches

F. Summary and Conclusions

A. Introduction

Centralization of property rights is a key issue in the analysis of the distribution and effects of control rights in the same manner as the distribution of wealth is a key issue in the analysis of ownership rights. After

1. Plato, *The Laws,* Chapter 3, translated by A. E. Taylor.

278

many years of indifference, political economists are finally beginning to analyze questions about the determinants of the centralization of property rights and the impact of such patterns of property rights on the functioning of the economy.

Stemming from these concerns the purpose of this chapter is to explore the concepts of centralization and to show how they may be applied to the study of the economy as a whole. This task is carried out in three steps. I first examine a series of concepts and indices of centralization that have been proposed for use in empirical investigations of complex organizations and that may be of use in studying economic systems. Then I look at several important developmental propositions about centralization, i.e., propositions about the determinants of various types of centralization. Finally, I examine a series of impact propositions about centralization, i.e., propositions about the effect of particular kinds of centralization on the functioning of the economy.

Evidence for many propositions in the analysis is taken from previous results of this study, especially those dealing with control rights, so that this chapter has a summary nature. Because of the lack of detailed empirical materials permitting exhaustive exploration of a few aspects of centralization, this chapter is primarily a survey of a larger number of general problems and is thus a series of related notes on an extremely intricate topic. The case studies presented, especially on spatial and temporal centralization, are included not only for the results they yield but also as illustrations of a particular method of analysis.

B. Concepts or Indices of Centralization

1. General Approach

Centralization of property rights implies that a single decision-making unit (a person or a group) holds more property rights than another unit. The existence of property rights implies an asymmetric power relationship between individuals in which one individual forces or induces a second to do what he ordinarily would not for the benefit of the first. Centralization is defined here in terms of an inequality, rather than of organization structure, so that nonhierarchical organizations or systems can be studied, i.e., economies as well as enterprises.

Such an approach gives rise to many problems and requires a number of subtle distinctions.[2] Not only may different aspects of a relationship between individuals reflect different degrees of property centralization but

2. Two rigorous discussions of these matters that attack the troublesome problems of feedbacks between the ruled and the ruler are: Herbert A. Simon, "Notes on the Observation and Measurement of Political Power," in

even a given aspect may reflect centralization according to one index and decentralization according to another index. In the discussion below I focus on only a small group of problems that are most relevant for the analysis of economic systems.

It is helpful to begin discussion by focusing first on power or control and the ways it can be exercised. "Control" is used in a broad sense, i.e. not only the ability of a superior to direct the actions of a subordinate *ex anti* but also the ability to correct such action *ex post* if it has deviated from some norm. There are three basic ways in which one person can exercise control over another.

First, control can be exercised by the property-holder narrowing the set of decisions that can be made by the other person. The most extreme case is, of course, when only one choice can be made, i.e., an order or command in which if obedience is not forthcoming, sanctions are invoked which are more unpleasant than fulfilling the order.

Second, control can be exercised by the property-holder changing the value that another person places on a particular choice. This can be done in a direct fashion, such as setting prices for inputs or outputs to influence production or investment choices; or it can be done by propagandistic or educational means in order to change the inner values (or "objective function") of the subordinate individuals; or it can be done by placing in particular positions only personnel whose evaluations of alternatives correspond to what is desired.

Third, control can be exercised by the property-holder determining the manner in which another person goes about making a choice, e.g., by influencing the way in which the subordinate searches for alternatives or the information he uses in deciding between alternatives or the method he uses to calculate value.

From this point of view centralization depends not on which of the three types of controls (hereafter designated "coercive," "incentive," and "ideological" controls) are exercised but rather on their intensity. An oft repeated administrative ideal found in the business literature, that a multi-

---

his *Models of Man* (New York: 1957), pp. 62–78; and John Harsanyi, "Measurement of Social Power, Opportunity Costs and the Theory of Two-Person Bargaining Games," *Behavioral Science,* VII, 1/1962, pp. 67–80. Although both Simon and Harsanyi employ a rigor that is notably lacking in most other discussions of power, it is difficult to imagine situations in which social scientists would have enough information to employ their various definitions. More specifically, there appears to be a trade-off between analytical precision in defining power and information with which empirical content can be given to the analysis. In this chapter I am examining situations for which much information is lacking; and in order to make any empirical evaluation of centralization, I am forced to use an approach with less precision that I would desire.

divisional enterprise must be "decentralized in operations, centralized in controls" implies, according to my approach, centralization via incentive or ideological controls, combined with a highly effective information system and use of coercive controls only as a last resort.

Much can be said about these three types of controls and their interrelations. For instance, using contemporary China as a case study Skinner and Winckler have argued that in systems experiencing rapid change, administrative emphasis on one of these three types of controls (their classification is slightly different) shifts in a systematic fashion over time.[3] More relevant for the purposes at hand, however, is an exploration of specific concepts or indices by which centralization can be empirically measured so that we can say something definite about centralization in particular economies.

2. Ten Concepts of Centralization in Search of a Social Scientist

One finds a bewildering variety of specific concepts or indices of centralization in the social science literature that have some relation to the asymmetric relationship discussed above. In order to organize discussion, it is useful to consider such concepts or indices of centralization under three headings: those dealing with aspects of control directly; those focusing on participation; and those emphasizing structural properties of the system. The various concepts or indices of centralization are not necessarily parallel or of equal importance; further, there is some degree of overlap. Nevertheless, the concepts are sufficiently different and useful to warrant brief discussion. Although a recitation of definitions is tedious, the reader should be assured that I try to employ all in the empirical analysis below.

a. *Concepts or indices of centralization focusing directly on control.* (i) Centralization is manifested in the degree of detail in which effective commands or instructions are issued by higher to lower decision-making units.[4] The less detailed the commands, the greater amount of discretion a lower unit can exercise. This concept of centralization is clearly related

3. William Skinner and Edwin Winckler, "Compliance Succession in Rural Communist China: A Cyclical Theory," in Amitai Etzioni, ed., *Complex Organizations: A Sociological Reader,* 2nd edition (New York: 1969), pp. 410–38.

4. These commands or instructions must be effective, i.e., obeyed, or else we have situations described by János Kornai [*Overcentralization in Economic Administration* (translated by John Knapp) (London: 1959)] in which "formal" centralization was combined with a certain degree of "actual" decentralization because many orders were totally ignored and uninforced.

to the narrowing of the set of choices (coercive controls) of the lower units. To illustrate this concept I present data in the discussion concerning the number of "plan positions" and of centrally rationed goods in several East European nations.

(ii) Centralization is manifested by a high degree of vertical versus horizontal interaction of members of an organization.[5] Vertical interaction denotes dealings between subordinates and superiors within an organization hierarchy; horizontal interaction is between members who have no formal power relationships and between whom all deal from positions of equality. The frequency of performance review of a subordinate by his superior is a manifestation of vertical interaction; collegiality of decision-making is a manifestation of horizontal interaction. This concept of centralization is based on the assumption that a higher degree of vertical than horizontal interaction permits greater coercive controls to be exercised and that a greater degree of horizontal than vertical interaction permits greater decision-making by the individual involved; it is thus related to but not the same as the previous concept.

(iii) Centralization is manifested when decisions are made or responsibility is placed or initiative is taken or control is exercised at a high level of the structure of the system. On the other hand, the more autonomous the subunits of an organization are from higher administrative levels or the more autonomous the organizations within a system, the more decentralized the system. As a simple example, consider a federal system of government: the higher the percentage of public expenditures that are made at the federal rather than the local level the more centralized the system. This approach to centralization raises a number of difficulties, not only conceptually[6] but also empirically and it requires the investigator to distinguish carefully between "formal" responsibility and actual decision-making. (For instance, an organization in which initiative is exercised and decisions are made at a lower level of the hierarchy, after they are formally "cleared" by higher administrative levels may be effectively decentralized if such approval is relatively automatic.) This concept of centralization covers the use of not only coercive but also incentive and ideological controls; it is designated in the discussion as "hierarchical centralization."

b. *Concepts or indices of centralization focusing on participation.* (iv) Centralization is manifested in or measured by the routinization of jobs, that is, the degree to which activity is structured through the careful de-

---

5. This approach toward centralization is outlined by Kornai, pp. 191–99.

6. Certain such difficulties are discussed in greater detail in Appendix A-14.

lineation of competencies and through the establishment of standard operating procedures so that a person has little immediate choice as to what task he should perform and how he should do it.[7] This concept of centralization reflects not only the narrowing of the choice set facing an individual but also the specification of the procedures by which decisions are made.

(v) Centralization is manifested by low participation or influence of the members of an organization in decision-making concerning important organization policies. This concept of centralization is related to but not the same as hierarchical centralization; it focuses on the degree to which individuals can affect the control that is exercised over them.[8] For instance, an enterprise with an effective workers' council would, according to this definition, be more decentralized than a similar enterprise without such participation of workers in managerial decision-making. This participation or influence can take many forms and is difficult to measure; many empirical organization studies have been based on subjective appraisals of the "degree of participation" that particular organization members at different levels of the hierarchy feel that they and others can exercise. The Maoist model of intense participation of all organization members (the "mass line") is thus one of high decentralization according to this concept.[9]

A variant of this approach has been used by those approaching centralization in terms of the degree to which the operations of a system are determined by interaction and participation of the various members in contrast to operations determined by messages from the outside environment.[10]

This concept of centralization focuses on feedback between levels of a system; although it is most directly seen in relation to the choice set exercised by individuals, incentive and ideological controls may also be involved.

(vi) Centralization is manifested by the exercise of fewer property

7. Several more operational definitions along these lines are used in a study by D. S. Pugh, *et al.,* "Dimensions of Organization Structure," *Administrative Science Quarterly,* XIII, June 1968, pp. 65–105. Detailed job descriptions and formal operating procedures may also be dimensions of centralization unrelated to each other. (See Appendix A-16.)

8. A more operational definition of this dimension of centralization is presented by Jerald Hage and Michael Aiken, "Relationship of Centralization to Other Structural Properties," *Administrative Science Quarterly,* XII, June 1967, pp. 72–93.

9. The Maoist ideal, if not the reality, is analyzed brilliantly by Franz Schurmann, *Ideology and Organization in Communist China* (Berkeley: 1970), 2nd edition.

10. This concept of centralization is developed by Thomas Marschak, "On the Comparison of Centralized and Decentralized Economies," *American Economic Review,* LIX, May 1969, pp. 525–32.

rights within a system, other things remaining the same. This approach to centralization focuses not only on the degree of participation of members of a system in particular decisions but also on the scope of these decisions which, in turn, depends on the size of the set of exercised property rights. Thus in two systems with the same resources and number of people, the system in which more property rights are exercised (occurring, for instance, when the resources of the system are used more fully) is considered more decentralized.[11] This extension of the concept of centralization is, at first sight, counter-intuitive, not only with regard to the variability of property rights within a given system but also with regard to its relationship with participation. Therefore, a brief explication is in order.

Talcott Parsons has noted:

> The dominant tendency in the literature [on power], for example [Harold] Lasswell and [C.] Wright Mills, is to maintain explicitly, or implicitly that power is a zero-sum phenomenon, which is to say that there is a fixed quantity of power in any relational system and hence any gain of power in the part of A must by definition occur by diminishing the power at the disposal of other units B, C, D . . . . There are, of course, restricted contexts in which this condition holds, but . . . it does not hold for total systems of sufficient level of complexity.[12]

The set of property rights in an organization can expand by increasing the effective use of physical resources (e.g., technical changes leading to greater effectiveness in the use of resources, or instruments of coordination becoming more effective through faster communication so that more decisions can be made, or uncertainty and other barriers to effective decision-making being reduced). Alternatively the set of property rights can expand by increasing the use of psychic resources through increasing motivations to participate and strengthening feelings of participation in decision-making by members of the organization. That is, the exercise of power often involves use of some resource by a superior to a subordinate in return for compliance of an order of the former by the latter. Since such dispensed resources can consist of approval, affection, or other intangibles, the quantity of which is presumably not limited, then effective control can increase when such intangibles are used in a better fashion.

11. Arnold S. Tannenbaum [*Control in Organization* (New York: 1968), p. 32] examines on a theoretical basis two organizations, within each of which every member has the same degree of power. He labels the organization in which the average property rights are low as "anarchy" and the organization in which the average property rights are high as "polyarchy."

12. Talcott Parsons, "On the Concept of Political Power," *Proceedings of the American Philosophical Society,* CVII, March 1963, pp. 232–3.

> An increase in affectional ties among members [e.g., morale] may lead to the growth of social approval as a resource. . . . Hence social systems composed of persons who like one another can, in principle, engage in a greater amount of exchange of approval for compliance than a system composed of persons who are indifferent to one another.[13]

Increased participation is not necessarily a subjective phenomenon: In organizations certain decisions are simply not consciously made which, if participation in decision-making were increased, would be made. On a trivial level a decision to replace a broken chair may neither be affirmatively nor negatively made; the chair is simply not replaced because no one thinks about it. Examples of the phenomenon at a much more significant level can be easily found in the business administration literature.[14]

This notion of centralization is related to the three types of control in the same manner as the more limited definition of participation discussed above. Defining decentralization in terms of increasing the total power and participation of organization's members leads to the argument that the attempt by East Germany to improve the effectiveness of its economy by increasing the degree of participation in decision-making by people at all levels of the economy was a decentralization.

c. *Concepts or indices of centralization focusing on the structure of the system.* (vii) Centralization is manifested when the operations of a system or an organization are carried out primarily in one place rather than dispersed over the entire geographical area embraced by the system. This concept is based on the notion that the sharing of control by individuals from a wide number of places (which, in turn, may represent quite different interests) means more decentralization than when control is exercised by individuals from a single area that may not have such a diversity of interests. Such "spatial centralization" is examined for a set of economies with different economic systems later in the chapter.

(viii) Centralization is manifested by low vertical mobility within a system, which means that positions with great property rights are held

---

13. Tannenbaum, p. 15.

14. A much more important example of this increase in the set of property rights can be seen in the autobiography of Alfred P. Sloan, Jr., *My Years with General Motors* (New York: 1963). As President of G.M. (which has an industrial production larger than any East European nation except the Soviet Union), Sloan instituted an information system which not only allowed greater coordination of decisions at lower levels but also permitted certain decisions to be made at various levels which were totally neglected before.

by a few people over a long span of time. This approach is also used below to examine the centralization of an organization in terms of the lack of rapidity of changes in relative power of particular subunits of the organization. Part of this notion of centralization is based on the idea that it takes time to learn to exercise particular property rights, so that less control can be exercised by leaders if the turnover of leaders is fast; and part of this notion is based on the simple idea that with a rapid turnover power is shared by a larger number of individuals. This concept of centralization is designated below as "temporal centralization."

(ix) Centralization is manifested by a high degree of functional specialization, which occurs when the exercising of particular functions is placed in one man or department.[15] For instance, we say that the personnel functions are centralized in an organization when each division is no longer able to make its own decisions on such matters but must take the commands or negotiate with a central personnel agency. This dimension indicates the degree of subunit independence (or, from the opposite side, the degree of subunit dependence) on other subunits or higher administrative levels. While this concept of centralization certainly refers to the restructuring of choice sets among the subunits of organizations and a distinct narrowing of such choices of particular subunits, the primary emphasis is on the structure, or type of choices, rather than the amount of choices open to particular decision-makers.

(x) Centralization is manifested in a system by the existence of large organization units that control many resources; within an organization, centralization is manifested when the major subunits of the organization are relatively large (rather than consisting of a larger number of smaller units). This definition of centralization focuses on macro-structural properties of a system. It is frequently found in discussions of the alleged "organizational revolution" of industrial societies where it is argued that centralization in the economic system is increasing because the sizes of the various organizations such as enterprises, unions, pressure groups, and so forth are increasing.[16] Such a concept seems to rest on the notion that with increasing organizational size, autonomy of decision-making of most individuals decreases (i.e., more control in some form is exercised over them) and also, perhaps, on the assumption that the heads of the organizational units or the major subunits under consideration effectively exercise control. This concept of centralization raises a num-

---

15. This approach to centralization is argued by Herbert A. Simon, *et al., Public Administration* (New York: 1956), Chapter 12, pp. 260–80.
16. For instance, this approach to centralization appears to be adopted by Marion J. Levy, Jr., *Modernization and the Structure of Societies,* Vol. I (Princeton: 1966), especially pp. 16–18 where he defines centralization.

ber of difficulties, not the least of which are the snares in linking the centralization concept to the shape of the administrative hierarchy (which defines the sizes of subunits.)[17]

d. *Concluding observations.* The list of ten concepts or indices of centralization is not exhaustive, for the term has been used in other ways as well; further, the list does not contain all the variants of particular concepts or indices.[18] Nevertheless, the list seems to cover those definitions or indices that are most useful in the study of economic systems and are consistent with my basic approach. Usages of the concept of cen-

17. Usually those trying to link centralization with the shape of the administrative hierarchy do not argue centralization in terms of subunit size, although this seems nevertheless to be a key notion. In any case, the theoretical arguments lead to quite diverse views on the matter.

According to some observers such as Blau (Peter M. Blau, *et al.,* "The Structure of Small Bureaucracies," *American Sociological Review,* XXXI, April 1966, pp. 179–92), a flat administrative pyramid with a large average span of control indicates centralization because the high administrators are closer to those who actually carry out their commands, can interfere more easily, and receive less distorted information.

According to most other observers, a tall administrative hierarchy with a small average span of control indicates centralization since superiors can more easily watch a few rather than a large number of subordinates and, moreover, have more time to spend on individual decisions (arguments implicit in the definition of centralization given above). One detailed empirical study of this matter is by Thomas L. Whisler, *et al.,* "Centralization or Organizational Control: An Empirical Study of its Meaning and Measurement," Tannenbaum, pp. 283–307. Although the shape of the administrative hierarchy is not without interest, I do not think that the problem of centralization can be easily attacked in this manner.

18. One variant of the participation approach is contained in a pioneering article by Thomas Marschak ("Centralization and Decentralization in Economic Organization," *Econometrica,* XXVII, July 1959, pp. 399–430) in which centralization is said to be manifested when there is less iteration in the decision-making process between subordinate and superior, i.e., there is less interaction between the top decision-makers and lower echelons who supply crucial information and who carry out orders. For instance, a political system featuring less frequent elections is, according to this approach, more centralized than one with a great many elections. Similarly, an organization in which the top managers receive information from lower units, make a decision, and send down unalterable orders is more centralized than organizations in which top managers send down tentative plans and then revise them at least once before sending down unalterable orders. This concept of centralization seems based on the notion that iteration between top and bottom levels within an administrative hierarchy allows greater influence on the decision by lower echelon by means of greater participation. However, such a concept of centralization may seem partly at odds with that defining centralization in terms of vertical versus horizontal interaction, and also in terms of frequency of performance review. Such a conflict is more apparent than real, since this interactive definition refers primarily to the process of arriving at decisions, while the other two definitions refer more to the giving of orders.

tralization that are inconsistent with my approach, e.g., centralization defined in terms of the way in which control is exercised[19] or in terms of bureaucratization,[20] are omitted from further mention.

I find it strange that the organization theory literature on centralization has focused primary attention on control manifested through the narrowing of the choice sets of subordinates rather than on control manifested through the manipulation of values or procedures, although the latter two methods of control, particularly in political systems, are just as important. Furthermore, most concepts of centralization in the organization theory literature are defined in terms of hierarchical organizations although, as organization theorists quite readily admit, this is only one specific type of organization. Moreover, much of the organization literature on centralization never seems to have transcended the rather narrow sets of concerns that gave rise to organization theory as a separate discipline in the first place.

Although the logical or conceptual differences of the ten definitions or indices should be clear, their empirical connections deserve brief exploration.

3. Relationships between Concepts or Indices of Centralization

To what extent are the various concepts of centralization empirically related? Surely an organization can have a centralized pattern of property rights with regard to certain decisions and a decentralized pattern with regard to other decisions. For instance, during the "mobilization phase" of early Soviet industrialization in the late 1920s, some industries were administered in an extremely centralized fashion while others were operated on a highly decentralized basis.[21] Or in a recent study of decentraliza-

19. It is sometimes argued in the literature of Eastern Europe that reliance on "indirect" incentives (i.e., manipulation of prices), rather than on "direct" incentives (i.e., commands) represents a decentralization *per se*. If the two methods are used to induce the same response on the part of the subordinate, then this is not a decentralization, according to my definition. Historically, however, the move from direct to indirect incentives has been accompanied by a decentralization according to other concepts.

20. One spurious index of centralization that is often used in the organization literature is the ratio of workers in administration to workers in production. Although this is an interesting phenomenon to investigate (see especially Appendix B-11), it seems more related to the particular industry or to bureaucratization than to centralization, at least according to the ten definitions outlined above.

21. This is analyzed in a fascinating article by John Michael Montias, "Types of Communist Economic Systems," in Chalmers Johnson, ed., *Change in Communist Systems* (Stanford: 1970), pp. 117–34. In the mobilization phase, hierarchically transmitted commands were relatively few except in the priority industries. Plans were initiated "from below" and the

tion in fifty-three state employment security agencies in the United States in the 1960s, Peter Blau found no correlation between delegation of authority to lower officials in hiring procedures, delegation of budget decisions, or influence exercised by lower officials in agency policy-making.[22]

But with regard to single areas of decision-making, it is possible that the degree of centralization according to one concept or index may or may not be related to that according to another concept. The empirical studies of a number of different types of complex organizations show quite clearly that certain concepts of centralization (e.g., centralization in terms of job routinization and hierarchical centralization) show no empirical correlation and that other concepts of centralization (e.g., centralization in terms of functional specialization) are related to some concepts (in this case, centralization in terms of job routinization) but not to others (e.g., hierarchical centralization).[23]

One way to investigate this matter is to study a set of organizations in terms of the various definitions of centralization and then to see which indices show positive or negative relationships with each other. Although some empirical evidence on these matters is available, the data extend to only a few concepts or indices of centralization and much remains to be done before conclusive answers can be given.

C. Developmental Propositions about Centralization

Distinguishing ten definitions of centralization is a pleasant academic parlor game, but the exercise has a more serious purpose, namely to develop a series of propositions about property relations. Developmental propositions deal with the determinants of the centralization of property rights or with factors influencing the change in centralization of particular

overall plan seemed to serve as a loose framework rather than as a set of operational directives. It can be argued that centralization in the nonpriority industries was great but manifested by means of the manipulation of values so that managers made decisions according to the public interest rather than to more limited interests. If this is true, then centralization was manifested in a different way by quite different means; on the other hand, I'm not sure how effective this attempted manipulation of values actually was or, indeed, how strongly Soviet leaders really exercised such activities to fulfill a conscious design.

22. Peter M. Blau, "Decentralization in Bureaucracies," in Mayer Zald, ed., *Power in Organizations* (Nashville: 1970), pp. 150–74. Blau defined centralization in terms of the hierarchical level on which certain decisions are made, an improvement over the more mechanical definition of centralization that he presented in his article "The Structure of Small Bureaucracies," discussed in note 17.

23. The recent literature on these matters is reviewed in Appendix A-16.

systems; such propositions form the focus of analysis of this section. Impact propositions deal with the effects or consequences of the degree of centralization on the functioning of systems and are discussed in Section E.

The expanding literature in the field of organization theory on the determinants of various dimensions of centralization should have great relevance for the analysis of economic systems. Unfortunately, organization theorists have not yet produced very coherent evidence on these matters: Part of the difficulty lies in the poor quality of the data; part lies in relatively crude statistical techniques, especially in the handling of more than one independent variable; and part lies in the inadequacy of theory about these matters. For those interested, recent empirical studies of the determinants of centralization in complex organizations are briefly summarized in Appendix A-16.

The mining and manufacturing sector of an economy can be considered a complex organization and in this section I examine its centralization according to various concepts or indices.[24] In the first two subsections there are brief case studies of the determinants of spatial and temporal centralization in order to use the results for future discussion and also to show the ways in which such research on developmental hypotheses concerning centralization could be carried out in the future. In the third and fourth subsections I examine ways in which the "economic system" and the level of economic development influence centralization according to the ten concepts and indices of centralization discussed above. Although many parts of this section are more of a survey of problems than a catalogue of answers, a number of confusions can be cleared up and certain definite and useful conclusions drawn.

1. Determinants of Spatial Centralization in Mining and Manufacturing

Spatial centralization is manifested when the operations of a system or an organization are carried out primarily in one place rather than dispersed

---

24. A number of organizational studies have used various materials from censuses of manufacturing to argue various issues concerning centralization, but I have had difficulty in determining exactly what some of their variables have measured and, as a result, have been unable to include their results in this brief survey. Such studies include: Jack P. Gibbs and Harley L. Browning, "The Division of Labor, Technology, and the Organization of Production in Twelve Countries," *American Sociological Review,* XXXI, February 1966, pp. 81–92; and William A. Rushing, "Organizational Size, Rules, and Surveillance," in Joseph A. Litterer, ed., *Organizations: Structure and Behavior,* 2nd ed., Vol. I (New York: 1969), pp. 432–40. A number of other studies using data from censuses of manufacturing have focused on spans of control, relation of white-collar to blue-collar workers, and other

over the entire geographical area embraced by the system. It is an aspect of centralization that lends itself easily to empirical analysis and several international comparisons of such centralization have appeared in recent years.[25] Close attention to this matter is important, not only because the equalization of industrial development among geographical regions is an important policy goal for many governments, but also because some theorists are pointing toward processes of spatial centralization as paradigmatic of all important processes of centralization.[26]

Do economies in which all important investment decisions are made or approved by a central state organization have a greater or lesser degree of spatial centralization than market economies or economies with a lower degree of state investment participation?[27] Since state participation in investment decisions was much greater in any East European nation (with the possible exception of Yugoslavia) than in any West European nation, this should not be a difficult question to answer. If we look at the East European literature on these matters, however, a curious ambivalence can be discerned that complicates answering this question.

On the one hand, East European policy-makers have proclaimed their adherence to the idea that industrial development should gradually become equalized among regions, not only to avoid the regional "disproportions" that allegedly characterize capitalism but also to minimize the social costs of uprooting people in a rural area in one part of the nation and sending them to work in industry in another part. Furthermore, they have noted that it is impossible for a nation to march to communism if certain parts of the country are greatly lagging in industrial development. They also argue that regional equalization of industry can be achieved only through conscious planning and, conversely, cannot be obtained by

such issues that, as I note above, have little relationship to the question of centralization of property rights.

25. Two such studies of the spatial centralization of nations are: Jeffrey G. Williamson, "Regional Inequality and the Process of National Development: A Description of Patterns," *Economic Development and Cultural Change,* XIII, July 1965, Part II, pp. 1–84; and Iwan S. Koropeckyj, "Equalization of Regional Development in Socialist Countries: An Empirical Study," *Economic Development and Cultural Change,* XXI, October 1972, pp. 68–86.

26. See especially Manfred Kochen and Karl W. Deutsch, "Toward a Rational Theory of Decentralization: Some Implications of a Mathematical Approach," *American Political Science Review,* LXIII, September 1969, pp. 743–49.

27. Although most industrial investment in Eastern Europe (except Yugoslavia) is subject to the approval of various central bodies, it must also be noted that in most West European nations, 40 to 60 percent of investment is financed by various government organs which presumably have some decision-making power. (This matter is discussed in detail in Angus Maddison, *Economic Growth in the West: Comparative Experience in Europe and North American* [New York: 1964].)

reliance on the "anarchic forces" of the market.[28] Finally, avoidance of manufacturing concentration in several regions has certain advantages for national defense purposes, to which Eastern Europeans should not be blind.

On the other hand, East European policy-makers have also proclaimed their desire to obtain the fastest possible industrial growth rate for the entire economy. With a given amount of investment funds, faster growth may be achieved by investing in areas where social overhead capital has already been built and where it is not necessary to train an entirely new labor force which has never been exposed to modern manufacturing methods. In other words, there may be a trade-off between growth and regional equality such that more rapid growth precludes regional equalization of mining and manufacturing. In addition, because central investment funds are allocated in a bargaining process, representatives from more industrialized areas around the capital may have a better chance of obtaining such funds than those from distant and unindustrialized regions.

Since theoretical considerations can be used to argue either side of the question of whether regional equalization of industry is greater or less in the East than in the West, empirical analysis of the type presented below must be used to resolve the question.

To explore empirically the spatial distribution of mining and manufacturing, we could examine either relative differences of value-added in these sectors on a per capita basis for all regions or relative differences in the percentage of the population engaged in these sectors (which I designate as the "industrialization indicator") in the various regions. Results using the two measures appear highly correlated[29] and since data only for the industrialization indicator are relatively abundant for countries in both the East and the West, this measure was chosen for use.

Few serious problems arise in the collection of data. Pains were taken to include all parts of the labor force in mining and manufacturing (including, in the East European nations, the labor force in industrial producer cooperatives and private industry) to eliminate systematic bias arising from this source. Although the definition of the manufacturing sector is slightly broader in the data used for East Europe, this should not significantly affect the results.[30]

28. These arguments are discussed in greater detail by Koropeckyj.
29. This is demonstrated empirically by Koropeckyj.
30. The East European data include the labor force of certain utilities which are excluded in the data for the West. Although this should give the East European results a slight bias toward regional equality (presumably the distribution of utilities is regionally more equal than manufacturing), the results should not be sufficiently affected since this part of the labor force is very small compared to the rest in manufacturing. It would also be desirable

In condensing the data for making the most meaningful comparisons, three statistical considerations must be taken into account. First, if some aggregate measure such as the coefficient of variation is used to measure the dispersion of the industrialization indicator, the results are affected by the number of regions into which the nation is divided.[31] To circumvent this problem, all nations were divided into nine regions by joining contiguous districts into regions of roughly equal population size.[32] Several nations have data for fewer than nine regions and, therefore, had to be eliminated. Second, it would be useful to have a statistic that allows us to determine whether a change in the industrialization indicator is due to a shift in population or to a greater increase in the labor force employed in mining and manufacturing. The coefficient of variation was therefore scrapped for a statistic described in the next paragraph. Finally, in order to avoid any biases introduced by comparing periods with different technological influences on the process of spatial centralization, I tried to obtain data for a decade interval from the mid-1950s to the mid-1960s for all nations. The relevant data with countries arranged according to descending per capita G.N.P. (measured at the middle of the decade interval) are presented in Table 8–1.

The nine regions in each country were arranged according to descending industrialization ratios and a line was drawn which divided them into two groups roughly equal in population; aggregate industrialization ratios were then calculated for the two groups and compared. Information is lost by this procedure, but comparability is gained. The results in the first column of statistics show the ratio of industrialization ratios of the industrially more developed to the less developed areas. For instance, if the industrialization indicator in the more developed set of regions was

---

to make the comparisons only for manufacturing, but regional data for manufacturing alone are not available for most East European nations.

31. Both Williamson and Koropeckyj measure the degree of dispersion of industrialization between regions by the coefficient of variation uncorrected for the number of regions. The effects of consolidation can be shown for the United States for which such coefficients of variations of the ratio of manufacturing labor force to the population can be easily calculated:

	1955 coefficient of variation	*1965* coefficient of variation	*Ratio 1965 to 1955*
48 states and Washington, D.C.	.481	.428	.890
9 regions	.383	.311	.811

32. The Soviet Union had to be omitted from the comparisons for this reason because data on the industrial labor force in years a decade apart are available only on a republic basis, and one republic accounts for one-half of the population (the RSFSR) and a second republic accounts for roughly one-half of the remainder (the Ukraine).

TABLE 8-1

Indicators of Spatial Centralization in Mining and Manufacturing[a]

Country	Time Period	Industrialization Indicator at Beginning of Period	Ratios of Data in More Developed to Less Developed Regions		
			Relative Change in Industrialization Indicator	Relative Growth of Population	Relative Growth of Labor Force in Mining and Mfg.
Capitalist nations					
United States	1955–65	1.923	.861	.946	.815
Switzerland	1956–66	1.633	.876	1.031	.903
Sweden	1955–65	1.384	.987	1.010	.997
Canada	1955–65	2.208	1.034	1.057	1.093
West Germany	1955–65	1.679	.853	1.076	.918
Norway	1955–65	1.936	.855	1.048	.896
Belgium	1955–64	1.445	.762	1.004	.765
Netherlands	1950–60	1.278	1.031	1.030	1.062
Japan	1955–65	1.737	1.156	1.239	1.477
Italy	1951–61	3.034	1.045	1.045	1.092
Greece	1951–61	1.925	.977	1.173	1.146
Socialist nations					
Czechoslovakia	1955–65	1.466	.967	.941	.910
East Germany	1955–65	3.008	.988	1.011	.999
Hungary	1957–67	2.918	.759	1.059	.803
Poland	1955–65	2.117	.815	1.022	.834
Bulgaria	1959–68	1.783	.765	1.027	.785
Romania	1956–65	1.801	.971	.981	.953
Yugoslavia	1957–67	1.576	.965	1.009	.974

a. All nations were divided into nine regions except Yugoslavia, for which data for only eight regions were available. The various statistics are defined and discussed in the text; exact definitions, however, can easily be given in symbolic form. Let L = the labor force in mining and manufacturing; P = population; subscripts v and u designate the developed and underdeveloped regions of the nation, and subscripts t and t-1 designate the two time periods. The industrialization indicator is designated I = L/P. The four ratios for which data are presented are:

$$I_v/I_u; \quad (I_{v,\,t}/I_{u,\,t})/(I_{v,\,t-1}/I_{u,\,t-1}); \quad (P_{v,\,t}/P_{u,\,t})/(P_{v,\,t-1}/P_{u,\,t-1}); \quad \text{and} \quad (L_{v,\,t}/L_{u,\,t})/(L_{v,\,t-1}/L_{u,\,t-1}).$$

The source of data and other notes are presented in Appendix B-25.

10 percent and in the less developed regions was 5 percent, then a ratio of 2.000 is entered in the table. We should not expect these ratios to be related to any economic variables in the mid-1950s since geographical, historical, and political (e.g., war) factors would greatly influence the results. And, indeed, regression experiments with the data indicate that the relative industrialization indicators are related neither to per capita income, economic system, population, density of population, or other variables that I tried (singly or together).

Equalization of industrialization (or spatial decentralization) occurs when the industrialization indicator of the less developed regions increases faster than this indicator for the more developed regions. A comparison of relative ratios of change is presented in the next column, where any number below 1.000 indicates a trend toward regional equalization and any number above 1.000, the reverse. If, for instance, the relative industrialization indicator in the first column of data were 2.000 in the first year and 1.500 in the second year, the number .750 would be entered in the table, from which we could see that spatial decentralization had occurred.

In most nations spatial decentralization (or regional equalization of industry) had occurred. This process was most marked in Hungary, a nation with a relatively high initial degree of regional inequality. In the few nations where spatial centralization occurred, the process was not very extensive.[33] In order to isolate the underlying determinants, a large number of regression experiments were performed, with numerous variables (discussed below) tried either singly or together. The results can be easily summarized.

First of all, the process of spatial centralization does not seem to be systems-determined. That is, the process of spatial decentralization was not significantly different in rate among the East European nations, where governmental participation in investment decision-making was considerably greater than in the West, than among the Western nations. These negative results were not changed when Yugoslavia was dropped from the sample. Although East European policy-makers apparently made investment decisions resulting in a slight spatial decentralization, the performance of the East is no different than that of the West where market forces played a more important role.

Second, although previous investigators have hypothesized a rela-

33. The statistic for Japan may be somewhat misleading since it is the only nation for which the degree of aggregation of the regions made a great deal of difference. If forty-six regions are used, the relative change in the industrialization indicator in Japan was roughly one. Thus spatial centralization remained relatively constant if we look at small districts, but increased if we look at larger regions, a situation which is certainly possible but which did not occur in any other nation.

tionship between level of economic development and spatial centralization, no such tendency could be found. More specifically, it has been argued that in early stages of industrialization (at least in capitalist nations), spatial centralization occurs and that spatial decentralization begins to occur only after industrialization is well under way. Using the dollar value of per capita G.N.P. as a measure of development, no such pattern could be detected.

Third, no relationship between the rate of spatial decentralization in mining and manufacturing with any other economic variable could be found. To fish for empirical associations, I fed into the regression such variables as density of population, total population, population growth, labor-force growth, and initial level of the spatial centralization ratio; no statistically significant relationships could be found with these variables, either singly, together, or in various combinations with per capita income and an economic systems variable. Certain obvious political factors did not seem to play a role either, for nations with important ethnic minorities (e.g., Switzerland, Canada, Belgium, Czechoslovakia, Romania, and Yugoslavia) do not seem any different than the rest; and nations in which political leaders placed particular (verbal) emphasis on regional equalization of industry (especially Italy and Yugoslavia) appear no different either. It is also interesting to note that regional orientation of governmental decision-making organs (e.g., East Germany followed in a modified fashion between 1958 and 1963 a version of the Soviet *sovnarkhoz* experiment) seems to have made no difference either.

In the third and fourth column of statistics are relative rates of change of the population and industrial labor force in the more and less developed regions of the country. Any ratio greater than one indicates that the population (or labor force) grew faster in the more developed areas. For instance, if 50 percent of the population were in the more developed areas in the initial year and 60 percent were there in the final year, 1.200 would be entered in the table. If there were no population shift between the two regions, we would expect the relative growth ratio to be slightly less than unity because the rate of natural increase of the population is usually higher in the less developed areas. The same type of statistical analysis is carried out for the labor force in mining and manufacturing.[34]

Regression experiments reveal that the relative regional growth of population in the more developed regions was greater in the capitalist nations than in the socialist nations; and, moreover, that this process occurred to a greater extent in the nations with lower levels of economic

34. The algebraic relationship between the second, third, and fourth columns (designated in this note as B, C, and D) can be easily expressed: $B = D/C$.

development (per capita G.N.P.). A similar but more ambiguous result is also obtained in examining the relative regional growth of the labor force in mining and manufacturing in the two systems.[35] This suggests that the process of spatial decentralization of mining and manufacturing which was roughly equal in capitalist and socialist nations was accompanied by a greater relative shift in population in the former group of nations. It must be emphasized that we cannot be sure about this matter (more particularly, we cannot tell whether these results occurred because of migration or because of different patterns of natality and mortality in economically more and less developed areas in the two economic systems) until we carry out a close demographic analysis which is difficult with the scanty data for some East European nations.

Although negative results are never as exciting as positive results, one conclusion is important: the impact of economic system or high governmental participation in investment decision-making is quite unclear and previous dogmatism on the subject appears unwarranted. In the field of spatial decentralization of mining and manufacturing, words and institutions are apparently much weaker than deeds; as yet, we have little knowledge of the actual determinants of this type of centralization.

2. Determinants of Temporal Centralization in Mining and Manufacturing in the West

Temporal centralization focuses our attention on the degree to which particular individuals or organizations hold leading positions over long periods of time. With this concept of centralization we can examine the degree to which large enterprises in one period maintained their relative importance in the entire mining and manufacturing sector over time. The use of enterprises as the unit of analysis is based on the assumption that there is sufficient continuity in control over individual enterprises that such temporal comparisons are meaningful. This topic of temporal patterns of relative importance of large enterprises has received considerable attention from economists who have looked at this phenomenon in order to determine the "dynamism" of competition or the "dynamism" of the organization of industry.

---

35. Several regression results are presented in Appendix B-29. Regression experiments were made using a variety of independent variables such as industrialization indicator in the initial period, population density, population growth, growth of labor force in mining and manufacturing, economic system, total population, and per capita G.N.P. With regard to the regressions with the relative growth of labor force as the dependent variable, serious questions arise as to whether the capitalist and socialist nations are drawn from the same statistical universe and, for this reason, the various regression results are not explored in detail.

For the United States, data are available about the relative sizes of the largest enterprises for a sixty-year time period, and for several Western European nations, relevant data are readily accessible for a postwar decade. Unfortunately, no East European data could be located so that the comparisons made must be intra-system, rather than inter-system. For the United States the set of big businesses includes 100 largest enterprises; and for the other countries the sample of largest enterprises is proportionately smaller. (Determination of the "set of big businesses" is discussed in Chapter VI.) Relevant statistics on temporal centralization are presented in Table 8–2.

In the first column of statistics are data showing the percentage of assets of mining and manufacturing enterprises in the set of big businesses that were also in this set the decade before. If the group of enterprises in the set remained exactly the same, the statistic would be 100 percent; if every enterprise in the set of big businesses was completely different, the statistic would be 0 percent.

The data show clearly that for the United States, the percentage of assets of mining and manufacturing enterprises in the set of big businesses that was accounted for by the enterprises in the set a decade before has risen over the half century. This means that the relative importance (measured in assets) of new enterprises entering the set of big businesses has been declining over time. Although this measure of temporal centralization is easy to compute, it is not completely adequate since it says little about changes in relative asset shares within the set of big businesses, i.e., whether the relative importance of enterprises remaining in "big business" over the decade has greatly changed.

One way to measure stability of position within big business is to calculate the coefficient of variation (standard deviation divided by mean asset share of all enterprises in the sample of that nation) of asset share between the beginning and the end of the decade; such data are presented in the next two columns.[36] For the United States, this coefficient of variation declined between 1909 and 1929, remained at a low plateau until 1958, and then rose between 1958 and 1968. Thus between 1909 and 1958, the results indicate a decline in relative movement among enter-

36. Let us assume that the coefficient of variation is 40 percent. If we assume that the change in asset shares roughly approximates a normal distribution, then we can use this datum for the following statements: For an enterprise among the top "big businesses" with an asset share of A, there is a 68 percent probability that A will change over the decade less than 40 percent (i.e., A ± .40 A); and a 95 percent probability that there will be a 78 percent change in asset share (i.e., A ± .78 A). There are other methods of analyzing this problem (e.g., regression analysis is used by David Mermelstein, "Large Industrial Corporations and Asset Shares," *American Economic Review*, LIX, September 1969, pp. 531–42), but interpretation of the results using my approach is simpler.

TABLE 8–2

Indicators of Mobility of "Big Business" in Four Western Nations[a]

Country	Years for Which Comparisons Are Made	Percentage of Assets of Big Businesses in Later Year Accounted for by Big Business in Earlier Year	Coefficient of Variation of Share in Big Business in Later Years *Vis-à-vis* Earlier Year		Enterprise Disappearing because of Mergers	
			No adjustment	Adjusted	Percentage of enterprises	Percentage of assets involved
United States	1909–19	52%	112%	112%	1%	1.1%
	1919–29	50	76	76	11	7.3
	1929–35	73	32	54	4	2.4
	1935–48	70	41	31	0	0.0
	1948–58	71	36	36	0	0.0
	1958–68	87	60	60	5	2.0
France	1956–57/ 1966–67	75	75	75	10	7.6
Germany	1957–66	86	55	62	9	7.0
United Kingdom	1953–54/ 1964–65	90	38	35	6	2.2

a. The coefficient of variation is an indication of the degree to which the share coefficients of assets of individual big businesses changed over time. It was calculated from the list of big businesses after adjustments for mergers and dissolutions. A standard deviation of change of asset share was calculated for the enterprises between the early and later years; the ratio of this standard deviation to the average asset share of individual big businesses is the coefficient of variation. The adjusted figure is a rough adjustment so that decade intervals could be compared for all nations and at all times. Sources and methods are discussed in Appendix B-27.

prises in the set of big businesses and thus an increase in temporal centralization. This conclusion parallels the results obtained from the more simple measure presented in the first column. However, the coefficient of variation measure indicates a temporal decentralization between 1958 and 1968, which, as I argue below, seems to be due to differential merger activities among the enterprises in the sample with enterprises outside the set of big businesses (mergers or dissolutions within the set of big businesses are taken into account in the calculations) and has little to do with the classical idea of the "dynamism" of capitalism.

For Western Europe, such long time-series comparisons could not be made; nevertheless, comparisons can be made for recent years and certain rough conclusions drawn. First, temporal centralization was least in France and greatest in the United Kingdom, with West Germany in the middle. Both France and Germany showed slightly less temporal centralization in the decade running from the mid-1950s to the mid-1960s than the United States. Although the relative positions of French and German enterprises may come as a surprise, the differences between the two nations are not great; the high temporal centralization for the United Kingdom parallels the widely held and discussed belief that the United Kingdom industrial system lacks dynamism.[37] The relative importance of the largest enterprises between the two comparison dates was quite high in all three countries; on the other hand, the degree of change of asset shares within this group also seems relatively high, at least in France and West Germany.

In interpreting these temporal centralization results in terms of the "dynamism" of capitalism, certain precautions must be exercised. Certainly the relatively low mobility of enterprises into the "big business" category can be interpreted in terms of increasing permanence of a small group of extremely large enterprises. However, the coefficients of variation of share within this group can be traced to several different factors. If each big business maintained its share of the specific industries in which it is engaged but if certain industries grew at very much different rates than others, then the relative asset shares of big businesses would change. Similarly, if certain big businesses merged with a large number of small enterprises while others did not, relative asset shares of big businesses would change because of differential merger activity. Finally, of course, a high coefficient of variation of asset share could actually reflect the phenomenon we are trying to measure, namely differential change in asset growth because of differential response to market oppor-

---

37. Other types of evidence on this matter are presented by various authors in Richard Caves, ed., *Britain's Economic Prospects* (Washington, D.C.: 1968).

tunities. The merger activity within the set of big businesses was probably paralleled by mergers between big businesses and enterprises outside this set, and I strongly suspect that this is the reason why the coefficient of variation of asset shares was high at the same time that the relative importance of assets of enterprises remaining in the set of "big businesses" between the two comparison dates was also rising.[38]

From this discussion about temporal centralization several conclusions can be drawn. First, temporal centralization appears to have increased over time which, in turn, suggests that temporal centralization is linked with long-term processes of industrialization. Since enterprise size in absolute terms (see Chapter VI) was also increasing at the same time, there may be some causal connection here as well. Second, at a single point in time, temporal centralization does not appear strongly related with the level of industrialization. This may be due to the fact that temporal centralization can be strongly affected by a number of different factors such as merger activities of large firms and governmental policies toward such mergers, factors which may change over time in a systematic manner but at different rates so that cross-section analyses do not reveal causal factors. Third, the appearance of the same enterprises in the set of "big businesses" decade after decade suggests that certain crucial aspects of industrial activity are not taken properly into account in the neoclassical analysis of economic activity; more specifically, enormous size appears to endow an enterprise with longevity that is not accounted for with traditional theories of competition.

38. The change in market shares of large enterprises has been statistically analyzed by Irvin M. Grossack, "Toward an Integration of Static and Dynamic Measures of Industry Concentration," *The Review of Economics and Statistics,* XLVII, August 1965, pp. 301–8; and Michael Gort, "Analysis of Stability and Change in Market Shares," *Journal of Political Economy,* LXXI, February 1963, pp. 51–63. Although both studies covered only the 1947–54 period, they showed little change in market shares in individual industries, a phenomenon that paralleled the relatively small change in four-digit, four-firm concentration ratios. Although such dynamic data are not available for a later period, the continued stability of the four-digit, four-firm concentration ratios suggests that the dynamic stability continued.

The influence of diversification on corporate growth for the 1960–65 period has been empirically studied by Charles H. Berry, "Corporate Growth and Industrial Diversification," (unpublished paper). His preliminary results show that although growth in corporate assets are positively related to increases in diversification (some of which may have come about through mergers), the relationship is not strong and, furthermore, there are a number of other explanatory variables which seem more important. On the other hand, more than two-thirds of all important industrial mergers (which have been increasing in importance every year) can be classified as conglomerate, according to the Federal Trade Commission (*Large Mergers in Manufacturing and Mining, 1948–67* [Washington, D.C.: 1968]).

3. The "Economic System" as a Determinant of Centralization

In the previous two subsections case studies of various determinants of particular types of centralization were explored. In the next two subsections the impact of particular determinants on the various types of centralization are examined. Because of the nature of the problems and the lack of much important information, the conclusions in the discussion below must be more tentative than those drawn above.

In the following pages I investigate the impact of "economic system" on centralization. Quotes are placed around "economic system" because I mean this term to be considered according to conventional labels of such systems; in Chapter IX I argue that defining economic systems in terms of the degree of centralization is often useful.

The basic question for exploration is: In what ways are socialist "centrally planned economies" more centralized than capitalist "market economies"? Although seemingly trivial, this question is difficult to answer and requires a comparison of a set of East European and of Western economies using the various concepts or indices of centralization discussed above. Moreover, it requires consideration not only of the East European economies during the 1950s but also in their postreform operations as well.

Rather than plunging directly into the comparisons, it seems useful to consider briefly some basic relationships between ownership and centralization to see at a general level if this particular aspect of property rights affects centralization in a systematic manner.

a. *Ownership and concepts of centralization.* On a micro-economic level, ownership appears to have certain distinct relationships with different concepts of centralization. One group of investigators found in the United Kingdom that hierarchical centralization is greater in publicly owned enterprises than in privately owned enterprises, a finding in line with their general conclusion that organizations dependent on other organizations of a broader scope have greater hierarchical centralization than autonomous organizations (e.g., an industrial establishment would manifest less hierarchical centralization if it were a single establishment enterprise, rather than part of a multi-establishment enterprise).[39] Another investigator found that in Israel publicly owned enterprises had greater cen-

39. D. S. Pugh, *et al.,* "The Context of Organization Structures," *Administrative Science Quarterly,* XIV, March 1969, pp. 91–114; and Yitzhak Samuel and Bilha F. Mannheim, "A Multidimensional Approach toward a Typology of Bureaucracy," *Administrative Science Quarterly,* XV, June 1970, pp. 216–28.

tralization in terms of job standardization and routinization than privately owned enterprises, but this result has not been found in studies of other nations.[40] One explanation for greater centralization in publicly owned enterprises that organization theorists have offered is that such enterprises are usually manager-dominated and, according to empirical studies, owner-dominated enterprises show less hierarchical centralization than privately owned but manager-dominated enterprises.[41] (If there are only a few managers but many owners, owner-dominated enterprises may show less centralization in another way, namely a greater number of people participating in important decision-making.) The results of these studies, while interesting, may not replicate with international comparisons since national administrative traditions may be quite different; nevertheless, they are suggestive.

On a macro-economic level, as I argued in Chapter I from a sample of West European nations, the degree of public ownership appears correlated with the degree of governmental planning and administration of the economy, which suggests centralization. The correlation admits, however, of a number of exceptions. Further, the evaluation of "governmental planning and administration" was made from a survey of expert opinion and the exact criteria on which they based their judgments were not specified. It is time, therefore, to make our own judgments about these matters using explicit criteria. To facilitate discussion I start backwards on the list of concepts and indices of centralization that are presented above.

b. *"Economic system" and structural concepts of centralization.* Four structural concepts of centralization were defined above, but for spatial centralization I have already shown that economic system does not appear to play a role, either in the cross-section or in the time-series analysis. For temporal centralization, data with which to make meaningful comparisons are not available. Therefore, we must focus our attention on centralization defined in terms of the existence of large organizational units and in terms of functional specialization.

Comparisons between East and West regarding large industrial units were made in Chapters V and VI and we have much evidence on which to draw. Holding market size constant, we saw that the average sizes of both industrial establishments and enterprises are larger in the

40. Samuel and Mannheim found a positive relationship; but no significant relationship is reported by Pugh, *et al.,* "The Context . . . ." It is interesting that Samuel and Mannheim found the least centralization in terms of job routinization in enterprises owned by the labor unions, while the privately owned enterprises scored roughly between the union owned and the publicly owned enterprises.

41. Pugh, *et al.,* "The Context . . . ."

East than in the West. However, is comparison of the absolute size of production units proper or is the really critical comparison the degree of enterprise or establishment agglomeration? At this point it is not necessary to answer this question since agglomeration on both the enterprise and the establishment level appear greater in the East as well. We must also note that supra-enterprise decision-making organizations in the East (associations) also appear larger in most cases than in the West (e.g., cartels), but empirical evidence on this matter is fragmentary. However, two important exceptions of this last generalization in the East are Hungary and Yugoslavia, where such organizations do not play an important role; this comparison of supra-enterprise organizations thus only applies between market economies in the West and centrally administered economies of the East.

For centralization defined in terms of functional specialization, little empirical evidence is available. If we broaden the concept of functional specialization to include specialization of production of a particular good by a small number of decision-making units (so that indicators of industrial concentration can be used in the analysis) then we can pursue this line of inquiry. Despite the possibilities for competition in Eastern Europe that are outlined in Chapter VII (competition between enterprises that are centrally and noncentrally directed; and competition by means of extra-branch production), it seems clear that the mining and manufacturing sectors in East Europe (except Yugoslavia) show a greater degree of monopoly than in the West and thus the industrial structure in the East is more centralized than in the West. However, for Yugoslavia I presented evidence in Chapter VI that the average concentration ratio is roughly the same as that in Sweden and that it also does not appear out of line with other nations of similar market size in the West. Since "socialism" does not exclude Yugoslav "market socialism," the higher centralization according to this concept of production specialization in the East does not appear to be so much a factor of system (defined in terms of ownership) as a factor of history, namely the imposition of the Soviet model of socialism on these small East European economies.

Using structural concepts of centralization, the East European nations appear more centralized only with regard to the size of organizational units. With regard to functional specialization or spatial centralization, there do not appear to be significant differences in the East and the West that can be attributed directly to ownership of the means of production.

c. *"Economic system" and participation concepts of centralization.* Three participation concepts of centralization were defined above. For centralization defined in terms of the routinization of jobs, we have no empirical evidence that would link "economic system" to centralization.[42] For centralization in terms of total property rights exercised in the system, we also have a similar dearth of comparable data. For centralization in terms of participation in decision-making, comparable data do exist for several countries but it is doubtful that valid generalizations based on these case studies covering all nations in the East and the West can be made.[43] Although we do not have sufficient information to generalize about differences between the East and the West using the three participation concepts of centralization, we can make some interesting distinctions regarding the pre- and post-reform economic systems in Eastern Europe.

As I argued in Chapter VII, an important aspect of the economic reforms in most of the East European nations was improving information-flows by increasing the informational content of prices and by improving the quality of dialogue between the center and the production units which plays such an important part in the administration of the economy. In particular, the East German emphasis on "economic levers" (policy instruments activated by informational feedbacks from the enterprises) showed not only a "cybernetic" approach but also an awareness of the importance of active participation by lower level units.

For centralization defined in terms of the total set of property rights, we can add an additional insight. The various administrative stream-linings, by attempting to release enterprise managers from "petty tutelage from above," tried to encourage managers to make decisions in certain areas that had been previously neglected; by releasing individual initiative the total volume of decisions made by the managers and central government together was to rise.

Although we can not make East-West comparisons using participation concepts of centralization, we can say that in this regard the East European economic reforms (excepting perhaps Romania) appeared to represent a decentralization. As I indicated in Chapter VII, many of the projected reforms were not carried out and detailed information is not

42. It is possible to argue that the requirements of technology transcend system in this regard and the nations in East and West should be just the same. Such a contention is disputed by new-left economists who argue that economic systems can generate technologies that either increase or decrease job routinization so that technology is not an independent variable.

43. For instance, examples of workers' councils can be found in both the East and the West (Adolf Sturmthal, *Workers' Councils* [Cambridge, Mass.: 1964]) but relatively few capitalist or socialist nations have such institutions so that "economic system" cannot be linked to this type of participation. Investigations of participation in decision-making are seldom published for the East European nations and the only studies I have been able to locate that permit comparisons between East and West are for the United States and Yugoslavia: see particularly Josip Zupanov and Arnold S. Tannenbaum, "The Distribution of Control in Some Yugoslav Industrial Organizations as Perceived by Members," in Tannenbaum, pp. 91–109.

available to allow us to assess the degree to which such decentralization was realized.

d. *"Economic system" and control concepts of centralization.* Three control concepts of centralization were defined above: centralization in terms of the administrative levels at which certain decisions are made (hierarchical centralization), the degree of detail of commands, and the extent of vertical interaction. Evidence is available for comparisons using all three concepts.

Several obvious factors point toward greater hierarchical centralization in the socialist than in the capitalist nations. In terms of scope, decision-making at the highest levels of government regarding mining and manufacturing production is very much more ambitious in most East European nations than in the West, a conclusion based on the much more limited nature of short- and long-run economic plans in the West. Further, "government regulation" in the West covers a much narrower area than in most nations in the East. Finally, government investment plans in the West leave more to individual decision-makers at a lower level than in most Eastern nations.

One problem, raised in Chapter III, emerges at this point: To what extent does actual decision-making parallel formal decision-making in Eastern Europe? Do the higher levels merely "ratify" decisions made at lower levels? Does the central governmental apparatus act merely as a supply agent or a market research agent for enterprises in the East? Although some decisions in East European industry undoubtedly occur through the give and take between enterprises and higher organs, the existence of managerial bonuses manipulated from above and (except in Yugoslavia and Hungary) material balances and rationed goods suggests that higher organs are trying to impose their will on the enterprises. Complaints by industrial managers in the East European press suggest that if the material balance and rationing systems were removed, the pattern of production would be different. Thus the conventional wisdom (in both the East and the West) that in East Europe greater initiative in production is taken by the government and more conscious and effective control (effective in the sense that choice sets by subordinates are affected) is exercised by decision-making units above the enterprises seems to reflect the true state of affairs. Let those who dispute this greater hierarchical centralization in the East offer more adequate counter-evidence than a few isolated and unqualified statements by economists from East Europe that are plucked from the literature.[44]

44. This issue of formal versus effective centralization has been raised by Paul Craig Roberts, *Alienation and the Soviet Economy* (Albuquerque: 1971). His empirical evidence in support of the proposition that in East

For centralization defined in terms of the detail of commands we can, in general, say that the East European nations (except Yugoslavia and possibly Hungary) appear more centralized than nations in the West. But is this a temporary phenomenon? Are the East European nations, as often alleged, becoming less centralized in this respect over time? To answer these questions some quantitive evidence is fortunately available so that in a crude way we can measure changes in the degree of detail of commands over time.

Perhaps the most revealing information deals with "plan positions," the number of product groups covered in the national plan. Closely related to this is the number of centrally rationed inputs, which are administratively linked to the plan. In addition, information is available on the number of material balances, the physical balances of supply and demand for different product groups drawn up by the planners. This gives some indication of the degree of disaggregation on which the administrators are working.[45] For East Germany and Poland such data are presented in Table 8–3.

Looking first at plan positions, the situation in East Germany showed considerable differences over the years. An important decline in plan positions occurred between 1955 and 1957 (which was reversed in the next decade) and again in 1967 (which was reversed after the abandonment of many of the reforms in 1969–70) so that the situation in 1972 was roughly the same as in 1963 before the reforms began. From the vantage point of the enterprise this represented no decentralization; from the vantage point of the State Planning Commission, the highest planning organ, this did represent a decentralization since the plan positions set forth at the center declined and those of the middle level of administration (the associations) increased.[46]

European economies, power really lies in the hands of the enterprise is, unfortunately, impressionistic and is based on isolated and unqualified statements found in a small part of the East European economic literature.

45. Two precautionary notes must be added. First, changes in the number of material balances or rationed goods may reflect either a change in scope or a change in the degree of aggregation. Although both represent a change in hierarchical centralization, the former seems more significant. Unfortunately, data are not available to distinguish these two cases for East Germany and Poland. Second, use of these data is based on the assumption that the degree of aggregation or scope of the material balances or rationed goods reflects some operational difference in the management of the economy. If a single aggregated balance for steel is "approved" but ten working balances for individual types of steel are also "informally" handed down to lower organs, then the "reduction" in balances has no real significance. Again, reliable information on such matters is extremely difficult to find. The data in Table 8–3 are presented in the unsubstantiated belief that they reflect actual differences in the operation of the economy.

46. For a brief discussion on the meaning of "centralization" in a three-tiered hierarchy, see Appendix A-14.

TABLE 8–3

Material Balances, Plan Positions, and Centrally Rationed Inputs in East Germany and Poland, 1954–1970[a]

A. East Germany

Year	State Planning Commission, Economic Council and Ministries	V.V.B.s (associations)	Other Central Organs and Trade Organs	Subtotal	Local Organs	Enterprises	Total
Material balances							
1956	1000 —————————		?	?	?	?	?
1959	570	370	2000	2940	330	0	3270
1963	1188	507	3366	5061	33	98	5192
1964	874	2192	2173	5239	46	168	5453
1965	436	4886	679	6001	2	350	6353
1966	233	4792	455	5480	4	456	5940
1967	138	4504	371	5013	8	1024	6045
1972	c. 300	c. 4800	?	?	?	?	5800
Plan positions							
1955	955 —————————		0?	955	0?	0?	955?
1956	810 —————————		0?	810	0?	0?	810?
1957	440 —————————		0?	440	0?	0?	440?
1959	560	0?	0?	560	0?	0	560?
1963	816	0	0	816	0	0	816
1964	719	45	85	849	0	0	849
1965	329	375	40	744	0	15	759
1966	167	529	76	772	0	21	793
1967	40	112	16	168	0	8	176
1972	300	?	?	?	0	?	800

Centrally rationed inputs

1954	330–483
1955	688
1957	553
1959	408–426
1960	363

B. Poland

Year	Total Material Balances (apparently central level)	Centrally Rationed Inputs
1955	2000–3000	1575
1957	?	1088
1958	?	455
1960	?	325
1963	?	400
1964	1600	416
1965	?	463
1966–70	?	400–450

a. For East Germany the data come from Frederic L. Pryor, *The Communist Foreign Trade System* (Cambridge, Mass.: 1963), p. 285; Michael Keren, "Concentration and Efficiency in Eastern European Reforms," in Morris Bornstein, ed., *op. cit.*, Table 2; and Michael Keren, "The New Economic System in the GDR: An Obituary," forthcoming. Certain problems of comparability arise between the data for 1954–1959 and 1963–1972; in addition, alternative estimates, which are slightly different, can also be found. For the purposes for which the data are used in the text, these data problems should not affect the conclusions. For Poland the data come from *Ekonomika przemysłu* (Warsaw: 1966), cited by Janusz G. Zielinski in a forthcoming monograph on the Polish economy.

The centrally rationed inputs in East Germany showed roughly the same pattern as the plan positions between 1955 and 1960, namely a decline. In Poland the centrally rationed inputs fell drastically between 1955 and 1958, the years bracketing the notable Polish experiments, and have remained roughly the same ever since.

In Poland the series on material balances appeared to parallel the series on centrally rationed inputs. In East Germany the situation was much more complicated since the number of material balances remained roughly constant from 1963 to 1972 but the distribution among agencies changed as the share administered by the highest organs declined and the share of the associations increased markedly.

From such data two theoretical conclusions can be drawn. First, the perspective from which centralization is viewed (from the enterprise or from the highest organs) is important to specify since results may differ from these vantage points. Second, changes in planning instruments (plan positions) and the administrative instruments (material balances and centrally rationed inputs) do not necessarily parallel each other. This latter conclusion also has implications for comparisons between nations, for we should not suspect that the quantitative relation between the two instruments would be the same. And, indeed, in the early 1960s the number of centrally rationed inputs was roughly the same in East Germany and Poland, even though the number of material balances was considerably greater in the former nation. The planning instruments are a facet of the information-flows and the administrative instruments are an aspect of the distribution of property rights; the relationship between the centralization of property rights and of information and implications for the economy are discussed in greater detail in Chapter IX.

The most important empirical conclusion to be drawn from these data is that the economic reforms in the sixties of East Germany and Poland, both of which were administrative streamlinings designed to decentralize administration by increasing participation, showed little decentralization in terms of administrative instruments, at least from the vantage point of the enterprises. That is, decentralization in terms of the detail of commands and decentralization in terms of participation do not appear correlated.

Scattered data on material balances and plan positions are also available for other East European nations,[47] but since comparability is

47. Certain data for Bulgaria, Czechoslovakia, Hungary, and the Soviet Union may be found in T. Cholinski, *et al., Gospodarka zapasami w krajach socjalistycznych* (Warsaw: 1967), cited by Zielinski. The international comparability of these data leaves something to be desired, especially since the data for the Soviet Union differ by a factor of several-fold from other data I have been able to obtain from an American expert on Soviet material planning, Professor Herbert Levine.

unclear only two generalizations can be made. First, by the measure of centrally rationed inputs or material balances, Hungary and Yugoslavia had a much greater decentralization in the late 1960s than the rest of the East European nations since these administrative devices were essentially eliminated. Second, according to both these indicators, the Soviet Union appeared more centralized than the other East European nations.[48] This is especially remarkable because the Soviet Union has a much larger and complex economy than these other nations and centralized administration should be relatively more costly.

For the last concept of centralization—centralization defined in terms of vertical versus horizontal interaction—it seems clear that any nation relying on a market mechanism is more decentralized than an economy with a central economic administration. Thus with the exception of Yugoslavia and Hungary, the East European nations were more centralized than nations in the West. The East European economic reforms (except, perhaps, in Romania) in the sixties did lead to some decentralization in this regard since, as I pointed out in Chapter VII, greater stress was placed on horizontal interaction. The adoption by Hungary of a type of market allocation system was an especially dramatic step in this direction.

Comparisons using the three structural concepts of centralization lead us to the conclusion that centralization is greater in the socialist nations (with the possible exceptions of Hungary and Yugoslavia) than in the capitalist nations. The economic reforms in East Europe led to some decentralization in terms of greater horizontal interaction, but not in terms of the degree of detail of commands, at least from the perspective of the enterprises for the two countries for which we have data.

e. *Some brief observations.* From this gallop through the ten concepts or indices of centralization, three sets of conclusions can be drawn.

First, for those concepts or indices of centralization for which data are available, the economies of the East (excepting Hungary and Yugoslavia) appear for the most part markedly more centralized than the economies of the West. This conclusion is drawn from the comparisons of centralization in terms of the existence of large organizations, functional specialization, decision-making at high levels of the economy, the details at which commands are issued from above, and vertical interaction. For spatial centralization no systemic differences appeared and for the various participation concepts we have little evidence that the East European economies are more centralized.

48. From the sources cited in the previous note, the Soviet Union appears to have more than several thousand centrally rationed inputs.

Second, centralization in the postreform economies in Hungary and Yugoslavia is very much more difficult to guage in relation to Western nations. For instance, differences in the degree of hierarchical centralization in the Yugoslav and, let us say, the French economy (which has been characterized by considerable governmental interference in production decisions) may be very small indeed. These two exceptions to the conclusion that economies in East Europe are markedly more centralized than those in the West make us ask if the high degree of East European economic centralization is due to the ownership of the means of production, or to other factors such as national traditions of administration,[49] or to outside political reasons (such as the forced acceptance of the Soviet model of administration), or to the existence of administrative legacies (such as holdovers from Stalinism, or, less dramatically, to the existence of extremely large enterprises in Hungary as a holdover of minireforms in Hungary before the major 1968 reform.)

Thus the question—Is the degree of centralization of control rights related to the degree of public ownership?—must be approached extremely cautiously. Perhaps all we can say from the available evidence is that there is an empirical link between governmental ownership and centralization but that this relation appears weak and can be outweighed by other political-economic factors. Although this conclusion is not flashy enough to print on manifestoes or embroider upon banners, it should be borne in mind when reading the many dogmatic discussions about such matters in which ideological rather than empirical evidence is presented.

Third, the economic reform drives in Eastern Europe in the sixties represented decentralizations (except perhaps in Romania), but it must be emphasized that the type of decentralization varied considerably among nations. For one group, including East Germany, Poland, and the Soviet Union, aims of the reform included decentralization defined according to participation and in terms of greater horizontal interaction. For a second group, including Yugoslavia and Hungary, aims of the reform included dismantling of previous administrative allocation mechanisms and moving closer to market allocation methods, changes which represented a decentralization in terms of hierarchical control.

4. The Level of Economic Development as a Determinant of Centralization in the West

The centralization of an economy may be influenced not only by its "economic system" but also by its degree of economic development. In Chap-

49. On national traditions of administration, see Michel Crozier, *The Bureaucratic Phenomenon* (Chicago: 1964), Part IV; or David Granick, *The European Executive* (Garden City, N.Y.: 1962).

ter III, I presented evidence that although the distribution of income and wealth in the West may be becoming somewhat more equal over time, the distribution of certain control rights is becomingly increasingly less equal. With the various concepts and indices of centralization discussed above, we can now explore this question more systematically.

One extremely important phenomenon must be immediately noted: The level of economic development (as measured by per capita G.N.P.) can affect the degree of centralization differently in a single nation over time than among a group of nations at a single point in time. For instance, the centralization of public expenditures (as measured by the share of total public expenditures accounted for by the central government) appears *directly* related to the level of economic development in studies of nations over long periods of time, but *inversely* related to the level of economic development when nations are compared at a single point in time.[50] For the various concepts and indices, centralization in the mining and manufacturing sector appears more highly correlated with the level of economic development when time-series rather than cross-section data are examined.

Before examining relationships between centralization and economic system to validate this generalization, it is useful to clear up certain problems regarding system size and centralization since system size and the level of economic development are often correlated, at least when examining the manufacturing and mining sector over time. To make the analysis more concrete, I use the example of enterprise size and centralization.

a. *Enterprise size and enterprise centralization.* For centralization defined in terms of administrative levels at which certain decisions are made, certain analytic difficulties arise in examining small and large enterprises since it is not specified whether we are measuring hierarchical centralization from the top or the bottom of the hierarchy. Let us suppose, for example, that five "small" enterprises merge to form a multi-divisional or conglomerate "large" enterprise. A new top hierarchical level is grafted on top of the five formerly independent enterprises (now called "divisions") but the new top management decides to "decentralize" so that the major "operating decisions" will be made on the divisional level. Since the managers of the divisions must still refer certain decisions upward which the previous "small" enterprise managers had made for themselves, the division managers have lost relative power, at least in certain areas of decision-making. Furthermore, it is likely that employees

50. The reasons underlying this phenomenon are analyzed by Frederic L. Pryor, *Public Expenditures in Communist and Capitalist Nations* (Homewood, Ill.: 1968), especially Chapter 2.

within the division have lost certain property rights since the empirical evidence showed that "dependent organizations" (organizations that are part of larger organizations) are operated with greater hierarchical centralization than autonomous organizations. Now it is true that the new top manager participates less in operational decisions than the former top managers of the five constituent enterprises, so that in this trivial sense there has been hierarchical decentralization. Nevertheless, since a new hierarchical level has been created and since hierarchical levels below the new top have lost relative power *vis-à-vis* higher administrative levels, a very real hierarchical centralization has occurred.

This type of argument runs counter to the analysis of some economists such as John Kenneth Galbraith who place the real power of enterprises in the hands of technicians below the manager and on whom the manager is dependent for information and technical advice.[51] According to Galbraith's approach, the increasing size of enterprises is accompanied by a greater dispersion of power and a greater amount of power is placed in the collective hands of the technicians. But there are lower and higher levels of technicians (in a very real sense, the division managers of the example cited above are technicians as well) and power can still shift more into the hands of the higher technicians. Galbraith's approach seems to erase all notion of organizational hierarchy.

Another link between enterprise size and the degree of control exercised by managers can be viewed by examining the planning systems of large and small enterprises. Without long-range planning, it is difficult for an enterprise manager to impose his will on subordinates since in particular crises (which might have been avoided with the use of such plans), the immediate requirements of the situation are often extremely compelling and the manager is forced to ratify decisions by lower echelons that deal with the crises. With long-range planning, such operating crises are supposed to decrease and, moreover, the top manager can more easily guide the solution of particular crises since he has a longer time perspective with which to view the situation. Effective long-run planning is thus an instrument leading to hierarchical centralization.

An implicit assumption in the business literature is that the degree of long-run planning differs among enterprises of different sizes and thus hierarchical centralization is linked to average enterprise size. However, data to test this cliché show that for two of the three types of long-run planning for which we have information, namely the setting of conceptual and mission goals and the setting of specific goals (e.g., sales of different products, financial goals, goals for manufacturing operations, etc.), there is no significant difference between small and large United States enter-

51. John Kenneth Galbraith, *The New Industrial State* (Boston: 1967).

prises. Only for the setting of specific strategies do the large enterprises show longer time horizons.[52]

For centralization in terms of vertical interaction, as manifested by frequency of review of performance of subordinates by superiors, we can also investigate differences between large and small enterprises. Interesting data are available on the frequency with which operating units of enterprises submit seven different types of reports upwards to the main office. They show no statistically significant differences between large and small enterprises for any of these different types of reports.[53]

This brief discussion concerning enterprise size and centralization can be quickly summarized. Enterprise size is associated with centralization in the sense that an additional hierarchical level has been added at which certain decisions are made which were previously made at lower levels. On the other hand, enterprise size does not appear associated with centralization as manifested by longer planning horizons or by frequency of vertical interaction. Such results suggest caution in generalizing about relationships between size of the entire mining and manufacturing sector and its centralization.

b. *Economic development and structural concepts of centralization.* Evidence on the relation of economic development and centralization is available for all four structural concepts of centralization.

For centralization defined in terms of the existence of large organizational units in the economy, we can draw upon the evidence on establishment and enterprise size presented in Chapters V and VI. The data for Western nations show that the average size of both production units appears positively related to the level of economic development over time, but not at a single point in time. Thus centralization defined according to organizational size in an absolute sense appears at least to be positively associated with economic development when time-series data are used.

But is this structural concept of centralization best reflected by a measure of the absolute sizes of enterprises or by the degree of agglomeration (which is the average size of production units in comparison to the entire mining and manufacturing sector)? If the latter measure is more satisfactory, then generalizations are more difficult to make. The establishment data show that per capita income and agglomeration are positively related when cross-section data are used, but are inversely related when time-series data are examined. The enterprise data show that per capita income and agglomeration are not correlated in the cross-section data, but a comparable generalization cannot be developed for time-series

52. For the data underlying these generalizations, see Appendix A-17.
53. For the data underlying this generalization, see Appendix A-17.

since sufficient data are not available. If we define agglomeration somewhat differently in terms of the relative importance of the largest 50 or 100 enterprises, then a positive relation between the degree of agglomeration and the level of economic development can be seen for some, but not all, nations.

Thus for this particular concept of centralization no final conclusion is possible because different indicators yield quite different results. The choice of the best of the two indicators cannot be resolved without taking us too far afield.

For centralization defined in terms of functional specialization, little direct evidence is available. If we follow the procedure of the previous subsection and broaden this concept to include the degree to which production of particular goods is concentrated in a few enterprises, then definite conclusions can be drawn. As I showed in Chapter VI, the degree of monopoly does not appear related to the level of economic development either among nations at a single point in time or in individual nations over time.

For temporal centralization, I present evidence (Section C-2) that such centralization appears to be increasing in the United States and I argue that the same is probably true for other Western nations. Evidence on too few nations is available for any cross-section generalizations to be made.

Finally, for spatial centralization I show (Section C-1) that at least in the postwar period, no relation between the level of economic development and centralization can be found at a single point in time; over time, however, most nations in the sample showed a spatial decentralization.

Of the four structural concepts of centralization, a positive relationship with the level of economic development is found with the time-series data for temporal and spatial centralization and in some aspects for centralization in terms of large organizational units. Using cross-section data, no important relationships between economic development and centralization are found for these concepts. For other structural concepts or measures of centralization, the results show no important relationships between centralization and development.

c. *Economic development and participation concepts of centralization.* Two of the three participation concepts of centralization permit interesting relations to be drawn between centralization and economic development.

For centralization defined in terms of the routinization of jobs, certain evidence is available. The sociologist Robert Blauner argues that the beginning of industrialization is accompanied by an increase in the routinization of jobs, especially through the introduction of assembly line techniques; in later stages of industrialization, however, assembly line jobs become a smaller share of total jobs in mining and manufacturing and work dealing with continual flow processes permitting considerable individual freedom increases in relative importance.[54]

Blauner's argument is a synthesis of the views of two very diverse streams of judgments about the effects of industrialization on job routinization: One stream may be said to stem from Adam Smith who saw the increasing division of labor accompanying industrialization creating men whose work consisted of one or two simple operations and who became as a result "as stupid and ignorant as it is possible for a human creature to become."[55] The other stream may be said to stem from C. H. Saint-Simon and Karl Marx and is much more optimistic, viewing industrialization as leading to the elimination of both physical and mental drudgery through the mechanization of all heavy work and the automatization of all repetitive work so that a full human potential will be realized.

The empirical evidence on these matters leaves much to be desired. Nevertheless, industrialization (and economic development) appear to be accompanied both over time and among a group of nations at a single point in time with a rising share of jobs in the mining and manufacturing sector requiring considerable education because discretionary decision-making is necessary. Such evidence also suggests that economic development is indeed accompanied in both time-series and cross-section views with a decline in the routinization of jobs after a certain level of industrialization has been reached. The speed of such de-routinization may increase, especially if experiments to eliminate rigid assembly line processes (such as those being carried out by the Volvo company in Sweden) prove successful.

For centralization defined in terms of participation in decision-making, many different phenomena can be examined. I have already mentioned that rising education levels accompanying economic development suggest greater participation while, at the same time, the larger enterprise size suggests less participation (at least at the formerly highest levels before mergers took place). For a more important participation phenomenon—namely the separation of ownership and control—we can draw upon the evidence presented in Chapter III to make some additional inferences about centralization and development.

If an enterprise is administered by an owner-manager, participation by others in important enterprise decision-making may be quite limited. As the enterprise grows in size, not only do the number of executives but also the number of owners increase as well, so that during this stage the

54. Robert Blauner, *Alienation and Freedom* (Chicago: 1964).
55. Adam Smith, *The Wealth of Nations,* Book 5, Chapter 1, Part III, Article II.

group of people both inside and outside the enterprise who participate in decision-making grows; this represents a decentralization. But such decentralization continues only until the number of decision-makers becomes sufficiently large that delegation of important decision-making powers to a small group of managers occurs. Indeed, if the enterprise reaches a very large size and the stock holdings have been splintered among many individuals, then owner participation in decision-making may disappear. Thus the refocusing of enterprise decision-making and the decline of stockholder influence represents a centralization.

If control of a group of enterprises passes from the managers to a group of finance capitalists, an even further centralization in terms of participation in decision-making has occurred, which is similar to the centralization occurring with the merging of previously independent companies.

From the evidence presented in Chapter IV, control appears to have shifted over time from owners to managers in three leading capitalist nations. Thus the level of economic development and centralization in terms of this aspect of participation in decision-making appear positively correlated. As I also noted, further centralization in terms of a shift of power from the managers to a smaller group of finance capitalists was judged to be problematic.

Cross-section generalizations about the relationship between the separation of ownership and control and economic development cannot be made because of lack of data. However, since this separation is due in great part to the large absolute size of enterprises and since the absolute size of enterprises does not appear related to economic development among nations at a single point in time, it is doubtful that a correlation between the separation of ownership and control (and thus participation in decision-making) and per capita income could be found even if the data were available.

For centralization defined in terms of the set of property rights exercised within the system, it is almost tautological to assert that economic development is accompanied by decentralization. This is because economic development is often defined in terms of the goods and services produced in the economy and the "extension of significant choices" in the spheres of consumption and production.

To conclude, centralization in terms of job routinization and of the size of the set of property rights within the system appears inversely related to the level of economic development with both the cross-section and the time-series data. Centralization in terms of participation in decision-making appears directly related to the level of economic development over time, at least with regard to the separation of ownership and control, but is probably not positively related with development among nations at a single point in time.

d. *Economic development and control concepts of centralization.* For two of the three control concepts of centralization, the available evidence relating centralization and development is impressionistic.

For centralization defined in terms of the detail of commands, we must distinguish two stages of the development of capitalism. In the first stage industrialization was accompanied by the dismantling of detailed mercantilistic and guild regulations concerning manufacturing operations. After several decades or more had elapsed, the pendulum appeared to swing in the opposite direction; and governmental control of industry, primarily of an "indirect" nature, began to increase. For instance, in the United States over the last half century there has been a proliferation of particular regulatory measures (e.g., pure food and drug laws, automobile safety standards, antidiscrimination laws) that have been labeled (and libeled) in the conservative press as "creeping socialism"; and in other capitalist nations a similar development has occurred. This positive relationship between centralization and economic development over time may not appear in comparisons among a group of capitalist nations at a single point in time, e.g., the United States may have less centralization along these dimensions than France.

For centralization defined in terms of vertical versus horizontal relationships, sufficient information of a systematic nature, other than that discussed in the previous paragraph, is not available for additional generalizations to be made.

For centralization defined in terms of the level at which certain decisions are made or initiative is taken, discussion can be brief. The growth of large decision-making units ("large" defined in an absolute sense) that has accompanied economic development over time, as I pointed out, points toward a positive correlation of hierarchical centralization and economic development. As also noted, such a correlation does not appear in the cross-section data.

In short, time-series evidence points toward a positive relationship between economic development and centralization defined either in terms of the detail in which commands are issued or in terms of the hierarchical level at which important decisions are taken. Such relationships are not observable in the cross-section data.

e. *Some brief observations.* From this welter of evidence several conclusions can be drawn.

First, according to many concepts and indices centralization appears to be correlated *over time* with the level of economic development. More specifically, positive correlations are found between development and temporal centralization as well as centralization in terms of the detail of commands, the separation of ownership and control, and of the hierarchical level at which important decisions are taken. Negative correlations are found between development and centralization in terms of job routinization and of the size of the set of property rights within the system. For other concepts and indices, either ambiguities arise or no important relationship can be found.

Second, the relationship between centralization and the level of economic development appears much more problematic *at a single point in time.* Correlations are found for only two concepts of centralization, namely in terms of job routinization and the size of the set of property rights. In other cases either no important relationships are found or, for several concepts of centralization, no evidence is available.

The difference in time-series and cross-section relationships of centralization and economic development is probably due in large part to the great influence of political and cultural factors in slowing down or speeding up the changes in centralization that are correlated with economic development over time. That is, the relationships of centralization and development are observable over long time spans when the basic economic forces have a chance to assert themselves strongly, but in the short run these forces can be masked by political factors. A secondary influence on centralization occurs through the relationship of market size and size of production units: size of production units is correlated with economic development over time but not at a single point in time.

D. Speculations about a Relationship between Income Equality and Centralization

A theme from the above discussion and from other chapters of this study can now be related. From evidence presented in Chapter IV we saw that the equality of income has slowly increased over time in capitalist nations at the same time as one type of centralization (stemming from the separation of ownership and control) of control rights has increased. We now see that this inverse relationship between the equality of income and the equality of control rights (centralization) holds for most concepts or indices of centralization when examining time-series evidence.

From a previous subsection, I argued that most socialist nations have greater centralization of control rights than capitalist nations and I presented evidence in Chapter III that the inequality of income is less in the former group of countries. Again an inverse relation between equality of income and equality of control rights is found, this time using cross-section evidence.

Two smaller bits of relevant evidence also warrant mention. During the Czechoslovakian discussions on economic reforms during the mid-1960s, the reformers wanted not only to decentralize the economy but also to widen wage differentials, claiming that a decentralized economy cannot work effectively with great labor income levelization. During the Romanian discussions on economic reforms, in which certain steps toward centralization (transfer of certain decision-making powers from the enterprise to the association) may have outweighed steps toward decentralizations, high officials emphasized the importance of reducing labor income differentials.

For preindustrial economies, it has been argued[56] that inequalities of income accompanied inequalities in control rights. What could underlie the reversal of this relationship that has occurred in industrial economies? Four possible reasons may be offered. Cynically one might argue that real income is hidden in highly centralized economies through the existence of perquisites and other valuable privileges accompaning power; thus the greater equality of *monetary* incomes in centralized economies is merely an illusion and that equality of *real* incomes and control rights are positively related. It can also be argued that greater centralization implies greater standardization, especially of labor incomes, so that large disparities of payment for the same type of work or the development of local monopolies of particular labor groups can be suppressed. It also seems plausible that greater centralization may lead to greater implicit threats of coercion so that income incentives are not necessary to induce desired types of behavior. And finally, the more centralization in an organization, the harder it is for wage and bonus setters to get *reliable* information on individual performance and, hence, the more equal the pay. (This is related to the observation that centralized organizations appear to rely more on seniority than merit for setting salary scales.) All of these arguments appear to have merit; unfortunately, empirical evidence to investigate any of them is extremely difficult to obtain at the present time.

One piece of counter-evidence must also be admitted. From the mid-1950s to the late 1960s in the Soviet Union, there was a marked decrease in the degree of income inequality at the same time that the economy was experiencing some decentralization, at least along certain lines. It could be argued that this is an exception to our rule because it represented a retreat from an historically unique situation, i.e., Stalin was one of the

56. Max Weber, *General Economic History* (New York: 1966) (originally 1923), Part IV.

few state administrators in history who was able to obtain firm control over both the distributions of income and control rights so that in both spheres he could impose extreme inequality.

Any relationship that can be established between income equality and centralization of control rights which is valid in most industrialized nations regardless of economic system is extremely important to the development of the field of political economy.[56a] Before this relationship can be empirically confirmed, it is necessary to study closely changes in income inequality that accompanied the rise and fall of the East European economic reforms of the 1960s. Such a task is not easy, but validation of generalizations of this importance that embrace most nations is worth the effort.

E. Impact Propositions about Centralization

In the discussion up to now I have focused on certain concepts or indices of centralization and their determinants. Although the centralization of property rights has intrinsic interest and, indeed, can be considered as an important desideratum with which to evaluate the success of economic systems, it is also useful to study the influence of such centralization on the rest of the economic system. This is a difficult problem area and the discussion below is of the nature of a brief survey. After discussing certain theoretical issues, I review one aspect of the empirical literature on centralization, namely the impact of centralization of economic systems on various performance indicators.

1. Some Theoretical Approaches

Propositions about the influence of centralization according to various concepts or indices are discussed from a theoretical standpoint in a wide number of social science disciplines; and a wide number of writers, ranging from Plato (whose ideas on overcentralization are presented at the head of this chapter) and ancient Chinese theoreticians[57] to the editorial

56a. While this book was in press I came across a sociological analysis by Frank Parkin [*Class Inequality and Political Order: Social Stratification in Capitalist and Communist Societies* (London: MacGibbon and Kee, 1971)] that raised these issues in a much different context.

57. In Lewis Maverick, ed., *Economic Dialogues in Ancient China: The Kuan-Tzu* (New Haven: 1954), one finds a wide variety of propositions about the good and bad effects of various types of centralization. For instance, with regard to spatial centralization in mining and manufacturing, it was noted: "A country can not be effectively governed when its wealth is not spread throughout the nation. A nation cannot be effectively governed when the industrial arts are not respected throughout the nation . . . ."

writers of any daily newspaper, have discoursed on such matters. To a great extent, the lack of specification of which dimension of centralization is under discussion has vitiated many such analyses.

Exploration of the impact of the centralization of property rights can be found especially in the literature in the fields of management, organization theory, and economics. Some notion of the types of approaches can be gained by a brief sampling from the literature in these same three fields.

In the management literature, there is considerable discussion about the various advantages and disadvantages of centralization. A typical analysis is presented in Table 8–4. Although the author's concept of centralization is not at all clear, I believe that he is referring primarily to hierarchical centralization.

This list is set up in an interesting manner in order to present a relatively complex set of considerations. Other sources focus primarily on the advantages or disadvantages of some type of unspecified centralization or decentralization alone, a procedure that permits a greater number of propositions[58] but not necessarily greater analytic depth. In many cases it is difficult to see exactly what concept or index of centralization the author has in mind, the chain of logic with which the author derived the propositions, or the manner in which one might put to empirical test such propositions.

In the organization theory literature, propositions about the advantages and disadvantages of centralization or decentralization also seem to abound.[59] Although these are often framed with greater sophistication than in the management literature, there is often greater naiveté in content: the idea of an optimal degree of centralization is replaced with the notion that centralization or decentralization *per se* is good or bad![60]

---

58. For instance, a long list of propositions is presented by William T. Morris, *Decentralization in Management Systems* (Columbus: 1968), pp. 18–22. In addition, there are a number of surveys of opinions businessmen have about the effects of centralization, e.g., Helen Baker and Robert R. France, *Centralization and Decentralization in Industrial Relations* (Princeton: 1954).

59. Lists of propositions can be found in many places, e.g., Jerald Hage, "An Axiomatic Theory of Organization," *Administrative Science Quarterly*, X, December 1965, pp. 289–320; or James D. Thompson, *Organizations in Action* (New York: 1967).

60. One often finds propositions such as: "Except where there is a high degree of complexity, organizations which have a high degree of centralization with regard to tactical decisions are more likely to have a high degree of effectiveness." [James L. Price, *Organizational Effectiveness: An Inventory of Propositions* (Homewood, Ill.: 1968)]. Unless one assumes that few organizations have too high a degree of centralization, the proposition makes little sense. The literature is, unfortunately, filled with this kind of proposition.

TABLE 8–4

Hypothesized Advantages and Disadvantages of Different Configurations of Property Rights[a]

Centralized Organization

Advantages	Disadvantages
1. Uniformity of standards and activities among organizational units. 2. Utilizing the talents of outstanding executives by the entire organization. 3. Uniformity of decisions. 4. Consistency of operating. 5. Cost savings due to elimination of overlapping or duplicated activities.	1. Stretching communication lines to the breaking point. 2. Excessive demands on executives' time. 3. Undesirably "personalizing" management policy by concentrating authority in a few hands. 4. Forcing top executives to develop a breadth of interest that is beyond their capacity.

Decentralized Organization

Advantages	Disadvantages
1. More manageable scope of operations. 2. Development of more executives capable of decisive action in setting and administering policy. 3. Shortening lines of authority and communication, thus increasing efficiency. 4. Vesting decision-making responsibility in the individuals closest to situations. 5. Creation of more chains of promotions.	1. Lack of uniformity in policy and procedures. 2. Difficulty in finding executives able and willing to assume primary responsibility. 3. Acceptance of second rate executives in top jobs, simply because they are available and in line. 4. Poor coordination between decentralized units. 5. Interunit rivalry interfering with operations.

a. This list was drawn up by the Research Institute of America and cited by Aaren Uris, "Centralization versus Decentralization," in Franklin G. Moore, ed., *A Management Sourcebook* (New York: 1964), pp. 261–7.

In any case, only a few of the many hypothesized relationships have been tested.

In the economic literature, several approaches can be found. There is a large body of literature dealing with the effect on behavior of particular types of market structure which, in turn, can be linked to particular types of centralization.[61] In addition, a number of mathematical models

61. These are summarized in Frederic M. Scherer, *Industrial Market Structure and Economic Performance* (Chicago: 1970); or William G. Shepherd, *Market Power and Economic Welfare: An Introduction* (New York: 1970).

of centralization have been constructed and the efficiency of organizations with different degrees of centralization and in different economic environments (e.g., existence of externalities, large economies of scale, and so forth) have been analyzed.[62] Such models are, of course, extremely abstract and do not lend themselves easily to empirical testing; and those propositions that can be tested are usually intuitively obvious.

In these three literatures much remains to be done before rigorous and nonobvious propositions that are empirically testable can be presented. This has not prevented, however, empirical testing of particular propositions that may not have rigorous theoretical bases but which contribute, nevertheless, to our knowledge of the subject.

2. Some Empirical Approaches

In the literature of organization theory, a large number of empirical studies investigating the effects of various types of centralization on organizational activity can be found; although many of these deal with small group experiments or case studies,[63] many have been carried out on different types of large complex organizations.[64] In the economic literature, numerous empirical studies on the effect of market structure on enterprise behavior have been made and these are summarized in any competent text in the field of industrial organization.[65] However, none of the studies are very helpful in analyzing the effect of various types of centralization on the performance of economic systems and a very much cruder approach must be adopted.

Let us start with the conclusion noted above that before the economic reforms of the sixties, the Eastern European nations (except Yugoslavia) appeared more centralized than capitalist market economies,

---

62. For instance, Leonid Hurwicz, "Optimality and Informational Efficiency in Resource Allocation Processes," in Kenneth Arrow, *et al.,* eds., *Mathematical Methods in the Social Sciences* (Stanford: 1959); Hurwicz, "Conditions for Economic Efficiency of Centralized and Decentralized Structures," in Gregory Grossman, ed., *Value and Plan* (Berkeley: 1960), pp. 162–83; Hurwicz, "Centralization and Decentralization in Economic Processes," in Alexander Eckstein, ed., *Comparison of Economic Systems* (Berkeley: 1971); or Thomas Marschak. A different approach is presented by Oliver E. Williamson, *Corporate Control and Business Behavior* (Englewood Cliffs: 1970); although Williamson does not deal with centralization according to most concepts or definitions (he assumes a constant relationship between span of control and organizational effectiveness, which means that hierarchical centralization is assumed constant), he does handle problems of hierarchical "shape" which is related to centralization in a structural sense.

63. A summary of many of these can be found in Hage.

64. Some major studies are summarized briefly in Appendix A-18.

65. E.g., Scherer or Shepherd.

as measured by most concepts and indices of centralization. If centralization played a critical role in the functioning of the economy, some insight into the impact of centralization can be gained by comparing the economic performance of a set of nations in the East and the West. Such a method of analysis suppresses the distinctions about centralization that were so carefully made and explored in earlier sections of this chapter. Moreover, such comparisons are relatively uncontrolled in the sense that they do not permit the isolation of particular types of centralization that act as the most important factors underlying any discovered differences between systems. However, such comparisons do permit the cumulative effects of different types of centralization to be noted together and thus allow some notion of the empirical magnitudes involved in the exploration of the impact of centralization to be gained.

Surveying the results of comparisons of relative economic performance in the East and the West has importance in regard not only to centralization, but also to the ideological "battle of the 'isms' " which, contrary to some, is still quite alive. The results also provide perspective for the many types of East-West comparisons that were presented in the previous chapters.

Statistical problems facing anyone making comparisons of the economic performance of nations in the East and the West are extremely difficult. Although there is a vast East European literature on East-West comparisons (which has been increasing considerably in quality),[66] I have chosen to survey those studies which are most explicit about the handling of the most difficult methodological problems such as the particular adjustments to the data to make them comparable. For better or worse, such studies are mostly the work of American or West European economists. In the survey below, I look first at relative static efficiency, then turn to economic growth, dynamic efficiency, economic fluctuations, structure of production, and structure of consumption.

With regard to static economic efficiency there are, as far as I know, no full-scale East-West comparisons. A number of pilot studies have been carried out between pairs of nations, usually the Soviet Union and the United States.[67] In these studies the problem is usually framed in terms

66. A useful survey of Eastern European comparative work is by Alexander Erlich, 'Eastern' Approaches to a Comparative Evaluation of Economic Systems," in Alexander Eckstein, ed., pp. 301–35. Recent empirical work by East European economists focuses primarily on economic growth rates, fluctuations in production, and, to a certain extent, structure of production.

67. Such studies include: Joseph S. Berliner, "The Static Efficiency of the Soviet Economy," *American Economic Review,* LIV, May 1964, pp. 480–89; Abram Bergson, *Planning and Productivity under Soviet Socialism* (New York: 1968); Abram Bergson, "Comparative Productivity and Efficiency in

of total factor productivity, i.e., the relative outputs of the two countries if their factor endowments (capital and labor) were the same. The most extensive such study shows that Soviet outputs per unit of "total" input is roughly 30 to 60 percent that of the United States and thus appears to be less efficient. Such studies have received considerable criticism. From a theoretical viewpoint, there are some nightmarish problems of index number construction so that the meaning of these results is somewhat problematic.[68] From an empirical viewpoint, several economists have pointed out that certain West European nations such as Italy (which has the same level of economic development as the Soviet Union) have roughly the same relative total factor productivity *vis-à-vis* the United States as the Soviet Union so that the greater static efficiency of the United States compared to the Soviet Union may be less a function of economic system than of level of development.[69] Indeed, such global studies of static efficiency are based on the assumption that all nations are utilizing the same technological knowledge (i.e., have the same production function), an assumption which undoubtedly biases the results.[70] Such studies also employ narrow definitions of efficiency that do not take into account particular social costs or nonincluded factors of production.[71]

In addition to these global studies of static efficiency, there are also a number of "partial" studies focusing on particular sectors or particular problems such as the relative wastage of capital in inventories, use of particular inputs such as steel or fuels, underutilization of labor, and so forth.[72] Although these generally indicate greater static efficiency of the

the U.S.S.R. and the U.S.A.," in Alexander Eckstein, ed., pp. 161–219; and Edwin M. Snell, "Economic Efficiency in Eastern Europe," in Joint Economic Committee, Congress of the United States, *Economic Developments in Countries of Eastern Europe* (Washington, D.C.: 1970).

68. See especially Evsey Domar, "On the Measure of Comparative Efficiency," in Eckstein, ed., pp. 219–33 and the following "Comment" by Bergson, pp. 233–41.

69. This has been pointed out by Domar, and Phillip Hanson, "East-West Comparisons and Comparative Economic Systems," *Soviet Studies,* XXII, January 1971, pp. 327–44. See also Abram Bergson, "East-West Comparison and Comparative Economic Systems: A Reply," *Soviet Studies,* XXIII, October 1971, pp. 296–301.

70. For instance, total factor productivity appears highly correlated with labor productivity.

71. Such social costs include pollution or psychological degradation of the workers, etc. Excluded factors of production are land (which none of the studies takes into account) or people not in the labor force who wish to work but who have given up looking for employment.

72. These studies include Snell; Robert W. Campbell, "A Comparison of Soviet and American Inventory-Output Ratios," *American Economic Review,* LXVIII, September 1958, pp. 549–65; Boris P. Pesek, "Soviet and American Inventory-Output Ratios Once Again," *American Economic Re-*

West, they are open to the obvious criticism that they focus on just a small part of the total efficiency picture.

Discussion on relative static efficiency in centralized and non-centralized economies is thus in a very curious position. On the one hand, there is a great deal of theoretical evidence that suggests that the centralized economies of Eastern Europe have less static efficiency than the Western market economies.[73] And it is easy enough to catalogue hundreds of examples of grotesque waste and inefficiency in East Europe.[74] And yet, on the other hand, there is no convincing evidence on an aggregative level that such differences actually exist between the two sets of nations. Part of this is due undoubtedly to the crudeness of our statistical tools; part is due to the fact that extensive studies of many nations have not yet been carried out; and part of this may be due to the fact that the differences in efficiency may actually be very small. I do not believe that the total factor productivity approach will ever yield very convincing results of differences between the two sets of nations, especially because of the very great importance of index number problems. A more promising approach appears to be through the comparison of production interrelations as shown in comparable input-output tables and preliminary work along these lines reveal no important differences.[75]

With regard to economic growth (excluding for the moment considerations of investment rates) there is a growing body of literature comparing performance in East and West Europe. The major problem in making such comparisons arises because the governmental calculation of indices is quite different in the two groups of nations and incomparabilities occur unless extremely time-consuming adjustments are made to

---

view, LXIX, December 1959, pp. 1030–33; Alfred R. Oxenfeldt and Ernest Van den Haag, "Unemployment in Planned and Capitalist Economies," *Quarterly Journal of Economics*, LXVIII, February 1954, pp. 43–60.

73. For a rigorous discussion see Abram Bergson, *The Economics of Soviet Planning* (New Haven: 1964).

74. An interesting catalogue for the Soviet Union is presented by Naum Jasny, "A Note on Rationality and Efficiency in the Soviet Economy," *Soviet Studies*, XII, April 1962, pp. 321–33. It must also be noted that studies of inefficiency have been made for the United States; see, for instance, the comments of Edward F. Denison, *The Sources of Economic Growth in the United States and the Alternative before Us* (New York: 1962).

75. A number of different kinds of questions can be explored with such data. For instance, have the East European centrally planned economies adopted technologies that minimize linkages between industrial branches in order to avoid disruption caused by interbranch coordination problems? Preliminary investigations by the Economic Commission for Europe. "Comparative Analysis of Economic Structures by Means of Input-Output Tables," *Economic Bulletin for Europe*, XXIII, January 1972, pp. 59–76, suggest that this is not the case. Unfortunately, the E.C.E. did not correct the tables for price distortions, and the results must therefore be considered tentative.

take these statistical differences into account.[76] A problem of interpretation of the results also arises because economic growth is not independent of the level of development. For semiindustrialized or industrialized nations, economic growth appears inversely proportional to the level of development:[77] thus Bulgaria is growing faster than Poland which is growing faster than Czechoslovakia; and Japan is growing faster than West Germany which is growing faster than the United States. If we hold per capita incomes constant and compare similarly calculated G.N.P. growth indices for the nations in East Europe and in the O.E.C.D., no significant differences in growth rates between the East and the West can be found for the postwar period.[78] This result, surprising as it may appear, is more readily understandable when we realize that growth rates for almost all European nations have reached unprecedented heights in this period of "economic miracles."

With regard to dynamic efficiency (economic growth, taking into account the investment rate), most empirical studies have found the market economies of the O.E.C.D. performing somewhat better than the centralized economies of East Europe. Three types of methodologies in these studies have been employed. In a recent study, Abram Bergson compared the growth of G.N.P. per employed worker to the share of investment in the economy and concluded that a given percentage of economic growth is brought about by a greater amount of investment in Eastern Europe than in O.E.C.D. nations.[79] Others have tried to measure growth in total factor productivity (growth in output per unit of some weighted average of labor and capital) and have found somewhat greater

76. There is a large and boring body of literature on these problems. In comparing growth of aggregate production, two immediate problems arise. First, the East European sectoral weights (weights for the volume indices for each sector) are based on a price system that undervalues agriculture (the slowest growing sector) and overvalues mining and manufacturing (the fastest growing sector). The comparisons cited below for the most part are based on Western recalculation of East European data. For nonadjusted comparisons, see Economic Commission for Europe, *Some Factors in Economic Growth in Europe during the 1950s* (Geneva: 1964).

77. This is demonstrated by Branko Horvat, "Relation between the Rate of Growth and the Level of Development," Indiana University, International Development Research Center Working Paper No. 13, April 1972.

78. Results of preliminary experiments holding other factors constant (e.g., "special environmental" factors impeding growth) have not proved interesting.

A number of comparative studies of growth rates in the East and the West have been made that yield the results discussed in the text. See especially Maurice Ernst. "Postwar Economic Growth in Eastern Europe, A Comparison with Western Europe," in Joint Economic Committee, Congress of the United States, *New Directions in the Soviet Economy,* Part IV (Washington, D.C.: 1966); or Abram Bergson," Development under Two Systems," *World Politics,* XXIII, July 1971, pp. 579–618.

79. Abram Bergson, "Development under Two Systems."

productivity in the West; such studies, however, are open to some criticism with regard to estimates employed.[80] An allegedly more adequate procedure than either of these two types of studies is to calculate aggregate production functions and then compare coefficients for various nations in the East and the West, but this is a difficult task that is fraught with great statistical and theoretical problems. Further, the available evidence is quite conflicting.[81] For instance, one study for the Soviet Union showed relatively low elasticities of substitution of labor for capital (*vis-à-vis* the United States) which indicates that the Soviet Union has an absorption problem of new investment and has been running into diminishing returns;[82] studies for other East European nations have not revealed such results. The calculation of aggregate production functions for East Europe is just in the early stages of research, index number problems influencing the calculated coefficients have not been completely overcome, and we have some distance to go before important generalizations can be drawn from the results.

A number of comparative studies of market and centrally administered economies have also focused on macro-economic fluctuations of such variables as total national product, production in different sectors, foreign trade, and public expenditures.[83] In general, these studies have

80. Bela Balassa and Trent J. Bertrand, "Growth Performance of Eastern European Economies and Comparable Western European Countries," *American Economic Review*, LX, May 1970, pp. 314–31. For other insights, see Bela Balassa, "The Dynamic Efficiency of the Soviet Economy," *American Economic Review*, LIV, May 1964, pp. 490–505; Ernst; and Snell.

81. Through 1971, the English language literature included a number of studies. For the Soviet Union the most complete study is Martin L. Weitzman, "Soviet Postwar Economic Growth and Capital-Labor Substitution," *American Economic Review*, LX, September 1970, pp. 676–93; see also Earl R. Brubaker, "Synthetic Factor Shares, the Elasticity of Substitution, and the Residual in Soviet Growth," *Review of Economics and Statistics*, LII, February 1970, pp. 100–4; and Charles R. Blitzer, "The Elasticity of Substitution and the Retardation of the Soviet Growth Rate," *Review of Economics and Statistics*, LII, February 1970, pp. 104–8.

For East Europe most of the studies were not yet published by the end of 1971. These included Oldřich Kýn and Ludmila Kýnová, "Aggregate Production Functions for Czechoslovakia and Poland," paper presented at the Econometric Society meeting in Detroit, December 1970; Jan Vaňous, "Aggregate Production Functions for the Czechoslovak Economy," unpublished paper, Haverford College, 1971; Alan A. Brown and Egon Neuberger, "Dynamic L-Shaped CES Functions in Eastern Europe," paper presented at the Southern Economic Association, Miami, 1971; and Charles S. Rockwell, "Growth and Technical Progress in the Socialist Enterprises of Yugoslavia: A Cobb-Douglas Analysis using Extraneous Estimators," Yale University, Economic Growth Center Discussion Paper No. 91, July 1970.

82. See especially Weitzman; Brubaker; and Blitzer.

83. These include: George J. Staller, "Fluctuations in Economic Activity: Planned and Free-Market Economies, 1950–59," *American Economic Review*, LIV, June 1964, pp. 385–95; George J. Staller, "Patterns of Sta-

shown either no significant differences between the two sets of nations or else somewhat greater fluctuations in Eastern Europe. Although these results may seem extremely surprising, such studies encounter few statistical or theoretical problems and confidence can be placed in these results.

With regard to the structure of production and consumption, comparative empirical work is just beginning. We know that in the centrally administered socialist economies the industrial sector has received a larger share of resources than in the capitalist nations and that within the industrial sector, heavy industry produces relatively more than light industry in the East in comparison to the West.[84] Such a phenomenon reflects, of course, the higher rate of investment and the more closed economies of Eastern Europe. Of much greater interest is the degree to which the structure of production corresponds to product desires of consumers and, in addition, the degree to which the goods produced are distributed to the people who want them. In more technical terminology these are questions of consumer sovereignty and consumer choice.

In the conventional Western wisdom, the centrally planned economies do not have consumer sovereignty but they do have a high degree of consumer choice. If one scans the economic literature of Eastern Europe, the contention about the lack of "real" consumer sovereignty is often disputed but, on the other hand, most East European economists have hundreds of anecdotes about the misallocations on the retail level so that the assumption about consumer choice seems dubious.

There is some empirical and theoretical evidence that the correspondence between the structure of production and consumer desires is far from optimal in the centrally administered economies, e.g., the presence of queues, the importance of a highly differentiated sales tax (that drives a wedge between production and consumer wants), and so forth.[85]

---

bility in Foreign Trade: OECD and Comecon, 1950–63," *American Economic Review,* LVII, September 1967, pp. 879–88; Egon Neuberger, "Is the U.S.S.R. Superior to the West as a Market for Primary Products," *Review of Economics and Statistics,* XLVI, August 1964, pp. 287–93; Frederic L. Pryor, *Public Expenditures . . . ,* Chapter 7; and Branko Horvat, *Business Cycles in Yugoslavia* (translated by Helen M. Kramer) (White Plains: 1971), Chapter 13 (published in *Eastern European Economics,* IX, March-April 1971).

For interesting theoretical statements of the problem, see Horvat, *Business Cycles in Yugoslavia;* Alexander Bajt, "Investment Cycles in European Socialist Economies: A Review Article," *Journal of Economic Literature,* IX, March 1971, pp. 53–64; and Josef Goldmann and Karel Kouba, *Economic Growth in Czechoslovakia* (White Plains: 1969).

84. Paul Gregory, *Socialist and Nonsocialist Industrialization Patterns: A Comparative Appraisal* (New York: 1970).

85. These turnover taxes are not short-term devices used to equate supply and demand but remain for long periods of time; for instance, in the Soviet Union the product classes on which high and low turnover taxes were placed in the 1930s were roughly the same as those in the 1950s. [Lists of

But such phenomena also exist in the West. Measuring the relative lack of correspondence between consumer desires and production patterns is further complicated by the degree to which the economy produces "useless" commodities for consumption which people "do not really want."[86] Such problems may make empirical comparisons of consumer sovereignty impossible; on the other hand, data are being published that will permit some comparisons of consumer choice—or the efficiency of the retail system—to be made between nations with different economic systems.[87]

The results of this survey of empirical comparisons of systems performance are quite different from what one might expect from ideological evidence or, for that matter, from the cold war screeds of both the East and the West. Particularly the similarity in static efficiency and in G.N.P. growth rates may come as a surprise. The difference in aggregate fluctuations and in dynamic efficiency may also be unexpected.

Most strikingly, the difference in economic performance between the centrally administered economies of East Europe and the capitalist market economies of the West are for the most part either nondiscernible or discernible but small for the first four performance criteria mentioned above. For other performance criteria (consumer choice and consumer sovereignty) quantitative comparisons for the various economies have not

---

tax rates can be found in Franklyn D. Holzman, *Soviet Taxation* (Cambridge, Mass.: 1955), Chapter 6; and Daniel Gallik, *et al., The Soviet Financial System,* Foreign Demographic Analysis Division of the Bureau of the Census, International Population Statistics Reports P-90, No. 23 (Washington, D.C.: 1968), Chapter 6.]

86. This doctrine of "useless" goods and services comes in two versions: a mild version presented by John Kenneth Galbraith, *The Affluent Society* (Boston: 1958); and a harsh version that is argued by Paul Baran, *The Political Economy of Growth* (New York: 1957), Chapter 2. Baran not only consigns gadgets to the category of "useless" but also many services such as those supplied by retailers and ministers. [Arguments about "uselessness" can cut both ways especially if low quality consumer products are being produced; further, East European autos used to have useless "tailfins," all of the stores employ retail clerks, and there is empirical evidence (Pryor, *Public Expenditures . . .* , p. 131) that the per capita number of ministers and priests in the United States is equal to the per capita number of full-time communist party officials in the Soviet Union who serve, in a manner of speaking, a priestly function.

87. The lower the degree of consumer choice (the less efficient the retail system), the more time people must spend shopping, other things being equal. Now certain comparable data on shopping times of citizens in a number of European nations in both the East and the West are available from an international study of time budgets that was carried out under the sponsorship of UNESCO by Alexander Szalai and survey research organizations from many countries. My own preliminary analysis of the data suggests that shopping times are roughly 20 percent greater in East Europe than in West Europe, other things (per capita income and retail clerks per capita) held constant. Much further work needs to be done on this problem.

yet been published. This lack of great difference between the systems has some important implications for the theory of convergence between economic systems and these matters are discussed in considerable detail in Chapter IX.

Of course, it must be added that individual economies showed very great differences within each group. Some of these differences were undoubtedly due to causal relationships between particular features of the economy (e.g., level of economic development) and the different performance indicators. And other differences were brought about by different policies pursued by the top decision-makers in the various nations.[88] Variation of performance among nations of the same system was often as great or greater than variation between systems.

As noted in the introduction of this survey of empirical comparison of systems performance, we have been dealing with two groups of nations between which there are great differences according to almost all definitions or indices of centralization. But because the economies of Eastern Europe were quite similar until the recent economic reforms (except, of course, that of Yugoslavia), there was very little independent variation of different types of centralization among the Eastern nations so that it is difficult to decide which type of centralization might account for differences in performance. That is, in isolating the effects of centralization by looking at the economic performance of a set of nations in the East and the West, considerable problems of multicollinearity arise. If the East (and the West) European economies become increasingly different, statistical analysis of causal links between different types of centralization and performance may become easier.

F. Summary and Conclusions

In these empirical notes on the centralization of control rights, a great deal of material from a number of different areas is covered; in addition, the reader has been forced to march through ten concepts or indices of centralization more times than perhaps desired. But these various indices of centralization are as important to control rights as measures of the inequality of income are to ownership rights—and both are vital aspects of a study of property in its broadest meaning. Several major arguments of this chapter deserve further emphasis.

88. An example of an excellent comparative study that brings in such factors is Edward F. Denison and Jean-Pierre Poullier, *Why Growth Rates Differ: Postwar Experience in Nine Western Countries* (Washington: D.C.: 1967).

First, the concept of "centralization" is multidimensional and a number of different meanings can be attached to the term. The theoretical discussion covered various concepts or indices of the term. These were divided into definitions focusing directly on control, on participation, and on structural properties; other groupings of the concepts or indices are also imaginable. The various concepts or indices are not only different in logic but also often do not occur together in practice and their inter-relations must be determined empirically.

Second, a number of different determinants can be specified for the various concepts or indices of centralization. Special case studies of spatial and temporal centralization are presented to show how such analyses can be carried out. Although economic "system" (defined in terms of ownership of the means of production) appeared to be a deter-minant of a number of different types of centralization, after the economic reforms in Eastern Europe in the mid- or late 1960s this relationship became less certain as some socialist nations opted for market coordina-tion of production. For certain types of centralization, (e.g., spatial centralization), economic "system" appears to play no role at all. The level of economic development also appears to have a causal role in most types of centralization, but this link can be seen most clearly in exami-nation of time-series evidence; the relationship between centralization and the level of economic development is obscured in the cross-section evidence by political and cultural forces.

Third, evidence is presented to show a relationship between the equality of income and centralization. More specifically, nations showing greater centralization according to most concepts or variables also appear to have a more equal distribution of income, other things remaining equal. In other words, there appears to be an inverse relationship between income equality and equality of control rights.

Fourth, the link between the performance of an economy and the degree of centralization is difficult to determine. Comparisons between the centrally administered socialist economies of East Europe and the capitalist market economies of the O.E.C.D. nations reveal either no differences at all (static efficiency and growth rates) or else only very small differences (economic fluctuations and dynamic efficiency). It should be added that the results of the comparisons for individual per-formance indicators are quite surprising—at least they were to me—and suggest that much of the conventional wisdom on these matters in both the East and the West is incorrect.

Many of the results reported in this chapter are quite tentative, for empirical analysis of centralization is just in its infancy. Certainly the subject should form an important part of the core of any extensive theory of property. But it should also be clear that such studies are not easy to carry out and that conceptual and empirical nightmares abound. If the payoff in terms of the intellectual contribution of such studies does not provide a sufficient inducement for scholars, then perhaps the increasing political interest that is being paid to questions of centralization may provide the requisite incentives for further research.

CHAPTER IX

Property and Economic System

> The power of a man . . . is his present means
> to obtain some future apparent good.
>
> Hobbes[1]
>
> To act morally means to act out of pure
> awareness of duty . . . regardless of whether
> reality will yield to our desires.
>
> Kolakowski[2]

A. *Introduction*

B. *Property and Other*
   Systemic Elements
   1. Three Elements of an
      Economic System
   2. A Structural Viewpoint
   3. A Process Viewpoint

C. *The Problem of Convergence*
   of Economic Systems
   1. The Convergence Position
   2. The Nonconvergence
      Position

D. *Toward a Theory of Property*

A. *Introduction*

The empirical studies in this book have focused on particular aspects of economic systems that concern property. The purpose of this chapter is to place the various propositions about property in a broader context. To carry out this task I focus on three problems.

The first is defining and exploring several important elements of a functioning economic system other than property and examining their interrelations. The analysis is carried out from a structural viewpoint, looking at particular types of consistency problems of the system; and from a

---

1. Thomas Hobbes, *Leviathan,* Part I, Chapter 10.
2. Leszek Kolakowski, *Toward a Marxist Humanism: Essays on the Left Today* (New York: 1968), p. 116.

336

process viewpoint, looking at particular methods of coordinating decisions and actions in various parts of the system.

The second problem is examining the alleged convergence of economic systems and analyzing the way in which various propositions about property discussed in the previous chapters can give new and useful insights to this issue. In particular, I argue that the case of convergence is both empirically and theoretically insufficient and that the anticonvergence case is more convincing.

And the third problem is placing the positive theories of property developed in this book into a perspective in which certain important moral or normative issues can be raised.

B. Property and Other Systemic Elements

1. Three Elements of An Economic System

The concept of "economic system" is almost impossible to define exactly. An economic system includes all those institutions, organizations, laws and rules, traditions, beliefs, attitudes, values, taboos, and the resulting behavior patterns which directly or indirectly affect economic behavior and outcomes.[3]

In analyzing economic systems, it seems useful to distinguish three major structural elements: (1) the structure of property; (2) the structure of motivation (i.e., what are the goals of important property right holders or decision-makers and what are the incentives to which they respond); (3) the structure of information (i.e., what information is available to the various property right holders and what types of information networks link these decision-makers to one another). Before defining these systemic elements more carefully and looking at their interrelations, several important aspects of this approach must be made explicit.

The three structural elements are not the only factors influencing the performance of an economy. To carry out a complete analysis we must also take into account environmental factors (e.g., natural resources, the international trade situation, the level of technology) and policy factors (policies followed not only by the government but by important economic organs as well).

It should be clear that the three structural elements are interdepen-

---

3. This definition is modified from that proposed by Tjalling C. Koopmans and John Michael Montias, "On the Description and Comparison of Economic Systems," in Alexander Eckstein, ed. *Comparison of Economic Systems* (Berkeley: 1971), pp. 32–3. Several of the ideas in this section about the three structural elements of economic systems were developed by Egon Neuberger and myself in an unpublished joint essay, "A Conceptual Framework for Analyzing Economic System."

dent with, rather than independent of, each other. For instance, the long-term goals pursued by the most important property-holders (decision-makers) can greatly influence the structure of the information system which, in turn, can affect the process of production coordination. Or the distribution of decision-making power among various individuals influences the information system, the incentive system, and even the hierarchy of goals. Or the information structure may affect the distribution of property, the structure of goals and motivation, and the coordination of production. Nevertheless, separating these three elements does permit certain crucial interactions to be viewed more systematically, an advantage which I hope to make apparent.

Finally, the set of concepts advanced can be used not only to analyze the economy as a whole, but also major institutions that compose the economic system. I have tried to define the elements to apply to many different types of systems so that comparative analysis can be more easily carried out on all levels.

a. *The structure of property.* Important aspects of the structure of property include the degree and pattern of nationalization, the distribution of ownership, the separation of ownership and control, the industrial structure and the sizes of decision-making units in production, and various aspects of the centralization of control rights. All of these have been subject to analysis in previous chapters.

b. *The structure of motivation.* Goals and incentives are aspects of motivation which are well known to be vital links in understanding the transformation of property rights and informational inputs into effective actions. Yet comparative empirical study of such motivations in different economic systems has been very neglected. This is primarily due, I believe, to several major difficulties of analysis.

First, it is difficult to discover what these goals and incentives really are. Announced goals, either in the form of published "plans" or "personal statements," may not represent the actual goals of top decision-makers. As noted in Chapter IV, considerable confusion still exists about differences in motivation of owner-managers and hired managers of industrial enterprises. Disputes about motives influencing decision-making are rampant in the literature of economic history[4] or economic anthropology.[5] Although various techniques can be used to isolate norms and

4. For instance, on the special motives underlying the operations of French family enterprises in the nineteenth century, a donnybrook among historians has taken place. Among the contestants on opposing sides are Alexander Gerschenkron and David B. Landes.

5. Considerable differences of opinion exist about the motivational structures of different types of agricultural units such as feudal manors, slave

relevant motivational factors (e.g., questionnaires, content analyses of speeches or writings,[6] depth interviews, "revealed preference" methods, and so forth), each gives rise to well-recognized problems.

Second, it is difficult to distinguish societal norms (both on a general level and with regard to specific roles) and personal interests (including consciously held goals, incentives provided by the economic system for personal gratification, and unconscious motives such as the need for achievement).[7] If societal norms are different, the same incentives may result in quite different decisions in different economic systems. Two examples illustrate this point. In capitalist economies societal norms are often different during war and peace and the behavior of enterprise managers may vary considerably in these two periods, even though the incentives facing the managers are quite similar. Or in East Europe the East Germans have been able to make a hierarchically centralized economy work considerably better than the Czechoslovaks and the primary cause may be differences in the national ethos, especially in regard to views toward authority and the willingness to accept commands.[8]

Third, additional analytic difficulties arise from the fact that certain norms may not be held by all members of the system. For example, if

plantations, plantations employing free labor, "capitalist" farms, and so forth. Although there are many propositions about the differences, few have been adequately tested, at least to my knowledge. Although there were ferocious debates about these matters in the Continental economic literature, especially dealing with the theory of the peasant economy, there seems to be little awareness or interest of such matters in the Anglo-American economic literature, even after the recent resuscitation of the works of A. V. Chayanov in English translation.

6. Two interesting examples of empirical research along these lines for nations in both the East and West are: Robert C. Angell, "Social Values of Soviet and American Elites: Content of Elite Media," *Journal of Conflict Resolution,* VIII, December 1964, pp. 130–86; and David C. McClelland, *The Achieving Society* (New York: 1967), paperback ed.

7. There are a number of extremely different conceptual problems in distinguishing different aspects of values, norms, goals, motives, and "self-interest" which are discussed in an incisive manner by Talcott Parsons, "The Motivation of Economic Activities," *Essays in Sociological Theory, Pure and Applied* (Glencoe, Ill.: 1949), Chapter 9. Parsons emphasizes that "self-interest" embraces a number of motives including self-respect, recognition by others, enjoyment of activities for their own sake, sensual pleasures, and aesthetic interests. Similarly "goals" and "incentives" are complex concepts.

8. In most cases such "psychological" types of analyses are quite unsatisfactory because they are seldom very adequately documented. In the East German-Czechoslovakian comparison, references to the differences in national character as manifested by, let us say, Zuckmayer's *The Captain from Kopenick* and Hašek's *The Good Soldier Schweik* may be suggestive but they are hardly convincing. However, almost every East European economist whom I queried about differences in economic performance of East Germany and Czechoslovakia pointed first to differences in the national ethos of the two countries; there may actually be something to this national ethos argument.

property rights in the manufacturing sector are shared between the productive units and the government, then it is necessary to consider possible conflicts of goals and interests between these groups. An analysis of the economy of Nazi Germany in the 1930s without close attention to such factors would make unintelligible many aspects of the evolution of the economic system.[9] Although conflicts of goals between governmental organs and production units and the role of particular incentives in determining the outcome have received considerable empirical attention in the literature on regulated industries in capitalist nations,[10] the results of such studies have not, for the most part, been assimilated by specialists in economic systems.

A final difficulty is theoretical: Assuming that we know the goals and motivation of a population, what could we predict about the behavior of the entire system? Although we can say many useful things about the behavior of individual units,[11] we are far from an understanding of the collective behavior of all units. How would, for instance, three different economies composed respectively of merchants, soldiers, and holy men respond differentially to a wheat scarcity? We have precious few testable hypotheses about such matters.

c. *The structure of information.* Analysis of the structure of information[12] includes not only investigation of the channels of information and the

9. Such an analysis of conflicts of interest has been carried out in an exemplary fashion by Arthur Schweitzer, *Big Business in the Third Reich* (Bloomington, Ind.: 1964).

10. One particularly useful investigation is by George J. Stigler and Claire Friedland, "What Can Regulators Regulate? The Case of Electricity," *The Journal of Law and Economics*, V, October 1962, pp. 1–16.

11. Several different types of literature are devoted to this problem. One is in the field of industrial organization and deals with questions of enterprise behavior under various types of governmental regulations. Good examples of this literature include: H. Averch and L. Johnson, "The Firm under Regulatory Constraint," *American Economic Review*, LXX, December 1962, pp. 1052–69; or L. G. Telser, "On the Regulation of Industry," *Journal of Political Economy*, LXXVII, November-December 1969, pp. 937–52. Another is in the field of planning dealing with the effects of particular incentive schemes for socialist enterprises. Good examples of the literature include: János Kornai and T. Lipták, "A Mathematical Investigation of Some Economic Effects of Profit Sharing in Socialist Firms," *Econometrica*, XXX, January 1962, pp. 140–61; or Edward Ames, *Soviet Economic Processes* (Homewood, Ill.: 1965). Another is in the field of "collective economics" and deals with decision-making in cooperatives. Examples of this literature are cited in Chapter I, note 39. A general survey of many such problems is by Oliver E. Williamson, *The Economics of Discretionary Behavior: Managerial Objectives in a Theory of the Firm* (Chicago: 1967).

12. Some economists, such as Thomas Marschak ("On the Comparison of Centralized and Decentralized Economies," *American Economic Review*, LIX, May 1969, pp. 525–32), have argued that the structure of property and

types of information that are transmitted, but also the processes of obtaining, transmitting, storing, retrieving, and processing information. It should not be surprising that in an economy such as that of the United States, the resources devoted to the information system are a large share of the G.N.P. and, over time, are increasing faster than the G.N.P.[13] As a rule, the more complex the technological processes of an economy, the wider its assortment of goods and services, and the finer its division of labor, the more information-intensive it becomes.

Information inputs to decision-makers in comparable positions (e.g., enterprise managers) in different economic systems vary enormously in quantity, quality, and type. In market economies managers base decisions not only on price information but also market research data, consumer intentions surveys, stock market reports, tax analyses, general news about congressional actions, and so forth.[14] In centrally administered economies managers base their decisions on plan data, different types of commands and incentives, informal messages from other enterprise managers about availability of supplies, and so forth.

Information channels also provide an important clue on the functioning of an economy. As noted in Chapter VII, the industrial hierarchy in centrally administered economies can be organized in basically four different ways, following respectively the "production principle," the "territorial principle," the "functional principle," or the "conglomerate principle." Each of these organizational principles has been adopted in at least one centrally administered economy.[15] The extent to which these princi-

information are not distinct since the only way we have, for instance, of determining the hierarchical centralization of property rights is by studying the patterns of information-flows. Although study of the information-flows may be one way of analyzing the structure of property rights, it is not the only valid way. Further, my definitions of informational centralization and hierarchical centralization of property rights are sufficiently distinct that one could occur without the other. (An empirical example is given in the discussion of Table 8–3.) Thus, although the structure of property rights is reflected in certain types of patterns of information-flows, there is a good deal more about the structure of information that we wish to know as well.

13. Data on these matters are presented by Fritz Machlup, *The Production and Distribution of Knowledge in the United States* (Princeton: 1962).

14. These ideas are particularly stressed in János Kornai, *Anti-equilibrium* (Amsterdam: 1972).

15. Soviet experience with the "functional principle" in the early thirties is discussed by David Granick, *Management of the Industrial Firm in the U.S.S.R.* (New York: 1954). Since then the Soviet Union has followed the "production principle" except for an experimental fling from 1958 to 1965 with the "territorial principle." According to various commentators (Leo Huberman and Paul M. Sweezy, *Socialism in Cuba* [New York: 1969], p. 84, and Roberto M. Bernardo, "Managing and Financing the Firm," in Carmelo Mesa-Lago, ed., *Revolutionary Change in Cuba* [Pittsburgh: 1972], pp. 185–208), the Cubans are experimenting with the "conglomerate principle," pri-

ples are adopted can be determined by studying the channels of information. Moreover, the functioning of these information channels has, I believe, considerable influence on the performance of these economies.[16]

Centralization is a critical notion in the analysis of information. Intuitively, the concept of decentralization of information suggests that each decision-making unit concerns itself only with the effect of its actions (or the *actions* of others) on itself and that it has no direct information about the processes or internal structures of other decision-making units.[17] More formally, an information structure containing messages pertaining only to price and quantity data relevant to buying and selling, in which the senders are indifferent to the identity of the receiver and *vice-versa* (i.e., where the sender would transmit the same message to any interested buyer or seller) may be defined as decentralized. An information structure containing, let us say, data representing an enterprise's production or cost function, or where messages in a hierarchical structure are "addressed" to particular receivers (i.e., where the senders are interested in the identity of the receiver) may be defined as centralized. These definitions thus focus on content and channels of information, rather than on informational sources.[18]

---

marily in the form of large vertically integrated enterprises (called "combinados").

As discussed in Chapter VII, information can also flow in a number of parallel channels (from the enterprise to the top of the hierarchy *via* the party, the secret police, the accounting agency, the production ministry, the banking system, the regional authorities, economic news-gathering agencies, and so forth). Chinese experience with such parallel channels is discussed by Franz Schurmann, *Ideology and Organization in Communist China* (Berkeley: 1970), 2nd ed.

16. The relative advantages and disadvantages of the production versus the regional principles in the Soviet Union are well analyzed in a qualitative manner by Peter Wiles, *The Political Economy of Communism* (Cambridge, Mass.: 1962), Chapter 8; and mathematically by Michael Keren, "Industrial versus Regional Partitioning of Soviet Planning Organization," *Economics of Planning,* IV, 3/1964, pp. 143–60. These kinds of issues are discussed in almost every management textbook.

17. These ideas are developed in much more rigorous detail by Leonid Hurwicz, "Optimality and Informational Efficiency in Resource Allocation Processes," in Kenneth Arrow, *et al.,* ed., *Mathematical Methods in the Social Sciences, 1959: Proceedings of the First Stanford Symposium* (Stanford: 1960), pp. 27–45. Hurwicz later changed his definition of informational centralization in his article "On the Concept and Possibility of Informational Decentralization," *American Economic Review,* LIX, May 1969, pp. 513–5 where he restricts information of decentralized systems to those cases where communication is confined only to commodity-dimensional messages. The usefulness of this revised definition, of which I am dubious, is disputed by Bela Balassa and Abram Bergson, "Discussion," *American Economic Review,* LIX, May 1969, pp. 525–38.

18. In a completely perfect market, sources of information (e.g., price or exchange rate data) may be highly centralized and yet the information transfers of the system, from the standpoint of the above definition, may be completely decentralized.

According to this approach any hierarchically centralized system has a certain degree of information centralization (since various types of control instruments utilized by the center require attention to the identity of the sender and, moreover, messages from the center may not contain just information concerning buying and selling) but there are varying degrees of information centralization consistent with a given degree of hierarchical centralization. For instance, a centrally administered economy in which the center relied exclusively on indirect incentives (such as changing prices) would be informationally more decentralized than a system in which the center controlled the enterprises by direct commands to individual productive units. Similarly, a centrally administered economy in which the enterprises were required to send up information relating to just a single point on their production functions (e.g., the marginal cost of producing a designated output) would be informationally more decentralized than an economy in which the enterprises were required to send up complete information about their production functions.

Distinguishing the structures of information and property and defining the centralization of information in the manner discussed above has several advantages. First, it permits a distinction to be made between the centralization of property and of information which allows as I show below, a useful classification of allocation mechanisms to be constructed. Second, both the definitions of centralization of information and of property are independent of the production function in the economy and of particular aspects of the economic environment. Such a separation is useful if we wish to pinpoint whether performance according to some economic indicator is due to centralization in the system or to environmental or technological considerations that lie beyond the reach of human intervention (in the short run). Third, both quantitative and qualitative measures can be devised to measure centralization of both property and of information.[19] I try to demonstrate more concretely the advantages of this particular approach toward economic systems in the discussion below.[20]

19. A crude empirical analysis is presented in Table 8–3 where the number of material balances and rationed goods for East Germany and Poland are compared. Much more elaborate empirical analyses can also be carried out. Quantitative measurement of information centralization can be made from exploration of the relative importance of horizontal versus vertical channels of communication, or direct versus indirect means of steering the economy; of course, measurements would have to be taken of such dimensions of information-flows from the standpoint of various decision-making units in the economy such as enterprises. Qualitative judgments could also be made, e.g., observing merely the direction of change regarding reliance on price changes or other indirect control instruments. For instance, the greater reliance on fluctuating prices in Hungary after the 1968 reform (see Chapter VII) represents information decentralization.

20. A number of theoretical studies have been made of the degree to which economic efficiency can be achieved in informationally centralized and

d. *"Structural analysis" and economic problems.* Two types of analyses flow from the separation of property, motivation, and information structures. We can examine inconsistencies in economic systems that arise from the interaction of these structural elements. By "inconsistency" I mean irrationality of behavior to achieve a given goal, either because of some failure of a necessary input or else because of some conflict with another goal. Such a structural approach provides useful insights into the operation of the system although emphasis is placed primarily on negative aspects. We can also try to link the ways in which traditional types of economic functions (e.g., the production of a particular set of goods, the distribution of income, and so forth) are fulfilled through the interaction of these three structural elements over time. Such a process approach emphasizes positive aspects of the system.

Clearly both types of analyses are necessary for a full understanding of the functioning of a system. In Section B-2 I discuss various aspects of the structural approach; in Section B-3 I turn to the process approach.

2. A Structural Viewpoint

a. *A static view of interaction difficulties.* In order to show in a concrete manner how an analysis of interaction difficulties can be carried out, I draw a number of examples from the East European economic experience (most of which are discussed in greater detail in Chapter VII) to serve as illustrations. This does not mean that such an analysis is confined solely to socialist economies for, indeed, a similar analysis could be carried out for capitalist economies as well. The three structures define six different types of interaction difficulties (i.e., six different pairs or types of interactions) and the examples below are organized to illustrate each type.

(i) Motivation-information inconsistencies: A bonus system based on sales at arbitrary fixed prices may be inadequate for the economy to achieve an efficient allocation of resources if such prices encourage the "wrong" production or production processes. In certain socialist nations such as Bulgaria and Poland, price reforms lagged many years behind administrative reforms and, in a situation with decentralized authority (i.e., hierarchical decentralization) and irrational prices, the center can hardly expect that its notions about the proper output and input mix will be carried out. Similarly, in both capitalist and socialist economies adequate charges are not made to companies dumping wastes into the air or

---

decentralized structures in a number of articles by Hurwicz and others. The propositions discussed below in the text focus on more concrete issues.

the streams and, as a result, pollution occurs that may result in an inefficient allocation of resources.[21]

(ii) Motivation-property inconsistencies: Several types of phenomena may be discussed under this rubric. First, there are those difficulties arising from insufficient power (or policy tools) to achieve desired goals.[22] For instance, the postreform East German economy ran relatively smoothly and plan goals were realized until 1968 and 1969 when plan goals were considerably increased; these higher goals were not fulfilled which led to a hierarchical recentralization and a change in the property structure. In Yugoslavia policy-makers were unable to achieve their goals with a system of guided market socialism and, as a result, the system of market interventions in the late fifties and early sixties (the Yugoslav "visible hand") was allowed to wither.[23] Among capitalist nations the property structure is such that few governments have the policy tools to halt inflation. Second, there are certain unanticipated consequences of utilizing property rights in order to attain a particular goal that leads to conflicts with other goals that a group is pursuing. For instance, decentralizing investment decision-making power in an economy to increase efficiency may lead most to investment placed in a single region with considerable social overhead capital, a result running contrary to other goals regarding dispersion of productive units throughout the land. Many difficult political problems centering around this dilemma have arisen in Yugoslavia.

(iii) Motivation inconsistencies: This covers problems arising not only from inconsistencies in overall goals (e.g., between maximum growth and spatial dispersion of industry that are discussed in Chapter VIII) but also from inconsistencies between incentives and goals at various levels of an administrative hierarchy. Although much ingenuity has been used in devising bonus schemes that bring about consistency between the goals of the center and the enterprises, inconsistencies inevitably arise and the more complex the system (e.g., as in the Soviet Union), the greater the possibilities of such inconsistencies arising since it becomes more difficult to predict exactly what the enterprise manager will do.

21. The central government in Czechoslovakia has been the only one, as far as I know, to worry sufficiently seriously about these polution problems to attack them on a national scale: It introduced a nationwide pollution tax in its economic reforms of 1967. Unfortunately, I have seen little systematic evidence of the way in which this pollution tax system has been administered or its effectiveness in discouraging pollution.

22. Such inconsistencies are analyzed in an illuminating fashion by Jan Tinbergen, *Economic Policy: Principles and Design* (Amsterdam: 1956).

23. See especially Egon Neuberger, "The Yugoslav Visible Hand: Why Is It No More?" in Janet G. Chapman and Chou Shun-hsin, eds. *The Economics of the Communist World,* forthcoming.

Other inconsistencies arise between performance goals and goals about specific institutional forms in which economic activity is carried out. In the area of foreign trade in Eastern Europe, the goal of the "foreign trade monopoly" for its own sake hindered the realization of the goal of a more effective pattern of exports and imports, and this was a major motive in the important changes of the foreign trade system that occurred in most East European nations during the late 1960s.

(iv) Property-information inconsistencies: This type of difficulty arises when the information available to the decision-maker is not sufficient for effectively exercising power. A decision-maker may have the proper tools for carrying out his goals, and, indeed, the proper information may be available somewhere in the system, but if information channels are so structured that the data do not reach him in time, or reach him in a distorted manner, or if he is unable to process correctly the information, then serious problems arise. For instance, one of the major objections to the material balancing system (which is still employed in a majority of East European nations as a planning and allocation tool to bring supply and demand of particular goods into alignment) was that proper information was not obtained quickly enough, that this information was distorted, and that it was not processed correctly. It was the distortions in the information system brought about by deliberate enterprise overestimation of costs that led to the mismanaged Czechoslovakian price reform which led to the enterprises ending up with very much higher amounts of liquid funds than were planned or were consistent with stable prices.

(v) Property inconsistencies: Several types of such difficulties can be specified. First, formal property rights may overlap so that effective coordination may be impossible. In certain cases of economic reforms, notably Czechoslovakia and Bulgaria, the formal powers assigned to the enterprise and the intermediate associations overlapped, and unresolvable conflicts arose. (In Czechoslovakia this inconsistency was publicly recognized and the associations began to be stripped of their powers in 1968; in Bulgaria, most commentators on the reforms either seemed unaware of such problems or chose to minimize them and it is not surprising that such confusion strengthened the hand of the centralizers and led, in a few years, to a hierarchical recentralization.) Second, particular decision-making units may have virtually no property rights and, at the same time, great formal responsibilities. For instance, in Poland the associations were supposed to have considerable powers but, in actuality, such powers have seemed so limited that certain commentators in the Polish press have begun to wonder whether such units were even necessary.

(vi) Information inconsistencies: These difficulties occur when conflicting signals are received by decision-makers. One case arises when there are parallel structures of power (e.g., party and government) and when information transmitted by them is different, a situation arising often in the prereform planning hierarchies in Eastern Europe.[24] Another case arises when planning is carried out in physical terms by production ministries and in financial terms by the ministry of finance so that enterprises receive conflicting plans from these two higher authorities, a situation also arising often in the prereform planning hierarchies in Eastern Europe.[25]

b. *Interaction difficulties and economic system.* Examples of these six types of inconsistencies can be multiplied almost infinitely; a more systematic approach focuses on the different kinds of inconsistencies that are associated with particular types of economic systems. To show this more clearly let us, for the moment, define socialist economic systems in terms of the relative hierarchical centralization of property rights (a property element) and in terms of the relative emphasis on material incentives to encourage production (a motivation element).[26] Possible examples of the four different socialist economic systems thus defined are shown in Table 9-1. The classification of China and Cuba is tentative; hence the question marks.[27]

It should be evident that the types of controls exercised by central governmental organs (the three types of controls were defined in Chapter VIII) differ considerably in the four different socialist economic systems: Incentive controls would be more heavily used in a hierarchically decen-

24. Such information inconsistencies may also have certain extremely important positive results; such a case is argued by Reinhard Bendix, "The Cultural and Political Settings of Economic Rationality in Western and Eastern Europe," in Gregory Grossman, ed., *Value and Plan* (Berkeley: 1960), pp. 245–65.

25. Another type of inconsistency arises in certain countries where foreign trade planning was carried on by both production and foreign trade authorities. Documentation of these conflicts is provided by Frederic L. Pryor, *The Communist Foreign Trade System* (Cambridge, Mass.: 1963), p. 62. I do not know the degree to which these various plan inconsistencies have survived the economic reforms of the various nations.

26. A problem of interpretation of "material incentives" arises, for in countries such as Cuba and China which have "deemphasized" such incentives, wage differentials were apparently greater than in the Soviet Union. (Evidence from formal wage schedules on these matters is presented by Carmelo Mesa-Lago, *The Labor Sector and Socialist Distribution in Cuba* [New York: 1968], pp. 110–11; the materials cover the early 1960s.) By "deemphasis of material incentives" I mean where large bonuses are not given for surpassing production targets set from above or where large monetary gains are not obtained for producing particularly scarce items.

27. In placing China in its particular position, I am following the interpretation of Schurmann; for Cuba, I am following the interpretation of René Dumont, *Cuba: Est-il socialiste* (Paris: 1970) when he speaks of the militarization of the Cuban economy. (The army is an example of a hierarchically centralized organization that deemphasizes material incentives.)

TABLE 9–1

*Examples of Socialist Economic Systems Defined in Terms of
Hierarchical Centralization of Property and Material Incentives*

	Property Structure	
Motivation Structure	*Hierarchically Relatively Decentralized*	*Hierarchically Relatively Centralized*
Material incentives for production relatively emphasized	Yugoslavia	Soviet Union
Material incentives for production relatively unemphasized	China?	Cuba?

tralized economy with material incentives; commands would be more heavily used in a hierarchically centralized economy with little emphasis on material incentives; ideological controls would be more heavily used in an economy that is hierarchically decentralized with little emphasis on material incentives; and the most "even mix" of controls would probably occur in a hierarchically centralized economy with emphasis on material incentives.

Such an approach has considerable relevance to the analysis of structural inconsistencies, for different types of inconsistencies would occur in the four different economic systems. For instance, given the difficulty of setting up a pollution tax, motivation-information inconsistencies regarding pollution might be more prevalent in Yugoslavia than in China, where antipollution measures might be more easily implemented through ideological manipulation. However, property inconsistencies in the nature of overlapping and conflicting powers might be more serious in Cuba than in Yugoslavia.

I believe that the taxanomic exercise in Table 9–1 can be used as a starting point for a systematic generation of testable propositions about the operations of different economic systems with regard to structural inconsistencies. This, in turn, would give us greater insight into the variability of economic performance of different economic systems. The examples provided in the discussion should give an indication of the type of propositions that could be developed.

3. A Process Viewpoint

The structures of property, motivation, and information must have some internal coherence if production outputs are to be coordinated with production inputs, and if the desires of those wishing to buy particular goods and services are to be brought into some alignment with those producing such goods and services. These coordination processes can be conceptualized in a number of different ways; the scheme discussed briefly below has the advantage of embracing a wide number of actual economies and, in addition, a number of proposed economic systems as well.

a. *Examples of coordination processes.* One method of classifying coordination processes is to consider various combinations of centralized and decentralized information and property structures. In such an exercise, the motivation structure remains a hidden participant whose consistency with the systems discussed below must be assumed for any of the coordination processes to work. Although such an approach defines economic systems only at a very abstract level, such a typological exercise is quite useful in gaining an overall view of economic systems as a whole. The four possible combinations are presented in Table 9–2.

Each of the types of economic systems outlined in the table deserves brief comment.

(i) A number of different types of coordination processes can be envisioned for those cases in which both the information and the property structures are decentralized. The perfectly competitive market system where coordination is obtained by the famous invisible hand is an obvious example, although, of course, no such economy in a pure form ever actually existed. In primitive economies, a different type of coordination mechanism occurs where every participant follows closely the actions he or his family predecessors took in the past; where economic interdependencies are relatively small; and where if the motivation structure is properly attuned such economies have retained their basic forms for centuries. Another type of coordination mechanism occurs with both decentralized information and property structures through institutionalized bargaining between large decision-making units. An example of such a bloc economy (discussed briefly in Chapter VII) is the foreign trade system of Eastern

TABLE 9–2

Examples of Coordination Processes

	Property Structure	
Information Structure	*Hierarchically Decentralized*	*Hierarchically Centralized*
Decentralized	Market, tradition, or bargaining	Iterative administration
Centralized	Indicative administration	Central administration

Europe where the pattern of trade is determined in large part in yearly bilateral negotiations between representatives of each nation.[28] Of course, there is a wide variety of ways in which such bargaining can be structured, depending on the type of units involved and the relative degree of interdependence. Concerning feedbacks between the producer and consumer units in these various types of coordination processes, the situation can differ. In a market economy there is, of course, constant feedback between producers and consumers. In the bargaining situation, the feedback periods can vary, and in the East European foreign trade system certain contacts between the yearly major bargaining sessions were undertaken to take care of any unforeseen changes. And in the traditional system, the feedback period is quite undetermined until more is specified about the system.

(ii) The case where both property and information structures are relatively centralized, I designate as central administration; one obvious example is found in Weber's classic description of a bureaucracy.[29] Several different types of coordination mechanisms may be operative within such a central administration. For instance, the center can send to the peripheral units a series of commands based on some rough and ready informal planning procedures, and then meet every "crisis" by a set of new commands. This type of administration requires a considerable feedback of information from the periphery to the center. Or the center may attempt to coordinate the economy by a comprehensive formal plan based on elaborate information processing about preferences, productive capacities, production functions, and the like that would be operative for some time. In this case, feedback between the periphery and the center does not need to take place so frequently, but the quantity and quality of data transmitted when this feedback does occur needs to be much greater. Various intermediate coordination mechanisms can also be designated, such as that used within the industrial sector of the Soviet Union under Stalin. In this system, coordination was attempted by means of a formal and extensive central plan and based on a highly centralized information system that used a rather primitive information processing technology and concentrated on achieving consistency rather than optimality. Since there were various incentives to transmit distorted information, adverse consequences resulting from such information deficiencies were counteracted by means of a set of manipulated indirect incentives and a supplementary priority system of allocation. For the supplementary control devices to operate, feedback had to be relatively frequent but the infor-

---

28. This is described in moderate detail in Pryor.

29. Max Weber, *Economy and Society,* trans. by Guenther Ross and Claus Wittich (New York: 1968).

mation did not need to be of particularly high quantity or quality while, at the same time, less frequent but more massive feedback of information occurred on a yearly basis at the time in which the annual plan was drawn up.

(iii) A coordination process featuring a hierarchically centralized structure of property but a decentralized information system I designate as iterative administration. In such cases, control of the economy is exercised by the center, often on the basis of a formal plan, but this control is exercised in a relatively indirect manner. The productive units are not merely passive senders of information and implementers of commands, as in the case of central administration, but instead are independent decision-makers which participate in the determination of output and/or prices.

The key feature of iterative administration, as the name suggests, is the existence of a continous dialogue between the center and the productive units, where each is engaged in making certain types of decisions and where the final outcome is the result of the interaction between them. A number of iterative administration systems are discussed in the economic literature, the best known example of which is Oskar Lange's model of market socialism.[30] In this proposal the center announces the prices of goods and services, the enterprises respond with production that maximizes profits (assuming certain constraints are met) and then the center changes the prices according to changes in the level of inventories. We must assume, of course, that the center is manipulating prices in a manner to obtain a *different* pattern of production than would occur under market conditions; for otherwise, the Lange central planner would be merely a bureaucratic "market surrogate." (This latter system would be classified in the same box of Table 9–2 as market economies since the government would exercise little conscious influence on the allocation of resources and, as a result, the property structure would be decentralized.)

If we allow a certain degree of centralization of information (so that particular points on the production function are sent by the producing units to the center), then we can include under the rubric of iterative administration those schemes embodying the Dantzig-Wolfe decomposition principle[31] or other schemes such as the Kornai-Lipták two-level plan-

30. Oskar Lange, "On the Economy Theory of Socialism," in Benjamin E. Lippincott, ed., *On the Economic Theory of Socialism* (Minneapolis: 1938). It must be noted that Lange's model is in no sense complete since he did not analyze the motivational structure on the part of either the center or the productive units that would insure that the decision-making rules he established would actually be carried out, as many of Lange's critics (especially Friedrich von Hayek) have noted.

31. George B. Dantzig, *Linear Programming and Extensions* (Princeton: 1963), Chapter 23.

ning system.[32] (Using the Dantzig-Wolfe scheme, the center sends down prices for particular production factors and goods and the enterprises send up data on the demand for the factors or goods in question as well as total cost data, and certain procedures are followed by decision-makers at both the center and the enterprise until the conditions for an optimal output structure are met: Using the Kornai-Lipták system, the center sends down certain goals in physical units, the producers send up marginal cost data, and iteration occurs until optimality is reached.) Another type of iterative administration scheme is when there is a division of decision-making power between the center and the enterprises with the center determining the amount of investment and the sectoral distribution of investment funds (by using differential interest rates or investment auctions) and allowing a market for consumption goods to function without interference, as long as the constraints set by the investment decisions are met. The crucial interactions come in the responses of enterprises to the central investment decisions, and the responses of the center to the actions of the enterprises.

(iv) The final case—where information is centralized but property rights are hierarchically decentralized—I designate as indicative administration. In such a situation the center prepares orientation figures on the basis of internal information supplied by the enterprises, but the enterprises are free within limits to accept or reject these orientation figures as the basis of their actions in the future. Such a system is claimed to have a number of advantages.[33]

First, such an indicative system may aid the process of dynamic adjustment to some set of equilibrium prices and outputs by speeding up the process; this assumes, of course, that producers put some credence in the plan and adjust their decisions accordingly. Although problems of dynamic adjustments would not arise with such great force in situations where future markets for each commodity existed, this is not realized in any actual economic system. Without such future markets, various types

32. János Kornai, *Mathematical Planning of Structural Decisions* (Amsterdam: 1967), Appendix H. A number of additional schemes of this nature have been proposed including G. M. Heal, "Planning Without Prices," *Review of Economic Studies,* XXXVI, March 1969, pp. 347–63; or E. Malinvaud, "Decentralized Procedures for Planning," in E. Malinvaud and M. O. L. Bacharach, eds., *Activity Analysis in the Theory of Growth and Planning* (London: 1967), pp. 170–208. Certain approaches along these lines are also contained in the public finance literature or the industrial management literature, e.g., Andrew B. Whinston, "Price Guides in Decentralized Organization," in William W. Cooper, *et al.,* eds., *New Perspectives in Organizational Research* (New York: 1964).

33. The following three paragraphs are based on a much more extensive analysis by J. N. Wolfe, "Planning by Forecast," in D. C. Hague, ed., *Price Formation in Various Economies* (New York: 1967), pp. 153–69.

of adjustment problems arise that may lead to under- or over-production, cobwebs, or other undesirable performance.

Second, indicative administration may reduce risk, especially in investment, and thus lead to a rise in productivity through the use of more specialized machinery and greater investment.

Third, credible forecasts by a central planning body, combined with some statements of governmental policy, provide incentives to producers to investigate investment opportunities that they might ordinarily have missed. This, in turn, may lead to greater efficiency by taking certain aspects of dynamic comparative advantage into greater account.

If we turn, for a moment, to actual economic systems, we see certain aspects of such indicative administration in France. However, the actual situation is much more complicated since there is considerable use of manipulated incentives to induce the productive units to behave in accord with the planned goals. The large amount of investment actually carried out by the government, the important control of industrial credit exercised by the government through its banks, and the possible tacit and not-so-tacit agreements between large producers give the plan a certain force that ordinary indicative administration may not have.[34] In other words, it is no accident that there was greater similarity between the plan goals and actual performance in those sectors in which the government had the greatest control over investment.[35] Japan has also had a type of indicative administration but with very different results: The economy has grown very much faster than anticipated and differences between plan goals and actual production in different sectors have varied wildly. Part of this seemed to be due to technical faults of the various indicative plans; part was due to the lack of coordinated ministerial action based on the plan; and part seemed to be due to producers ignoring the plan.[36] In any case, the generalized market research carried out through indicative administration may have dysfunctional as well as functional elements.

It is particularly difficult to generalize about the feedback mechanisms in an indicative administration if the type of indicative plan—its scope, detail, and horizon—has not been specified. In the literature, indi-

34. These issues are discussed in much greater detail by Vera Lutz, *Central Planning for the Market Economy* (London: 1969); Stephen S. Cohen, *Modern Capitalist Planning: The French Model* (Cambridge, Mass.: 1969); John and Anne-Marie Hackett, *Economic Planning in France* (Cambridge, Mass.: 1963); or Geoffrey Denton, *et al., Economic Planning and Policies in Britain, France, and Germany* (London: 1968).

35. This is empirically demonstrated by Armand M. J. Van Nimmen, "French Planning: An Essay in Evaluation," Ph.D. dissertation, Columbia University, 1967.

36. See especially Shigeto Tsuru, "Formal Planning Divorced from Action: Japan," in Everett E. Hagen, ed., *Planning Economic Development* (Homewood, Ill.: 1963).

cative administration is generally analyzed in terms of long-run planning, with indicative plans redrawn in intervals of more than three years. But certainly, feedback between the real world and the indicative administrators can occur more often.

All four types of coordination processes can be more closely analyzed in terms of self-regulating systems if the particular types of decisions made by the various important units are more clearly specified. Since we have not yet specified the structure of motivation, nor have we designated very specifically the structures of property or information, except along the dimension of centralization-decentralization, the four coordination processes must be considered as very abstract representations with many vital economic problems defined away. Actual economies are, of course, much more complex affairs, in which it is necessary to investigate many dimensions of property, information, and motivation before a clear understanding of the operation of the system can be gained. Further, different processes of coordination can coexist not only in different sectors, but also within the same sector. One example of the latter situation occurs where certain "threshold phenomena" are observable, i.e., where one type of coordination process is employed until certain variables reach critical levels (when a "crisis" becomes too severe) and then other coordination processes are substituted.

Once other dimensions of property are brought into the analysis, other types of coordination mechanisms can be defined. The literature on such coordination mechanisms is vast and most of the theoretical models have been formulated without explicit recognition that theories of property are involved, just as we do not need to know explicitly about theories of prose in order to converse. By making the role of the structure of property more explicit, however, a broader perspective on this complicated literature may be gained.

b. *Economic mechanisms within economic processes.* Analyzing an economic system in terms of its coordination processes requires viewing the economy from a highly abstract standpoint; some of the complexity of the system can be analyzed at a lower level of abstraction by examining particular economic mechanisms that occur within the overall coordination processes. Such mechanisms must be examined not only in terms of the structures of property and information, but also of motivations and goals. Cyclical fluctuations of particular economic variables provide excellent illustrations of such economic mechanisms.

Of course, certain types of cyclical fluctuations of aggregate production are related to the environment of the system rather than to the system itself. Examples of these environmental factors influencing fluctuations include the relative importance of agriculture or foreign trade in the economy, the level of technology (e.g., introduction of fodder crops in England in the eighteenth century reduced the variability of the cattle stock between the summer and winter), and certain capital investments (e.g., irrigation systems reduce production fluctuations in agriculture).[37]

Different types of cycles can be generated within a system, depending on information and decision lags and the motivation structure. For instance, certain types of investment behavior lead to accelerator-multiplier cycles that can be specified and found in market economies; and certain types of investment behavior by managers of socialist enterprises lead to inventory cycles that can be specified and found in centrally administered economies.[38] Similarly, interactions between trade and investments leading to cyclical performance can be found in both centrally administered and market economies.[39] For indicative or iterative administration, much less is known about such macro-economic instabilities.

Various types of micro-economic fluctuations (e.g., cobwebs) have been both theoretically defined and empirically analyzed for market economies, and such cyclical performance also exists in centrally administered economies. Stalin, for instance, seemed well aware of the possibilities of such cyclical behavior arising from economic chain reactions occurring from inbalances in supply and demand.[40]

Particular mechanisms can also be specified for the transmission of

37. The relationships between economic development and stability of aggregate production within particular sectors can be easily seen from data presented by George J. Staller, "Fluctuations in Economic Activity: Planned and Free Market Economies, 1950–1960," *American Economic Review,* LIV, June 1964, pp. 385–95.

38. Such inventory cycles are explored by Josef Goldmann and Karel Kouba, *Economic Growth in Czechoslovakia* (White Plains: 1969); and by Josef Goldmann in a forthcoming essay, "Growth Rate Fluctuations in Central and East European Economies." Czechoslovakia appears to have had greater inventory cycles than East Germany and I wonder if the cause may be traced to differences in the motivation structure of managers in the two nations rather than to explicit differences in the property systems.

39. See especially Alan A. Brown, "Toward a Theory of Centrally Planned Foreign Trade," in Alan Brown and Egon Neuberger, *International Trade and Central Planning* (Berkeley: 1968); and John M. Montias, "Socialist Industrialization and Trade in Machinery Products," in the same volume.

40. In a remarkable statement, Stalin once noted: "There, in the capitalist countries . . . the errors of single capitalists, trusts, syndicates, or this or that capitalist group are corrected through the elementary force of the market. . . . . No really important error, no considerable overproduction, no appreciable discrepancy between production and . . . demand can occur in the capitalist countries without the mistakes, errors, and discrepancies being corrected by this or that crisis. . . . With us it is quite different. Every important disturbance in trade or in production, each error in calculation in our economy does not end with just a partial crisis, but affects the whole economy." (Cited without reference in "Soll oder Muss," *Der Aussenhandel,* III, 22, 1953, pp. 507-8.)

inflationary forces, for the directing of investment funds or, as I showed in Chapter IV, in the distribution of wealth through marriage and inheritance. Economists interested in mechanisms in socialist economies could profitably draw from the literatures of organization theory and of business administration to help them isolate mechanisms appearing in centrally administered systems.

Of course, much remains to be explored in the coordination processes and the economic mechanisms that are embodied within these processes. Nevertheless, this discussion should give the reader some flavor of the problem as well as a greater appreciation of the importance of close attention to the property structure in order to carry out such an analysis.

C. The Problem of Convergence of Economic Systems

The concept of property plays a crucial role in a number of broad issues such as the sources of alienation, the role of ideology, and the convergence of economic systems. Considerations of the convergence of economic systems is quite directly related to a number of issues raised in this and previous chapters and is discussed below in detail.[41]

The convergence of economic systems has been debated on so many levels of analysis and by so many people taking into account so many different economic, sociological, and political considerations that it is difficult to gain a view of the most important theoretical issues.[42] This difficulty is compounded by the unfortunate neglect of most participants to define very precisely what they mean by "convergence of economic systems."

By "convergence of economic systems" I mean trends in different economies that are narrowing differences in the structures of property, information, and motivation. Others have analyzed "convergence" in terms of the existence of particular institutions, or in terms of policies or goals pursued in the economy, or in regard to the official ideology, or in terms of policy instruments employed by the central government, or even in regard to the performance of the economy; but these approaches seem either incomplete or misleading.

Rather than reviewing all the twists and turns of the various arguments for or against convergence, I am going to attempt a more synthetic

41. Some brief notes on these other issues may be found in Appendix A-18: Property and Alienation; and Appendix A-19: Property and Ideology.

42. Aside from the sources cited in this discussion, most of the important relevant English language economic literature on convergence is cited in one of the four essays on convergence (by Bornstein, Spulber, Stuart and Gregory, and Weber and Seidl) in Hans Raupach, ed., *Jahrbuch der Wirtschaft Osteuropas* (Munich: 1971).

analysis. The argument below proceeds in two steps. First, I explore the basic positions on which the convergence case rests, bringing in whenever possible relevant empirical materials. Second, I restate the anticonvergence case in terms of the approach outlined in the previous pages focusing on the three systemic elements, and I attempt to demonstrate that this is the most coherent way to analyze the various issues of the convergence debate.

1. The Convergence Position

Among the myriad of arguments used to advance the convergence case, several basic lines of argumentation can be separated. Each is briefly discussed below, after which the role of empirical studies related to the question of convergence is brought under critical scrutiny.

a. *The "perfectionist" case.* One group, which I designate the "perfectionists," has an optimistic belief in progress and posits a notion of perfectibility toward which all societies are heading.[43] Such a theoretical stance, held by various groups since the French *philosophes,* can be argued in a number of ways.

Perfection can be viewed in simple moral terms and springs from some basic notion either about what man "should be" or what man "really is." In the first case, movement is viewed in terms of an upward progression; in the second case, in terms of man realizing his basic essence. The instrument for this movement can be attributed either to outside forces (e.g., God) or to some earthly force such as the rise of education and leisure that allows man to perceive this moral idea or inward essence more readily. Economic development, by releasing man from an overriding concern about sheer physical survival, provides the necessary and sufficient conditions either for moral improvement or the growth of rationality (with, of course, the aid of computers and other data processing machinery) that brings about the closer realization of the perfectibility of man and society.[44]

This argument assumes that there is one single perfect state of man and society; against this position two major objections can be raised. First, there may be several different types of utopia, corresponding to the different temperaments and cultures of their inhabitants. Second, this po-

43. For a brilliant review of this position, see Ian Weinberg, "The Problem of the Convergence of Industrial Societies: A Critical Look at the State of a Theory," *Comparative Studies in Society and History,* XI, January 1969, pp. 1–15.
44. The perfectionist case reads a little like an economic version of Tolstoy's famous first line to *Anna Karenina,* "Happy families are all alike; every unhappy family is unhappy in its own way."

sition assumes a gradual ideological convergence—a convergence in the general world views, values, and intellectual systems—of the world's population which does not look very promising, at least in the foreseeable future.[45]

The perfectionist position focuses on the very long run—say a century from now—for which little social scientific evidence can be given. It seems best, therefore, to leave such matters to the theologians and poets, and turn to arguments for which social science evidence can be used more systematically.

b. *The economic determinist case.* The economic determinists hold that there is a strong consistency between societies at a given level of economic development (i.e., that the level of development is a major determinant of economic system) and that societies will become more alike as differences in the level of development disappear. As noted (note 77) in Chapter VIII, there is some empirical evidence that among the more developed nations, differences in gross national products are gradually narrowing (i.e., per capita G.N.P.s of the poorer nations within this group are growing more rapidly than those of the richer nations). Thus, one major premise of the case of the economic determinists appears to be realized, at least among the richer nations. Other types of empirical evidence used in such arguments include the alleged decline of diversity between peoples and economies as industrialization proceeds. From a theoretical side, the deterministic aspects of the case for convergence can be argued from three separate positions: the structural-functional, the evolutionist or stage theory approach, and the Marxist, each of which is briefly outlined below.

(i) The structural-functional position, as exemplified by sociologists such as Talcott Parsons or Marion Levy,[46] argues that there are certain functional prerequisites for a highly developed economy that narrow the possibilities within which the structure of an economy can vary. For instance, on the cognitive level such economies must be characterized by rational, rather than traditional, outlooks on the part of its population (i.e., scientific rationality as opposed to superstition or the belief that past methods should determine present methods). Membership in decision-making groups must also be on the basis of achievement, rather than ascription (e.g., kinship). Moreover, performance of economically rele-

45. With regard to ideological convergence or, what is the same thing, the "death of ideology," see Appendix A-19.

46. Talcott Parsons, *The Social System* (Glencoe, Ill.: 1951); or Marion J. Levy, Jr., *Modernization and the Structure of Society* (Princeton: 1966). There are many variants of the structural-functional case that are not explored here; my only purpose is to outline briefly the logic of the position.

vant tasks must be highly specific, rather than diffuse (i.e., the societal division of labor must be highly complex and individuals must fulfill an increasingly narrow range of economic tasks in order for the system to grow to higher levels of development). A variant of the structural-functional position occurs in an empirical analysis of property rights of one hundred precapitalist societies where I show that particular levels of economic development are prerequisities for particular property rights to occur.[47] Other variants of the structural-functional position, usually quite implicit, occur in the argument of John Kenneth Galbraith and W. W. Rostow insofar as these are used to support the convergence position.[48]

Three peculiarities of the structural-functional position must be noted. First, there is the assumption that with a rising level of economic development, the functional prerequisities become more confining so that diversity among economies necessarily declines; the validity of this assumption is not at all obvious. Second, the more specific the structural-functional arguments are carried, the more controversial they become, especially with regard to very particular societal configurations such as the pattern of family organization, the organization of production units, the rights of an educated elite (or meritocracy), and so forth. While most of us can assent to structural-functional arguments on a very abstract level, more concrete applications of this argument raise many more doubts. Third, structural-functional propositions are often extremely difficult to test and, in many cases, are stated in a manner that makes them almost tautologically true.

(ii) The evolutionist position rests on the assumption that with a given level of technology, certain institutional configurations are required for greater political or economic power; further, a nation must adopt these institutional configurations (e.g., a particular pattern of centralization of property rights) or perish as a national unity. History is thus viewed as a series of stages, each dominated by particular configurations that become adopted by those nations aspiring for power.[49] This position appears in a more specific garb in the argument that central economic administration (or, given a different ideological orientation, the lack of

47. Frederic L. Pryor "Property Rights and Economic Development," *Economic Development and Cultural Change,* XX, April 1972, pp. 406–37.

48. E.g., John Kenneth Galbraith, *The New Industrial State* (Boston: 1967); or W. W. Rostow, *The Stages of Economic Growth* (Cambridge, England: 1960). These are, of course, only two well-known examples; less well known but perhaps of equal or greater persuasiveness are such books as Clark Kerr, *et al., Industrialism and Industrial Man* (Cambridge, Mass.: 1960).

49. A number of stage theories do not, however, have such a competitive logic; for a general review of various stage theories, see Bert F. Hoselitz, "Theories of Stages of Economic Growth," in Bert F. Hoselitz, ed., *Theories of Economic Growth* (Glencoe, Ill.: 1960), pp. 193–238.

central economic administration) leads to greater economic growth and that sooner or later, a survival of national integrity requires adoption of the "progressive" institutions. The evolutionist argument is sometimes used in connection with the structural-functional position in order to provide a mechanism that makes the necessary conditions for an institution also sufficient conditions for the existence of that institution.[50]

(iii) The Marxist position views the process of economic growth in terms of a dynamic relationship between two factors within the mode of production: the economic base (which includes property relations, particularly with regard to ownership; these property relations are sometimes designated the "relations of production") and the forces of production (which include the level of technology, the resources of the society, and the means of production in the economy). The mode of production determines the societal "superstructure" (which includes the law, art, and politics of the society).[51] Several different types of relationships can be distinguished between the forces of production and the relations of production. For the forces of production to develop, the relations of production must be in a particular configuration. At particular phases of history when radical changes in the relations of production have occurred, the productive forces can develop quickly; and at other points in history, the relations of production become fetters on the development of the forces of production and economic growth is retarded until these relations of production become radically changed as part of the inexorable process of history.

The Marxist position combines both the structural-functional and the evolutionist arguments: Particular relations of production are functional prerequisites for development; and only those economies survive that have the highest degree of development which, in turn, requires in some cases radical change in the property relations. Marx did not clearly foresee that socialist economies (in the sense that the means of production are publicly owned) would arise in nations that were considerably less developed than the leading capitalist nations. Given the present economic systems of the world, modern Marxists argue that in the far future convergence will certainly occur since all economies will become communist; in the near future, however, such convergence is not likely

50. A particular case of this is discussed at the end of Pryor, "Property Rights. . . ."

51. Several doctrinal difficulties arise in the placement of the various factors in the entire schema. I am trying to follow the ideas outlined by Karl Marx, "Preface," *A Contribution to the Critique of Political Economy,* ed. by Maurice Dobb (New York: 1970), originally published in 1859. My interpretation is similar to that of Oskar Lange, *Political Economy* (London: 1963), Chapter 2; it must be noted that different interpretations have also been given.

since neither the current capitalist or socialist nations will radically change their property relations without a great deal of turmoil and stress since the ruling class in each society would seriously resist such changes.[52] In any case, convergence occurs only with the closing of the levels of development of various societies and the common adoption of the communist mode of production.

c. *The interdependence case.* A third and final group of theorists argue convergence on the basis of a homogenization that comes about through lower costs of transportation and communication and greater interdependence. Just as nation-states have become more homogeneous over time, so the world will become in the future; the "Americanization" of Western Europe is but one of many signs of this process. The greater interdependence of nations encourages a drive toward unity that can, in part, be realized through greater conformity in ideology and institutions. The global village that is resulting from newer and cheaper mass communication methods both causes and presupposes a greater cultural and economic uniformity.

This interdependence position, which is usually the least rigorously argued, combines certain elements of the perfectionist case and the evolutionist case, adding a certain sociological determinism to leaven the discussion. As in the perfectionist case, it assumes a "death of ideology"; as in the evolutionist position, it seems to assume that the most productive institutions will be copied by all nations.

d. *Relevant empirical studies.* Evidence used to verify a particular convergence theory depends, of course, on the way in which the theory is framed. Nevertheless, in most cases certain types of basic trends are generally referred to that are considered correlates of economic development. These deserve brief attention.

From both time-series and cross-section analysis we know, for instance, that economic development is accompanied by a shift of the labor force from agriculture to manufacturing to particular services (Petty's law);[53] that the share of income spent on food decreases (Engel's law);

52. If one held rigidly to a theory of stages, then it is not clear that a centrally administered economy for a nation at a relatively low level of development is necessarily the most productive institutional arrangement and that for rapid economic growth, a capitalist stage is first necessary. Needless to say, Soviet and other modern Marxists do not hold this view but argue instead that in all cases, socialist production is more efficient than capitalist production.

53. Evidence on this and other propositions discussed below is presented by Simon Kuznets, *Modern Economic Growth, Structure, and Spread* (New Haven: 1966).

that production extends to a much greater variety of products, total input-output tables become more dense (more squares in the matrix are filled);[54] and that the share of government expenditures rises to some upward limit of the G.N.P. (Wagner's law).[55] In capitalist economies we know with economic development that the capital/labor ratio rises, that the capital/output ratio and the organic composition of capital do not greatly change,[56] and that the share of labor income in the total national income rises slightly over time (Chapter IV). We also know with economic development that birth and death rates fall, that the proportion of highly trained or educated workers increases, and that the division of labor becomes more complex. From time-series, but not cross-section evidence, we know that the sizes of establishments and enterprises in manufacturing are related to the level of economic development (Chapters V and VI); and evidence suggests that enterprise size is, in certain ways, related to managerial power (Chapter IV). Many more propositions relating development to certain economic variables have been demonstrated.

A number of political and sociological considerations are also related to the level of economic development. We know, for instance, that the rise of the nuclear family is associated with economic development (at least up to a certain point), and that certain patterns of urbanization are associated with increasing economic development.[57] We have certain evidence that "strength of democratic institutions" may have some relation to development and that political mobilization seems associated with development as well.[58] Many more correlations can, of course, be cited.

Those arguing the anticonvergence position can, I believe, safely concede that many of the correlates of economic development cited

54. This is discussed by Wassily Leontief, "The Structure of Development," *Scientific American,* September 1963; and Hollis B. Chenery and T. Watanabe, "International Comparisons of the Structure of Production," *Econometrica,* XXVIII, October 1958, pp. 487–521.

55. This "law" is discussed at considerable length in Frederic L. Pryor, *Public Expenditures in Communist and Capitalist Nations* (Homewood, Ill.: 1968), Chapter II.

56. See Kuznets. The organic composition of capital is the capital stock divided by labor income which equals the capital/output ratio divided by the labor share of national income, both of which remain relatively constant.

57. A large number of these propositions are summarized by Robert M. Marsh, *Comparative Sociology* (New York: 1967).

58. A number of authors have argued this dubious proposition, e.g., Seymour M. Lipset, *Political Man* (Garden City: 1960); G. A. Almond and S. Verba, eds., *The Politics of Developing Areas* (Princeton: 1960); Kuznets, Chapter 8. Other studies are summarized by Marsh. The most statistically sophisticated study of this sort is by Irma Adelman and Cynthia Taft Morris, *Society, Politics, and Economic Development* (Baltimore: 1967), which uses factor analysis and finds a cross-section relationship, but not a relationship over time (at least between 1950 and 1964).

above are probably going to extend in the future. Of course, the occurrence of a particular relationship—even in all nations now existing—does not prove by itself that a necessary and sufficient relationship exists between economic development and the variable in question; nevertheless, such evidence combined with a number of theoretical arguments generally makes a convincing case. For instance, I am gladly willing to concede that economic development is accompanied by an ever increasing division of labor that requires an increasing level of different technical skills and that the communist utopia, in which individual specialization within the division of labor is abolished, seems highly unrealistic.[59] And I believe that certain institutional arrangements such as the factory are probably here to stay for several centuries and that a return to the putting-out system of production may not occur in the foreseeable future.[60] What is worth pointing out is that a great many important economic phenomena are *not* related to the level of economic development and also deserve consideration.[61]

59. According to Marx and Engels, *The German Ideology,* (Moscow: 1968), Chapter 1, p. 45: "[I]n communist society, where nobody has one exclusive sphere of activity but each can become accomplished in any branch he wishes, society regulates the general production and thus makes it possible for me to do one thing today and another tomorrow, to hunt in the morning, fish in the afternoon, rear cattle in the evening, criticise after dinner, just as I have a mind, without ever becoming hunter, fisherman, shepherd, or critic."

In the most coherent Marxist interpretation of the future communist society that I have seen, Ernst Mandel (*Marxist Economic Theory* [New York: 1968], Chapter 17) reinterprets this to mean that technology will succeed in abolishing all routine work and will liberate research and thought from all material slavery. As an example of this spontaneous revolt of man against the tyranny of the division of labor, Mandel points to the huge development of amateur, do-it-yourself activities. Although it is undoubtedly true that certain aspects of the division of labor are stultifying for human development, this does not necessarily mean that things will become better in the future. I have not yet seen any Marxist argument to show convincingly that technology will develop differently in the future than it has in the past. And if the communist utopia does appear within our lifetime, I definitely do not want Ernst Mandel to take out my tonsils or build a bridge for me, despite his impressive erudition.

60. In an unguarded moment, Weinberg, p. 14, presents the opposite case when he argues: "For all we know, the structural arrangements common to the pioneer [industrial] nations such as the centralized factory, the industrial city, and the [skilled] labor force may simply not be characteristic of some latecomer processes of industrialization."

61. A much stronger position is taken by Robert C. Stuart and Paul R. Gregory, "The Convergence of Economic Systems: An Analysis of Structural and Institutional Characteristics," in Raupach, ed., pp. 425–43, who argue that convergence can be meaningfully argued only in terms of variables that are not related to economic development. That is, if two sets of economies differ in institutions and also differ over time in terms of such variables as the relative importance of foreign trade in the economy, the sectoral distribution of production or investment, or the relative importance of services,

The empirical case for convergence of economic systems is also argued in terms of changes in institutions or in the use of particular policy tools that are occurring in the East and the West. For instance, most developed capitalist nations are engaging in economic planning and regulating the economy on both a macro- and a micro-economic level, primarily through the use of indirect policy tools (use of taxes and subsidies, or monetary and fiscal policy), although resort to direct interventions is also occasionally taken. On the other hand, the East European nations have started to put a scarcity price on capital (an interest rate), have placed more emphasis on managers' achieving profit goals based on actual sales, and are using more indirect (and fewer direct) measures of control.[62] Although this certainly represents a decreasing of the differences between capitalist and socialist economies, Wiles has noted that this may be more indicative of a dropping of revolutionary nonsense, rather than the start of a long-term trend to eliminate all systemic differences.[63] The critical question is, of course, how far this narrowing of differences will occur.

Finally, the empirical case for convergence is sometimes argued on a number of nonexistent "trends" that deserve brief mention. Some observers have alleged to see a certain "creeping socialism" in the West but the signs of this are far from clear: The degree of nationalization has not appreciably increased in the last two decades (a matter discussed below and in Chapter II); further, the share of public expenditures in the G.N.P. has remained roughly constant in many nations. Some analysts have also detected the rise in a special type of collectivism in the West, namely a split between owners and managers and increasing enterprise agglomeration and monopolization so that managerial power is con-

---

then they have not converged. On the other hand, if the two sets of economies differ in institutions but do not differ with regard to such performance variables unrelated to economic development, then the sets of economies have converged in all important respects. Although I have considerable sympathy with this approach it seems incomplete in two respects. First, if all important variables are related to the level of economic development, the convergence or nonconvergence is defined in terms of trivial phenomena. Second, economies may differ in performance not only because of economic system or the level of economic development, but also because of other variables such as size of domestic market, or climate. Therefore, performance variables must be selected that are not related to these variables as well.

62. This is argued by Jan Tinbergen, "Do Communist and Free Economies Show a Converging Pattern?" in Morris Bornstein, ed., *Comparative Economic Systems* (Homewood, Ill.: 1965), pp. 455–64; and H. Linnemann, J .P. Pronk, and J. Tinbergen, "Convergence of Economic Systems in East and West," in Morris Bornstein and Daniel Fusfeld, eds., *The Soviet Economy: A Book of Readings,* 3rd ed., (Homewood, Ill.: 1970), pp. 441–61.

63. I use Wiles for rhetorical support rather than substantive support, since he has, in a series of articles and speeches between 1962 and 1969, taken almost every position in favor of, and against, convergence that can reasonably be advanced.

stantly expanding.[64] However, such simple views of agglomeration and monopolization are exploded in Chapter VI. With regard to Eastern Europe, those viewing the changes toward market socialism in Hungary and Yugoslavia as harbingers of change for the entire socialist camp have, in many cases, probably not based their opinions on any knowledge of economic reforms in East Germany, Romania, or the Soviet Union, where market socialism has been explicitly rejected. Finally, political arguments for convergence, based on a rise in political repression in the West and a decline in the East, also appear weak: Although "repression" may be increasing somewhat in certain capitalist nations, the reverse is the case in other capitalist nations; similarly, the political liberalization in Eastern Europe has not extended very far in most countries[65] and it is quite uncertain whether any such changes will be permanent—witness the reversals of the Khrushchev or Dubček liberalization measures under Brezhnev and Kosygin.

2. The Nonconvergence Position

After a brief review of some invalid arguments for nonconvergence, I would like to link the problem of convergence with the notion of economic system argued in the beginning of the chapter and to present what I feel are some valid arguments for doubting the convergence of economic systems within the foreseeable future.

a. *Some invalid arguments.* Generally speaking, Marxists reject any idea that capitalist and socialist economies are converging and point toward convergence only in the far future when all nations are communist.[66] A number of arguments I believe to be invalid are employed.

First, there are a number of arguments of the type "the form is similar but the content is different" that are mere semantics, e.g., in socialism one labors for oneself and society, while in capitalism one labors only for the capitalist. Of equal intellectual vacuity are such arguments as: In so-

64. This fallacious view is forcefully argued by Stanislav Andreski, *Elements of Comparative Sociology* (London: 1964), Chapter 24.

65. An interesting set of comparisons is by Zbigniew K. Brzezinski and Samuel P. Huntington, *Political Power: U.S.A./U.S.S.R.* (New York: 1964), who try to document the great differences between the two systems. For some interesting sociological remarks about East European political "liberalization," see Andreski, Chapter 23.

66. The most notable exception to this generalization is that of the academician Andrei D. Sakharov, *Progress, Coexistence and Intellectual Freedom* (New York: 1968), pp. 71–81. I suspect that these views concerning convergence of economic systems, although argued by a physicist, are supported by a number of other intellectuals in the Soviet Union who have not been able to publish their ideas.

cialism there is only production for use, while in capitalism there is only production for profit. These, I believe, can be dismissed without argument.

Second, there are a number of much more serious arguments about the nature of conflicts in the society. More specifically, the class conflict is supposed to characterize capitalism, now and forever more; while in socialism, contradictions are nonantagonistic and no divisions of interest between different social groups develop. This view is not universally held in Eastern Europe, and a number of thoughtful East European analysts have pointed to the existence and even desirability of interest or stratum conflicts.[67] This, of course, is a difficult problem to discuss, especially since the determinants of the way in which societies cleave are far from clear; e.g., in the United States during the 1960s, cleavages appeared more importantly along racial than economic class lines while in other nations such as Sweden in the early 1970s, it was white-collar versus blue-collar workers.[68] Although this argument about conflict between workers and capitalists may be a correct characterization of capitalism of some countries in some periods, as a general characterization of cleavages in capitalist economies, it does not seem valid.

b. *A structural approach.* Let us consider the structures of property, motivation, and information and look briefly at the ways in which economies in the East and West are different and are changing.

With regard to the structure of property, both divergent and convergent elements in the East and West can be observed. One type of property configuration is, of course, the distribution of ownership, especially between the public and private sectors. Is there any evidence that public ownership will greatly increase in coming years in the West or that private ownership will greatly increase in Eastern Europe? The arguments about basic economic "contradictions" in either groups or nations forcing such changes in ownership appear to be based less on changes in the actual patterns of ownership in these nations (see Chapter II) than on either theoretical consideration based on relatively abstract political economic theories or on a certain optimism that important groups in the particular nation will finally see the "true light" and force changes. Cer-

67. Two well-known analysts of such issues in Eastern Europe are the late Polish economist Oskar Lange, *Political Economy*, pp. 44–5, who spoke of strata conflicts in socialism; and the Hungarian politician turned sociologist, Andras Hegedus, who recognizes strata conflicts and believes them beneficial to society. [For a summary of the latter's ideas see "Hegedus, His Views and His Critics," *Studies in Comparative Communism*, II, April 1969, pp. 121–47.]

68. Sweden faced a bizarre "white-collar strike" as a result of certain wage levelization measures in the early part of 1971.

tain predictions by non-Marxists of reprivatization in Eastern Europe that are based on the slight increase of private small-scale handicraft and services appear to be indulging in fiction; and Marxist arguments concerning the breakdown of capitalism are hardly more rigorous. Although anything can happen in the next fifty years, the possibility of radical changes in the degree of public or private ownership among the economically developed or semideveloped nations of the world does not seem very great. Along this ownership dimension, therefore, convergence between economic systems does not appear imminent in the foreseeable future in most nations. It must be further added that considerable changes in the *distribution* of ownership holdings *within* the private sector in the capitalist nations could occur; some important circumstances for such changes were analyzed in Chapter IV using a simulation model.

Forces influencing other dimensions of the structure of property sometimes lie outside the realm of human influence (e.g., the separation of ownership and control in capitalist nations), sometimes result from deliberate human choice (e.g., hierarchical centralization in many East European nations), and sometimes occur as the consequence of "semiconscious" human choice (e.g., the helter-skelter enterprise consolidations in Hungary and Czechoslovakia before the economic reforms in the sixties). Although, as I noted in Chapter VIII, the level of economic development has a considerable long-run influence on various aspects of centralization, the major differences in various aspects of centralization between the East and West appear to be the result of conscious political choice. Are there compelling economic reasons that would lead to the choice of a particular degree of some aspect of centralization?

As I argued in the brief comparative survey of economic performance of nations with greater and less centralization in the last part of Chapter VIII, the performance differences between systems do not appear to be great. Although there is considerable variability among nations in the same group, the intragroup differences are either not significant or small in most cases. In addition, the theoretical analysis of the economic impact of centralization is very underdeveloped. Thus there does not appear to be any hard scientific evidence, either empirical or theoretical, that unambiguously points to the economic desirability of a high or low degree of centralization. The variety of attempted economic reforms in East Europe appears in part due to the lack of compelling reasons to choose a relatively centralized or decentralized system.

If nations face equally desirable choices about the degree of centralization of property rights along different dimensions, then convergence depends on how many choices are available. If a wide spectrum of choices is available, then convergence between the economic systems in East and West Europe could occur in the sense that the degree of centralization (according to the various concepts) of the nations i.ı each group will fall along a spectrum such that there is a large overlap between the two sets of nations. However, if nations face only several discrete choices about the degree of centralization in order to maintain a coherent economic system, then it is possible for reasons of historical inertia that most East European nations will choose a highly centralized system while the reverse choice will be made in the West for the same reason. Thus convergence will not occur. The critical question is the degree to which nations face a spectrum of choices of centralization or just a few major alternatives in selecting or changing an economic system.

In the analysis of the economic reforms in East Europe in the sixties, evidence is brought forward that nations do not face a spectrum of choices but rather that several discrete choices must be made if the economic system is to have coherence. I argued that "mixed economies" tended to be unstable and move either toward more centralized or decentralized property patterns. Since the evidence was fragmentary, this conjecture is tentative. If I am correct about this matter, then economic systems are pushed into several general molds, within which only minor variations can be made without adversely affecting economic performance.

This conclusion means that economic systems would converge only if all nations in the East and West would select the same general mold, but, as I indicated above, there are no compelling economic reasons (i.e., reasons based on economic performance) for such a choice. Although some nations in Eastern Europe may approach the decentralized property pattern of the West by adopting some type of market socialism system, I see no important economic forces that would influence all East European nations to make a similar choice. A similar argument applies for Western nations adopting highly centralized economic systems, even if their predominant mode of property ownership might change.

Before turning to convergence in the structure of motivation I would like to emphasize that the considerations discussed in the above paragraphs directly contradict the arguments of some economists such as Nobel laureate Jan Tinbergen, who forsees a convergence of systems to an "optimum regime."[69] Tinbergen appears to argue that there is one optimal economic system that lies between those of the East and West and that nations in both parts of the world are gradually moving toward it. His primary evidence is the increasing degree to which national gov-

69. See Tinbergen's articles in note 62; Jan Tinbergen, "The Theory of the Optimum Regime," in his *Selected Papers* (Amsterdam: 1959); or his "Some Suggestions on a Modern Theory of the Optimum Regime," in C. H. Feinstein, ed., *Socialism, Capitalism, and Economic Growth: Essays Presented to Maurice Dobb* (Cambridge, Eng.: 1967), pp. 125–32.

ernments are beginning to use the same type of policy tools to achieve their economic goals which, in turn, are also becoming more similar. Leaving aside for a moment this notion of a convergence of goals[70], this argument is strongly rooted in the notion that a "mixed economy" is not only viable and stable but performs better than much more centralized or decentralized systems. This is open to some doubt, I believe. Although Yugoslavia is often used as an example of such a successful mixed economy, especially since it has a high growth rate of aggregate production, it should be noted that it also had the greatest aggregate production fluctuations, the highest unemployment rate, one of the most persistent inflations, and one of the most chronic balance of payments problems of any nation in Europe. Moreover, the Yugoslavian economic system appears to be becoming increasingly less "mixed," even though it maintains public ownership of the means of production. In other words, a "mixed" economy may combine the worst features of both centrally administered and market economies, and not their best. Although a scientific resolution of these matters has yet to be made, I believe that the fragmentary evidence points to this possibility, rather than that of an "optimum regime" lying between the East and West. This conclusion is controversial and admits honest differences of opinion.

The structure of motivation is ultimately, I believe, a more important phenomenon to consider when analyzing convergence than the structure of property, even though the structure of property greatly influences the goals, incentives, and aspirations of participants in the economy. National values differ and this may strongly affect economic institutions. For instance, Americans and Japanese have a number of different values concerning family structure, concentration of economic power, and paternalism such that even if their levels of economic development were roughly similar, their respective economies might have quite different types of organizations (such as factories) within any given set of "functional prerequisites."[71]

70. Revulsion by men of good will against the crudity of the debate in the 1930s and 1940s of the "grand alternative of the 'isms' " led in the West to the opposite extreme in the 1950s and 1960s of the "spectrum of system choices," the "death of ideology," and the convergence hypothesis. I discuss some of my objections to the "death of ideology" below and in Appendix A-19.

71. An interesting study of differences in Japanese and American values is by Charles Morris, *Varieties of Human Value* (Chicago: 1956). Ways in which these value differences are manifested in production units are analyzed by J. C. Abegglen, *The Japanese Factory: Aspects of its Social Organization* (New York: 1958). Although it can be argued that many of the differences between Japanese and American values and, hence, the operation of factories, will disappear with a closing of the level of economic development between the two nations, this remains to be seen.

If we recognize that conditions of economic scarcity are going to continue for the foreseeable future and leave discussions of the era of general plenty (which comes under various labels such as the land of Cockaigne or the era of full communism) to social science fiction writers, then we cannot achieve all of our goals and must worry about trade-offs between goals. It is not at all clear that when faced with trade-offs between individual freedom and individual equality, all nations would make the same choice. To make the matter more concrete, in Chapter VIII I suggest that nations may face a choice between hierarchical centralization of property rights and equality in the distribution of monetary income. If this trade-off actually exists (which is far from proven), then national predispositions in the United States may lead toward greater stress on hierarchical decentralization while the opposite decision might be made in East Germany.

Even more serious trade-offs occur where the total amount of income is involved. For instance, Cuba has laid great emphasis on moral as opposed to material incentives for workers and, as a result, productivity has suffered.[72] Once the level of economic development in nations rises far above the level of minimum subsistence so that destitution is banished, nations may choose particular institutions that are economically less efficient but that maximize some other goal. In one important sense, economic constraints become less important (i.e., that sheer physical survival is not imperiled) as economic development proceeds. The common notion that the political integrity of a nation is imperiled if it does not have the highest possible per capita G.N.P. is one of those bizarre implicit political assumptions that has never been proven. Its relevance in an era when the leading superpowers have the ability to kill the entire world's population ten times over seems particularly doubtful.

Although such trade-offs may theoretically be open to nations, the degree to which such choices are recognized or acted upon differs from country to country. The argument advanced by Marxists that capitalist economies are somehow less capable of recognizing or acting upon such choices seems particularly hollow in the light of the performance of most East European nations. In point of fact, the economic, political, and social systems in all nations are profoundly conservative in the sense that all contain strong mechanisms for their own continuance. The miserable performance of most economies with regard to one pressing problem of our era recognized as a problem by scientists literally decades ago—pollution—has little relation to economic system (defined in any way one

72. See, for instance, the remarks of Wassily Leontief, "A Visit to Cuba," *New York Review of Books,* August 21, 1969; and "The Trouble with Cuban Socialism," *New York Review of Books,* January 7, 1971.

cares to).[73] The evidence advanced to prove that one type of economic system is more or less conservative than another is far from convincing and, at the present time, we must consider this an open question.

With regard to the structure of information, numerous configurations are possible. Although political dimensions of information are extremely controversial (e.g., how much should a central government be allowed to know about the "private" lives of its citizens), economic dimensions appear to engender less heated disputes. But as noted in the previous section, the structure of information plays a crucial role in the coordination processes of an economy and, whether it is explicitly recognized or not, the structure of information is a critical element in the choice between varieties of market, centrally administered, indicative administered, or iterative administered systems. As awareness of the costs and benefits of particular types of feedback mechanisms grows, the structure of information may also become an explicit subject of controversy in the economic literature and, after some lag, may reach the political arena. Although the increasing use of the market in several East European nations implies a convergence of information structures, in other nations of Eastern Europe a different tendency is occurring. Since the structure of information depends vitally on the internal operations of decision-making units and since we know so little about such processes, we can say little about convergence or divergence of economic systems that is based on any type of systematic appraisal of the facts in this area.

By examining trends in the structures of property, goals and incentives, and information of various economies in the East and West, we are converting the question of convergence or divergence of economic systems from a unidimensional to a multidimensional question. We can thus bystep the sterile discussion of "systems are or aren't converging" to an analysis of the ways in which economies are and aren't becoming more alike. The approach also forces us to consider much more carefully the impact of various aspects of economies on their performance in order to judge whether there are compelling economic reasons for change. Finally, we are also impelled to consider more carefully differences in the goals and aspirations of different groups in these economies and their ability to achieve their ends. Although such an approach to the question of convergence of economic systems makes the discussion more tepid, scientific truth may be further advanced: A scalpel is often of more use to surgery than an ax.

73. Those believing that pollution problems are due primarily to private ownership of the means of production or to irrational planning should examine a case study by Marshall I. Goldman, *The Spoils of Progress: Environmental Pollution in the Soviet Union* (Cambridge, Mass.: 1972).

D. Toward a Theory of Property

In this final section I would like to summarize concisely the basic lines of argument in this book and then to comment briefly on the future development of a theory of property. Since the development of a positive theory of property depends in part on the need for such theory, it is necessary to discuss several important moral or normative dimensions of a theory of property as well.

The type of analysis pursued in this book focuses attention on institutions of which property, in a broadly defined sense, is a fundamental element. Two types of basic questions have been asked: What are the forces influencing the rise, development, and continuance of particular property relations? And what are the effects or impact of particular property relations or institutions on the course of economic activity?

Developmental propositions about the pattern of property rights include the analysis in Chapter II of different determinants of public ownership of the means of production, the simulation model in Chapter IV relating particular marriage and inheritance institutions to the distribution of income and wealth, the examination in Chapters V and VI of the determinants of the sizes of establishments and enterprises in manufacturing, and the analysis in Chapter VIII of different influences on particular aspects of the centralization of property rights. Impact propositions about the pattern of property rights include the exploration in Chapter IV of the role of ownership in the distribution of total incomes, the examination in Chapter VII of the influences of particular configurations of property rights on further institutional changes in Eastern Europe, and the analysis in Chapter VIII of the role of system in spatial centralization and particular types of economic performance. Depending on one's point of view, certain discussions can be considered to focus upon either developmental or impact propositions; e.g., the simulation model in Chapter IV shows determinants of the distribution of wealth, which are developmental hypotheses, but it also shows the effect of particular institutions on a performance variable and is thus an impact proposition as well.

In both developmental and impact studies, it is necessary to use both sophisticated theory and refined statistical tools and in this respect we are limited. With regard to theory we are bound, for the most part, to a modification of analytic tools and theories either developed from traditional economic analyses of market economies or borrowed from other disciplines. The analytical tools used in this book such as the simulation model for the study of changes in the distribution of income, or the study of average sizes in the examination of establishments and enterprises are relatively primitive. The statistical techniques employed—primarily regression analysis—also leave something to be desired. But we must use whatever is at hand for the time being; although there is a limit to the degree to which we can fruitfully borrow from other disciplines, we are far from reaching this point.

If we are to learn more about economic institutions, their development and their effects, if we are to develop deeper knowledge about institutional prerequisites for high standards of living and the degree to which we can vary institutions to achieve goals other than this single goal, then we must begin much more intensive empirical study of economic institutions in general and property in particular. A positive theory of property that is more than empty theoretical phrases cannot be developed until we plunge much more deeply into empirical analysis than hitherto. Programmatic appeals to use this or that particular method of analysis or to focus on this or that particular problem are quite useless if no empirical work is ever carried out. Approaching empirical analysis of economic phenomena with the concept of property allows a great many disparate phenomena to be analyzed together; although the subject matter of the various studies in this book appear at first glance to be widely different, they all deal with property and have relevance for each other, as I have tried to indicate in this and the previous chapters.

Underlying the notion of property in this book is that of economic power. Hobbes' idea of the ultimate nature of power that is cited at the beginning of this chapter, namely to be able to obtain some desired goal in the future, puts a moral element on the concept that I have avoided up to now. But morality does not imply moralism; that is, Kolakowski's dictum (also cited at the chapter head) that morality means blindly following one's immediate moral perceptions regardless of consequence and possibility of realization is quite incorrect. It is the assessment of our various moral goals and the degree to which they are mutually exclusive, it is a recognition that conflicts between moral goals are inevitable (and that trade-offs with costs are involved), that represents a truly moral use of economic power. Those arguing that recognition of trade-offs is the first step toward immorality are acting on a premise about lack of conflict between moral goals that is, I believe, unrealistic.

Thus if we wish to change the economy in any effective manner in order to realize more perfectly any particular goal, then often we must have a knowledge of institutions and property relations that is a difficult but important duty to obtain. Advocates of blind action without regard to whether the future will conform to their wishes are following Kolakowski, but not necessarily Hobbes. Such partisans of action will, of course, have little power of persuasion on those with any stake in the *status quo;* but they can, of course, cause considerable turmoil and confusion. Although confusion is not necessarily bad, it may deflect our attention from progressive changes in society which are quite feasible and which might be generally accepted.

Although scientific analysis of property relations existing now or in the past can reveal only part of the information needed for policy-making, we can, at least, avoid certain mistakes and realize some goals more effectively if such studies are made and utilized. Although an adequate all-embracing positive theory of property lies far in the future, greater empirical and theoretical attention to property at the present time may not only bring about the realization of such a theory but, at the same time, may be of assistance in bringing about a future economic system in which we will want to live and make such theories.

APPENDIX A-1

Some Notes on the Definition of Property and Property Institutions (for Chapter I, Part B)

A. *Explication of Definition*

The definition of property advanced in Chapter I is: Property is a bundle of rights or set of relations between people with regard to some good, service, or "thing"; such rights must have economic value and must be enforced in some societally recognized manner.

This is a broad definition that focuses on positive rather than moral rights, i.e., it emphasizes the choices open to an individual and the direct constraints that limit his actions rather than rights which a person "should" have (such as the right of free speech) or some right which a person "legally" has, but which he can not enforce. The definition concerns, in other words, those rights from which predictions of behavior can be based. Since economics deals with the implications of individuals maximizing their perceived self-interests with constrained choice sets in the areas of production, distribution, and consumption the appropriateness of this concept of property to economic analysis should be quite apparent.[1]

I claim no originality in the conceptual exploration below of the definition of property for much of the discussion follows standard jurisprudential thought. However, certain distinctions drawn by property lawyers or political theorists (e.g., between "property" and "property rights" or rights *in rem* and *in personam*) are irrelevant to economic analysis and are not discussed, while other aspects of property that have considerable economic importance (e.g., valuation) but are not stressed in jurisprudential analysis of property are emphasized. In other words, the concept is defined for use in economic analysis.

1. "Bundle"

A particular property can consist of one or more single rights. The term "bundle" is chosen as a neutral term and should not be interpreted to mean that the various rights associated, let us say, with some tangible object have any connections with each other. Indeed, one of the purposes of a theory of property is to determine which particular rights are generally held together.

Examples of single property rights are quite common. For instance, person P may have the right to cross a given piece of land "held" by person Q, although P may be unable to exercise other rights attached to such land (e.g., the right to build a house on it, graze cattle on it, or collect rent from it). If Q tries to prevent P from exercising his single right (in this case, an ease-

1. This aspect of property is particularly stressed by Armen Alchian [B5].

ment), P can prevent Q's obstruction through legal action. Similarly P, by virtue of his position in an organization, may have the right to drive the company car home at the end of the day and use it for his personal pleasure, although he may have no rights in determining what kind of car it is, or who drives it during the day. In this second case the mechanism by which P enforces his right does not fall in the formal legal sphere administered by the government but is part of the authority sphere of a private organization in which obstructionists may ultimately be prevented from their action by being fired. A property right possessor can have such a small part of the bundle of rights associated with some good, service, or "thing" that some have argued he can even suffer from particular types of psychological estrangement from his property![2]

A person can possess a number of property rights with regard to some good, service, or "thing"; indeed, he may come close to possessing all such rights such that the only limitations on his set of choices may be certain general injunctions from the state (e.g., zoning laws) or from society (e.g., the building of huge "graven images" on his land). So many property rights can adhere to such a seemingly simple article as a canoe that the only practical method of structuring behavior in society to minimize friction might be the apportionment of at least a subset of such rights to particular individuals or groups.[3] No society has yet been discovered, not even the most simple hunting and gathering society, in which such a parceling of property rights leading to differential economic advantages does not occur.[4] Such considerations underlie the reasoning of those who have argued that "primitive communism" could never have occurred and that property rights held on a subsocietal basis are a functional prerequisite for societies to survive.[5]

Among the bundle of rights defining some property, numerous subsets of rights are often singled out for particular attention. In the text I have focused upon income rights and control rights, but other types of rights can be designated, depending on the analytic purpose of the investigator.

2. *"Rights or Set of Relations"*

A large and rich literature concerning the concept of "rights" could be consulted at this point; and a large number of different types of rights defined by lawyers (e.g., claims, powers, privileges, and immunities)[6] could be defined. But for the purpose of this study, two aspects of the concept are necessary to

2. This charming idea comes from David T. Bazelon ("What is Property," in his [B25, Chapter 2] with whom I find myself usually in strong disagreement.

3. An interesting discussion of property rights in canoes is presented by Bronislaw Malinowski, "Melaneasian Economy and the Theory of Primitive Communism," [B167] Chapter 2. For a brilliant survey of property in primitive societies, see A. Irving Hallowell, "The Nature and Function of Property as a Social Institution," in [B107] Chapter 12.

4. See Melville J. Herskovits, "Land Tenure: Hunters, Herders and Food Gatherers," [B108] Chapter 12; or John H. Dowling, "Individual Ownership and the Sharing of Game in Hunting Societies," [P2], LXX, June/ 1968, pp. 502–7.

5. See especially Malinowski [B161] for this type of argument. Much of the difficulty in this debate lies in different definitions of "property" and "communism" used by the participants.

keep in mind. First, A's claim on B (or A's right) in regard to some good, service, or "thing" (hereafter designated as C) implies that B has a duty toward A with regard to C; similarly A's competence over B with regard to C implies that B is subjected to the dispositions of A concerning C. Further, these rights or competencies can be defined either positively or negatively (e.g., A has no claim over B in regard to C). Second, as I discuss below these rights, claims, or competencies are enforceable and are not merely "abstract."

Such distinctions between types of rights (or sets of relations) are sometimes useful in analyzing other legal distinctions. For instance, Soviet law places great importance on the difference between "personal" and "private" possessions: "personal" possessions are homes, toothbrushes, clothing, etc. which a person has for his own or his family's personal use and which are not employed for the purpose of obtaining income; while "private" property are items such as machines or land which, through the employment of workers, can be used for producing goods or services from which profit can be extracted. (Soviet law in regard to personal possessions is quite similar to such law in the United States;[7] on the other hand, Soviet law limits the amount of private property which a person may possess.) All this really means is that in the Soviet Union a disability is attached to land, machines, and buildings in regard to profit-making activities that precludes certain property claims that are generally recognized in Western nations such as the United States.

3. *"Good, Service, or 'Thing'"*

Property relations between people can be with regard to corporeal objects such as land or machines or buildings or in terms of an incorporeal "thing" that has economic value such as: franchises (claims to the production or selling of particular goods and services); patents (a power to prevent others from producing a particular good within a certain time period); occupational licenses (the privilege to practice a certain profession); scenic easements (an immunity preventing others from destroying a view on a particular piece of land); or claim to collect social insurance benefits after reaching a certain age. Many of these rights are granted or sold by governments and the economic importance of such incorporeal rights emerging from the state is immense, even in nominally "capitalist" economies where the governmental role is considered to be "small."[8]

Although property is defined primarily in terms of a triadic relation (A's relationship to B with regard to C), one side of this triad is sometimes semantically suppressed in discussion of certain rights in personal services. For

6. Extensive classifications of different rights are presented by Wesley Newcomb Hohfield, "Some Fundamental Legal Concepts as Applied In Legal Reasoning," [P71, XXIII, Nov./1913, pp. 16–59]; Roscoe Pound, "Legal Rights," [P30, XXVI, Oct./1915, pp. 92–116]; C. Reinhold Noyes, [B198]; and Alf Ross, "The Legal Modalities," in [B223, Chapter 2]. All of these authors emphasize the different aspects of a right (or duty) when viewed from the opposite side of the relationship.

7. This is discussed by Harold J. Berman [B34].

8. Some important aspects of the legal and economic implications of particular incorporeal rights are analyzed for the United States in an extremely provocative article by Charles Reich, "The New Property," [P71, LXXIII, April/1964, pp. 733–87]. This was written when Reich was still content to be a legal scholar.

instance, society may grant a husband the right to force his wife to carry out certain productive tasks under penalty of divorce if she fails to comply. To avoid the awkwardness of saying that the husband (A) has a property right in his wife (B) for her to perform a service (C), which makes the whole relationship sound more impersonal than it may actually be, certain circumlocutions are used which emphasize just the bond between husband and wife. Although this employment of the property concept may have repugnant overtones, this should not detract from the usefulness of this analytic approach.

4. "Economic Value"

"Economic value" is used in its broadest meaning. On the production side, it includes opportunity costs (the losses in production of any good or service arising from the use of such inputs for other types of production) and changes in production resulting from changed methods of production. On the consumption side "economic value" includes welfare arising from consumption and any changes in welfare resulting from substitution of one consumption good for another, a redistribution of income, a change in production, and so forth. Although a person possessing a particular property right obtains some net positive economic gain, he might not be the only person to gain; further, the net gain may not appear first in the form of money. But in any case, some economic value is involved in the process.

One obvious indicator of value is, of course, the exchange value, i.e., the price that something can be sold for on the market place. Such value accrues not only to goods and services but also to incorporeal things. Economic values can also be transferred even when no money or markets exist by use of particular "exchange or barter equivalencies."

Other types of property rights can not be sold or exchanged (or "alienated") but still have a positive economic value that can be imputed.[9] Sometimes the imputation can be made from the price of an associated object or service, e.g., an inalienable tax advantage on a particular piece of land is reflected in its price being higher than an equivalent piece of land. Or a nontransferable license to practice a profession can be valued as the difference between what a person could earn with and without such a license. Or the right to use the automobile of an enterprise for personal use can be valued at the foregone costs of providing transportation for such purposes in the next least expensive manner. If the particular nontransferable property relates to something used in production, then imputation of the economic value of the right can be made from some estimate of the opportunity cost which, in turn, is derived from information on the price of the produced good, the prices of other inputs of production, and information about the various processes of production open to the manufacturer.

In economies where there are no market prices (i.e., most very primitive economies) such evaluations must be carried out in terms of certain goods, e.g., the rights adhering to the person financing the building of a canoe can be valued in the additional share of the fish catch that is allotted him than is given other members of the crew.

For property rights to exist, a certain positive part of the economic value of a right must potentially be realizable by the possessor. Such realization depends partly on enforcement of property rights (which is discussed below)

9. Valuation problems are analyzed at length by Alchian, [B5].

and partly on the technological, financial, and social ability of the possessor to exercise his right. That is, realization depends vitally on the instruments of the possessor to exercise his will.

In certain cases the instrument of realization is merely the human body of the property holder; in other cases machinery and modern technology must be employed. In some cases the major instrument is the ability to give orders to others, while in other cases such instruments are the ability to manipulate incentives of others.

Most relationships between individuals that have property aspects also have social, political, religious or other aspects as well. This coexistence of property rights with other relations makes the analysis at the same time more interesting and more difficult. In particular cases, of course, the property aspects are completely subordinate to these other considerations (e.g., in France, a husband was permitted by law until 1924 to beat his wife, a right which could be exercised to induce the wife to engage in certain productive activities; and until 1945, a French woman could not hold elective office even though it was doubtful many could be elected)[10] but in such situations the economic values involved are very small.

5. *"Enforced in a Socially Recognized Manner"*

The enforcement of property rights is a critical aspect of their existence. The sanctions against person B violating person A's property rights can be initiated through formal legal procedures in which the coercive powers of the government are invoked and, indeed, such sanctions are used in numerous situations including the enforcement of contract or of statutory law. Or if the property right violation occurs within a bureaucratic organization, sanctions can be initiated by appealing to those with greater authority who have the power to cut salaries or to remove personnel. Or if the violation of property rights occurs in particular social situations, sanctions such as ostracism, use of physical violence, or denial of particular privileges that are granted by the group can be exercised.[11] The "social" aspect of enforcement means that all rights have a public element.

It must be emphasized that the sanctions initiated must be socially recognized. When governmental sanctions are initiated in an illegal manner (e.g., when governmental powers are invoked through bribery), the situation does not involve property rights under my definition. Similarly, cases where goods and services are allocated through force, violence, deceit, and crime of individuals acting on their own are not amenable to analysis of property rights. Finally, the particular territorial claims of animals (e.g., the sweet call of a bird is really a warning to other birds of its species to stay away from a particular territory) are not enforced in a socially recognized manner (since animals do not have a "society," a prerequisite of which is extensive symbolic interactions) and, therefore, can not be considered a property relation.[12]

10. These and other horror stories about the legal status of French women come from John L. Hess, "French Mothers to Get Equal Say in Raising Children," [P47, April 17, 1970, p. 8].

11. For a discussion of such sanctions in primitive societies, see Hallowell, [B107].

12. Protagonists of this position that animals have "property" include: Ernest Beaglehold, *Property: A Study in Social Psychology* (London: Allen

On the other hand we must also note that certain powers to dispose over certain goods, services, or "things," no matter how obtained, become "legitimized" in particular situations. In such cases, property rights are established.

The enforcement of property rights is intimately connected with the institutional structure of the society and the values of the members of that society. Many possible types of property rights are not recognized by societies (e.g., in the United States I do not have a property right in my freedom of speech because no court would ever enforce a contract in which I sold that right to another person; indeed, in certain cases such a contract is called blackmail and brings penalty to the buyer). A number of difficult problems arise in trying to decide whether a particular relationship is a property right, but these boundary cases need not detain us from analyzing those situations in which property aspects are quite apparent to all.[13]

B. A Typology of Property Rights

There are a great many ways of classifying types of property rights, but for the purpose of making economic analyses, one instructive approach is to examine the ways in which such rights are received, used, and disposed of. In particular, three important questions can be distinguished:

First, how is a particular property right acquired? Two major possibilities occur. Such rights can be obtained through *exchange* of some type (e.g., through purchase or barter or through some type of reciprocal transfer of goods). Other types of property rights are obtained by *assignment,* i.e., either through inheritance or by virtue of membership in particular groups or by delegation by some person who is the "ultimate possessor."

Second, how is the right held? Some property rights can be held in an *absolute* fashion, so that they can not be taken away by anyone. Others, however, are held in a *conditional* fashion and can be taken back at particular times when certain tasks or responsibilities are not properly fulfilled. The holding of property rights includes either the use of particular goods, services, or "things" or merely the receiving of income from the property.

Third, how is the right disposed of? Certain rights are *alienable* and can be sold, given away, or destroyed. In other cases, the rights are *inalienable* so that the holder can not dispose of the right as he wishes but is forced to transfer it (if he so wishes) in only a particular way and only to particular people.

From these sets of considerations, eight different combinations can be specified which not only provide convenient boxes for classifying particular types of rights but which, as I suggest in the text, have analytical importance as well. These are presented in Table A-1.

Some of the combinations appear unlikely to occur with any frequency,

---

and Unwin, 1931) [B26]; and Robert Ardrey, [B13]. Such false analogies confuse, rather than aid, analysis.

13. Questions involving determination of socially recognized enforcement procedures are difficult to handle in certain cases, particularly in cases where a particular property right is legally recognized (i.e., "on the books") but is not actually enforced or in cases where a major group in the society does not recognize a particular right (e.g., a Moslem group may recognize a particular franchise to sell meat while a Hindu group in the same society may not).

e.g., a particular property right that is acquired only by purchase but which can be held only at the pleasure of a superior authority could lead to some obvious abuses by the superior and would probably in most circumstances hold little attraction to a potential buyer;[14] similarly, a right held conditionally would probably seldom be alienable, especially those that are exercised by virtue of membership to a group.

TABLE A-1

Combinations of Particular Types of Property Rights

Acquiring	Holding	Disposing	Comments
exchange	absolute	alienable	a subspecies: "absolute rights" (see below)
exchange	absolute	inalienable	uncommon
exchange	conditional	alienable	unlikely
exchange	conditional	inalienable	unlikely
assignment	absolute	alienable	uncommon
assignment	absolute	inalienable	a subspecies: "corporate rights" (see below)
assignment	conditional	alienable	unlikely
assignment	conditional	inalienable	a subspecies: "stewardship rights" (see below)

A right that is purchased but which is inalienable would appear to be uncommon since such an arrangement, if extensively exercised, would lead to its own disappearence, i.e., lead to a situation where all rights are acquired by assignment such as inheritance. Similarly, a system where rights are obtained by assignment but which are alienable could, in certain circumstances, lead to a situation where most rights are obtained through exchange.

It should be emphasized that these assessments of "unlikely" and "uncommon" are in the nature of hypotheses based on some simple theoretical considerations. Once criteria for "uncommon" and "unlikely" are more specifically developed, they could be empirically tested.

Certain combinations of types of rights have important economic significance and deserve greater attention.

One type of right which is obtained by purchase, exercised in an absolute fashion, and can be alienated is what I call an "absolute right." A classic definition of a bundle of such rights is that it consists of ". . . that sole and despotic dominion which one man claims and exercises over the external things of the world, in total exclusion of the rights of any other individual in the universe."[15] In a world of such rights one of the important functions of property ". . . is to draw a boundary between public and private power. Property

14. An example of such a case is an oil property that permits a very generous depletion allowance for tax purposes but this privilege is in imminent danger of being revoked by the legislature.

15. This definition comes from Blackstone's *Commentaries,* II, I, p. 2, and is cited by Noyes [B198, p. 297]. Noyes also points out how Blackstone later modified this definition because it did not fit the actual pattern of property rights, Such a notion of property is based, of course, on the Roman idea of *dominium.*

draws a circle around the activities of each individual or organization. Within that circle, the owner has a greater degree of freedom than without. Outside, he must justify or explain his actions, and show his authority. Within, he is master. . . ."[16] Thus "property" and "privacy" are strongly related.[17] A *laissez faire* market economy of small capitalist enterprises approaches a world of "absolute rights" but, of course, a pure case has never been realized in history.

A subspecies of the rights which are obtained by assignment, exercised in an absolute fashion, and are inalienable, are what I call "corporate rights." In such a situation a group exercises such rights together and a person participates in the exercising of the rights by virtue of his membership in the group.[18] A small-scale example of such "corporate rights" occurs in producer cooperatives where the group decides together through some type of voting system who shall join the group, who shall be removed from the group, and what types of activities should be carried out with the manpower and the assets of the group. The guild system existing in certain feudal economies, or the Yugoslavian Workers' Councils, or the Israeli kibbutzim approach a world of "corporate rights" although again no pure cases of corporate right systems have been recorded.

Finally, a subspecies of the rights which are obtained by assignment, exercised in a conditional fashion, and are inalienable are what shall be called "stewardship rights."[19] In this case the property rights of use of one person or group are delegated to a particular person (or steward) who exercises such rights subject to varying kinds of conditions. In certain cases the stewardship rights are firmly embedded in the legal structure and the reciprocal rights of the steward and the ultimate possessor are clearly defined; in other cases, however, the separation of "ownership" and "control" occurs in an informal fashion and the obligations of the steward are quite ambiguous, especially in those situations where the ultimate possessors can not effectively monitor the activities of the steward. A large-scale example of a world of such stewardship rights is a hierarchically organized centrally planned economy. These stewardship rights are particularly difficult to explore since the analyst runs into a number of severe methodological problems resulting in paradoxes that have puzzled scholars for several centuries.[20]

I have singled out these three different types of rights because economies appear to function differently according to their relative mix in actual situations. Some evidence is presented in Chapter IV about the differential behavior of enterprises managed by owners and by professional managers who do not have an ownership interest. And there is theoretical evidence that

16. Reich, note 8, p. 771.

17. In regard to the Soviet Union, such a relationship is analyzed by George Kline, " 'Socialist Legality' and Communist Ethics," [P45, VIII (1963), pp. 21–34].

18. Property rights that a person possesses by virtue of his citizenship in a particular nation constitute a subset of those rights discussed under the concept of *imperium*.

19. This term implies greater initiative than the term "custodial rights" which is used for the same idea by Tjalling C. Koopmans and John M. Montias, "On the Description and Comparison of Economic Systems," in [B71].

20. One aspect of this problem is discussed through an analysis of a number of paradoxes arising in the master-servant relationship by G. W. F. Hegel in his *Phenomenology of Spirit*.

enterprises managed by a single owner and enterprises that function as product cooperatives act quite differently in particular situations.[21]

C. Property Institutions

"Institution" is a difficult concept to define with exactitude. For the purpose of discussion let us consider institutions as "social relations and norms that are stable and sanctioned." This approach suggests that property is an institution *per se*. But associated with property are other institutions, especially the procedures, and rules by which conflicts between individuals concerning property are contained, that deserve brief comment.

The "recognition" of property rights stems in part from the type of evidence to be used to define such rights and the effective methods by which threats to invoke the enforcement mechanism allow certain property rights to be used without recourse to adjudication. In many cases unambiguity is a crucial factor. For instance, the building of a fence to delineate a particular garden plot serves as an unambiguous sign to trespassers about where particular property rights begin. Inscription of deeds permits more difficult cases to be adjudicated. In bureaucratic organizations, elaborate manuals of procedures and organizational plans serve to minimize conflicts in property rights among members and as a basis of adjudication of such disputes from above. Of course, it is often not desirable to delineate property rights very exactly so that such rights can be exercised by people who have sufficient cunning or charisma to take advantage of the situation—a process which gives organizations (especially universities with ossified administrations) or societies certain flexibility. Nevertheless, it should also be clear that in other cases unambiguity about the boundaries of particular rights might serve to generate disputes that could prove dysfunctional for the society as a whole.

Defining and enforcing boundaries of property rights are not, of course, easy matters and a great many problems arise in particular cases such as public goods (where property rights of use can be enjoyed by more than one person at the same time for little or no additional cost and where it is difficult to prevent such multiple use, e.g., radio broadcasts or defense services created by an effective ICBM system, etc.). Other such cases arise with consumption or production externalities. These fall into a special class of cases in which the exercising of property rights by one person affects crucially the exercising of property rights by others and problems in obtaining a just distribution of real welfare among individuals or groups becomes acute.[22]

By analyzing carefully the costs of defining and enforcing particular types of property rights, a number of interesting propositions can be generated about the occurrence or pattern of such rights. One example of such a theory arises from Cheung's analysis of the relative costs of quit-rent and sharecropping contracts in different situations of uncertainty and his hypothesis about major factors influencing the relative distribution of these two types

21. The classic statement of this argument is by Benjamin Ward, "The Firm in Illyria: Market Syndicalism," [P3, XLVIII, Sept./1958, pp. 566–89]. This argument has been modified by a number of following articles that are cited in Chapter I, note 39.

22. These problems are analyzed in a classic article by R. H. Coase, "The Problem of Social Costs," [P38, III, Oct./1960, pp. 1–44].

of contracts in agriculture;[23] another example arises in the analysis of slavery that I present elsewhere.

Transferring of rights also gives rise to areas of disputes. Some rights can be obtained through some type of exchange (e.g., market exchange, or bartering, or particular types of reciprocal relationships) in which disputes concerning exchange rates or fulfillment of agreements arise. Other types of property rights are obtained by assignment" (i.e., either through inheritance, which requires particular rules for eligibility and division among heirs), or by membership in particular groups (which focuses our attention on the rules of admittance into such groups). Gift exchange, which is a particular type of assignment, does not seem to raise many problems where adjudication of disputes becomes necessary since it is voluntary. The reverse aspect of transfer is the disposition of property rights and such matters are either at the discretion of the possessor or limited by particular restrictions (e.g., inalienable inheritance rights which impose some rule of transfer upon the possessor) surrounding which disputes may arise.

The manner in which certain rights in a particular good, service, or thing are shared also gives rise to certain critical institutions. Of course, certain property rights are held in an absolute fashion by a person and can not be taken away by anyone. But others, however, are held in a conditional fashion such that mechanisms exist through which property rights are withdrawn from the possessor at particular times or when certain tasks and responsibilities are not met. Such mechanisms may consist primarily of the exercise of authority on the part of a superior in the same administrative hierarchy or may be considerably more elaborate such as review boards, court hearings, and so forth. Or rights may be exercised jointly by two or more people and institutions arise through which disputes between the sharers can be resolved. Such institutions can be various types of voting mechanisms or devices for arbitration; if rights are jointly exercised by two or more levels of an administrative hierarchy, highly complex multi-level iterative systems can evolve that serve to bring opposing proposed courses of action into alignment.

Since the resolution of disputes about property rights is intimately connected with the very existence and exercise of those rights, a complete economic theory of property must take these carefully into account. Some attempts along these lines have been made in the analysis of the impact of economic development on a set of different institutions influencing the delineation of rights (such as the formal inscription of deeds) and the transfer of rights (particularly inheritance regulations).[25] In Chapter IV of this study I try another type of analysis of such property institutions, namely to trace the impact of particular property transfer rules on the size distribution of property and income in the entire society.

D. Ownership, Scale of Production and Economic System

As noted in the text, economic systems are often defined in terms of the prevailing mode of ownership. In this section I would like to extend this classifi-

23. Steven N. S. Cheung, "Transaction Costs, Risk Aversion, and the Choice of Contractual Arrangements," [P38, XII, April/1969, pp. 23–43].

24. See Frederic L. Pryor, "Property Rights and Economic Development," [P16], XX, April/1972, pp. 406–36.

25. Pryor, [P16].

cation in another dimension and to give some actual examples to show such relationships between ownership and labels of economic system more clearly.

Let us start with economies with three possible patterns of ownership:[26] predominantly private ownership ("capitalism"), predominantly government ownership ("socialism") and predominantly nongovernmental, nonprivate ownership such as cooperatives (for simplicity, I shall consider in this category only producer cooperatives where corporate rights are exercised). Such a threefold distinction blurs the importance of other types of property rights and to show how this ownership definition of economic system can be enriched by including another type of pattern of property rights, a simple two-dimensional definitional schema can be constructed.

As a second dimension let us consider the importance of the size of the unit over which productive decisions are made, i.e., the scale of control over productive units.[27] In the table below, "small" designates productive units such as handicraft shops and small enterprises; "medium" designates large enterprises and industrial branches; and "large" designates most or all of the entire manufacturing sector of the nation. With three different distinctions of scale of control and of ownership, a ninefold classification of economic systems can be constructed and is presented in Table A-2.[28]

"Primitive capitalism" designates those economies which are composed of a large number of small private enterprises. Historically, such cases have been characterized by direct participation of the owners in industrial management and the coordination of production between enterprises by a market mechanism. "Advanced capitalism" occurs where the scale of production enterprises is considerably larger. Historically such systems have been characterized by a split between ownership and management (with a hired steward exercising certain nonownership rights concerning the use of the productive assets).[29] Marxists and others have also argued that this type of system is accompanied by cartelization or monopolization of production, a conjecture that receives empirical attention in Chapter VI. "Etatism" occurs when the government or some semigovernmental group exercises the most important rights of control (or makes the most important production decisions) even though the productive units are "owned" by private individuals. (Examples include the Nazi economy or, for that matter, most wartime capitalist econ-

26. I am omitting from consideration economically less developed economies where the principle forms of wealth are property in land or slaves and am considering only those economic systems where the most important form of productive assets is property in machines and structures.

27. Objections can be raised that size of productive unit is not the proper criteria for classification of economic systems in the same way that size is not used as a classification principle in zoology. But this is a false analogy for two reasons. First, size is really a proxy for the level of the industrial hierarchy on which the most important production decisions are made (i.e., a measure of centralization in a particular meaning). Second, the limited purpose of this exercise is to show the relationship between various labels of economic systems that take into account ownership of the means of production which already exist in the economic literature.

28. The construction of this table was considerably influenced by the analysis of Peter Wiles [B270], Chapter I, although on certain points we hold quite different views.

29. On this point I am, of course, following the hypothesis of A. A. Berle and Gardiner C. Means [B33]. Such matters are discussed empirically in much greater detail in Chapter IV.

TABLE A-2

Designations of Economic Systems Based on Ownership and Scale of Control

Predominant Mode Ownership	Private	Producer Groups	Governmental
State control of predominant productive units			
Small	"primitive capitalism"	"producer cooperatism"; "guild socialism"	"municipal socialism"
Medium	"advanced capitalism"	"syndicalism"	"commission socialism" or "socialism by government boards"
Large	"etatism"	"full communism"	"bureaucratic socialism" or "Stalinism"

omies.) A more descriptive word for such economic systems might be "state capitalism" but unfortunately this has become a term of abuse among socialists who apply this label to economies that call themselves "socialist" but that they do not like (e.g., certain Yugoslavs have applied this term to the Soviet Union). In all "private ownership" economies, as the scale of control over production decision increases, there appears to be a shift from absolute right systems toward stewardship and corporate right systems. The system of coordination of production decisions shifts from a market to various types of bureaucratic and bargaining procedures.

Among economic systems where producer-group ownership predominates, a similar spectrum can be viewed. Where units of production are very small, I designate the system as producer-cooperatism; for somewhat larger units of production, the system has sometimes been called guild socialism. An example of the former is the agricultural sector in Israel (or at least that part with the kibbutzim); and of the latter, the manufacturing sector of Yugoslavia (where enterprise policies are made by Workers' Councils and profits are shared by all workers and employees). Coordination of production between units can be achieved by various devices, of which the market mechanism or some modification thereof appears the most simple. Where decision-making units are larger and perhaps cover an entire industrial branch, we have "syndicalism" in which entire industries are owned and controlled by the workers and employees. Although certain economies have syndicalist elements, none have approached very closely such a system.[30] Where the entire

30. In this connection the three nations that come immediately to mind are Portugal, Spain, and Fascist Italy, for in all three cases some powers are (or were) exercised by industrial councils with representatives from labor and from enterprise owners. Nevertheless, the actual powers of such boards appears to be (have been) small. For instance, Portugal—which has the most highly developed syndicalist ideology and also had the longest period (over forty years) to institute such a system under the leadership of Salazar—falls far short of allowing such syndicalist arrangements much importance. [This

economy is owned and corporately managed by the workers and employees, I use Wiles' term of "full communism." How such a system would work and, indeed, whether it could function without quickly losing its element of corporate control and becoming bureaucratic socialism (see below) is a question that I leave to the reader. In any case we have no historical examples of economies controlled by large-scale producer groups and, therefore, I can say little on an empirical level about how corporate rights become exercised in situations with large productive units.

Governmental ownership usually implies extensive stewardship arrangements since property rights in government-owned enterprises are seldom exercised in a corporate fashion by the voters or by all government personnel. Where the productive units are small, I have chosen to designate the system as "municipal socialism" since city government ownership of utilities is probably the most widespread example of such a case. This generic term also includes those cases where the central government owns a wide number of small productive units all over the country, but allows the property rights of use to be exercised by the individual enterprise managers (e.g., a Lerner-type market socialism situation). In these situations, production is coordinated by means of a market mechanism. With larger scale production units, we have situations where entire industries are governmentally owned and are operated as trusts by government boards or commissions (e.g., the United Kingdom Coal Trust). Coordination of production between various units can be achieved by a variety of methods. "Bureaucratic socialism" or "Stalinism" (the most prominent historical example) occurs when the entire economy is run as a single enterprise, with the stewardship rights exercised within a single administrative hierarchy.

As I discuss in the text, economic systems can be defined along a great number of other dimensions. Nevertheless, this little definitional exercise permits us to see more clearly the relationship between a number of designations for economic system that frequently appear in the literature, especially those involving ownership. And in this brief discussion a number of questions are also raised (especially concerning the changing ways in which production decisions between productive units are coordinated when the scale of these units increases and when the mode of ownership changes) that deserve further research.

APPENDIX A-2

A Measurement of the Extent of the Government Sector in the United States from 1950 through 1966 (for Chapter I, Part C)

The following table is an experimental attempt to quantitatively measure changes in the "government sector" in the United States.

---

is argued by A. Ramos Pereira, "L'economie portugaise face au modèle de la libre concurrence," in [B84], Vol. II, pp. 147–81.]

TABLE A-3

The Extent of the Government Sector in the United States
as a Percentage of National Income

Date	Adjusted Purchases of Goods and Services					
	Government (direct)	Government enterprises	Regulated Industries, Value-added	Subtotal	Government Transfer Payments	Total
1950	14.0	1.9	18.8	34.7	5.9	40.6
1951	18.5	1.8	18.6	39.0	4.2	43.1
1952	22.1	2.0	18.1	42.2	4.1	46.3
1953	23.0	2.0	17.2	42.2	4.2	46.3
1954	21.4	2.0	17.2	40.5	4.9	45.4
1955	19.5	2.0	16.2	37.7	4.9	42.5
1956	19.5	1.9	16.0	37.5	4.9	42.4
1957	20.4	2.0	15.8	38.3	5.4	43.7
1958	22.2	2.2	16.7	41.0	6.6	47.6
1959	21.1	2.1	15.8	38.9	6.2	45.2
1960	21.0	2.2	16.0	39.2	6.4	45.6
1961	22.0	2.2	16.1	40.3	7.1	47.4
1962	22.3	2.2	15.6	40.0	6.8	46.9
1963	22.2	2.3	15.4	39.8	6.8	46.7
1964	21.8	2.2	14.8	38.8	6.6	45.5
1965	21.3	2.2	14.7	38.2	6.6	44.8
1966	22.0	2.2	14.5	38.6	6.6	45.2

The regulated industries in the table include agriculture; railroads, airplanes, pipelines and other regulated branches of transportation; electricity, gas, telephone, telegraph, radio and T.V. broadcasting and other regulated branches of utilities and communications; commercial banking and insurance; and certain natural resource industries such as crude oil, natural gas production, and anthracite coal. The entire list of industries is presented by Kaysen and Turner [B132, pp. 289 ff]. I have included only the value added by these industrial branches since government regulations apply primarily to their outputs, not inputs.

The government transfer payments are to individuals and exclude interest payments and other similar expenditures.

The major statistical problem in calculating such a table is to eliminate double counting between different sectors, e.g., the sales or purchases between the government, government enterprises, and regulated industries. This was accomplished using a two-step procedure.

(1) With the aid of a 1958 input-output table, such double counting as a percentage of total purchased goods and services by the government directly and by government enterprises was calculated.

(2) These ratios were assumed to hold for all the years covered in the table.

All data used in the calculation came from various issues of [P65].

APPENDIX A-3

Relative Importance of Consumer and Producer Cooperatives (for Chapter II, Part C)

TABLE A-4

Ratios of Economically Active Working in Consumer and Producer Cooperatives to Total Economically Active in Different Sectors of the Economy

Sector	France 1954	Poland[b] 1960	Yugoslavia 1953	Finland[c] 1965	East Germany[b] 1964	Israel[e] 1959	Soviet Union[d] 1959	Bulgaria 1956
Total	1%	6%	8%	10%	19%	21%	31%	43%
Utilities	6	0	0	2	0	0	0	0
Transportation, communication	0	3	0	2	0	22	0	0
Service, public administration	0	1	1	15	0	12	1	1
Construction	1	6	0	3	18	27	0	2
Mining and manufacturing	1	14	4	6	4	17	7	6
Commerce and finance	2	44	18	24	26	15	8	0
Agriculture, forestry, fishing	a	1	11	7	81	48	66	65

a. Estimate made for total.

b. Manufacturing and mining are defined slightly differently in the two parts of the table.

c. Ratios are calculated from GNP rather than labor force data.

d. In the following years, many of the producer cooperatives outside of agriculture were converted into state enterprises.

e. Histradrut and Kibbuzim enterprises are included as cooperatives.

f. Ratios are slightly overstated because labor force concept covers only 94 percent of economically active. Sources of data for these tables and methods of estimation are given in Appendix B-2. Typographical signs designate that the branches marked were combined in the original data.

TABLE A-5

Ratios of Economically Active Working in Consumer and Producer Cooperatives to Total Economically Active in Different Branches of Mining and Manufacturing

Branch	ISIC Number	West Germany 1950	France 1954	Norway[f] 1953	East Germany[b] 1964	Finland 1963	Bulgaria 1958	Hungary 1966	Poland[b] 1960	Israel[e] 1965
Total		0%	1%	5%	5%	6%	6%	12%	14%	15%
Mining and quarrying	10–19	0	1*	0	0	1	0*	0*	0*	21
Food processing	20	4	5	26	13	44	3**	0**	31**	21*
Beverages	21	1	6	0	4	1	3**	0**	31**	21*
Tobacco products	22	0	0	0	0	0	3**	0**	31**	21*
Textiles	23	0	0	2	5	2	5	1	6	2
Clothing and footwear	24	0	0	0	5	4	29	3	39	6
Lumber products except furniture	25	0*	0**	5	13*	5	0	24†	17†	23**
Furniture	26	0*	0**	1	13*	3	12	24†	17†	23**
Paper products	27	0**	0	0	2	0	0	11	15	8
Printing	28	0**	0	11	2	1	4	0	25	13
Leather products except shoes	29	0	0	0	12	0	21	3	37	8
Rubber products	30	0	0	0	0	0	3	3‡	9	0
Chemicals	31	0	0	1	1	2	3	3	9	10
Petroleum and coal products	32	0	0	0	0	2	0*	0*	0	0
Stone, glass, clay products	33	0	1*	0	2	0	1	2	0	0
Primary metals	34	0	0	0	0	0	0	0	10	26
Metal products except machinery	35	0	0	0	0	1	8	15	16	14
Machinery except electrical, transport	36	0	0	0	5	2	2***	8	4	21
Electrical goods and machinery	37	0	1	0	5	0	2***	3	6	16
Transport equipment	38	0	0	1	0	1	2***	1	5	20
Miscellaneous	39	0	0	0	2	2	3	50	37	7

See Tables A-4 for all notes.

APPENDIX A-4

Analysis of Components of Variation of Personal Income
(for Chapters III and IV)

Symbols and notation:

Y = total personal income $\bar{k}$ = mean value of K
P = property income $\bar{i}$ = mean value of i
W = work income   Var (i) = variance of i
i = rate of return on wealth   Cov (i,k) = covariance between i and k
k = wealth   r (i,k) = correlation coefficient between i and k

Definitions:

Y = P + W
P = ik
r (i,k) = Cov(i,k)/[Var(i),Var(k)]$^{\frac{1}{2}}$ (This is a standard definition of the correlation coefficient.)

Important Relationships:

1. Var(Y) = Var(P) + Var(W) + 2 Cov(P,W) =
       Var(P) + Var(W) + 2r(P,W)/[Var(P),Var(W)]$^{\frac{1}{2}}$

2. Var(P) = $\bar{i}^2$ Var(k) + $\bar{k}^2$ Var(i) + 2$\bar{i}\bar{k}$ Cov(i,k)
This is a standard first approximation to the variance of a product. A more exact relationship is given by Leo A. Goodman, "On the Exact Variance of Products" [P40, IV Dec./1960, pp. 708–13].

3. Var(P) = $\bar{i}^2$ Var(k) + $\bar{k}^2$ Var(i) + 2$\bar{i}\bar{k}$ Cov (i,k) +
             2$\bar{i}$E$_{12}$ + 2$\bar{k}$E$_{21}$ + E$_{22}$ − Cov(i,k)^2
Where E$_{mn}$ = Expected value [(i − $\bar{i}$)^m (k − $\bar{k}$)^n]

     The same analysis can be made for work income where the two components are work done (labor hours) and return per work hour.

APPENDIX A-5

Some Institutional Approaches to the Distribution
of Income (for Chapter III, Parts B and C)

The purpose of this appendix is to survey ways in which institutional approaches have been used or in some cases could be used in the study of the size distribution of income to generate testable propositions. I start with a discussion of the "barriers approach," which is based on the use of standard price theory. Then I turn to bargaining and bureaucratic models which are based on other considerations. The discussion ends with brief mention of a variety of other approaches that may prove fruitful in future work on income distribution problems.

A. The Barriers Approach

1. A Theoretical View

"Barriers" are defined as those institutions that prevent a society from achieving a perfectly competitive economy in the markets of both goods and production factors. Barriers can either increase or decrease the inequality of personal income and, before turning to a number of concrete examples, it is useful to examine these matters in an abstract manner.

To see how barriers may increase the inequality of personal income, let us imagine an economy composed of a number of regions, between which there are no flows of information, goods, or factors of production. The different regions could have different production functions, could be using different technologies, and could have very different factor productivities and payments. For the nation as a whole, factor returns could vary enormously from region to region and the size distribution of income would as a result be quite unequal.

If we lift the barriers to information flows and allow the regions to adjust their methods of production (without changing amounts of labor or capital in any region), then there still would be a high variation in factor returns since the ratios of capital to labor would vary greatly among regions. Nevertheless, we would expect an inverse relationship in the various regions between the amount of a factor and its return (since all regions would share the same technical knowledge and be on the same production function) and, according to the analysis of components of income variations outlined in Appendix A-4, this negative correlation would lower the overall variation in factor payments (i.e., the third term in the second formula of Appendix A-4 would be negative) and, hence, the variations of total income would be less.[1]

If we further allow goods and factors to flow between regions freely and allow for adjustments to this new situation (while keeping the overall levels of capital and labor constant), then the size distribution should probably become even more equal since factor returns in the various regions would become much more equal.[2]

Particular barriers can also decrease the inequality of income; these arise primarily from certain kinds of social discrimination in situations requiring several kinds of skills. For instance, if occupancy of positions where

1. Average factor incomes would be higher and, according to the analysis of income variance in Appendix A-4, this would act in a direction to offset the decrease in income variation. However, this influence would probably be quite weak and not completely offset the forces acting in the opposite direction.

2. Complete factor price equalization need not be assumed here for the conclusion to hold true. The phenomenon described in the above footnote would also occur here as well but probably would be very weak.

the marginal productivity of high-ability individuals is extremely high is restricted to certain groups whose members do not necessarily have the highest abilities in the society, then the income from these positions would be less than if they were occupied by more capable individuals. In other words, a meritocracy may lead to a more unequal income distribution than before.[3] (I refer to income inequality as measured at one point in time; compared to a meritocracy, restriction of high paying positions to a single group might yield a higher inequality of income over generations, where income units are families and their descendants.)[4]

Certain barriers can either increase or decrease the inequality of income, depending on the particular parameters of the system. Such barriers arise, for instance, in cases where there is migration of production factors between two areas where factor incomes and variations in factor incomes are quite different. A classic concrete case is the migration from rural to urban areas, but the entire problem can be analyzed mathematically in a quite general way.[5]

2. Some Examples

The importance of particular barriers can be seen in any of the many studies of the determinants of income variation.[6] Although a complete inventory and evaluation of all possible barriers influencing the size distribution of income would be an enormously extensive and difficult research project,[7] a brief summary of certain major barriers might show the outlines such work could take and, at the same time, would make more concrete some of the above considerations.

a. Barriers to the flow and application of knowledge. A large variety of institutional barriers to the dissemination and flow of information can be designated. Information can be blocked on the origin side by rules of secrecy, lack of adequate media, or lack of incentives for transmission. On the receiving side information can be blocked by language barriers, inadequate data gather-

3. This conclusion has been noted by many, e.g., Melvin Reder, "A Partial Survey of the Theory of Income Size Distribution," in [B238, pp. 205–55], who states, "A 'meritocracy' may be more than just an aristocracy, but it is not clear that it will be more egalitarian."

4. I would like to thank Peter Mieskowski for his discussion on this point. It must be noted that for a precise answer to be given, we must take into account a number of factors concerning the inheritability of ability and the effect of income on the development of a home environment encouraging children to develop such abilities.

5. Various cases are analyzed by Simon Kuznets, "Economic Growth and Income Inequality," [P3, XLV, March/1955, pp. 1–28]. A more general mathematical analysis is given by Henri Theil, "Migration and Its Effect on Per Capita Income Inequality: Maxwell's Demon on Ellis Island," [B249, pp. 114–20].

6. E.g., F. Gerald Adams, "The Size of Individual Income: Socio-Economic Variables and Chance Variation," [P56, XL, Nov./1958, pp. 309–98); or J. Conlisk, "Some Cross-Section Evidence on Income Inequality," [P56, XLIX, Feb./1969, pp. 115–18).

7. The only full scale attempt to evaluate the influence of particular barriers on a national level is by Edward F. Denison, [B67], but this study deals primarily with the effect on total income, rather than its distribution.

ing mechanisms (e.g., market research, productivity missions, etc.), or lack of incentives for obtaining such information. Although information may flow freely other barriers may prevent its application or use. These include: reverence for tradition and traditional production methods; patents and other devices to prevent utilization; lack of complementary factors for applying information (e.g., capital, the proper types of labor or resources, etc.); or lack of incentives for such utilization. It is, of course, difficult to measure quantitatively the effects of barriers to the flow of information for the nation as a whole, but numerous case studies attest the importance of such barriers in particular situations.[8]

b. Barriers to the movement of goods and factors of production. Barriers to movement include all those preventing single goods or factors from going to the area of highest price or payment; a usual result of such barriers is wide dispersions of prices for the particular goods or factors over the economy under examination and a greater inequality of income. These barriers to movement are somewhat different from barriers to opportunity which act to increase the equality of income and which are discussed in the next subsection.

In a perfect market with free flow of goods and factors, factor prices are equalized under a variety of circumstances. If factors are prevented from moving freely, then it has been argued that the flow of goods will still bring about such factor price equalization.[9] Nevertheless, the circumstance under which such an equalization occur are highly specialized and unlikely to occur in real life; therefore, it seems worthwhile to examine in greater detail the particular barriers to movement of production factors. Two general classes of barriers are useful to distinguish: those acting to discriminate and those acting to incarcerate.

In regard to the movement of labor, discriminatory institutions include labor monopolies (e.g., closed-shop unions or other types of noncompeting groups); patterns of social discrimination (e.g., against Negroes, or women, or foreigners, or particular ethnic or religious groups) which force such workers to work in situations where complementary factors are less and labor returns are lower[10] (other types of social discrimination are discussed below); or particular types of taxes on specified labor groups so that their net factor returns are lower. Institutions acting to incarcerate labor include ties of tradition, family, or caste; various types of legal restrictions on mobility arising from serf or slave relationships; or institutions to reduce incentive for mobility (e.g., when an employee in a United States company is bound to his

---

8. Several of these factors are analyzed on a national level by [B67]. For an excellent comparison of information flows between systems in a particular industry, see Richard Judy, "The Case of Computer Technology," in [B262, pp. 43–73].

9. E.g., Paul Samuelson, "International Factor Price Equalization Once Again," [P18, LIX, June/1949, pp. 181–97]; or [B13, Chapter 4 and Appendix].

10. If those discriminated against were not paid their marginal productivity in some work situation, then such a situation would perhaps be better analyzed using bargaining theory. For instance, we know from many sources (e.g., [B141, Chapter 3]) that average incomes of Negroes and whites in the United States are quite different. The degree to which this is due to barriers to mobility, barriers to opportunity (e.g., obtaining education), or to a bargaining situation has not yet been determined.

enterprise by a large accumulation of nontransferable pension fund rights or the passbook system in the Soviet Union that requires particular approvals before agricultural workers can migrate to the cities.)

In regard to the movement of capital, discriminatory institutions include various types of monopolies (either "natural" or government created), prohibitions on the use of outside capital (e.g., in certain situations in postwar Japan), governmental policies to prevent capital inflows into particular sectors (e.g., defined limits on capital investments in agriculture appeared to have been applied in the Soviet Union in the early part of the plan era), or special taxes on particular types of capital. Incarceratory institutions are usually governmentally established and include a variety of different types of capital export barriers.

Barriers to the flow of goods may change "real" factor incomes by changing the relative prices of goods and services consumed by factor income receivers. Discriminatory institutions include monopolies, differential sales taxes and various types of import barriers; incarceratory institutions include export tariffs and quotas.

c. Barriers to opportunity. The discussion of barriers to movement implicitly assumes that production factors embody a single attribute that is used in the production process. If we view "capital" or "labor" as composed of many attributes so that income going to the factor depends on the attributes that are available and used, the correlation between attributes held and used by particular factors, and the relationship between output and combinations of attributes (e.g., work may be a multiplicative product of two attributes[11]) are the major determinants of income.

A barrier to opportunity exists when not all attributes can be used or when not all potential attributes can be developed. Examples of the first type are: when particular labor groups capable of fulfilling managerial positions are denied the chance in all situations; or when strict seniority systems are used which prevent the most capable of occupying top positions until they are past their prime. An example of the second type of barrier to opportunity are when a person is denied access to educational institutions or on-the-job training because of failure to meet irrelevant entrance requirements such as membership in a particular social group, adequate financial support (and an imperfect capital market so that sufficient funds can not be borrowed) or proper political attitudes. The lack of a home environment which encourages personal development could also be considered as a barrier to opportunity of this second kind. These examples have concerned labor; it is also possible to consider such barriers for capital. For instance, it could be argued that lack of institutions for contract enforcement prevent the attributes of capital from being developed, i.e., discourage investment; however, such types of arguments run a certain risk of anthropomorphizing capital and will not be further pursued.

The barriers to opportunity of labor act to forestall a meritocracy and, therefore, may serve to decrease inequality of income. In this way they differ

11. Such an approach to income distribution is analyzed by A. D. Roy, "The Distribution of Earnings and of Individual Output," [P18, Sept./ 1950, XL, pp. 489–505]; Jan Tinbergen, "On the Theory of Income Distribution," [P68, LXXVII, 2/1956, pp. 155–75]; and others.

from the barriers to information and the barriers to movement which clearly affect the income distribution in the direction of inequality.

B. Bargaining Models

Under the rubric of "bargaining models" I classify those theories that reject the marginal productivity theory of factor payment and rely instead on the outcome of particular clashes between groups to determine relative average payments to the groups in question. The size distribution of income is then affected in two different ways: Obviously, the larger the difference between average incomes in the two (or more) competing groups, the greater the inequality of personal income, other things remaining the same. Also clearly, if the dispersion of income within the two groups is different, then the relative share of total income received by the group with the largest dispersion also affects the overall size distribution of income.[12] For instance, since the size distribution of individual property incomes is much more unequal than labor income, the relative importance of these factor incomes affects total income inequality.

Although the groups specified by the various bargaining theories differ from theory to theory, all of them bear a family resemblance in that the exact distribution of group payments cannot be determined by attention to economic factors alone but must be supplemented by different types of sociological and political analyses. Such an approach focuses particular attention on the actions of government, for almost no economic or political policy undertaken by the government is neutral in regard to average group incomes or the size distribution of income. On the other hand, reliance on political and sociological forces makes such theories extremely difficult to test and often empirical studies utilizing such theories degenerate into merely *post facto* rationalizations.[13]

Two types of bargaining models are discussed below: Those focusing on the share of labor and property income are designated as "class-struggle" models; and those isolating other bargaining groups are lumped together in a residual category. As I have little to add to these bargaining models, this section is in the form of an annotated survey.

1. Class-struggle Models

The writings of Marx and Engels are the *locus classicus* of the many variants to the class-struggle models that have been proposed. Marx separated short-

12. Such cases are analyzed by the sources cited in note 5.

13. This difficulty has led to some outspoken criticism of the entire bargaining approach. For instance, in regard to the share of income between labor and property, Melvin Reder ("Alternative Theories of Labors' Share," in [B2, pp. 182–3]) has written: "No theory has ever been offered that relates in a testable manner either factor prices or profit margins to such forces as bargaining power, oligopoly agreements, etc. Indeed, these forces have not been defined in such a way that we could ever know when they had increased or decreased except by looking at their alleged effects. Needless to say, this makes it impossible to refute or confirm any statement about the effect of these forces on the variables . . . whose behavior they are supposed to explain." Although I believe that Reder has overstated his argument, it has a strong grain of truth.

and long-run forces, and in his analysis of the latter, he saw relative factor shares as the resultant of two types of forces. On the one hand, as productivity rises in the long run, the rate of surplus value rises and the share of labor income in the national income declines as labor income remains at the level where workers are just able to reproduce themselves. The existence of the industrial reserve army of unemployed, which is created in the normal process of economic growth, prevent the wage rate from ever rising much above this "subsistence level" except for short periods during booms. On the other hand, this "subsistence level" is historically determined and can vary from place to place and from time to time depending on particular noneconomic forces[14] which neither Marx nor Engels analyzed in detail. The indeterminacy in factor income shares arises because a rising subsistence level can offset the rising level of surplus value and the relative strengths of these two forces were not analyzed. Since there is little evidence that the share of labor income is declining - indeed, most studies show exactly the reverse[15] - a number of variants to the Marxist model have been proposed.

One popular variant rejects the notion of wages falling to some type of subsistence level and instead focuses attention on the institutions through which workers mobilize their efforts to wrest higher wages from their capitalist and to obtain a greater share in total national income. Economists have made great efforts to analyze empirically the effects of labor unions and a large number of empirical studies (discussed briefly below) have been carried out to measure their impact.

A second variant, which has been propounded with vigor by Kenneth Boulding and Nicholas Kaldor, looks at the relative income shares of property and labor and their interaction with investment and growth. The major linkage occurs through differential propensities to save of wage recipients and profit receivers and the saving and dividend policies of corporations; once these are specified and the total amount of saving is designated, factor income shares are determined.[16]

A final well-known variant was proposed by Kalecki who linked the share of property income to the degree of monopoly and argued that as the degree of monopoly increases, profit markups and hence the total share of profits in the national income would rise.[17]

As mentioned above, problems of verification are considerable. If, as in

14. Karl Marx [B173, Vol. I, Chapter 6]: "The number and extent of his [the worker's] so-called necessary wants, as also the mode of satisfying them, are themselves the product of historical development . . . In contradistinction therefore to the case of other commodities, there enters into the determination of the value of labor power a historical and moral element."

15. These matters are discussed in detail in Chapter III.

16. Kenneth Boulding, "The Fruits of Progress and the Dynamics of Distribution," [P3, XLIII, May/1953, pp. 473–83]; o. Nicolas Kaldor, "Alternative Theories of Distribution," [P57, XXIII, March/1956, pp. 83–100]. Further work by the "Cambridge School" economists have developed this theme and have pointed out certain logical difficulties of the marginal productivity theory of factor incomes (this development is surveyed by G. C. Harcourt, "Some Cambridge Controversies and the Theory of Capital," [P35, VII, June/1969, pp. 369–405]) from a theoretical, rather than an empirical perspective.

17. Michael Kalecki, "A Theory of Long Run Distribution of the Product of Industry," [P48, V, June/1941, pp. 31–41] or [B127, Part I]. There are a number of different versions of this theory.

the original Marxist model, factor income shares are indeterminate, then the theory can not be tested unless some other characteristic, e.g., the degree of fluctuation of property and labor income shares, can be deduced from the model. Unfortunately, such alternatives tests have not yet been proposed.

On the other hand, hypotheses about the impact of labor unions on wage and profit shares in the national income can be tested, albeit with difficulty. Over twenty empirical studies, including both cross-section and time-series have been published on the impact of unions in the United States and, in general, they indicate that the wages of union member *vis-à-vis* nonunion workers are somewhat higher, other things remaining equal.[18] However, this does not necessarily imply that they have wrested a higher income share in the national product. Studies on this latter question are considerably scarcer but available evidence reveals no observable impact of unions.[19] Even if one holds the position that the major impact of unions has been to prevent labor's share of the national income from declining, such results are extremely damaging to Marxist notions unless one frames the hypothesis in an extremely long-run perspective so that it can be argued that the available econometric evidence covers only short-run phenomena.[20]

Unfortunately, the factor share theories of Boulding and Kaldor have not been econometrically tested in any convincing fashion. Preliminary tests are not, however, very encouraging.[21] Kalecki's theory about the degree-of-monopoly influencing factor income shares also has yet to be empirically demonstrated, but preliminary tests are negative.[22] Although class-struggle models may have a certain intuitive appeal, their usefulness in analytic work dealing with income shares of labor and property has yet to be demonstrated. However, such ideas have had usefulness in serving to stimulate the study of the incidence of taxes on labor and property income in order to gauge the influence of the struggle between these two groups in the legislative arena.

2. *Other Types of Bargaining Models*

A "sociological theory" of income distribution has been put forward by Jean Marchal and Jacques Lecaillon.[23] They distinguish between various types of

18. Most of these are conveniently summarized and analyzed in [B152].

19. The most thorough study is [B233].

20. Such a long-term theory is difficult to test because of data deficiencies; however, certain studies that do present very long-term time-series do not offer much support for such an hypothesis. For instance, in a study of five nations, E. H. Phelps-Brown and Margaret H. Browne [B208, p. 321] conclude: "We can establish no firm conclusions about the effect of union strength, therefore, by comparing the historical situation before and after the extension on unions."

21. Melvin Reder in [B2] assigns "reasonable" savings coefficients to labor and property income and tests the results against a savings function not distinguishing between these two types of income to show that the Kaldorian savings hypothesis has no additional explanatory power. Although such an attempt does not provide conclusive evidence on the matter, such a pseudo-econometric sensitivity analysis is an extremely useful exercise to show how such a profit theory could be tested.

22. Evidence on this matter is reviewed in Appendix A-6.

23. A complete theory is promised to be published in [B169, Vol. IV]; bits of the theory can be found (in English) in Jean Marchal, "The Construction of a New Theory of Profit," [P3, XLI, Sept.,/1951, pp. 599–665];

income receivers such as industrial (and commercial) entrepreneurs, agricultural entrepreneurs, rentiers, unskilled workers, clerks, and "cadre," show that each is a particular sociological type which receives a different "kind" of income, and posit a general struggle of all groups against each other for a larger share in national income. This is a variant of the "noncompeting groups" approach that does not invoke marginal productivity considerations. Certain evidence on differences between average incomes among white- and blue-collar workers arising from international comparisons that may not be explicable on grounds of traditional supply and demand forces offers some positive evidence, but the theory has not yet been put to serious statistical test.

A number of economists have emphasized the importance of clashes between particular sectors of the economy (e.g., agriculture, manufacturing, and services) or between different regions of a nation (often identified with a particular industrial sector) to obtain larger income shares.[24] Particular attention is paid to the effects of government economic policy as a resultant of these sectoral or regional clashes. For instance, Peron in Argentina used exchange rate and commercial policies to raise the relative incomes of industrial over agricultural workers; the revocation of these measures following his removal greatly changed the relative income position of these two groups.[25] Changes in tax and subsidy policies may have important regional impacts (e.g., between the South and North in the United States before the Civil War) and changes in credit policies can greatly affect both regional and sectoral incomes as well as the relative position of particular income groups (as in Chile during the 1950s and 1960s).[26]

None of these theories discussed above is determinate in the sense that predictions can be made about relative average group incomes such that we can directly link institutions to the size distribution of income. But they may prove useful supplements where governmental policy has had a measureable impact on the income distribution.

3. A Final Comment on Bargaining Theories

Although the marginal productivity theory of income determination is built on a number of questionable assumptions, it has proven relatively successful in giving some rough indication of relative factor income shares. Although there are a number of grave statistical problems in fitting production functions to aggregate data, reasonable predictions about factor shares can be obtained. Nevertheless, such a theory tells us little about the size distribution of income. If we can prove that average group incomes are really determined through a bargaining process, then we will have more information about the

---

Marchal and Lecaillon, "Is the Income of the 'Cadres' a Special Class of Wage," [P55, LXXIII, May/1958, pp. 166–82]; and Lecaillon and Marchal, "Wage-Structure and the Theory of the Distribution of Income: The French Pattern," in [B121, pp. 71–156]. See also R. Gendarme, "Reflections on the Approaches to the Problems of Distribution in Underdeveloped Countries," [B168, pp. 361–88].

24. Such a theory has been implicit in a number of writings; it has been explicitly developed by Markos Mamalakis, "Public Policy and Sectoral Development: A Case Study of Chile, 1940–1958," in [B163, pp. 1–200]. Results of a conference on this theory are reprinted in [P43, V, Spring/1970].

25. [B69] and [B266].

26. [B163].

inequality of the distribution of personal income. This point, however, has not yet been reached.

C. A Bureaucratic Model

The basis of this model was posited two centuries ago by Adam Smith who wrote: "The wages of labour vary accordingly to the small or great trust which must be reposed in the workmen. . . . Such confidence could not safely be reposed in people of a very mean or low condition. Their reward must be such, therefore, as may give them that rank in the society which so important a trust requires."[27] From this hypothesis a number of economists have constructed useful models of income determination.[28]

For our purposes one important verification of this hypothesis appears when we examine modern corporations and observe that those superior in rank usually receive higher salaries than those below them. A useful model of organizational salaries can be constructed by making two simplifying assumptions: Both the span of control (i.e., the number of men subordinate to a single superior) and the ratio of the salary of a subordinate to his immediate superior remain constant at all levels of the organization hierarchy.

From these assumptions two extremely useful propositions can be derived: the salary of the head of an organization varies directly with the scale of his organization; and the distribution of income follows a Pareto distribution with the coefficient of inequality a simple function of the span of control and the ratio of superior to subordinate salaries.[29] For both of these propositions considerable empirical evidence is at hand.[30]

Before these propositions can be used to generalize about the income distribution of an entire nation, two additional considerations must be mentioned. First, there is theoretical and empirical evidence that the average span of control is not constant among enterprises but rather varies directly with the size of the organization, i.e., the larger the enterprise, the larger the span of control.[31] Second, the labor income distribution for the entire nation will follow a Pareto distribution in only two obvious cases: when a nation is composed of a single enterprise; or when all enterprises in a nation have the same number of employees. If we must contend with a distribution of enterprises, then we must add a series of different-sized Pareto distributions (i.e., different in the degree of inequality and a different highest income) to form a distribution of personal income for the entire nation and this complicates matters. For instance, in comparing the distribution of labor incomes in East and West, we must take into account the results from Chapter VII that the East

27. [B235, Book I, Chapter 10].
28. The relevant literature is briefly summarized by Reder in [B238, p. 219]. Often this consideration enters under the rubric of the "Scale of Operations Effect."
29. These propositions are rigorously derived by Lydall [B158, pp. 125–33 and Appendix 4].
30. Relevant studies are summarized by Lydall [B158] and Reder in [B238].
31. Both theoretical aspects and certain empirical materials are presented by Louis R. Pondy, "Effects of Size, Complexity, and Ownership on Administrative Intensity," [P1, XIV, 1/1969. pp. 47–60].

European nations have larger size enterprises and a smaller variation in size than in the West.[32]

Since a rounded model embodying the interrelations between the size distributions of incomes and enterprises has not yet been constructed by mathematical economists, it is impossible to test any empirical hypothesis and we are left only with conjectures.[33] Additional phenomena, namely the lower wages paid to workers by smaller enterprises and establishments (see below) must also be taken into account. Nevertheless, this link between the consumption and production sides of property is an extremely interesting phenomenon that must be accounted for by any general positive economy theory of property; furthermore, the requisite data on size distribution of wages and of enterprises for testing any derived hypotheses are readily available.

D. Other Institutional Considerations

There are, of course, a large number of other types of institutional theories, the most interesting of which are briefly listed below.

In a number of contexts many authors have argued that institutional agglomeration (the relative employment of the largest enterprises *vis-à-vis* the total labor force or the extent to which the labor force is represented by a small number of unions; or the level at which wage negotiations are carried on, i.e., plant, enterprise, industrial, or national level) acts to make labor incomes more equal as a by-product of a pursuit of standardization. That is, large enterprises with establishments in many areas and industries do not differentiate wages and salaries to the extent to which the individual labor markets might allow. Similarly, unions representing workers in many establishments try to narrow intraestablishment and area differentials.[34]

If, on the other hand, enterprises are highly agglomerated in only one branch of manufacturing or if only part of the manufacturing labor force is unionized, then labor income inequality may increase. On the enterprise side this comes about because of the well-known phenomenon that large enter-

32. Lydall [B158] implicity assumes that the sum of these various Pareto distributions is another Pareto distribution and provides as support evidence that the upper tail of the distribution of labor income in nonagriculture sectors follows a Pareto distribution in most Western nations. He finds, however, that such data for Eastern Europe (he uses Hungary, Czechoslovakia, Poland and Yugoslavia; I found similar results for Bulgaria and the Soviet Union) more closely approximates a log normal distribution and argues that this is due to paying managers according to their work output, rather than their responsibility, a conjecture which is based on Marx's formula [B174] for income payments in the first phase of communism rather than any knowledge of East European practices. Although this is an ingenious explanation, it seems specious and the real differences may lie elsewhere, e.g., the fact that bonuses to high income recipients may not be included in the East European data.

33. The linkage between the size distribution of enterprises and of income was first extensively examined by Ronald Tuck [B256]. His approach and mine differ in the directions of causation assumed between these two phenomena.

34. Albert Rees, [B216].

prises generally pay higher average wages to workers than small enterprises.[35] On the union side this might come about because union members obtain higher incomes at the expense of nonunion workers and, indeed, many labor economists have laid more weight on this factor than on an equalization of wages through the narrowing of inter-plant or geographical wage differentials.[36]

Economists have also argued that income inequality is greatly affected by societal values and attitudes, e.g., toward risk[37] or toward social class mobility.[38] That is, societies create certain institutions that reflect particular value positions (e.g., that minimize risk or maximize social class mobility), and these in turn affect income distribution. Obviously some of these institutions are related to the barriers discussed above.

In regard to income distribution in less developed nations, it has been often argued that as a society is closer to the biological subsistence level, the size distribution of income is more equal (at least in the lowest income brackets) because a lower limit is defined by the starvation limit.[39] Of course, such a proposition assumes that societies are unwilling to allow personal income to fall below the subsistence limit for individual families, an assumption which unfortunately is not always true in a number of situations. It has been noted that the larger the extended family and the group within which income is shared, the less unequal will be the distribution of income among individual members of that society after intra-familial redistributions take place.

35. The impact of the phenomenon on the distribution of Japanese labor incomes is analyzed by [B158, pp. 194–9]. Tibor Scitovsky ("A Survey of Some Theories of Income Distribution," in [B58, pp. 15–30]) argues that accompanying the increasing size of enterprises is a decreasing inequality in labor income because the demand for people in the top few positions in an enterprise decrease *vis-à-vis* the demand for those in subordinate positions and thus differentials are decreased. A number of counterarguments can be given, however, and the validity of Scitovsky's argument has yet to be empirically demonstrated. Some have attributed this wage differential between large and small enterprise to the higher degree of relative monopoly of the former, but comparisons of relative wages of enterprises in the U.S.A. and Canada which have different degrees of monopoly (David Schwartzman, "Monopoly and Wages," [P11, XXVI, Aug./1960, pp. 428–38]) casts doubt on this interpretation.

36. [B216, pp. 96–9]; or [B152, Chapter 9].

37. This is argued with considerable ferociousness by Milton Friedman, "Choice, Chance, and the Personal Distribution of Income," [P39, LXI, Aug./1953, pp. 277–90].

38. The importance of social class in determining a person's income is emphasized by Lydall [B158, pp. 135–6] who wrote: "At every stage, socioeconomic class exercises a bias toward improving the chances of the upper class child. His genetic endowment, on the average, is higher; his environment is better ordered and gives greater stimulus and opportunity to his development; his schooling is of better quality and more prolonged; he is encouraged to prepare for a superior profession or occupation, and the financial obstacles are less; and his opportunity of appointment and promotion are often favorably influenced by personal and family connections. While pure chance factors are important, the position within a given generation, in all countries, is that a child's career and its life earnings, are largely determined by the class into which it is born."

39. A simple mathematical model of this matter is presented by Reder in [B238].

Other propositions deal with the existence of "institutionally determined" wage limits with other factor incomes derived as residual shares.[40] Unfortunately, the less developed the society, usually the less reliable are data on the size distribution of income; therefore, many such propositions must remain untested.

APPENDIX A-6

Empirical Evidence on Kalecki's Theory of Factor Income Shares (for Chapter III, Part B)

Kalecki [B127] focused critical attention on the degree of monopoly as the most important determinant of relative factor income shares. He framed his definition of monopoly in terms of a cost markup which makes certain versions of this theory tautologically true. In order to avoid such problems, I am redefining monopoly in terms of concentration ratios.

In the industrial organization literature there are a number of studies showing a positive relationship between profit rates and concentration which do not quite serve our purpose. Collins and Preston [B57] have also shown the relationship between the degree of monopoly and profit markups, which comes closer to Kalecki's approach. Nevertheless, such studies do not necessarily prove that the property income share increases over time as monopoly increases since the excess profits of the more monopolistic industries may be gained at the expense of profits in other industries. Therefore, another approach is called for.

As noted in Chapter VI, the degree of monopoly in the United States manufacturing sector has remained roughly the same since the early 1900's and the share of labor income in manufacturing value added has remained roughly constant as well, once we take into accounts shifts in branch structure (Robert Solow, [P3, XLVIII, Sept./1958, pp. 618–32].) The relationship is consistent with Kalecki's theory but is not a particularly strong piece of evidence.

A stronger experiment can be made with some international comparisons by comparing the average degree of monopoly in manufacturing for the country as a whole and the share of property income in this sector as well. Data on the degree of monopoly come from Chapter VII; data on the labor share (i.e., wages and salaries) of manufacturing value-added can be obtained from [G79] and [G80], from which the share of property income can easily be derived. (Data on the share of property income in the entire national income are presented in Table 3–2.) In order to avoid peculiarities appearing in a single year, property income shares were calculated by averaging such

40. An extremely interesting model of the "institutional wage" is presented by Edgar O. Edwards, [B73].

ratios for four years in the 1960s (or, when appropriate data were not available, for 1958 and 1963). The countries were ranked by degree of relative monopoly and by relative share of property income in manufacturing value added and compared. For an eight-nation sample (seven nations when Yugoslavia is excluded) no positive relationship was obtained. Since Kalecki did not specify other factors to be taken into account, his theory does not appear very useful in explaining international differences in factor income shares.

APPENDIX A-7

Determination of the Speed of Convergence to an Equilibrium Income Distribution (for Chapter IV, Part B)

Because of the influence of random factors in the inheritance-marriage simulation program, the generated income distribution do not completely converge to a single income distribution, but rather to a band of income distributions around the equilibrium. A number of curve-fitting methods were attempted in order to derive the equilibrium distribution but these proved unsatisfactory and the following alternative method was adopted.[1]

First, an unweighted average and standard deviation of the Gini coefficient of income equality were calculated for the last five generations in the thirty generations simulation. The sixth to last Gini coefficient was then tested to see if it fell within the .95 confidence limit of the calculated average. If this was the case, then the unweighted average and standard deviation were recalculated to include this datum and the next Gini coefficient was examined in like manner. The process was stopped when the examined coefficient did not meet the test; the number of generations was then determined, and average coefficient for the other indicators of inequality (e.g., the standard deviation of the logarithms of income, the share of income accounted for by the top 10 percent, etc.) were recorded.

Then, with the calculated standard deviation of the Gini coefficient from the above process, I started from the first generation to see at what generation the Gini coefficient had a significant chance of belonging to the calculated equilibrium. When this point was reached, the generation number was recorded. The conversion point was considered to lie between this point and the earliest generation to be included in the calculation outlined in the first step.

Such a procedure is based on the assumption that the income distribution converges by and large within thirty generations. Whether such a convergence occurred at all was determined by visual inspection of the entire series of calculated Gini coefficients.

1. This is a modification of a method suggested by Richard N. Cooper, to whom I would like to express my thanks.

APPENDIX A-8

Additional Results of the Equilibrium Income Distribution Using the Simulation Model (for Chapter IV, Part B)

TABLE A-6

Measures of Equilibrium Income Distributions Assuming Differential Fertility Rates

Assumptions: No net capital formation; no capital or income redistributions; standard deviation of random element is .15; labor share of national income is 75 percent; rich and poor families are the top and bottom 25 percent on the income distribution while the middle class are the 50 percent of the families inbetween.

Fertility Pattern and Inheritance Rules	Number of children Rich	M.C.	Poor	Marriage Rules No-choice Gini Coef.	No-choice S.D. of Logs. of Income	No-choice Income % of Top 10%	Limited-choice Gini Coef.	Limited-choice S.D. of Logs. of Income	Limited-choice Income % of Top 10%	Equal-choice Gini Coef.	Equal-choice S.D. of Logs of Income	Equal-choice Income % of Top 10%
	2	2	2									
Primog.				.307	.383	34.4%	.308	.428	34.2%	.297	.446	33.5%
Compr.				a	a	a	.064	.116	11.9	.060	.110	11.8
Eq. div.				a	a	a	.064	.116	11.9	.060	.110	11.8
	3	2	1									
Primog.				.309	.385	34.5	.309	.385	34.4	.306	.431	34.3
Compr.				.075	.135	12.5	.074	.136	12.5	.076	.137	12.6
Eq. div.	1	2	3	.074	.132	12.6	.069	.123	12.4	.074	.132	12.7

TABLE A-6 *(continued)*

Measures of Equilibrium Income Distributions Assuming Differential Fertility Rates

Assumptions: No net capital formation; no capital or income redistributions; standard deviation of random element is .15; labor share of national income is 75 percent; rich and poor families are the top and bottom 25 percent on the income distribution while the middle class are the 50 percent of the families inbetween.

Fertility Pattern and Inheritance Rules	Marriage Rules								
	No-choice			Limited-choice			Equal-choice		
	Gini Coef.	S.D. of Logs of Income	Income % of Top 10%	Gini Coef.	S.D. of Logs of Income	Income % of Top 10%	Gini Coef.	S.D. of Logs of Income	Income % of Top 10%
Number of children **Rich M.C. Poor**									
2 2 2									
Primog.	.308	.382	34.2	.308	.423	34.2	.298	.459	33.4
Compr.	.303	.380	33.7	.304	.421	33.8	.301	.453	33.7
Eq. div.	.308	.383	34.1	.300	.420	33.6	.295	.443	32.9
1 3 1									
Primog.	.310	.386	34.2	.306	.429	34.1	.300	.442	33.7
Compr.	.306	.383	34.0	.305	.404	33.9	.295	.453	33.8
Eq. div.	.308	.386	33.9	.302	.427	33.6	.295	.443	33.2
3 1 3									
Primog.	.310	.386	34.3	.306	.424	34.1	.303	.432	33.9
Compr.	.168	.296	15.6	.160	.283	15.3	.135	.239	14.4
Eq. div.	.168	.296	15.5	.158	.280	15.1	.130	.234	14.4

a. If the system starts from a highly unequal distribution of wealth, the equilibrium distribution of income is equal to its original value. If the system starts from a relatively equal wealth distribution where high-ability people with no property might marry low ability people with property (since they would be next to each other on the income scale), then the equilibrium income distribution would be highly equal.

APPENDIX A-9

Equilibrium Gross National Products in the Simulation Experiments (for Chapter IV, Part B)

TABLE A-7

Equilibrium Gross National Product with Different Savings Functions[a]

Assumptions: All families have two children; standard deviation of random element is .15; labor share of national income is 75 percent; no negative saving; no technical change.

Abbreviations: S = personal savings; Y = personal income; $\overline{Y}$ = average income; z = a constant

Variations	Marriage Rules and Inheritance Rules					
	No-choice		Limited-choice		Equal-choice	
	Primo- geniture	*Equal Division*	*Primo- geniture*	*Equal Division*	*Primo- geniture*	*Equal Division*
	S = Yz; any income or capital redistribution					
z = 1.5	114	114	114	114	114	114
z = 2.0	126	126	126	126	126	126
z = 2.5	136	136	136	136	136	136
	$S = (Y - \overline{Y})z$					
No redistributions						
z = 2.0	79	78	79	75	79	71
z = 2.5	85	84	85	79	85	73
z = 2.0, income redistributions of R percent						
R = 0.0%	79	78	79	75	79	71
R = 30.0	70	69	70	65	70	57
R = 60.0	58	57	58	55	58	47
R = 90.0	37	36	37	34	37	31
z = 2.0, capital redistributions of R percent						
R = 0.0%	79	78	79	75	79	71
R = 30.0	70	70	70	66	70	58
R = 60.0	58	58	58	54	58	52
R = 90.0	47	48	49	48	47	47

a. For the equilibrium G.N.P.s using the nonlinear saving function, production at the 30th generation was used as the equilibrium value.

TABLE A-8

Equilibrium Gross National Products with Different Fertility Rates and Population Growth[a]

Assumptions: Standard deviation of random element is .15; Cobb-Douglas production function with labor share of national income as 75 percent; no technological change: no income of capital redistribution; no negative savings; rich and poor are top and bottom 20 percent of income distribution respectively.

Basic parameters:[b] 50 families; 25 generations

Abbreviations: S = personal savings; Y = personal income; $\overline{Y}$ = average income; z = a constant

Fertility Patterns and Inheritance Rules			Marriage Rules								
			No-choice			Limited-choice			Equal-choice		
Number of Children			Primo-geniture	Compro-mise	Equal Division	Primo-geniture	Compro-mise	Equal Division	Primo-geniture	Compro-mise	Equal Division
Rich	M.C.	Poor	$S = Yz, (z = 2.0)$			$S = Yz, (z = 2.0)$					
3	2	2	535	535	535	535	535	535	535	535	535
2	2	3	535	535	535	535	535	535	535	535	535
						$S = (Y - \overline{Y})z, (z = 2.0)$					
3	2	2	337	314	298	336	309	281	336	271	252
2	2	3	337	335	335	336	331	328	336	282	288

a. For the equilibrium, G.N.P. production at the 25th generation was used as the equilibrium value.

APPENDIX A-10

The Effects of the Educational System on the Income Distribution in the East and West (for Chapters III and IV)

The effects of education on individual earnings and the influences of human capital on the distribution of labor incomes have been intensively studied over the past decade.[1] Although we do not have adequate comparable data on the distribution of human capital in the East and West, certain broad generalizations can nevertheless be made.[2]

In regard to primary and secondary education there appears to be no statistically significant difference in enrollment rates (full-time primary and secondary school pupils as a percentage of the school age population) or pupil/teacher ratios in East and West Europe, once we standardize for differences in per capita income.[3] It appears, however, that the East European nations have a somewhat higher percentage of young adults receiving degrees in institutions of higher learning than in the West although the evidence is somewhat mixed on this account.[4] In the West there are financial barriers for children from lower income classes to attend universities; in some countries in the East, there are political barriers against children from bourgeois backgrounds. Although it appears that the social class composition of university students more closely approximates that of the population in the East, between certain pairs of nations in the East and West for which data are available, such differences in social class composition seem small or negligible.[5]

Such evidence suggests that although the distribution of primary and secondary education in the two groups of nations may be roughly' similar, certain differences appear for higher education. More precisely, the distribution of higher education may be somewhat more unequal in the West (because the percentage of the population with higher education is lower) and,

1. For a brilliant survey, see Jacob Mincer, "The Distribution of Labor Incomes: A Survey with Special Reference to the Human Capital Approach," [P35, VIII, March/1970, pp. 1–27].

2. [B158, p. 211] attempts one type of comparison between the East and West regarding the inequality of the distribution of education which, unfortunately, uses relatively poor data and which is not standardized for per capita G.N.P. The paragraphs below are an alternative approach which is based on comparable data and which is standardized for per capita G.N.P. but which, on the other hand, does not completely describe the phenomena we are investigating.

3. This is the result of a regression analysis of data for both 1956 and 1962 that is presented by [B214, pp. 192 ff].

4. In [B214, pp. 195 ff.], problems arise because the results of a regression analysis differ greatly, depending on whether the United States is included or excluded from the sample.

5. [B214, Appendix E-15]. The two pairs of nations for which comparable data are available are the United States and the Soviet Union, and West and East Germany.

moreover, the West may have somewhat greater barriers of opportunity for such education. Nevertheless, the evidence on the matters is mixed and, furthermore, the differences do not appear to be sufficiently great to be an important determinant for differences in the inequality of individual labor incomes.

APPENDIX A-11

Details of the Study of Conglomerate Mergers on Market Shares (for Chapter IV, Part B)

A. The Sample

Lists of mergers of large corporations for 1961 were obtained from [G98]; for 1966 from [P44, I, Jan/1967]. Only those mergers where the acquiring enterprise was listed in the *Fortune* list of the 500 largest manufacturing enterprises were included. Further, only mergers were recorded where the acquired enterprise's financial data were listed in [B189]. Finally, all horizontal or vertical mergers were eliminated so that the list contained only conglomerate mergers. The criterion by which horizontal mergers were distinguished was whether the two enterprises produced goods in the same or related three-digit industries. Vertical mergers were determined on a more subjective basis — whether the products of one enterprise potentially could be used as inputs for production by the second.

B. Data on Market Share Changes

I first attempted to obtain data on changes in market share following merger by writing to various relevant trade associations. Of the 150 or so letters sent out, I received only three useful replies. Therefore, another approach was called for.

A letter of enquiry was sent to the sales vice president or president of every acquiring enterprise in which two questions were asked: Were many product lines dropped? And has the market share of those product lines that have been maintained changed since year of acquisition? An explanatory note was appended that in situations where market share increased in certain lines and decreased in others, the judgment should be made according to relative importance of the various lines, i.e., to changes in total product sales *vis-à-vis* changes in total sales of all relevant industries.

Of the letters covering valid mergers (mergers that actually took place or where the acquired company was not sold again within the next few years; the basic lists of mergers proved somewhat inaccurate), the response rate was roughly 48 percent.

C. Calculations

For market share changes in the five years preceding the merger, only a rough estimate could be obtained. The following method of estimation was employed: Sales data of the acquired company were compared against growth of value of shipments for the corresponding three-digit industry which were obtained from [G85, various issues]. For certain companies which produce goods in many industries, the sum of value of shipments in the corresponding four-digit industries was used as the basis of comparison instead. In other cases where these procedures did not prove possible to carry out, I employed a modified method using industrial value-added data instead. For companies which had experienced mergers, sales of subsidiaries, or major changes in their accounting practices in this period, comparisons were made for a shorter time interval so that company growth would not be biased by these institutional or accounting factors. In certain cases where such mergers or corporate changes had appeared almost every year, no estimate of relative growth of company sales could be obtained.

So very few enterprises dropped product lines of the acquired enterprise that this part of the analysis did not appear fruitful to pursue.

No adjustments were made to the replies submitted by the companies regarding changes in market share of the acquired enterprise after merger.

D. Results

For the two years the following results were obtained: See table A-9, page 412.

E. Sources of Bias

There seem to be two important sources of upward bias so that the data show a higher change in market share than actually occurred. First, companies with a decline in market share of the acquired enterprise might be more hesitant about answering the questionnaire than companies with a more successful record. Second, high officials in a particular company may have a more rosy view of their firm's market behavior than the true facts warrant (a "halo effect"). Sources of downward bias did not seem important.

In comparing the few trade association replies with the company replies, no conclusion can be drawn. In one case the trade association reported a decrease in market share when the company reported an increase; in a second case, exactly the reverse was true.

TABLE A-9
Changes in Market Shares of Companies Acquired by Conglomerates

Market Share Change in Five Years Preceding Merger	Mergers in 1961				Mergers in 1966			
	Market share in 1970 vis-à-vis year of merger				Market share in 1970 vis-à-vis year of merger			
	Decreased	Roughly Same	Increased	Total	Decreased	Roughly Same	Increased	Total
Decreased	0	1	2	3	0	2	4	6
Roughly same	0	0	0	0	0	1	2	3
Increased	1	0	2	3	1	5	5	11
Undetermined	0	1	2	3	1	4	2	7
Total	1	2	6	9	2	12	13	27

APPENDIX A-12

Size Distributions of "Big Businesses" (for Chapter VI, Part C)

TABLE A-10

Quartile Share of Labor Force Employment of the Top "Big Businesses"[1]

Country	Date	Percentage of Labor Force of Total Top "Big Businesses"			
		1st Quartile	*2nd Quartile*	*3rd Quartile*	*4th Quartile*
United States	1968	59%	19%	13%	9%
Japan	1966	57	19	13	11
West Germany	1965	64	19	10	6
United Kingdom	1964/65	53	23	15	9
France	1966	56	20	14	10
Italy	1965	70	14	9	6
Spain	1965	47	24	17	12
Sweden	1964	37	26	20	17
Belgium	1966	54	24	14	8
Switzerland	1966	57	19	15	9
Austria	c. 1966	43	27	17	13

1. The table is computed from data on individual enterprises obtained from: [P25, LXXIX, 6/1969], [B210], [B251], and [P21, Numbers 606, 609, 618, 633, 641, 646, and 662]. In each list of enterprises only predominantly mining and manufacturing enterprises were chosen. For certain cases estimates of employment for particular enterprises had to be made. The data for Belgium are for "capitaux propre" rather than employment; for other countries for which such data on "capitaux propre" and employment were available, roughly the same results were obtained using both indicators of enterprise size. These data contain several major sources of inconsistencies: First, most enterprises appear to have included workers and employees in foreign subsidiaries but I can't be sure that this rule was followed in every case. Second, the handling of workers and employees in independent subsidiaries or partially owned subsidiaries is not clear.

The data for the various countries (arranged according to descending value of total G.N.P.) show quite a distinct pattern: The top quartile of enterprises employs roughly 56 percent of the total; the second quartile, 21 percent: the third quartile, 14 percent; and the fourth quartile, 9 percent. There is no systematic deviation from this pattern either according to total G.N.P. or per capita G.N.P. in the nations forming the sample. This suggests that the size distribution curve of the top "big businesses" is roughly the same in all countries. Further, the top two quartiles employ about 77 percent of total

employment and the top quartile employs about 73 percent of the employment of the top half. Thus the tail of the distribution appears to approach
that of geometric series.[2]

APPENDIX A-13

Comparisons of the Numerical Results of Concentration and Agglomeration Ratios (for Chapter VI, Parts C and D)

Since concentration ratios are available for only a small number of nations,
it seems useful to see if some substitute can be devised so that more nations
can be brought into the comparison. One possible alternative measure is the
"agglomeration" ratio, which is the share of a particular industry that is
accounted for by an average size enterprise. Although the agglomeration ratio
can be calculated from either output or input measures, only the latter are
available for many nations.

In a narrowly defined industry the two measures should give roughly the
same results. On an aggregate level, however, the weighted concentration
indices measure a particular facet of competition while the aggregate agglomeration ratio measures a phenomenon that reflects not only the share of a particular market but also vertical and conglomerate production of the enterprise
as well. Since both concentration and agglomeration are related to the size of
the domestic economy, it seems likely that nations would rank roughly the
same using the two different indicators. To resolve the question we can make
a statistical experimentation which is presented in Table A-11.

Although the rankings from the concentration ratios show a rough
similarity with those derived from the agglomeration ratios, there are also
many differences. The Kendall rank order correlation measures between the
concentration ratio rankings and the agglomeration ratio rankings are, respectively, .39, .56, and .39, none of which is statistically significant at the .05
level.

The two nations that differ most greatly in rank using the two indices
are Italy and Japan. Italy has the lowest relative concentration but a middling
level of agglomeration, which suggests that agglomerative enterprises (i.e.,
enterprises producing in many different markets) play a relatively important
role in the economy. Japan, on the other hand, has a roughly average concen-

2. The employment share of the first quartile as a percentage of the
first two quartiles is roughly 95 percent that of the employment share of the
first two quartiles as a percentage of the top four quartiles. After performing
the necessary statistical tests, this difference turns out greater than one would
expect by change (.05 level); therefore, in the text I say that the two ratios
approach, rather than equal, each other.

TABLE A-11

Aggregate Concentration and Agglomeration Ratios[a]

Country	Weighted Four-digit Concentration Ratios (U.S. Weights; Incl. Regional Industries)			Agglomeration Ratio × 10,000						
					Arithmetic Average		Entropy Measure		Niehans Measure	
	Date	Data	Rank	Date	Data	Rank	Data	Rank	Data	Rank
Italy	1961	.89	1	1961	.37	5	1.43	3	11.4	5
France	1963	.93	2	1963	.35	4	1.53	4	9.0	4
West Germany	1963	.94	3	1962	.21	3	.96	2	5.0	2
United States	1963	1.00	4	1963	.13	1	1.92	5	8.0	3
Japan	1962	1.14	5	1963	.16	2	.68	1	4.3	1
Netherlands	1963	1.23	6	1962	1.10	6	3.56	6	18.2	8
Yugoslavia	1963	1.47	7	1963	4.21	9	7.23	9	13.0	6
Switzerland	1965	1.63	8	1965	1.28	7	3.64	7	14.3	7
Belgium	1963	1.66	9	1962	1.61	8	5.97	8	28.8	9

a. The weighted concentration ratios come from Table 5–11. The agglomeration ratios are based on employment data and were derived in the process of calculating Table 4–7.

tration ratio but low agglomeration ratios, which suggests that agglomerative enterprises are relatively less important in Japan than one would suspect. (Since the Zaibatsu provide for coordinating of manufacturing activities above the enterprise level, this may indicate a deliberate designation of specialization in particular products to individual enterprises in such industrial groups.)

Further experiments can also be performed on these two sets of ratios. We can disaggregate and compare weighted concentration ratios and agglomeration indices by two-digit manufacturing industries. The rankings of industries using the two sets of ratios are quite different. The leather and leather products (excluding shoes) branch shows a relatively low degree of concentration and a relatively high degree of agglomeration, suggesting that enterprises producing in this sector are quite large and produce a variety of other products as well. The metal products and the machinery branches appear exactly the opposite — their concentration is relatively higher than their agglomeration, which suggests that enterprises in these branches are highly specialized and produce only a very narrow range of products.

The conclusions drawn from such experiments is quite clear: the two different ratios can not be used as substitutes. Further, comparisons of the results using both ratios yields additional information on the structure of industry which may be of considerable use to the analyst.

APPENDIX A-14

Some Aspects of Centralization in a Three-tiered Hierarchy (for Chapters VII and VIII)

Description of relative changes in the holding of property rights among members of a hierarchy raise a number of definitional problems, three of which are explored briefly below.

(1) Relative changes in centralization from the standpoint of organizational structure can occur in a number of different ways. If we assume that the total amount of property rights remains the same, twelve possible patterns of change can be envisioned in a three-tiered hierarchy, of which several could bear the descriptive label of "centralization." These are presented in Table A-12, where a plus indicates an increase in property rights at a particular level and a minus, the reverse.

If we define centralization as a shift in property rights from the bottom to the top of the hierarchy, it should be clear that there are three kinds of centralization (columns 1, 2, and 3), with the most thorough centralization in column 1 and the least thorough in column 3.

Decentralization is, of course, the reverse process and is shown in columns 4, 5, and 6. The most thorough decentralization appears in column 4; the least thorough, in column 6.

TABLE A-12

Possible Changes of Property Rights in a Three-tiered Hierarchy

	1	2	3	4	5	6	7	8	9	10	11	12
President	+	+	+	−	−	−		+		−	−	+
Intermediate level	−		+	−		+	+	−	−	+	+	−
Rank and file	−	−	−	+	+	+	−		+		−	+

"Semicentralization" occurs when there is an upward shift in the holding of property rights between any two adjoining levels; the two cases are pictured in columns 7 and 8; "semidecentralization" is the reverse phenomenon and is pictured in columns 9 and 10.

"Positive intermediation" occurs when the intermediate decision-making units gain property rights at the expense of the highest and lowest units, as shown in column 11. "Negative intermediation" occurs when the intermediate units lose power at the expense of the highest and lowest units, as pictured in column 12.

(2) An aspect of centralization from the standpoint of the decision-making process can also be illustrated using a similar approach. Let us assume that we can quantitatively measure the extent of the set of property rights of an organization that are held at different levels of the administrative hierarchy so that we can draw control graphs. Three examples are presented in Chart A-1.

The first distribution of property rights has been found in a number of United States business enterprises; the second, in certain United States labor unions; and the third, in local chapters of an American women's voluntary organization (the League of Women Voters).[1] At least in the first two, a measure of "relative" centralization or decentralization can be gained by measuring the slope of the line.

CHART A-1

"Control Graphs" in Three Organizations[a]

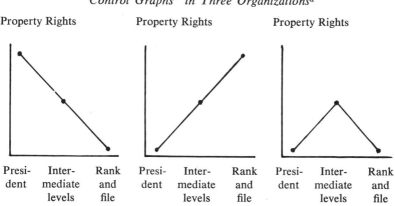

| Property Rights | Property Rights | Property Rights |

| Presi-
dent | Inter-
mediate
levels | Rank
and
file | Presi-
dent | Inter-
mediate
levels | Rank
and
file | Presi-
dent | Inter-
mediate
levels | Rank
and
file |

a. I am using the approach of Tannenbaum [B246], substituting "property rights" for his term "control."

1. For such studies see [B246].

For organizations similar in size, the size of the set of property rights exercised by each level of the hierarchy can be such that the line of property rights of one organization might lie completely above that of another. In this situation, we have a greater degree of decentralization in a very special sense that is briefly examined in Chapter VIII. Empirical evidence from a large number of different types of organization has led Tannenbaum to conclude that organizational effectiveness is much more strongly influenced by heights of the line rather than its slope.[2]

(3) One last aspect of centralization from the standpoint of individuals deserves brief mention. It is perfectly possible for the amount of property rights exercised by a single individual to decrease, even though the property rights exercised by the collectivity of individuals at that particular hierarchical level increase. For instance, the rank and file of an organization could be given a much wider sphere of decision-making but, at the same time, their jobs could be much more standardized so that individually they exercise much less discretion. In this case we have centralization from the standpoint of individuals but decentralization from the standpoint of organizational structure. This is discussed in Chapter VIII.

APPENDIX A-15

Empirical Relations between Dimensions of Centralization (for Chapter VIII, Part B)

In the organization theory literature in the last decade, a number of analyses have isolated various dimensions of centralization and investigated whether they are correlated with each other. The results of these investigations are briefly summarized below.

Some investigators have examined the relationship between different dimensions of centralization in similar types of organizations. For instance, Hage and Aiken examined sixteen health and welfare agencies and found that centralization in terms of participation in decision-making by organization members at low administrative levels was related to hierarchical centralization but that the correlations of these two dimensions of centralization with other dimensions or indices such as a high routinization of jobs or a high degree to which subordinate performance is examined by superiors were not

2. [B246].

strong or were even nil.[1] Marshall Meyer found in a study of 254 governmental (municipal, county, and state) financial administrations that "authority of a person" (which seems related to hierarchical centralization and also, perhaps, centralization in terms of functional differentiation) was not related to "authority of office" (which is roughly similar to centralization in terms of standardization and routinization of jobs).[2] Peter Blau in his study of employment security agencies found centralization (in terms of routinization of jobs) to be related to hierarchical centralization in certain areas of decision-making, but not in others.[3]

Empirically different dimensions of centralization can also be shown in studies of different types of organizations. In an elaborate factor analysis of sixty-four variables for forty-eight different types of organizations, Pugh and his collaborators found four major unrelated clusters of organizational characteristics, of which one is the "structuring of activities" (centralization in terms of high standardization of jobs, formalization of procedures, etc.) and another the "centralization of authority" (hierarchical centralization).[4] Furthermore, centralization in terms of functional specialization (which formed part of the cluster of "structuring of activities") was also negatively related to "centralization of authority." Richard Hall examined ten organizations in different fields and found that hierarchical centralization, centralization in terms of job routinization and standardized procedures, and centralization in terms of functional differentiation are not related to each other; however, later studies with a larger sample cast some doubt on this conclusion.[5]

1. Jerald Hage and Michael Aiken, "Relationship of Centralization to Other Structural Properties," [P1, XII, June/1967, pp. 72–93]. The relationship between the four variables can be easily summarized. (I am using their table of partial correlations since, unlike the authors, I think this a more important indication of relationship; a double plus or minus means strong relationship; a single plus or minus means weak relationship.)

Centralization measures	A.	B.	C.	D.
A. Low participation in decision-making by lower echelon members		++	+	−
B. High level of hierarchy at which decisions made	++		o	+
C. High modification of rights and duties of positions (low routinization)	+	o		++
D. High degree to which subordinates checked by superiors	−	+	++	

2. Marshall W. Meyer, "The Two Authority Structures of Bureaucratic Organization," [PI, XII, Sept./1968, pp. 211–28].

3. Blau, "Decentralization in Bureaucracies," in [B276, pp. 150–74].

4. D. S. Pugh, *et al.*, "Dimensions of Organization Structure," [P1, XIII, June/1968, pp. 65–105].

5. Richard H. Hall, "The Concept of Bureaucracy: An Empirical Assessment," [P4, LXIX, July/1963, pp. 32–41]. In a later study of twenty-five organizations (Richard H. Hall and Charles R. Tittle, "A Note on Bureaucracy and Its 'Correlates,'" [P4, LXXII, Nov./1966, pp. 267–72), these measures of centralization did form a relatively good Guttman scale, which suggests that they are really different aspects of the same variable. This discrepancy between results is difficult to explain but may lie in the small sample used in the first paper.

Comparisons between these various studies is often quite difficult since some investigators use "objective" measurements while others rely on the perceptions of the participants of the organization ("subjective" measurements); nevertheless, both objective and subjective indices may be measuring the same phenomenon. For instance, Whisler, *et al.* investigated seventy-three departments within a large insurance enterprise and showed that perceived hierarchical centralization was correlated with hierarchical centralization as measured by the inequality of compensation.[6]

Several simple conclusions can be drawn: First, centralization of property rights consists of a number of dimensions that are not necessarily empirically related to each other; at the very least centralization in terms of job routinization seems not only unrelated, but quite possibly even a substitute for hierarchical centralization. Both of these dimensions are included among those uses of the concept of centralization that are directly related to the act of control; without doubt some of the definitions of centralization that are only indirectly related to the act of control form other nonrelated dimensions. Only much more intensive empirical analysis can determine whether or not my designated dimensions of centralization cluster around a smaller number of more basic components of centralization.

Second, in analyzing the development of centralization or the impact of centralization on the functioning of the economy, it is necessary to specify which dimension of centralization is being discussed. Failure to follow this simple advice has vitiated much of the theoretical discussion on the topic.

APPENDIX A-16

Propositions about Centralization: Results of Empirical Studies (for Chapter VIII, Part E)

In this brief summary discussion focuses first on developmental propositions (i.e., propositions about the origin, development, or continuance of centralization) and then on impact propositions (i.e., the effect of centralization on the functioning of the system). For the most part only the results of recent empirical research are reported.

A. Developmental Propositions

I begin with an examination of the relationship between centralization and particular organizational variables (such as age of organization, size, and vertical height of administrative bureaucracy), then turn to the link between

6. Thomas Whisler, *et al.,* "Centralization of Organizational Control: An Empirical Study of its Meaning and Measurement," in [B246, pp. 283–307].

centralization and various task and technology variables (complexity of production processes, mechanization, work flows, and uncertainties) and finally end with a short examination of centralization and several labor force variables. Since empirical research in the organization theory literature has focused on only a few of the many concepts of centralization, this review of research is relatively brief.

A number of studies show that the age of organizations appears inversely related to hierarchical centralization: the older the organization, the less the hierarchical centralization.[1] These results seem to run contrary to studies of voluntary organizations purporting to demonstrate an "iron law of oligarchy"[2] but the different results may depend partly on the fact that different types of organization (industrial enterprises as opposed to political parties or other voluntary organization) are under study. None of the studies I have seen have shown any relationship between organizational age and centralization defined in terms of routinization of jobs.

The size of organizations, as measured either by inputs (such as work force) or outputs, appears to influence particular dimensions of centralization in quite different ways. Several studies demonstrate that increasing organizational size is directly related to centralization in terms of job routinization or standardization.[3] Size also appears directly related to centralization in terms of functional differentiation.[4] On the other hand, evidence on the relationship between organizational size and hierarchical centralization is quite mixed, with some investigators finding little relationship and others finding either positive or negative correlations.[5]

The relationship between the number of vertical levels of authority in administrative hierarchies (which is related to but not the same as the size of the organization) and the centralization of property rights does not appear very clear. To be sure, centralization in terms of job routinization seems directly related to the number of vertical levels.[6] But the evidence on the relationship between vertical levels and hierarchical centralization is quite mixed (although more studies show a negative correlation).[7]

1. See especially D. S. Pugh, *et al.,* "The Context of Organization Structures," [P1, XIV, March/1969, pp. 91–114]; Thomas L. Whisler, "Measuring Centralization of Control in Business Organizations," in [B39]; and Yitzhak Samuel and Bilha F. Mannheim, "A Multidimensional Approach toward a Typology of Bureaucracy," [P1, XV, June/1970, pp. 216–28].

2. Reference is made here, of course, to Robert Michels, [B184].

3. Pugh, *et al.,* "The Context . . ."; Samuel and Mannheim; Richard H. Hall, "The Concept of Bureaucracy: An Empirical Assessment," in [P4, LXIX, July/1963, pp. 32–41].

4. Pugh, *et al.,* "The Context . . . ." Certain contrary evidence is offered by Hall.

5. Pugh, *et al.,* "The Context . . . ," and Hall, find no relationship; Peter M. Blau, "Decentralization in Bureaucracies," in [B276, pp. 150–74] finds a positive relationship between size and centralization regarding budget decisions and a negative relationship regarding personnel decisions; Alfred D. Chandler, Jr. [B51] finds a hierarchical decentralization as production volume and diversity increases.

6. Pugh, *et al.,* "The Context . . . ."

7. Pugh, *et al.,* "The Context . . . ." find no relationship; on the other hand Peter Blau, "Decentralization in Bureaucracies," and Marshall W. Meyer, "The Two Authority Structures of Bureaucratic Organization," [P1, XII, Sept./1968, pp. 211–28] find negative relationships.

Turning from organization variables to task and technology variables, a number of correlates with centralization have been observed. Greater organizational complexity is usually accompanied by decentralization as manifested by participation of lower echelon personnel in decision-making.[8] Evidence is more mixed with regard to organizational complexity and hierarchical centralization, although on balance it appears that hierarchical centralization is less in highly complex organizations or organizations producing a large diversity of products.[9]

Centralization also seems affected by the type of work carried out by the organization. Certainly more routine work leads to greater centralization, manifested not only by routinization of jobs but also by the levels of administration on which important decisions are made.[10] Evidence on the impact of the type of technology of manufacturing (in terms of unit production, mass production, or process flow production) is for most dimensions of centralization extremely mixed and no conclusions can be drawn.[11] Similarly, evidence on the relationship of mechanization of administration and centralization, particularly with regard to the impact of computers, is also highly mixed and again no definite conclusions can yet be drawn.[12]

Considerable theoretical work has focused on the relationship of the work environment (variability of inputs, uncertainty of outputs, uncertainty of sales) but relatively little adequate empirical evidence is available.[13] If highly rapid changes in technology of product markets are occurring, certain case study materials suggest that hierarchical decentralization occurs.[14]

Considering finally the relationship between centralization and important labor force variables, several propositions or correlations deserve attention. A number of analysts have argued that a more highly educated labor force

8. Jerald Hage and Michael Aiken, "Relationship of Centralization to Other Structural Properties," [P1, XII, June/1967, pp. 72–93].

9. Hage and Aiken show a positive relationship between hierarchical centralization and most but not all measures of organizational complexity. On the other hand, a negative relationship is supported on a general level by Pugh *et al.,* "The Context . . ." and in a specific context by Robert W. Ackerman, "Influence of Integration and Diversity on the Investment Process," [P1, XV, Sept./1970, pp. 341–51]. The evidence supporting the negative relationship seems more convincing.

10. Jerald Hage and Michael Aiken, "Routine Technology, Social Structure, and Organization Goals," [P1, XIV, Sept./1969; pp. 366–76]; and Richard H. Hall, "Intraorganizational Structural Variation: Application of the Bureaucratic Model," [P1, VII, Dec./1962, pp. 293–308].

11. Studies showing some relationship include those by Samuel and Mannheim, and Joan Woodward, [B275]. Contrary evidence is supplied by Pugh, *et al.,* "The Context . . ." and David J. Hickson, D. S. Pugh, *et al.,* "Operations Technology and Organization Structure: An Empirical Reappraisal," [P1, XIV, Sept./1969, pp. 378–97].

12. According to the evidence presented by Blau, "Decentralization in Bureaucracies," increasing computerization is associated with increasing decentralization; contrary evidence is more informally presented by various authors (especially Whisler) in [B195].

13. These issues are analyzed on a theoretical level by James D. Thompson [B250]. Michel Crozier [B62], especially Chapter 6; and Charles Perrow, "A Framework for the Comparative Analysis of Organizations," [P5, XXXII, April/1967, pp. 194–208].

14. Alvin Toffler [B253] emphasizes this theme especially in his analysis of the emergence of "ad-hocracies" (Chapter 7).

leads to greater decentralization along many dimensions and, indeed, some of the recent empirical evidence supports this contention.[15] Others have argued that the greater the shared values between the top and lower echelons, the greater the decentralization but the supporting evidence is more in the nature of case studies and theoretical arguments than large-scale organization comparisons.[16] Labor force considerations can also be derived from a number of propositions discussed with regard to organization and task and technology variables.

In short, the available empirical evidence on the determinants of centralization that might be of interest in the analysis of economic systems is neither very extensive nor, unfortunately, very conclusive.

B. Impact Propositions

Some of the difficulties of linking the performance of organizations to their centralization are discussed in the text. In the organization theory literature some attention has been paid to these matters, but the empirical studies are few and far between.

Several studies purport to show a positive relationship between various dimensions of centralization and organizational adaptiveness. For instance, in a cross-section study of thirty-two schools with regard to 183 educational innovations (representing "progress"), one educator found that a much higher percentage of such innovations with regard to teaching had been adopted by the schools operating in hierarchically decentralized school districts.[17] Or in a study of sixteen social welfare organizations over a five-year period, several investigators found a definite correlation between decentralization, in terms of participation of lower level employees in decision-making, and the degree of organizational change.[18]

On the other hand, in situations where great structural changes are required, it is well known that organizations often hierarchically centralize to be able to carry out such tasks. During war time, for instance, when the structure of production must be rapidly changed, few nations have recently relied on the price mechanism but rather have used direct commands and command mechanisms indicating hierarchical centralization to make these changes. The same sorts of considerations are often given for nations wishing to increase rapidly their growth rates, e.g., with respect to priority industries during the first five-year plan, the Soviet Union was highly hierarchically centralized.

15. Blau, "The Structure . . . ," and Woodward, offer evidence on this matter but their empirical measures leave much to be desired. Hage and Aiken, "Relationship . . . ," show that high professional training is accompanied by high participation (low centralization) and a high degree of control of decisions of subordinates by their superiors (high centralization).

16. R. S. Milne, "Mechanistic and Organic Models of Public Administration in Developing Countries," [P1, XV, March/1970, pp. 57–67] cities case study materials on these matters. On a more theoretical level certain issues are analyzed by numerous analysts including James G. March and Herbert A. Simon [B167].

17. François S. Cillié [B54].

18. Jerald Hage and Michael Aiken, "Program Change and Organizational Properties, A Comparative Analysis," [P4, LXXII, March/1967, pp. 503–19].

Although it is not completely clear that such centralization resulted in greater change than would have occurred with a lesser degree of centralization, the burden of proof seems to be on those who wish to prove the reverse.

From such mixed evidence two conclusions are possible. Either different types of changes can be most effectively achieved by centralization or decentralization along particular specified dimensions; or the empirical evidence regarding relationships between centralization and adaptability to change is conflicting and much more evidence is needed. Possibly both interpretations are correct.

A definite relationship seems to exist between centralization and dissatisfaction with work or one's fellow employees. One study of sixteen social welfare organizations showed that feeling of disappointment with career and professional development were directly related to hierarchical centralization, lack of participation in decision-making, and routinization and standardization of jobs; a similar pattern was also obtained for dissatisfaction in social relations with supervisors and fellow employees.[19] If we consider centralization in terms of organization size, a number of studies show job dissatisfaction and centralization correlated.[20] It is well known that strikes, labor problems, and low morale are found more often in large production establishments than small, and that low morale is often associated with highly routinized jobs or highly frequent performance reviews.

The relationship between efficiency and centralization is extremely difficult to judge since many studies define efficiency in terms of productivity or profits so that economies of scale affect the results. Now if we measure hierarchical centralization in terms of size of organization, then the relatively large literature on the relationship or lack of relationship between enterprise size and profitability becomes of interest.[21] But until we can obtain some independent measure of economies of scale in such industries, we can not determine whether to attribute the results to such scale factors or to considerations of differential efficiency.[22]

In the organization literature there are a number of highly careful studies of efficiency or organizational effectiveness and centralization, defined in terms of hierarchical centralization and in terms of the amount of total power within organizations.[23] Almost all of these studies show that centralization in

---

19. Michael Aiken and Jerald Hage, "Organizational Alienation: A Comparative Analysis," [P6, XXXI, Aug./1966, pp. 497–507].

20. For instance, Seigio Talacchi, "Organization Size, Individual Attitudes, and Behavior: An Empirical Study," [P1, V, Dec./1960, pp. 398–420].

21. One extensive recent study is by Marshall Hall and Leonard Weiss," Firm Size and Profitability," [P57, XLIX, Aug./1967, pp. 319–31]; another study is by Larner [B148]. For an extensive review, see [B228, Chapter 4].

22. One way to circumvent such difficulties is to study the performance of the same organization under centralized and decentralized regimes. One interesting macroeconomic experiment with the performance of the Yugoslav economy during periods in which hierarchical centralization was quite different is carried out by Thomas Marschak, "Centralized versus Decentralized Resource Allocation: The Yugoslav 'Laboratory'," [P55, LXXXII, Nov./1968, pp. 561–87].

23. These are presented by Tannenbaum [B246]. Although these studies are highly suggestive, the statistical methods of analysis leave much to be desired, particularly in his handling of the relative degree of hierarchical centralization.

terms of total power, rather than hierarchical centralization, is the crucial variable in determining efficiency or effectiveness.

It is, of course, difficult to set up statistical experiments to determine the impact of different types of centralization. Since there may be an optimum degree of centralization, we must test for nonlinear relationships between centralization and efficiency so that an optimum can be determined; further complications arise because the optimum degree of, let us say, hierarchical centralization may depend partly on technical parameters of the industry, partly on the environment within which the enterprise functions, and partly on national or regional traditions or the quality of the labor force. These difficulties may account for the relative sparseness of relevant literature exploring the interrelations between centralization and performance on an empirical basis.

APPENDIX A-17

Centralization and Temporal Aspects of Enterprise Behavior (for Chapter VIII, Part E)

The discussion in this appendix centers on two temporal aspects of enterprise behavior: the frequency of performance review and the time horizon of planning. In both cases analytic attention is focused on the impact of enterprise size upon these variables.

A. Frequency of Performance Review

Centralization can be defined in terms of highly frequent reviews of a person's performance by his superiors in a hierarchy, so that the time span during which the subordinate can make decisions at his own discretion without accounting for his actions to others becomes a crucial variable.[1] This index is related to the boundaries of the choice set of the individual and touches on two concerns that often appear in the business literature: individual responsibility and the "centralization of control." An organization with more frequent examinations of performances on the part of its members is thus considered more centralized.

It is well known that within manufacturing enterprises, such performance reviews occur more frequently at bottom levels of the administrative hierarchy than at higher levels.[2] We can compare relative centralization of

---

1. This concept is analyzed and discussed in much greater detail by Elliott Jaques [B124, especially pp. 32–42].
2. [B124].

different enterprises by comparing the frequency of performance review at the same level and examine the effects of one possible determinant upon this, namely enterprise size.

The basis of the empirical analysis is a survey of administrative practices in twenty-five multidivisional or conglomerate corporations in mining and manufacturing in the United States that replied to a questionnaire of the corporate planning project of Swarthmore College.[3] Questions were asked about the frequency with which operating units (divisions) must submit reports upward to the main office. To show the influence of size, I have divided all corporations into two groups: those with sales ranging from $9 million to $97 million ("small corporations") and those with sales ranging from $118 million to $8,382 million ("large corporations"). Relevant data are presented in Table A-13.

TABLE A-13

*Average Interval of Time of Reports from Operating Units
to the Main Office*[a]

Type of Report	25 Corporations Total	13 Small Corporations	12 Large Corporations	Significant Differences (.05 level) between Large and Small Corporations
Cash balances	2.2 weeks	2.4 weeks	2.0 weeks	No
Bookings	2.6	2.5	2.7	No
Production shipments	2.6	2.6	2.6	No
Profits	3.7	3.8	3.6	No
Marketing/sales analyses	7.8	8.1	7.5	No
Number of employees	8.2	4.5	12.3	No
Research and development progress	11.1	13.4	9.2	No

a. The averages were calculated only for those enterprises indicating such reports are sent; however, almost every enterprise used all seven of these reports. A two-tailed test for differences between sample means is employed. For performance reports on both the number of employees and on progress in research and development, the standard deviations are extremely large.

The table reveals relatively few differences between the small and the large corporation with regard to frequency of performance review. Within the sample of twenty-five multidivisional or conglomerate enterprises, the small corporations show a slightly less frequent review of cash balances and

3. This project was directed and carried out by Mr. Jon Lax and I would like to thank him for his permission to use the data. Questionnaires were sent to 108 conglomerates and multidivisional enterprises, of which twenty-five usable answers were received. I have retabulated the results and interpreted them in a somewhat different manner than Mr. Lax.

of research and development progress and a somewhat more frequent review of bookings and number of employees than large corporations. In not one case is the difference between large and small enterprises statistically significant and we must conclude that enterprise size is not a determinant of this aspect of centralization, at least within the range covered in the table.

It would, of course, be extremely useful to examine the number of different reports that operating units must send upward and the degree of detail in which they are specified. It would also be useful to examine the results for separate industries since different industries may be characterized by different degrees of risk and other variables that could influence the frequency of performance review. Unfortunately, the available data of the corporate planning project do not permit such an analysis.

We have, unfortunately, no comparable data on the frequency of performance reviews in enterprises of other nations although, in principle, such data would not be difficult to gather. For the East European nations we have a great deal of anecdotal evidence on the frequency with which performance reports are requested, but such evidence does not lend itself to quantitative analysis such that we could compare enterprises in different systems to determine the impact of the system on this dimension of centralization. I suspect, however, that enterprise size is not a determinant of this aspect of centralization in other nations as well, at least as long as the enterprise sales are larger than a prespecified minimum. And I further suspect that few differences would be found for this aspect of centralization between enterprises in East and West, i.e., that this type of centralization is largely dictated by technological factors. These suppositions require further empirical investigation.

B. Time Horizon of Planning

If long-range plans have any operational content, then the time horizon of planning reflects the extent to which high executives in the enterprise attempt to exercise control over the future development of their organization. An operational long-run plan allows these decision-makers to deal with a problem with fewer constraints than if the problem were unanticipated and a short-run "crisis" occurred. Thus a longer time horizon of planning may reflect greater centralization of an enterprise. The conventional wisdom on these matters suggests that larger corporations have longer time horizons of planning and are thus more centralized and it is this proposition for which relevant data is presented in Table A-14.

For those enterprises not carrying out such long-range planning, a planning horizon of one year (corresponding to the budgeting period) was assigned. A two-tailed test is employed to determine the significance of the differences between the sample means, which means that we are testing the proposition that no differences exist between large and small enterprises. If a one-tailed test is used (which means that we are testing the proposition that large enterprises do not have longer time horizons than small enterprises), then a statistically significant difference exists between large and small enterprises with regard both to specific strategies and actual targeting.

It must be noted that determination of the statistical difference between large and small corporations depends not only on the differences between the two groups but also on the variation within each group.

For the most general type of long-run planning, namely conceptual and

TABLE A-14

Time Horizons of Enterprise Long-range Plans[a]

Type of Long-range Planning	25 Corporations Total	13 Small Corporations	12 Large Corporations	Significant Difference between Large and Small Corporations
Conceptual and mission goals	5.5 years	5.4 years	5.5 years	No
Specific strategies	3.9	3.3	4.6	Yes
Actual targeting	2.4	1.9	3.0	No

a. These data come from the Swarthmore Corporate Planning Project.

mission goals, both small and large enterprises appear roughly the same. Similarly, there are no statistically significant differences between small and large enterprises with regard to targeting of particular goals (e.g., sales of particular products, financial goals, goals for manufacturing operations, etc.). Only for specific strategies do large corporations have significantly larger time horizons.

Thus the conventional wisdom about enterprise size and time horizons of planning does not appear validated. If these long-run plans are more than mere slips of paper and if they are based on appraisals of the future that permit effective decision-making, then centralization in this regard does not appear to be related to enterprise size.

APPENDIX A-18

Property and Alienation[1] (for Chapter IX, Part C)

The concept of "alienation" appears in discourse about man in society on four different levels which, for convenience, I label the ontological, ethical, psychological, and economic. The ontological aspect concerns the essence of

1. Aside from the primary sources cited below, I especially benefited from reading the following secondary sources: Shlomo Avineri [B15]; Daniel Bell, "The Debate on Alienation," in [B145, pp. 195–211]; Bert F. Hoselitz, "Karl Marx on Secular and Social Development," [P12, VI, Jan./1964, pp. 142–63], and P. C. Roberts [B219].

man and the role of alienation as an essential element of man's activity.[2] The ethical aspect of the concept deals with the difference between man as he ought to be and man as he is in present society.[3] The psychological aspect concerns the feelings of powerlessness, meaninglessness, normlessness (anonomie), estrangement from society, and self-estrangement that are experienced by men.[4] The economic aspects of alienation are those concrete conditions or institutions in society that are manifestations of alienation or that bring about alienations in the ontological, ethical, or psychological meaning of the term; the economic aspects are, as it were, bridges between the "real world" and the other definitions of the term. Alleged manifestations of alienation include the production of goods for sale on the market ("commodity production"), the existence of property income, the division of labor, the powerlessness of a worker to determine the conditions of his work, the fetishism of commodities, and the presence of competition rather than cooperation between men.[5]

In order to explore the relationship between property and alienation I would like to examine the relationship between property and these alleged manifestations of alienation. From such an analysis we can also see relationships between alienation on an economic level and the ontological, ethical, and psychological approaches. In order to organize discussion, I examine below the influence of economic development on the various economic manifestations of alienation, then turn to more concrete relationships of the structure of property and alienation, and end with a brief discussion of alienation and the coordination mechanism of society.

2. Hegel, who popularized but did not invent the concept, argued that the Idea realizes itself (develops consciousness of its essence) by alienating its content and returning from that alienation. With regard to man, Hegel noted that through activity man creates something that is outside of himself; this alienation of man from man results in development because by such activity and by using the results of this activity for particular purposes, man defines and realizes himself as a human being, so that generic and historic man come closer together. Thus alienation is part of man's being and, at the same time, is the tool by which man develops himself.

3. The ethical meaning of alienation and a relatively clear-cut view about what man should be is contained in the writings of Erich Fromm (e.g., "Marx's Concept of Man," in [B86, pp. 1–87] which, it must be added, seems to be more about Fromm's own ideas than Marx's).

4. This is the classification of Melvin Seeman, "On the Meaning of Alienation," [P6, XXIV, Dec./1959, pp. 783–91]. He also has some interesting empirical work showing that these various psychological dimensions are not well correlated with each other or with certain consequences with regard to action that have been predicted from them; one such study of his is "On the Personal Consequence of Alienation in Work," [P6, XXXII, April/1967, pp. 273–86].

5. These manifestations were drawn from Karl Marx and Friedrich Engels, [B178]; Karl Marx, [B175]; and other early writings. Avineri [B15] presents an interesting argument of the way in which these early ideas about alienation are brought back in a different form into Marx's later writings such as *Capital*.

It can be argued that only one of these five manifestations of alienation is the true Marxist meaning of the term; for instance, Roberts [B219] claims that it is "commodity production." Rather than enter a debate on "what Marx really said," I choose below to examine all of these alleged manifestations in order to explore the relationships between alienation and property.

(1) The level of economic development has a strong influence on property relations[6] and, in addition, can influence directly the abovementioned economic manifestations of alienation in a number of ways. On the one hand, the higher the level of development, the less man is at the mercies of nature (the realm of necessity) and the more man is able to manipulate his physical environment for his own purposes (the realm of freedom): In this regard powerlessness is reduced. On the other hand, accompanying a rising level of development (at least up to the present time) is an increasing division of labor and a rise of the wage system.[7]

With regard to the increasing division of labor, work can become meaningless as the number of different products which a single man produces is reduced; as the degree to which he works on a whole product, rather than a part, decreases; and as the number of stages of production in which he participates becomes smaller.[8] In addition, the division of labor results in a splintering of man's perception of reality by giving him only a partial view of the social process; moreover, man develops only partial interests, i.e., interests in particular parts of the social process, rather than the process as a whole. Marx extended the argument one more step: Through such mechanisms the division of labor seems to gain an independent life of its own that stands over and above the lives of the individuals who compose it.[9] It should be clear that because of adverse psychological effects, too great a division of labor may lower productivity, rather than increase it, as American businessmen are beginning to find out. It has been argued that the adverse effects stemming from an extensive division of labor might be modified in three quite different ways: carrying out particular social engineering measures to give the worker a greater sense of the entire social-economic process and his place in it; sacrificing a certain degree of productivity in order to reduce the division of labor; and developing new technologies in order to reduce the division of labor. The feasibility and efficiency of any of these measures is open to considerable debate.

6. A number of these relationships are explored empirically by Frederic L. Pryor, "Property Rights and Economic Development," [P16, XX, April/1972].

7. In both [B179] and [B175] Marx viewed the division of labor and the wage system as aspects of the property system.

8. This approach is adopted as the basis of an empirical sociological examination of alienation in four industries in a brilliant book by Robert Blauner [B36].

9. One forceful exposition of this position is given by Marx and Engels, [B179, pp. 44–5] who argued: ". . . further, the division of labor implies the contradiction between the interests of the separate individual or the individual family and the communal interest of all individuals who have intercourse with one another. And indeed, this communal interest does not exist merely in the imagination, as the "general interest," but first of all in reality, as the mutual interdependence of the individuals among whom the labor is divided. And finally, the division of labor offers us the first example of how, as long as man remains in natural society, that is, as long as a cleavage exists between the particular and the common interest, as long, therefore, as activity is not voluntarily, but naturally, divided, man's own deed becomes an alien power opposed to him, which enslaves him instead of being controlled by him. For as soon as the distribution of labour comes into being, each man has a particular, exclusive sphere of activity, which is forced upon him and from which he cannot escape."

The development of the wage system is alleged to encourage competition rather than cooperation between workers. Further, by putting a price on man, Marx argued that man is reduced to the role of a commodity and, hence, is treated as a means, rather than an end.

(2) The structure of property rights can also be a source of alienation. One facet is, of course, ownership: the worker owns neither the product he helps to make nor the means of production with which he works in such economic systems as capitalism. But, in a very real sense, such an ownership situation is also the case in Eastern European nations as well, where the worker gets no share of the profits (except in Yugoslavia) and feels that he has no *direct* ownership stake in either the means of production or the actual product. One measure that could be used in both capitalist and socialist economies to reduce this form of alienation is profitsharing schemes.

A second facet relates to the ability of a worker or employee to influence the general policies guiding the productive unit in which he is employed. Part of this problem stems from the massive scale on which production is now carried out: the voice of a single worker in an enterprise of 20,000 is scarcely audible.[10] Another part stems from the hierarchical organization of property rights within an organization[11] which can not, in any real sense, be relieved by a labor union that negotiates with the management but which is also too large for a worker's voice to be heard.

A final facet of the relationship between the structure of property and alienation refers to the ability of the worker to influence his immediate environment of work and his own work schedule, e.g., the pace of his work, the freedom of his physical movement, the use of his varied skills, and so forth. Part of this is a function of the technology of the industry in which the worker is engaged and alienation stemming from this factor differs greatly between printers (craft work), textile workers (machine-tending technology), auto workers (assembly line technology) or chemical workers (continuous process technology).[12] And another part of this problem stems from the organization and supervision of work, especially with regard to hierarchical and other types of centralization that may differ greatly among enterprises.

(3) The coordination mechanisms of the society are a third and final major source of the manifestations of alienation. This can be viewed from the political-economic level, e.g., competition rather than cooperation between citizens is stressed.[13] This can also be seen in more traditional economic

10. The effects of sheer organizational size on performance in a number of different types of organizations is explored empirically in several studies and summarized by R. W. Rivans, "Industrial Morale and Size of Unit," [B89a, pp. 295–301].

11. An empirical investigation of this is carried out by Michael Aiken and Jerald Hage, "Organizational Alienation: A Comparative Analysis," [P6, XXXI, Aug./1966, pp. 497–507].

12. Blauner [B36].

13. Marx argued in his essay "Zur Judenfrage," [B180, Vol. 1, p. 370] in the following manner: "The political emancipation is changing man, on the one side, from being a member of bourgeoise society, from the egoistic, privatized individual; on the other side, from being a citizen, from being merely a law-abiding person. Only when the actual individual recovers the abstract citizen from himself and as an individual man becomes a member of the human species in his daily life, in his individual work, and in his individual relationships, only when man recognizes and organizes his own strengths

terms, e.g., of a market mechanism standing over and above individuals such that all social relations are reified; money appears to represent all values;[14] and man is forced to prostitute himself for his daily bread.[15] In addition, Marx argued that the market rules man in another way: the worker is driven to work that he hates by the whip of hunger while the capitalist is driven to accumulate in order to maintain his position; in both cases human potential (defined ethically) is not realized. It should be clear that nonmarket coordination mechanisms can also lead to similar types of alienation. Man can also be reduced to the role of things or means in bureaucratic coordination processes, and bureaucratic powers and privileges can represent as insidious a reduction of human values as money. In addition, competition and strife are not necessarily ruled out in such nonmarket cases: merely the arena for such activity is changed.

From such a catalogue of forces underlying the manifestations of alienation, three major problems of scientific analysis arise:

First, the ontological and ethical conceptions of alienation are really beyond the sphere of scientific enquiry. The only empirical questions that can really be answered are: Do such alleged manifestations of alienation really exist? What are the relationships between these manifestations and various psychological dimensions of alienation? And finally, what are the relationships between these manifestations of alienation and particular behavior? Answering the first question requires, among other things, a careful analysis of the structure of property rights. Answering the second question is more difficult, but can be accomplished in part by various sample survey techniques.[16] The third question, which is the most crucial in terms of where the economic system is heading, is most difficult to answer and relatively few empirical studies have focused on such issues.[17]

Second, to what extent can the various negative aspects of alienation be modified? A number of extreme positions have been taken on this issue. Classical Marxists assert that alleviation is impossible until the era of general material abundance and the initiation of communism. Others have argued that minimization is hardly possible because there is an inevitable conflict between instinct and civilization, or creativity and social institutions, the

as social forces so that such social forces are no longer separated from political forces, only then has human emancipation been achieved."

14. In his "Power of Money in Bourgeois Society," [B175] Marx declared money to be the "pimp between man's needs and the object of those needs."

15. The great many sexual images regarding alienation lead Lewis Feuer ("What is Alienation? The Career of a Concept," in [B239, pp. 127–48]) to the idea that Marx's earliest meaning of alienation was primarily sexual and to be considered part of Marx's love lyrics of his student days and other juvenilia; Feuer presents abundant textual evidence to support this strange position.

16. Studies using such techniques include Aiken and Hage; Blauner; and Seeman, "On the Personal Consequences . . . ."

17. One interesting attempt in this direction is by Clark Kerr and Abraham Siegel, "The Interindustry Propensity to Strike — An International Comparison," in [B135], in which alienation-inducing aspects of work are used as determinants of strike action. Unfortunately, the analysis is a little *post hoc*. Another attempt is by Seeman, "On the Personal Consequences . . . ."

resultant of which is inevitably alienation.[18] The scientific issues underlying the original question turn on the economic, political, and social determinants of a high income economy; or, more specifically, the degree to which a high level of economic development is necessarily dependent on particular structures of property, motivation and goals, and information.

A third and final problem deals with the role of ideology. Given a particular economic system, one important aspect concerning the degree to which psychological alienation may be present is the ideology of the person involved. In other words, alienation depends partly on a person's perception of the society. For instance, a worker may view the labor market as a manifestation of freedom in that he can change his job at any time, his choice of work is not dictated by personal dependence on one particular person (which, for instance, is not the case in the army where a person can not easily quit) and the possible choices open to him are almost limitless. On the other hand, another worker may feel that the labor market is demeaning to him as an individual and that he is little better than a prostitute selling her body. Depending on particular ideological positions, psychological dimensions of alienation may be very differently affected by the same "concrete manifestation of alienation."

APPENDIX A-19

Property and Ideology (for Chapter IX, Part C)

In order to analyze certain important relations between ideology and property, it is necessary first to distinguish the three most important ways in which "ideology" is defined: a basic world view or framework of analysis; a set of values with which to evaluate societal events; and an intellectual system derived within the basic world view and incorporating the set of values so as to lead to a semicoherent set of opinions on which to base action. Each of these meanings deserves brief discussion.

Ideology as a basic world view seems to coincide with Mannheim's definition of a "total conception of ideology."[1] Such a world view includes our categories of thought, the ways we view societal causation, our perceptions of what men and society really "are," our basic feelings about the purposiveness of history, our conception of the world as a unity or not, and

---

18. The instinct versus civilization view is argued forcefully by Sigmund Freud [B85] and has been carried forward by psychoanalysts ever since. The creativity versus social institutions seems to be standard fare for most of mainstream American sociology.

1. Karl Mannheim, [B165, Chapter 2]. Others have referred to ideology as political discourse on its most general, formative level — which seems to be roughly the same thing.

so forth. That is to say, our world view defines the mental framework in which we place the various factors of our existence and the basic processes by which we analyze such facts. In order to show more concretely what I mean, I present in Table A-15 five examples of such basic world views, and the implication of these views for understanding the direction and manner in which change occurs, the role of leaders and of politics, and the place of property rights in the functioning of the system. It must be added that many holding particular world views may have little explicit consciousness of these views, even though they may make judgments on the basis of these world views every day.

Ideology as a set of values with which an individual judges societal events is a second meaning of the concept. For instance, most people have relatively explicit values with which they judge the legitimacy of certain types of property rights. A utopia is the projection of such values into an ideal society and is, primarily, an ethical construct.

Ideology as an intellectual system created within the basic world view and incorporating certain explicit values to arrive at certain conclusions about society is a third perception of the concept. This definition seems to be that used by Daniel Bell, who noted "What the priest is to religion, the intellectual is to ideology."[2] Or what Raymond Aron referred to as the "pseudo-systematic formulation of a total vision of the historical world."[3] This intellectual system, which can be sufficiently embracing to include a philosophy of history, a theory of man's role in the present, an image of the future, and propositions about how to change the present in the "proper" direction can be used for a number of purposes; its propagandistic role to persuade people to follow a particular course of action may have led to the pejorative connotations of the term.

From this threefold way at looking at ideology, a number of propositions and implications can be drawn, of which several of particular importance to property are listed below.

First, ideologies at all three levels do not necessarily need to be based on verified facts or empirically determined norms and, indeed, part of the strength of particular ideologies may depend on the fact that they can't be empirically verified. Underlying certain ideologies may be particular ethical or metaphysical perceptions that act to filter "facts" and "events" so as to arrive at quite different views than others. For example, different individuals may have quite different views with regard to the impact of a particular dimension of centralization which, although systematic, have little basis in actual empirical results. That is, on the basis of our basic world view, our values, and our intellectual constructions, we can and do make empirical judgments about particular phenomena that are not derived from evaluation of any particular facts on the matter but that serve as a basis of action anyway.

Second, social scientific and ideological thought do *not* differ in that values enter the latter, but not the former; for, in truth, values enter in both. The critical distinction revolves on the manner in which values enter. In both, values enter in the perception and selection of "facts" with which to support particular arguments. But the standards for validation of arguments is quite

2. Daniel Bell, "The End of Ideology in the West," in Chaim Waxman, ed., [B263, p. 82].
3. Aron, cited by Chaim Waxman, "Introduction," in [B263, p. 3].

TABLE [A.1]

Examples of World Views[a]

	Basic Metaphor of Society	Direction and Way in Which Change Occurs	Role of Leader and Politics	Place of Property Rights
Feudal	Society as a hierarchy or body with lower and higher parts.	Little change, but that which occurs directed by the spirit of the people following natural laws of growth.	Leader guides societal processes and change by means of long experience and knowledge of spirit and traditions.	Property rights held on the basis of fulfilling reciprocal obligations. Property rights hierarchically controlled.
Administrative (managerial, technocratic)	Society as an organization responding to central direction.	Change occurs through direction of managers; politics subordinated to administration.	Leader is chief administrator and social engineer, assuring order through drawing up of plans and decrees.	Property rights restricted by laws and administrative measures, which can be changed by administrators according to the public interest.
Liberal	Society as the resolution of competing forces.	Change occurs through change in competing forces which brings about new equilibrium.	Leader enforces rules of competition. Parliament arrives at most effective policies through rational debate. (Ideas of market-place).	Minimal public infringement on property rights, except to set up rules of game.
Marxist	Society as a dialectic process within an historical context.	Change occurs through contradiction of production forces and production relations.	Leader is agent of dominant class which, when historical conditions are appropriate is overthrown.	Property rights are dependent on development of productive forces and change as society changes.
Fascist	Society as the result of deeds performed by an elite.	Change occurs through a change in will and consequent noble deeds.	Leadership is exercised through carrying out of acts and deeds and must, for this reason, be venerated and followed.	Property rights are maintained only by these strong enough to fight for them and win.

a. This table was drawn from the discussion of Mannheim, [B165, Chapter 3]; nevertheless, I have made a number of additions and changes.

different.[4] Or to put the matter differently, social science is an ideology that specifies certain empirical methods of validation and certain ways in which discourse may be carried on which, in particular cases, has had considerable success (measured according to its own criteria).

Third, the particular belief that "ideology is dead" or that "liberal civilization begins only when the age of ideology is over"[5] misses the point that all individuals have ideology in all three senses of the word and that the lack of ideological conflict is not necessarily good. Although such conflict could cease to occur because everyone is happy and in agreement on all matters, it could also cease because such conflict is politically smothered by the government or society. On the other hand, ideological conflict may serve an extremely useful function, for ideological conflict can arise with an increase in doubt, stemming from rapid and disorienting changes in society or from the discovery of new facts that require new ways of thinking to bring theory and practice in closer congruence. Similarly, ideological conflict arises when the aspirations of particular groups are not realized and such conflict can arise in a variety of other circumstances and is harmful to society only if there are no ways — short of extreme bloodshed — to resolve them or when the positions argued are pursued with sufficient intolerance that no compromise is possible.

Turning now to ideological disputes about property, we must separate conflicts over different aspects of property. In previous eras ownership of the means of production was the most controversial aspect of the debate, but other aspects are increasingly reaching the arena of public discussion.

With regard to ownership of the means of production, the controversy seems to have declined. In the United States, none but extremely small parties with little following call for a major change. In Western Europe, certain

4. This is argued nicely by Stephen Rousseas and James Farganis, "American Politics and the End of Ideology," in Waxman, p. 218, in the following manner:

The hope or the belief, that the end of the ideological case of mind will permit us to view the real world uncolored by any value judgments is nothing but the delusion of an unsophisticated positivism; which is, in essence, a flight from moral responsibility. For facts are themselves the product of our viewing "reality" through our theoretical preconceptions which, in turn, are conditioned by the problems confronting us. And the theoretical precepts which determine the relative facts of a particular view of "reality" are not themselves entirely value free. Social theories, in short, are the result of our concern with specific problems. And social problems, at bottom, are concerned with ethical goals. Social theorists, furthermore, differ in their value judgments and thus differ in theoretical constructions of "reality." They differ, that is, in the problems they see, or, what amounts to the same thing, they see a given problem in different ways. Consequently, they differ as to the facts relevant to a given problem. There is, in other words, a selectivity of facts in the analysis of social problems. Some facts included in one approach are excluded in another, and even those held in common may, and usually do, differ in the weight given to them and in their theoretical and causal interrelations.

5. Lewis Feuer, "Beyond Ideology," in [B263, p. 66]. Clifford Geertz once noted, "We may wait as long for the 'end of ideology' as the positivists have waited for the end of religion." (Cited by Joseph LaPalombara, "Decline of Ideology: A Dissent and an Interpretation," in Waxman, [B263, p. 341].)

socialist parties have become disenchanted with public ownership as a party goal (e.g., the British Labour Party),[6] some have disavowed it explicitly as a plank in their party platform (e.g., the West German Social Democratic Party), and others have softpedaled the issue (e.g., the Italian Communist Party).[7] The issue has, therefore, been backed primarily by political parties on the extreme left of the political spectrum. As noted in Chapter II, nationalization has not greatly moved forward in Western Europe after the first few years following the end of the war. Certain reasons may be adduced for the decline of interest in ownership as a political goal, of which the two most important are the rapid rise in real income of all families and the gradual equalization of income during the process.

Ideological disputes concerning other aspects of property such as the proper degree of centralization along various dimensions are much more difficult to discuss, in part because such matters have received relatively little attention except when framed in highly misleading terms (e.g., the "market" versus "planning") or except in very specific circumstances. Several aspects of such discussion deserves particular attention.

First, much of the terminology of such discussion is ambiguous, with constant switching from one dimension of centralization to another without much explicit awareness that this is occurring.

Second, as shown in Chapter VIII, we have relatively little "hard" social science evidence on either the determinants or the impact of various types of centralization. Although this state of affairs should make the subject ripe for more ideological debate, where empirical evidence is not so important, the various questions have not been framed with sufficient precision to permit this type of discussion either. Much of the hard won evidence on the question of centralization has come in the course of making business decisions and is not readily transferable because of the particular natures of special cases.

Third, until the debate about centralization reaches public attention in the form of the "distribution of power" with particular alternatives to the present situation clearly outlined, little change should be forthcoming. That is, in the West people seem to accept the centralization of property with an astoundingly fatalistic attitude, considering such matters to be beyond human intervention.

6. C. A. R. Crosland, [B61].
7. LaPalambara in [B263].

Statistical Notes

APPENDIX B-1

Calculation of Per Capita Gross National Products in a Common Currency (for all Chapters)

The basis of the calculations used throughout the text is a set of estimates made for the mid 1950's in which all goods and services produced in particular nations were valued in terms of corresponding goods and services in the United States. In cases where this could not be done, a rougher estimation procedure was carried out. Full details are contained in [P19, July/1966] and [B214, Appendix B-3].

These results were updated for the different years contained in the tables by multiplying the dollar value by the change in per capita G.N.P. as measured by constant price estimate in the particular national currency.

APPENDIX B-2

Sources and Methods for the Nationalization Estimates (for Chapters I and II)

1. Austria: These estimates were made by Dr. Anton Kausel of the Oesterreichisches Institut fuer Wirtschaftsforschung, to whom I would like to express my appreciation. Publicly owned industry includes enterprises owned by the nationalized banks. The ratios are calculated on G.N.P. data, rather than labor force data. Another set of estimates using G.N.P. data can be found in [P29, Oct./1964].

2. Bulgaria: The basic data come from [G8]. The armed forces are not included.

3. East Germany: The basic data come from [G25]. The half-state enterprises are included as part of the public sector. Manufacturing includes industrial handicrafts. A rough estimate was made of economically active in the "security sector" (uranium mines, police, army and other military units) and are included at appropriate places.

4. Finland: The basic data come from [G18, 9/1966, p. 63]; [G19, 1965]; and data submitted by the Central Statistical Office. For Table 3–1, labor value-added, rather than labor force, form the basis for calculating the nationalization ratios.

5. France: The data come from [G21, various issues] and [G22]. For the sectoral ratios in Table 3–1, a number of estimates had to be made pri-

marily in transportation and communication on the basis of incomplete information. 1954 establishment data were used as the numerators of the ratios for the sectors, but the denominators were derived from more complete data on the economically active accordingly to slightly different definitions. For the branch ratios in Table 3–2, establishment data were used for both sides of the fraction.

6. Greece: The data come from [G29] plus information supplied on public enterprises by the Ethnike Statistike Hyperesia.

7. Hungary: The data come from [G32, 1966].

8. Israel: For the economic sectors the data come from [B77]. The army was estimated at 57,000. The calculations for the service and for the commerce and finance sectors are rough estimates made by disaggregating a combined class and then adding in the estimate for the army. For the branches in manufacturing and mining, the data come from [G38].

9. Japan: The basic data come from [G43, 1964]. For the sector estimates the military are excluded but the resulting incomparability with the rest of the nations should be small. For the public sector neither of the two series presented in the yearbook is complete and, therefore, the larger number was chosen in each case. For the branch ratios, establishment data were used exclusively.

10. Norway: The data for Table 3–2 come from [G50] and unpublished information on publicly owned establishments supplied by the Statistical Bureau. For several branches certain small estimates had to be made. For Table A-4, the data come from [G49], which, however, understates economically active population by about 6 percent so that the ratios are slightly overstated.

11. Poland: The basic data come from [G56, 1962] and [B212]. Manufacturing includes industrial handicrafts.

12. Sweden: The basic data come from [G66, various years] and [G70]. To census data on economically active in various public establishments were added employees of corporations that were 50 percent or more owned by the government. These corporations were classified according to sector and branch from their products listed in [G70].

13. Soviet Union: The basic data come from census materials reproduced in [G94, pp. 44–61] and, for commerce, were supplemented by data from [B93]. In using the 1959 census, certain difficulties arose. Industry, construction, transportation, and communication are not broken down and are 13.8 percent higher than employment reported in the yearly series; therefore, the yearly data for each of these categories was adjusted upward by this percentage. Collective farmers not engaged in agriculture were assigned to manufacturing and considered as employed by cooperatives. Artisans were assigned to services. Personnel in cooperative trade were estimated from turnover data on various types of trade.

14. Switzerland: The data come from materials supplied by the Eidgenössisches Statistisches Amt.

15. United Kingdom: Data on labor force come from [P20, 11/1960]; data on economically active in the public sector come from materials supplied by the Central Statistical Office.

16. United States: The data come from [G87, Vol. 1, Part 1, Table 1–214].

17. West Germany: The data come from [G26, Nos. 23, 27, 44, 45, and 55] and [G27, 1954]. The data on the public sector omit the Volkswagen

Werke (which was technically owned by no one) and may also incompletely cover other wholly owned corporations as well.

18. Yugoslavia: The basic data come from [G107] and [G108, 1955] and are believed to exclude military forces.

APPENDIX B-3

Estimation of Capital/Labor Ratios
(for Chapters II and VI)

Deriving the rank order of capital/labor ratios in various branches of manufacturing and mining presents difficulties both in regard to theory and to appropriate data.

On the theoretical side a number of economists have demonstrated that if the elasticities of substitution between labor and capital are different from unity, then capital/labor ratios may differ according to the ratio of the rate of interest to the wage of labor so that an industry that is more capital intensive *vis-à-vis* another at a particular ratio of factor return may be less capital intensive at a different ratio (on this matter see [B188]). This difficulty did not prove of great importance, however, for the pattern of relative capital intensity is quite similar in all countries, i.e., very high coefficients of concordance were obtained for all three measures of capital intensity.

On the empirical side it was difficult to obtain comparable data on the capital stock for various countries with which to make the calculations and data for only six capitalist and six socialist nations could be located. Further, definitions of the capital stock differed considerably. Although I tried to obtain data on the gross value (value excluding depreciation) of fixed capital (i.e., building and equipment), the data for certain nations included land and for other nations the handling of depreciation was obscure. For most of the socialist countries the data also only covered the nationalized enterprises and large cooperatives and excluded handicraft and private productive units. In spite of these differences the pattern of capital/labor ratios was quite similar among the various nations and the results for the capitalist and socialist nations separately were highly correlated.

Nevertheless, it appeared worthwhile to derive several alternative measures to see how much the pattern of relative capital intensity varied when different measurements were used. The results are persented in Table B-1.

The three measures present a very similar pattern: the Kendall rank order correlation coefficient between the ranks of the capital/labor ratios and the energy and electricity measure are both .73; and the correlation coefficient between the ranks of the latter two measures of capital intensity is .82. We can, therefore, put some reliance on any of the three measurements; since the capital/labor ratio is the most direct measure of capital intensity, it is used in the text.

TABLE B-1

*Rank Orders of Capital Intensity of Different Branches
in Mining and Manufacturing*

ISIC Number	Branch of Industry	Capital/ Labor Ratio	Energy Con- sumed per Worker and Employee	Electricity Consumed per Worker and Employee
32	Petroleum and coal products	1	1	2
27	Paper and paper products	2	5	4
34	Primary metals	3	2	3
31	Chemicals	4	4	1
10–9	Mining and quarrying	5	6	6
21	Beverages	6	7	8
33	Stone, glass, clay products	7	3	5
30	Rubber products	8	9	7
20	Food processing	9	8	9
22	Tobacco products	10	16	18
23	Textiles	11	10	10
35	Metal products except machinery	12	12	13
38	Transport equipment	13	13	12
28	Printing and publ.	14	20	20
36	Machinery except electrical, transport	15	15	14.5
39	Miscellaneous	16	17	16
37	Electrical goods and machinery	17	18	14.5
25	Lumber products except furniture	18	14	11
29	Leather products except footwear	19	11	17
26	Furniture	20	19	19
24	Clothing and footwear	21	21	21
	Number of nations in sample	12	17	21
	Coefficient of concordance	.7876	.7909	.7686

(All are statistically significant at .05 level.)

A. Sources for Capital/Labor Ratios

Australia: [G3].
Bulgaria: [G7, 1966].
Czechoslovakia: [G12, 1966].
East Germany: [G25, 1967].
Hungary: [G32, 1965].
Japan: [G44].
New Zealand: [G48].
Poland: [G56, 1967].
Portugal: [G59].
South Africa: [G61].
United States: The estimate was made from data from [G106, 1963] and [G104] for fourth quarter 1963.

Soviet Union: The basic data come from [B255]. This was supplemented by data from Treml, "The 1959 Soviet Input-Output Table Reconstructed," in [G97]; [G95]; and [G75, 1960 and 1961].

B. Sources for Other Data

The data on energy and electricity per worker and employee come from [G79], supplemented for Yugoslavia by [G108].

APPENDIX B-4

Measurement of Enterprise Capital Requirements in Mining and Manufacturing (for Chapter II)

Data on the capital requirements of average size enterprise for various branches of manufacturing and mining are not available, but estimates can be made. The data used in the text were derived from the following simple three-step procedure.

Data on the rank order of enterprise size as measured by the number of workers and employees were obtained from Appendix B-19; depending on how the average is calculated, there are several slightly different rank orderings. Second, the rank order of the capital/labor ratios in the various branches were taken from Table B-1. Finally, the two sets of rank orders were multiplied and new ranks were calculated from the products, a procedure that is based on the identity: average labor force in enterprise times capital per worker equals capital stock in enterprise. Although multiplying ranks has certain disadvantages, the results should serve as a useful first approximation. Relevant data are given in Table B-2 for three different measures of average size; it is noteworthy that the series are very similar and that it makes little difference which series is taken for the calculation in Appendix B-6.

TABLE B-2

Rank Orders of Capital Requirements for Average Size Enterprises[a]

ISIC Number	Branch of Industry	Capital Requirements using Various Measures of Size		
		Arithmetic Average	*Entropy Index*	*Niehans Index*
10–9	Mining and quarrying	6.5	6	6
20	Food processing	13	13	13
21	Beverages	8.5	10	11
22	Tobacco products	4.5	4.0	7

23	Textiles	11	11	12
24	Clothing and footwear	20	20	19
25	Lumber products	18	18	18
26	Furniture	21	21	21
27	Paper and paper products	4.5	4.0	4
28	Printing and publishing	16	16	16
29	Leather products except shoes	19	19	20
30	Rubber products	6.5	8	9
31	Chemicals	3	4.0	3
32	Petroleum and coal products	1	2	2
33	Stone, glass, clay products	8.5	9	10
34	Primary metals	2	1	1
35	Metal products except machinery	5	15	15
36	Machinery except electrical, transport	4	14	14
37	Electrical goods and machinery	2	12	8
38	Transport equipment	0	7	5
39	Miscellaneous products	7	17	17

a. A decimal in the rank ordering indicates a tie. For further calculations, the capital requirements using the arithmetic average of employee size are used.

APPENDIX B-5

Correlation Matrix for the Independent Variables for the Nationalization Tests (for Chapter II)

TABLE B-3

Correlation Matrix for Independent Variables for the Nationalization Tests (Kendall coefficients)

Variables	1	2	3	4	5	6
6 Volume of branch sales to all industries						1.00*
5 Volume of branch sales to government					1.00*	.24
4 Weighted four-digit concentration ratios				1.00*	.46*	.12
3 Percentage of branch sales to government			1.00*	.36*	.74*	.07
2 Workers and employees in average size enterprise		1.00*	.05	.54*	.14	.35*
1 Fixed capital in average size enterprise	1.00*	.75*	—.08	.42*	.04	.38*

An asterisk denotes statistical significance at the .05 level.

APPENDIX B-6
Measurements for the Nationalization Tests (for Chapter II)

TABLE B-4
Rank Orders of Industrial Branches According to Five Criteria

ISIC Number	Branch of Industry	Share of Production in Branch Bought by:		Value of Branch Prod. Bought by Gov't.	Value of Branch Products Used as Intermediate Goods	
		Gov't. Sector	Gov't. Sector + Utilities Trans. and Commun.		Absolute Amount	Share of Prod. Total Branch − Exports
10–9	Mining and quarrying	11	1	9	3	2
20	Food processing	17	17	11	5	17
21	Beverages	20	19	19.5	18	18
22	Tobacco	21	21	21	21	21
23	Textiles	18	18	17	4	9
24	Clothing and footwear	13	11.5	13	19	19
25	Lumber products expt furn.	19	20	19.5	13	1
26	Furniture	7	9	10	20	20
27	Paper products	12	11.5	12	8	4
28	Printing	2	3	6	14	12
29	Leather products except shoes	15	16	18	17	11
30	Rubber products	10	5.5	16	15	8

31	Chemicals	9	10	4	2	6
32	Petroleum and coal products	3	14	3	7	7
33	Stone, glass, clay products	14	13	14	10	5
34	Primary metal	16	15	15	1	3
35	Metal products	8	8	7	6	10
36	Machines except electrical, transport	5	5.5	2	9	14
37	Electrical goods and machinery	6	4	5	12	13
38	Transport equipment	1	2	1	11	15
39	Miscellaneous	4	7	8	16	16
	Number of countries in calculation	6	6	6	8	7
	Coefficient of concordance	.68	.66	.67	.74	.48
	(all statistically significant at .05 level)					

These data were derived from input-output tables for the following eight nations:
Belgium, France, West Germany, Italy, and Netherlands: [G16] for the years 1959 and 1960 (West Germany only).
Japan: [G43, 1966, pp. 478–83] for the year 1963.
United Kingdom: [G77] for the year 1954.
United States: [P65, XLIV, Sept./1965, pp. 33–9] for the year 1958.

APPENDIX B-7

Experiments in Correlation with "Heavy" and "Light" Industry (for Chapter II)

TABLE B-5

*Rank Orders of "Heaviness Ratings" and Other Variables
and Important Correlations*

ISIC Number	Branch of Industry	"Heaviness Ratings"	Degree of U.S. Unioniza-tion 1958	Relative Wages	Degree of National-zation
22	Tobacco products	1	7	15	8
32	Petroleum and coal products	2	2	1	3
31	Chemicals	3	17	3	5
38	Transportation equipment	4	5	4	2
30	Rubber products	5	4	10	17
34	Primary metals	6.5	1	2	4
36	Machinery except electrical, transport	6.5	12	5	6
37	Electrical goods and machinery	8	11	9	10
10–9	Mining and quarrying	9	8	6	1
33	Stone, glass, clay products	10	3	13	9
27	Paper and paper products	11	6	8	13
28	Printing and publishing	12	16	7	7
39	Miscellaneous industries	13	20	14	18
20	Food processing	15.0	13.5	16	12
23	Textiles	15.0	21	20	14
35	Metal products	15.0	9	12	16
21	Beverages	17	13.5	11	11
29	Leather goods except shoes	18	15	19	21
24	Clothing and footwear	19	10	21	20
25	Lumber products except furniture	20	18.5	18	15
26	Furniture	21	18.5	17	19

Correlations between "Heaviness Ratings" and Other Variables

Variable	Kendall Rank Order Correlation Coefficient
Degree of United States unionization, 1958	.43*
Relative wages	.58*
Degree of nationalization	.53*
Capital/labor ratio	.41*

An asterisk designates statistical significance at the .05 level.

Sources and Methods

The "heavy-light ratings" were calculated as a weighted average of rank of number of workers and employees in an average size enterprise (arithmetic average), rank of amount of capital in an average size enterprise, and rank of average degree of monopoly. The first two variables received weights of 1; the third variable received a weight of 2. The rankings come from Appendices B-19, B-4, and B-26. Since no estimate of the average concentration ratios in mining and quarrying was available, it was assumed that this ratio was the same as in the stone, glass, and clay branch of manufacturing.

The data on the relative degree of unionization come from [B152], Chapter VII. For certain branches the average degree of unionization was estimated by calculating weighted averages of the individual subbranches; for mining and quarrying, the degree of unionization in 1953 was used, and for beverages and food processing, the relative degree of unionization for each branch was considered equal to the combined total of these two branches.

Relative wage data come from Chapter III.

Data on relative degree of nationalization come from Chapter II.

Other Notes

The relative wages derived from a sample of nineteen Western nations is much more highly correlated with relative wages in the United States (Kendall coefficient = .86) than the relative degree of unionization in the United States in the various manufacturing and mining branches (Kendall coefficient = .39). This suggests that economic factors related to the various industries (e.g., average level of skills, degree to which female labor can be utilized, and so forth) are more important determinants of relative industrial wages than relative unionization.

APPENDIX B-8

Average Wages and Salaries in Different Branches of Mining and Manufacturing (for Chapters II and III)

The various computations contained in Table 3–3 and the regression on wage dispersion are quite insensitive to the exact definition of average wages. For instance, quite similar results are obtained if average wages of operatives, rather than all workers and employees, are used.

In the regression explaining wage dispersion omitting or including the United States makes little difference to the results. The regression is calculation with a transformation into natural logarithms to minimize the effect of extreme points.

Sources and Comments

The data for the Western nations come from [G79] and were obtained by dividing the total wages and salaries by the number of workers and employees. For some nations years on either side of 1963 were used.

For Bulgaria the data come from [G7, 1967] and cover only state industries (i.e., cooperatives are excluded) in 1965.

For Czechoslovakia the data come from [G12, 1966] and cover only blue-collar workers in 1965.

For East Germany the data come from [G25, 1967] and cover workers and employees only in the socialist sector in 1965.

For Hungary the data come from [G79] and are for 1964.

For Poland the data come from [G57] and are for 1956.

For the Soviet Union the data are for 1959 and come from [B255], supplemented by sources listed in Appendix B-3. The basic source of data presents a similar picture to that in [B129]: data in the former source are in considerably greater branch detail while the latter source focuses primarily on wage patterns over time.

For Yugoslavia the data come from [G108] and are for 1963.

APPENDIX B-9

Sources and Methods for Calculating Distributions of Labor Earnings (for Chapter III)

The data for Austrialia, Austria, Belgium, Canada, Czechoslovakia, Denmark, Finland, France, West Germany, Hungary, Japan, New Zealand, Poland, Spain, Sweden, the United Kingdom, the United States, and Yugoslavia come from Lydall [B158]. I have omitted the Netherlands because of certain incomparabilities. For Hungary I recalculated the estimates using somewhat different data and obtained almost exactly the same results.

The data for the Soviet Union were estimated in a simple three step manner. Data on blue-collar wages in manufacturing are presented in a graph form by M. Mozhina, "Izmeneniia v raspredelenii promyshlennykh rabochikh SSSR po razmeram zarabotnoi platy," [P10, 10/1961, pp. 18–25]. I took readings of this graph, plotted a cumulative wage curve (using log-probability paper) and obtained almost exactly the same decile and quartile ratios as Mozhina presents (respectively 3.29 and 1.85 for the ratio of wages in the 90th and the 10th deciles; and the ratio of wages in the 75th and 25th decile). (My thanks to Janet Chapman for sending me a copy of this article and other information; a rough copy of the crucial graph is presented in [G83], Chapter 8, p. 40). From another Soviet source ([B217] p. 43), we are told that the ratio of wages and salaries for men and women in the entire economy at the

90th and the 10th deciles is 4.2, in comparison to labor income differentials using the "standard definition." Mozhina data understate the differentials by excluding salaries and also earnings in nonmanufacturing sectors, while the other datum overstates the differentials by including the earnings of women and also wages and salaries in the farm sector (i.e., state farms).

I estimated the labor income distribution by adjusting the curve derived by the Mozhina data so that the ratio of the wages and salaries in the 90th and 10th deciles was 4.2. After the decile readings were obtained, further adjustments were carried out so that the bias caused by a more inclusive coverage was eliminated following Lydall's adjustment procedures.

Data for wages and salaries of all employed workers and employees for Bulgaria and East Germany come respectively from [G7, 1967, p. 70] and [G83, chapter 9, p. 23]. Both of these contain a bias for greater dispersion than the "standard definition" because they include the wages and salaries of women and workers on state farms; therefore, they were adjusted accordingly.

Certain scattered data are also available for Romania [B101, pp. 124–5] and [B245, pp. 290–1] but there are too many uncertainties to allow their use in the table.

In all cases the conversion of the data to the "standard definition" represents only a first approximation and, for this reason, the results in the text are stated in terms of probability.

TABLE B-6

Regression Formulae for Nonagricultural Labor Income Data

	N	R^2
$\ln X_5 = 5.811 + .057^* \ln P - .163^* S - .137^* \ln Y/P$		
$\quad\quad\quad (.019) \quad\quad (.050) \quad\quad (.058)$	21	.55*
$\ln X_{10} = 5.665 + .042^* \ln P - .108^* S - .126^* \ln Y/P$		
$\quad\quad\quad (.014) \quad\quad (.037) \quad\quad (.043)$	21	.56*
$\ln X_{75} = 4.138 - .041^* \ln P + .068^* S + .083^* \ln Y/P$		
$\quad\quad\quad (.009) \quad\quad (.023) \quad\quad (.027)$	21	.67*
$\ln X_{85} = 3.936 - .047^* \ln P + .173^* S + .089 \ln Y/P$		
$\quad\quad\quad (.017) \quad\quad (.043) \quad\quad (.050)$	21	.58*
$\ln X_5 = 6.403 - .153^* S - .141^* \ln Y/P$		
$\quad\quad\quad (.060) \quad\quad (.069)$	21	.32*
$\ln X_{10} = 6.101 - .100^* S - .130^* \ln Y/P$		
$\quad\quad\quad (.044) \quad\quad (.051)$	21	.33*
$\ln X_{75} = 3.717 + .061 S + .086^* \ln Y/P$		
$\quad\quad\quad (.033) \quad\quad (.039)$	21	.26*
$\ln X_{85} = 3.449 + .164^* S + .093 \ln Y/P$		
$\quad\quad\quad (.051) \quad\quad (.059)$	21	.38*

where:

$\ln$ = natural logarithm;

X = wages and salaries in a specified percentile in a cumulated wage distribution;

S = economic system (= 0, capitalist; = 1, socialist);

P = population (in 1,000 people);

Y/P = per capita income valued in dollars;

N = number of observations in sample;

R^2 = coefficient of determination.

An asterisk denotes statistical significance at the 0.05 level.

APPENDIX B-10

Relative Prices of Capital and Labor in Europe and America (for Chapter V)

The calculation was made for 1955 in the following manner. First, an estimate was made to determine how many units of foreign currency of various nations $100 of investment goods (construction plus equipment) would sell for in different nations. (The relevant data come from [B92, p. 40].) This was then multiplied by the prevailing interest rate of the nation (taken as either the rate of discount or the rate on government bonds, whichever was higher; the data come from [G35, X, Jan./1957]) to determine the price of capital. The price of labor was taken as the average hourly wage rate of men and women in manufacturing (data come from [G34, 1958]). Comparing the United States, the United Kingdom, Denmark, and Italy (whose per capita incomes stood in the relationship: 100; 64; 56; 35), the derived ratios of the price of capital to the price of labor stood in the ratio 100: 600: 700: 2000.

APPENDIX B-11

Operatives and Office Workers in Mining and Manufacturing (for Chapter V)

TABLE B-7

Rank Orders of Ratios of Operatives to Total Workers and Employees[a]

ISIC Number	Brand of Industry	Rank (Lowest Ratio Has the Highest Rank)	
		West	*East*
10–19	Mining and quarrying	6	9
20	Food processing	13	17
21	Beverages	18	18
22	Tobacco	9	5
23	Textiles	2	2
24	Clothing and footwear	1	1
25	Lumber products except furniture	4	10
26	Furniture and fixtures	5	8
27	Paper and pulp products	8	6.5
28	Printing and publishing	19	11
29	Leather	3	3
30	Rubber	15	6.5
31	Chemicals	21	16

32	Petroleum and coal products	20	13
33	Stone, glass, clay products	7	4
34	Primary metals	11	12
35	Metal products except machinery	10	14
36	Machinery except electrical, transport	16	19
37	Electrical goods and machines	17	20
38	Transport equipment	14	21
39	Miscellaneous	12	15
Number of nations in sample		18	7
Coefficient of concordance		.50	.49

The two rank orderings have a Kendall rank order correlation coefficient of .56 which is statistically significant at the .01 level.

a. The data come from [G79], supplemented in a number of cases by various national sources.

APPENDIX B-12

Sources of Data for Time-series Comparisons of Industrial Establishments and Enterprises (for Chapter V)

Establishments

1. Australia: 1907 data [G2]; 1961/62 data [G4].
2. France: 1906 data [G23]; 1962 data [G17].
3. Germany: 1907 data [G24]; 1961 data [G27] supplemented by [G15, 2/1965].
4. South Africa: 1918/19 data [G64]; 1961/62 data [G61].
5. Switzerland: 1905 data [G71]; 1965 data [G72].
6. United States: 1909 data [G92]; 1963 data [G85].

Considerable effort was made to locate detailed data on employment in industrial establishments for the pre-World War I period for all European nations. With the exception of Belgium ([P23, 6/1966], which includes only blue-collar workers) such data could not be located.

In each case the detailed data were grouped as close as possible to the ISIC two-digit classifications and in such a manner that the detailed industrial classifications at both points in time for a single nation were comparable. For most nations, several of the ISIC classes had to be combined.

Enterprises

1. Germany: 1907 data [G24, Volumes 214–22]; 1961 data [G27].
2. Norway: the Norwegian figures were estimated from data presented by [B265, p. 82].
3. Sweden: data for both years come from [G67, p. 54].
4. United States: the data on the book assets on the largest 100 manufacturing and mining enterprises come from the list presented by Norman R. Collins and Lee E. Preston, "The Size Structure of the Largest Industrial Firms, 1909–1958," [P3, LI, Dec./1961, pp. 1005–11]. From these lists I removed all enterprises primarily engaged in distribution and other activities outside of manufacturing and mining and, in order to bring the number of enterprises back to one hundred, estimated the assets of the companies just below the dividing line. Data on the book value of the capital stock come from Daniel Creamer, *et al.* [B60, p. 325]. Small adjustments were made to the Creamer datum for 1937 to derive the 1935 capital stock. Collins and Preston use IRS data on the capital stock and show a rise in the share of the 100 largest corporations between 1909 and 1919 but the Creamer series is much more refined and yields a different result.

The series for manufacturing enterprises alone come from FTC estimates published in [G91, 1969, p. 479].

An alternative series can be estimated from IRS data (e.g., see Morris Adelman, [G100, Part 1, p. 339]) which reveals a similar picture.

APPENDIX B-13

Relative Establishment Size in Mining and Manufacturing (for Chapter V)

TABLE B-8

Average Rank Orders of Establishment Size in the West[a]

ISIC Number	Branch of Industry	Average Rank Orders			
		Arithmetic Average	Entropy Index	Niehans Index	Percentage of Labor Force in Establishments Over 1000
10–19	Mining and quarrying	10	8	7	3
20	Food processing	13	14	14.5	16
21	Beverage	14	15	16	18
22	Tobacco	2	4	5	12
23	Textiles	9	10	10	9
24	Clothing and footwear	18	18	18	17
25	Lumber products except furniture	20	20	19	19
26	Furniture and fixtures	21	21	21	20
27	Paper and pulp	8	9	11	10
28	Printing and publishing	16	16	14.5	14
29	Leather products except shoes	19	19	20	21
30	Rubber	3	3	3	4
31	Chemicals	7	6	6	7
32	Petroleum and coal products	5	7	9	8
33	Stone, glass, and clay products	12	12	12	11
34	Primary metals	1	1	1	1
35	Metal products except machinery	15	13	13	13
36	Machinery except electrical, transport	11	11	8	5
37	Electrical goods and machinery	6	5	4	6
38	Transport equipment	4	2	2	2
39	Miscellaneous	17	17	17	15
	Number of nations in sample	23	23	23	14
	Coefficients of concordance	.89	.86	.80	.54

a. The nations from which the rankings are derived are presented in Table 6-4.

TABLE B-9

Average Rank Orders of Establishment Size in East Europe[a]

ISIC Number	Branch of Industry	Average Rank Orderings			
		Arithmetic Average	Entropy Index	Niehans Index	Percentage of Labor Force in Establishments Over 1000
10–19	Mining and quarrying	3	3.5	3	3
20, 21, 22	Food, beverage, tobacco	14.5	12.0	12	13
23	Textile	4	5	6.5	5
24	Clothing	11	12.0	10	11.0
25, 26	Lumber products and furniture	13	15	16	15
27	Paper products	8	8.5	9	9
28	Printing and publishing	12	12.0	14	14
29	Leather products	10	10	11	11.0
30, 31, 32	Rubber, chemical, petroleum, products	6.5	6.5	5	6
33	Stone, glass, clay products	14.5	14	13	11.0
34	Primary metals	1	1	1	1
35	Metal products except machinery	9	8.5	8	8
36	Machinery except electrical, transport	6.5	6.5	6.5	7
37	Electrical goods and machinery	5	3.5	4	4
38	Transport equipment	2	2	2	2
39	Miscellaneous	16	16	15	16
Number of nations in sample		3	3	3	3
Coefficients of concordance		.92	.92	.89	.92

a. The rankings are derived from data for Hungary (1966), Poland (1960) and Yugoslavia (1963). Appropriate data of establishment size for the other East European nations could not be located. Ranks with decimal points indicate tie scores.

It should first be noted that the rankings are very similar for the three coefficients in each of the tables. The coefficients of concordance of the three rankings in Tables B-8 and B-9 are respectively .97 and .98. Both of these are statistically significant at the .01 level.

In comparing the rank ordering of establishment size between nations in the East and West, it is necessary to recalculate the Western data so that the same combination of industries is obtained; in several cases this recalculation reverses the average rank orders of two nations. The Kendall rank order correlation coefficients for the entropy, Niehans, and percentage coefficients between the two groups are respectively .64, .74, and .68, all of which are statistically significant at the .01 level.

APPENDIX B-14

Sources of Data on Establishment Size (for Chapter V)

Austria: [G5].
Australia: [G4].
Belgiuum: [G17].
Canada: [G11].
Denmark: [G14].
Finland: [G20].
France: [G17].
Greece: [G29].
Hungary: [G32, 1966].
Ireland: [G36].
Israel: [G38].
Italy: [G40], supplemented by [G17].
Japan: [G42].
Netherlands: [G17].
New Zeland [G48].
Norway: [G51].
Poland: [G58].
Portugal: [G59].
South Africa: [G61].
Spain: [G65].
Sweden: [G69]. An adjustment was made so that both workers and employees
    were included.
Switzerland: [G72].
United Kingdom: [G76].
United States: [G86].
West Germany: [G27], supplemented by [G15].
Yugoslavia: [G108].

APPENDIX B-15

Relative Enterprise Size in Manufacturing and Mining (for Chapter VI)

In a manner similar to the establishment rankings, the enterprise rankings for the three indicators are very similar in both tables. (Table B-10 and B-11 on pages 457-58.)

In order to compare the rank orderings of enterprise size in the East and West, it is necessary to recalculate the Western data in order to have the same industrial groups as are in the East European nations. The Kendall rank order coefficients for arithmetic, entropy, Niehans, and percentage coefficients are respectively .77, .62, .65 and .60, all of which are statistically significant at the .01 level.

APPENDIX B-16

Sources of Data on Enterprise Size (for Chapter VI)

Belgium: [G17].
Bulgaria: [G7].
Czechoslovakia: [G12].
East Germany: [G25].
France: [G17].
Greece: [G29].
Hungary: [G32].
Italy: [G17].
Japan: [G42]. Tobacco products and ordinance industries are omitted.
Netherlands: [G17].
Poland: [G56].
Portugal: [G59].
Romania: [G60].
Switzerland: [G72].
U.S.S.R.: [G75].
United States: [G88].
West Germany: [G27, 1964].
Yugoslavia: [G109].

TABLE B-10
Average Rank Orders of Enterprise Size in the West[a]

ISIC Number	Branch of Industry	Average Rank Orderings			
		Arithmetic Average	Entropy Index	Niehans Index	Percentage of Labor Force In Enterprises Over 1000
10–19	Mining and quarrying	8	7	6	6
20	Food processing	13	13	13	13
21	Beverages	14	15	17	17
22	Tobacco products	2	2	5	3
23	Textiles	9	9	10	10
24	Clothing and shoes	18	18	18	18
25	Lumber products except furniture	20	20	19	19
26	Furniture and fixtures	21	21	21	21
27	Paper products	10	10	11	11
28	Printing and publishing	17	17	16	15
29	Leather products except shoes	19	19	20	20
30	Rubber products	5	8	7	8
31	Chemicals	4	5	4	4.5
32	Petroleum and coal products	1	4	8	4.5
33	Stone, glass, and clay products	12	12	12	12
34	Primary metals	3	1	1	1
35	Metal products	15	14	14	16
36	Machinery except electrical, transport	11	11	9	9
37	Electrical goods and machinery	6.5	6	3	7
38	Transport and equipment	6.5	3	2	2
39	Miscellaneous	16	16	15	14
	Number of nations in sample	10	10	10	9
	Coefficients of concordance	.74	.73	.65	.62

a. The sample of nations is presented in Table 6–4.

TABLE B-11

Average Rank Orders of Enterprise Size in East Europe[a]

ISIC Number	Branch of Industry	Average Rank Orderings			
		Arithmetic Average	Entropy Index	Niehans Index	Percentage of Labor Force in Enterprises Over 1000
10–19	Mining and quarrying	2	2	2	1
20, 21, 22	Food, beverage, tobacco	12	14	14	14
23	Textile	5	6	7	4
24	Clothing	13.5	13	10	10
25, 26	Wood products and furniture	15	15	15	13
27	Paper products	7	7	9	7
28	Printing and publishing	13.5	16	16	16
29	Leather products	16	9	8	11
30, 31, 32	Rubber, chemical, petroleum products	8	8	5.5	8
33	Stone, glass, clay products	9	10	11.5	9
34	Primary metals	1	1	1	2
35	Metal products except machinery	10	12	13	12
36	Machinery except electrical, transport	6	5	5.5	6
37	Electrical goods and machinery	3.5	4	4	5
38	Transport equipment	3.5	3	3	3
39	Miscellaneous	11	11	11.5	15
	Number of nations in sample	5	5	5	5
	Coefficients of concordance	.70	.59	.55	.62

a. The nations composing the sample are Czechoslovakia, 1965 (this year was chosen because it preceded some very hurried consolidations that took place in 1966); East Germany, 1966; Hungary, 1966; Poland, 1960 (this year was chosen so that comparability with the establishment data could be obtained); and Romania, 1966 (only centrally directed state enterprises are included). For Czechoslovakia, East Germany, and Romania, only state enterprises are included. Yugoslavia was not included because government policy is aimed to encourage primarily single establishment enterprises and the comparisons in the table are made to shed light on administrative economies of multiestablishment enterprises.

APPENDIX B-17

Variation in Enterprise and Establishment Size in the West (for Chapters V and VI)

TABLE B-12

Rank Orders of Coefficients of Variation of Size[a]

ISIC Number	Branch of Industry	Establishments			Enterprises		
		Arithmetic Average	Entropy Index	Niehans Index	Arithmetic Average	Entropy Index	Niehans Index
10–19	Mining and quarrying	1	1	1	1	5	7
20, 21, 22	Food, beverage, tobacco	10	9	10	13	7	10
23	Textiles	9	10	12	10	10	9
24	Clothing and shoes	13	13	14	11	14	4
25, 26	Lumber products, furniture	12	16	15	15	16	8
27	Paper products	7	11	16	8	4	3
28	Printing	16	15	11	16	15	14
29	Leather products	11	14	9	6	2	1
30, 31, 32	Rubber, chemical, petroleum products	5	2	3	4	3	11
33	Stone, glass, clay products	15	12	13	12	13	15
34	Primary metals	3	5	7	7	11	16
35	Metal products	14	8	5	14	12	2
36	Machinery except electrical, transport	6	6	8	5	8	13
37	Electrical goods and machinery	4	4	4	3	6	12
38	Transport equipment	2	3	2	2	1	6
39	Miscellaneous	8	7	6	9	9	5
	Number of nations in sample	23	23	23	10	10	10

a. Size is measured by number of workers and employees in an average size unit. The highest coefficient of variation (standard deviation divided by the mean) has rank number 1; the lowest, 16.

Because the percentage of labor force in productive units has an upward limit (100 percent), the coefficients of variation are difficult to interpret and are not presented. Certain of the classes are grouped so that comparisons can be made with data from the East European nations.

APPENDIX B-18

Relative Degrees of Multi-establishment Enterprises in Mining and Manufacturing (for Chapter VI)

TABLE B-13

Rank Orders of Enterprises Size/Establishment Size Ratios

ISIC Number	Branch of Industry	Average Rank Orderings		
		Arithmetic Average	*Entropy Index*	*Niehans Index*
10–19	Mining and quarrying	3	4	5
20	Food processing	7	8	3
21	Beverages	11.5	14	15
22	Tobacco	1	1	2
23	Textiles	13	13	8
24	Clothing and footwear	15	15	14
25	Lumber products except furniture	16	17.5	16
26	Furniture and fixtures	20	21	21
27	Paper and pulp	11.5	11	9
28	Printing and publishing	18	16	18
29	Leather products except shoes	19	20	20
30	Rubber and rubber products	8.5	9	12
31	Chemicals	4	2	4
32	Petroleum and coal products	2	6	13
33	Stone, glass, and clay products	8.5	12	6
34	Primary metals	6	3	7
35	Metal products except machinery	21	19	17
36	Machinery except electrical, transport	14	10	10
37	Electrical goods and machines	5	5	1
38	Transport equipment	10	7	11
39	Miscellaneous	17	17.5	19
	Number of nations in rankings	10	10	10
	Coefficients of concordance	.43	.43	.28

Although the coefficients of concordance are lower than those obtained in most of the other investigations of this study, they are all statistically significant at the .01 level. The Kendall rank order correlation coefficients between the three rankings are also statistically significant.

In order to compare the rankings of Poland and Hungary with the results from the West, it is necessary to recalculate the Western data and combine ISIC classes so that the series are more comparable. The results of such comparisons are presented in Table B-14.

Although the relative rankings of the enterprise size/establishment size ratios are significantly related when the size variable is a simple arithmetic

TABLE B-14

*Comparisons of the Relative Enterprise Size/Establishment Size Ratio
Rankings of Hungary and Poland with the West*

Kendall Rank Order Correlation Coefficients
(Number of Ranks: 16)

Nation	Arithmetic Average	Entropy Index	Niehans Index
Hungary (1966)	.43*	.18	.22
Poland (1960)	.49*	−.19	−.10

average, this does not prove the case when the size indicators are either the entropy or the Niehans index.

For the three indicators of size, the relative rankings of the enterprise size/establishment size ratio for Hungary and Poland have Kendall rank order correlation coefficients of .29, .11, and .21; thus the degree of multi-establishment enterprises in different industrial branches does not appear significantly related in these two nations.

Data for the ratio of enterprise size/establishment size where the size variable is the percentage of the labor force in production units over one thousand are not presented because the upward limit (100 percent) of both the numerator and denominator make the results difficult to interpret.

APPENDIX B-19

Relationships between Establishment Size in Manufacturing and Other Variables (for Chapter V)

TABLE B-15

*Relationships between Establishment Size in Manufacturing
and Other Variables[a]*

Regressions with G.N.P.	S	R²
$\ln A = 3.054 + .096^*\ln Y$	23	.32
(.031)		
$\ln E = 1.713 + .222^*\ln Y$	23	.53
(.045)		
$\ln N = -.557 + .405^*\ln Y$	23	.56
(.078)		
$\ln P = -.516 + .198^*\ln Y$	14	.44
(.064)		

Property and Industrial Organization

Regressions with Agglomeration Variables

$\ln A' = 4.040 + .561^* \ln (Y/Z) - 1.035^* \ln Y - .227 \ln X$ 23   .96
           $(.144)$ $(.060)$ $(.131)$

$\ln E' = 2.473 + .517^* \ln (Y/Z) - .869^* \ln Y - .062 \ln X$ 23   .94
           $(.152)$ $(.063)$ $(.138)$

$\ln N' = .164 + .359 \ln (Y/Z) - .597^* \ln Y + .241 \ln X$ 23   .82
          $(.229)$ $(.094)$ $(.207)$

where A = arithmetic average establishment size;
      E = entropy index of establishment size;
      N = Niehans index of establishment size;
      P = percentage of manufacturing labor force in establishments over 1000;
      A′ = arithmetic average establishment size divided by manufacturing labor force;
      E′ = entropy index divided by manufacturing labor force;
      N′ = Niehans index divided by manufacturing labor force;
      Y = gross national product calculated with dollar price weights;
      Z = population;
      X = ratio of nonagricultural merchandise exports to value-added in mining and manufacturing;
      S = number of nations in sample;
      R^2 = coefficient of determination.

   a. Other regressions are presented in Table 5–5.

APPENDIX B-20

Relationships between Enterprise Size in Manufacturing and Other Variables (for Chapter VI)

TABLE B-16

Relationships between Enterprise Size in Manufacturing and Other Variables[a]

Regressions with G.N.P.	S	R^2
$\ln A_m = 2.146 + .154^* \ln Y$ $(.042)$	10	.62*
$\ln E_m = -2.850 + .516^* \ln Y$ $(.085)$	10	.82*
$\ln N_m = -5.020 + .724^* \ln Y$ $(.107)$	10	.85*
$\ln P_m = -7.336 + .339^* \ln Y$ $(.065)$	9	.80*

Table B-16, *continued*

Relationships between Enterprise Size in Manufacturing and Other Variables[a]

Regressions with G.N.P., Per Capita G.N.P., and Export Ratios

	S	R^2
$\ln A_m = 1.662 + .225 \ln (Y/Z) + .088 \ln Y - .038 \ln X$	10	.70*
(.193) (.093) (.161)		
$\ln E_m = -3.765 + .488 \ln (Y/Z) + .357 \ln Y - .137 \ln X$	10	.86*
(.383) (.185) (.320)		
$\ln N_m = -8.160 + .325 \ln (Y/Z) + .796* \ln Y + .532 \ln X$	10	.94*
(.351) (.170) (.294)		
$\ln P_m = -9.871 + .311* \ln (Y/Z) + .368* \ln Y + .283* \ln X$	9	.97*
(.120) (.064) (.109)		

Experiments with Size Variables including Mining Enterprises

	S	R^2
$\ln A_{mm} = 2.283 + .148* \ln Y$	10	.57*
(.045)		
$\ln E_{mm} = -2.659 + .509* \ln Y$	10	.81*
(.088)		
$\ln N_{mm} = -4.787 + .715* \ln Y$	10	.83*
(.114)		
$\ln P_{mm} = -6.636 + .303* \ln Y$	9	.75*
(.066)		
$\ln P_{mm} = -8.054 + .414* \ln (Y/Z) + .211* \ln Y$	9	.87*
(.177) (.065)		

Experiments with Agglomeration Variables

	S	R^2
$\ln A_m' = 3.965 - .779* \ln Y$	10	.92*
(.080)		
$\ln E_m' = -1.031 - .417* \ln Y$	10	.61*
(.118)		
$\ln N_m' = -3.201 - .209 \ln Y$	10	.29
(.116)		
$\ln N_m' = -5.537 + .775* \ln (Y/Z) - .400* \ln Y$	10	.58*
(.355) (.130)		

where:

A = arithmetic average of enterprise size;
E = entropy index of enterprise size;
N = Niehans index of enterprise size;
P = percentage of labor force in enterprises over 1000;
m = manufacturing enterprises only;
mm = manufacturing and mining enterprises;
' = agglomeration index (average size enterprise divided by labor force);
Y = gross national product calculated with dollar price weights;
Z = population;
X = ratio of nonagricultural merchandise exports to value-added in mining and manufacturing;
S = number of nations in sample;
R^2 = coefficient of determination.

a. Other regressions are presented in Table 6-6.

APPENDIX B-21

Relationships between Share of Labor Force in Largest Enterprises and Other Variables (for Chapter VI)

TABLE B-17

Relationships between Share of Labor Force in Largest Enterprises and Other Variables[a]

	S	R^2
ln T200 = −3.710 + .328* ln (Y/Z)	11	.43
(.127)		
ln BB = −11.868 + .586* ln Y + .505* ln X	10	.88
(.092) (.195)		
ln BB = −11.028 + .464* ln (Y/Z) + .316* ln Y	10	.86
(.204) (.076)		
ln BB = −9.178 + .407* ln Y	10	.76
(.080)		

where:
    T200 = share of labor force in mining and manufacturing employed by the top 200 enterprises (domestic branches only);
    BB = share of labor force in manufacturing and mining employed by the top "big businesses" (defined in Chapter VII);
    Y = G.N.P. calculated with dollar price weights;
    Z = population;
    X = ratio of nonagricultural exports to value-added in mining and manufacturing;
    S = number of nations in sample;
    R^2 = coefficient of determination.

    a. The data for T200 and BB come primarily from estimates derived from the sources cited in Appendix B-16, plus an estimate for Sweden.

APPENDIX B-22

A Detailed Description of the Calculation of the Weighted Concentration Indices (for Chapter VI)

The basic data were comparable concentration ratios for a number of four- and five-digit industries for eleven foreign nations plus a complete set of four- and five-digit concentration ratios for the United States.
In order to simplify discussion, the following symbols are used:

$UC5_i$ = the concentration ratio in a five-digit industry i in the United States;

$FC5_i$ = the concentration ratio in the foreign country that is comparable to $US5_i$;

$UC4_i$ = the concentration ratio in a four-digit industry that includes industry i in the United States;

$FC4_i$ = the concentration ratio in the foreign country that is comparable to $US4_i$;

$UU2$ = weighted two-digit concentration ratio for the United States for the particular sample, using United States value-added weights;

$FU2$ = weighted two-digit concentration ratio for the foreign nation for the particular sample, using United States value-added weights;

$UUT2$ = weighted two-digit concentration ratio for the United States for all industries in that classification, using United States value-added weights (one set of these were calculated using all industries, another set excluding regional industries).

For each country the foreign five-digit ratios were first "converted" into four-digit ratios by using a simple method. For those industries in which only one pair (i.e., comparable United States and foreign ratios) of five-digit concentration ratios was available, the foreign ratio was adjusted by multiplying by $(UC4_i/UC5_i)$ and was then paired with $UC4_i$. Where several pairs of five-digit ratios were available, a weighted average (using value of shipment weights) was first calculated and then the foreign weighted average was adjusted by multiplying by $(UC4_i/$U.S. weighted five-digit average).

The calculated two-digit weighted averages give the desired relationship between the United States and foreign ratios, but they can not be considered to reflect satisfactorily the absolute degree of concentration since the sample of industries is not necessarily representative. Therefore, both the $UU2$ and the $FU2$ data were adjusted by multiplying by $(UUT2/UU2)$. The results were then used to calculate the final weighted averages.

When the averages using the foreign weights were calculated, one additional problem arose since I had no complete set of foreign ratios with which to calculate an aggregate corresponding to $UUT2$. If we assume that the adjusted $FU2$ average (i.e., $FU2 \times UUT2/UU2$, which I designate by the letter X) reflects the *level* of concentration for the whole two-digit branch, then we can adjust both the foreign-weighted United States and foreign two-digit weighted averages by multiplying both by (X/foreign-weighted foreign two-digit weighted average). While this procedure is the best we can do with the available data, it does leave something to be desired if we are interested only in this result alone. However, the reason for the exercise is to gain some idea of possible index number effects by comparison with the United States weighted results and, therefore, the major purpose is served.

The selection of industries classified as "local" or "regional" or other adjustments made with the United States data were based on the calculations of William G. Shepherd [B231, Appendix Table 8]. Similar calculations for local or regional industries in the various European nations could not be carried out because of lack of data.

The ranking of weighted two-digit concentration ratios shown in Table 2–3 presented similar problems of estimation as the aggregate ratios, but were calculated in a slightly different way using the following four-step procedure. First, all industries classified as "local" in the United States were excluded from the sample. Second, binary sets of weighted two-digit ratios were calculated for the United States and each foreign nation using United States value-added weights. Third, each pair of United States and foreign weighted concentration ratios for the various two-digit industries was adjusted by multiplying by z/y (where z is the weighted two-digit concentration ratio for the United States including *all* four-digit industries after making adjustments taking into account biases due to the presence of regional and local industries and other peculiarities in that two-digit industrial branch; and where y is the weighted two-digit concentration ratio for the United States for the particular two-digit comparison between the United States and the specific foreign nation.) This adjustment was made because the selection of industries in the binary comparisons was not random. (Starting the binary comparisons by excluding regional industries would have left too small a sample for some two-digit industries.) Finally, the adjusted foreign concentration ratios and the full-sample United States ratios were ranked and the concordance coefficient (which was .51 for the twelve nation sample) was determined to be statistically significant.

APPENDIX B-23

Sources of Data for Concentration Ratios (for Chapter VI)

Belgium, West Germany, Netherlands: The concentration ratios were calculated by the E.E.C. and presented by Jacques Houssiaux in [G101, pp. 3957–96]. These data were supplemented in several cases by estimates made by Joseph Miller of Indiana University. The branch weights come from [G15, J-A/1967].

Canada: The concentration ratios come from Gideon Rosenbluth [B222, p. 90 and Appendix A]. Those ratios given for just three firms were adjusted in the following manner: three- and four-firm concentration ratios by individual industries that were given by Rosenbluth were compared and a curve was fitted. This relationship between three- and four-firm concentration ratios was then used to adjust those three-firm ratios for which no four-firm ratios were calculated. Branch weights were estimated from data from [G79a] and [G10].

France: The concentration ratios come from Houssiaux, [G101], and from Jacques Loup, "La concentration dans l'industrie français, d'après le recensement industriel de 1963: la structure des marchés," in [P22, XXIV, Feb./1969, pp. 17–239]. The two-digit weighted concentration ratios were calculated with value of shipment weights since value-added weights were not available. The branch weights come from [G15, J-A/1967].

Italy: The concentration ratios were calculated from employment data by size class following a technique described by Joe S. Bain [B18, pp. 27–9]. The basic data come from [G41]; the branch weights come from [G15, J-A/1967].

Japan: The concentration ratios come from [G45]; the branch weights come from [G80].

Sweden: The concentration ratios come from [G68]. The basic set of statistics are concentration ratios by industrial branches (Table 2, pp. 86–95); these were supplemented by ratios for products according to the Brussels classification (Table 3, pp. 95–110). The former table was based on value of shipment data and had value-added weights supplied; the latter table was based on physical shipments data and had gross sales information supplied. The gross sales data were converted into value-added weights by applying the United States ratios of these two magnitudes. Certain estimates were also made in those cases where concentration ratios for more than four firms were presented. The branch weights come from [G69].

Switzerland: The concentration ratios were calculated according to the Bain method (see notes for Italy) from employment data by size group presented in [G73]. The data are not completely comparable with those of the other nations because of the Swiss practice of isolating those firms that produce in a great many industries and placing them in a special category entitled "Verbindung," a procedure that may greatly affect the calculated concentration ratios particularly in the machinery branches. The branch weights are from [G72].

United Kingdom: The basic data for the concentration ratios come from [B76, Appendix B]. Where three-firm concentration ratios are given, estimates for four-firm ratios were made using the relationship found for Canada and described above; where five- and six-firm ratios are presented, estimates of four-firm ratios were made using the Bain method. Branch weights were estimated from data from [G79a] and [G78].

United States: The concentration ratios come from [G99]; the branch weights in manufacturing come from [G86].

Yugoslavia: The concentration ratios come from Joel Dirlam in [G101, pp. 4482–95]. Although the original source could not be located, a similar table is published by Izak Drutter, "Tržišni aspekti koncentracije," in [B74, Table 13]. One misprint was corrected. Branch weights come from [G108].

APPENDIX B-24

Additional Relationships between Concentration Ratios of Different Nations (for Chapter VI)

TABLE B-18

Additional Relationships between Concentration Ratios of Different Nations with Certain Adjustments[a]

		S	R^2
Belgium	$F = .298 + .700*U$ (.226)	36	.22*
Canada	$F = .242 + .922*U$ (.199)	32	.42*
France	$F = .021 + .837*U$ (.135)	44	.48*
West Germany	$F = .083 + .820*U$ (.099)	65	.52*
Italy	$F = .006 + .953*U$ (.139)	34	.60*
Japan	$F = .166 + .672*U$ (.165)	38	.31*
Netherlands	$F = .251 + .466U$ (.251)	15	.21
Sweden	$F = .433 + .573*U$ (.107)	53	.36*
Switzerland	$F = .332 + .465*U$ (.150)	34	.23*
United Kingdom	$F = .237 + .522*U$ (.111)	69	.25*
Yugoslavia	$F = .585 + .144 U$ (.226)	15	.03

where:
  U = Four-firm, four-digit concentration ratios in the United States;
  F = Four-firm, four-digit concentration ratio in the specified foreign nation;
  S = Number of concentration ratios in the sample;
  R^2 = Coefficient of determination.

   a. The four-firm, four-digit concentration ratios exclude all United States regional or local industries. In addition I have excluded all industries in which the concentration ratio in either country is .05 or less or .95 or more; this is to avoid the source of error discussed in footnote 58 of Chapter II, which arises because the concentration ratios are bounded by absolute limits of 0.00 and 1.00. Similar results to Table B-18 occur when the concentration ratios in either country of .10 or less or .90 or more are removed.

APPENDIX B-25

Sources and Methods of Calculating Spatial Centralization Statistics (for Chapter VIII)

Regional data on population and on labor force in manufacturing and mining establishments (including private, cooperative, and publicly owned establishments) were collected for as many economically developed and semideveloped nations as possible. For most nations such data are readily available although in certain cases, noted below, comparability problems arise.

In order to avoid the bias discussed in the text, I combined the regional data in each country so that nine large regions were formed. Three rules for combining regions were followed: (1) Only contiguous regions would be combined; (2) each large region would be roughly similar in population; (3) whenever possible, regions with ethnic similarity would be combined (e.g., separately Czech and Slovak regions). Although a number of countries had to be eliminated since data for at least nine regions could not be located, the final sample consisted of seventeen nations which is quite sufficient for my general purpose.

Ratios of labor force in manufacturing and mining to population (the "industrialization indicator") were calculated for each region, with a high ratio designating a more industrialized region. I then ordered the regions in each nation according to their descending rank of industrialization indicator and drew a line dividing the regions into large groups of roughly equal population but with one group of regions having higher and the other group of regions having lower industrialization indicators. The statistics presented in Table 9–1 in the text were then calculated.

A large number of regressions were calculated to isolate the determinants of the various statistics, but few turned out to have statistically significant coefficients of determination. Regressions on subsamples of capitalist and socialist nations were also run with similar discouraging results.

Sources of the Data

1. Belgium: The data come from various issues of [G6] and [P23].
2. Bulgaria: The data come from various issues of [G7].
3. Canada: The data come from various issues of [G9]; employment in mining in 1965 had to be estimated. The population data for both early and late years are one year later than labor force data.
4. Czechoslovakia: Data for economically active in manufacturing and mining in 1961 come from [G13]; labor force in 1955 and 1965 were calculated by means of regional labor force indices presented in [G12, 1967, p. 205]. The definition of manufacturing and mining is somewhat broader than for the Western nations. Population data for both early and late years are one year later than labor force data and come from various issues of [G12].

5. East Germany: The data come from various issues of [G25] and include state, cooperative, and private establishments in manufacturing, mining, and industrial handicrafts. The definition of manufacturing and mining is somewhat broader than for the Western nations.

6. Greece: The data come from [G29] and various issues of [G30]; the labor force data include only those in manufacturing.

7. Hungary: The data come from [G33] and various issues of [G32]. The labor force data include state, cooperative, and private establishments and were partly estimated. The definition of manufacturing and mining is somewhat broader than for the Western nations.

8. Italy: The data come from various issues of [G40a].

9. Japan: The data come from various issues of [G43].

10. Netherlands: The data come from various issues of [G46].

11. Norway: The data come from various issues of [G52].

12. Poland: The data come from various issues of [G56] and the labor force data include state, cooperative and private establishments in industry and industrial handicrafts. A number of small estimates had to be made. The definition of manufacturing and mining is somewhat broader than for the Western nations.

13. Romania: The data come from various issues of [G60] and the labor force data include state, cooperative, and private establishments in industry and handicrafts. The definition of manufacturing and mining is somewhat broader than for the Western nations and, in addition, the handicraft sector include some services as well.

14. Sweden: The data come from various issues of [G66] and are supplemented by other official sources.

15. Switzerland: The data come from various issues of [G74]. The population data for both early and late years are one year earlier than the labor force data.

16. United States: The data come from various issues of [G91].

17. West Germany: The data come from various issues of [G27].

18. Yugoslavia: The data come from various issues of [G109]. Serbia is divided into three separate subregions.

APPENDIX B-26

Sources of Data on Ownership and Control
(for Chapters IV and VIII)

Private ownership is when one individual or group of persons controls 80 percent or more of the voting shares of an enterprise; majority ownership, 50 to 80 percent of the voting shares; minority control, 15 to 50 percent of the voting shares; control through a legal device, when a controlling block of stock is owned by another company, or institution, or is voted by a nominee;

and management control is when no person or group owns more than 15 percent of the voting shares. In known cases where a group owning less than 15 percent of the voting shares is able to effectively exercise control, this is reclassified as minority control.

In carrying out an empirical investigation, considerable problems arise in defining a "group." Certain investigators have attempted to surmount this problem by looking at the stock holdings of the twenty largest holders; while others have used more subjective methods. The data in the table from all three nations have used the latter method.

Sources

1. The United States data comes from Robert Larner [B148] who, in turn, took 1929 data from Berle and Means [B32]. The dividing line between minority control and managerial control is 20 percent for the 1929 data and 10 percent for the 1963 data. One other large scale analysis of this problem was carried out by the United States Temporary National Economic Committee [G105], but these data are disputed by Robert Aaron Gordon [B97] and Larner [B148].
2. The United Kingdom data come from data presented by P. Sargent Florence [B83], who classified the enterprises according to the holdings of the twenty largest stockholders. From the fifty largest enterprises in each year, I reclassified his data using the method followed by Larner [B148]. The data presented by Florence (especially Tables V-A, V-B and the tables in Appendices A and B) are not completely sufficient for this task and in a number of cases doubts can be raised about the classification. Managerial control was defined where the top twenty stockholders held less than 30 percent of the voting shares and where no single owner held more than 15 percent.
3. The data for Australia come from Edward L. Wheelwright [B267] who followed a method similar to that of Berle and Means [B33]. Among the top twenty enterprises were two enterprises which Wheelwright did not classify (because of peculiarities in the voting procedures) which I attempted to place in the proper classification on the basis of the data supplied. A study of the configuration of ownership and control in Australian industries was carried out a decade later by Wheelwright and Miskelly [B268], which revealed relatively little change.

APPENDIX B-27

Sources and Methods of Calculating Enterprise Mobility Coefficients (for Chapter VIII)

A. *Method*

The first step was to prepare lists of big businesses according to assets (only sales data were available for West Germany) for the various nations for roughly decade intervals. The lists were restricted to firms primarily engaged in manufacturing and mining, with financial, trade, transportation and other such enterprises eliminated. One hundred enterprises were chosen for the United States; following the techniques described in Chapter VI for determining the size of the "set of big businesses," fifty-three were selected for Germany; forty-eight for the United Kingdom; and twenty-nine for France.

Second, considerable efforts were expended in determining which enterprises disappeared because of mergers or appeared because of dissolutions. For purposes of comparisons an enterprise that was formed from three enterprises on the list in the previous period was considered as three enterprises and the list for the later year was correspondingly reduced by two enterprises. A similar procedure was followed for dissolutions.

Most of the data in Table 9–3 was calculated from ratios of the assets of the individual enterprises in the list to the total assets of the set of big businesses for the specific country in the designated year.

B. *Sources*

1. United States: data for 1909–58 come from Norman R. Collins and Lee E. Preston, "The Size Structure of the Largest Industrial Firms, 1909–1958," [P3, LI, Dec./1961, pp. 986–1011]. For 1958–68 the data come from [P25, July/1959 and May 15/1969].
2. United Kingdom: the 1953/54 data come from [B197]; the 1964/65 data, from [B251].
3. France: the French data for 1956/57 come from Houssiaux [B119]; for 1966/67, from [P21, 633, Oct. 28/1967].
4. West Germany: the 1957 data are for sales, rather than assets, and come from [P26, Nov. 7/1959, p. 5]; the 1966 data are for sales as well and come from [P26, Sept. 9/1967], as reported in [G101, pp. 3817–20].

C. *Interpretation of Statistics*

The coefficient of variation of share in big business in the later year *vis-à-vis* the earlier year is an indication of the degree to which the share coefficients of assets of individual enterprises of big business change over time. The coefficient is calculated from the list of big businesses after adjustments for mergers and dissolutions. If a big business in a later year was not among the big businesses of the earlier year, its change in asset share is considered equal to its asset share in the later year. A standard deviation of change of asset share was calculated and the ratio of this to the average asset share of individual big businesses in the later year is presented in the table.

The "adjusted" coefficient of variation is an attempt to estimate the coefficient of variation on a decade basis by assuming that the change from year to year is similar. Thus if the period covered in the comparison is eight years, the calculated coefficient of variation of share for the decade is estimated by multiplying the eight-year statistic by 1.25.

Glossary

The following nontechnical definitions give only the meanings of the terms as they are used in this study. For more complete and precise definitions, particularly for the statistical terms, the reader must turn to the technical literature. All terms defined in this glossary are italicized.

Agglomeration ratio: the ratio of the number of workers and employees in an average size production unit to the number of workers and employees in the relevant industry.

Alienation: this is defined and discussed in Appendix A-18.

Association: an administrative unit in many East European economies between the ministries and the production enterprises.

Big Business: a specified number of the largest enterprises in mining and manufacturing. The particular number of enterprises is determined from the ratio of the labor force in mining and manufacturing in the particular nation to that in the United States. Thus if West Germany has one-fourth the labor force in mining and manufacturing as the United States has and if 200 *big businesses* are under consideration for the United States, then the largest 50 such enterprises are examined for West Germany.

Capitalism: an economy in which most of the means of production are privately owned.

Centralization: ten definitions are provided in Chapter VIII, Section B of which three are given here: *hierarchical centralization* refers to decision-making at higher levels of an administrative hierarchy; *spatial centralization* refers to the dispersion of mining and manufacturing over all areas of a nation; *temporal centralization* refers to the degree to which there is a rapid turnover in the set of large enterprises.

Coefficient of concordance: a statistic ranging from 0.0 to 1.0 that indicates the degree to which a series of rank orderings are similar. A coefficient of 1.0 means that all of the rank orderings are exactly alike; a coefficient of 0.0 indicates a totally random pattern.

Coefficient of determination: a statistic indicating the percentage of variation between a set of points that is explained in terms of specified independent variables in a *regression*. If all points fall along the *regression line*, the coefficient of determination is 1.0 or -1.0 depending on whether the relationship is direct or inverse. If the independent variables can not be used to explain any of the variation in the points, the coefficient of determination is 0.0.

Coefficient of variation: the ratio of the *standard deviation* to the arithmetic average.

Concentration ratio: a measure of the degree of monopoly that is usually calculated by determining the ratio of the value of sales of the top products of a particular product or group of products. A *four-firm, four-digit concentration ratio* is calculated from the sales of the top four enterprises and refers to products falling within a "four-digit" range in an *industrial classification.*

Conglomerate merger: the merger of two enterprises that do not produce the same range of products and that do not produce products used as intermediate products in the production process of the other enterprises.

Consumption unit: the decision-making unit that directs decisions about the amount and type of personal consumption of individuals. This can be the individual himself, his family, or the government.

Corporate rights: Property rights that are exercised by a group together.

Cross-section study: a study of some variable at a single period of time in a number of different instances, e.g. the average sizes of enterprises in a number of countries at roughly the same time, in contrast to a *time-series study.*

Dependent variables: see *Regression.*

Dollar value G.N.P.: see *Gross national product.*

Economies of scale: economies of scale occur when the amount of production factors (land, labor, and capital) are all increased by some fraction and total production increases by more than that fraction.

Enterprise: a business organization consisting of one or more *establishments* under common ownership and control.

Entropy index: a measure of average size that more heavily weights large size units than an arithmetic average. The formula is given in Chapter VI.

Establishment: a business or industrial unit at a single physical location that produces goods or services. It can consist of several "plants" or "factories," as long as they are located together and under a single management.

Gini coefficient: a measure of inequality that is calculated from a Lorenz curve. The units under examination (families, individuals) are lined up according to the variable under examination (e.g., income, wealth) from smallest to largest. The Lorenz curve indicates the percentage of the total variable that is accounted for by a given percentage of the units under examination (e.g., 25 percent of total income is accounted for by 40 percent of the poorest families). The Gini coefficient is the ratio of the area bounded by a line indicating complete equality and the calculated Lorenz curve to the total triangle of the construction.

Gross national product (G.N.P.): the total amount of goods and services produced in an economy. The *dollar value G.N.P.* is the gross national product where all goods and services are valued at the dollar prices in the United States.

Heavy industries: see *Light industries.*

Hierarchical centralization: see *Centralization.*

Ideology: this is defined and discussed in Appendix A-19.

Independent variable: see *Regression.*

International Standard Industrial Classification (ISIC): a classification of industries set out by United Nations statisticians. "Two-digit" industries are broad classifications of products such as food processing or transportation equipment production. "Three-digit" industries are more narrowly defined, e.g., meat packing or motor vehicle production. "Four-digit industries" are still more narrowly defined, e.g., sausage production or automobile production.

Kendall rank order correlation coefficient: a statistic showing the degree of correlation between two rank orderings. If the rank orders are exactly the same or exactly opposite, the Kendall rank order correlation coefficient is respectively 1.0 or −1.0; all other coefficients fall within this range. A coefficient of 0.0 indicates that the two rankings are not at all related.

Light industries: industries characterized by small average size enterprises (in terms of inputs) and low degrees of market concentration, in contrast to *heavy industries* that are characterized by large average size enterprises and high degrees of market concentration. These heavy and light industries are discussed in detail in Chapter II.

Market socialism: a *socialist* economy in which goods and services are allocated through a market and central planning of current production plays a very small or nonexistent role.

N.a.: not available.

Nationalization ratio: the ratio of economically active population in government-owned establishments or facilities to the total economically active in the relevant sectors.

Niehans index: a measure of average size in which large sizes are given more weight than in either an arithmetic average or an entropy index. A formula is given in Chapter VI.

Normative theory: a theory dealing with the ways in which particular goals or ends can be achieved in the best possible way. Attention is focused on the "ought," rather than the "is."

Ownership: a particular property right giving a claim to income resulting from the use of a particular good, service, or "thing" under consideration.

Positive theory: a theory dealing with actual behavior of variables rather than with desired behavior. Attention is focused on the "is" rather than the "ought."

Primogeniture: an inheritance arrangement with all the wealth going to one child in a family.

Production unit: either a production *establishment* or *enterprise.*

Property: a bundle of rights or set of relations between people with regard to some good, service, or "thing"; such rights must have economic value and must be enforced in some societally recognized manner. This definition is analyzed in detail in Appendix A-1.

Property institution: procedures by which conflicts between individuals concerning property rights are contained, i.e., the standards of normal procedures that serve as reference points in any dispute over property and the procedures by which disputes can be adjudicated.

Regression: the calculation of the relationship between variables when the functional form is specified. A *simple linear regression* is the calculation of the relationship between two variables which are linked in a simple linear form ($y = a + bx$) where y is the *dependent* or *explained variable,* x is the *independent* or *explanatory variable,* and A and B are the calculated regression coefficients. In the diagram the regression line is estimated by the method of least squares, i.e., coefficients 'a' and 'b' are calculated so as to minimize the square of the distance from the actual observations to the calculated line. A *multiple regression* is when more than one *independent variable* is used. A diagram illustrating some of these concepts is presented on page 477.

Simulation model: when the behavior of a set of variables is not studied by algebraically solving a set of equations but rather by studying either arithmetically or mechanically the behavior of the system containing the variables under various conditions.

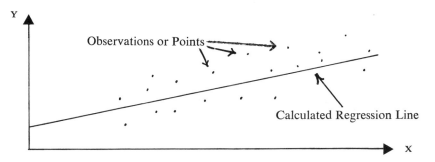

Socialism: an economy in which most of the means of production is publicly owned.

Spatial centralization: see *Centralization.*

Standard deviation: a measure of the dispersion of observation around the arithmetic mean of these observations. It is calculated by taking the square root of the sum of the squares of the distance of the various observations from the arithmetic mean divided by the number of observations.

Standard error: this is the standard deviation of an estimated *regression coefficient.*

Statistical significance: in testing the significance of an estimated statistic (e.g., an arithmetic mean) we are asking about the probability that it is different from some given value, usually zero. The range of significance is determined by the standard deviation or standard error of the statistic and a probability statement of the following kind: the changes are less than one out of twenty (or one out of a hundred) that the estimated value of the statistic is the same as the given value.

Temporal centralization: see *Centralization.*

Time-series study: a study of a variable over a period of time, in contrast to a *cross-section* study.

Bibliography

Periodicals

P1. *Administrative Science Quarterly*. Ithaca: Cornell University Graduate School of Business and Public Administration, quarterly.

P2. *American Anthropologist*. Washington, D.C.: American Anthropological Association, six times a year.

P3. *American Economic Review*. Nashville, Tenn.: American Economic Association, five times a year.

P4. *American Journal of Sociology*. Chicago: University of Chicago Press, six times a year.

P5. *American Political Science Review*. Washington, D.C.: American Political Science Association, quarterly.

P6. *American Sociological Review*. Washington, D.C.: American Sociological Association, six times a year.

P7. *Antitrust Bulletin*. New York: Federal Legal Publications, Inc., quarterly.

P8. *Applied Statistics*. London: Royal Statistical Society, three times a year.

P9. *Der Aussenhandel* (now *Sozialistische Aussenwirtschaft*). East Berlin: Verlag Die Wirtschaft, monthly.

P10. *Biulleten' nauchnoi informatsii: Trud i zarabotnaya plata*. Moscow: Nauchnoissled, Institut truda, monthly.

P11. *Canadian Journal of Economics and Political Science* (now *Canadian Journal of Economics*). Toronto: Canadian Economic Association, quarterly.

P12. *Comparative Studies in Society and History*. New York: Cambridge University Press, quarterly.

P13. *East Europe*. New York: Free Europe, Inc., monthly.

P14. *Eastern European Economics*. White Plains: International Arts and Sciences Press, quarterly.

P15. *Econometrica*. New Haven: Econometric Society, quarterly.

P16. *Economica*. London: London School of Economics, quarterly.

P17. *Economic Development and Cultural Change*. Chicago: Research Center in Economic Development and Cultural Change, quarterly.

P18. *Economic Journal*. Cambridge, Eng.: Royal Economic Society, quarterly.

P19. *Economics of Planning*. Oslo: Norwegian Institute of International Affairs, three times a year.

P20. *Economic Trends*. London: Central Statistical Office, monthly.

P21. *Enterprise*. Paris: weekly.

P22. *Études et conjoncture*. Paris: Institut national de la statistique, monthly.

P23. *Études statistiques et économétriques*. Brussels: Institut national de statistique, monthly.

P24. *Explorations in Economic History*. Yellow Springs, Ohio: Antioch Press, quarterly.

P25. *Fortune*. New York: Time Inc., monthly.

P26. *Frankfurter Allgemeine Zeitung*. Frankfurt: daily newspaper.

P27. *Human Organization*. Lexington, Ky.: Society for Applied Anthropology, quarterly.

P28. *Human Relations.* New York: Plenum Publishing Co., six times a year.

P29. *Information zu aktuellen Fragen der Sozial-und Wirtschaftspolitik.* Vienna: Institut fuer angewandte Sozial-und Wirtschaftsforschung, monthly.

P30. *International Journal of Ethics* (now *Ethics*). Chicago: University of Chicago Press, quarterly.

P31. *International Labour Review.* Geneva: International Labour Office, monthly.

P32. *Journal of Asian Studies.* Coral Cables, Fla.: University of Miami, Graduate School, five times a year.

P33. *Journal of Conflict Resolution.* Ann Arbor: Center for Research on Conflict Resolution, quarterly.

P34. *Journal of Economic History.* New York: Economic History Association, quarterly.

P35. *Journal of Economic Literature.* Nashville, Tenn.: American Economic Association, quarterly.

P36. *Journal of Finance.* New York: American Finance Association, five times a year.

P37. *Journal of Industrial Economics.* Oxford: Basil Blackwell, three times a year.

P38. *Journal of Law and Economics.* Chicago: University of Chicago Law School, twice a year.

P39. *Journal of Political Economy.* Chicago: University of Chicago Press, six times a year.

P40. *Journal of the American Statistical Association.* Washington, D.C.: American Statistical Association, quarterly.

P41. *Journal of the Royal Statistical Society.* London: Royal Statistical Society, quarterly.

P42. *Kyklos.* Basel, Switzerland: Kyklos Verlag, quarterly.

P43. *Latin American Research Review.* Washington, D.C.: Latin American Studies Association, three times a year.

P44. *Mergers and Acquisitions: The Journal of Corporate Venture.* New York: Mergers and Acquisitions Inc., six times a year.

P45. *The Natural Law Forum.* Notre Dame, Ind.: Notre Dame Law School, irreg.

P46. *The New York Review of Books.* New York: three times a month.

P47. *The New York Times.* New York: daily newspaper.

P48. *Oxford Economic Papers.* London: Oxford University Press, three times a year.

P49. *President Magazine.* Tokyo: Diamond Time Inc., monthly.

P50. *Problems of Communism.* Washington, D.C.: Government Printing Office, six times a year.

P51. *Proceedings of the American Philosophical Society.* Philadelphia: American Philosophical Society, six times a year.

P52. *Proceedings of the Industrial Relations Research Association.* Madison, Wisc.: Industrial Relations Research Association, annual.

P53. *Psychometrika.* Princeton: Psychometrika Society, quarterly.

P54. *Public Interest.* New York: Basic Books, Inc., quarterly.

P55. *The Quarterly Journal of Economics.* Cambridge, Mass.: Harvard University Press, quarterly.

P56. *The Review of Economics and Statistics.* Cambridge, Mass.: Harvard University Press, quarterly.

P57. *The Review of Economic Studies.* Edinburgh: Oliver and Boyd Ltd., quarterly.

P58. *Schweizerische Zeitschrift fuer Volkswirtschaft und Statistik.* Bern: Schweizerische Gesellschaft fuer Volkswirtschaft und Statistik, quarterly.

P59. *Scientific American.* New York: Scientific American Inc., monthly.

P60. *Slavic Review.* Seattle: American Association for the Advancement of Slavic Studies, quarterly.

P61. *Sociometry.* Washington, D.C.: American Sociological Association, quarterly.

P62. *Southwestern Journal of Anthropology.* Albuquerque: University of New Mexico, quarterly.

P63. *Soviet Studies.* Glasgow: University of Glasgow, quarterly.

P64. *Studies in Comparative Communism.* Los Angeles: University of Southern California, quarterly.

P65. *Survey of Current Business.* Washington, D.C.: U.S. Department of Commerce, monthly.

P66. *Swiss Review of World Affairs.* Zurich: Neue Zuercher Zeitung, monthly.

P67. *Transactions of the New York Academy of Sciences.* New York: New York Academy of Sciences, eight times a year.

P68. *Weltwirtschaftliches Archiv.* Kiel, Germany: Institut fuer Weltwirtschaft, quarterly.

P69. *Western Economic Journal.* Los Angeles: Western Economic Association, quarterly.

P70. *World Politics.* Princeton: Center of International Studies, Princeton University, quarterly.

P71. *Yale Law Journal.* New Haven: Yale Law School, eight times a year.

P72. *Yorkshire Bulletin of Economic and Social Research.* York, England: University of York, twice a year.

P73. *Zeitschrift fuer die gesamte Staatswissenschaft.* Tuebingen, Germany: J. C. B. Mohr, quarterly.

P74. *Zeitschrift fuer Nationaloekonomie.* Vienna: Springer-Verlag, irregular.

Publications of Governmental and Intergovernmental Organizations[1]

G1. Australia: Commonwealth Bureau of Census and Statistics. *Official Year Book of the Commonwealth of Australia.* Canberra: annual.

G2. ———: Commonwealth Bureau of Census and Statistics. *Production, Bulletin No. 2: Summary of Commonwealth Production Statistics.* Melbourne: Government Printer, n.d.

G3. ———: Commonwealth Bureau of Census and Statistics. *Secondary Industry, 1959–60,* Bulletin No. 54. Canberra: 1962.

G4. ———: Commonwealth Bureau of Census and Statistics. *Secondary Industry, 1961–62,* Bulletin No. 56. Canberra: 1963.

G5. Austria: Oesterreichisches statistisches Zentralamt. "Ergebnisse der nichtlandwirtschaftlichen Betriebszaehlung, 1964, 1. Teil," *Beitraege zur oesterreichischen Statistik,* No. 171. Vienna: 1968.

G6. Belgium: Institut national de statistique. *Annuaire statistique de la Belgique.* Brussels: annual.

1. Some more common governmental periodicals are listed above.

G7. Bulgaria: Tsentralno statistichesko upravleniye pri Ministerskiya sŭvet. *Statisticheski godishnik na Narodna republika Bŭlgariya.* Sofia: 1960.

G8. ———: Tsentralno statistichesko upravleniye pri Ministerskiya sŭvet. *Prebroyavane na naselenieto v Narodna republika Bŭlgariya na 1.XII. 1956 godina,* Vxl. IV. Sofia: 1960.

G9. Canada: Dominion Bureau of Statistics. *Canada Year Book.* Ottawa: annual.

G10. ———: Dominion Bureau of Statistics. *General Review of Manufacturing Industries of Canada, 1954.* Ottawa: 1957.

G11. ———: Dominion Bureau of Statistics. *General Review of Manufacturing Industries of Canada, 1961.* Ottawa: 1965.

G12. Czechoslovakia: Státní statistický úřad. *Statistická ročenka Československé socialistické republiky.* Prague: annual.

G13 ———: Vydala Ústředuí komise lidové kontroly a statistiky. *Sčítání lidu, domů a bytů v Československé socialistické republice k l. březnu 1961,* Vol. II. Prague: 1965.

G14. Denmark: Det Statistiske Department. *Virksomhedernes størrelsesfordeling, personel, ejerforhold m.v.: Erhvervstaellingen 1958.* Copenhagen: 1963.

G15. European Economic Community. *Industrial Statistics.* Brussels: quarterly.

G16. ———. *Input-Output-Tabellen fuer die Laender der Europaeischen Wirtschaftsgemeinschaft.* Brussels: October/1964.

G17. ———. *Statistische Studien und Erhebungen: Endgültige Ergebnisse des Industriezensus von 1963,* 2/1969. Brussels: 1969.

G18. Finland: Central Statistical Office. *Bulletin of Statistics.* Helsinki: monthly.

G19. ———: Central Statistical Office. *Statistical Yearbook of Finland.* Helsinki: annual.

G20. ———: Suomen Virallinen Tilasto. *Vuoden 1953: Liikeyrityslaskenta,* Vol. I. Helsinki: 1960.

G21. France: Institut national de la statistique et des études économiques. *Annuare statistique de la France.* Paris: Presse Universitaire de France, annual.

G22. ———: Institut national de la statistique et des études économiques. *Les établissements industriels et commerciaux en France en 1954.* Paris: Presse Universitaire de France, 1966.

G23. ———: Ministère du travail et de la prévoyance sociale. *Résultats statistiques du recensement général de la population,* Volume 1, 2nd part. Paris: Imprimerie nationale, 1910.

G24. Germany: Kaiserliches Statistisches Amt. *Statistik des Deutschen Reiches,* Vols. 214–222. Berlin: Putthammer and Muehlbrecht, 1910.

G25. ———: German Democratic Republic (East Germany): Staatliche Zentralverwaltung fuer Statistik. *Statistisches Jahrbuch der Deutschen Demokratischen Republik.* East Berlin: annual.

G26. ———: German Federal Republic (West Germany): Statistiches Bundesamt. *Statistik der Bundesrepublik Deutschland.* Mainz and Stuttgart: Kohlhammer Verlag, irregular.

G27. ———: German Federal Republic (West Germany): Statistisches Bundesamt. *Statistisches Jahrbuch fuer die Bundesrepublik Deutschland.* Mainz and Stuttgart: annual.

G28. Greece. Ethnike Statistike Hyperesia. *Résultats du récensement de la population et des habitations effectué le 19 mai 1961*, Vol. I and III. Athens: 1964, 1968.

G29. ———: Ethnike Statistike Hyperesia, *Résultats du récensement des industries manifacturières, artisanat et des industries extractives.* Athens: 1965.

G30. ———: Ethnike Statistike Hyperesia. *Statistical Yearbook of Greece.* Athens: annual.

G31. Hungary Központi Statisztikai Hivatal. *A magyar népgazdasag ágazati kapcsolatainak mérlege, 1959 évben.* Budapest: 1961.

G32. ———: Központi Statisztikai Hivatal. *Statisztikai évkönyn.* Budapest: annual.

G33. ———: Központi Statisztikai Hivatal. *Területi idösorok.* Budapest: 1969.

G34. International Labour Office. *Yearbook of Labour Statistics.* Geneva: annual.

G35. International Monetary Fund. *International Financial Statistics.* Washington, D.C.: monthly.

G36. Ireland: Central Statistics Office. "Analysis of the Census of Industrial Production 1963," *Irish Statistical Bulletin,* supl. Dublin: March/1968.

G37. ———: Central Statistical Office. *Statistical Abstract of Ireland.* Dublin: S.O., annual.

G38. Israel: Central Bureau of Statistics. "Establishments and Employed Persons in Industry by Branch—May 1965," *Census of Industry and Crafts,* Publ. 2. Jerusalem: 1966.

G39. ———: Central Bureau of Statistics. *Statistical Abstract of Israel.* Jerusalem: annual.

G40. Italy: Instituto centrale di statistica. *Annuario di statistiche industriale.* Rome: annual.

G40a. ———: Instituto centrale di statistica. *Annuario statistico italiano.* Rome: annual.

G41. ———: Istituto centrale di statistica. *4° Censimento generale dell' industria e del commercio,* Vol. III, Industrie, Tomo 1, *Impresse.* Rome: 1966.

G42. Japan: Bureau of Statistics. *1963 Establishment Census of Japan.* Tokyo: 1965.

G43. ———: Bureau of Statistics. *Japan Statistical Yearbook.* Tokyo: annual.

G44. ———: Ministry of International Trade and Industry. *Census of Manufacturing, 1964.* Tokyo: 1968.

G45. ———: Tokihiki Iinkai. *Nihon no sangyo shucho.* Tokyo: 1964.

G46. Netherlands Central Bureau of Statistics. *Statistical Yearbook of the Netherlands.* s'Gravenhage: annual.

G47. New Zealand: Department of Statistics. *New Zealand Official Yearbook.* Wellington: annual.

G48. ———: Department of Statistics. *New Zealand Industrial Production 1963–64.* Wellington: August/1965.

G49. Norway: Statistisk Sentralbyrå *Bedriftstelling 1963.* Oslo: 1967.

G50. ———: Statistisk Sentralbyrå. *Industristatistikk 1964.* Oslo: 1966.

G51. ———: Statistisk Sentralbyrå. *Industristatistikk 1966.* Oslo: 1968.

G52. ———: Statistisk Sentralbyrå. *Statistisk årbok.* Olso: annual.

G53. O.E.C.D. *Labor Force Statistics, 1956–66.* Paris: 1968.

G54. ———. *Manpower Statistics, 1950–62.* Paris: 1963.

G55. ———. *National Accounts of the O.E.C.D. Nations, 1958–67.* Paris: n.d.

G56. Poland: Głowny urząd statystyzny. *Rocznik Statystyczny.* Warsaw: annual.

G57. ———: Głowny urząd statystyzny. *Statystyka przemyslu 1958 (Statystyka Polski,* Zeszyt 41). Warsaw: 1960.

G58. ———: Głowny urząd statystyczny. *Statystyka przemysłu 1964 [Statystyka polski materiały statystyczne,* Zeszyt 1 (123)]. Warsaw: 1966.

G59. Portugal: Instituto nacional de estatística. *O inquérito industrial de 1957–59, Volume geral.* Lisbon: n.d.

G60. Romania: Direcţia Centrală de Statistică. *Anuarul statistic al R.P.R.* Bucharest: annual.

G61. South Africa: Bureau of Statistics. *Industrial Census 1961–62,* Report 303, and 304. Pretoria: Government Printer, 1968.

G62. ———: Bureau of Census and Statistics. *Statistical Yearbook.* Pretoria: annual.

G63. ———: Bureau of Census and Statistics. *Thirty-Fifth Industrial Census, 1951–52.* Report No. 206. Pretoria: 1954.

G64. ———: Office of Census and Statistics. *Statistics of Production.* Pretoria: Government Printing and Stationary Office, 1921.

G65. Spain: Servicio sindical de estadistica. *Estadisticas de produccion industrial 1965.* Madrid: 1966.

G66. Sweden: Central Bureau of Statistics. *Statistical Abstract of Sweden.* Stockholm: annual.

G67. ———: Finansdepartementet. *Ägande och inflytande inom det privata näringslivet,* Koncentrationsutredningen V. Stockholm: 1968.

G68. ———: Finansdepartementet. *Industrins struktur och konkurrensförhållanden,* Koncentrationsutredningen III. Stockholm: 1968.

G69. ———: Statistika centralbyran. *Industri 1965,* Sveriges officiella statistik. Stockholm: 1967.

G70. ———: Utgiven av handelsdepartment. *Statliga företag.* Stockholm: 1966.

G71. Switzerland: Eidgenössisches Departement des Innern, Statistisches Bureau. "Ergebnisse der eidg. Betriebszählung von 9. August 1905," *Schweizersiche Statistik,* Vol. 176. Bern: 1911.

G72. ———: Eidgenössisches statistisches Amt. *Eidgenössische Betriebszählung Sept. 1965, Betriebe,* Band 2, Statistische Quellenwerke der Schweiz, Heft 410. Bern: 1967.

G73. ———: Eidgenössisches statistisches Amt. *Eidgenössische Betriebszählung, September 1965,* Band 1, Statistische Quellenwerke der Schweiz, Heft 409. Bern: 1967.

G74. ———: Eidgenössisches statistisches Amt. *Statistisches Jahrbuch der Schweiz.* Basel: annual.

G75. U.S.S.R.: Tsentral'noyê statisticheskoye upravleniye. *Narodnoyê khoziaistvo SSSR.* Moscow: annual.

G76. United Kingdom: Board of Trade. *The Report of the Census of Production 1958,* Part 133. London: H.M.S.O., 1960.

G77. ———: Board of Trade and Central Statistical Office. *Input-Output Tables for the United Kingdom, 1954;* Studies in Official Statistics 8. London: H.M.S.O., 1961.

G78. ———: Central Statistical Office. *The Index of Industrial Production.* London: H.M.S.O., 1959.

G.78a. United Nations. *The Growth of World Industry, 1938–61.* New York: 1963.

G79. ———: *The Growth of World Industry, 1953–65.* New York: 1967.

G80. ———: *The Growth of World Industry, 1967 ed.* New York: 1968.

G82. ———: *Yearbook of National Account Statistics.* New York: annual.

G83. ———: Economic Commission for Europe. *Incomes in Postwar Europe: A Study of Policies, Growth, and Distribution.* Geneva: 1967.

G84. ———: Economic Commission for Europe. *Some Factors in Economic Growth in Europe during the 1950's.* Geneva: 1964.

G85. U.S.A.: Bureau of the Census. *Annual Survey of Manufacturers.* Washington, D.C.: G.P.O., annual.

G86. ———: Bureau of the Census. *1963 Census of Manufacturing,* Vol. I. Washington, D.C.: G.P.O., 1966.

G87. ———: Bureau of the Census. *1960 Census of Population.* Washington, D.C.: G.P.O., 1964.

G88. ———: Bureau of the Census. *1963 Enterprise Statistics,* Part I. Washington, D.C.: G.P.O., 1968.

G89. ———: Bureau of the Census. *Historical Statistics of the United States.* Washington, D.C.: G.P.O., 1960.

G90. ———: Bureau of the Census. *Sixteenth Census of the United States: 1940.* Washington, D.C.: G.P.O., 1943.

G91. ———: Bureau of the Census. *Statistical Abstract of the United States.* Washington, D.C.: G.P.O., annual.

G92. ———: Bureau of the Census. *Thirteenth Census of the United States,* Vol. VIII, *Manufacturing 1909.* Washington, D.C.: G.P.O., 1913.

G93. ———: Bureau of the Census. *United States Census of Population: 1950, Special Reports.* Washington, D.C.: G.P.O., 1955.

G94. ———: Congress, Joint Economic Committee. *Annual Economic Indicators for the U.S.S.R.* Washington, D.C.: G.P.O., 1964.

G95. ———: Congress, Joint Economic Committee. *Current Economic Indicators of the U.S.S.R.* Washington, D.C.: G.P.O., 1965.

G96. ———: Congress, Joint Economic Committee. *Economic Developments in Countries of Eastern Europe.* Washington, D.C.: G.P.O., 1970.

G97. ———: Congress, Joint Economic Committee. *New Directions in the Soviet Economy.* Washington, D.C.: G.P.O., 1966.

G98. ———: Congress, Select Committee on Small Business, U.S. House of Representatives. *Mergers and Superconcentration.* Washington, D.C.: G.P.O., Nov./1962.

G99. ———: Congress, Subcommittee on Antitrust and Monopoly, U.S. Senate. *Concentration Ratios in Manufacturing Industry, 1963.* Washington, D.C.: G.P.O., 1966.

G100. ———: Congress, Subcommittee on Antitrust and Monopoly, U.S. Senate. *Economic Concentration,* Part V, *Concentration and Divisional Reporting.* Washington, D.C.: G.P.O., 1966.

G101. ———: Congress, Subcommittee on Antitrust and Monopoly, U.S. Senate. *Economic Concentration,* Part 7A, *Hearings.* Washington, D.C.: G.P.O., 1968.

G102. ———: Department of Commerce. *Survey of Current Business.* Washington, D.C.: G.P.O., monthly.

G103. ———: Federal Trade Commission. *Large Mergers in Manufacturing and Mining; 1948–67.* Washington, D.C.: G.P.O., 1968.
G104. ———: Federal Trade Commission and Security and Exchanges Commission. *Quarterly Financial Reports for Manufacturing Firms, Fourth Quarter 1963.* Washington, D.C.: G.P.O., 1964.
G105. ———: Temporary National Economic Committee. *Distribution of Ownership in the 200 Largest Nonfinancial Corporations,* Monograph No. 29. Washington, D.C.: G.P.O., 1940.
G106. ———: Treasury Department, Internal Revenue Service. *Statistics of Income.* Washington, D.C.: G.P.O., annual.
G107. Yugoslavia: Savezni zavod za statistiku. *Popis stanovništva 1953,* Knjiga V. Belgrade: 1960.
G108. ———: Savezni zavod za statistiku. *Yugoslav Industry 1963 (Statistički bilten 421).* Belgrade: 1963.
G109. ———: Savezni zavod za statistiku. *Statistički godišnjak S.F.R.J.* Belgrade: annual.

A Selected List of Books

B1. Abegglen, J. C. *The Japanese Factory: Aspects of its Social Organization.* New York: Free Press of Glencoe, 1958.
B2. Abramovitz, Moses, ed. *The Allocation of Economic Resources.* Stanford: Stanford University Press, 1959.
B3. Adelman, Irma and Morris, Cynthia Taft. *Society, Politics, and Economic Development.* Baltimore: Johns Hopkins Press, 1967.
B4. Akademiya nauk SSSR, Institut ekonomiki. *Politicheskaia ekonomiia uchebnik.* Moscow: Gos. izd. polit. lit., 1955.
B5. Alchian, Armen. *Some Economics of Property.* Rand Corporation Paper P-2316. Santa Monica, Calif.: May 26/ 1961.
B6. Allen, R.G.D. *Macroeconomic Theory.* New York: Macmillan, 1967.
B7. Almond, G. A. and Verba, S., eds. *The Politics of Developing Areas.* Princeton: Princeton University Press, 1960.
B8. Alton, Thad P., et al. *Czechoslovak National Income and Product in 1947–48 and 1955–56.* New York: Columbia University Press, 1962.
B9. ———, *Hungarian National Income and Product in 1955.* New York: Columbia University Press, 1963.
B10. ———, *Polish National Income and Product in 1954, 1955, and 1956.* New York: Columbia University Press, 1965.
B11. Ames, Edward. *Soviet Economic Processes.* Homewood, Ill.: Irwin, 1965.
✗B12. Andreski, Stanislav. *Elements of Comparative Sociology.* London: Weidenfeld and Nicolson, 1964. ✗
B13. Ardrey, Robert. *The Territorial Imperative.* New York: Atheneum, 1966.
B14. Arrow, Kenneth, et al., eds. *Mathematical Methods in the Social Sciences.* Stanford: Stanford University Press, 1959.
B15. Avineri, Shlomo. *The Social and Political Thought of Karl Marx.* Cambridge, England: Cambridge University Press, 1968.
B16. Azrael, Jeremy R. *Managerial Power and Soviet Politics.* Cambridge, Mass.: Harvard University Press, 1966.

B17. Bagiotti, Tullio, ed. *Essays in Honor of Marco Fanno*. Padua: University of Padua, 1966.

B18. Bain, Joe S. *International Differences in Industrial Structure*. New Haven: Yale University Press, 1966.

B19. Baker, Helen and France, Robert R. *Centralization and Decentralization in Industrial Relations*. Industrial Relations Section, Department of Economics and Sociology. Princeton: 1954.

B20. Balassa, Bela. *The Theory of Economic Integration*. Homewood, Ill.: Irwin, 1961.

B21. Banton, Michael, ed. *The Revelance of Models for Social Anthropology*, Association for Social Anthropology Monograph No. 1. London: Tavistock Publ., 1965.

B22. Baran, Paul. *The Political Economy of Growth*. New York: Monthly Review Press, 1957.

B23. ———, and Sweezy, Paul. *Monopoly Capitalism*. New York: Monthly Review Press, 1966.

B24. Baumol, William. *Business Behavior, Value, and Growth*. New York: Macmillan, 1959.

B25. Bazelon, David T. *The Paper Economy*. New York: Vintage Books, 1963.

B26. Beaglehold, Ernest. *Property: A Study in Social Psychology*. London: Allen and Unwin, 1931.

B27. Becker, Abraham S. *Soviet National Income, 1958–64*. Berkeley: University of California, 1969.

B28. Becker, Rudolf. *Sowjetische Lohnpolitik zwischen Ideologie und Wirtschaftsgesetz*. Berlin: Duncker und Humblot, 1965.

B29. Bellerby, J. R., *et al. Agriculture and Industry: Relative Income*. London: Macmillan, 1956.

B30. Bergson, Abram. *Planning and Productivity under Soviet Socialism*. New York: 1968.

B31. Bergson, Abram. *The Structure of Soviet Wages*. Cambridge, Mass.: Harvard University Press, 1944.

B32. ———, and Kuznets, Simon, eds. *Economic Trends in the Soviet Union*. Cambridge, Mass.: Harvard University Press, 1963.

B33. Berle, Adolf A. and Means, Gardiner C. *The Modern Corporation and Private Property*. New York: Macmillan, 1933.

B34. Berliner, Joseph S. *Factory and Manager in the U.S.S.R.* Cambridge, Mass.: Harvard University Press, 1957.

B35. Berman, Harold J. *Justice in the U.S.S.R.* New York: Vintage Books, 1963.

B35a. Blair, John M. *Economic Concentration: Structure, Behavior, and Public Policy*. New York: Harcourt, Brace, Jovanovich, 1972.

⋋B36. Blauner, Robert. *Alienation and Freedom: The Factory Worker and His Industry*. Chicago: University of Chicago Press, 1964.

B37. Bogdanov, Aleksander (A. A. Malinovskii). *Tektologiya, vseobshchaya organizatsionnaya nauka*. Peterburg, Moscow: Izdt. Z. I. Grzhebina, 1922.

B38. Bornstein, Morris, ed. *Comparative Economic Systems*. Homewood, Ill.: Irwin, 1965.

⋋B39. ———. *Plan and Market: Economic Reforms in Eastern Europe*. New Haven: Yale University Press, 1973.

B40. ———, and Fusfeld, Daniel. *The Soviet Economy: A Book of Readings*, 3rd edition. Homewood, Ill.: Irwin, 1970.

B41. Boulding, Kenneth. *The Organizational Revolution*. New York: Harper, 1953.

B42. Brown, Alan and Neuberger Egon. *International Trade and Central Planning*. Berkeley: University of California Press, 1968.

B43. Brown, J. F. *Bulgaria Under Communist Rule*. New York: Praeger, 1970.

B44. Brown, Murray, ed. *The Theory and Empirical Analysis of Production*. New York: Columbia University Press for N.B.E.R., 1967.

B45. Brzezinski, Zbigniew K. and Huntington, Samuel P. *Political Power: U.S.A./U.S.S.R.* New York: Viking Press, 1964.

B46. Burgess, Leonard R. *Top Executive Pay Package*. New York: Free Press of Glencoe, 1963.

B47. Burnham, James. *The Managerial Revolution*. New York: John Day, 1941.

B48. Campbell, Robert W. *The Economics of Soviet Oil and Gas*. Baltimore: Johns Hopkins Press, 1968.

B49. Caves, Richard, ed. *Britain's Economic Prospects*. Washington, D.C.: Brookings Institution, 1968.

B50. Centre européen de l'enterprise publique. *Les entreprises publiques dans la Communauté Economique Européenne*. Paris: Dunod, 1967.

B51. Chandler, Alfred D., Jr. *Strategy and Structure*. Cambridge, Mass.: MIT Press, 1962.

B52. Chapman, Janet G. and Chou, Shun-hsin, eds. *The Economies of the Communist World*. (forthcoming).

B53. Cheung, Steven N. S. *The Theory of Share Tenancy*. Chicago: University of Chicago Press, 1970.

B54. Cillié, François S. *Centralization or Decentralization: A Study of Educational Adaption,* Contributions to Education No. 789. New York: Teachers College, Columbia University, 1940.

B55. Clark, Colin and Struvel, Geer, eds. *Income and Wealth, Series X: Income Redistribution and the Statistical Foundation of Economic Policy.* New Haven: International Association for the Study of Income and Wealth, 1964.

B56. Cohen, Steven S. *Modern Capitalist Planning: The French Model*. Cambridge, Mass.: Harvard University Press, 1969.

B57. Collins, Norman R. and Preston, Lee E. *Concentration and Price-Cost Margins in Manufacturing*. Berkeley: University of California Press, 1968.

B58. Conference on Income and Wealth. *The Behavior of Income Shares: Selected Theoretical and Empirical Issues*. Princeton: Princeton University Press for N.B.E.R., 1964.

B59. Cooper, W. W., *et al., eds. New Perspectives in Organization Research*. New York: Wiley, 1964.

B60. Creamer, Daniel, *et al. Capital in Manufacturing and Mining,* Princeton: Princeton University Press for N.B.E.R., 1960.

B61. Crosland, C.A.R. *The Future of Socialism*. New York: Macmillan, 1957.

B62. Crozier, Michel. *The Bureaucratic Phenomenon*. Chicago: University of Chicago Press, 1964.

B63. Dahl, Robert A. and Lindblom, Charles E. *Politics, Economics, and Welfare*. New York: Harper and Brothers, 1953.

B64. Dahrendorf, Ralf. *Class and Class Conflict in Industrial Society*. Stanford: Stanford University Press, 1959.

B65. Dantzig, George. *Linear Programming and Extensions.* Princeton: Princeton University Press, 1963.

B66. Davis, Lance and North, Douglass. *Institutional Change and American Economic Growth.* (forthcoming).

B67. Denison, Edward F. *The Sources of Economic Growth in the United States and the Alternatives before Us.* New York: Committee for Economic Development, 1962.

B68. ———, and Poullier, Jean-Pierre. *Why Growth Rates Differ: Postwar Experiences in Nine Western Countries.* Washington, D.C.: Brookings Institution, 1967.

B69. Diaz-Alejandro, Carlos F. *Exchange-Rate Devaluation in a Semi-Industrialized Country: The Experience of Argentina, 1951–61.* Cambridge, Mass.: M.I.T. Press, 1965.

B70. Domhoff, G. William. *Who Rules America?* Englewood Cliffs: Prentice-Hall, 1967.

B71. Eckstein, Alexander. *Comparison of Economic Systems.* Berkeley: University of California Press, 1971.

B72. Edwards, Allen L. *Techniques of Attitude Scale Construction.* New York: Appleton-Century-Croft, 1957.

B73. Edwards, Edgar O. *Work Effort, Investable Surplus and the Inferiority of Competition.* Yale Economic Growth Center Discussion Paper No. 64.

B74. Ekonomski institut. *Problemi privredne koncentracije.* Zagreb: 1964.

B75. Engels, Friedrich. *The Origin of the Family, Private Property, and the State.* New York: International Publishers, n.d.

B76. Evely, R. and I.M.D. Little. *Concentration in British Industry.* Cambridge, Eng.: University Press, 1960.

B77. Falk Project for Economic Research in Israel. *Sixth Report, 1961–63.* Jerusalem: 1964.

B78. Fédération générale du travail de Belgique, *Holdings et democratie économique.* Brussels: 1956.

B79. Feinstein, C. H. *Domestic Capital Formation in the United Kingdom, 1920–38.* Cambridge, Eng.: University Press, 1965.

B80. Feiwel, George. *The Soviet Quest for Economic Efficiency.* New York: Praeger, 1967.

B81. Florence, P. Sargent. *Investment, Location, and Size of Plant.* Cambridge, Eng.: University Press, 1948.

B82. ———. *The Logic of British and American Industry.* London: Routledge and Paul, 1953.

B83. ———. *Ownership, Control and Success of Large Corporations.* London: Sweet and Maxwell, 1961.

B84. Frei, Rudolf, ed. *Economic Systems of the West.* Basel: Kyklos Verlag, 1959.

B85. Freud, Sigmund. *Civilization and its Discontents.* New York: Norton, 1962.

B86. Fromm, Erich, ed. *Marx's Concept of Man.* New York: Ungar, 1969.

B87. Galbraith, John Kenneth. *The Affluent Society.* Boston: Houghton Mifflin, 1958.

B88. ———. *American Capitalism: The Concept of Countervailing Power.* Boston: Houghton Mifflin, 1952.

B89. ———. *The New Industrial State.* Boston: Houghton Mifflin, 1967.

B89a. Galenson, Walter and Lipset, Seymour Martin, eds. *Labor and Trade Unionism.* New York: Wiley, 1960.

B90. Gallik, Daniel, *et al. The Soviet Financial System: Structure, Operations, and Statistics.* U.S. Bureau of the Census, International Population Statistics Report, Series P-90, No. 23. Washington, D.C.: G.P.O., 1967.

B91. Georgescu-Rogen, Nicholas. *Entropy and Economic Processes.* Cambridge, Mass.: Harvard University Press, 1971.

B92. Gilbert, Milton, *et al. Comparative National Product and Price Level.* Paris: O.E.C.D., 1958.

B93. Goldman, Marshall I. *Soviet Marketing.* New York: Free Press of Glencoe, 1963.

B94. Goldsmith, Raymond W. *Financial Structure and Development.* New Haven: Yale University Press, 1969.

B95. ———. *The National Wealth of the United States in the Postwar Period.* Princeton: Princeton University Press, 1962.

B96. ———, and Saunders, Christopher, eds. *The Measurement of National Wealth:* Income and Wealth, Series VIII (International Association for Research in Income and Wealth). London: Bowes and Bowes, 1959.

B97. Gordon, Robert Aaron. *Business Leadership in the Large Corporation.* Washington, D.C.: Brookings Institution, 1945.

B98. Granick, David. *The European Executive.* Garden City, N.Y.: Doubleday, 1962.

B99. ———. *Management of the Industrial Firm in the U.S.S.R.* New York: Columbia University Press, 1954.

B100. ———. *Soviet Metal-Fabricating and Economic Development.* Madison: University of Wisconsin Press, 1967.

B101. Grindea, Dan. *Venitul naţional în Republica Socialistă România.* Bucharest: Editura stiinţifica, 1967.

B102. Gromov, I. and Kamenetskiy, V. Ya. *Proizvidstvennoye ob'edin' eniye v SSSR.* Moscow: Izd. "Ekonomika," 1967.

B103. Grossman, Gregory, ed. *Value and Plan.* Berkeley: University of California Press, 1960.

B104. Hackett, John and Ann-Marie. *Economic Planning in France.* Cambridge, Mass.: Harvard University Press, 1963.

B105. Hagen, Everett E., ed. *Planning Economic Development.* Homewood, Ill.: Irwin, 1963.

B106. Hague, D.C., ed. *Price Formation in Various Economies.* New York: St. Martin, 1967.

B107. Hallowell, A. Irving. *Culture and Experience.* Philadelphia: University of Pennsylvania Press, 1955.

B108. Herskovits, Melville J. *Economic Anthropology.* New York: W. W. Norton, 1952.

B109. Hildebrand, George H. and Liu, Ta-Chung. *Manufacturing Production Functions in the United States, 1957.* Ithaca: New York State School of Industrial and Labor Relations, Cornell University, 1965.

B110. Hilferding, Rudolf. *Das Finanzkapital.* Frankfurt: Europäische Verlagsanstalt, 1968.

B111. Hoffman, Walther G. *Die branchenmaessige Lohnstruktur der Industrie: Ein intertemporaler und internationaler Vergleich.* Tuebingen: J. C. B. Mohr, 1961.

B112. ———, *et al., Das Wachstum der deutschen Wirtschaft seit der Mitte des 19. Jahrhunderts.* West Berlin: Springer Verlag, 1965.

B113. Holzman, Franklyn D. *Soviet Taxation.* Cambridge, Mass.: Harvard University Press, 1955.

B114. Horowitz, David, ed. *Marx and Modern Economics.* New York: Monthly Review Press, 1968.

B115. Horowitz, Irving Louis, ed. *The New Sociology: Essays in Social Science and Social Theory in Honor of C. Wright Mills.* New York: Oxford University Press, 1964.

B116. Hoselitz, Bert F., ed. *Theories of Economic Growth.* Glencoe, Ill.: Free Press, 1960.

B117. Hough, Jerry. *The Soviet Prefects: The Local Party Organs in Industrial Decision-Making.* Cambridge, Mass.: Harvard University Press, 1969.

B118. Houssiaux, Jacques. *Le pouvoir de monopol.* Paris: Sirey, 1958.

B119. ———. *Les 500 plus grandes sociétés françaises.* Paris: Sirey, 1958.

B120. Huberman, Leo and Sweezy, Paul M. *Socialism in Cuba.* New York: Monthly Review Press, 1969.

B121. Hugh-Jones, E. M. *Wage-Structure in Theory and Practice.* Amsterdam: North Holland Publishing Co., 1966.

B122. Hulburt, Virgil L. *Uses of Farm Resources as Conditioned by Tenure Arrangements.* North Central Regional Publication No. 151, Nebraska College of Agriculture Research Bulletin 215. Nebraska: 1964.

B123. Isard, Walter. *General Theory: Social, Political, Economic and Regional.* Cambridge, Mass.: M.I.T. Press, 1969.

B124. Jaques, Elliott. *Measurement of Responsibility.* London: Tavistock Publishing, 1956.

B125. Jasny, Naum. *Essays on the Soviet Economy.* New York: Praeger, 1963.

B126. Johnson, Chalmers, ed. *Change in Communist Systems.* Stanford: Stanford University Press, 1970.

B127. Kalecki, Michal. *Theory of Economic Dynamics.* London: Allen and Unwin, 1954.

B128. Kanovsky, Eliyahu. *The Economy of the Israeli Kibbutz.* Cambridge, Mass.: Harvard University Press, 1966.

B129. Kaplan, Norman. *Earnings Distributions in the USSR.* Santa Monica: Rand Memorandum RM-6170, Nov. 1969.

B130. Kaser, Michael. *Comecon,* 2nd ed. London: Oxford University Press, 1967.

B131. Katzarov, Konstantin. *The Theory of Nationalization.* The Hague: Martinus Nijhof, 1964.

B132. Kaysen, Carl and Turner, Donald F. *Antitrust Policy: An Economic and Legal Analysis.* Cambridge, Mass.: Harvard University Press, 1959.

B133. Kemp, Murray. *The Pure Theory of International Trade.* Englewood Cliffs, N. J.: Prentice-Hall, 1964.

B134. Kendall, Maurice G. *Rank Correlation Methods.* New York: Hafner, 1962.

B135. Kerr, Clark. *Labor and Management in Industrial Society.* Garden City, N.Y.: Doubleday, 1964.

B136. Keynes, John Maynard. *Essays in Persuasion.* New York, 1932.

B137. Kolaja, Jiri. *Workers' Councils: The Yugoslav Experience.* New York: Praeger, 1965.

B138. Kornai, János. *Antiequilibrium.* Amsterdam: North Holland Press, 1972.

B139. ———. *Mathematical Planning of Structural Decisions.* Amsterdam: North Holland Publishing Co., 1967.

B140. ———. *Overcentralization in Economic Administration,* (trans. by John Knapp). London: Oxford University Press, 1959.

B141. Kravis, Irving B. *The Structure of Income: Some Quantitative Essays.* Philadelphia: University of Pennsylvania, 1962.

B142. Krupp, Hans-Juergen. *Theorie der personellen Einkommensverteilung.* Berlin: Duncker und Humblot, 1968.

B143. Kuusinen, O. W., *et al. Fundamentals of Marxism-Leninism.* Moscow: Foreign Language Publishing House, n.d.

B144. Kuznets, Simon. *Modern Economic Growth: Rate, Structure, and Spread.* New Haven: Yale University Press, 1966.

B145. Labedz, Leopold, ed. *Revisionism: Essays on the History of Marxist Ideas.* New York: Praeger, 1962.

B146. Lampman, Robert J. *The Share of Top Wealth Holders in National Wealth, 1922–56.* Princeton: Princeton University Press for N.B.E.R., 1962.

B147. Lange, Oskar. *Political Economy,* Vol. I. London: Pergamon, 1963.

B148. Larner, Robert J. *Management Control and the Large Corporation.* New York: Dunellen, 1970.

B149. Lenin, V. I. *Imperialism, The Highest Stage of Capitalism.* Moscow: Progress Publ., 1968.

B150. Levy, Marion J., Jr. *Modernization and the Structure of Societies.* Princeton: Princeton University Press, 1966.

B151. Lewellen, Wilbur G. *Executive Compensation in Large Industrial Corporations.* New York: Columbia University Press for N.B.E.R., 1968.

B152. Lewis, H. Gregg, *Unionism and Relative Wages in the United States.* Chicago: University of Chicago Press, 1963.

B153. Lippincott, Benjamin E., ed. *On the Economic Theory of Socialism.* Minneapolis: University of Minnesota Press, 1938.

B154. Lipset, Seymore M. *Political Man.* Garden City, N.Y.: Doubleday, 1960.

B155. Litterer, Joseph A., ed. *Organizations: Structure and Behavior,* 2nd ed. New York: Wiley, 1969.

B156. Lundberg, Ferdinand. *The Rich and the Super Rich.* New York: Lyle Stuart, 1968.

B157. Lutz, Vera. *Central Planning for the Market Economy.* London: Longmans, 1969.

B158. Lydall, Harold. *The Structure of Earnings.* Oxford: Clarendon Press, 1968.

B159. Machlup, Fritz. *The Production and Distribution of Knowledge in the United States.* Princeton: Princeton University Press, 1962.

B160. Maddison, Angus. *Economic Growth in the West: Comparative Experience in Europe and North America.* New York, 20th Century Fund, 1964.

B161. Malinowski, Bronislaw. *Crime and Custom in Savage Society.* New York: Harcourt Brace and Co., 1926.

B162. Malinvaud, E. and Bacharach, M. O. L., eds. *Activity Analysis in the Theory of Growth and Planning.* London: Macmillan, 1967.

B163. Mamalakis, Markos and Reynolds, Clark Winton. *Essay on the Chilean Economy.* Homewood, Ill.: Irwin, 1965.

B164. Mandel, Ernst. *Marxist Economic Theory.* New York: Monthly Review Press, 1968.

B165. Mannheim, Karl. *Ideology and Utopia,* trans. by Louis Worth and Edward Shils. New York: Harcourt, Brace and Co., 1951.

B166. March, James G., ed. *Handbook of Organizations.* Chicago: Rand McNally, 1965.

B167. March, James G. and Simon, Herbert A. *Organizations.* New York: Wiley, 1958.

B168. Marchal, Jean and Ducros, Bernard, eds. *The Distribution of National Income.* New York: St. Martin's Press, 1968.

B169. Marchal, Jean and Lecaillon, Jacques. *La répartition du revenue national,* Vol. IV. Paris: forthcoming.

B170. Marris, Robin. *The Economic Theory of "Managerial Capitalism."* New York: Free Press of Glencoe, 1964.

B171. Marsh, Robert M. *Comparative Sociology.* New York: Harcourt, Brace and World, 1967.

B172. Marshall, Alfred. *Industry and Trade.* London: Macmillan, 1920.

B173. Marx, Karl. *Capital,* Vols. I, II, III. Moscow: Foreign Language Publishing Co., 1961.

B174. ———. *Critique of the Gotha Program.* New York: International Publishers, 1938.

B175. ———. *The Economic and Philosophic Manuscripts of 1844,* ed. by Dirk J. Struik. New York: International Publishers, 1964.

B176. ———. *Grundrisse der Kritik der politischen Oekonomie.* East Berlin: Dietz Verlag, 1953.

B177. ———. *Precapitalist Economic Formations,* ed. by Eric J. Hobsbawm. New York International Publishers, 1965.

B178. ———. *Zur Kritik der politischen Oekonomie,* ed. by Karl Kautsky. Berlin: Dietz Nachfolger, 1924.

B179. ———, and Engels, Friedrich. *The German Ideology.* Moscow: Progress Publ., 1968.

B180. ———, and Engels, Friedrich. *Werke.* East Berlin: Dietz Verlag, 1961.

B181. Mason, Edward S., ed., *The Corporation in Modern Society.* New York: Atheneum, 1966.

B182. Meade, James E. *Efficiency, Equality, and the Ownership of Property.* London: Allen and Unwin, 1964.

B183. Menshikov, Stanislav. *Millionaires and Managers: Structure of U.S. Financial Oligarchy.* Moscow: Progress Publ., 1969.

B184. Michels, Robert. *Political Parties,* tr. Eden Paul and Cedar Paul. Glencoe, Ill.: Free Press, 1949.

B185. Miller, Walter G., *et al. Relative Efficiencies of Farm Tenure Classes in Intrafirm Resource Allocation.* North Central Regional Publ. No. 84, Iowa Agricultural Experimental Station Bulletin 461. Iowa: 1958.

B186. Mills, C. Wright. *The Power Elite.* New York: Oxford University Press, 1956.

B187. ———. *The Sociological Imagination.* New York: Grove Press, 1961.

B188. Minhas, Bagicha Singh. *An International Comparison of Factor Costs and Factor Use.* Amsterdam: North Holland Publishing Co., 1963.

B189. Moody's Investors Service. *Moody's Industrial Manual.* New York: annual.

B190. Moore, Franklin G., ed. *A Management Sourcebook.* New York: Harper and Row, 1964.

B191. Morgan, James N., *et al. Income and Welfare in the United States.* New York: McGraw-Hill, 1962.

B192. Morris, Charles. *Varieties of Human Value.* Chicago: University of Chicago Press, 1956.

B193. Morris, William T. *Decentralization in Management Systems.* Columbus: Ohio State University Press, 1968.

B194. Musgrave, Richard A., ed. *Essays in Fiscal Federalism.* Washington, D.C.: Brookings Institution, 1965.

B195. Myers, Charles A., ed. *Impact of Computers on Management.* Cambridge, Mass.: M.I.T. Press, 1968.

B196. National Institute of Economic and Social Research. *A Classified List of Large Companies Engaged in British Industries.* London: Dec./1955.

B197 Nelson, Ralph. *Concentration in Manufacturing in the Development of the United States.* New Haven: Yale University Press, 1963.

B198. Noyes, C. Reinhold. *The Institution of Property.* New York: Longmans, Green, and Co.: 1936.

B199. Orcutt, Guy H., *et al. Microanalysis of Socio-economic Systems: A Simulation Study.* New York: Harper, 1961.

B200. Pack, Howard. *Structural Change and Economic Policy in Israel.* New Haven: Yale University Press, 1971.

B201. Parsons, Talcott. *Essays in Sociological Theory, Pure and Applied.* Glencoe, Ill.: Free Press, 1949.

B202. ———. *The Social System.* Glencoe, Ill.: Free Press, 1951.

B203. Patinkin, Don. *Money, Interest, and Prices.* Evanston, Ill.: Row, Peterson and Co., 1956.

B204. Peacock, Alan T., ed. *Income Redistribution and Social Policy.* London: Jonathan Cape, 1954.

B205. Pejovich, Svetozar. *The Market-planned Economy of Yugoslavia.* Minneapolis: University of Minnesota Press, 1966.

B206. Perlman, Mark. *Labor Union Theories in America.* Evanston: Row, Peterson and Co., 1958.

B207. Perlo, Victor. *The Empire of High Finance.* New York: International Publishing Co., 1957.

B208. Phelps-Brown, E. H. and Browne, Margaret H. *A Century of Pay.* London: Macmillan, 1968.

B209. Polanyi, Karl, *et al. Trade and Market in Early Empires.* Glencoe, Ill.: The Free Press, 1957.

B210. President Magazine. *The President Directory 1967: Japan's 500 Leading Industrial Corporations.* Tokyo: 1967.

B211. Price, James L. *Organizational Effectiveness: An Inventory of Propositions.* Homewood, Ill.: Irwin, 1968.

✗ B212. Prochazka, Zora and Combs, Jerry W., Jr. *The Labor Force of Poland.* U.S. Bureau of the Census, International Population Statistics Report, Series P-20, No. 20. Washington, D.C.: G.P.O., 1964.

B213. Pryor, Frederic L. *The Communist Foreign Trade System.* Cambridge, Mass.: M.I.T. Press, 1963.

B214. ———. *Public Expenditures in Communist and Capitalist Nations.* Homewood, Ill.: Irwin, 1968.

B215. Raupach, Hans, *et al. Jahrbuch der Wirtschaft Osteuropas,* Vol. 2. Munich: Guenter Olzog Verlag, 1971.

B216. Rees, Albert. *The Economics of Trade Unions.* Chicago: University of Chicago Press, 1962.

B217. Rimashevakaia, N. M. *Ekonomicheskoi analiz dokhodov rabochikh i sluzbashchikh.* Moscow: Ekonomika, 1965.

494

Property and Industrial Organization

B218. Roberts, David. *Executive Compensation*. Glencoe, Ill.: Free Press, 1959.
B219. Roberts, Paul Craig. *Alienation and the Soviet Economy*. Albuquerque: University of New Mexico Press, 1971.
B220. Robinson, E.A.G., ed. *Economic Consequences of the Size of Nations*. New York: St. Martins, 1960.
B221. ———. *The Structure of Competitive Industry*. New York: Harcourt Brace, 1932.
B222. Rosenbluth, Gideon. *Concentration in Canadian Manufacturing Industries*. Princeton: Princeton University Press for N.B.E.R., 1957.
B223. Ross, Alf. *On Law and Justice*. London: Stevens and Sons, 1958.
B224. Rostas, L. *Comparative Productivity in British and American Industry*. Cambridge, England: University Press, 1948.
B225. Russett, Bruce, *et al. World Handbook of Political and Social Indicators*. New Haven: Yale University Press, 1964.
B226. Sakharov, Andrei D. *Progress, Coexistence and Intellectual Freedom*. New York: Norton, 1968.
B227. Schaller, Howard, ed. *Public Expenditure Decisions in the Urban Community*. Baltimore: Johns Hopkins, 1963.
B228. Scherer, Frederic M. *Industrial Market Structure and Economic Performance*. Chicago: Rand McNally, 1970.
B229. Schumpeter, Joseph. *Capitalism, Socialism, and Democracy,* 3rd ed. New York: Harper and Bros., 1950.
B230. Schweitzer, Arthur. *Big Business and the Third Reich*. Bloomington: Indiana University Press, 1964.
B231. Shepherd, William G. *Market Power and Economic Welfare*. New York: Random House, 1970.
B232. ———. *Economic Performance under Public Ownership*. New Haven: Yale University Press, 1965.
B233. Simler, Norman J. *The Impact of Unionism on Wage-Income Ratios in the Manufacturing Sector of the Economy*. University of Minnesota Studies in Economics and Business, No. 22. Minneapolis: University of Minnesota Press, 1961.
B234. Simon, Herbert A., *et al., Public Administration*. New York: Knopf, 1956.
B335. Smith, Adam. *Wealth of Nations*. New York: Modern Library, 1937.
B236. Smith, James. "Income and Wealth of Top Wealth Holders in the United States, 1958," Ph.D. dissertation, University of Oklahoma. Ann Arbor: University Microfilms, n.d.
B237. Smith, Robert S. and de Vyver, Frank T., eds., *Economic System and Public Policy: Essays in Honor of Calvin Bryce Hoover*. Durham, N.C.: Duke University Press, 1966.
B238. Soltow, Lee, ed. *Six Papers on the Size Distribution of Wealth and Income*. New York: Columbia University Press for N.B.E.R., 1969.
B239. Stein, Maurice and Vidich, Arthur, eds. *Sociology on Trial*. Englewood Cliffs: Prentice-Hall, 1963.
B240. Steindl, Josef. *Random Processes and the Growth of Firms: A Study of the Pareto Law*. New York: Hafner Publishing Co., 1965.
B241. Stigler, George. *The Organization of Industry*. Homewood, Ill.: Irwin, 1968.
B242. Stouffer, Samuel A., Guttman, Louis, *et al. Measurement and Prediction*. Princeton: Princeton University Press, 1950.

B243. Summers, Robert. *An Econometric Investigation of the Size Distribution of Lifetime Average Annual Income.* Technical Report No. 31, Department of Economics, Stanford University. Stanford: 1956.

B244. Sweezy, Paul. *The Present as History.* New York: Monthly Review Press, 1953.

B245. Taigăr, Simion. *Veniturile populatiei si nivelul de trai in R.P.R.* Bucharest: Editura politica, 1964.

B246. Tannenbaum, Arnold S., ed., *Control in Organization.* New York: McGraw-Hill, 1968.

B247. Textor, Robert B. *A Cross-Cultural Summary.* New Haven: HRAF Press, 1967.

B248. Thalheim, Karl C. and Höhmann, Hans-Herman, eds. *Wirtschaftsreformen in Osteuropa.* Cologne: Verlag Wissenschaft und Politik, 1968.

B249. Theil, Henri. *Economics and Information Theory.* Chicago: Rand McNally, 1967.

B250. Thompson, James D. *Organizations in Action.* New York: McGraw-Hill, 1967.

B251. Times of London. *The Times 300: A Guide to Leading Business in Britain and Europe.* London: 1965.

B252. Tinbergen, Jan. *Economic Policy: Principles and Design.* Amsterdam: North Holland Publishing Co., 1956.

B253. Toffler, Alvin. *Future Shock.* New York: Random House, 1970.

B254. Torgerson, Warren S. *Methods of Scaling.* New York: Wiley, 1958.

B255. Treml, Vladimir G. *The 1959 Soviet Intersectoral Flow Table.* Research Analysis Corporation Technical Paper RAC-TP-137. Washington, D.C., Nov./1964.

B256. Tuck, Ronald. *An Essay on the Economic Theory of Rank.* Oxford: Blackwells, 1954.

B257. Udy, Stanley H., Jr. *Organization of Work.* New Haven: HRAF Press, 1959.

B258. Universities-National Bureau Committee for Economic Research, ed. *Business Concentration and Price Policy.* Princeton: Princeton University Press for N.B.E.R., 1955.

B259. Vanek, Jaroslav. *The General Theory of Labor-Managed Market Economies.* Ithaca: Cornell University Press, 1970.

B260. Van Nimmen, Armand M. J. "French Planning: An Essay in Evaluation." Ph.D. dissertation, Columbia University, 1967. Ann Arbor: University Microfilm, 1970.

B261. Veblen, Thorstein. *Absentee Ownership and Business Enterprise in Recent Times.* New York: August Kelly, 1964.

B262. Wasowski, Stanislaw, ed. *East-West Trade and the Technology Gap: A Political and Economic Appraisal.* New York: Praeger, 1969.

B263. Waxman, Chaim, ed. *The End of Ideology Debate.* New York: Simon and Schuster, 1968.

B264. Weber, Max. *Economy and Society,* trans. by Guenther Ross and Claus Wittich. New York: Bedminister Press, 1968.

B265. Wedervang, Fröystein. *Development of a Population of Industrial Firms.* Oslo: Universitetsforlaget, 1964.

B266. Weisskoff, Richard. "Income Distribution and Economic Growth: An International Comparison." Ph.D. dissertation, Harvard University. Cambridge, Mass.: 1969.

B267. Wheelwright, Edward L. *Ownership and Control of Australian Companies*. Sidney: Law Book Co., 1957.

B268. Wheelwright, Edward L. and Miskelly, Judith. *Anatomy of Australian Manufacturing Industry*. Sidney: Law Book Co., 1967.

B269. Wiener, Norbert. *The Human Use of Human Beings: Cybernetics and Society*. Boston: Houghton-Mifflin, 1950.

B270. Wiles, Peter. *The Political Economy of Communism*. Cambridge, Mass.: Harvard University Press, 1962.

B271. Wiles, Peter. *Price, Cost, and Output*. New York: Praeger, 1963.

B272. Williamson, Oliver E. *The Economics of Discretionary Behavior: Managerial Objectives in a Theory of the Firm*. Englewood Cliffs: Prentice Hall, 1964.

B273. Williamson, Oliver E. *Corporate Control and Business Behavior*. Englewood Cliffs: Prentice-Hall, 1970.

B274. Wittfogel, Karl. *Oriental Despotism: A Comparative Study of Total Power*. New Haven: Yale University Press, 1957.

✗ B275. Woodward, Joan. *Industrial Organization: Theory and Practice*. London: Oxford University Press, 1965.

✗ B276. Zald, Meyer, ed. *Power in Organizations*. Nashville: Vanderbilt University Press, 1970.

Index of Persons

Abegglen, J. C., 369n
Ackerman, Robert W., 422n
Adams, F. Gerald, 393n
Adelman, Irma, 362n
Adelman, Morris, 151n, 182n, 199n, 211n, 452
Aiken, Michael, 283n, 418, 422n–24n, 431n–32n
Alchian, Armen, 375n, 378n
Alexander, C. F., 67
Almond, G. A., 362n
Alton, Thad P., 76n–77n
Ames, Edward, 30n, 261n, 340n
Andreski, Stanislav, 365n
Angell, Robert C., 339n
Ardrey, Robert, 380n
Aristotle, 35
Aron, Raymond, 124, 434
Arrow, Kenneth, 325n, 342n
Averch, H., 30n, 340n
Avineri, Shlomo, 429n
Azrael, Jeremy R., 124n

Bacon, Francis, 3–4
Bagiotti, Tullio, 199n
Bain, Joe S., 4n, 175n, 199n, 467n
Bajt, Alexander, 331n
Baker, Helen, 323n
Balassa, Bela, 248n, 257n, 261n, 330n, 342n
Baran, Paul, 71n, 118n, 332n
Baumol, William J., 30n, 122n, 170n
Bazelon, David T., 376n
Beaglehold, Ernest, 379n
Becker, Abraham S., 77n
Becker, Rudolf, 80n
Bell, Daniel, 434
Bellerby, J. R., 76n
Bendix, Reinhard, 347n
Bergson, Abram, 73n, 75n, 80n, 266n, 326n–28n, 329, 342n
Berle, Adolf A., 29, 115, 120, 385n, 471
Berliner, Joseph S., 30n, 326n
Berman, Harold J., 377n
Bernardo, Roberto M., 341n
Berry, Charles H., 301n
Berry, R. Albert, 112n
Bertrand, Trent J., 330n
Bjorksten, John, 176n
Blair, John M., 176n, 182n, 211n
Blake, William, 132
Blau, Peter M., 287n, 289n, 419, 421n–23n
Blaug, Mark, 69n

Blauner, Robert, 316–17, 430n–32n
Blitzer, Charles R., 330n
Bogdanov, Aleksander, 172n
Bonini, C. P., 147n
Bornstein, Morris, 125n, 261n, 309n, 364n
Boulding, Kenneth, 29, 172, 397–98
Brezhnev, Leonid, 365
Brown, Alan A., 218n, 330n, 355n
Brown, J. F., 217n, 276n
Brown, Murray, 137n
Browne, Margaret H., 398n
Browning, Harley L., 290n
Brubaker, Earl R., 330n
Brzezinski, Zbigniew, 365n
Burgess, Leonard R., 122n
Burke, Richard V., 276n
Burnham, James, 115

Campbell, Robert W., 125n, 327n
Caves, Richard E., 173n, 300n
Ceauşescu, Nicolae, 237n
Chandler, Alfred D., Jr., 421n
Chapman, Janet G., 274n, 345n, 448
Chayanov, A. V., 339n
Chenery, Hollis B., 362n
Chervenkov, Valko, 275n
Cheung, Steven N. S., 29, 30n, 383, 384n
Chevalier, Jean-Marie, 120
Chiu, John S., 122n, 127–28
Cholinski, T., 310n
Chou Shun-hsin, 274n, 345n
Cillié, François S., 423n
Clark, M. Gardner, 80n
Clayton, E. M., 31n
Cline, William R., 30n
Coase, R. H., 383n
Cohen, Stephen S., 353n
Collins, Norman R., 403, 452, 472
Conlisk, J., 393n
Cooley, David E., 127–28
Cooper, Richard N., 404n
Creamer, Daniel, 452
Crosland, C. A. R., 26n, 437n
Crozier, Michel, 312n, 422n
Cullen, D. E., 79n

Dahl, Robert A., 276n
Dahrendorf, Ralf, 115
Dante, 1, 34
Dantzig, George, 270n, 351n
Deane, Phyllis, 70n
de Bernonville, 70n

Subject Index

administration: costs and establishment size, 143–45; economies of, 169–78; indicative, 349–54; iterative, 351–52; reforms in East Europe, 220–21

agglomeration: and "big business," 195–97; and centralization, 315–16; degree of, 135, 143, 213; and economies of scale, 182; and enterprise size, 463; and establishment size, 156, 462; institutional, 401; and market size, 186, 213

agglomeration ratio: compared with concentration ratio, 414–16; defined, 474

aggregate production functions, 330

agriculture: and distribution of income, 76–77; and labor-force measures, 16

alienation, 428–33

allocation, central, 229–31

American values, 369; *see also* United States

antitrust legislation, 211

armed forces: and labor-force, 16; nationalization of, 51

asset revaluation, 251–53

associations: bonus system of, 266; defined, 222, 474; in East Europe, 222–28; investment decisions by, 269; major functions of, 234

Aufsichtsrat, 26

Australia: establishment size in, 153, 154, 157; labor earnings in, 83; ownership and control in, 119; public ownership and labor in, 14

Austria: big business in, 413; establishment size in, 157; labor earnings in, 82; nationalization ratios for, 46–47; public ownership and labor in, 15; public-expenditure ratio, 21; socialism indicators for, 23

autonomy, and centralization, 282

averages, various types of, 150–53

bank loan charges, 251–53

banks, investment decisions by, 268–69

bargaining, 396–400

barriers: environmental, 141–43, 172, 179–81; and income distribution, 392–96

Belgium: big business in, 413; centralization in, 294; concentration ratios for, 202–7, 415, 468; distribution of labor earnings in, 82; employment by enterprises in, 185, 196; establish-

ment size in, 157; multi-establishment enterprises in, 174; property income in, 72; public ownership and labor in, 14; socialism indicators for, 23

big business: defined, 474; and enterprise size, 195–97; mobility of, 299–301, 472–73; share of labor force employed by, 196; size distributions of, 413–14

bloc economy, 228–29, 349–50

bonus systems, 260–66, 344

Bulgaria: associations in, 226; centralization in, 294; cooperatives in, 389–90; cost calculations and price formation in, 250–60; decision-making in, 231–32, 236; distribution of labor earnings, 83; economic reforms in, 217–77; employment by largest enterprises, 196; employment size changes, 223; employment size of enterprises, 192; foreign trade of, 246–49; incentive systems in, 260–66; interaction difficulties in, 344, 346; nationalization ratios for, 46–49, 59; public ownership and labor force in, 15; public-expenditure ratio for, 21

bundle, defined, 375–76

bureaucracies: decision-making in, 24–27; income distribution in, 400–1

business. *See* big business

Canada: centralization in, 294; concentration ratios for, 202–7, 468; distribution of labor earnings in, 82; establishment size in, 157; property income in, 72; public ownership and labor in, 14; socialism indicators for, 23

capital: accumulation, 101–8; associations' control over, 234; charges on, 251–53; to labor ratios, 440–42; relative prices in Europe and America, 450; requirements for enterprises, 442–43

capital intensity: and establishment size, 139–40; rank orders of mining and manufacturing branches, 441

capitalism: advanced, 385–86; centralization in, 302–12, 319; decision-making in, 117–18; definitions of, 385–86, 474; dynamism of, 300; how distinct from socialism? 11–12; industrialization in, 319; and ownership, 11–12, 385–87; primitive, 385–86

cartels: and competition, 205; East European associations as, 225–28